An Empire of Books

AF653945

An Empire of Books

The Naval Kishore Press and the Diffusion of the Printed Word in Colonial India

Ulrike Stark

permanent black

Published by
PERMANENT BLACK
Himalayana', Mall Road, Ranikhet Cantt,
Ranikhet 263645
perblack@gmail.com

Distributed by
ORIENT LONGMAN PRIVATE LTD
Bangalore Bhopal Bhubaneshwar Chandigarh
Chennai Ernakulam Guwahati Hyderabad Jaipur
Kolkata Lucknow Mumbai New Delhi Patna
www.orientlongman.com

Copyright © 2007 Ulrike Stark

ISBN 81-7824-196-X
ISBN 978-81-7824-261-3

Typeset in Naurang
by Guru Typograph Technology, Dwarka, New Delhi 110075
Printed and bound by Manipal Technologies Limited, Manipal

FSC www.fsc.org MIX Paper | Supporting responsible forestry FSC™ C043100

For

Jana, Nina,

Dhruv and Nikhil

Contents

Acknowledgements

The right books always seem to find me at the right time. My first encounter with books printed by Naval Kishore in nineteenth-century Lucknow took place in the mid-1990s. I had recently joined the South Asia Institute of Heidelberg University and was looking for a suitable topic for a postdoctoral research project when, one day, a librarian asked me to inspect a box of old, dusty, and brittle Hindi and Urdu books stacked away in the basement of the Institute Library. The contents of the box turned out to be nothing less than a treasure. Instead of being discarded, the books moved several floors up into my office. They formed the starting point of a fascinating journey into the history of the book in South Asia and became the subject of a *Habilitationsschrift* submitted to Heidelberg University in 2004.

During the years I spent in researching and writing this book, I have received much invaluable advice and support from a great many people. I am deeply indebted to Professor Monika Boehm-Tettelbach for years of mentorship, constructive advice, and inspiration. She was always there to guide and support me with formidable scholarship and critical insights. I owe her more than words can express.

A large number of colleagues and friends have provided critical comments, advice, and assistance. In particular, I would like to thank Dr Ravi Ahuja, Mala Al-Farooq, Dr Georg Berkemer, Dr Christoph Emmrich, Dr Harald Fischer-Tiné, Lila Hüttemann, Dr Jörg Gengnagel, Dr Anindita Ghosh, Dr Christina Oesterheld, Dr Thomas Lehmann, Amtul Manan Tahir, Professor Fateh Muhammad Malik, Professor Jamal Malik, Dr Margrit Pernau, and Dr Srilata Raman.

I owe special thanks to Professor Vasudha Dalmia for support and encouragement over the years and for inviting me to Berkeley at a critical time. In Benares, the late Dr Dhirendranath Singh readily shared his formidable knowledge of Hindi print culture with me.

In Lucknow I have to thank many people for their outstanding support and hospitality. Many families spontaneously welcomed me into their homes and provided me with an unforgettable experience of Lakhnavi food and Lakhnavi *tahzib*. I am deeply grateful to the family and descendants of Munshi Naval Kishore, particularly Rani Ram Kumar Bhargava, Dr Ranjit Bhargava, and his wife Shrruti Bhargava for their interest in and support of my work. Dr Ranjit Bhargava not only wholeheartedly supported my project and gave me permission to work on the premises of the Naval Kishore Estate (Raja Ram Kumar Book Depot), but also put some rare private papers at my disposal and shared family memories with me. Shrruti Bhargava welcomed me into the family and fed me during long hours of archival research.

I would like to thank Nasir Abid for first introducing me to his beautiful city and giving me a glimpse of Sarshar's Lucknow; he helped establish contacts and opened many doors. Archival doors were also miraculously opened by the late Ashok Priyadarshi. Mrs Nirmala Sharma provided hospitality and made me feel at home in her guesthouse.

Very special thanks are due to Ram and Dee Advani for their support, affection, and encouragement since my first visit to Lucknow in 1996. As for so many scholars who come to Lucknow, Ram Advani's bookshop has been a refuge and a haven for me. I consider myself fortunate to have found a brother and very dear friend in him.

I am deeply grateful to my friends who gave me shelter, food, and encouragement during my research trips to India and England: Anshu and Sanjiv Narayan and their family provided me with a second home in Delhi; Kathleen Lawless, the late Burhan Tufail, Henie Lustgarten, and Phil Weitzman have been wonderful hosts during many visits to the British Library.

I am greatly indebted to the librarians and staff of various libraries and archives for their courtesy and efficiency in handling all manner of enquiries: the South Asia Institute Library (Heidelberg), the British Library (London), the Indian Institute Library (Oxford), the National Archives (New Delhi), the Nehru Memorial Museum and Library (New Delhi), the Uttar Pradesh State Archives (Lucknow), the Amiruddaula Public Library (Lucknow), and the Library of the Nadwat al-ʿulama (Lucknow). Dr Graham Shaw at the British Library, Elizabeth Krishna at the Indian Institute, and Nusrat Naheed at the Amiruddaula Public Library were especially generous with their time and knowledge.

Lila Hüttemann, Dr Indra Sengupta-Frey, Dr Guriqbal Sahota, and Rajeev Kinra read parts of this book in draft and offered valuable advice and suggestions. I owe special thanks to Kate Sullivan and Arnab Dey for their careful and perceptive reading of the entire manuscript and to Michaela Dimmers for helping me with illustrations, layout and much more. Bao Do with his enormous expertise in computing and layout worked miracles in transforming my manuscript into a publishable book at a critical time. Professor Clinton Seely provided valuable assistance in getting the manuscript ready for publication. Jason Grunebaum has been very generous with his time, and patiently assisted me in putting the finishing touches on the book. Dwaipayan Sen did a great job helping me compile the index.

I am grateful to the Humanities Division of the University of Chicago and especially Dean Danielle Allen for their generous financial support in getting this book published.

Lastly, I owe very special thanks to my wonderful family and friends who provided encouragement and emotional support over the years. You kept me grounded and in remembrance of the things that are really important in life.

Note on Transliteration and Conventions

For the sake of readability, no diacritical marks have been used for personal and geographical names, nor for Indian terms that have become part of the English language. Indian language names and scripts also appear without diacritics. For personal names, modern transliteration has been used, except in the case of some famous figures who are still better known by contemporary forms (e.g. Rammohan Roy). The English forms of some Indian place-names (e.g. Lucknow, Benares, Delhi, Calcutta) have been retained. The state of Avadh also often appears in its old British spelling, 'Oudh', especially when colonial institutions are discussed (e.g. Oudh Educational Department).

A special difficulty of this study is that it deals with terms and book titles in five different languages, namely Hindi, Urdu, Sanskrit, Persian, and Arabic. To use a different transliteration system for each language would have made it thoroughly unreadable, while confusing the reader unnecessarily. For this reason I arrived at a compromise. Words in Hindi and Sanskrit are transliterated according to the systems used in R.S. McGregor's *Oxford Hindi–English Dictionary* and M. Monier-Williams' *Sanskrit–English Dictionary*. For Sanskrit terms the inherent vowel 'a' has been retained (hence *Rāmāyaṇ* in Hindi and *Rāmāyaṇa* in Sanskrit). Transliteration of words in Urdu, Persian, and Arabic follows the system used in J.T. Platts, *A Dictionary of Urdū, Classical Hindī, and English* with some minor modifications. The Persian *iẓāfat* is indicated by -e. The same word may sometimes be transliterated variously, depending on whether it occurs in a Hindi or Urdu context.

There exists a baffling variety of contemporary spellings for the name of the central character of this book, Munshi Naval Kishore (correctly transcribed as Navalkishor in Urdu and Navalkiśor in Hindi). Some of these represent 'corrupt' English pronunciation. The publisher himself signed his name 'Newul Kishore' in English documents. In opting for Naval Kishore I have chosen a compromise between the most common variant and the principles of modern transliteration.

Throughout this book Naval Kishore Press (NKP) titles issued from Lucknow, Kanpur, and Lahore have been marked by an asterisk preceding the year of publication. The date after the asterisk indicates the year of *first* publication from the NKP only, and often does not coincide with the first printed edition of a given title. Also, despite my best efforts, the publication dates given for NKP first editions may not always be accurate, for the firm did not keep a complete and accurate record of its early imprints dating from *c.* 1858–65. To complicate matters, lithographed and typeset versions of the same text, as well as reprints in different format, were often announced as 'first' editions, while reprints of other publishers' titles were generally designated as 'second' editions on NKP title pages.

Unless otherwise indicated, all translations from the original Hindi and Urdu are my own.

Tables

Illustrations

Glossary

ʿālim	a learned man, in particular one learned in Islamic legal and religious studies
ashrāf	(pl. of *sharīf*); honourable people, the well-born. Muslims whose ancestors were immigrants in the subcontinent
darbār	a levee or public audience held by an Indian prince, or by a high-ranking British official
qānūngo	a subordinate official in the Mughal and British revenue administrations
ḥakīm	a physician in the Greek–Islamic tradition
jāgīr	an assignment to a noble of the land revenue from one or more villages in lieu of salary
madrasah	a secondary school or college for Muslims
maktab	an elementary school in which Persian, Urdu, and Quranic recitation is taught
marṡiya	an elegy; a lament, usually composed in commemoration of Imam Husain
maṡnavī	a lengthy narrative poem in the rhyme scheme AA, BB, CC, etc.
munshī	a writer; secretary
mushāʿira	a gathering of poets; a poetic contest
pān	a digestive preparation using betel leaf as its base
pāṭhśālā	a Sanskrit primary school
qaṣbah	a small country town, often the seat of Muslim gentry
raʾīs	a man of wealth and respectable position; a commercial magnate

sant	a pious person; a term used for North Indian saint poets who believed in an unqualified and non-incarnate Ultimate Being
sarrishtadār	the head Indian officer in a collector's office or court of justice
shāgird	a pupil, or apprentice to a poet of established reputation
taḥṣīl	a revenue subdivision of a district
taḥṣīldār	a district official in charge of a *taḥṣīl*
ta<u>*kh*</u>*alluṣ*	a poet's pen name
taʿalluqdār	in Avadh, a large landholder who collected and paid revenue to the administration from his own lands as well as from other landholders
ta<u>*z*</u>*kirah*	a collective biography of saints or poets
ʿulamā	pl. of *ʿālim*; the learned
vaidya	a practitioner of Ayurveda
wāso<u>*kh*</u>*t*	a lyric genre
zamīndār	a landholder

Abbreviations

AECR	*Appendix to the Education Commission Report. Report by the NWP&Oudh Provincial Committee*
AUS	*Annual of Urdu Studies*
DIPL	Nabi Hadi, *Dictionary of Indo-Persian Literature*
DPI	Director of Public Instruction
ECR	*Education Commission Report*
EI	*Encyclopaedia of Islam. New Edition*
GRPI	*General Report on Public Instruction*
HLHH	J.H. Garcin de Tassy, *Histoire de la Littérature Hindouie et Hindoustanie*, vols I–III
JPHS	*Journal of the Punjab Historical Society*
JRAS	*Journal of the Royal Asiatic Society*
LLH	J.H. Garcin de Tassy, *La Langue et la Littérature Hindoustanies. Revue Annuelle*
MAS	*Modern Asian Studies*
NAI	National Archives of India, New Delhi
NKP	Naval Kishore Press
NWP	North-Western Provinces
OAR	*Oudh Administration Report* (later called [*Annual*] *Report of the Administration of the Province of Oudh*)
OIOC	Oriental and India Office Collections, British Library
PGNWP	Proceedings of the Government, North-Western Provinces
QLP	Quarterly Lists of Publications
RA NWP&Oudh	*Report of the Administration of the North-Western Provinces and Oudh*

RPE Oudh	*Report upon the Progress of Education in the Province of Oudh*
RPIR	*Report on Publications Issued and Registered*
SRGNWP	*Selections from the Records of Government. North-Western Provinces*
SVN	Selections from Vernacular Newspapers (also called Native Newspaper Reports and Notes on the Press)
SVNP	Selections from Vernacular Newspapers of the Punjab
TUH	Rahman ʿAli, *Taẕkirah-e ʿulamā-e Hind*
UPSA	Uttar Pradesh State Archives, Lucknow

Introduction

The promise of the history of the book is simply this, that it will not tolerate a simplistic or reductionist understanding of the relationship between culture and society.

—David D. Hall, *Cultures of Print*

The history of the book in India is a history largely untold. This study is an attempt to shed light on the social, cultural, and material aspects of book production in nineteenth-century North India. During this transitional period in Indian history, a new institution arose in the urban literary-cultural sphere, signalling the triumph of print: the commercial publishing house. Through a case study of the Naval Kishore Press of Lucknow (est. 1858), the largest Indian-owned printing press and publishing house in the subcontinent at the time, this study investigates the impact of the commercial book trade on the diffusion and laicization of knowledge, and on processes of intellectual formation, modernization, and cultural renaissance in North India. More specifically, it explores the role of a singularly influential and prolific publisher in the production, transmission, and canonization of printed texts in the North Indian languages of Hindi and Urdu during a decisive moment in their shared and divided history.

In focusing on an Indian publishing house, this study enters a fascinating world of artisanal, scholarly, literary, and entrepreneurial talent. Book printing and publishing in nineteenth-century India was a venture as much entrepreneurial as intellectual. I trace a history which starts from the rise of the Naval Kishore Press and concludes with its position as the most successful business enterprise in nineteenth-century Indian publishing. In doing this, I am as interested in the economics of book production as in what has been called the 'human face' of the book trade (Isaac/McKay 1999). Print generated new professions and introduced a distinctive figure into the colonial public sphere: the commercial printer-publisher. This book aims to show, through a famous example, that the foremost pioneers in Indian commercial publishing were not just savvy businessmen. Rather, they were men deeply engaged in the intellectual and literary life of their time who shared its larger cultural, cognitive, and social concerns.[1] The more successful among them combined learning, cultural expertise, and antiquarian interests with craftsmanship and a keen sense of business. Exercising the various roles of entrepreneur, publicist, literary patron, philanthropist, disseminator of knowledge, and educator, the great icons of early Indian publishing—Fardunji Sorabji Marzban in Bombay, Munshi Harsukh Rai in Lahore, Maulvi ᶜAbdul Rahman Khan in Kanpur, Mustafa Khan and Munshi Naval Kishore in Lucknow—assumed importance not only as early industrialists but also as intellectual pathbreakers and intermediaries. In investigating the life and career of one of them, I seek to explore the motivation of such men generally—people for whom printing and publishing was not just a business but a vocation.

The policy, success, and impact of the Naval Kishore Press (hereafter NKP) are inextricably linked to its founder-proprietor, whose multifaceted life presents an extraordinary tale of fortune. Munshi Naval Kishore (1836–95), the central character of this book, set out as a journalist and printer; his fame, however, rests on his achievement in both general and scholarly publishing. To narrate his life is to narrate the story of an Indian Hindu who participated in the revival of Hindu traditions while acting as one of the foremost promoters of Islamic learning and preservers of the Arabic and Indo-Persian literary heritage in the subcontinent. Naval Kishore belonged to the North Indian service gentry. He embodied the synthesis of Indo-Muslim and Hindu learned traditions in an exemplary fashion—most poignantly captured in Khvaja Abbas Ahmad's succinct characterization of him as a 'Muslim pandit and Hindu maulvi'. Yet Naval Kishore also belonged to the new generation of Indians who had received some Western education and been exposed to ideas of Western enlightenment rationality. Underlying his self-perception was a strong sense of the publisher's cultural mission in society. This was to shape the policy of his firm in such a way that it combined capitalist principles of profit making and increasing turnover with literary and cultural patronage. This policy accounted for the development of the NKP as a vibrant intellectual meeting place, where scholars and literati of various backgrounds would gather and interact.

[1] To date, virtually nothing is known about female participation in the early North Indian publishing trade, perhaps the sole exception being that of Mallika, the cultured young Bengali protégé and companion of Bharatendu Harishchandra, who collaborated with the great Hindi author in his literary ventures. Harishchandra set up a small publishing house and bookshop for her (Madan Gopal 1972: 174; Dalmia 2004).

It is the dual nature of the publishing house—as a modern, capital-oriented industrial enterprise and an important site of intellectual, literary, and scholastic pursuits—which this books seeks to explore. Book publishing at the NKP—whether in Arabic, Persian, Sanskrit, Hindi, or Urdu—was never inspired by the profit motive alone. Rather, it was informed by the twin objectives of revitalizing India's cultural and literary heritage and of contributing to Indian modernity through the diffusion of knowledge and education. Combining commercial with educative, scholastic, and aesthetic aims, such a policy followed the imperatives of cultivation and entertainment; it included literature both 'high' and 'low' and sought to address the scholarly elite and the general reading public alike. How these objectives were achieved will form a major concern of my book.

Through an investigation of the internal structures and external relationships of the publishing house, I attempt to reconstruct the process by which the 'House of Naval Kishore' set about creating a distinct identity for itself. The period under review spans the years from 1858 to 1895. The first date marks the establishment of the firm, which, conveniently enough, coincides with a transformative moment in Indian history. The second date marks the death of Naval Kishore, which brought to a close a major phase in the history of the publishing house.

While drawing inspiration from the genre in which much publishing history is written, this book is only in part a conventional 'house history', for it also seeks to address larger questions of the transformations in literary culture and learned practice induced by commercial printing. Often cited, a comment made by the Urdu cultural historian Abdul Halim Sharar in his famous swan song of Lakhnavi culture *Lucknow: The Last Phase of an Oriental Culture* still remains one of most poignant formulations of the vast and lasting impact of the NKP on the North Indian literary and cognitive domain: 'The Newal Kishore Press is still the key to the literary trade. Without using it no one can enter the world of learning' (Sharar 1975: 108).

With its focus on the second half of the nineteenth century, this book is not a study of the shift from oral to written culture.[2] Nor is it primarily concerned with the transition from manuscript or scribal culture to print culture initiated in Hindi and Urdu at the turn of the nineteenth century.

[2] For the interface of orality and literacy see, e.g., the classic study by Walter J. Ong (Ong 1982) and the works authored and edited by Jack Goody (Goody 1968; 1986; 1987; 2000).

Instead, it addresses a third paradigm shift in the history of print in India, which I call the 'commercialization' of print. The term 'commercialization', as used here, refers to a number of parallel and interconnected processes that shaped the regional-language book trade from around the 1840s: the introduction of new reproduction techniques and the ensuing shift to industrialized mass production; the decline in production costs and the concomitant possibility of reduction in book prices; the transition from European to large-scale Indian ownership, agency, and investment in the book trade; the rise of the marketplace as a dominant force in literary culture; the emergence of commercial genres; and, finally, the creation of a new class of professional authors. In short, commercialization describes the transformation of the printed text from artifact and cultural asset into a cheap and easily available consumer commodity. As such, it is intimately linked to wider economic, social, and cultural shifts induced by colonialism—notably, the dawning of the age of industrial capitalism, the spread of colonial literacy and formal education, and the rise and economic empowerment of an Indian educated middle class.[3]

Preparing the Ground: Towards a History of the Book in India

Much has happened since Elizabeth Eisenstein, in her seminal work on print culture *The Printing Press as an Agent of Change* (1980), decried 'the persistence of a venerable philosophical tradition of proud ignorance

[3] Focusing on commercialization and industrial mass printing does not mean ignoring the highly complex ways in which print and oral cultures continued to coexist throughout the century, both contesting and complementing each other. Heeding Roger Chartier's warning against a 'too simplistic opposition between oral culture and scribal or print culture' (Chartier 1984: 231), recent research has increasingly stressed the need to overcome the orality *versus* print dichotomy. Scholars have highlighted the fact that print did not replace orality, but supplemented it. Sheldon Pollock points to the 'often simultaneous orders of oral, manuscripts and print cultures' (Pollock 2003: 15), while Stuart Blackburn, in his investigation of printed folklore in Tamil Nadu (Blackburn 2001; 2003), makes a strong case against the traditional idea of the mutual exclusivity of print and orality. The notion of an inimical relationship between print and oral cultures, he contends, is closely linked to other misconceptions: one being a 'pristine' oral culture later 'polluted' by print, and another what he calls the 'untenable dichotomy' between orality and modernity. His argument regarding Tamil folklore—that print, 'far from widening the gap between literary and oral culture, actually bridged it and brought them together in the form of printed folklore' (ibid.: 3)—finds a North Indian parallel in the creative interface of orality and print existing for popular forms of musical drama (Hansen 2001) and narratives of the

concerning material and mechanical phenomena' (Eisenstein 1980: 24). The history of the book has since developed into a thriving discipline which encompasses not only analytical bibliography and cultural history, but also the material, economic, and legal aspects of book production and distribution, the professional practices of the industry, and 'the after-life of books as seen through reading practices, libraries and the operation of the book market' (Maclean 1999: 12). Although the study of the printed book dates back much further, its academic beginnings in the West are taken to lie in the 1950s and are generally associated with Lucien Febvre and Henri-Jean Martin's pathbreaking *L'Apparition du Livre* (1958, trs. into English as *The Coming of the Book)*. Accompanying the rise of book history as a distinct area of scholarly investigation has been a steadily increasing number of competing methodologies pertaining to analytical and descriptive bibliography, history, the sociology of knowledge, literary and reception studies, and so forth, which at one point prompted Robert Darnton to speak of an 'interdisciplinarity run riot' (Darnton 1982: 67).

A quarter century later, the multiplicity of methodologies remains, while the sheer amount, high quality, and depth of scholarly investigations into European book history is overawing. Classic studies of European print culture have tended to view the transition from manuscript to print culture as a 'communications revolution' and have described the printed book as an intellectual ferment that effected major cultural, social, and political transformations. Identifying increased dissemination, standardization, and fixity as the main features of print culture, Eisenstein in particular has laid much stress on 'the preservative powers of print' (Eisenstein 1980: 51–159). Her mechanistic interpretation of print culture has been challenged most forcefully by Adrian Johns in his compelling study of 'print in the making' in early modern England (Johns 1998). Focusing on prevailing practices of piracy and unauthorized printing, Johns opposes Eisenstein's key concept of 'intrinsic fixity' to the 'uncertainty' of early print culture. He does so by highlighting issues of the reliability of printed knowledge—a reliability that authors and scholarly printers often found hard to obtain. His argument that print entailed not one but 'many cultures', and that these cultures of the book were themselves 'local in character' (Johns 1998: 30), underpins the necessity of studying print cultures in their particular geographic, social and cultural contexts.

Persian/Urdu *dāstān* and *qiṣṣa* genre. *Qiṣṣa*s were refashioned in print, while also circulating 'back and forth between oral narration, print, and performance' (Sangari 2004: 215).

Although considerably removed in time and space, Johns's fundamental concern with the reliability and authoritativeness of early printed texts is of direct relevance to the South Asian context, as has been demonstrated by Francis Robinson in his seminal essays on the adoption of print by nineteenth-century Indian Muslims (Robinson 1993; 1996). In India, it was during the second half of the century that the transition from 'uncertainty' to 'fixity' first took place, with printer-publishers like Naval Kishore standing at the juncture of early and modern, i.e. commercial, print culture with its mass production technologies. Yet fixity was never absolute. As Frances Pritchett has shown through the example of the *qiṣṣa*, some genres resisted fixity and continued to show a high degree of textual fluidity even after they were consigned to print (Pritchett 1985: 34–5).

Compared to the huge number of excellent empirical and theoretical studies on the history of the book in the West, book history in South Asia is still in its formative phase. Despite a general consensus that print, in its twin manifestations of the newspaper and the printed book, was crucial to the project of Indian modernity and effected major transformations in the cultural, literary, and political domains, scholars of South Asia have only recently begun to respond to the immense challenge posed by the history of the book in Indian regional languages. A persistent trend has been concentration on the newspaper and periodical press—according to Veena Naregal the 'most suitable site to analyse the structure of exchanges and meanings of publicity established through print' (Naregal 2001: 190). Given the intimate nexus between the spread of print and the development of modern regional-language journalism, most research has in turn focused on the socio-political impact of the press and its role in the diffusion of public knowledge, in generating critical opinion, and in shaping Indian nationalism.[4] But few critics have acknowledged the pivotal function of the newspaper media in expanding interest in the printed word prior to the emergence of the 'cheap book' trade.

Compared with the sustained scholarly interest in the press media, the history of the book has received little, and very uneven, attention. While the advent and early phase of book printing in India have been relatively well documented, no comprehensive account has been offered of the development of the commercial book trade and industrialization of the print medium in Indian regional languages in the nineteenth century.[5] This is not surprising in light of the fact that India still lacks a

[4] See, e.g., Khare 1964; Chakraborti 1976; Sharma 1996; Narain 1998.

[5] See, e.g. Priolkar 1959; Diehl 1964; Rhodes 1969; Kesavan 1985–97; Shaw 1981 and 1998; Rohatgi and Godrej 1989; Ross 1999.

'national' book history.[6] Fortunately, however, this neglect is beginning to show signs of waning. For instance, a relatively recent volume entitled *Print Areas. Book History in India* (2004) promises to be the first in a series of studies devoted to the systematic exploration of book history in India.

The fact that academic contributions to the history of the book in India and, more specifically, in Hindi and Urdu, are still limited in number naturally does not make the task any easier. The study of the printed book in the subcontinent continues to pose particular problems to researchers. The difficulties confronted include the scarcity of basic empirical data on just about every aspect of production, transmission, and consumption. Factual knowledge of material, infrastructural, and operational aspects of the regional-language book trade, of author–publisher and publisher–bookseller relations, of readership and consumption practices is still limited. Seldom extant, Indian publishers' and booksellers' archives are not readily accessible and lie mostly untapped. British official records, our principal source of publication data, are not always reliable and in their concern with statistics provide only a limited insight into the operations, networks, and underlying motivations of indigenous publishers. In this situation, research has tended to focus on book-producing and disseminating institutions with a recorded history—early European and missionary printing presses, government colleges, schoolbook and translation societies. North India's indigenous publishing houses have received little scholarly attention, despite their pivotal role in shaping a market for the Hindi and Urdu book.[7] To my knowledge there exist only two monographs on early Indian publishing houses in the Hindi and Urdu region (Singh 1986; Shams Badauni 1995).

The history of the book cuts across established academic disciplines and has been accurately described as 'polyvocal' and 'inevitably interdisciplinary'. While one might observe with Darnton that scholars of book history in Indian regional languages still find themselves 'crossing paths in a no-man's-land located at the intersection of a half-dozen fields of study' (Darnton 1982: 65), it seems more apt to point out that this very

[6] For a pioneering work in Indian book history, dealing with Bengali, see Khan 1999.

[7] For nineteenth-century India there exist no clear-cut lines between printer and publisher, their differentiation into separate institutions occuring only in the twentieth century. For reasons of simplicity the terms 'printing press', 'press', and 'publishing house' will be used interchangeably throughout this book to refer to the kind of business enterprise that prepared, printed, and issued books for public distribution or sale.

multidisciplinarity has in fact greatly energized the study of book history in South Asia. Significant impulses have been received from disciplines concerned with the study of nationalism, popular cultures, and the formation of Indian public opinion. Recent debates on the Habermasian public sphere and on Benedict Anderson's influential concept of nationalism (Anderson 1983) have naturally foregrounded issues pertinent to print. Anderson's articulation of the role of 'print-capitalism' in the emergence of the 'imagined community' of the nation posited the creation of 'national print-languages' and 'monoglot mass reading publics' as a powerful factor in forging national identities.[8] His argument has since been qualified in a number of important ways by, among others, Anthony D. Smith, who cautions against overgeneralizing the power of the printed word in societies that possessed various other means of public mobilization.[9] Yet, even while the various critiques of Anderson must be acknowledged here, his concept of 'print capitalism' cannot and will not be dismissed altogether. Print capitalism, in its most basic sense of the 'convergence of capitalism and print technology', is nicely exemplified by the House of Naval Kishore, whose role in shaping the North Indian printing industry has been with good reason compared to that of the legendary J.N. Tata in the Indian steel industry (Nagar 1991). 'Print capitalist' appears to me to be a particularly apt epithet for an individual who built up India's largest publishing concern from scratch, combining the roles of single largest employer in the North-Western Provinces and Oudh, founder-editor of

[8] According to Anderson, print cultures shaped nationalist ideologies in a threefold way: they created 'unified fields of exchange and communication', gave a new 'fixity' to the language which over time helped 'to build that image of antiquity so central to the subjective idea of the nation', and created new 'languages-of-power' that were different from the older administrative vernaculars (Anderson 1991: 44–5).

[9] 'The portrayals of the nation that stirred people into action were oral, audial and visual rather than literary, a matter of symbols, songs, images, reports and rituals' (Smith 1998: 139). This important point has been raised in a different context by Peter Burke who, outlining the importance of the new print media for Lutheran reform in sixteenth-century Germany, stresses the fact that the *true* mass media at the time were still oral and visual ('The Public Sphere—Past and Present', public lecture at Heidelberg University, 25 June 2002). For further criticism of Anderson, see Chatterjee 1993: 4–6; Tønnesson and Antlöv 1996: 6–9; Bayly 1996a. Dilip Menon (Menon 2002), in a study of lower caste Malayalam novels, vehemently rejects Anderson's 'axiomatic twining' of the nation and the novel, arguing that rather than 'narrating the nation', lower-caste novels were more concerned with addressing questions of fashioning the self, of caste collectivity, and religious imagination in the face of colonial modernity.

North India's most influential Urdu daily newspaper, large landed proprietor, and pioneering investor in new businesses such as the Lucknow Paper Mills.

The Publishing House and the Literary System

Robert Darnton's often-cited 'communications circuit' has provided a classic analytic model for theorizing the life cycle of a book through the stages of production, transmission, and consumption (Darnton 1982).[10] While the communications circuit has recently come under critique for being too rigid, overly deterministic, and lacking contextualization, cultural theory has offered a more dynamic methodology for the study of book history in the form of the Pierre Bourdieu's influential 'fields of cultural production' (Bourdieu 1993). In Bourdieu's theory the literary field is a 'relatively autonomous' structured space which has its own specific 'laws of operation' but is embedded within and subject to the indirect influences of a larger field of power. Bourdieu's articulation of the literary field has been called a 'radical contextualization'. As a theory of context it offers a framework that not only encompasses the various agents operating in the field of literary production but also the changing social, economic, political, and technological conditions by which it is affected.[11] The internal organization of the field, Bourdieu contends, is marked by hierarchical structures and a fundamental opposition between two sub-fields, namely 'restricted production' (small-scale avant-garde publishers who invest in works of literary and aesthetic value, believe in 'art for art's sake', and are concerned with the excellence of their craft) and 'large-scale production' (commercially oriented publishers, who invest in the mass production of saleable texts and measure value in purely financial terms). From being 'functionaries' in Darnton's model, publishers and other cultural intermediaries in Bourdieu's theory advance to being 'symbolic brokers in the field' who can confer cultural status on a given text and assert 'principles of cultural legitimacy' (McDonald 1997: 20).

[10] Envisaging the different segments and agents in the book's life cycle from a 'holistic' viewpoint, the communications circuit maps its journey from the author to the publisher, printer, bookseller, etc. to the reader. The circuit runs full cycle from reader back to author, since writers are themselves readers who address implicit readers and respond to reviews.

[11] This paragraph draws on the insightful discussion of Darnton's and Bourdieu's theory offered by Peter D. McDonald (McDonald 1997: 9–21).

In theorizing the role of the publishing house, this book also draws on another methodological framework that highlights contextualization, notably Peter U. Hohendahl's articulation of the 'institution of literature'. Theoreticians of the 'institution' have variously used the term to designate concrete, material organizations on the one hand and 'ideological formations'—that is, a wider set of rules, values, norms, and practices—on the other. Taking into account these various uses, Hohendahl, in his study of mid-nineteenth century German literary culture (Hohendahl 1989), has advocated the concept of the institution as a helpful analytical category for exploring the inner coherence between literary and social history. Drawing on concepts of the public sphere, in which the institution of literature is embedded, his approach is concerned with the conditions under which textual production and consumption occur.[12] Hohendahl stresses the historicity of the institution of literature. His theory of 'institutionalization' outlines the formation of a network of interacting sub-institutions in the literary domain. It allows us to view the publishing house as an institutional space operating within a discursive and interactionist sphere of other sub-institutions involved in literary production and transmission. Depending on their nature, function, and agenda, these act as authorities, controlling agents, or innovators in questions of literary tradition and canon formation.

In the South Asian context, Francesca Orsini has successfully drawn on Hohendahl's useful conceptual framework in her study of the Hindi public sphere in 1920–40. She demonstrates how educated Indians advanced their political, social, and literary agendas through creating institutional spaces (Orsini 2002). In applying the theory of the institution to the literary field of nineteenth-century North India, we encounter structures (sub-institutions) specific to the colonial situation, such as Orientalist scholarship, the Anglo-Indian press, and the colonial education system. Thus, of particular interest to this study is the question of how, within this institutional configuration, the publishing house interacted with other sub-institutions—indigenous scholarship, literary associations, public libraries, the 'vernacular' press, colonial education and its school curricula, and so on.

[12] 'The publicly grounded institution of literature is subject to indirect pressures exerted by political and economic issues on the public sphere. Traditional literary history, which is oriented towards authors, works, or genres, cannot contribute much to the institutional character of literature and thus can comprehend diachronic processes only as isolated series of events' (Hohendahl 1989: 45). See also Hohendahl's influential *The Institution of Criticism* (1982).

As research on print culture in the West has shown, histories of publishing houses are not limited to author–publisher relations, editorial practices, and sales and marketing, but have contributed to our understanding of various material, socio-historical, economic, and organizational aspects of cultural production. In the exploration of nineteenth-century Hindi and Urdu literary culture, the role of the publisher is an understudied area. Breaking new ground in that sense, this book proceeds from the assumption that the commercial publishing house assumed a dual function within the literary field that was both reflective and innovative. The successful publisher's choices not only *responded* to readership tastes and reflected processes of canonization as well as current trends in literary activity, they also *shaped* these processes. In selecting, rejecting, and revising manuscripts, publishers were, as Leslie Howsam suggests, 'astute interpreters' of contemporary tastes or, more metaphorically, 'canaries in the coal-mines of the contemporary culture, testing the atmosphere in which they were doing business' (Howsam 1998: 13). Publishers also influenced tastes: new editions, frequent reprints, cheap formats, and serialization had a direct bearing on enhancing the audience of a given text. The imprint of a publisher could invest a book with prestige; a contract with a reputed publishing house could be a step in an author's canonization.

In probing how the publishing house interacted with other institutions within the broader configuration of the institution of literature, this book is also concerned with the radical shifts in structures of patronage generated by print. The rise of the printed book coincided with the gradual dissolution of traditional patronage systems that centred around the court and that were shaped by a strong bond between the poet or writer, his royal patron, and his audience of connoisseurs. Within such milieux authors had depended on their wealthy patrons for financial security and social prestige. With the coming of print and the decline of courtly patronage, literature acquired new organizational forms. Mass printing technology not only altered the relationship among the participants in literary production, it also changed the function of the book. In metropolitan Britain, as much as in colonial India, the printing press was put to 'utilitarian' ends, the colonial state emerging as one of the principal patrons of the printed book. More than mere intermediaries between author and reader, publishers now rose to become important literary patrons.

Another principal new source of patronage was the reader. While private patronage continued to be of importance, printed products were increasingly sustained by a new Indian consumer class. With the book's gradual transformation into a commercial commodity, literary production and transmission were for the first time subsumed to the forces of the marketplace, the fate of a literary work and its author depending on its saleability and reception (Das 1991: 38–9).

That Naval Kishore was at the same time a scholarly, literary, and general publisher has major implications. In Bourdieu's terms, he spanned the two sub-fields of 'restricted' and 'large-scale' production.[13] His policy of offering the literary canon of classic authors to a large public in inexpensive and linguistically accessible formats, for example, was a means of reconciling the traditional concept of cultivation of the mind with the capitalist principle of profit-making. While literary studies in the areas of Hindi and Urdu have traditionally tended to focus on 'high' culture, in recent times the stimulating impact of interpenetrating studies of popular and print culture has entailed a shift of attention towards 'popular' and 'lowly' genres. My investigation into a commercial publishing house cuts right across these distinctions. In it, the boundaries between 'high' and 'low', and 'elite' and 'popular' literature are often blurred. In trying to bring the printed book within the reach of the broadest possible audience, Indian commercial publishers catered for both the upper and the lower end of the market. Although much of the literature viewed here belongs to the domain of high culture, including a broad selection of Hindi and Urdu literary and religious classics, the commercial use of print also entailed the mass production of various forms of 'cheap' chapbook literature and an often undiscussed but significant body of non-belletristic texts—religious and mythological tracts, medical and astrological manuals, song books, legal forms and almanacs. While located outside the canon of high textuality, these staples of the commercial book trade were widely consumed across castes and classes. In exploiting their sales potential, a 'respectable' publisher of Naval Kishore's means and stature was no different from the many small and 'cheap' presses operating in the world of popular print. Consequently, the term 'literature' will be used here throughout in a general, inclusive sense, comprising both literary and 'non-literary' textual genres.

Literacy, Readership, and Consumption

An important aspect of book history is concerned with literacy and the practice of reading. To say that print culture had a profound impact on

[13] Indeed, as McDonald points out, the two sub-fields are an 'idealized opposition', while in actual practice 'few agents are ever exclusively committed to a single position in the field' (McDonald 1997: 14). Rather, they occupy positions which combine the two perspectives in various degrees.

literacy is a truism, but since few scholars have hitherto taken up the formidable task of tracing the nature of this development in the South Asian context, we know little about the exact mechanisms at work. It is one thing to acknowledge the impact of print on literacy, and quite another to trace the precise modes and processes by which new readerships were constituted. With its focus on aspects of production and transmission, *An Empire of Books* is not intended to and indeed cannot be an examination of readership and reading practices. Yet some of the analytical problems posed by the categories of literacy and the reading public are addressed here because they have a direct bearing on my concern with the nature, extent, and limits of commercial publishing.

In the subcontinent the printed book entered, and came to flourish in, a world deeply imbued with oral traditions: it coexisted and interacted with old and strong oral cultures. At the same time, India boasted a rich and highly refined manuscript culture. A helpful concept in understanding the impact of printed texts and their generally high valorization in the Indian context is the distinction between literacy and 'literacy awareness', introduced by C.A. Bayly in his *Empire and Information* (1996). Even if pre-colonial and colonial Indian society was largely non-literate, it was also, as Bayly argues, 'a society acutely aware of literacy, where even the poor could gain access to writers and readers at a cost', and where illiteracy 'did not preclude sophistication in using others' learning' (Bayly 1996: 13, 38). The power and prestige of writing and the written word was acknowledged not only by the literate castes but by a much larger section of the population. Even to the illiterate, the printed book could constitute an object of veneration and seem a prized possession.[14]

Literacy, as a category of analysis, remains problematic in several respects. For one thing, it is difficult to give a close estimate of the size of the literate public in nineteenth-century North India, given the scanty statistical evidence. As research in the Bengal region has shown, even in the pre-colonial period basic literacy among non-elite castes may have been more widespread than has been generally assumed (Ghosh 1998: 187). In this context, one is well advised to remember Roger Chartier's articulation of the 'wide range of reading abilities' existing between literacy and illiteracy (Chartier 1984: 236–7). The problems surrounding the issue of literacy are already fully evident in the colonial Census Reports, our principal statistical source. A predominantly rural region,

[14] The educationist Raja Shiva Prasad reports an encounter with a villager who proudly showed him a missionary tract 'which a Padri Sahib had given him at Ballia fair, and which he had kept with the greatest care possible, doubly covered, for his son when he was of school-going age.' *AECR* 1884: 316.

the North Indian plains showed a generally lower level of literacy than the coastal regions. Yet various factors—such as the development of commerce, the level of patronage exercised by indigenous rulers, and the concentration of scribal and merchant castes—accounted for significant sub-regional variation. According to the NWP Census of 1872, male literacy was around three per cent, while female literacy was close to nil.[15] The 1881 Census listed 6.6 per cent of the male population in the province as 'literates' or 'scholars', an expression of British officials grappling with the need to further distinguish between the functionally and fully literate. At 6.4 and 6.6 per cent, literacy among Hindus and Muslims was almost equal and stood in stark contrast to the high literacy of 51.6 per cent prevailing among Jains. Furthermore, there was a marked urban-rural divide. The condition of life among the rural population offered little opportunity or incentive for acquiring more than basic reading skills. Literacy was naturally much higher among the urban population and was reinforced by the impact of formal education.[16] Of special significance in the present context is the subtle but important distinction between literacy and habitual book reading (Altick 1957: 31). An Indian trader who knew how to read and write in the Mahajani script may not have taken to reading literary works. A rural government school pupil, having acquired some basic reading skills over a year or two of schooling, may never have bought a book in later life and could even have lost the ability to read through lack of practice.

Female literacy is another issue that needs to be addressed. Attitudes towards female literacy and education underwent dramatic change in the course of the century, and had a direct bearing on the number of literate women and their reading habits. During the early nineteenth century the notion of female literacy was surrounded by strong fears and social taboos. Traditional superstitions invoked the harmful effects of a woman's knowledge of how to read and write—moral depravity, failure to secure a husband, or even widowhood (Borthwick 1984: 60–1; Forbes 1996: 33). Over time, perceptions changed: under the combined influence of colonial literacy schemes, social reform, and Indian nationalism the ability to read and write came to be regarded by many as a useful asset, indeed

[15] *NWP Census 1872, Vol. 1*: 31–2. In Avadh literacy was even lower.

[16] In 1881 the proportion of school-going boys in the age group five to nine ranged from 12 percent in Aligarh to 19 percent in Lucknow. *Report on the Census of the NWP&Oudh and of the Native States of Rampur and Native Garhwal*, . . . 1881: 91–3.

a requirement, in a young woman's religious and domestic education (Chatterjee 1993). The British introduced the first textbooks for girls; Indian support came from reformist literati. The powerful plea for female literacy made by Nazir Ahmad in *Mirāt al-ʿarūs* (The Bride's Mirror, *1869)—the first bestseller and presumably the first piece of modern fiction widely consumed by female readers of Urdu—was reiterated by Altaf Husain Hali in *Majālis an-nisā* (Assemblies of Women, 1874).[17] Indian nationalism propagated the new ideals of companionate marriage and the enlightened mother who, on the strength of her education, was a capable manager of domestic affairs and educator of her children, the future builders of the nation.

While the habit of book reading gradually ceased being condemned as harmful per se, attitudes towards female reading remained deeply ambivalent. Even Indian advocates of female education nourished latent fears of 'wrong reading' that would bring out women's supposedly innate immorality and perfidious character (Sangari 1999: 147–63). Raja Shiva Prasad's testimony before the Education Commission of 1882 is a case in point. Eager to refute colonial stereotypes of the backwardness of Indian women, he contended that Indian women were 'more educated, more intelligent, more free . . . than the Europeans have any idea of', while at the same time cautioning that he knew of 'cases where women have gone astray by knowing how to read and write'.[18] As long as such patriarchal anxieties prevailed, books 'suitable for women' remained confined to a prescriptive and carefully monitored canon of textbooks and didactic works. Small in number and restricted by patriarchal ideology, the potential of the 'female market' in North Indian languages, I would suggest, was too limited to be commercially exploited in the period under review. Unlike Britain or even contemporary Bengal, in North India it was not before the turn of the century that publishers began to target the Hindi and Urdu female readership as a distinct and commercially viable market. Having said this, it is important to note that women, both as readers and listeners, did exist as a category in publishers' minds for a wide range of non-gender-specific publications. Women had access to and were eager consumers of the products of print culture to a much larger degree than literacy figures suggest.[19]

[17] Minault 1986; 1998: 38–55.

[18] *AECR* 1884: 323.

[19] For an illustration of this point, see Sangari 1999; Ghosh 2002; Joshi 2002.

What *do* literacy figures, unsatisfactory though they are as evidence, tell us then? Mostly, that to focus only on the low levels of literacy reveals very little about contemporary Indian readers' consumption of printed texts. A much more promising approach has been adopted by Priya Joshi in her fascinating account of the Indian consumption of the British novel in late-nineteenth-century India (Joshi 2002). Joshi analyses consumption patterns through a study of library holdings and borrowing practices. In the process she convincingly argues against the use of class as an analytic category in defining readership.

By contrast, other critics invoke class in their exploration of heterodox reading cultures defined by gender, community, and social status. No doubt, as cheap printed matter became more accessible, the reading public expanded to include larger sections of the lower social strata, who in turn shaped their own print cultures. Departing from a critique of the dominant analytical framework for studying Bengali culture—which has remained 'primarily concerned with middle class intellectuals' and 'dominant print culture shaped by the educated elite'—Anindita Ghosh has brought the lower-class reader into focus (Ghosh 2002). Her study of the popular commercial publishing trade in mid- to late-nineteenth-century Bengal suggests that the number of lower-middle-class urban and rural homes which consumed popular forms of printed literature was much larger than is usually assumed. Numerous 'cheap' presses in Calcutta's Battala area thrived on the tastes of these petty bourgeois readers, running a brisk trade in popular print which even surpassed the limited output of the city's more 'respectable' presses. Ghosh highlights the importance of this 'small book' trade in resisting the dominant cultural and literary norms that the 'culturally chauvinistic' *bhadralok* (genteel middle classes) tried to impose on non-elite groups.[20]

While I follow Joshi in rejecting a class-based classification of readership, this book throughout makes reference to the 'common reader', 'general reading public', and 'mass reading public'. I am fully aware that these terms constitute highly problematic analytical categories. The 'mass reading public', particularly, can only be a contextualized heuristic device. Given the fact that the Indian masses lacked both the education and the economic means to read and buy books, we can hardly speak of a mass reading public in the sense described by R.C. Altick in his seminal *The English Common Reader* (1957). To cite a famous example from

[20] For the 'disciplining' of popular print on the part of the *bhadralok*, see also Roy 1996.

British publishing history, Charles Dickens's *Pickwick Papers* created the first genuine British mass audience for literature with a circulation of 40,000 within the first five months of serialization in 1836 (Hughes/ Lund 1995: 151). Circulation figures for Indian periodicals are, of course, a far cry from this. Yet the gulf is much less evident when it comes to first print runs of belletristic works, where a figure of *c.* 1000 copies was frequently found in both the British metropolis and India.

Within the specific limits of the Indian context, the term 'mass reading public' can still make sense if we do not take it as a numerical variable to be measured against the entire population, but as a category indicative of the transformation in the size and nature of the literate audience which was brought about by the combined effects of colonial literacy and the commercialization of print. As I aim to show in this book, the common reader and the mass reading public certainly existed as potential categories in commercial publishers' minds. The connotation of 'mass' in India was simply different, referring to thousands rather than tens of thousands. In their immediate concern with the expansion of the reading public, a principal aim of Naval Kishore and his confreres was to bring printed literature to the people. Publishers deployed special advertising strategies and invested in promotional schemes to attract the broadest possible audience. Successful commercial publishing not only meant enlarging the number of readers by satisfying existing tastes and shaping new ones, it also meant inducing more and more people to buy books. Here, the financial factor was crucial. As will be shown, the NKP's policy of popularizing the printed book—a policy firmly based on reprints of classics, translations, and inexpensive books in small formats—was key to the firm's success.

In this context, Naval Kishore's patronage of the public library, another novel institution in the colonial literate sphere, assumes significance. Even if few in number and confined to urban spaces, public libraries were important multiplicators of print. Unlike Europe, in contemporary India the reader who did not want to regularly invest in books had limited avenues for cheap access to books. The flourishing railway libraries system of Victorian England, with its cheap pocket editions, did not have its Indian counterpart at this time, while commercial circulating libraries with their fresh arrivals from England catered almost exclusively to Europeans and the English-educated Indian elite. As Joshi has shown, British publishing firms carefully cultivated the colonial marketplace. In the wake of Macmillan's highly successful Colonial Library Series (est. 1886), all major British publishers at some point started their own

Foreign, Colonial, or Imperial library series (Joshi 2002: 94). For readers of Indian languages no such facilities existed. In this situation, the newly emerging public libraries and the reading rooms of colleges and learned societies assumed an important role in cultivating the reading habit.

The history of the public library system in northern India remains to be written.[21] In the metropolis the appalling lack of public library facilities had been brought to public notice in 1848. After a heated debate, the controversial Public Libraries Bill was passed in 1850, levying a rate in support of public libraries (Altick 1957: 224). When, in its wake, the scheme of setting up public libraries was placed on the colonial agenda, it found immediate support among the Indian educated elite . In trying to assess the role of public libraries in creating larger audiences, one has to remember that they not only functioned as institutionalized sites for private reading and public lecturing but also as book-borrowing facilities, making more books available to more readers at very little cost. This said, it is important to understand that public libraries at the time were not 'public' in the modern sense of the word—of giving free access to everybody. The term typically refers to a subscription library maintained and managed collectively by the subscribers and sustained by government grants (Mishra 1979: 22).

The foregoing discussion raises the question of whether there was a print 'revolution' in nineteenth-century India. Outlining historical continuities and the evolutionary aspect of intellectual transformation, C.A. Bayly has pointed to the existence of sophisticated systems of written social communication in the pre-print era. Print in itself did not create an information revolution, contends Bayly; rather, 'it speeded up the velocity and range of communication among existing communities of knowledge' (1996a: 243). Scholars in literary studies have highlighted the persistence of pre-print forms of textuality and tend to agree that the putative print revolution was not a generic revolution. Leaving aside the new surge of textbook literature, the most common types of books produced were similar to those in the pre-print era. The basic tendency, as

[21] The first permanent public library in India was set up in Calcutta in 1818, when the private holdings of the college library of Fort William were made available to the general public. For the first time a collection of 8341 printed books and almost 3000 manuscripts was made accessible not only to Europeans but to 'literary men in general in India'. Part of its holdings later merged into those of the Calcutta Public Library opened in 1836 (Kopf 1969: 187–9; Joshi 2002: 53–9). For early circulating and public libraries in Bengal, see Ohdedar 1966; Kabir 1987; for Maharashtra, see Mahajan 1984. Misra 1979 provides a general overview of the development of public libraries in India.

Blackburn has argued, was not to produce new genres or texts, but rather 'to reproduce more texts in old genres'. Orsini has offered a poignant formulation of print culture as '*genres reproduced* and *genres introduced*' (Orsini 2004: 435–6).[22]

In its concern with commercial publishing, *An Empire of Books* proposes to look at the print 'revolution' as a quantitative rather than qualitative or generic shift. It argues that one of the most 'revolutionary' aspects of print was that, once it reached the stage of commercialization, it provided a hitherto unknown general access to the products of written culture among literate audiences. India's legendary richness in manuscripts easily allows one to forget that, for the average Indian reader, manuscripts were expensive and hard to come by, as borne out by perennial contemporary complaints. This, to a certain extent, also holds true for the printed book in its early phase. The step from the rare and costly manuscript to the mass-produced printed book—costing barely one-tenth the price of a manuscript, if not less (Davis 1983: 16) and available through a rapidly expanding network of distribution sites and agents—was indeed revolutionary. To illustrate this point: Naval Kishore, an Indian publisher of Hindu origin, was most likely the world's first publisher to issue in 1868 a finely printed Qurʾan at the sensational price of Rs 1, 8 *as.*, thus bringing the holy book within reach of an unprecedented number of ordinary Muslims. While general accessibility remains to a certain extent a theoretical construct and does not imply that every Indian at all times had books within his reach or could actually afford to buy them, commercial mass printing altered power configurations within the cognitive and literary domain. Knowledge was no longer the preserve of small elites but expanded into the public realm.

To study a publisher's production and sales figures can help to establish the general popularity of an author or genre, and possibly to infer the canonical status of a given text, yet it reveals little about the composition of the readership in terms of religious affiliation, class, and gender. Likewise, the study of a commercial publishing house cannot enlighten us about individual tastes, consumption practices, and a book's impact,[23] but may provide valuable insights into consumption *trends* and thus help

[22] See also Bayly 1996a: 242.

[23] As Jonathan Rose suggests, one should be wary of the assumption, 'widely shared among students of popular culture', that the influence of a given book is 'directly proportional to its circulation' (Rose 1995: 205). The sensational Victorian novelist G.W.M. Reynolds, arguably the most widely read author in England at the height of his career (and a favourite with Indian readers, too), easily outsold Charles Dickens in the metropolitan market, but failed to register in contemporary Victorian

provide answers to the vexed question of the circulation of printed books. As we will see, contemporary British officials and Indian observers differed widely in their assumptions about the impact of the printed book on reading behaviour (Chapter 1). Modern critics, too, depending on their academic background and agenda, tend to disagree in their assessments. While Pollock cautions that in the subcontinent the printed book remained, and continues to remain, 'out of the reach of many people' (Pollock 2003: 22), Joshi invokes an India 'in which Indians passionately, powerfully, and persistently read—and often wrote—seemingly everything that the empire of print purveyed and made available' (Joshi 2002: 280). Indeed, there is ample evidence that more reading was done than the bare circulation of newspapers or sales figures of books would suggest. While it is impossible to determine how many readers or listeners were reached by a given book, the printed book introduced new cultural practices, allowing for both individual and shared reading.[24] Critics have pointed to the importance of prevailing practices of shared reading and reading aloud in providing access to literary and print culture among non-literates. Like newspapers and periodicals, books were read to household members, friends, and menials or to wider audiences in public settings. Even conventional forms of recitation located in the traditional domain of religious public performance started to make use of the printed text.[25] Against this backdrop, Ghosh's questioning of the assumption that literacy is a necessary precondition for identifying consumers of print literature (Ghosh 2002: 4332) seems particularly relevant.

The issue of readership then leaves us with more queries than answers. Much rigorous empirical research needs to be done before we can say what and how much was being read by whom. For Hindi and Urdu, especially, the study of consumption, reading practices, and reader response remains a huge scholarly enterprise which will require the collective

reader surveys of favourite authors and did not secure a place among canonized authors in English literature.

[24] James Long, in his 1859 survey of the Bengal book trade, calculated that there were six million readers or listeners for over 600,000 copies of Bengali books issued in 1857, at the rate of 10 persons per book. His estimate for newspapers was about the same, with 2950 copies being read by approximately 30,000 readers. No similar estimates exist for North India. In 1853, 39 newspapers and periodicals were circulated in the NWP in a total of 1839 copies. In the following year, circulation had gone up to 3223 copies and would continue to rise rapidly.

[25] See, e.g., Long 1859; Roy 1996: 46; Metcalf 1990: 21; Naregal 2001: 31–2; Ghosh 2002.

effort of a body of scholars. Such an investigation must necessarily draw on very different sources from the ones on which this book is based, and include a survey of private testimonies—autobiographies, memoirs, letters, the proceedings of literary associations, the inventories and borrowing records of public libraries, and so on.

Indigenous Responses to Print

Commercial publishers operated in and negotiated a field of conflicting opinions in relation to print. Members of the English-educated Indian elite generally welcomed the printing press as an agent of enlightenment, progress, and social change. On establishing the first 'modern' school in Benares, Jai Narayan Ghoshal, an ex-superintendent of the Calcutta police, rich merchant, and convert to Christianity, in 1818 requested the London Church Missionary Society to send a printing press to Benares, judging it one of the 'most effectual means' for 'enlightening the mind' of his countrymen. Without the possibility of multiplying and dispersing textbooks and treatises on different subjects throughout the country, he contended, 'the progress of knowledge must be very slow, and the Hindus long remain in their very fallen state, which is a very painful consideration to a benevolent mind'.[26] Some forty years later, the foremost Benares educationist Raja Shiva Prasad so highly estimated the importance of print that, in his widely used alphabetical primer *Varṇamālā* (Garland of Letters, 1860), he inserted under the letter 'ch' an illustration of a printing press (*chāpe kī kal*) amidst the familiar drawings of animals and vehicles. Among Muslim intellectuals, Sayyid Imdad Husain, editor of the *Dehlī Urdū Akhbār,* showered praise on colonial officials in 1853 for having introduced the first printing presses in Delhi, thereby encouraging his countrymen to set up their own presses and participate in the diffusion of knowledge. 'May God increase their number every day', he piously hoped.[27] Noting that the printing press had brought all sorts of learned books within easy reach of 'the common people', the great Bharatendu Harishchandra asserted in 1883 that it had doubtless led to 'the dawning of a new age for mankind' (Harishchandra 1989: 564). In Bengal, the anglophile Brahmo Samajist Bholanauth Chunder went as far as claiming

[26] Cited in Long 1848: 70. Ghoshal's application included a request for one or two suitable missionaries to be sent along as supervisors of the press, 'men of learning who may be able to satisfy the inquiries of the learned of this ancient city on subjects of science and history as well as of religion.'

[27] *Dehlī Urdū Akhbār* of 8 August 1853. I am grateful to Margrit Pernau for providing me with the original text of the editorial.

that 'Nothing less than Hindoostan ought to be given away to the English in grateful reward for their introducing the *art of printing*' which, he enthusiastically asserted, was 'emancipating thousands of minds from the yoke of a superstition that held us as brutes for centuries' (Chunder 1869: 229).

While such a view was certainly not shared by many, the enthusiasm that print generated did not remain confined to the progressive and modernizing sections of society. Print also made inroads into the milieux of traditional education and religious orthodoxy, overcoming religiously and socially grounded reservations. A potent means of propagating ideas and exerting influence, print was adopted by the orthodox and reformers, by traditionalist, revivalists, and modernists. It cut across boundaries, providing a powerful example of the limitations of the outdated traditionalist–modernist dichotomy. Generating a vast corpus of tract and pamphlet literature, it shaped the dissemination of religious knowledge and had a profound impact on the nature of religious teaching. As scholars of Indian Islam have shown, reformist Muslims were among the first to avail themselves of the printing press (Metcalf 1982; Robinson 1993, 1996, 2001). Print was crucial to the spread of Islamic reformist ideas, opening up a whole new discursive sphere of religious debate. Avril Powell, in her compelling study of the religious interface between Christian missionaries and Muslims in pre-Mutiny India, has demonstrated the great familiarity of leading Indian ʿulama with printed translations of the Bible and missionary tracts, which shaped the Christian–Muslim encounter (Powell 1993). The use of printed texts on both sides, often assuming the proportion of pamphlet wars, enlarged the audiences of traditional forms of public religious disputation (*munāẓara*) beyond local confines.

Among those concerned with the impact of print on contemporary Hinduism, William Pinch has outlined how, within Hindu sectarian groups, the popularization of print encouraged processes of self-reflexivity and led to an 'increasing doctrinal self-consciousness' in bringing to light and juxtaposing the variety of local, often conflicting, exegeses. In the process, principal sectarian texts were reinterpreted and put to a specific use (Pinch 1996: 54). Following the example of both Christian missionaries and Bengali reformers, Hindu religious leaders, while steeped in the world of oral transmission, recognized the power of the printed word and began to exploit it to propagate their views. Perhaps the most salient example is that of Swami Dayanand Sarasvati, founder of the Hindu reformist Arya Samaj. Jordens reports an angry outburst of the Swami who, when touring the Punjab in the 1870s, found that not a single printed copy of the Veda could be procured in the town he was visiting, while missionaries were busy translating and selling cheap editions of the Bible in every regional language. Dayanand seized, if somewhat belatedly, the opportunities provided by print: he established his own press and started seeing his lectures and teachings into print, thus turning from public speaker to 'publicist of the pen' (Jordens 1978: 166).

Yet the Indian reaction to print was not without its ambivalences. There were reservations even among those modernizing sections of the intelligentsia who welcomed print and availed themselves of its possibilities. In opening up an easy and cheap avenue to knowledge, print challenged exclusivist elite notions of higher learning. Its impact on traditional religious education, especially, was seen as a mixed blessing. Sayyid Ahmad Khan, commenting on Shah ᶜAbdul ᶜAziz's Urdu translation of the Qurʾan, remarked in the 1840s: '[At present] every commoner believes himself to be a scholar and every ignoramus regards himself as a learned man. Merely on the basis of having read a few chapbooks on religious issues and a translation of the Qurʾan, and that too in Urdu, with some ordinary teacher or just through his own effort, he considers himself as a jurist and an exegete and dares to preach and opine on issues.'[28] The great poet Mirza Ghalib, in a lighter vein, poked fun at a learned friend of his, insinuating that the latter owed his entire erudition to 'having purchased fifty rupees' worth of two-penny books' (Rahbar 1987: 127). Evidently, the general accessibility and democratizing trajectory of the printed book provoked latent fears about appropriations of elite knowledge by the populace.

Genteel traditions of learning were not the only issue at stake. Increasing attention has recently been paid to the larger divides between elite and popular cultural norms, reinforced by commercial print, which led to a project of sanitizing literary tastes and marginalizing popular cultures on the part of upper-class elites (Roy 1996; Gupta 2001). The colonial state, while deploying print as a vehicle of ideology and essential tool in education, had similar reservations about print, manifest in its preoccupation with 'taste' and 'refinement'.

Publishers and the Colonial State

Critics have looked at print as an instrument of colonial ideological domination, especially in the domain of education. Print, as Veena Naregal has pointed out, was not only a new communicative technology, it also

[28] Cited in Naim 2003: 17. The quote is taken from Sayyid Ahmad Khan's *Ās̤ār aṣ-ṣanādīd* (first published in 1847).

signified 'a shift from prevailing assumptions about the distribution of cultural and political power' (Naregal 2001: 4). At the cultural level it introduced 'radical shifts in assumptions about language, literacy and the "literary"' (ibid.: 146). Rather than focusing on print only as a colonial project, *An Empire of Books* seeks to examine an Indian publisher's own cultural and literary agendas. Nonetheless, the relationship between publisher and colonial state remains central to this book.

The rise of the NKP roughly coincided with a major shift in colonial education policy following Charles Wood's Education Despatch of 1854. In a clear departure from the anglicist policy laid out in Macaulay's infamous Minute on Education and the ensuing English Education Act of 1835, it ushered in a new era in colonial education marked by the official promotion of the modern regional languages and their literatures.[29] The policy shift provided a distinct impetus to the nascent domestic publishing industry in Hindi and Urdu. Publishers were widely co-opted into the colonial literacy and education project. To the colonial state, itself a large player in the publishing field, Indian commercial publishers were both collaborators and financial rivals. The state had a vested interest in encouraging private agency, which was to be duly instrumentalized in favour of the British civilizing mission. At the same time, it needed to assert its claims to cultural hegemony, and its economic interests through keeping a check on the extent of agency and the proliferating operations of indigenous printer-publishers, especially in the lucrative and highly competitive textbook sector. As will be shown, state control over the publishing trade happened via three powerful mechanisms: licensing, censorship, and patronage.

Marked by cooperation and contestation, the publisher–state interface provides a salient example of the transactional character of the colonial encounter at large. In making this point a guiding assumption of this book, I follow recent approaches that replace the old interpretive model of colonialism as an 'oppressive structure', or as a one-way relation of dominance and conquest, by a theory of transaction (Trivedi 1993; Joshi 2002). Indian publishers engaged with the state in a dynamic relationship that, if by no means symmetric or egalitarian, was based on continuous negotiation, dialogue, and exchange. This transactional character powerfully illustrates Eugene Irschick's formulation of the creation of knowledge as a 'dialogic process' (Irschick 1994).

[29] Aimed to create an Indian anglicized elite, the English Education Act made the promotion of European literature and sciences the primary object of British educational efforts and decreed that all educational funds were to be employed on English education alone.

These concerns will in various degrees inform the individual chapters of this book. Chapter 1 looks at North Indian print culture in its wider historical perspective. It traces the emergence of the printed book in Hindi and Urdu from its beginnings to the phase of commercialization, introducing several important figures and centres in early publishing. It also addresses issues of state intervention in the book trade—press legislation, registration, and obscenity laws. Chapter 2 is devoted to the biography and public life of Munshi Naval Kishore. The commercial history of the NKP is outlined in Chapter 3. Chapter 4 examines the relationship between the House of Naval Kishore and the colonial state, describing the nature and extent of collaboration in official and textbook printing and highlighting various areas of contestation. Chapter 5 takes a look within, probing the publishing house as an intellectual space and outlining the NKP's contribution in the field of scholarly publishing. Chapter 6 looks at a second cornerstone of the House of Naval Kishore, and a publishing success of a different kind, namely its Urdu newspaper *Avadh Akhbār*. Chapter 7, finally, examines the publisher's engagement with Hindi literature and literary tradition.

This Introduction would not be complete without alerting the reader to some limitations of this book: scholars of Urdu literature will immediately notice that it devotes a special chapter to Hindi but does not contain a separate chapter on the Urdu publications of the NKP. Given the firm's outstanding importance in Urdu publishing and the 'inestimable services' (Russell 1992: 86) it rendered to Urdu literature, this calls for an explanation. The reasons have mainly to do with the genesis of this book. My academic background is in Hindi literature, and I thus first conceived it as an investigation into a little-acknowledged aspect of NKP publishing, namely the firm's promotion of Hindi and Sanskrit literature.[30] Approximately a third of NKP publications are works in Hindi (including Khari boli, Brajbhasha and Avadhi) and Sanskrit. However, it soon became apparent that this was too limited an approach. To adopt the broader perspective of a book historian and probe the history and

[30] This neglect of the NKP has to do with a general trend in Hindi literary studies, which for the nineteenth century have tended to concentrate on Benares, Allahabad, and Agra, focusing on Bharatendu Harishchandra (1850–85) and other prominent figures of his literary coterie. Developments in Hindi literature outside these established centres have received much less attention, especially if they happened in a place like Lucknow, a city traditionally associated with Indo-Muslim and Urdu culture. Further, one has to note that studies of Hindi literature in the nineteenth century, if not text-immanent, often focus on issues of cultural, political, and social ideology. By contrast, there is a paucity of empirical work on the material, technological, and organizational aspects of the literary sphere.

impact of the publishing house seemed an undertaking of much greater pertinence to the study of literary culture and intellectual history in nineteenth-century India. As a result, this book, while concerned with both Hindi and Urdu, shows a certain bias for the former and may occasionally be seen to falter when it comes to assessing aspects of Urdu literary culture.

The second reason for not delving deeper into Urdu is the problem of sheer quantity. To narrate the story of the NKP *and* offer a detailed account of the firm's Urdu publications is well beyond the scope of a single book. Given the awesome total of an estimated 5000 titles published by Naval Kishore during his lifetime, of which over 2000 are in Urdu, even a superficial analysis of this large body would have blown this book to an unpublishable size.[31] Besides, a substantial number of monographs and papers on the House of Naval Kishore is already available to Urdu-reading scholars and students. To leave the complex task of presenting an in-depth study of the firm's Urdu publications to an expert in the field seemed all the more advisable in light of the fact that a large portion of NKP Urdu titles consists of Islamic literature—religious classics in translation, treatises in the Islamic sciences, sectarian tracts and pamphlets, works of Sufi mysticism—which call for contextual analysis by a scholar of South Asian Islam rather than of literary studies. To compensate for this lack, I have included an extensive appendix of NKP Urdu publications in the hope that this will encourage further research by those interested in Urdu.

This said, the book does reflect as much as possible the huge and important literary, linguistic, religious and cultural undertaking that Urdu publishing at the NKP presented. It does so in a deliberate attempt to overcome a well-established academic tradition—partly rooted in the historic dichotomization of Hindi and Urdu—to deal with the two languages and literatures separately. Such separation has, both inadvertently and deliberately, reinforced the existing divide. One of the most important insights in writing this book has been that to view Naval Kishore's engagement with India's past and present literary cultures from an exclusive 'Hindi' or 'Urdu' perspective would be a highly dissatisfactory and misguided undertaking. Such an approach, moreover, would fail to give an authentic and adequate picture of the cultural notions and intellectual

[31] The NKP comprehensive catalogue prepared by Prag Narayan in 1895 included 4500 titles. Not listed in it are titles printed at the firm's Kanpur and Lahore branches. Their number is estimated at another 500 (Siddiqi 1981: 15).

climate that informed the policy of the House. As Orsini has argued with much insight, a study of Hindi publishing 'would necessarily have to be one of Hindi *and* Urdu publishing, for they were part of an osmotic literary system' (Orsini 2002: 68). As the present investigation into a Lucknow-based publishing house seeks to show, her argument holds all the more true for the nineteenth century. Underlying the NKP's policy was a strong notion of a cultural continuum between the Hindi and Urdu literary spheres, which, despite internal shifts in emphasis and external contestations, was never dismissed.

A similar shortcoming of this study concerns the vast and important contribution made by the NKP to book publishing in Persian and Arabic. Given my linguistic limitations, I could only scratch the surface of the firm's pioneering and formative influence in diffusing religious, literary, and scientific knowledge in the classical Oriental languages. The House of Naval Kishore engaged in the commercial mass production of Arabic and Persian books at a time when printing in the Middle East was still in its infancy, and thus developed a thriving export business. Its large corpus of religious and secular texts in Arabic and Persian made a distinct impact in India and the larger Islamic world. As one observer asserts, 'Even an Islamic country was not able to stimulate the history of Islam in the same way as did the Naval Kishore Press' (Siddiqi 1981: 17). This outstanding contribution to Islamic publishing still awaits proper evaluation.

A particularly aggravating circumstance in the making of this book, sadly familiar to those studying Indian print culture, was the paucity of primary sources. Despite the NKP's historical significance, nothing has survived of the publisher's archives but for a few stray documents. In the absence of account books and ledgers, business correspondence and private papers, this study was undertaken without the very documents that constitute the most important sources for the book historian. The more or less regular coverage in colonial records of various aspects of NKP commercial activity could only partly fill this lacuna. As a result, basic questions concerning the publisher's interaction with booksellers and traders, his financial statements and sales records, the motivation underlying promotional schemes and their nature and scope, and so on, can only be answered tentatively. Equally frustrating, the central issue of author–publisher relations, which makes for so much compelling and insightful writing on publishing and the book trade in Victorian England, could only be addressed in a most rudimentary fashion. It remains to be seen whether this book can provide some encouragement to future researchers to take up the complex task of reviewing the fascinating history of early Hindi and Urdu publishing from the perspective of authors.

One final point: in giving publication details of a large number of original works or translations in Persian, Sanskrit, Hindi, and Urdu, this study at times borders on a descriptive bibliography. I am fully aware that this can be tedious, especially for readers with a more general interest in Indian book history. Yet to insist on bibliographical detail seemed a methodological imperative in view of the fact that publication data on nineteenth-century books in Indian languages are not easy to come by and usually have to be collected in a painstaking process from a variety of sources.[32] Much solid and meticulous bibliographical groundwork needs to be done to provide the empirical underpinnings for a more systematic theoretical discussion of the history of the book in South Asia. In assembling data that have not been recorded earlier in an English-language source, the present book is an attempt in this direction. In order not to overburden the text, a good deal of the bibliographical information has been relegated to the various appendices. The aim in compiling these is to offer a database of Hindi and Urdu imprints amenable to future analysis.

[32] For example, James F. Blumhardt's important catalogues of Hindustani and Hindi printed books in the library of the British Museum fail to list publishers' names.

1
The Coming of the Book in Hindi and Urdu

The introduction of print to India dates back to the year 1556, when Portuguese Jesuit missionaries set up the first printing press in Goa.[1] Two decades later, the first book in an Indian language and script appeared in the form of the *Doctrina Christam* (1577), a Tamil translation of a Portuguese catechism prepared by the Jesuit Henri Henriques.[2] By contrast, it was not until the last decades of the eighteenth century that northern India saw a similar turning point in its cultural history when, for the first time, the introduction of movable type fonts enabled the production of printed matter in Arabic, Persian, Bengali, Urdu, and Hindi on Indian soil. This momentous event marked the 'real advent of print' in the East and North of the subcontinent. It was followed by another revolutionary development in the 1820s, when the introduction of lithography opened up the realm of print to Indian agency, allowing for widespread Indian ownership of printing presses. At the technological level, these innovations together formed the starting point for the emergence of the Indian-language press and the printed book in Hindi and Urdu.

Several explanations have been offered as to why the North Indian Muslim rulers showed no apparent interest in the printing press, despite the early presence of Jesuit missionaries at the Mughal court and the vigorous interaction of the court with European scholars and travellers. The sophistication of manuscript production and culture under Mughal rule may have been a disincentive, preventing the adoption of print technology. The prestigious and influential establishment of professional copyists, the monopoly maintained by cheap and easily accessible bazaar

[1] The first books printed in India are said to be Antonio de Quadros's *Conclusoes* (1558) and Gaspar de Leao's *Compendio spiritual da vida christa* (1560). For the early history of printing in India, see Priolkar 1959 and Kesavan 1986.

[2] For a detailed account of early books in Tamil, see Blackburn 2003: 26–72.

writers, ritual objections to printing religious texts, and politically motivated hostility to the press among indigenous rulers have been cited as further impediments.[3] Francis Robinson also cogently points to the valorization of oral transmission in Islamic tradition, which had to be compromised only when Islam came under attack from various sides in the nineteenth century (Robinson 1993; 1996). In addressing the important question of why, at that point, Indian Muslims adopted print technology with so much vigour and at a much faster pace than other Islamic populations, Robinson persuasively argues that in the colonial situation print was for Indian Muslims a powerful weapon in counteracting the combined threat of colonial rule, Christian proselytizing, and a Hindu majority population.[4] At a time when Islam was perceived to be under threat, print became crucial in asserting Islamic identity; it was key to broadcasting religious knowledge and fostering a deeper understanding of Islamic traditions among Indian Muslims. Indian ʿulama used the new technology of print to compensate for the loss of political power: 'If Islam could no longer be supported by the swords of Muslim princes, it could now be supported by the enhanced religious understanding of Muslims themselves' (Robinson 1996: 72).

Serving as a preliminary to our study of the NKP, this chapter will look at the phenomenon of print in modern North Indian languages in its wider historical context. The first sections will sketch the history of the Hindi and Urdu printed book from the time it was ushered into life and raised by colonial scholar-administrators and Christian missionaries, to the time it reached adulthood and flourished under Indian aegis. In tracing this process, the focus will be on the Indian agents at the heart of book production, that is the printer-publishers of East and, subsequently, North India. Having looked at several early centres of print in the NWP and Avadh, the later sections probe the emergence of commercial print culture in the post-1857 period. The social background of some North Indian printer-publishers will be explored. The final section will outline the conditions imposed on the domestic publishing trade by colonial rule and describe some of the specific difficulties that Indian publishers encountered in their profession on account of state regulation.

[3] Bayly 1996a: 238. Priolkar cites instances of Brahminical rejection of print on acount of issues such as fear of pollution: it was feared that printing ink contained animal fat that would defile the texts (Priolkar 1958: 128–9). However, this difficulty could easily be solved by substituting vegetable oil for unclean animal fat (Diehl 1973: 122–3).

[4] For the adoption of print in various parts of the Islamic world, see Atiyeh 1995.

The printed book features prominently in a number of processes marking Indian modernization. The emergence of Hindi and Urdu as modern print languages and the concomitant development of the regional-language book trade coincided with their rise in the North Indian public sphere in a mutually stimulating process. Print culture shaped the public sphere even as it was shaped by it. Urdu and Hindi were put to new public uses via processes that relied heavily on print, while these uses in turn generated an increasing demand for printed literature in the modern languages. The new print media generated modes of 'public' opinion and participation and facilitated the formation of collective identity.[5] They also opened up new ways of acquiring, managing, and diffusing knowledge, which were equally essential to modern political, social, and cultural discourse. Together, print and the 'vernacularization' of education induced far-reaching changes in the cognitive and literary realms.

From the late eighteenth century, Urdu began to gather prestige as the lingua franca of the educated classes and gained momentum as a prose idiom. Urdu got a great boost in 1837 when it replaced Persian as the language of the court and administration in the NWP. Preceding and accompanying its new public status of 'official vernacular' was the acceptance of Urdu as a language of religious expression and a vehicle of rationalist and scientific discourse. Avril Powell has shown how printed texts came to form an essential element of the early Christian–Muslim encounter (Powell 1993). The circulation of the *Mīzān al-ḥaqq* (Balance of the Truth, 1835) and other influential tracts by a German pietist missionary, Karl Hermann Pfander, provoked a series of refutations on the part of Lucknow's leading ʿulama, marking the beginning of 'an era of prolonged tract warfare between Islam and Christianity in northern India' (ibid.: 172–3). Print came to be closely intertwined with Islamic revival. Muslim traditionalists and reformers were pre-eminent in making use of the print media to publish religious classics and their own contemporary writings. In the process, Urdu gained ground as the language of an original religious literature. The first translations of the Qurʾan into Urdu, undertaken in the late eighteenth century by Shah ʿAbdul Qadir Dehlavi and Shah Rafiuddin Dehlavi, the sons of the great Muslim thinker Shah

[5] The mutual stimulus of the Indian-language press and the creation of public opinion can first be witnessed in the socio-religious controversy over sati in the 1830s. The sati debate gave an enormous impetus to the Indian press and generated a number of short-lived journals that acted as mouthpieces of either orthodox or reformist opinion.

Waliullah of Delhi, had constituted an important landmark in the acceptance of Urdu as a religious idiom. They provided the impetus to much further translation activity, initiating a proliferation of religious texts in Urdu which, from the late 1820s, began to circulate in print.[6] This widespread dissemination of religious and scientific classics in the modern idiom was 'clearly key to the effectiveness of the reformist movement' (Metcalf 1982: 206).

As a new means of disseminating Islamic knowledge and reformist thought across a broader section of society, mass-printed Urdu texts had a profound impact on religious education. Circulated in print from the 1820s, an influential reformist text such as the *Taqwiyat al-īmān* (Strengthening of the Faith) not only marked the beginning of an original religious literature in Urdu, but was able to reach far larger audiences of readers and listeners than had ever been known before. By opting to write in simple Urdu its author, Shah Muhammad Ismaʿil, explicitly addressed himself to a large new audience of 'ordinary' Muslims (Metcalf 1982: 200–1). By the late 1850s, cheap tracts and pamphlets churned out by Indian presses were making inroads into traditional Islamic education. As Robinson has argued, the mass-produced printed text, while initially strengthening the position of the ʿulama, ultimately undermined their authority. In breaking the ʿulama's monopoly over the transmission of knowledge, print gradually induced religious change (Robinson 1993: 245).

The nineteenth century saw the consolidation and linguistic codification of Urdu and Hindi as modern literary idioms, a process in which printed textbooks produced under missionary and colonial aegis played an important part. The rise of the modern languages generated a flurry of translation activity on the part of literary and scientific societies, scholars, and literati, who sought to revive old and propagate 'modern' knowledge through the printed word in Urdu, and increasingly, in Hindi. With nascent Hindu nationalism and revivalism, Hindi was assigned an important new role as the vehicle of a distinct Hindu consciousness and was soon to challenge the position of Urdu (Dalmia 1996). In the literary domain within both languages the shaping of a literary canon was under way. The emergence of new literary genres, such as the modern novel and discursive prose writing, was closely linked to new publication formats in the print media.

[6] Metcalf 1982: 199–215; Russell/Khurshidul Islam 1994: 31. For the translation of the Qurʾan into Urdu, see also *HLHH* I: 76–87.

Despite the centrality of the printed book in these processes, research on the history of the book in Hindi and Urdu has been fragmentary and uneven. That the earliest phase of Hindi and Urdu printing in the subcontinent is comparatively well documented is largely due to the efforts of Graham Shaw, who, alongside his pioneering study, *Printing in Calcutta to 1800* (1981), contributed a series of seminal essays.[7] Urdu publishing in the nineteenth century has received a fair amount of attention in the pioneering works of Imdad Sabiri, Muhammad ᶜAtiq Siddiqi, Nazir Ahmad, and Nadir ᶜAli Khan, who painstakingly collected data on individual printing presses from all over northern India.[8] These studies and compilations contain a mine of valuable information for the book historian. None of them has so far been translated into English.

The picture looks more dismal for the history of the book in Hindi. Information on the early spread of Hindi printing in the Hindi-speaking region is especially hard to come by. While missionary and official efforts have received some attention (Vedalankar 1969), there is hardly any work that explores Indian involvement in early Hindi book production. This is of course owing to the fact that the North Indian book trade was for a long time dominated by Persian and Urdu, with Hindi printing constituting only a secondary activity for most presses. A full-fledged Hindi print industry only developed from the late 1860s. As a result, the period 1830–60 stands out as a largely undocumented 'dark area', within which the long-awaited third volume of B.S. Kesavan's *History of Printing and Publishing in India* (1997) is a telling example. Contrary to its claim to cover the 'Origins of printing and publishing in the Hindi heartland', it fails to provide any substantial insights into the development of Hindi publishing during precisely the period 1830–57, passing more or less directly from Fort William College and the Calcutta presses to the post-1857 scenario. Moreover, Kesavan's study contains much inaccurate information.

The first classificatory overview of Hindi books, attempted by Mataprasad Gupta in 1947, is equally lacking, in that it covers a period beginning only from 1867 (Gupta 1947). To gather reliable data on early imprints in Hindi, one needs to resort to the holdings of libraries, private collections, and other bibliographical source material and from these

[7] Shaw 1989, 1991, 1994, 1997a &b, and 1998.

[8] Sabiri 1953 and 1973; Siddiqi 1957 and 1962; Ahmad 1985: 104–55; Khan 1990. By contrast, the standard works on early Urdu journalism by ᶜAbdus Salam Khurshid (Khurshid 1963; 1964) and Nadir ᶜAli Khan (Khan 1991) are available in English.

deduce a history. This was the approach adopted by Krishnacarya in his pioneering study *Hindī ke ādimudrit granth* (1966), the first systematic attempt at a bibliography of early printed books in Hindi. While Krishnacarya's work remains unsurpassed in many ways,[9] his periodization of Hindi printing into three periods—(1) Lalluji period (1801–22), (2) Missionary period (1822–44), and (3) Shiva Prasad period (1845–70)—appears problematic. Although his effort to highlight the contribution of individual figures is commendable, he grossly overstates the role of Lalluji Lal (d. 1825) and Raja Shiva Prasad (1823–95) in the domain of print. Undoubtedly, both were eminent figures in nineteenth-century Hindi literature, but dubbing Lalluji the 'Caxton of India' is as fallacious as calling Shiva Prasad the leading force in Hindi printing up to 1870.

A more convincing classification of major periods in early Hindi printing has been offered by Dhirendranath Singh in his pioneering study of the Khadgavilas Press of Bankipur (Patna), the first influential literary publishing house in Hindi, which rose to fame as the publisher of Bharatendu Harishchandra (Singh 1986). In distinguishing between three periods—(1) Missionary period (1800–58), (2) Naval Kishore period (1858–80), and (3) Khadgavilas period (1880–1926)—Singh was the first to highlight the role of individual Indian publishers in shaping Hindi print culture. He was also the first to point to the central importance of the NKP in Hindi publishing during the second half of the century, a formative stage in the development of modern Hindi literature. Although Singh's periodization favours the misconception that the NKP's heyday was over by 1880, it clearly underscores the pivotal role of the Lucknow press in commercial Hindi printing for a period stretching more than three decades.

What did the landscape of Hindi and Urdu printing look like before the middle of the nineteenth century, before large commercial publishers like Naval Kishore entered the scene? What were the circumstances under which early printer-publishers operated, and what was the size and scope of book production? In drawing on a variety of English-, Hindi-, and Urdu-language sources, the following account seeks to give a brief sketch of the early phase of printing and publishing in the North Indian languages, moving in subsequent stages from Calcutta and its environs to the Hindi–Urdu region. As we will see, in early Hindi and Urdu book

[9] The most voluminous modern compilation which purports to be a comprehensive bibliography of Hindi imprints from the beginning to 1964 is the *Hindī-sāhitya-sāriṇī* (1971) issued from the Hoshiarpur Vishveshvaranand Institute. It follows a generic rather than chronological arrangement of titles and is utterly defective in its documentation of pre-1870 imprints.

production, success and failure came in equal measure: encountering severe financial difficulties, many of the early Indian private and commercial printer-publishers were forced to relive the experiences of their European precursors in the late eighteenth century.[10] Even though lithography opened up the realm of print to Indians by greatly reducing costs, for more than one North Indian pioneer of print the words uttered by the French-born Calcutta printer Haji Mustapha at the end of his career would become a prophesy: 'Printing in this country requires a young man and a rich one, and I am neither' (cited in Shaw 1981: 27).

1.1 Early Printing in Hindi and Urdu

The earliest known specimens of printing in Nagari, and in the Perso-Arabic script used for Urdu, hail from Europe. Specimens of Nagari first appeared in books printed in Europe from 1625 onwards, while movable Nagari types were cast in Rome as early as 1740.[11] Benjamin Schultze's translation of the New Testament into Urdu (Dakkhini) was printed in Halle in 1758 using Arabic type. When, in the late eighteenth century, movable types first came into use in the northern part of the subcontinent, it was in Calcutta, the youngest of the presidency towns and seat of the East India Company administration, that printing in various Indian languages really took off. Calcutta was not only a trading place of a cosmopolitan character; under Governor General Warren Hastings it also became a stronghold of Orientalist scholarship which centred around three important institutions—the Calcutta Madrasah (est. 1781), the Asiatic Society of Bengal (est. 1784), and, later, under Hastings' successor Marquess Wellesley, Fort William College (est. 1800).[12] Although Madras was the first of the colonial metropolises to print books in an Indian

[10] The line of demarcation between 'private' and 'commercial' printer is particularly difficult to draw for the early phase of printing in North India. I largely follow the definition of a 'private' press proposed in Ransom 1963, that is, a press reserved for personal and not public use, usually set up in a private residence or the buildings of an association, for which financial gain is clearly secondary to literary, scholarly, artistic, and typographic pursuits.

[11] The first known printed book to make use of Nagari types is the *China monumentis illustrata* (Amsterdam 1667) by the renaissance scholar Athanasius Kircher, which contains a description of the entire Devanagari syllabary supplied by the Jesuit missionary Heinrich Roth. The earliest specimens of printing from movable metal types in Nagari can be found in the *Alphabetum Brammhanicum seu Indostanum universitatis Kasi* (Rome 1771). For early Nagari printing in Europe, see Shaw 1997a.

[12] For a detailed account of these institutions, see Kopf 1969.

language, notably Tamil (Blackburn 2003: 58), from the 1780s onwards Calcutta developed into the largest centre of printing in South Asia. It was here that the printed book in Hindi and Urdu first saw the light of day.

The beginning of regional-language printing in Bengal is generally associated with the Orientalist scholar-official and pioneer of Indian typography Charles Wilkins (1750–1836). Wilkins had come to Calcutta in 1770 as a writer in the East India Company's service. At the governor general's request and with the assistance of the Bengali blacksmith Pancanan Karmakar, he cast the earliest known fonts of Bengali type in 1778. They were used to print Nathaniel Halhed's *A Grammar of the Bengal Language* (1778). As superintendent of the newly set up Company's Press, he also manufactured an elegant font of *nastaʿlīq* types used to print Francis Gladwin's *A Compendious Vocabulary, English and Persian* (1780), Francis Balfour's *Inshā-yi Harkaran* (The Forms of Herkern, 1781), and a plethora of other works in Persian. Wilkins did not, however, cast any Nagari font until his return to England in 1786.[13] The credit for preparing the first Nagari founts used for printing in India goes instead to the Chronicle Press, one of the earliest commercial presses of Calcutta, established jointly by Daniel Stuart and Joseph Cooper in 1786. The two Englishmen set up a type foundry where Bengali, Nagari, and Persian types were cast. In 1789 the Chronicle Press issued a volume of the *New Asiatick Miscellany*, which contained some Sanskrit verses and an ode (*rekhta*) by the Dakkhini poet Wali Gujarati in the Devanagari script. These verses not only constitute the first known instance of a Nagari fount having been successfully cast in India; Wali's ode also stands out as the first Urdu literary text to be printed in India (Shaw 1981: 32). The Chronicle Press assumes importance in the early history of Hindi and Urdu printing in several respects: it issued John Gilchrist's *Dictionary, English and Hindoostanee* (1786–90) and his *Grammar of the Hindoostanee Language* (1796); its Nagari and *nastaʿlīq* fonts were used to print a number of celebrated works, such as *Ulfaz udwiyeh* (1793), a *materia medica* containing a large number of names printed in Nagari. Around the same time, Peter Spalding, type-founder at the East India Company's Calcutta mint, also began to cast *nastaʿlīq* and Nagari fonts. His Nagari types were used for printing translations of government

[13] Wilkins's Persian types were described as having come 'from his hands in so perfect a state of beauty, as hardly to admit improvement' (cited in Khan 1999: 62). His Nagari font was first used after 1800 to print his *Grammar of the Sanskrit Language* (1808) and several other grammars. Further details in Shaw 1981: 34.

regulations and first appeared in an Indian newspaper in the *Calcutta Gazette* of June 1796 (Shaw 1981: 33–4).

The year 1800 marks a major turning point in the history of print in Hindi and Urdu with the simultaneous establishment of the Baptist Mission at Serampore and the College of Fort William in Calcutta. A training academy for young British civil servants, Fort William College began producing a vast array of classical and modern-language grammars, lexicons and textbooks for the instruction of its students (Das 1978:154–64), while the Serampore Mission engaged in the huge venture of spreading the scriptures and edifying Christian literature in the regional languages of India. Common to these efforts, whether of an evangelical, educational, or academic thrust, was their reliance upon, and trust in, the power of the printed word.

Missionary Printing

The relatively late introduction of print in the North Indian regional languages is partly a consequence of the East India Company's policy of 'non-interference' in religious matters. Until 1813 it forbade the initiation of missionary activities within its territories. Prior to that, it was only in the Danish enclave of Serampore that the Baptist missionaries William Carey, William Ward, and Joshua Marshman could engage in proselytization and start to spread the gospel in printed form. Opened in 1802, the Serampore Mission Press soon grew into the largest printing press in South Asia, inaugurating a period in the history of Indian-language printing that was dominated by missionary activity. While print was central to proselytization, missionary printing also made a pioneering contribution in the field of vernacular education. Besides translations of the Bible and Christian tracts, missonaries produced a plethora of textbooks, grammars, dictionaries, and other educational works. The output of the Serampore Mission Press alone was immense: despite a devastating fire in 1812 that destroyed the press and valuable manuscripts, a total of over 212,000 volumes in forty different Indian languages were issued from Serampore between 1801 and 1832 (Grierson 1903: 241).

Missionary printing received a great boost when the Charter Renewal Act of 1813 opened India to missionary activity. However, the Company continued to invoke its neutrality in religious matters and remained hostile to proselytization; missionary activity, therefore, was still considerably impeded (Powell 1993: 80). In view of this, the dimensions of missionary publishing during its early phase are all but astounding: the legendary Baptist Mission Press in Calcutta (est. 1818), an institution closely linked to the Calcutta School Book Society, reportedly published, by 1820, a total of 710,000 volumes in various languages.[14] The Calcutta Auxiliary Bible Society (est. 1813), within three decades of its establishment, issued vernacular versions of the Christian scriptures in over half a million copies (Long 1848: 511).

Missionaries were eminent pioneers of Hindi and Urdu print culture. After 1820 there was a gradual expansion of missionary activity into the upper Gangetic region. The opening of missions in the towns and urban centres of the north-west was accompanied by the establishment of printing presses, notably the Surat Mission Press (1820), American Mission Press in Ludhiana (1836), Mirzapur Orphan Press (1838), Allahabad Mission Press (1838), Sikandra Orphanage Press (1840), and Muzaffarnagar Mission Press (1846). Together with the simultaneously emerging tract and school book societies, these institutions generated a huge number of printed texts for use in missionary and government schools, making a profound impact on the spread of literacy. Indeed, it was through the two pillars of missionary activity, romantically invoked in a Christian journal as 'the schoolhouse rising in the desert' and 'the creative crash of the printing press, as it pours forth its intellectual bounties', that a large number of Indians first became acquainted with the printed word in their mother tongue.[15] By 1868 the North India Tract and Book Society (an amalgamation of the Benares and Agra tract societies) had alone produced Hindi and Urdu tracts in almost 180,000 copies. The complex ideological and pedagogic implications of this spate of Christian literature have been dealt with elsewhere and need not be reiterated here.[16] It may suffice to point out one consequence of missionary engagement in Hindi and Urdu printing: in following an ideologically determined policy to address Hindus and Muslims separately through publications in Nagari and the Urdu script, missionary printing was a first step in cementing the separation of the two languages (Dalmia 1997: 170).

Missionary printing also introduced important improvements in the quality of book production. The achievements of the paper mill of the Serampore Mission Press will be discussed later. Its type-foundry, established in 1803 and run by Wilkins's former assistant Pancanan, made significant progress in the production of oriental fonts. The various

[14] Details in M.H. Khan 1999: 233–47; Kesavan 1997: 155.

[15] *Madras Christian Instructor and Missionary Record*, September 1844 (cited in Viswanathan 1989: 81).

[16] See, e.g., Ingham 1956; Viswanathan 1989.

Nagari fonts cast at Serampore—no less than forty-five were reported to have been destroyed in the fire of 1812 (Shaw 1997a: 129)—remained in demand for a long time, supplying presses in wide parts of north and central India, as also in Calcutta and Bombay, the two principal centres of early Nagari printing. It was only much later that the Serampore types were superseded by the more refined and elegant 'Bombay type' produced at Javaji Dadaji's Nirnay Sagar Press after 1869.

Remarkable improvements were also made with regard to the founts used for printing in Persian and Urdu. Nonetheless, the Serampore Mission Press continued to import Persian founts from England. Urdu typography was still in its infancy: owing to the scarcity of suitable founts, nearly all Urdu books printed in India before 1800 were in *nastaʿlīq*. The *naskh* character, which lent itself much better to movable type-printing and was much used for oriental printing in England, only made its appearance in India when it was popularized by missionary printers and schoolbook societies. Among those who favoured it for its appearance and ease of learning (Ahmad 1985: 107–8) was John Gilchrist of the College of Fort William—an institution that maintained close ties with the Serampore Mission Press.

The Hindustani Department at Fort William College

The first books in Hindi and Urdu were not issued from the Serampore Mission Press but from Calcutta. The beginning of book printing in the North Indian languages, much like the history of their modern literatures, is associated with Fort William College and the name of John Borthwick Gilchrist (1759–1841). Gilchrist, a Scotsman who had entered the Company's service as an assistant surgeon in 1782, had already gained a reputation as a scholar and skilled linguist of Urdu when he was appointed supervisor of the College's Hindustani Department in 1801. He emphasized the importance of modern spoken idioms as vehicles of communication. He initiated the preparation of a substantial number of Urdu and Hindi texts, many of them adaptions or translations of the Persian and Sanskrit classics.[17] His intent in popularizing Urdu—or Hindustani, as the language was usually referred to by him—transcended the functional needs of the college and was directed at a more general revitalization of the language. As he wrote in 1803:

[17] For an overview of the publications of Fort William College, see S.K. Das 1978: 68–78.

> I shall engage soon to form such a body of useful and entertaining literature in that language as will ultimately raise it to that estimation among the natives which it would many years ago have attained among an enlightened and energetic people . . . May not we then reason thus from analogy, that the Hindoostanee will ascend as high on the Indian scale . . . as the English has done in a similar predicament in our own country.[18]

To this end, Gilchrist set up the Hindustani Press in 1802. The press produced several celebrated works which not only figure prominently in the history of modern Urdu prose, but also constitute the earliest printed books in Urdu. The first two, appearing in 1802, were Mir Amman's *Bāgh o bahār* (The Garden and the Spring), a prose rendering of the famous Persian tale of the Four Dervishes, and *Bāgh-e Urdū* (Garden of Urdu), a translation of Saᶜdi's *Gulistān* by Mir Sher ᶜAli 'Afsos'. Subsequent publications included a prose adaptation of Mir Hasan's famous *Maṣ̤navī Siḥr al-bayān* entitled *Naṣr-e Benazīr*, and *Guldasta-e Ḥaidarī,* the first *taẕkirah* of Urdu poets in the Urdu language to be published (Pritchett 2003: 880).

Despite his predilection for Hindustani, Gilchrist also recognized the importance of what he identified as '*hindavī*' or '*bhākhā*', a 'vulgar' or 'rustic' style which he associated with the spoken idiom of the Hindus. His giving employment to a number of '*bhākhā*' munshis, who were to teach and prepare texts in Hindavi, has been viewed as a decisive step in institutionalizing the dichotomization of Urdu and Hindi into autonomous linguistic entities. It formed the starting point for the establishment of a separate literary corpus for Hindi and nourished the future concept of mutually exclusive literary canons of Hindi and Urdu (Dalmia 1997: 164–9). In the present context, Gilchrist's measure is significant in that it entailed the publication of the earliest-known printed books in Hindi and the Nagari script. Issued at his instance from various Calcutta presses in 1802, these were *Siṃhāsan battīsī*; *Mādhunal*, being a Hindi version of a Brajbhasha narrative by Motiram; and *Śakuntalā nāṭak* from the Brajbhasha of Nevaj.[19] A fourth title, a Nagari-script edition of the *Marṣ̤iya* (elegy) by Mir ᶜAbdullah 'Miskin', illustrates the fact that the division between Hindi and Urdu was not yet a clear-cut one. Among other texts simultaneously issued in Nagari and Urdu-script versions

[18] *Proceedings of the College of Fort William, Home Misc. Series.* Vol. DLIX, June 27, 1803: 256 (cited in Kopf 1969: 83).

[19] Krishnacarya 1966: 12–13; Kesavan 1997: 184–5. For a discussion of these texts on linguistic grounds, see Vedalankar 1969: 52–63.

were *Siṃhāsan battīsī* and *Baitāl paccīsī*, two popular folk narratives of Sanskrit origin.

After 1803 Gilchrist's activities were continued by his successor William Hunter. As the new owner of the Hindustani Press, Hunter published some forty Urdu and twelve Hindi works, including the poetic collections of several famed eighteenth-century Urdu poets—*Dīvān-e Mīr Soz* (1810), *Intikhāb-e Saudā* (1810), and *Kulliyāt-e Mīr Taqī* (1811)—and also versions of popular *qiṣṣa*s such as the *Qiṣṣa-e Ḥātim Tāʾī* (1803). Publications in Hindi include the first (incomplete) edition of Lalluji Lal's *Premsāgar* (1803), Biharilal's *Satsaī* (1809), and Lalluji's *Rājnīti* (1809)—a Brajbhasha translation of the Sanskrit collection of fables, *Hitopadeśa*. Simultaneously, Hunter's own Urdu translation of the New Testament came out in a Nagari-script edition in 1805.[20]

Indian critics have tended to dismiss the importance of Fort William College texts in the development of modern Hindi and Urdu literature. The Urdu literary historian Muhammad Sadiq has denied this importance altogether, asserting that 'Fort William College did not enter as a formative factor in the development of modern Urdu prose' (Sadiq 1995: 291). Sisir Kumar Das, while also judging the impact of the texts produced at the college as being of little consequence, has nevertheless underlined their importance in the development of book printing in Indian languages (Das 1978: 79). Arguably, the initial impact of Fort William College publications was limited, the texts being designed for a non-Indian audience and at first hardly read outside the college. Yet it must not be overlooked that works such as Lalluji's *Premsāgar*, Mir Amman's *Bāgh o bahār*, and Maulvi Ikram ʿAli's Urdu version of *Ikhwān al-safā* (1811) subsequently gained immense popularity among Indian readers and, even if somewhat belatedly, came to figure among the most frequently reprinted works in the nineteenth century.[21] As Frances Pritchett has shown, narratives of the *qiṣṣa* genre—*Qiṣṣa-e Ḥātim Tāʾī*, *Siṃhāsan battīsī*, *Baitāl paccīsī*—especially, were eagerly picked up by the mass-publishing industry after 1850.[22]

[20] Further details on the Hindustani Press in Kopf 1969: 82 and 116–17. For a list of Fort William College publications in Urdu and Hindi, see Das 1978: 157–60.

[21] *Ikhwān al-safā*, an Arabic work on the early Islamic brotherhood of the 'Brethren of Purity', contains a collection of philosophical and allegorical discourses between men and animals. The Urdu translation was highly estimated among Orientalists for its pure and elegant style and was frequently translated into European languages (*HLHH* II: 8–10).

[22] Pritchett 1985: 20–36. As Ralph Russell has pointed out, it took almost thirty

From the book historian's perspective the importance of Fort William College in shaping the Hindi and Urdu book is incontestable. At a more technical level, the Hindustani Department's effort to standardize printed texts made a lasting impact on Indian literary practices in introducing principles of Western typography. The most important innovation was the use of punctuation marks. Other momentous changes in Indian writing systems were the insertion of spaces between words and indents to mark paragraphs. Although it would take some time for these innovations to be more widely adopted in Hindi and Urdu printing, Fort William College books provided the first model of a standardized system of arranging printed texts.

The early missionary, government, and European-run private or commercial presses played a key role in providing the impetus and opportunity for Indian participation in the arts of printing and publishing.[23] While owned and controlled by Europeans, these presses were usually operated by Indians. In giving training to local pressmen, compositors, and binders, they functioned as important multiplicators in spreading knowledge of printing technology. The early decades of the century were thus marked by a printing trade that was already heavily dependent on an Indian workforce and Indian expertise. By contrast, Indian ownership of presses was still scarce. Up until the 1820s press proprietorship remained by and large confined to Europeans. Of course there were famous exceptions—such as the enterprising South Indian Raja of Tanjore, Serfoji II, who possessed both the means and the intellectual curiosity to set up his own typographic press. It was first used for printing Sanskrit and Marathi works in 1805 (Shaw 1997). Around 1810 the Nizam of Hyderabad acquired a press as a 'curiosity of western technology', but apparently never used it (*EI* 6: 806). The first North Indian ruler to take an active interest in the new technology was Ghaziuddin Haidar of Avadh, who had a typographic press installed in Lucknow in 1817.

Previously, Fardunji Marzban, a learned traditional *mullah* from Surat and member of the affluent Parsi trading community of Bombay, had founded the first Indian-owned commercial press in western India in 1812. Marzban apparently began his career in books as a caretaker

---

years for the *Bāgh o bahār* to acquire sufficient popularity to warrant publication in the Urdu homeland. In Lucknow, the text was initially made the target of much ridicule on account of its very simple prose style. However, during the period 1850–79 it saw twenty-three different editions in the Urdu-speaking region and also appeared in several Nagari versions (Russell 1992: 84; 263).

[23] See also Kopf 1969: 114–15.

working in a compatriot's bookstore. Yet it was profits made from trading which allowed him to set up on his own as the first Gujarati publisher (Naregal 2001: 177–8). If Indians of humbler means and origin entered the realm of print at the time, it was usually owing to government patronage. Baburam, the pioneer among Indian printer-publishers in Calcutta, is a case in point. A Bengali Brahmin from Mirzapur, Baburam became associated with the Sanskrit Department of Fort William College. At the behest of the department's head, Henry T. Colebrooke, he opened the Sanskrit Press in 1807, becoming the city's first Indian press proprietor (Kopf 1969: 118). Under the patronage of the college, Baburam produced a substantial number of books in Sanskrit, Bengali, and Hindi. He was the first to print two of the most frequently reproduced Hindi texts, notably Lalluji Lal's *Premsāgar* (1810) in its first complete edition, and Tulsidas's *Rāmāyaṇ* (1811), in an edition prepared by Sadal Mishra. Backed by Fort William College, Baburam did brisk business and within a few years amassed a fortune estimated at Rs 400,000 (Diehl 1964: 71). Around 1815 he sold the Sanskrit Press to Lalluji Lal. Lalluji, whose role as a publisher has been eclipsed by his literary activities as *bhākhā* munshi in the college's Hindustani Department, continued to print texts prepared by himself and other munshis for the use of the college, while also undertaking some publishing on his own.[24] One of the first texts of old Hindi literature issued from his press in 1815 was *Vinayapatrikā* (The Petition to Ram), a devotional classic by Tulsidas. Lalluji remained actively engaged in the printing trade until the time of his retirement in 1824, when he had his press transferred to his native town, Agra. No imprints are recorded from the Sanskrit Press after 1824. In fact, it is extremely doubtful whether Lalluji ever had a chance to operate from Agra, for he died the year after.

By the 1820s Hindi and Urdu printing in Calcutta was coming into its own. Simultaneously, the first Indian-owned newspapers began to appear in the city. In 1822 Rammohan Roy (1774–1833) issued his celebrated Persian weekly *Mirāt al-A<u>kh</u>bār*, while another Bengali, Harihar Datt, launched the first Urdu paper, *Jām-e Jahān Numā*. Datt was no novice in journalism: he had previously served as editor to *Sambād Kaumudī*, a Bengali weekly established by his father Tarachand Datt. The chequered career of *Jām-e Jahān Numā*—which went from an Urdu to a biglot Persian–Urdu publication, was then temporarily published in separate Urdu

[24] Apparently Lalluji employed one Gurudas Pal as printer at the Sanskrit Press. The books issued from his press were sold by various Calcutta booksellers (Nair 1990: 47).

and Persian versions, and finally ended up as a Persian paper with an Urdu supplement—illustrates the still limited acceptance of Urdu as a language of journalistic prose writing. With no more than nine Indians among its twenty-six subscribers (1828), the paper catered largely for a European readership in both content and style. Rather than its high quality and the able editorship of Munshi Sadasukh Lal, it was government support to which *Jām-e Jahān Numā* owed its survival. No sooner was the support withdrawn than the Urdu supplement of the paper ceased publication.[25] The *Udant Mārtaṇḍ* or 'Rising Sun', the first Hindi paper appearing in Calcutta in 1826, did not fare any better. Its proprietor-editor, Pandit Jugal Kishore, a native of Kanpur and proceedings reader at the chief civil court of Calcutta, had clearly overrated the support that his target audience, the affluent community of Upper Indian businessmen settled in Calcutta, was willing to lend to the paper. His attempt to circulate the paper in the Hindi region was equally unsuccessful, with the Government refusing to support the paper through postal concessions. After a struggle of one and a half years to keep *Udant Mārtaṇḍ* alive, Jugal Kishore ended up bankrupt, with his property seized.[26] All that remained was for him to express frustration over the lack of reader support in one of his last editorials:

> Śudras serve and perform menial work, they have nothing to do with reading and writing. The Kāyasths learn Persian and Urdu and the group of Vaiśyas, after learning the alphabet, write account books, the Khatris sell cloth, they do not read or write and Brahmins assuming the form of "Kaliyugī Brahmans" have given up their studies. Who then should [buy and] read a Hindī newspaper? (Cited in Vedalankar 1969: 179)

Clearly, there existed no readership at the time to sustain periodical publications in Hindi or Urdu. By contrast, book publishing in the North Indian languages was developing into a viable commercial activity. After 1816 Calcutta witnessed the rise of several commercial type printing offices run by Indians.[27] Before long, printing no longer remained confined to the eastern metropolis but spread in a westward movement to the Doab region. Lalluji Lal's decision to ship his press to Agra in 1824 provides a nice image of the way in which Hindi and Urdu printing extended chiefly along the Ganges into north and north-western India. This process

[25] Nair 1990: 33–8; Khan 1991: 25–42.

[26] Nair 1990: 50–5.

[27] James Long's report listed 20 Persian and Urdu Presses existing in Calcutta in 1857.

was set in motion and much encouraged by the introduction of a new printing technique in the early 1820s—lithography, or drawing on stone.

1.2 The Impact of Lithography

The invention of lithography in the 1820s represents a watershed in the history of print in northern India. With its enormous impact on regional language printing, the introduction of the new technology would prove far more significant than the arrival of typography in the 1550s. Lithography was invented around 1798 by Alois Senefelder (1771–1834), a native of Prague residing in Munich. Within twenty years it was introduced into England and France. Even though it became widely accepted, lithography remained a subsidiary method of book printing in Europe, to be employed mostly for reproducing works of music and art (Scheglova 1999: 12). By contrast, the new technique met with immediate and overwhelming success in the subcontinent. Almost three times as many works were lithographed in India than in Europe during the period 1824–50 (Shaw 1998: 90).

It was only three years after the reputed London publisher Rudolph Ackermann had issued an English translation of Senefelder's treatise *A Complete Course in Lithography* (1819) that the new printing technology was first practised in India with some success by two Calcutta-based French artists, Jean Jacques Belnos and Philippe de Savignhac.[28] While the two Frenchmen produced specimens of lithographic engraving in 1822, the person generally credited with establishing lithography for purposes of book printing in India is James Nathaniel Rind, an assistant surgeon in the Bengal Medical Service. Returning from a period of sick leave in Scotland in 1822, Rind brought with him a lithographic press which was subsequently bought by the Bengal Government and officially established as the Government Lithographic Press on 1 April 1823. Soon afterwards, the Bombay Government followed suit, requesting six lithographic presses to be imported from England in 1824.[29] The new printing technique also attracted private investment and led to the establishment of the first commercial lithographic presses in the Presidency capitals. In 1823 Rind's former partner George Wood opened the Asiatic

[28] Senefelder's original *Vollständiges Lehrbuch der Steindruckerey* first came out from Munich and Vienna in 1818. The following section is largely based on Shaw 1998, who gives a detailed account of the French connection and the early phase of lithography in Calcutta; see also Cook 1989; Losty 1989.

[29] Shaw 1998: 94–9; on the early use of lithography in Bombay, see also Shaw 1989.

Lithographic Company's Press; similar firms followed in Bombay and Madras in 1826–7. Wood's press is important in several respects: unlike the government presses, which were primarily interested in the usefulness of lithography for reproducing maps (Cook 1989), it concentrated on the pictorial use of lithography. It was also the first to exploit in book form the versatility of lithography in reproducing the *naskh* and *nastaᶜlīq* scripts, leaving a profound impact on the subsequent use of lithography by Indian printers.[30] The first Indian-run lithographic press in Calcutta was opened in 1830 by the Muslim Faiz ᶜAli (Shaw 1998: 110–11).

Meanwhile, in 1826 the first upcountry lithographic press had been set up at Patna (Bihar) by the East India Company servant and amateur artist Sir Charles D'Oyly. From his press, later known as the Behar Amateur Lithographic Press, D'Oyly published a number of famous books of drawings (Losty 1989). In 1830 the Asiatic Lithographic Company's Press opened a branch in Kanpur and put it under the charge of Henry Archer. Archer, however, was soon to move on to Lucknow where, at the behest of the Nawab of Avadh, he established the city's first lithographic press in the same year.

Within a decade lithography thus spread from Calcutta right across Upper India. A crucial yet hardly explored corollary of this process was the shift to private Indian ownership of printing presses. Besides the Nawab of Avadh, one of the first Indians to own a lithographic press in the upper Gangetic region was Munshi Wajid ᶜAli Khan, who had left Hooghly in search of new opportunities and set up a newspaper press in Agra in 1833. It was not before the late 1830s that Indian press ownership became widespread in northern India. While inextricably linked to the advance of the new printing technology, the process was much enhanced by colonial legislation, notably the removal of earlier restrictive press and print laws through the liberal Metcalfe Act of 1835.

The advantages of lithography over printing from movable type were considerable: lithography was portable, easy to operate, and cost-effective; it allowed for faster reproduction and involved fewer material costs. Unlike type-printing, it did not involve expensive and sophisticated equipment, nor did it require a high level of expertise to master. It allowed even small-scale printers to simultaneously produce works in several languages, a fact of much consequence in the multilingual setting of nineteenth-century India. The low cost factor permitted many an enterprising Indian to set up his own shop. Moreover, lithography lent itself

[30] See Shaw 1998: 102–4 for the origin and contribution of the Asiatic Lithographic Company's Press.

particularly well to the reproduction of the aesthetically prestigious *nastaʿlīq* script; it was thus ideal for printing in Arabic, Persian, and Urdu. In this respect, it continued the manuscript tradition, a crucial cultural factor in its widespread acceptance across the subcontinent. The observations made by Ulrich Marzolph on the success of lithography in Iran are equally important in the North Indian context:

> Lithography offered itself as the logical continuation of manuscript production. This evaluation is, moreover, substantiated by what one may assume was the determined opposition of professional scribes to the technique of typography. While printing from movable type must have been perceived by them to gravely menace the eminent position of their traditional profession, lithography allowed for a smooth continuation of previous modes of book production while maintaining aesthetic standards and ensuring employment for the artists involved. Lithography even contributed positively to keeping the tradition of calligraphy alive, for it made written texts more accessible, thereby widening the circle of readership and stimulating demand. (Marzolph 2001: 15)[31]

Scholars of South Asian print culture, too, have emphasized the fact that lithography drew much of its cultural authority from its visible proximity to the manuscript tradition. Lithography, as Graham Shaw puts it, allowed for the 'mass-produced manuscript'; it was 'in essence, a link with the past. It combined the cultural attributes of the manuscript with the technical advantages of mass-production' (Shaw 1994: n.p.). The cultural factor was to play an important part in the adoption of print by Indian Muslims (Robinson 1996).

From a technical, economic, and cultural point of view, the new printing technology encouraged the emergence of autodidact printers. Lithography, in short, made 'Every Man his Own Printer', as the title of a contemporary English manual had it.[32] Hence the enthusiastic response it met throughout northern India. It was with the spread of lithography from Calcutta to the urban centres in the north-west—Patna, Benares,

[31] The spread of lithography in Iran, where it had been introduced by way of Russia, took place almost simultaneously with developments in India. The new technology became known in Iranian cities from the mid-1820s, the first known lithographed item being a Qurʾan produced at Tabriz in 1832–3 (Marzolph 2001: 13). However, Indian publishers soon surpassed Iranians in exploiting lithography for commercial printing, as suggested by the large holdings of nineteenth-century lithographed books from India in Iranian libraries.

[32] The wide appeal of lithography is also reflected in a title like W. Abraham's *Lithography in India. Being a few practical hints for the Indian amateur* (Bombay 1864).

Allahabad, Lucknow, Kanpur, Delhi, Agra, Meerut, and Lahore—and the concomitant rise of numerous, if mostly small-scale, indigenous presses that printing in Hindi and Urdu really took off. The importance of lithography as a prerequisite for widespread Indian participation in the book trade and the development of regional-language publishing cannot be overstated. Ultimately, it played a large part in the process of 'democratizing print in South Asia' (Shaw 1998: 89).[33]

An immediate effect of the mushrooming of Indian-owned presses in the NWP&Oudh was the flourishing of the Urdu press. Unlike Calcutta, where commercial presses survived on an existing demand for books, the first phase of printing in North India was characterized by a prevalence of newspaper presses.[34] Their emergence was much enhanced by the substitution of Urdu for Persian as a court and administrative language in 1837. In 1848 Marshman reported the existence of 17 lithographic presses in the NWP, which issued at least the same number of newspapers and periodicals.[35] By 1850 their number had risen to over 23, and 26 Urdu journals were said to exist (*LLH* 1850: 2).[36] While Urdu journalism flourished, the Hindi press only made its appearance in the Hindi heartland in 1845, with the *Banāras Akhbār*, and did not successfully establish itself until a quarter of a century later when Bharatendu Harishchandra launched his *Kavivacansudhā* (1868) and *Hariścandra-candrikā* (1874). The retarded growth of early Hindi journalism has been well documented and does not need further elaboration here. It is important to note, however, that Indian printer-publishers made numerous, if mostly abortive, attempts to establish Hindi journals right from the late 1840s.

[33] Orsini posits a hierarchy between typeset and lithographed Hindi books, stating that high-print-run government publications or books for wealthy patrons were printed (typeset), while books published on a smaller scale or issued by small commercial printers were lithographed (Orsini 2004: 437). While small printers could indeed hardly afford the high investment in typesetting machinery, my own probings into NKP Hindi imprints do not endorse her view.

[34] Ghosh relates the flourishing of the early Bengali book market to the strong tradition and popularity of manuscript writing in Bengal: 'To be economically viable . . . the safest item for the earliest commercial printers to publish was a book. The new vernacular presses simply built upon this existing relationship' (Ghosh 1998: 177). In 1878–9 only 26 papers were published in Bengal, as opposed to 591 in the NWP&Oudh (Gupta 2001: 269).

[35] *Friend of India* of 23 November 1848, cited in Vedalankar 1969: 183. Of the 19 newspapers in circulation in the NWP in 1848, five were in Persian, eleven in Urdu, and three in Hindi.

[36] In light of recent research findings, such estimates seem far too low and should be read with care.

At first, commercial printing and publishing in North India was largely confined to the urban sphere. Were it not for the exhaustive surveys compiled by Indian scholars, little would be known about indigenous enterprise in the printing business during the period 1830–57. As already noted, the history of early Hindi printing is very poorly documented and would be almost impossible to reconstruct but for the information contained in Urdu-language sources. As it is, determining the date of establishment or the lifespan of an Indian press is often quite difficult, with extant sources tending to give contradictory information. As a result, even an important landmark such as the date and place of publication of the first Hindi literary text printed in the Hindi heartland cannot be established with certainty. There is some agreement that the credit goes to a Tulsidas *Rāmāyaṇ* issued from the Asiatic Lithographic Company's Press in Kanpur in 1832.[37] This press has also been credited with printing the first Urdu book in the Urdu-speaking region, an edition of *Bāgh-o bahār* dating from the same year (Ahmad 1985: 139).

The following overview will sketch the growth of regional-language printing up until 1857 by looking at three principal sites of early book production in the Hindi–Urdu region: Agra, Lucknow, and Benares. While all three cities provide excellent illustrations of the nature and dynamics of this growth, each has its own distinguishing features. A fourth important centre of print in the region, the former Mughal capital of Delhi, has already been well researched for the period under review and is not therefore considered here.[38] However, we will revert to Delhi later, when exploring the social and professional background of some eminent pioneers of print in the NWP.

1.3 Printing in the NWP & Oudh Before 1857: Three Centres

Agra

Agra's rise to prominence as an urban centre dates back to the reign of the Mughal Emperor Akbar (r. 1556–1605), under whom the town came to flourish for a short period. Agra only regained its administrative

[37] Krishnacarya 1966: 22; Lutgendorf 1994a: 61. There is a curiously misinformed claim in Dh. Singh's otherwise excellent study that the first Hindi book lithographed in the Hindi heartland was a Tulsidas *Rāmāyaṇ* issued from Pandit Ramprasad Tivari's Kedar Prabhakar Press in Benares in 1819 (cf. Singh 1986: 43, 55).

[38] See, e.g., ʿAbdul Haq 1945; Spear 1951; Gupta 1981; Powell 1993; Pritchett 1995: 1–15; Minault 1999 and 2003; Pernau 2003.

importance in the early nineteenth century when, following the British annexation in 1803, it became the seat of the NWP provincial government and location of the *Ṣadr Divānī ʿAdālat* (Superior Revenue Court). From the 1830s onwards Agra was the site of intense missionary activity on the part of the American Presbyterian Mission and the Church Missionary Society (Powell 1993). Book printing was at first monopolized by the Agra School Book Society which, soon after its establishment in 1835, set up a printing press to engage in the production of missionary and educational works. The press could hardly keep pace with the rapidly increasing demand for textbooks in the provinces. After 1840 it was supported by the famous Secundra (Sikandra) Orphanage Press, established by the society's director W. Greenway and subsequently run by Rudolf Hoernle. The Orphanage Press was a flourishing business, operating six typographic and six lithographic presses. By 1845 it had distributed over 5,000 copies of Christian religious literature and a total of 16,000 copies of educational tracts in Hindi and Urdu. It also served as an important training institution to Indian printers, employing over fifty young men as apprentices or pressmen (Long 1848: 53–60). Meanwhile, the Agra Government had judged it expedient to no longer leave printing to missionaries, and set up its own press. Official printing in the city received much stimulus in the late 1840s, when Lieutenant Governor James Thomason introduced his pioneering schemes of mass primary education, directing his attention towards the establishment of vernacular schools and the production of elementary textbooks. A substantial amount of educational printing was undertaken at the Agra jail, whose prisoners 'were not only taught to read and write, but . . . worked some thirty or forty presses in the Jail itself, supplying Hindi and Urdu books by tens of thousands' (Long 1859: lxiii). Agra remained the main centre of official educational printing up to the 1850s, supplying the NWP with large numbers of English and vernacular textbooks. Implied in textbook production was a massive translation venture, in which textbook knowledge from English and other language sources was transferred into Hindi and Urdu. Since the scheme relied heavily on the mediation of Indian translators, these early textbooks constitute an important site of the discursive encounter between colonial empiricism—with its underlying concept of 'useful knowledge'—and Indian learning and literary forms.[39]

[39] For a discussion of two typical Hindi textbooks of the period, see Bayly 1996a: 235.

If the early Indian-owned presses in Agra were overshadowed by the overwhelming presence of missionary and official printing, they also profited from the latter. Job printing became an important source of income for the first local Indian print shops which, without exception, had started out as newspaper presses. Since the publication of a daily newspaper was not yet a commercially viable undertaking, the standard format adopted was that of a weekly. Even these weeklies, consisting of no more than a couple of handwritten and lithographed sheets, had few subscribers and depended heavily on government support and the patronage of Indian rulers for their survival. *Zubdat al-Akhbār*, a Persian paper issued from Agra's first privately owned printing press in 1833, was subsidized by five Indian rulers and a rich local merchant. On the strength of local patronage and under the able editorship of its proprietor Maulvi Wajid ʿAli Khan, the paper flourished; its circulation of 157 copies in 1848 was the second highest among newspapers in the NWP and the Punjab. By contrast, only two books are recorded as having been issued from the Zubdat al-Akhbar Press between 1833 and 1853. Both were authored by Wajid ʿAli Khan, who reportedly hoped to realize a gain of Rs 3500 from their sales. The first, *Maṭlaʿ al-ʿulūm va majmaʿ al-funūn* (1848), was a Persian encyclopaedia of the arts and sciences.[40] The second, *Guldasta-e anjuman*, was an Urdu grammar. Of the 250 copies printed in 1848, only 100 had been sold by the end of 1851 (Siddiqi 1962: 143–5).

Wajid ʿAli Khan's *Zubdat al-Akhbār* served as an important model for the emerging Urdu press at Agra. Much of the news it carried was reprinted in *Asʿad al-Akhbār*, one of Agra's first Urdu papers, owned by Munshi Qamaruddin Khan, an erstwhile *munshī* of the German Pietist Missionary Karl Hermann Pfander.[41] His Asʿad al-Akhbar Press (est. 1847) is typical of the approximately sixteen lithographic presses operated by Indians in Agra before 1857: initially centred around a newspaper, it made book printing an increasingly important additional business. Its first publication in book form, a pocket edition of the Qurʾan with an Urdu translation, came out in 1848. Although heavily priced at Rs 8, it realized over Rs 3250 in sales proceeds. Of the six books printed in 1849, five were Government or private commissions, the only press publication being an edition of Saʿdi's *Gulistān*. That Qamaruddin is

[40] Naval Kishore reprinted *Maṭlaʿ al-ʿulūm va majmaʿ al-funūn* in 1866, having acquired its copyright. Details in Khan 1991: 174–9; Sabiri 1953 (i): 73–7.

[41] For Qamaruddin, see Sabiri 1953 (i): 299–312. For an overview of Agra presses, see Khan 1990: 31–53.

recorded to have printed 'books' worth more than Rs 11,000 in 1850 is due to the printing of maps and official forms for the government. The yearly output of the press hardly ever exceeded ten titles, consisting mainly of Persian classics, religious or educational tracts in Persian or Urdu, *qiṣṣa*s and small prayer books in Urdu and, infrequently, Sanskrit. The first Hindi publication in 1851, printed in 350 copies, was an edition of Tulsidas's *Rāmāyaṇ*. Qamaruddin's perhaps most noteworthy publication of contemporary poetry, duly advertised in *Asᶜad al-Akhbār*, was the Persian *Dīvān* (1848) of Munshi Hargopal 'Tufta', a prominent pupil and associate of Mirza Ghalib (Siddiqi 1962: 147–53).

With its allure of government job work, by the 1850s Agra had become an increasingly attractive venue for Indian printer-publishers. Among those who were drawn to Agra was Babu Shivchandar Nath, the Bengali owner of the Jam-e Jamshed Press at Meerut. From there he had successfully issued *Jām-e Jamshed,* an Urdu weekly that enjoyed a circulation of over 100 copies. Upon his arrival in Agra in 1850, he secured a large government contract for textbook printing from Henry Stuart Reid, the new Visitor General of Schools in the provinces, allowing him to invest in some book publishing on his own. Shivchandar Nath's case exemplifies the risks implied in the heavy dependence of Indian printers on government patronage: in 1851 he derived most of his income from official contract work for textbook printing. When the contract was withdrawn in the following year, the number of books issued from his press dropped dramatically to only two items, one an Urdu almanac, the other an illustrated Hindi *Rāmāyaṇ*. While official patronage had accounted for his initial success, it also proved to be his ruin. In 1853 the Jam-e Jamshed Press was closed down (Siddiqi 1962: 159–61).

Official patronage often not only determined whether or not a press survived, it also proved a crucial factor in allowing presses to extend their activities from newspaper-printing to book publishing. The Nur al-Absar Press (est. 1852) of Munshi Sadasukh Lal is a case in point. Sadasukh Lal, a man well-versed in English, Hindi, and Urdu, was seemingly Babu Shivchandar's successor in receiving the patronage of Henry Stuart Reid. Having been alloted a fair amount of job work, his press thrived on educational printing. On the strength of government patronage Sadasukh Lal also maintained two weekly journals, *Nūr al-Absār* (Urdu) and *Buddhi Prakāś* (Hindi). Both were distributed to schools and colleges in the provinces. The extent of official support for these journals can easily be gauged from the fact that the government bought 200 copies of each paper, while private subscriptions barely amounted to 40 and

20 copies for the Urdu and Hindi versions respectively. Sadasukh Lal's papers were commended for their informative articles and their lucid style. Reid approvingly noted that, on his suggestion, the editor had filled his paper 'with interesting items of current news' and was about to introduce articles on 'History, Geography, Vernacular and Female Education' (cited in Vedalankar 1969: 186). Sadasukh Lal's career in publishing continued to rely on government patronage; in 1865 he was appointed Chief Government Translator and shifted the Nur al-Absar Press to Allahabad.

Two more local presses thrived on official patronage. One was the Mufid-e Khala᾿iq Press (est. 1856) of Munshi Shivnarayan 'Aram', who is known to the Urdu world as a publisher and correspondent of Mirza Ghalib. Shivnarayan had won a contract for printing the *Agra Government Gazette*. His two weekly journals, *Mufid-e Khalā᾿iq* (Urdu) and *Sarvopakārak* (Hindi), were heavily sustained by government subscriptions. The second was the Aftab-e ʿAlamtab Press (est. 1857) of Munshi Ganesh Lal, editor of the twin journals *Aftāb-e ʿĀlamtāb* and *Sūrajprakāś*. Unlike most of Agra's smaller presses, the aforementioned businesses were strong enough to survive the uprising of 1857, and resumed operations in 1858.

With the shift of the administrative capital to Allahabad and the establishment of a large government press there in 1858, Agra lost some of its former importance for official printing. Yet it seems, in a reversal of earlier circumstances, that it was precisely the absence of a government press and the decline of missionary activity in the city that opened up new avenues for an indigenous publishing industry to develop. It was only in the wake of 1857 that the city witnessed the dawn of non-educational book publishing. This is attested by the rise of some large Indian printing firms: besides Mirza Agha ʿAli's Ahmadi Press (est. 1864), the Mufid-e ʿAm Press (est. 1869) run by Ahmad Khan Sufi was to gain special importance for its paper *Mufid-e ʿĀmm* and its publications on Islamic literature, especially the reformist Ahl-e Hadis (Metcalf 1982: 204).

Lucknow

As the capital of an independent Indian state, with a flourishing intellectual and religious culture of its own and comparatively little direct colonial or missionary influence, Lucknow presents a markedly different case from Agra. While the impact of the British and European presence on the cultural concerns of the city has usually been dismissed as superficial,

Avril Powell attributes an 'unusual receptivity . . . to Western contacts' (Powell 1993: 56) to the Lucknow court. This is certainly true for new printing technology. Under the munificent patronage of the nawabs of Avadh, Lucknow saw the evolution of an eminent tradition of book printing well before it became a major site of modern commercial publishing. The introduction of print in Lucknow goes back to Nawab Ghaziuddin Haidar (r. 1814–27) who, presumably in 1817, founded Lucknow's first typographic press, the Matbaᶜ-e Sultani or Royal Press.[42] Rather than just one of the ruler's fancies, print technology can be seen as a logical continuation of the court's eminent patronage of scholarship and written culture, to which the magnificent royal library bore ample testimony. The Royal Press soon engaged in the production of scholarly and religious works. Among its first major imprints were *Haft qulzum* or 'Seven Seas', a Persian dictionary and grammar in seven volumes, compiled by the nawab's courtier Qabul Muhammad in 1820–2, as well as *Tāj al-lughāt*, a dictionary of Arabic into Persian. While these early imprints are significant in their own right, the real impetus to the development of a local print culture in Lucknow only came in 1830 with the advent of lithography. In this year the anglophile King Nasiruddin Haidar (r. 1827–37) invited Henry Archer, Superintendent of the Asiatic Lithographic Press at Kanpur, to shift his establishment to Lucknow. Archer readily complied, and in 1831 was able to present the king with what is presumably the earliest book lithographed in Lucknow, an Arabic commentary by al-Suyuti entitled *al-Bahjah al-Mardiyah* (Sprenger 1954: vi; Ellis 1894: 62).

Lithography in Lucknow did not remain confined to the royal court for long. From the late 1830s the new technology was taken up by private citizens. The strong impulse it provided to private and commercial enterprise is not only visible in the emergence of small-scale amateur presses but also in the establishment of some highly sophisticated and lucrative personal businesses. Very little is known about the background of the early printers of Lucknow and the extent to which the Royal Press played a part in their professional training. Nearly all of them were *ashrāf* Muslims of considerable means and learning. Maulvi Muhammad Husain, the pioneer among Lucknow printer-publishers, was a noted Islamic scholar who generally went by the name of Haji Harmain Sharifain. In 1837 he set up the Muhammadi Press where he assembled some

[42] The following paragraphs are largely based on Diehl 1973, Khan 1990: 305–25, and Khan 1991: 294–355. According to Khan, the very first book printed in Lucknow in 1819 was *Al-munāqab al-Ḥaidariya*, a praise of Ghaziuddin Haidar written in Arabic.

of the city's finest calligraphers, among them the famous Maulvi Hadi ʿAli who would later serve the NKP. In 1839 the city saw the establishment of its second principal press by Mustafa Khan, a rich glass merchant.[43] If ʿAbdul Halim Sharar is to be believed, Haji Harmain Sharifain was not uninvolved in the rise of the Mustafaʾi Press, which soon became his strongest competitor. The story, as told by Sharar, is that one day Mustafa Khan took some sheets to Haji Harmain Sharifain to be printed. The Haji was so rude to him that on returning home he decided to start his own press (Sharar 1975: 107). Born out of an impulse, the Mustafaʾi Press quickly rose to fame as one of the finest lithographic presses in northern India. The quality and artistic excellence of its Arabic and Persian imprints were said to be unsurpassed in the entire subcontinent. Run by an experienced merchant, it was also the most commercially successful of the early Lucknow presses.

The 1840s saw the emergence of two more presses operating on a larger commercial scale: the ʿAlavi Press of ʿAli Bakhsh Khan and the Muhammadi Press of Wali Muhammad. Together, these four firms came to account for almost two-thirds of the city's total book production (Diehl 1973: 120). In addition, there was a proliferation of smaller businesses. Aloys Sprenger, who from 1848 to 1850 was in Lucknow to catalogue the collection of Arabic and Persian manuscripts in the king's libraries, reports the existence of twelve private lithographic presses at the time (Sprenger 1854: vi). Nadir ʿAli Khan lists over twenty newly founded presses for the period 1839–57 (Khan 1990: 311–17).

Unlike other urban centres in the north-west, where early commercial printing revolved around newspapers, Lucknow printers, from the very outset, cultivated the art of the book. Headed by Mustafa Khan, they won fame for establishing an exquisite lithographic style distinctive of Lucknow. Causing the temporary abandonment of printing from movable type, lithography developed into an art in its own right. In its concern with aesthetics and its valorization of fine calligraphy, early book production in the city clearly reveals the dual influence of *navābī* court culture and Islamic scribal traditions. As Sharar narrates:

> At first printing was not undertaken on a commercial basis but purely as a private pursuit. The finest quality paper, highly appropriate for lithography, was used and the best calligraphists were employed at high salaries. They were shown great favour without any stipulations as to working conditions or how much they wrote in a day or whether they wrote anything at all. In the same way the printers were never asked how many pages they had

[43] Mustafa Khan was the son of Haji Muhammad Roshan Khan Ghafarullah al-Karim. His press was situated in Mahmudnagar.

> printed in a day. For the ink, thousands of lamps of mustard-oil were lighted to produce fine-quality lamp-black. Instead of acid, fine-skinned lemons were used and sponges took the place of cloth. In short, only the finest materials were employed. As a result, Persian and Arabic educational and religious books in the days of the monarchy could not have been printed anywhere else but in Lucknow, where they were produced irrespective of cost for discriminating eyes. (Sharar 1975: 107)

As the example of Lucknow shows, lithography did not simply supersede the traditional method of manuscript-writing. Rather, the two forms of book production coexisted for some time, with lithography drawing heavily on the manuscript tradition. Early lithographed books, whether in Arabic, Persian, and Urdu, or Sanskrit and Hindi, followed their respective manuscript traditions in the organization of their material as well as their textual, graphic, and artistic layout. At the same time, local practices did not remain untouched by the influence of European book-printing but underwent a gradual transformation, resulting in new graphic designs, formats, and arrangement of material. One of the more conspicuous innovations was the introduction of a separate title page and pagination (Scheglova 1999: 12–15). During the 1840s Lucknow printers developed a distinctive style of lithographic book format and title-page design that was visibly different from the style prevalent in Bombay and elsewhere. Its distinguishing feature, a horizontally oriented figure surrounded by an amply ornamented frame, would later be adopted by Naval Kishore for commercial book production (Scheglova 1999: 15). While ornamentation in these early books was usually in black and white, special hand-coloured copies were occasionally prepared on commission: an illustrated volume of Mir Amman's *Bāgh o bahār,* prepared for the Nawab of Rampur by the Murtazawi Press in 1843, had gold and colour on its pages. Even the uncoloured volumes of the edition were an object of pride for its editor, who praised the novelty of having a title page in white letters and stories printed in bold letters, 'looking like a garden with beds of flowers here and there' (Diehl 1973: 123–4).

The year 1849 saw a curious incident in Lucknow's printing history, when Wajid ʿAli Shah (r. 1847–56) ordered all presses in the city, including the Royal Press, to be shut down. This followed the publication by the Royal Press of a laudatory history of the royal family by Kamaluddin Haidar, a courtier and clerk at the Royal Observatory. The king's anger had presumably been incurred by the author's referral to an incident relating to Lord Hardinge's visit to Lucknow in 1847, when Wajid ʿAli Shah was required to wear English patent leather shoes to receive the

Englishman (Pemble 1979: 9). Local printers were badly affected by the king's drastic measure and were forced to move their establishments to the nearby town of Kanpur. Some of the more influential businessmen were able to defy royal orders and only shifted part of their presses to Kanpur (Diehl 1973: 118; Sprenger 1854: vi). When a few months later the ban was lifted and printing in the city resumed, it was under severe restrictions: the presses were only allowed to function under royal control; every published book had to bear the seal of the manager of the Royal Press (Khan 1991: 297). In the wake of the events of 1849, Lucknow lost two of its oldest and most renowned presses, the Muhammadi Press and Mustafa'i Press. Mustafa Khan, while maintaining his Kanpur branch, temporarily returned to Lucknow, only to shift his establishment to Delhi soon afterwards. By 1853 he was widely acknowledged as a large book dealer who commanded several sales agencies and whose books were 'in demand in innumerable circles' (cited in Khan 1991: 122). Another important consequence of Mustafa Khan's temporary shift to Kanpur was the rise of Kanpur's foremost commercial press, the Nizami Press. At Mustafa Khan's instance, his cousin, Maulvi ʿAbdul Rahman Shakir, had joined him in Kanpur and temporarily served at the Mustafa'i Press before he set up on his own in 1854. His Nizami Press quickly rose to prominence, producing more books than any other NWP press during the pre-1857 period. In attracting a large number of scholars and literati, it also anticipated the future role of Naval Kishore's press as an intellectual meeting place.[44]

The title pages of Lucknow or Kanpur imprints dating from 1849 to 1854 usually failed to state their place of publication, making their exact provenance impossible to determine. In 1854 Sprenger estimated the total number of books issued from both cities at *c.* 700 titles. Mustafa Khan alone published an impressive eighty works in 1853.[45] Sprenger did not fail to note that this spate of printed books had introduced far-reaching changes in both literary practice and religious education:

> Some of [the books] have gone through more than ten editions. The books most in request are of course school books and such other dialectical and religious tracts as every Mawlawy reads or pretends to read. But we already observe symptoms that the press is enlarging the narrow cycle of learning, and what is more important, that it extends education to all classes and even

[44] *SRGNWP* 1858. 'Note on natives presses and periodicals—1858': 49. Khan 1990: 235; 323–4.

[45] For a list of these titles, see Orsini 2004b.

> to ladies. Twenty years ago verses of the Quran were repeated as prayers and charms, and even the whole book was learned by heart, but without being understood, and the Sunnah was almost unknown; in our days people are gradually beginning to study the book, and I shall have to describe several commentaries on it in Arabic, Persian and Hindustany which have lately been published. . . . After the Musalmans had, several centuries ago, entirely lost sight of the original idea of their religion, they are now beginning to make their sacred books intelligible to all. This must lead to results analogous to those which the translation and study of the Bible produced in Europe. (Sprenger 1854: vi–vii)

Sprenger also commented on how print was giving rise to new textual genres and expanding the readership. Most remarkable was the rapid increase of 'periodical and light literature', including tales and religious works 'written expressly for ladies'. As he put it: 'Though the new literature which is rising has not much intrinsic value, things are progressing as rapidly and as healthily as they did in Europe, when the art of printing came first into vogue. The tendency is oriental and Mohammadan, but already a spirit of liberality is manifesting itself, which is the natural result of progress from school-learning and court refinement to a general civilization' (ibid.: vi–vii).

Yet for the early Lucknow publishing trade the period 1849–56 was not free of difficulties. The effects of the strict censorship in operation are most clearly visible from the absence of printed newspapers. These made a relatively late appearance, only with the British annexation of Avadh in 1856: no sooner had the reign of the Nawabs come to an end than at least seven Urdu papers were launched in Lucknow within a year.[46] Local journalism had only just made a promising start when the outbreak of the 'Mutiny' brought all efforts to an abrupt end. Its effects on Lucknow's early print industry were devastating. Only a few businesses—the Asafi Press of Beni Prasad, the ᶜAlavi Press of ᶜAli Bakhsh Khan, the Gulshan-e Mohammadi Press of Masahib ᶜAli and the Samar-e Hind Press of Pandit Baijnath—survived and resumed work after some time. Over a decade later, the number of printing presses operating in post-1857 Lucknow was still no more than fifteen.[47]

[46] See Khan 1991: 294–355 for a detailed account of early Lucknow papers. Khan and others mention an early *Lakhnaʾū Akhbār*, edited by the company chronicler Lalji in 1847. Presumably it was a handwritten newspaper in the *akhbārāt* style.

[47] I.e., Naval Kishore Press, Bhagvandin Press, Mustafaʾi Press, Gulzar-e Ahmadi Press, Samar-e Hind Press, Asadi Press, Gulzar-e Hind Press, ᶜAlavi Press, Gulshan-e Kashmir Press, Prakash-e Hind Press, Hasni Asna Ashree [= Isna-ᶜAshari] Press,

When, in the aftermath of 1857, the British started to grant licences to indigenous printers again, the first licence was given not to a local printer but to a young outsider who, significantly, was at once of Hindu origin and a newcomer to the city. The choice was to prove an apt one, for Munshi Naval Kishore would use the unique opportunity given to him to revolutionize the Lucknow book trade. Under British patronage he not only reintroduced typography and set commercial publishing in Arabic, Persian, and Urdu on a new footing; he also established Sanskrit and Hindi printing in the great center of Indo-Persian and Urdu culture.

Benares

Whereas pre-1857 Agra remained dominated by a strong Christian missionary presence and official publishing, Benares provides a classic example of how intimately Indian press ownership and the emergence of a local print culture were linked to the spread of lithography. The early printing shops that sprang up in the city from the mid-1840s were without exception lithographic presses. With its religious and economic importance as a pilgrimage site, excellence in Hindu scholarship, well-established patronage structures, and vibrant cultural life, Benares was predestined to become a centre of print in Sanskrit and Hindi, the languages associated with Hindu culture. It was indeed the first North Indian city to gain importance in non-educational Sanskrit and Hindi publishing. However, even in Benares it would take some time for a full-fledged Hindi print culture to develop. Although a medium of primary education, Hindi was still devoid of an official function and had not yet been assigned its future role as a vehicle of Hindu nationalism and revivalism. It would thus be wrong to assume that any of the commercial presses in pre-1857 Benares survived on Hindi printing alone. In fact none of them justly deserve to be called a 'Hindi press', for, much as in Agra, business was sustained by publishing government-sponsored journals in Urdu and Hindi, while the bulk of book printing was still undertaken in Persian and Urdu. As it was, the early printers of Benares struggled hard to make a living.

While there is some evidence suggesting the existence of printing presses in the city before 1840, up to the mid-1840s most print ventures

---

Kaliparshad's Press, Nasim Lucknow Press, Anjuman Press, and Sehr-e Samri Press (*OAR*, 1869–70: 145).

initiated at Benares were executed in Calcutta.[48] For instance, the famous Brajbhasha *Mahābhārat,* prepared under the aegis of the Maharaja of Benares, was printed at the Calcutta-based Shastra Prakash Press in 1829–30. The earliest Indian-owned press of Benares on which reliable information is available is the Benares Akhbar Press, opened in 1844 by the Maharashtrian Brahmin Govind Raghunath Thatte. Thatte's press is best known for launching the *Banāras Akhbār*, which is generally held to be the first Hindi or, correctly speaking, Nagari-script paper (its style was clearly Urdu) in the Hindi region. The paper was confined to local news, while also carrying serialized translations from Sanskrit law books. It was heavily patronized by the Raja of Nepal. Thatte's second paper, the Urdu weekly *Benares Gazette*, enjoyed higher subscriptions than the *Banāras Akhbār* but suffered from being poorly lithographed (to the extent that it was often barely legible) as well as from its editor's aggressive polemic against Christian missionaries. Following a case of libel in 1853, publication of the *Benares Gazette* was suspended.[49] In the present context, Thatte assumes importance as the first Benares publisher to issue a substantial number of books in Persian and Urdu, as well as some Hindi titles. Moreover, he was the city's first large commercial publisher of Sanskrit books. Despite its sizeable output, the Benares Akhbar Press (probably as a result of the libel case) was closed down in 1854. Thatte, with a resilience characteristic of early professionals in the book trade, joined the establishment of a compatriot.

The second important press of Benares was the Sudhakar Press (est. 1847), run by Pandit Rataneshwar Tivari, proprietor of the weekly *Sudhākar*. The paper, which drew its readership primarily from among the city's educated Hindus, opposed the language policy of the *Banāras Akhbār* and instead advocated chaste Sanskritized Hindi.[50] Its difficult and highly Sanskritized style, however, did not go down well even with Banarasi Hindus. A sharp decline in subscriptions after the first year

[48] This probably holds true for the publications of the Benares Tract Society, a missionary organization established in 1827 and reorganized in 1834 as a branch of the Calcutta Tract Society. It is said to have circulated 25,000 copies of vernacular tracts by 1836 (Vedalankar 1969: 106). Krishnacarya (1966) lists two early Hindi titles, namely the *Mānasdīpikā,* a famous commentary on Tulsidas allegedly printed in 1835, and a work called *Harirās* by one Udaykarn, printed in 1840. However, he does not give printers' names.

[49] Khan 1990: 101–4; 1991: 215–16.

[50] Of the *Sudhākar's* initial subscribers, 50 were Hindus, 22 Europeans, and two Muslims.

prompted a change in language policy and the introduction of a bilingual news column in Hindi and Urdu. The attempt was of no avail, the number of subscribers dipping even further (Siddiqi 1962: 83). It was only when the government came to the paper's rescue in 1852 that *Sudhākar* was able to survive, this time in a fortnightly format and with articles on scientific, educational, and literary subjects as a new feature. Given its precarious financial situation, the Sudhakar Press was hardly able to invest in book publishing. The few Hindi and Sanskrit books it issued after 1851 were nearly all commissioned by the Maharaja of Benares, whose patronage was an all-important force in the early development of a local print culture.[51]

Among the more successful print entrepreneurs of Benares was the Bengali Brahmin Kashidas Mitra, proprietor of the Kashi Press (est. 1851) and *Kāśī Yātrā Patrikā,* presumably the only Bengali paper published outside Bengal at the time. Catering to the city's sizeable Bengali community, the paper flourished. Its circulation rose from 92 to 130 copies within a year. Even more successful was its Urdu counterpart, *Aftāb-e Hind*, which came to enjoy the longest life among the early regional-language papers of Benares. If the Kashi Press fared better than most other local presses, it was because it operated along sound commercial lines. The way in which Kashidas advertised his services in *Aftāb-e Hind* suggests a keen sense of competitive marketing. The paper announced that anyone wanting a book or map printed in Bengali, Persian, Nagari, or English could get it done at the Kashi Press 'on more economical terms than in other printing houses' (cited in Khan 1991: 220).

The Kashi Press was the exception rather than the rule. A more typical illustration of the fate met by most early Benares presses is provided by the short-lived Bagh-o-Bahar Press (est. 1848), which was run jointly by Babu Kedarnath Ghosh and Kali Prasad. Having failed to establish *Mirāt al-ʿUlūm*, a monthly periodical that did not see more than three issues, the two men launched *Bāgh-o-Bahār.* It lived somewhat longer but in 1853 also had to be discontinued. Given its tight budget the Bagh-o-Bahar Press would not have survived even to that point had it not been for job work executed for the government and occasional commissioning by the Maharaja of Benares. In 1851 Kedarnath Ghosh announced that, due to want of purchasers, the small amount of book publishing undertaken at his press would have to be abandoned. Two years later the

[51] For a list of titles commissioned by the Raja of Benares in 1852, see Siddiqi 1962: 170.

press was closed down. Meanwhile, the editor of the short-lived *Mirāt al-ʿUlūm*, Harivamshlal (Harbanslal), had tried his luck in establishing a printing press of his own, the Mufid-e Hind Press (est. 1850). Again, his efforts were not met by much success. His paper *Zāʾirīn-e Hind* lost half its Indian subscribers after a year and began to depend solely on European subscriptions. It seems that Harivamshlal was forced to temporarily suspend operations in 1853. However, he showed much resilience and is reported to have still been running a press, possibly under a different name, in 1863.[52]

The case of Benares illustrates the limitations imposed on the early development of commercial print culture by the small size and purchasing power of the literate audience. Clearly, the difficulty for Indian printer-publishers was not to set up business but to remain in business. To launch a paper was relatively easy, to sustain it a much more difficult task. Frequent editorial complaints about defaulting subscribers and the general indifference of the Indian readership testify to the endless problems that raising subscriptions and sustaining sales caused.

If newspapers, in Khan's view, were the chief victims of poverty and economic depression (Khan 1991: 220), books fared even worse. For the average urban middle-class reader in the 1840s and 1850s the printed book was still an expensive commodity. In times of economic distress it was a luxury that could easily be foregone. As the example of Agra and Benares shows, few early commercial presses survived on book printing alone; instead, business was usually sustained by newspaper publishing. The Gulzar-e Hamesha Bahar Press (est. 1849) is another interesting example. Its proprietor, Virsingh Khatri, a scholar of local repute, had planned to set up a press with shareholders' money but found no support for his project. Undeterred, he set up shop on his own, making an impressive debut with sixteen different titles in Sanskrit, Persian, Hindi, and Urdu in 1849. His ambitions were thwarted when it turned out that his books sold very poorly and profits from sales in no way met production costs (Table 1.0). Virsingh complained—to no avail—that the public showed no appreciation of their learned compatriots' efforts to disseminate knowledge and information through print. In the following year his business was dissolved (Siddiqi 1962: 175–6).

[52] Several publications from the 'press of Harivamshlal' are listed in Krishnacarya and in official reports of 1862–3. In 1874 Harbanslal resurfaces as the manager of Pandit Gopinath Pathak's famous Benares Light Press (QLP, NWP 1874, fourth quarter).

TABLE 1.0

Books Published by the Gulzar-e Hamesha Bahar Press in Benares, 1849

Title	Subject	Language	Print Run	Price*	Copies Sold
Aṣṭādhyāyī	grammar	Sanskrit	300	1-4	3
Śikṣā	grammar	Sanskrit	300	0-2	2
Paraśvarī	astrology	Sanskrit	300	0-8	10
Mānus rahasī	literature	Hindi	100	0-3	5
Mahīman	ritual	Sanskrit	150	0-8	1
Meghadūta	poetry	Sanskrit	150	0-8	1
Pārthiva pūjan	ritual	Sanskrit	191	1-4	1
Majmuʿah-e cār āśtak	ritual	Sanskrit	100	0-1-6	21
Chāpek͟hānoṁ kā qānūn, pt. 1	law	Hindi	50	0-6	6
Chāpek͟hānoṁ kā qānūn, pt. 1	law	Persian	50	0-3	18
Chāpek͟hānoṁ kā qānūn, pt. 2	law	Persian	50	0-1-6	9
Mirāt al-mizān	grammar	Urdu	300	0-8	4
Dastūrāt ganj-e ḥisāb	arithmetic	Urdu	50	0-2	17
Tāʿlimāt-e-k͟haṭṭ-e gulzār	calligraphy	Urdu	100	0-1-6	–
Uday [?]	?	Hindi	100	–	–
Taṣvīrāt Sarasvatī	pictures	?	50	0-0-1	–

SOURCE: Siddiqi 1962: 175-6. *Price at which the book was sold to the public, given in rupees–annas–pies (1 anna = one-sixteenth of a rupee; 1 pie = one-twelfth of an anna).

According to official sources, prior to 1857 no less than five newspaper and eighteen other presses were operating in Benares.[53] As we have seen, information is largely confined to the former, while there is precious little documentary evidence on the early book-producing presses. For the time being, printing shops such as the Hariprakash Press, Ganesh Press, Divakar Press, and Kedarnath Prabhakar Press must remain mere names to us.

Since the impact of the 1857 uprising in Benares was less disruptive than elsewhere, a considerable number of the city's presses were able to resume work in 1858. During the following decades, the development of

[53] *SRGNWP* 1858. 'Note on native presses and periodicals—1858': 49.

book publishing into a viable commercial activity was accompanied by the rise of several large printing and publishing firms. By far the most influential establishments were the type press founded in 1857 by the British medical doctor E.J. Lazarus, known as Medical Hall Press or E. J. Lazarus & Co. Press, and the Benares Light Press set up in 1860 by Pandit Gopinath Pathak. Later, the Candraprabha Press (est. 1882?) run by Pandit Lakshmishankar Mishra, and the Bharat Jivan Press (est. 1885) run by Ramkrishna Varma were to gain special importance in Hindi and Sanskrit publishing.[54]

The preceding overview of three early centres of print in the NWP and in Avadh underscores the importance of localization in the study of Indian print culture. The emerging local print cultures of Agra, *navābī* Lucknow, and Benares were shaped by markedly different circumstances and featured different actors. Yet some important common denominators can be identified: prior to 1857 the number of viable and large-sized Indian publishing firms operating in North India was decidedly small. A large share of the book production in Hindi and Urdu still occurred outside the commercial market under missionary or colonial agency. A fair amount of book publishing was initiated and patronized by Indian rulers and nobles. The marketplace alone was not yet a force significant enough to sustain commercial publishing. A second point to note is that, being dominated by Persian and Urdu publications, the commercial book trade reflected official language use. With the exception of the occasional almanac, no Hindi imprints are recorded from Lucknow before 1857, while the number of non-educational Hindi titles issued from the private and commercial presses of Agra and Benares was still minimal. Besides a few select devotional classics (nearly all early Benares publishers relied on a pre-print favourite, Tulsidas's *Rāmcaritmānas*), publishers' output in Hindi was confined to popular forms of chapbook literature, including religious tracts, tales, folk dramas, and almanacs. This situation was to after dramatically when a number of changes ushered in the age of commercialization in the North Indian book trade.

1.4 The Age of Commercialization

Although the first commercial presses in North India date back to the late 1830s, the era of commercialization in Hindi and Urdu publishing, with its concomitant phenomenon of 'print capitalism', really only dawned

[54] See Appendices I and II for an overview of major Indian-owned Benares presses. For a more detailed discussion of print culture in Benares, see Orsini 2004a and 2004b.

in the second half of the nineteenth century. The boom of the Bengali print industry pre-dated it by nearly two decades. According to rough estimates made by the Reverend James Long, no less than 2,000,000 Bengali books had been printed by 1854, and a total of 8,000,000 by 1859 (Long 1859: [i]). So profound was the impact of print in Bengal that, by the second half of the century, the printing industry constituted one of the largest indigenous enterprises in Calcutta (Roy 1996: 30, 34). While no comparable figures exist for the NWP&Oudh, printing in Hindi and Urdu had definitely come into its own by the 1860s. In 1868, the first year of official registration, over 600,000 printed books were recorded in Hindi and Urdu. The number of private and commercial presses operating in the NWP had risen to fifty.[55] Two decades later, in 1888, over 110 presses were in operation. There was a marked concentration of presses in six urban centres—Benares, Allahabad, Lucknow, Aligarh, Agra, and Kanpur. During the period 1868–1900 these cities accounted for about 80 per cent of the total production in the provinces (King 1994: 41–2).

If lithography was paramount in enhancing print in the regional languages, it was only one of several technological factors preceding the boom of an indigenous print industry. A number of other technical innovations introduced in the subcontinent from Europe were essential in paving the way for industrial mass printing. The first was the replacement of the wooden press by the iron printing press invented by Earl Stanhope in 1803. Iron presses were quickly adopted in India. In the 1820s India's first lithographic printer James Rind printed from Ruthven's iron presses. Three decades later James Long attested to their widespread use in the Bengal region, noting that the wooden press had become a 'curiosity' (Long 1859: 12). Following the iron printing press, the invention of the steam-powered cylindrical printing press by the German engineer Friedrich Koenig in 1811 constituted a further epoch-making event. When the steam press was first adopted by the *Times* of London in 1814, it was hailed as 'the greatest improvement connected with printing since the discovery of the art itself' (cited in Steinberg 1996: 139). Replacing manpower by steam power, it raised the output of a press from approximately 300 to 1100 sheets an hour and lowered printing costs by twenty-five per cent.

While steam presses had become widespread in Britain by the 1840s, their adoption in India was slow. Even though steam engines had been utilized for various purposes since the early nineteenth century (a steam

[55] *PGNWP&Oudh. General Dept.*, 13 March 1869: 4.

engine, for example, was operating at the Serampore paper mill in 1820), the Indian print industry did not make use of the new technology until much later. Inhibiting the general use of steam-powered presses by Indian printers was the high expense involved. Given the cheapness of labour in India, the cost of a steam press was indeed prohibitive. When steam presses were at last adopted in the late 1880s, only the largest commercial firms could afford the investment: the Venkateshvar Press in Bombay, the Vangavasi Steam Machine Press in Calcutta, the Mufid-e ʿAm Press in Lahore, and the NKP in Lucknow were among the first Indian-owned firms to introduce steam printing. However, the revolutionary technology had attracted public attention as early as 1850, with *Asʿad al-akhbār* of Agra marvelling at the invention 'by the ingenious Europeans' of the new steam printing machine, which was reported to print no less than 25,000 copies of a paper in a day (cited in Khan 1991: 197).

A second crucial preliminary to the commercialization of print in northern India was the growth of the indigenous paper industry. Until mid-century the Serampore Paper Mill constituted the sole source of industrially manufactured paper for North Indian printer-publishers, who otherwise had to import expensive foreign paper from Europe. The difficult paper situation only changed in the 1870s, when the colonial government introduced special measures to stimulate the growth of the paper-manufacturing industry. It is a telling fact that the first paper mill in northern India owes its existence to the initiative of an Indian printer-publisher: none other than Naval Kishore, who seized the occasion to found a company of shareholders and establish the Lucknow Paper Mills in 1878–9 (see Chapter 3). The paper mill soon turned into Lucknow's largest industrial enterprise. It gave an enormous impetus to the printing trade in the north-west, functioning as the main supplier of inexpensive paper to printers in the NWP&Oudh and the Punjab. By 1888 the situation in industrial paper production had markedly improved. However, production remained confined to only nine big mills, of which five were situated in Bombay, two in Bengal, and one each in Lucknow and Central India (Watt 1892: 312).

One of the most important implications of the advance in printing technology and the growth of the indigenous paper industry was a considerable reduction in production costs and, consequently, the prices of printed matter. At the beginning of the century printed books were still very expensive. As noted by William Ward in 1818, an edition of the *Mahābhārat* cost as much as Rs 60, while the *Rāmāyaṇa* sold at Rs 24 (cited in Diehl 1964: 61). As Veena Naregal has shown for early Marathi books, even with differential pricing for 'whites' and 'natives', prices were hardly conducive to promoting the reading habit among Indians. Molesworth's *Maratha–English Grammar and Dictionary*, issued from the Bombay School Book Society in 1829, sold at a forbidding Rs 90 (Naregal 2001: 165). From mid-century the impact of industrialization on book prices becomes clearly visible. By 1860 the Bombay publisher Ganpat Krishnaji was able to advertise a 1700-page *Bhāgavata Purāṇa* for Rs 12. Similarly, the average price for a lithographed Hindi or Urdu almanac had dropped to 2 annas, i.e. only one-sixteenth of the price at which Fardunji Marzban had sold his first type-printed Gujarati almanac in 1814.

The emergence of the low-priced book in the Hindi and Urdu book trade can be dated roughly to the 1850s and 1860s.[56] The introduction of mass-produced cheap formats, sewed and bound in paper covers, resulted in a situation where, for the first time, books became an affordable commodity for a large section of the urban literate classes. The following Table 1.1 gives an indication of price patterns, listing books published from the NKP during the period 1863–87.

Various factors account for the great variation in sales prices: size, binding, and paper quality; whether the book was a publisher's production, a textbook, or a private commission; whether it was a first edition or a reprint; whether or not it contained illustrations. After the mid-1860s the prices of NKP publications slowly fell: for example, *Gulistān-e mutarjam*, an Urdu translation of Saʿdi's *Rose Garden*, went from Rs 1 for the first edition of 1867 to Rs 0-8-6 in 1875 (17th ed.), and declined to Rs 0-7-0 in 1882 (27th ed.). Similarly, Rajab ʿAli Beg's popular tale *Fasāna-e ʿajāʾib,* originally priced at Rs 0-12-0 in 1870, was sold at Rs 0-7-0 in 1875 (4th ed.), and at Rs 0-6-0 in 1882 (14th ed.). The NKP's 1876 reprint of *Durr al-mukhtār*, an authoritative law book by Hashkafi in Urdu translation, was already 25 per cent cheaper than the first edition issued from Muhammad Ahsan Nanautawi's Siddiqi Press four years earlier.[57]

To put these book prices into perspective, some figures relating to the late 1870s may be helpful: at the time, one rupee would buy 20 *ser* of

[56] In England, the price reversal process from a market dominated by books in the high-price category to one dominated by books in the low-price category took place somewhere in the period 1840–55. From 1855, low-priced books accounted for the largest percentage share in the English market, while expensive books went into a steady decline (Eliot 1995: 39–40).

[57] The respective prices for the voluminous edition of over 2200 pages being Rs 16 (Siddiqi Press: 1872) and Rs 12 (NKP: 1876).

TABLE 1.1

Price Patterns: Books Produced at the NKP, 1863–87

Date	Title	Language	Copies	Pages	Price*
1863	*Kulliyāt-e Ghālib*	Persian	?	566	5-0-0
1867	*Akbarnāma, 3 vols. (deluxe edition)*	Persian	275	1800	50-0-0
	Kulliyāt-e Mīr	Urdu	550	646	6-0-0
1868	*Zād al-ā<u>kh</u>irat, Tafsīr-e Qur'ān, 4 vols.*	Urdu	1100	1761	10-0-0
	Kulliyāt-e Momin	Urdu	1000	458	2-0-0
	Qiṣaṣ al-anbiyā	Urdu	1600	178	0-12-0
1869	*Bhāgavata Purāṇa*	Sanskrit	1375	2576	15-0-0
	Ā'īn-e Akbarī, 3 vols.	Persian	550	1238	30-0-0
	Mirāt al-ʿarūs	Urdu	3100	226	0-12-0
1870	*Fasāna-e ʿajā'ib*	Urdu	1100	178	0-12-0
	Rāmāyaṇ Tulsīkṛt	Hindi	1100	660	3-0-0
1872	*Dīvān-e Ẓafar*	Urdu	1000	670	2-8-0
	Kulliyāt-e Saudā	Urdu	500	490	2-0-0
1873	*Dīvān-e Ghālib*	Urdu	1250	104	0-4-0
1874	*Ṭibb-e Akbar*	Urdu	1250	782	2-8-0
	Gaṅgālahrī	Hindi	1125	22	0-0-9
	Zabān-e re<u>kh</u>tā	Urdu	1125	16	0-0-9
1875	*Kulliyāt-e Naẓīr Akbarābādī*	Urdu	1000	296	0-12-0
	Brajvilās	Hindi	1250	606	0-12-0
1876	*Āṣār aṣ-ṣanādīd*	Urdu	575	560	3-0-0
	Devībhāgavata	Hindi	1300	695	3-4-0
	Bihārī satsaī	Hindi	1200	233	0-7-0
1878	*Śivsiṃh saroj*	Hindi	325	485	1-4-8
	Gītāvalī saṭīk	Hindi	300	468	1-0-0
	Tarjuma-e Qānūn-e Shai<u>kh</u> Bū ʿAli Sīnā, vol. 1	Urdu	600	285	1-8-0
1882	*Viṣṇu purāṇa*	Hindi	300	342	0-12-0
	Maṣnavī Mīr Ḥasan (illust.)	Urdu	3000	54	0-1-9
	Hanumān cālīsā	Hindi	2500	8	0-0-3

Table 1.1 (*contd.*)

Date	Title	Language	Copies	Pages	Price*
1883	*Bījak Kabīrdās saṭīk*	Hindi	1200	552	1-4-0
	Naṣīr al-lughāt	Urdu	310	480	2-4-0
	Bhaktamāl saṭīk	Hindi	2400	386	0-12-0
1886	*Kavipriyā*	Hindi	1500	122	0-3-9
1887	*Mazāq al-ᶜārifīn tarjuma-e Iḥya᾿ ᶜulūm al-dīn*, 4 vols.	Urdu and Arabic	600	3010	10-0-0

*Price at which the book was sold to the public; given in rupees–annas–pies (1 anna = one-sixteenth of a rupee; 1 pie = one-twelfth of an anna).

split lentils (*dāl*), 16 *ser* of milk, or one *ser* of butter in the local Lucknow bazaar.[58] Among luxury items, one rupee would buy one *ser* of ready-made pickle or one *ser* of Lucknow's famous rose water essence. For one rupee you could get your watch cleaned or purchase 40 g of opium pills from the government-licensed opium vendor.[59] As for salaries, a compositor at the Allahabad Government Press earned a maximum of Rs 30 per mensem, a lithograph writer Rs 17.[60] A teacher employed in the Oriental Department of the Mohammadan Anglo-Oriental College in Aligarh received an average monthly salary of Rs 40, while first class students could win scholarships ranging from Rs 8 to 10 per mensem. By contrast, Nazir Ahmad, when embarking on a job in the dominions of the Nizam of Hyderabad in 1877, was initially offered a handsome salary of Rs 800 per month but was readily granted Rs 1200 on demand.[61]

Large print runs were another factor that brought prices down. During the early decades of the nineteenth century, books in Hindi and Urdu were usually printed in editions of 500 copies. This, for example, applies to the books issued from Fort William College. The Lucknow-based Mustafa᾿i Press in 1850 published twenty different works in Persian and Urdu in prints run of 500 or 600 copies each. Only three years later, average print runs had gone up to 1000 copies (Orsini 2004b: 111). By the early 1870s the institutionalization of formal education had created a

[58] 1 *ser* is approximately 1 kilo.

[59] All prices are calculated from Hoey 1880.

[60] *PGNWP&Oudh. General Dept.*, May 1877: 27.

[61] Shan Mohammad 1978 (2): 451, 96; Russell 1992: 115.

huge demand for educational titles, which sustained a flourishing government and private printing industry. Official estimates of an average first print run of educational works ranged from 3000 to 4700 copies. Much higher circulations were attained by alphabetical primers, which topped the list of educational bestsellers. *Akṣar dīpikā,* a Hindi alphabet book, was issued in a ninth edition of 100,000 copies in 1868, sold at 6 paisa each. Its Urdu counterpart *Tashrīḥ al-ḥurūf* enjoyed an even higher circulation. Naturally, the corresponding figures for non-educational works were much lower. These were estimated to command first editions of 700–900 copies on average.[62]

Large-scale commercial printing in Hindi and Urdu began relatively late. At first growth was slow, the number of printed books in Urdu rising from 217,153 to only 284,511 during the period 1868-84. With rapid advances in technology, increased official demand, and expansion of the readership, the growth rate picked up considerably during the last decades of the century and, at 548,030 Urdu books in 1900, had more than doubled. Hindi books displayed a similar growth pattern, except for an even slower start during the first period, the corresponding figures being 392,316 printed books in 1868, 399,882 in 1884, and a large 758,992 in 1900 (King 1994: 38–44).

In sum, the period 1868–95 showed a nearly fourfold quantitative increase in the production of Urdu books and a nearly threefold increase in Hindi books. The number of titles published in each language followed a similar growth pattern. Here, however, it is more difficult to establish reliable data on account of several imperfections in the sources. Official registration of books began in 1868 but during the first years was often incomplete (discussed below). The number of Urdu titles issued and registered in the NWP&Oudh increased from 214 in 1875, to 491 in 1885, to 560 in 1895. The corresponding number of Hindi titles was 121 in 1875, 295 in 1885, and 354 in 1895.[63] While books on law and religion were most numerous in Urdu, works on language and religion scored highest in Hindi, followed by poetry and history. Both languages showed a marked increase in fictional literature from the late 1880s onwards.

The importance of commercial publishing as a new branch of the colonial economy was for the first time documented in the NWP Census of 1872, which, in its occupational survey, contained a statement of professions connected with the book trade. Listed in the 'industrial class',

[62] *PGNWP. Educational Dept.*, March 1874: 19; *RPIR* 1874: 22.

[63] For growth patterns in Hindi and Urdu titles, see ch. 7, Table 7.1.

these so-called 'workers in books' (printers, newspaper proprietors, bookbinders, booksellers, inkmen, etc.) amounted to a total of 1981. The list counted three times as many booksellers as printers.[64] In the subsequent Census of 1881, by then including the province of Avadh, the ratio was inverted: while the number of booksellers had risen by a mere 10 per cent, the number of printers had shot up from 332 to 1657, greatly surpassing that of booksellers. This large increase was because of the inclusion of Lucknow printers as well as those associated with the Allahabad Government Press, which the earlier Census had failed to list. Booksellers, bookbinders, printers, librarians, newspaper proprietors, and copyists now came to a total of 2753 persons. Noting that this was 'a poor fraction among a population exceeding 44 millions!', the accompanying Census report made an unfavourable comparison with England, where 58 out of 10,000 people were said to be workers and dealers in books.[65] The corresponding figure for the NWP&Oudh was given as 1.2.[66] Over 65 per cent of them were located in the five urban centres of Agra, Allahabad, Benares, Kanpur, and Lucknow.

While these official figures provide some interest, they can hardly be regarded as accurate. Not only did they fail to include members of the book trade who ranged at the lower end of the social scale—notably pressmen, compositors, hawkers, and distributors—they also did not take into account those individuals for whom book copying or calligraphy was not a full-time occupation. Moreover, smaller towns like Meerut and Bareilly, which boasted a burgeoning print industry of their own, were not even taken into consideration. In retrospect, the figures seem much too low and as inaccurate as those given by Garcin de Tassy and other contemporaries, in terms of the number of indigenous lithographic presses operating during the first decades of Hindi and Urdu printing. Absent from official statistics were a large number of small private printing shops that often consisted of nothing more than a hand press set up at home. The figures reproduced in Table 1.2 below must therefore be read with caution.

Arguably, much of the intellectual and literary activity taking place in the realm of print escaped colonial statistics. Furthermore, official figures fail to shed light on a significant development: the easy accessibility of print to those living in small-town India, outside the urban centres. A

[64] *Census of the NWP&Oudh* 1882: 181.

[65] *Report on the Census of the N.-W. P. and Oudh and of the Native States of Rampur and Native Garhwal,* 1882: 108.

[66] Ibid.: 124.

more accurate impression of the changes wrought by commercial print culture can be gathered from contemporary testimonies such as that of George A. Grierson. To the great linguist and admirer of Indian literature the triumph of print was a mixed blessing:

> Large Native publishing-houses have risen in Lakh'naū, Banāras, and Paṭ'nā, from which have issued floods of printed works, old and new, good, bad, and indifferent. At the same time a mushroom growth of smaller establishments has sprung up all over Hindūstān, and there is now scarcely a town of importance which does not possess its printing-press or two. Every scribbler can now see his writings in type or lithographed for a few rupees, and too often he avails himself of the power and the opportunity. (Grierson 1889: 145)

TABLE 1.2

Number of Persons Engaged in the Book Trade in Urban Centres in the NWP&Oudh, 1881

	Booksellers	Bookbinders	Printers
Agra	46	40	101
Allahabad	49	30	638
Benaras	38	17	133
Kanpur	42	32	96
Lucknow	70	1*	400
Total	245	120	1368

SOURCE: Census NWP&Oudh 1881. *Supplement to the Report on the Census, comprising statistics of the tahsils . . .*, Allahabad 1882: 117–39. *This figure is obviously incorrect.

Printer-Publishers and their Social Background

Information on the social background, economic status, and motivation of the men associated with the nascent print industry in North India is still scarce. These printer-publishers came from a variety of backgrounds. Many belonged to the traditional scribal classes with a history in service and a cultural background in the Indo-Persian tradition. Unlike South or West India, where learned pandit-publishers played a decisive part in shaping regional-language print culture (Blackburn 2003; Naregal 2001), Brahmins were only one of the groups that dominated print in the North.

In the erstwhile Mughal territory, *ashrāf* Muslims, Kayasthas, and Khatris were equally important agents of the new print culture.

A characteristic pattern among Hindi and Urdu printer-publishers was that of 'men from families and/or castes with a literary heritage' who 'received some formal education and then learned the printing and newspaper business on-the-job training' (Kerr 1979: 286). Whether professionals or amateurs, many entered the world of print as journalists and newspaper editors. In this they differed markedly from those printer-publishers based in the metropolises of Madras, Calcutta, and Bombay, who usually received their training at missionary or government presses.[67] Pioneers like Munshi Naval Kishore, or his mentor Munshi Harsukh Rai (1816–90), exemplify a different pattern, in that they were men with journalistic leanings who were drawn into the realm of print through the newspaper business, having usually learned their craft in the establishment of a compatriot. Harsukh Rai had served as editor to *Jām-e Jamshed*, an Urdu journal of Meerut, before he shifted to Lahore in 1849 to set up his own shop and launch the Punjab's first Urdu paper in the form of *Koh-e Nūr*. It was here that Naval Kishore, in turn, served his apprenticeship in printing and journalism.

Few among these enterprising pioneers of print were endowed with the necessary financial resources and entrepreneurial talent that would allow them to turn their presses into viable publishing houses. Many, in fact, had no interest in doing so. The most conspicuous result of the rapid spread of lithography in northern India was the proliferation of small and short-lived newspaper presses that generally maintained a precarious existence on the brink of bankruptcy. Such was the allure of the newspaper press (and the degree of failure) that the educationist Raja Shiva Prasad remarked at one point: 'In this country a man not fit for any business undertakes one of the three professions—teaching, medicine or editing some newspaper.'[68] The proprietors of these small presses were often autodidacts who, willy-nilly, combined the jobs of writer, printer, and editor. Given the volatility and financial risks involved

[67] Gangakishore Bhattacharya, the first Bengali publisher, was a former employee of the Serampore Mission Press (Kopf 1969: 120). Ganpat Krishnaji, founder of Ganpat Krishnaji's Press in Bombay (est. 1831) was a pressman at the American Mission Press, who used his expertise to build up his own press-machinery and cast fonts in Marathi, Gujarati and Hindi. Javaji Dadaji Chaudhuri, a man of humble origin, worked at the American Mission Press and Times of India Press before he founded the famed Nirnaysagar Press in 1869 (Priolkar 1958: 102–3).

[68] *AECR* 1884: 316.

in the newspaper trade, its allure can hardly be explained by the hope of profits alone.

If not material gains, what then motivated Indian pioneers of print? For many, editing a vernacular paper constituted an intellectual pursuit rather than a commercial activity. Journalism, in Sudhir Chandra's telling phrase, was 'a mission rather than a profitable business' (Chandra 1992: 25), inspired by a variety of reformist, religious, educational, social, and political concerns. This in part also holds true for early book publishing. To the aspiring literate classes, print opened up new possibilities of cultural and political participation, of voicing individual and collective concerns. Whether in the form of journalism or book publishing, it was an agent of progress and change, and a potentially powerful weapon in colonial and indigenous debates over Indian modernity. Print afforded an opportunity to spread information, knowledge, and reformist thought on a supra-regional level. To many, it was a means of entering the fray of political, rationalist, and religious discourse and shaping 'public' opinion, be it in the name of a particular community, class, sect, or the general public.

With the commercialization of the publishing trade, print also began to offer new opportunities of subsistence which linked neatly with the traditional occupations of the scribal and clerical castes. As elsewhere, North Indian press proprietors fall into two main categories: professional printer-publishers who operated presses for their livelihood, and amateur or private printers, for whom book printing may have constituted a supplementary means of income but was most of all an intellectual pursuit, a reformist concern, or simply an artistic pastime. In the latter category we find a predominance of government servants who followed a regular job in the educational, judicial, or revenue sector and adopted printing as a sideline. The two categories frequently overlap, with many Indian intellectuals of public service or professional background embarking on temporary careers as 'professional' printer-publishers at some stage in their lives. Others took to printing after their retirement from public service.

As regards their educational background, North Indian printer-publishers characteristically combined a grounding in Indian literary and knowledge traditions with some exposure to Western education, usually received at one of the government colleges at Delhi, Agra, Benares, or Bareilly. In forging the career of many a future publicist and publisher, Delhi College (est. 1825) provided an especially significant impetus to the development of the printing profession in the North. A pioneering institution in combining Western and Oriental learning, the college set up its own press in 1845, from where it issued various journals, textbooks, and works of scientific literature (Minault 1999; 2003). Even prior to that, it produced several alumni who rose to prominence in the realm of print.

Among Muslims, editors and printer-publishers typically belonged to the high social strata of the *ashrāf*. Some came from highly respectable and learned families, who played an important part in the intellectual life of their time. The most salient examples are Sayyid Muhammad Khan and his younger brother Sir Sayyid Ahmad Khan, who belonged to one of the great service families of the Mughal empire. In 1841 Sayyid Muhammad established a lithographic press, from where, under the editorship of Sayyid ᶜAbdul Ghafoor, *Sayyid al-Akhbār* as well as a number of learned and poetical works by distinguished contemporaries were published—among them Ghalib's *Dīvān*. In turn, Sayyid Ahmad Khan maintained a small private press for some years, through which he supported the publication of scientific and literary works by the Scientific Society at considerable personal expense. The press, and printing material worth Rs 8,000, were later made over to the society (Muhammad 1978.1: 129). Another well-known figure among the pioneers of print in Delhi was Maulana Muhammad Baqir, a member of a Persian émigré family, who published *Dehlī Urdū Akhbār* (est. 1837), the first Urdu paper in Delhi, from his lithographic press.[69] Educated at Delhi College, Muhammad Baqir had taught there for some time before taking up a post in the collector's office. In his publishing work he was assisted by his father Maulana Muhammad Akbar, as also by his son, the eminent future literary critic Muhammad Husain 'Azad' (1831–1910), who, following his education at Delhi College, served as 'printer and publisher' at the Delhi Urdu Akhbar Press for some years (Pritchett 1995: 11–12).

Another remarkable Delhi College student who embarked on a short-lived career in print was Maulvi Karimuddin (b. 1822?). He belonged to a family of Sunni ᶜulama of Panipat. A prolific translator and author, Karimuddin is best known for his biographical anthology *Ṭabaqāt-e shuᶜarā-e Hind* (1847) and his history of India *Wāqiᶜāt-e Hind* (1863), a classic of colonial textbook literature.[70] In 1845 he and some partners

[69] For a discussion of the early years of the *Dehlī Urdū Akhbār*, see Pernau 2003. As Pernau has shown, Maulvi Muhammad Baqir was neither the founder-editor of the paper nor the original proprietor of the Delhi Urdu Akhbar Press. See also Khan 1991: 67–72.

[70] Powell 1999; Sabiri 1953 (1): 268–80.

set up the Rifah-e ʿAm Press with the express purpose of printing translations of difficult scientific works. Soon after, he also launched two Urdu journals, *Karīm al-Akhhār* and *Gul-e Raʿnā*, and began publishing a number of non-scientific Persian and Urdu books. However, he was frauded by his business partners and in 1848 had to close down his press, having sold its stock of books at a dumping price. He later embarked on a career in the Punjab education service.

A third future editor-publisher among Delhi College graduates was Munshi Muhammad ʿAzim who belonged to a reputed family of Muslim *pīrzāda*s (descendants of Sufi masters) from Mecca. He was trained as a compositor at the Delhi Gazette Press. In 1849 he established the Lahore Chronicle Press, from where he launched the *Lahore Chronicle*, the first English newspaper in the Punjab (Latif 1981: 342). Later he founded an influential Urdu paper in the form of *Panjābī Akhbār*.

Delhi College not only produced newspaper editors but also a distinguished publisher of Islamic literature in the person of Maulana Muhammad Ahsan Nanautavi, scion of a famous family of ʿulama closely connected with the Deoband *madrasah*.[71] The Nanautah family epitomizes the way in which reformist ʿulama availed themselves of print. Muhammad Ahsan's father, Maulana Mamluk ʿAli, was a highly reputed *ʿalim* who had worked as head teacher of Arabic at Delhi College. His cousin, the well-known religious leader and co-founder of the Deoband school Maulana Muhammad Qasim, took employment in 1850 in the Delhi Ahmadi Press (est. 1845), owned by his teacher Maulana Ahmad ʿAli Saharanpuri, a pioneering publisher of Islamic literature and the reformist teachings of Shah Wali Allah (Metcalf 1982: 77–8). After 1857 Muhammad Qasim went to Meerut, where he joined the Mujtabaʾi Press as a proofreader and collator. Later he became associated with the local Hashimi Press (est. 1859), from where he published a substantial number of Islamic works.[72] In turn, Muhammad Ahsan, having graduated from Delhi College, took up employment as head Persian teacher at Bareilly College. In 1862 he bought two lithographic presses, and, together with his brother Maulana Muhammad Munir, established the Siddiqi Press in Bareilly in order to bring out Arabic and Persian classics in translation, as well as a number of original religious works in

[71] The following information is largely based on Metcalf 1982.

[72] The Hashmi Press was owned by Maulana Hashm ʿAli, an associate of Muhammad Qasim, and run by his son Maulana Hakim Muhammad ʿUmar (Khan 1990: 372–3; Rizvi 1980: 83).

Urdu.[73] His multifaceted career—he was 'at once an *ʿalim*, a government servant, a writer, a newspaper editor, a book publisher, and a businessman' (Metcalf 1982: 242)—illustrates the versatility of Muslim ʿulama in making use of the modern print media. It also testifies to their new reliance on the printed word (increasingly in Urdu) in spreading religious tenets. Muhammad Ahsan's work was continued by his stepson ʿAbdul Ahad who, in 1886, acquired the distinguished Mujtabaʾi Press (est. 1863) in Delhi. Specializing in editions of the Qurʾan and Islamic literature, it achieved a stature second only to the NKP (ibid.: 243–4).

The Deobandi ʿulama were not the only religious leaders to embrace print; the Farangi Mahall family of Lucknow, if somewhat later, did likewise. Mention has already been made of Muhammad Yaʿqub, who published two influential journals, *Ṭ̤ilism-e Lakhnaʾū* and *Kārnāmah*, from the two presses he ran in Lucknow before and after the 'Mutiny'. Maulana Fakhruddin of Farangi Mahall worked for some time as a translator and editor of *Avadh Akhbār* at Naval Kishore's press. Yet, for the longest time, most of the works emanating from Farangi Mahall were printed outside Lucknow, at Delhi's Mujtabaʾi Press and at other presses run by 'ulama (Rizvi 1980: 84). It seems that it was only in 1894, with the establishment of the Yusufi Press by Maulvi Muhammad Yusuf, that Farangi Mahall began operating its own printing offices.

Among Hindus, unsurprisingly, it was the scribal community of the Kayasthas, followed by various Brahmin castes, which constituted by far the strongest presence in the book trade. Munshi Harsukh Rai, the doyen of Urdu printing and journalism in the Punjab, was a Bhatnagar Kayastha from Sikandarabad. Munshi Shivnarayan 'Aram', founder-proprietor of the Mufid-e Khalaʾiq Press, belonged to an affluent Kayastha family of Agra.[74] Like Naval Kishore, he had received his higher education in Persian and English at Agra College, but quite unlike the former he graduated from the college and went on to work there as a teacher of English before setting up his press. With his English education and employment in educational service, Shivnarayan corresponds to what

[73] Metcalf 1982: 243. British records generally name Muhammad Munir as the 'printer and publisher' at the Siddiqi Press. *Home Dept. Public Branch*. 9 Oct 1869; QLP, NWP 1869, second quarter.

[74] Shivnarayan's grandfather, Nazir Bansi Dhar, was a high court officer who invested his wealth in landholding. According to the testimony of Mirza Ghalib, whose family had long-standing connections with that of Bansi Dhar, the latter acquired a big estate 'which paid something like ten or twelve thousand rupees in land revenue to the government' (Russell/Islam 1994: 179).

C.A. Bayly has called the 'new munshi' (Bayly 1996a: 229–30): even while embarking on a career in publishing he remained closely tied to British patronage and served not only as a collaborator in educational schemes but also as a prime source of 'native opinion'. Another English-educated 'new munshi' who assumed the function of mediator-informant for the British was Munshi Sadasukhlal, the proprietor of the Nur al-Absar Press at Agra. His services to government were rewarded by his appointment to the post of Chief Government Translator. He shifted his press to Allahabad where it continued to thrive on official patronage. Little did it matter to Sadasukhlal that his journal *Nūr al-Absār* was no longer popular with the Indian public who regarded him as a turncoat (Bayly 1996a: 342): government support more than compensated for the decline in public subscriptions.[75]

The preponderance of Brahmins among Benares printer-publishers has already been noted. Unfortunately, no information is available on the background of these enterprising pandits hailing from Bengal, Maharashtra, or the Gangetic core region. Precious little is known about their individual motives and the specific circumstances under which they established their printing houses. While Dhirendranath Singh (1986) and, more recently, Orsini (2004a and b) have provided some valuable insights, this important chapter in the intellectual history of Benares remains unwritten. The sizeable number of learned Brahmins entering the publishing trade in Benares and elsewhere indicates that print was well compatible with their scribal and intellectual concerns.

Even Kashmiri Pandits could be seen to overcome the traditional aversion of their community towards commercial enterprise and enter the realm of print (Sender 1988: 164–5). Perhaps the first to do so was Pandit Moti Lal Kashmiri, who served as printer-publisher at the Delhi Urdu Akhbar Press in the 1830s. The most salient example, however, is that of Pandit Mukund Ram (1831–97), the founder-proprietor of the Mitra Vilas Press in Lahore (est. 1861). The son of a Kashmiri Brahmin priest of Srinagar, Mukund Ram provides a prime example of a self-made man who displayed a remarkable degree of enterprise and resourcefulness in his career. In 1848 he set out penniless for Lahore, where he opened a small calligraphy shop. According to his son, Kanhaiyalal, 'from his earning a[nna]s 2 a day he rose to be the *Chaudhri* (head man) of all the caligraphists of Lahore and transacted business of thousand rupees. From thence through the help and encouragement of the late

[75] 400 copies of *Nūr al-Absār* were taken by Government, while there were only 40 Indian subscribers. *PGNWP. General Dept.*, 10th June 1865: 65.

chief Pandit Radha Kishen, he was successful in establishing his press' (Kanhaiyalal n.d.: 6–7).[76] The account fails to mention that Mukund Ram derived a substantial amount of his income from serving as a calligrapher to Harsukh Rai's Koh-e Nur Press. The Mitra Vilas Press was established with the avowed purpose of publishing 'rare old MSS. and new works of distinguished scholars of Sanskrit of the rising generation' (ibid.: 10). Yet Mukund Ram's rise to prominence rested largely on his publications in Persian and Urdu. In 1870 he launched *Akhbār-e ʿĀm*, introducing the concept of a low-priced 'penny' paper in Urdu journalism.

Among the Kashmiri Pandits of Lucknow it was Pandit Kishan Narayan Zardchop, a former *taḥṣīldār* and the first president of the Lucknow Reform Club (Jalsah-e Tahzib), who initiated the move to the new print media with a view to fostering community interests. Upon his retirement in 1872, together with Pandit Sri Kishan Takru, he launched the monthly *Murāsala-e Kashmīr*, the first caste organ of the Kashmiri Brahmin community. The journal was first printed at the NKP; in 1875, however, the Kashmiri Pandits decided to set up their own press. It was named Bahar-e Kashmir Press after Shivnarayan 'Bahar', the late editor of *Murāsala* and a pivotal community member. Alongside the reformist journal *Mirāt al-Hind,* it issued a number of ephemeral writings expressing caste concerns.[77]

It was not only to the literate upper-caste elites that print offered new opportunities. With the industry's rapid commercialization in the second half of the century, the social background of those connected with the printing trade expanded to include men from humble origins as well. Anindita Ghosh has noted the influx, from the 1860s onwards, of non-scribal lower castes of smiths and artisans into the thriving Calcutta printing industry, which provided much better opportunities to them than their traditional occupation (Ghosh 1998: 180; 2002: 4332). While no comparable data exist for the NWP&Oudh, there is some evidence to suggest that in the North, too, people from lower social strata gradually began to avail themselves of the opportunities offered by print. This can be gathered, for example, from a rather disparaging comment made by DPI M. Kempson in 1874:

> Obviously, very little capital or enterprise is embarked in the printing and publishing trade. These are not the attributes of the class of natives who manage the business. Many of the publishers are poor and involved in debt, and keep up next to no establishment. Their stock consists in two or three

[76] See also Sender 1988: 216–17.

[77] Details in Sabiri 1953: 564–76; Sender 1988.

> lithographic stones and some coarse paper, with a rude Press for securing the impressions. Some of them are mere pressmen, who have learned the work in service, and have set up for themselves.[78]

Kempson professed to know of only one instance in which the lithograph work taught in jails had been utilized by an ex-prisoner as a means of livelihood. It is difficult to say whether he underestimated the impact of state prisons in providing training to large numbers of Indian pressmen. Printing had indeed become the most profitable branch of the colonial jail industries, with the central prisons in Agra and Lucknow running large typographic and lithographic departments.

While little is known about non-elite participation in the printing trade, by the 1880s a different and fairly heterogeneous social group comes into the foreground among Indian editors and publishers: writers and literati. Print had always constituted a natural attraction for the writer community, long before commercial printing, with its new genres of fictional literature, produced the 'professional' author who could live by his writing. Over the last decades of the century increasing numbers of aspiring authors were lured into setting up their own presses, more often than not at great financial risk. Many of them were largely ignorant of the practicalities of publishing and unable to effectively deal with the more mundane aspects of press proprietorship. The scholar-poet Pandit Mannalal Sharma 'Dvij', who in the early 1860s established the Kashi Sanskrit Press at Benares, was a notable exception in his successful career as a publisher of Sanskrit and Hindi works (Singh 1991). Rather more typical in their ephemeral attempts at press proprietorship were the writers of Bharatendu Harishchandra's literary circle. Harishchandra himself ran a small private press under the name of Harishchandra Chandrika Press for some time, but does not seem to have printed much apart from a few works authored by his father Gopalchand 'Girdhardas', a prolific Brajbhasha poet (Singh 1986: 76). While Harishchandra used the services of an array of publishers to publicize his writings, his own interest in print rested chiefly in deploying it as a journalistic medium. The way in which he availed himself of print as a publicist, essayist, and founder-editor of the influential pioneering magazines *Kavivacansudhā* (1868), *Bālābodhinī* (1874), and *Hariścandra-candrikā* (1874) provided an example to many literati: in 1876, the drama and fiction writer Shrinivas Das opened a small press in Delhi from where he launched a Hindi journal called *Sadādarś* and later published his *Parīkṣāguru* (1882), generally

[78] *RPIR* 1874: 24–5.

acclaimed as the first modern novel in Hindi. Pandit Ambikadatt Vyas followed suit and in 1883 set up a press in Bhagalpur to bring out his own writings as well as two journals. Other contemporary Hindi writers—Balkrishna Bhatt, Chaudhari Badarinarayan Upadhyaya 'Premghan', Pratapnarayan Mishra, Balmukund Gupta—turned to the new print media primarily to engage in a kind of journalistic writing that combined literary and patriotic concerns.[79] By contrast Devkinandan Khatri, the famed author of the first best-selling serial novel in Hindi, *Candrakāntā* (1892), used the income from his novel to found his own press. Churning out a continuous stream of fiction, his Lahri Press (est. 1898) flourished and became one of the foremost commercial presses in Benares (Orsini 2004b: 123–4).

The community of Hindi writers found a liberal benefactor in the person of Ramdin Singh, founder-proprietor of the Khadgavilas Press of Bankipur (Patna) in Bihar and the first major literary publisher in Hindi. Ramdin Singh, whose career has been excellently documented by Dhirendranath Singh (1986), belonged to a well-to-do family of Kshatriya *zamīndār*s of Ballia. While his own career as a writer was limited to authoring school textbooks, he was a lover of Hindi poetry and a great admirer of Bharatendu Harishchandra. In 1880 he gave up his humble job as a village schoolteacher and set up the Khadgavilas Press with the express purpose of promoting contemporary Hindi authors. In the tried fashion, the opening of his press was accompanied by the launch of a journal, *Kṣatriya Patrikā*. Belying its name, this was a literary rather than caste journal. However, it appealed enough to community spirits to receive the support of some affluent local rulers such as the Maharaja of Udaipur. In his aim to propagate Hindi literature Ramdin Singh spared no expense. He gave considerable financial assistance to Harishchandra, who made him his exclusive publisher and extolled him as 'a true and dear friend who is as passionately devoted to the advancement of Hindi as myself and is prepared to sacrifice his health, wealth and time to the cause of Hindi' (cited in Madan Gopal 1972: 155).

Although the Khadgavilas Press assumed prime importance in the early history of Hindi publishing, and despite the fact that Ramdin Singh made substantial profits which he invested in landed property (Gupt

[79] Their respective journals *Hindī Pradīp* (est. 1877), *Ānandkadambinī* (est. 1881), *Brāhmaṇ* (est. 1883), and *Bhāratmitra* (est. 1878) engaged in the critique of British rule in a more or less trenchant manner. While providing a forum for nationalist concerns, they also discussed literary issues and became important in the development of a modern Hindi prose style. See Mishra 1985; Chandra 1992.

1994: 31), he can hardly be reckoned among the new class of North Indian 'print capitalists'. As a Hindi literary publishing house, the production of his press was rather confined in size and scope. He could not vie with those large general publishers who offered a widely diversified range of mass-produced printed items in various languages and who had started to make huge profits.

What then distinguished a print capitalist like Naval Kishore from his humbler fellow workers in the publishing trade? It will be argued here that, rather than social background or educational opportunities, the roots of success lay in his ability to combine on the one hand the 'traditional' roles of the publisher as intellectual forerunner and connoisseur of elite and popular reading tastes, with on the other those of industrial entrepreneur, businessman, and modern employer. In the increasingly competitive market economy of colonial India—as perhaps in all other times as well—successful entrepreneurship, while by no means precluding literary and scholarly concerns, demanded the instincts of a businessman. Success as a publisher invariably presupposed the ability to secure government patronage—perhaps the most crucial financial factor in the growth of Indian printing firms at the time.

In this context, the success stories of Munshi Naval Kishore and Munshi Gulab Singh, founder-proprietor of the immensely successful Mufid-e ʿAm Press at Lahore (est. 1877), offer some interesting parallels. Both men belonged to a traditional middle-class background. Neither had large monetary resources when embarking on a career in print. Gulab Singh had worked as a schoolteacher and established a small printing shop to publish his own vernacular textbooks. Yet both publishers were from the outset on close terms with the colonial authorities. Starting off with educational printing and other contract work, their firms eventually flourished under official patronage. While Naval Kishore made his first large profit with a contract for printing the Urdu version of the Indian Penal Code in the 1860s, for Gulab Singh the commercial breakthrough came with a large printing contract for Census work in the 1880s. He subsequently rose to the position of official Government Publisher and Bookseller in the Punjab and was put in charge of the Government Book Depot.[80]

However, to fully understand the factors accounting for the rise of the most successful among North Indian publishers, it is not enough to record the impact of official patronage. One also needs to investigate the extent

[80] *Cyclopedia of India*, vol. 2: 324. *Thacker's Indian Directory* 1888.

and nature of a publisher's indigenous social and commercial networks. Naval Kishore's career, if extraordinary in many respects, exemplifies some of the typical dynamics in the making of an Indian print capitalist. Before turning to his life and career in the next chapter, it is necessary to take a closer look at the framework of colonial rule under which Indian printer-publishers operated. The legal measures and regulations introduced by the colonial state at various points in the nineteenth century affected not only the newspaper press but also the publishing and book trade, entailing both advantages and disadvantages.

1.5 Control *versus* Encouragement: Publishing under Colonial Legislation

The introduction of print in India at first gave rise to a vibrant newspaper press. By the 1820s the early Anglo-Indian journals of Calcutta were joined by the first Indian-language papers in expressing their critique of colonial policy and attacking its representatives. It was this increasingly recalcitrant newspaper press that constituted the original focus of colonial legislation on the printing trade. Faced with the double imperative of closely monitoring and at the same time nurturing the nascent Indian press, the colonial state reacted with a succession of measures that entailed alternating phases of liberal encouragement and strict censorship. While the implications of press laws and their adverse effects on the Indian-language press have been discussed at length elsewhere, a brief recapitulation of the salient legislation will be useful here to show the extent to which it impacted on the publishing and book trade.[81]

Even while receiving official encouragement, the 'native' press remained under close surveillance throughout the century. With book publishing, the situation was markedly different, for the utility of Indian enterprise in the field was widely acknowledged by the colonial state. As long as its output consisted predominantly of educational and religious works—as also of popular tales, astrological handbooks, almanacs, and other such ephemera—the indigenous book trade gave little reason for concern or direct intervention. Priya Joshi has noted the colonial authorities' 'remarkably sanguine' attitude towards print through much of the nineteenth century (Joshi 2002: 47). This attitude was partly based on the necessity of co-opting Indian publishers in the great utilitarian programme of disseminating 'useful' knowledge and Western enlightenment

[81] E.g. Barns 1940; Natarajan 1954; S. Ghosh 1998. The following overview is largely based on these works.

in Indian regional languages. After 1854 the colonial state, in its engagement with mass primary education, began to depend heavily on indigenous collaboration. In short, there were only two kinds of books that called for special scrutiny on the part of the authorities: seditious writings and, increasingly, literature of an 'obscene' or 'immoral' nature.

The first quarter of the nineteenth century was marked by controversies over censorship and freedom of the press that arose between the colonial authorities and the pioneers of the English language press in Calcutta. With the appearance of the first Indian-language papers after 1818, official attention shifted to the vernacular press, leading to the first confrontations with Raja Rammohan Roy and other champions of early Indian journalism. During that period book printers were able to operate in relative liberty. This was to change with the promulgation of the Press Ordinance of 1823 under Governor General John Adam. The Adam regulations imposed for the first time rigid restrictions on the press, making the establishment of a printing press subject to licence and introducing strict criteria for both the grant of a licence and the publication of printed matter. The authorities were invested with the power to immediately withdraw licences whenever it was deemed expedient. Infringement against any part of the regulations was met with severe fines and could lead to imprisonment and confiscation of the press. Foreboding the notorious Vernacular Press Act of 1878, the 1823 regulations directly targeted the increasingly vocal vernacular press and sought to introduce a distinction between Indian-owned papers and the English-language journals edited by Englishmen.[82] These regulations were vehemently opposed by Rammohan Roy, India's most eloquent advocate of a free press. When his appeal against them was rejected, he discontinued his weekly *Mirāt al-Akhbār* in protest.

The 1830s inaugured a new era of liberal policy under Governor General Lord William Cavendish Bentinck and subsequently Sir Charles Metcalfe. A firm believer in freedom of the press, Metcalfe perceived it as an integral part of the British civilizing mission and a prerequisite for legitimate government. In order to introduce a general law for the whole of India he had the 1823 ordinance repealed and replaced by Act XI of 1835. The liberal 1835 act came at a time when lithography was beginning to spread in North India. The combined effect was a surge in printing and publishing activity. While subject to heavy criticism, Metcalfe's liberalizing measures were endorsed by his successor, Lord Auckland.

[82] For a more detailed account, see Natarajan 1954: 21–7.

Meanwhile, British involvement in Indian education had been advanced by the appointment of a General Committee of Public Instruction in 1823 and the renewal of the East India Company's Charter in 1833, which entailed a rise in the educational grant. For the two next decades Anglicization, as laid out in Thomas Macaulay's Minute on Education (1835), remained the primary goal of colonial investment in education. It was only in the wake of the Education Despatch of 1854 that the colonial state turned to the instruction of the Indian masses. While English remained the language of higher education, the new policy of imparting primary and secondary education through the Indian languages entailed an unprecedented activity in official educational publishing. For the first time Indian printer-publishers directly profited from the scheme, for it involved a large amount of contract work.

The 'golden era' inaugurated by Lord Bentinck was to last until 1857, when the uprising greatly disrupted social and commercial life in urban North India. To counteract the seditious potential of the press, Lord Canning hastily enacted the so-called 'Gagging Act' in June 1857, reintroducing the licence system and renewing the strict censorship provisions of the Adam regulations of 1823. The government was given discretionary powers to grant and revoke licences at any time and to prohibit the publication of any newspaper, book, or printed pamphlet (S. Ghosh 1998: 123). Drastic as the new act was, it remained a temporary measure and was lifted after a year. While it led a number of Bengali publishers into trouble, it proved of little consequence in the NWP where the events of the uprising were disruptive enough in themselves to force most printing presses out of business.

When, in November 1858, the British crown took over direct government of India, a new and extended period of relative press freedom commenced under the reign of Queen Victoria. Whatever suspicions of the vernacular press the Rebellion had created, they were counterbalanced by pragmatic considerations, notably the pressing need to gain better insight into 'native opinion' and win over Indian publicists as allies in the tremendous task of restoring law and order as well as public confidence. Under Lord Canning a more lenient policy was adopted, in which encouragement and censorship were cautiously weighed against each other. Support for the new policy came from educational officers. Henry Stuart Reid, first DPI in the NWP, voiced a common opinion when pointing to the benefits of a *partial* encouragement of the vernacular press: 'The people must have newspapers of some kind or other', he asserted. 'The more respectable aided by the patronage of the Government drive the seditiously disposed Editors out of the field.'[83] The same trust in competition and the self-regulatory forces of patronage was echoed by James Long in his 1859 report on the native press in Bengal. Long openly warned against the dire consequences of too rigid a censorship, whose effects on 'good Government and sound education' could be nothing but 'suidical'. Instead, he advocated a more benevolent supervision: 'In the present position of India, the Native Press as the *exponent of the Native mind* ought to be attended to: if the *sound* part of the native press be encouraged by the Authorities, it will become the instrument of much good; if it be left in the hands of ill-designing ignorant men, it will be the source of much evil' (Long 1859: ii).

The policy adopted by the government in the wake of 1857 gave printers almost complete freedom. As a result, the domestic book trade flourished. Rather than resorting to the law, the colonial state increasingly relied on a new kind of mechanism to retain control over the activities of Indian publishers: government patronage became the single-most important means of rewarding 'loyal' editors and publishers, particularly those who collaborated in the colonial scheme of disseminating 'useful' literature. Withdrawal of patronage, on the other hand, proved an equally effective means of control: exercised relentlessly, it could see a publisher out of business. Legislation during the period was largely supportive of the growth of regional-language printing and of a regulative rather than restrictive kind. This is clearly evident in the most important law of the period, the 'Regulation of Printing Press and Newspaper Act XXV' of 1867 (renamed 'Press and Registration of Books Act' after its amendment in 1890).[84] Replacing the Metcalfe Act of 1835, it was primarily aimed at keeping the government informed about the activities and output of the mushrooming private and commercial presses. Yet, in formalizing the registration of books and consolidating intellectual copyright, it also gave a new degree of legal security to Indian publishers. This deserves to be looked at more closely.

Registration of Books and Copyright

As in metropolitan Britain, book registration and copyright protection in colonial India derived from mechanisms originally developed to control

[83] *Report on the State of Popular Education in the NWP for 1856/57 and 1857/58*: 38.

[84] For the wording of the 'The Press and Registration of Books Act (Amendment of 1890)', see Natarajan 1954: 74–80.

the press.[85] Copyright legislation in India dates back to the Indian Copyright Act of 1847 (Act XX of 1847), which was to affirm the application to India of the law obtaining in the British dominions, notably the Copyright Act of 1842 and the International Copyright Act of 1844.[86] Aiming to 'afford greater encouragement to the Production of literary works of lasting benefit to the World', the 1842 act centred on the copyright in books which was vested with the author (Law 2000: 164–5). In keeping with it, the Indian Copyright Act fixed the term of copyright at forty-two years from the date of publication, or at the natural life of the author and seven years thereafter, whichever period was longer. The act also forbade the import of foreign reprints of British books into England or her colonies. Proprietorship of copyright was formally assigned by an entry in the registry book. Publishers could claim copyright as first publishers of a given book or as proprietors of an author's manuscript from which a book was published.[87] The law, as Feather explains, was based on the clear assumption 'that copyright originated with the author, but that, because the author could only use the property thus created if it were shared with a publisher, the publisher was also afforded some protection' (Feather 1994: 147–8).

In Britain, as much as in her colonies, early copyright legislation proved unsatisfactory and was unable to keep pace with the changing relations between author, publisher, and bookseller in the rapidly modernizing world of print. Its deficiencies were most succinctly stated in the 1878 verdict of Queen Victoria's Copyright Commission: 'The law is wholly destitute of any sort of arrangement, incomplete, often obscure, and even when it is intelligible upon long study, it is in many parts so ill-expressed that no one who does not give such study to it can expect to understand it.'[88] While issues of copyright and piracy in nineteenth-century India have not been much studied, it can be said with some certainty that the law lagged behind practice. Lack of information on the legal provisions, for one, must have inhibited strict adherence to the law. With some Indian publishers barely aware of the content of the Copyright Act and others choosing to circumvent it, piracy and unlicensed reprinting of books must have been rampant. What certainly encouraged piracy was the fact that for a long time registering copyright was more honoured in the breach than the observance. Unlicensed reprinting was

[85] See Feather 1994 for a general historical survey of copyright in Britain.

[86] Thairani 1987: 1. See also *A Collection of Statutes Relating to India* 1899.

[87] *A Collection of Statutes* 1899: 195–206.

[88] 'Commissioners' Report of 1878, cited in Nowell-Smith 1968: 13.

most conspicuous in the case of widely used vernacular textbooks. The difficulty or absence of state enforcement did not help matters.

Copyright legislation also entailed some problems specific to the colonial situation. This is suggested by a petition addressed to the government by the Aligarh Scientific Society and British Indian Association in 1867, asking for an amendment to the 1847 act. Since the act did not exempt translations from copyright, the petitioners argued, it formed an 'insurmountable obstacle' to the society's objective of promoting modern Western knowledge through translation. To have to obtain the original author's sanction and pay a large copyright fee made such projects extremely difficult (Muhammad 1978.1: 288–90).

The significance of the 'Regulation of Printing Press and Newspaper Act XXV' of 1867 lies not only in its provision of an elaborate legal framework for the production and registration of books. For scholars of South Asian book history it has proved nothing short of a boon, for in its wake we find the first systematic attempt at a quantitative and qualitative registration of all literary and non-literary printed publications in Indian languages. Starting from 1868, the scheme initially took the form of *Quarterly Publication Lists* compiled separately for each province. These lists are a mine of invaluable data, providing details on a work's author or translator, its year and place of publication, subject, size, number of pages, edition, print run and sales price, on whether the book was typeset or lithographed, and on the proprietor of the copyright.[89] From 1874 the quarterly reports were summarized in the Home Department's yearly *Reports on Publications Issued and Registered in the Several Provinces of British India* (*RPIR*). Implied in them was an attempt to classify India's literary output by language and by principal generic categories that followed British criteria of what constituted 'noteworthy' literature: Arts, Biography, Drama, Fiction, History, Language, Medicine, Miscellaneous, Poetry, Politics, Philosophy (including Mental and Moral Science), Religion and Science (Mathematical and Mechanical). Unfortunately, the data contained in the reports are often unreliable. Figures are frequently distorted owing to a number of inaccuracies, such as the inclusion of illegitimate materials (time-tables, class lists, catalogues, etc.) and the exclusion of legitimate titles. Another problematic aspect is the failure to maintain a clear-cut distinction between books and 'tracts', the latter being sometimes included in the total of printed books and sometimes

[89] However, the reports were often compiled by British officials whose knowledge of the oriental languages and literatures was shallow. Hence, they are replete with transcription and translation errors, often to an inadvertently comic effect.

not.[90] Within data for a single year the statistics were skewed because of the omission of reprints; in another year the alleged 'indifference of publishers' towards registration was to blame.[91] Failure on the part of a large publisher to submit his titles in time could indeed result in a significant alteration of statistics. When, between 1879 and 1880, the total of books registered in the NWP&Oudh dipped from 541 to 409 titles, it was solely owing to the fact that Naval Kishore had not forwarded any books during the last quarter of 1880.[92] To further complicate matters, publishers often failed to state whether a title was a first edition or a reprint in new format. These imperfections notwithstanding, the data contained in the colonial reports present the most detailed and comprehensive documentation of the textual production of British India.

In stipulating that a copy of each registered title be deposited with the British Museum in London, the 1867 act also contributed significantly to the preservation of early printed books in South Asian languages. Most of the books have since gone into the British Library's Oriental and India Office Collections (OIOC), where they are accessible to scholars and researchers.

Finally, in formalizing registration, the 1867 act introduced some important changes in the physical appearance of nineteenth-century books. It stipulated that the name of the printer or publisher and the date and place of publication be printed legibly on the title page, allowing for a clear identification of the provenance of a given book or tract. This was a significant change from past practice, where books frequently bore no publication date or, as in the case of early printed Sanskrit books, lacked a title page—a legacy of the age of manuscripts. Another new feature on the title page was the copyright notice. The practice of official registration of books allowed for a public declaration of copyright by a simple statement of the 'name and residence of the proprietor of the copyright or of any portion of such copyright'.[93] Registration of copyright involved the payment of a fairly high fee of Rs 2 per title.

So alien, however, was the Western notion of protecting literary property to north Indian authors that they failed to respond to the new regulation. Authors in the Bengal region seem to have been far ahead of their compatriots in exercising their legal rights. As Long had noted in the 1850s, new Bengali works were generally rather highly priced when

[90] See also King 1994: 38–40.

[91] *PGNWP. Educational Dept.*, June 1873: 26; *RPIR* 1874: 21.

[92] *RPIR* 1879 and 1880.

[93] 'Press and Registration of Books Act, 1890', part 5, cited in Natarajan 1954: 78.

copy-wright, 'as various natives now find the composing of Bengali books profitable, and some authors draw a regular income from them' (Long 1859: 12). By contrast, almost a quarter of a century later, an NWP&Oudh report deplored that 'The advantages to be gained by the registration of copyrights are still but little known, or are imperfectly appreciated by native authors. Only 17 copyrights were registered last year, and all of these were copyrights owned by the Educational Department.'[94] With a mere two copyrights registered in Avadh in 1874, DPI John C. Nesfield resorted to special measures: in order to make the public acquainted with the advantages of having copyrights registered, he not only had a notice published in the *Educational Gazette*, but also, on receiving a book for registration, sent a note to the proprietor of the copyright advising him to have a copyright notice printed on the title page.[95] Nesfield's information campaign resulted in a temporary improvement, with ten copyrights registered during the course of the following year.[96] In the long run, however, it proved of little consequence: a decade later the percentage of registered copyrights, though considered to have 'considerably increased', still did not exceed a meagre six per cent of all registered titles.[97]

Suppressing 'Obscene' Literature

The colonial state exercised not only political but also moral surveillance. With the rise of Victorianism in the second half of the century, colonial concerns over 'immoral' and 'obscene' literature had specific implications for Indian publishers. Complaints about the alleged immoral character of specific genres of oriental literature both 'high' and 'low' were nothing new, but had been raised by Orientalists and British officials for some time.[98] Such perceptions drew on wider stereotypical notions of the 'lascivity' and 'unbridled sensuality' of an essentially 'decadent' East; underlying these were various colonial motives that ranged from moral indignation and puritanism to differing aesthetic sensibilities. However, it was not until the 1850s, when commercial print culture first began to allow the mass production and widespread distribution of popular

[94] *OAR* 1873–4: 96.

[95] *RPIR* 1874: 33.

[96] *OAR* 1875–6: 85. In the NWP, the number of registered copyrights during the same year was 17. *PGNWP. General Dept.*, October 1876: 8.

[97] *Report on the Administration of the NWP&Oudh*, for the year ending 31st March, 1886: 195.

[98] For details, see Ch. Gupta 2000: 93–4; 2001: 30–8.

forms of indigenous literature, that the colonial state felt compelled to react to the perceived 'obscenity threat' with legal measures.

By this time puritanical tendencies had gained momentum in Victorian England and were fast making their impact on colonial society. With shifting perceptions, 'Erotic' became a new classificatory category for Indian printed literature, as first evident in the series of reports on the Bengal book trade compiled by James Long for the government in the 1850s (Roy 1996). Significantly, legislation on obscenity in India appeared almost simultaneously with the 1857 Obscene Publications Acts in Britain, an act resulting from the crusading zeal of the early Methodist anti-vice societies.[99] While the British act was designed with a view to curbing the flourishing London underworld trade in pornographic books (later it served to ban some celebrated works of nineteenth-century European literature), obscenity laws in India initially did not target any specific literary genre.

The earliest Indian obscenity law was the Obscene Books and Pictures Act (Act I of 1856), which imposed a fine or imprisonment for the sale of obscene books or pictures.[100] Noting the case of 'one most hideously obscene book with its 20 most filthy pictures', of which over 30,000 copies had been sold within one year, Long was explicit in his satisfaction with the introduction of legal measures. 'The terror of the law against obscene publications is effecting what a regard to morality could not' (Long 1859: xxv), he asserted confidently. Following the 1856 act, legislation relating to obscenity was consolidated in the Indian Penal Code of 1860. Sections 292, 293, and 294 of the penal code prohibited the sale, distribution, import or printing of any 'obscene' book, pamphlet, picture, etc., as also the possession of the same for the purpose of sale or exhibition. Infringement of the law could result in imprisonment of up to three months or a fine, or both.

It is significant that the Penal Code did not define obscenity. Hence, extremely divergent material and literary genres could be classified as obscene (Gupta 2000: 89). Also, there was no attempt to distinguish

[99] Craig 1963: 40–53; Travis 2000: 4–9.

[100] The Act contained the following clause: 'Whoever, within the territories in the possession of the East India Company, of any shop, bazar, street, thoroughfare, highroad, or any place of public resort, distributes, sells or offers or exposes for sale or willfully exposes to public view, any obscene song, ballad, or works to the annoyance of others; shall, upon conviction, . . . be liable to a fine not exceeding hundred rupees, or to imprisonment with or without hard labour, for a period not exceeding three months, or to both' (cited in Roy 1996: 61).

between 'erotic' and 'obscene'. Rather, these terms were used interchangeably as evident from Long's terse statement: 'By Erotic is meant books abounding in obscene passages' (Long 1859: xxv). It was in no way required that a book deal as explicitly with sexual intercourse as the *Laẓẓat al-nisā* (Pleasure of Women)—a Persian version of the Sanskrit erotic classic *Kokaśāstra*—for it to be proscribed by government for its alleged indecency.[101] Any kind of work of an erotic or sensual nature prone to injuring Victorian sensibilities could theoretically be dismissed as 'obscene' or 'immoral'. As a result, the stigma of obscenity was frequently applied to works representing the most widely cherished of Indian literary genres, namely Urdu love lyrics and Hindi bhakti poetry. To F.B. Outram, Officiating Under Secretary to the NWP Government in 1858, this literature was a mere reflection of the general 'depravity' of Indian life and social conditions: '. . . it would be difficult to concoct books, more immoral in their tendency than the legends, traditions, and doctrines, which are instilled into the mind of every Hindoo by his spiritual guides, or the sensual aspirations which Mahomedanism delights in cherishing', he wrote. 'It is to be confessed too with sorrow, that Native Indian social life, even after 100 years of British efforts to establish decency, is about as prolific in wantonly degrading every-day circumstances, as the most prurient imagination could put in print.'[102]

Prior to the enactment of the Indian Penal Code, the NWP provincial authorities had limited themselves to excluding objectionable books from the educational curriculum, while largely refraining from exercising 'moral' censorship of a more pervasive kind. It was only when Matthew Kempson assumed the post of DPI in 1861 that publishers came under closer surveillance. An uncovenanted servant who had worked his way up the education service from private schoolmaster, Kempson has been portrayed as a much disliked and controversial figure (Powell 1999). He was clearly not overly sympathetic to indigenous enterprise in the book trade and generally confined his recognition to educational publishing, while remaining deeply distrustful of Indian publishers, whom he accused of withholding books 'of impure tendency' from registration.[103] No sooner had Kempson been assigned the post of DPI than he set out on a crusade

[101] The *Kokaśāstra,* also known as *Ratirahasya*, was a famed thirteenth-century sexual manual by Kokkoka. Its Persian version was published at least twice (Bombay 1869; Delhi 1873).

[102] *SRGNWP* 1858. 'Note on native presses and periodicals—1858': 43.

[103] *RPIR* 1876: 24.

to curb the spread of licentious literature in his province. Over time he advocated various measures to combat obscenity, the first and most lenient being increased patronage. In 1865 he urged that a larger share in textbook printing be given to Indian printer-publishers, who could hereby be turned into 'useful agents in education'. In the absence of such employment they were prone to 'fall back upon the issue of any rubbish they can find a market for'.[104]

Of rubbish Kempson saw plenty. Whole genres were subject to his wholesale condemnation: 'Whenever the term *Wasokht* occurs in the title . . . the subject matter is always of salacious tendency.'[105] He was particularly alarmed by the increasing number of Hindi translations of Persian and Urdu amatory poetry, a genre he unhesitatingly decried as 'trash'. The publication in 1863 of a Hindi version of Mir Hasan's immensely popular *Maṣnavī* from the Agra-based Ahmadi Press prompted him to urge government to establish an '*index expurgatorius*'.[106] The measure, he maintained, would be readily supported by 'all natives of respectability'.[107] Kempson's proposal met with little sympathy on the part of the government, which tried to restrain its overzealous servant, pointing to the impracticability of the suggested measure and the sufficiency of existing legal provisions. Since supply was stimulated by demand, the sober argument went, one could only hope for 'a general improvement in morality and literary taste'. It may not have escaped the authorities that Kempson's denigration of 'Mahomedan poetry' was not just a routine expression of the utilitarian contempt for poetry, but was nurtured by a more general prejudice against Muslim and Urdu culture. Indeed, in his report Kempson had explicitly stated that—

> The increase in the number of persons able to read their own vernacular has created a demand for books which illiterate and unprincipled printers meet with trash of this description, and it is a melancholy reflection that the vernacular, which we take to much pains in utilizing as an organ of education in the masses, should thus become a vehicle of immorality. It is almost incredible that a Hindu, capable of contrasting the principles of the English

[104] *PGNWP. General Dept.,* 10 June 1865: 81.

[105] *RPIR* 1877: 115.

[106] The reference is to Mir Hasan's *Siḥr al-bayān* (Enchanting Story, comp. 1785), a love poem generally considered to be one of the best examples of the *maṣnavī* genre. For a summary and discussion of the text, see Khurshidul Islam/Russell 1994: 69–94.

[107] *SRGNWP* 1864. 'Report on Native Presses . . . or the year 1864': 17.

> Government with the rule of his Mahommedan conquerors, should learn his own language with the aid and encouragement of the former and apply it to a revival of the latter.[108]

In the following year two small presses of Agra by the name of Mohammadi Press and Latafat Press came to his notice for issuing in large numbers a low-priced collection of erotic verse in Hindi called *Dil bahlāo* (Divert Your Mind). While invoking the morally corrupting effects of the book, in his report to government Kempson was more outspoken than before in his condemnation of the two Muslim publishers. Their offence called for draconian measures:

> The *Dilbahlao* . . . is bazar trash in the shape of ribald verses, some of them grossly indecent. It is stuff of this kind which arms native opposition to female education with its most powerful objections, and which poisons the minds of the youth in large towns. For one who reads, there are 100s who hear the libidinous suggestions and allusions. *The publishers are low Mahomedans, who eke out the profits of their presses by keeping up a supply of nastiness within the means of the poorest of their Hindoo fellow subjects.* The practice should be checked, and as the tracts bear the names of the presses, I hope his Honor will order revocation of licence in each case.[109] (emphasis added)

The government did not share Kempson's vision of the morally corrupt and corrupting 'Mahomedan' and in reply made it clear that there was no legal power to effect the withdrawal of licence of the Agra publishers. However, the offence was said to be punishable under the obscenity sections of the Indian Penal Code.

Kempson's strong anti-Muslim prejudice is further underscored by the fact that, in the same report, he let the well-known Hindu proprietor of the Mufid-e Khalaʾiq Press, Munshi Shivnarayan, get away with a rebuke for an identical offence. True, he noted with 'much regret' that a man of Shivnarayan's position and education had 'disgraced' his press through several objectionable publications, hereby 'lending [it] equally with the low Mahomedan publishers of Agra to pander to the vicious tendencies of his fellow townsmen by giving currency to this unwholesome trash.'[110] Yet he refrained from advocating special measures against

[108] *PGNWP. General Dept.*, 10 June 1865: 80.

[109] *SRGNWP* 1869. 'Publications registered at Curator's office, Allahabad': 244.

[110] Ibid.: 248. The titles in question were two Hindi versions of *Lailā Majnūn*, a love poem on the Radha-Krishna theme by Raskhan, and a piece of satirical poetry in the *bārah māsā* tradition entitled *Hīnu puruṣ kī bārah māsī* or 'Twelve Months of

Shivnarayan. The episode is important in that it exposes the practice of censorship as highly selective and illustrates British officials' arbitrariness in dealing with Indian publishers who had offended the law. Communal bias, as in Kempson, was not the only form of discrimination: while small-scale publishers could be prosecuted and fined on account of a single publication, those of high repute and influence generally had little to fear. Naval Kishore, too, repeatedly got away with an admonition. When in 1872 he was rebuked by the Avadh DPI for not maintaining 'sufficient supervision' over the class of books he published, he readily complied, promising 'to be very particular in future and to accept no book of an immoral tendency for publication.'[111] With this, the matter was settled. In another instance, regarding a popular collection of Urdu love tales called *Nauratan* (The Nine Gems), he equally gave in to official censorship. The fourth edition of 1882 contained an editorial notice to the effect that the text had been purged of all 'obscene expressions' contained in previous editions.[112]

1873 proved an especially difficult year for North Indian publishers and booksellers. Following the appointment of a committee in Calcutta that was to look into the matter of 'obscene' books, a list of objectionable works and their respective publishers was issued to the provincial governments. As a result several publishers and booksellers in the NWP and the Punjab were fined without prior notification. Not surprisingly, the books at stake were widely read works of poetry and romances such as Mir Hasan's above cited *Maṣnavī* or the famed Persian classic *Bahār-e danish* (Spring of Knowledge). While the matter created enough of a stir to be taken up by the Urdu press, the reaction of Indian commentators was rather subdued in nature. Some pointed to differing aesthetic concepts and moral sensibilities. Yet there was no general outcry at the notion that large parts of oriental literature were 'immoral'. Devoting an editorial to the question, the NKP's *Avadh Akhbār* was typical in offering an apologetic statement to the effect that just as exaggeration was regarded a merit rather than a defect in oriental literature, in the same way 'obscenity couched in a fine language' was considered 'quite an art among the eastern writers'.[113]

---

an Impotent Man'. All three titles were issued in large editions of 2000 or 2100 copies and sold for a few paisa.

[111] *RPE Oudh*, 1872–3: 120.

[112] QLP, NWP, 1882, fourth quarter.

[113] *Avadh Akhbār* of 26 September 1873, SVN 1873: 613.

This apologetic defence was in accord with a wider attitude among the new educated Indian middle class whose notions largely coincided with Victorian sensibilities when it came to questions of sexual representation in literature and art. Recent research has provided valuable insights into how educated Indians internalized the debate on obscenity.[114] As Charu Gupta has argued, the 'moral panic' that linked sections of the Indian middle class with their British counterpart worked in a reciprocal way. 'Such indigenous concern was not just a borrowing of Victorian morality', she contends. 'Indeed, British sensibilities were often shaped by indigenous perceptions' (Gupta 2001: 32). Indians responded to the 'obscenity threat' in a number of ways which had a bearing on both literary and wider cultural practices. Aiming 'to discipline the world of the printed text from within' (Roy 1996: 54), the middle classes embarked on a project to shape a new canon of respectable literature through a process of sanitation and the enforcement of a set of normative literary practices. In the process, forms of syncretic popular culture, especially women's cultural practices, were marginalized. Bengal witnessed a collective attempt of the educated *bhadralok* to suppress songs, rites, and other 'obscene' forms of women's popular culture (Banerjee 1989). In the Hindi region, Bharatendu Harishchandra excluded conventional Brajbhasha verse from his women's magazine *Bālābodhinī*, considering it too erotic for a female readership (Dalmia 1997: 247). Such an attitude was part of a gradual shift 'from the sensual to the virtuous' (Gupta 2002: 40)—later reinforced by Hindu nationalist notions of morality and propriety—that came to characterize much of canonized 'high' Hindi literature.

The debate on obscenity became closely intertwined with the language controversy over Hindi and Urdu. In decrying Urdu as a language of moral depravity, Hindi partisans drew on the same arguments as deployed by colonial officials like Kempson.[115] Raja Shiva Prasad's testimony before the Education Commission of 1882 provides a classic instance of how the 'purity' of Hindi religious literature was contrasted with the 'immorality' of Urdu amatory poetry. Emphasizing the high degree of learning among upper-class Hindu and Jain women, Shiva Prasad juxtaposed women who piously studied works such as the *Rāmāyaṇ*, *Sūrsāgar*, and *Brajvilās* with those wayward females who took to 'amorous and

[114] See Roy 1996 and, especially, Gupta 2000 and 2001.

[115] For a personification of Hindi and Urdu as virtue and vice in contemporary Hindi dramas, see King 1992.

vicious books, such as Mir Hasan ki Masnavi, Indarsabha, &c., to the very disgust of their parents and husbands, who find a good excuse thereby for discouraging female education.'[116] He also used the occasion to rail against *Bahār-e dānish* and other Persian classics used in schools, which, 'worse than anything—most amorous—spoil the character of the boys for their whole life, and lead them to the grossest sensuality.'[117] Ironically—and in a further illustration of how much moral panic had taken hold of the middle class imagination—Shiva Prasad's own compilation of Hindi selections *Guṭkā* (1867) came under attack from other witnesses appearing before the Education Commission. Pandit Dindayal Tivari, Deputy Inspector of Schools, and Babu Tota Ram, pleader at the Aligarh High Court, concurred in finding portions of *Guṭkā*, and above all *Padmāvat*, 'objectionable on moral grounds' and bound to have 'a demoralising effect on the minds of the students'.[118]

That the alleged licentiousness of Urdu literature should remain a favourite topic among supporters of Hindi is not surprising. A much more striking exemplification of the profound change in attitude taking place under colonial influence was the new denigration of Urdu poetry expressed by leading Urdu literati themselves. The novelist Nazir Ahmad (1831–1912) and the poet and critic Altaf Husain 'Hali' (1837–1914), both associated with the reformist Aligarh movement, concurred in their emphatic condemnation of classical Urdu and Persian poetry as depraved, linking its 'obscenity' to the cultural degradation of Indian Muslims. The spectacular scene introduced by Nazir Ahmad in his edifying masterpiece *Taubat an-Naṣūḥ* (The Repentence of Nasuh, 1874), in which his hero, Nasuh, in a deeply symbolic act burns his son's collection of classical poetry, has received some important scholarly comment.[119] Not surprisingly, *Taubat an-Naṣūḥ* was much liked by DPI Kempson, who personally translated it into English. Like Nazir Ahmad, Hali, in his influential *Musaddas* (1879), resorted to drastic language to decry the evil effects of degenerate Urdu poetry by calling it a 'filthy archive of poetry and odes, more foul than a cesspool in its putridity, [b]y which the earth is convulsed as if by an earthquake, and which makes the angels blush in heaven . . .' (Hali 1997: 193).

[116] *AECR* 1884: 323.

[117] Ibid.: 316.

[118] Ibid.: 177 and 340.

[119] Naim 1984a: 309–12; Pritchett 1995: 186–7. Pritchett offers a general discussion of the denigration of Urdu poetry at the hands of Nazir Ahmad, Azad, and Hali (ibid.: 169–83).

To what extent did these vibrant indigenous debates on obscenity affect Indian publishers and booksellers? It would seem that, to professionals in the book trade, the cultural and ideological implications of the obscenity debate were not a prime concern. What more immediately affected and vexed them was the absence of a clear policy on the part of the colonial authorities, which left it to their own discretion to publish or sell certain works at the risk of being prosecuted and fined. The booksellers of Lahore repeatedly addressed petitions to the government, asking for a clear definition of what was meant by 'obscene' books. While readily conceding that the Persian *Gulistān*, *Būstān*, *Bahār-e dānish*, and so forth, contained 'indelicate' passages, they put up a half-hearted defence in arguing that these works were not only 'the commonest form of oriental literature' but 'a vehicle of all kinds of instruction', which had always been used in schools.[120] The discrepancy between 'the estimation of the people' and the government was also noted in the *Āgra Akhbār*, which endorsed the petition of the Lahore booksellers in urging the authorities to publish a list of books considered obscene.[121] Naval Kishore's loyal *Avadh Akhbār* even went one step further in proposing that government purchase and destroy all copies of books pronounced immoral.[122] Yet several months later the paper adopted an entirely different stance, evoking the negative impact of government censorship on the marketplace. Allegedly, only almanacs and 'low treatises' were now to be found in booksellers' shops in the towns and cities. The publication of literary and scientific works was said to have been stopped, the trade in books 'at a stand-still'.[123] We must allow for a fair degree of hyperbole here, for even if the repercussions on the book trade were strongly felt by the publishers concerned, official publication statistics do not support the paper's claim. Nonetheless the *Avadh Akhbār*'s critique of government policy is significant in that it conveyed Indian resentment of the hegemonic intervention by a committee 'based in far-away Calcutta and consisting chiefly of Europeans' who decided over the fate of literary works. For the first time a claim was made for greater indigenous autonomy in judging literary and aesthetic matters. Unless able men from the north-western cities were invited to sit on the committee, the paper argued, there could be 'no hope of any good' coming

[120] *Panjābī Akhbār* of 21 March 1874, SVN 1874: 134.
[121] *Āgra Akhbār* of 30 July 1873, SVN 1873: 524–5.
[122] *Avadh Akhbār* of 26 September 1873, SVN 1873: 614.
[123] *Avadh Akhbār* of 3 March 1874, SVN 1874: 103.

from it.[124] Rather than adopting an authoritative stance, the government should hand over the task of revising Indian-language books to local associations.

The case of the 1873 controversy illustrates the contradictions of British policy in trying to suppress 'obscene' literature and the element of arbitrariness inherent in shifting official perceptions. The same books that were found objectionable in 1873 had been published under the British Registration Act for years. Assuming that these books were indeed obscene, the *Avadh Akhbār* sneered, it was strange 'that during the long period of 100 years, for which European civilization has been in progress in India, Government should have permitted their publication . . .'.[125]

In the absence of a list of proscribed works for the period under review, it is difficult to determine the precise extent of moral and literary censorship exercised by the colonial state. Nor can it be said how much individual Hindi and Urdu publishers were really affected by the restrictions it placed upon them. In this context it is interesting to note that heightened moral sensibilities did not prevent a revival of Orientalist interest in Indian erotics, which led to the discovery and translation of a number of important classical texts in Sanskrit.[126] This, however, was of little consequence to commercial publishers, for the texts were clearly not meant for general distribution among Indian audiences. The first English translation of the *Kāmasūtra*, printed in 1883 for the Hindu Kama Shastra Society of Benares, as well as its *editio princeps*, issued from Bombay's Nirnay Sagar Press in 1891, was designed 'for private circulation only'.[127] It is equally revealing that very few contemporary translations of erotic classics into Hindi and Urdu were consigned to print.[128] The wider cultural and social implications of literary censorship would warrant further study, especially with regard to the question of how, under the hegemonic impact of Western civilization, North India's educated elites participated in the stigmatization and marginalization of

[124] Ibid.

[125] *Avadh Akhbār* of 26 September 1873, SVN 1873: 613.

[126] See the preface by W.G. Archer in Comfort 1964.

[127] The Hindu Kama Shastra Society was a branch of the Kama Shastra Society founded in London in 1882 by Sir Richard Burton and F.F. Arbuthnot. The society also prepared a translation of the *Anaṅgaraṅga* ([2]1885), of which the first edition was reportedly printed in four copies only, 'for reasons best known to the printer' (Schmidt 1922: 30).

[128] By contrast, sex manuals and semi-pornographic books and pamphlets in Hindi flooded the market in the early twentieth century. See Gupta 2002: 52ff.

specific genres of their classical and modern literary traditions. Frances Pritchett has raised an important issue in highlighting 'the powerful, drastic act of cultural destruction' (Pritchett 1994: 187) implied in Nazir Ahmad's book-burning scene.[129]

As shown in the preceding section, restrictions imposed by the colonial state on the Indian book trade, through its licence system and acts of press censorship, affected the indigenous book publishing industry much less than it did the newspaper press. By and large, North Indian publishers suffered the negative consequences of colonial legislation only insofar as they were simultaneously involved in the newspaper trade. If publishers were at times adversely affected by colonial legislation, especially acts of moral censorship, the framework of state regulation imparted a high and lasting degree of legal security to the rapidly expanding and highly competitive print market. It consolidated proprietorial rights of both authors and publishers. It will be argued here that the advantages implied in colonial legislation outweighed its disadvantages. Bayly's observation that working within a colonial state 'both set limits to the development of local capitalists and provided them with access to new legal forms and commercial security' (Bayly 1992: 370) certainly holds good for the book trade. For many Hindi and Urdu publishers the security afforded by the legal framework and, in addition, the enormous possibilities arising from government patronage, were crucial in maintaining businesses and encouraging investments. The NKP, as will be shown in the next chapters, is a case in point.

Writers, Readers, Literacy: Colonial Perceptions

Even while British utilitarianism welcomed the advance of print in the modern languages as an essential vehicle of Indian modernization, colonial assessments of literary activity in Hindi and Urdu and the quality of contemporary authorship remained prejudiced through much of the nineteenth century. Attitudes were often patronizing, if not downright condescending. Noting the literate public in India to be not more than an

[129] The wider cultural context and implications of the paradigm shift in Urdu poetry in the wake of the 1857 Rebellion have been discussed by Frances Pritchett and Shamsur Rahman Faruqi in their introduction to the translation of Muhammad Husain Azad's canon-making history of Urdu literature *Āb-e ḥayāt* (1880; Azad 2001). Azad, who called for a new Urdu poetry and poetics modelled on English poetry, seems more equivocal in his condemnation of 'obscenity' than his contemporaries Nazir Ahmad and Hali.

'infinitesimal fraction' of the total population, F.B. Outram, Officiating Under Secretary to the NWP Government in 1858, set the tone for much future debate when he asserted that 'The attempt of Literature, good or bad, which finds its way into the Indian market, is to modern European ideas absurdly insignificant.'[130]

To remedy the dearth of literature and encourage contemporary authorship, in 1868 the NWP government issued its momentous call for useful books in the 'vernaculars', offering a reward to authors of 'meritorious' works, especially those suitable for a female readership. The profound impact of the Allahabad Government Gazette Notification on Urdu literature has been much commented on, particularly with regard to the highly influential series of didactic novels composed in response to it by Nazir Ahmad.[131] By contrast, the response among Hindi writers was rather subdued. Of the total of 1164 works submitted by 1874, only 208 were in Hindi. Half of the manuscripts were authored by Indian employees in the Education Department; only ten per cent were awarded a prize.[132] DPI Kempson could not but declare the notification a success and claim its popularity with the public. In actual fact, he remained deeply sceptical of the self-rejuvenating force of contemporary literature. The 'degree' of general culture to him was 'low' and certainly not conducive to erudition and authorship. 'There is little or no attempt at authorship except what is called forth by the hope of reward', he suggested.[133]

To depict contemporary literary culture as lacking innovation and unable to produce 'useful' knowledge was, of course, one of the strategies routinely employed to underpin the legitimacy of the British civilizing mission. The Allahabad Government Notification not only illustrates the utilitarian trajectory of official encouragement of literature, but also reflects a perennial colonial preoccupation with 'taste' and 'refinement', in which the 'vernaculars' seemed sadly lacking.[134] In establishing 'a standard of criticism . . . in matters of style, sentiment, and taste', the Notification was expected to have a canonizing effect.[135] This goal, in British eyes, was hardly ever met. The scheme of awarding prizes as a

[130] *SRGNWP* 1858. 'Note on native presses and periodicals—1858': 42.

[131] See Pritchett's afterword in Ahmad 2001. For the full wording of the Government Gazette Notification and a discussion of various prize book novels, see Naim 1984.

[132] *PGNWP. Educational Dept.*, October 1874: 68–70.

[133] *PGNWP. General Dept.*, June 1872: 36.

[134] For a discussion of colonial emphasis on introducing 'taste' and 'refinement' in modern Indian literatures, see Sangari 1999: 124–47.

[135] *PGNWP. Educational Dept.*, October 1874: 70.

form of government patronage was abandoned after only a few years. What remained was a lingering scepticism towards the potential of the modern languages to produce the kind of 'useful' and 'refined' literature that could form an effective tool of social and educational progress. Throughout the period 1868–95, the Home Department's yearly Publication Reports abound in statements to the effect that few new compositions were deserving of notice. The 1883 report, in a typical formulation, found 'no marked improvement either in literary activity or the quality of the works received'. At the same time, there was little or no appreciation for popular forms of indigenous narrative tradition. As long as British literature—eulogized by Macaulay as 'the brightest, the purest, the most durable of all the glories of our country, . . . so rich in precious truth and precious fiction, . . . which has exercised an influence wider than that of our commerce and mightier than that of our arms' (Macaulay 1880: 398)—provided the standard against which all other textual production was measured, disparaging attitudes towards much of the Indian folk literature persisted among colonial administrators. The assessment made by the Curator of the Lahore Government Book Depôt is by no means unusual:

> It is to be regretted that so very small a number of original works of general interest or translations of popular English books should be published. I am persuaded that this state of things will not improve until there is a greater desire for reading. Such a desire will not be excited as long as education is sought for solely on account of the return in rupees which it is expected to yield. The creation of a literature is not the work of one year or of ten years. No doubt that, as education increases among the masses, many books will be written, but, till there is a steadily growing demand for books of a stamp different from 'Sasi and Punnu', and the like, which are favourite reading of nine-tenth of those who are able to read, the Panjab will, I am afraid, continue without a literature.[136]

Others, if less condemnatory, were still resigned: 'One is glad to think that there is some demand for reading, however light', wrote one British observer in 1875.

As is evident from these statements, continuous dissatisfaction with the state of literary production in the modern languages was intimately linked to two other colonial perceptions: the first was the pessimism that had arisen from frustrated efforts in the field of education. In the 1880s, when printed books in Hindi and Urdu were flooding the marketplace

[136] *PG. Punjab. Educational Records*, March 1870: 11.

and an unprecedented number of writers, translators, and publishers were engaged in producing texts for public consumption, educational officers still painted a dismal picture, for neither colonial primary education nor the wide availability of cheap reading matter had resulted in a substantial rise in literacy rates outside the big urban centres. The second was the perceived absence of a reading culture in India. Critics have pointed to the central importance that representatives of the colonial state placed on reading. In the colonial imagination, writes Naregal, 'education proposed a system of learning centred on print and individual reading practices' (Naregal 2001: 145). Her view is endorsed by Joshi, who poignantly suggests that in the British imagination Indians in the British empire 'never really seemed to read at all' (Joshi 2002: 35). One of the most striking expressions of the notion that intellectual culture meant, per se, book culture and presupposed regular reading, can be found in J.C. Nesfield's educational report of 1883:

> In Indian shops there is nothing readable, that ever meets the eye: the shopkeeper's name and his prices can only be learnt by asking. There are very few house-holders in India who can afford to buy a newspaper: in towns [. . .] the number is less than 5 per cent.; and in villages nothing like a newspaper is ever seen. But even if the number of readers were a good deal larger than it is, it is admitted on all hands that the cheap Vernacular press of upper India is for the most part of questionable utility, and that the less the people allow themselves to be guided by it, the better. Surely it is somewhat premature to propose elaborate schemes for educating the masses of this country, until it has been ascertained that there is something for them to read. Such is the dearth of readers in this part of India, that even the best Vernacular newspapers, like the *Oudh Akhbār* (Urdu) or the *Kashi Patrikā* (Nagari) do not pay their own way, but are subsidized by Government. In point of fact the only readable matter, that meets the villager's eye, is an occasional court notice pasted on the trunk of a tree respecting some auction sale, or distraint of property for arrears of rent.[137]

In the absence of a culture of reading, rural India to Nesfield appeared to be an intellectual wasteland in which education was proving a futile enterprise. At the root of the dismal situation he not only saw the abject poverty of the rural population but also the failure of the colonial education project: linking literacy, the slow progress of public instruction, and the 'dismal' state of indigenous literature, he maintained, in a somewhat

[137] 'Results of primary education in the NWP&Oudh', *Calcutta Review*, vol. 76, 1883: 355.

convoluted argument, that the absence of a readership was due to the dearth of wholesome reading matter and vice versa. The cynical conclusion of the man who was soon to assume the post of DPI in the NWP&Oudh provides a superb example of colonial arrogance:

> The art of reading is at best only the instrument of knowledge, not knowledge itself; and if there is nothing for a man to read (as is the case with almost all the students from our primary schools), it is useless to put such an instrument into his hands. In a country like India, where a heap of refuse, a stagnant tank, a bullock cart or plough, a mud wall, a herd of lean pigs and lean cattle, are almost the only objects which a villager can see outside the precincts of his own hut, the want of books is not compensated, as it was in Athens, by the instructive or mind-expanding character of the scenes and events by which he is surrounded. His daily life consists of 'a narrow round of small but grinding vicissitudes,' which leave no margin for intellectual culture, or even for the conception of what such culture means.[138]

Such colonial attitudes, however disparaging, did not fail to leave their mark on the minds of Indian reformers. Often cited, Sayyid Ahmad Khan's reaction to his observation of the reading habits of the British working class during his 1869 visit to England provides a classic instance of the new Indian concern with mass literacy. 'The drivers of the various back Vehicles here constantly carry books or newspapers laid beneath their seats for their perusal while waiting for a fare', he wrote home. 'These men hold the same position in society here as do the Ekka drivers of Benares.' The lesson to be learnt was one of national importance: unless even the lowest classes were able to read and write tolerably, the great Muslim reformer contended, no nation could 'become civilized and enlightened, or rise to distinction' (cited in Muhammad 1978.1: 178–9).

The important question of the extent to which the printed book in Hindi and Urdu penetrated the rural market and impacted on non-urban society remains too complex an issue to be explored here.[139] Colonial attitudes, at all events, stand in marked contrast to indigenous perceptions,

[138] Ibid.: 369.

[139] The countryside was not altogether devoid of reading facilities. In Avadh, a scheme of village libraries was implemented in 1869. As a result, even a small place like Hardoi boasted its own teachers' library, which was supported by an annual government grant and furnished with over 1100 books and tracts. See *Fihrist-e kutub maujūda kutubkhāna mudarrisīn . . . muntasaqa sarrishta-e taʿlīm zila Hardoī suba Avadh* (Lucknow 1874, preserved in the OIOC).

which tended to view the impact of the printed book with much greater enthusiasm and optimism. We have already noted how traditionalists and modernists, religious reformers and the orthodox, all turned to the medium of print to spread their message in tracts and pamphlets and engage in new forms of printed communication. In urban and small-town North India, the growth of the Hindi and Urdu readerships and their expanding tastes generated an increasing demand for books on religion, poetry, and romance, but also on history, law, biography, geography, the sciences, and modern prose genres. The attraction of print knowledge can be witnessed in the sustained activities of literary and reform clubs in translating and disseminating scientific and learned works; in the emergence of public libraries and reading rooms; in the first private book collections among bibliophiles; and finally, towards the end of the century, in the appetite for entertaining fiction and the concomitant rise of the 'professional author'.[140]

Managed by the city's first literary and reform society Jalsah-e Tahzib, the Lucknow public library provides a good example of the kind of popularity that the products of print culture enjoyed among urban readers. Two years after its opening in 1868, the library was in a flourishing condition, boasting a collection of nearly 2000 volumes. 1011 books were lent out during the year, of which 100 were historical works, 106 fiction, 50 poetry, 125 moral treatises, 200 law books, and 330 miscellaneous publications.[141] When in 1874 the public library became the deposit library for the province of Avadh, its holdings grew to a total of over 4000 volumes. Its reading room was furnished with a large number of newspapers and periodicals in English and Urdu which, in emulation of the circulating library, were circulated among the society's members to be read and read out at home. As the Jalsah's secretary reported enthusiastically:

> Newspapers have been circulated amongst 5709 readers, against 4705 last year, and though the circulation has increased, yet the most prominent feature of the year has been, the incessant and pressing requests from members for Newspapers. There is no doubt that the Jalsah has accomplished one important task, that of creating a healthy taste for Newspaper reading, and of fostering an interest in what is going on in the world.[142]

[140] For the professionalization of Hindi authors, see Orsini 2004a: 443.

[141] *RPE Oudh*, 1870–1: 131.

[142] *Rept. of Public Instruction in Oudh*, 1872–3: 176. Again, British sources present very different assessments of the extent to which public libraries were patronized by the urban literate class. Noting that public libraries were 'rarely made use of by

A good way to challenge and qualify the bleak picture that colonial observers painted of Indian consumption is by investigating the vibrant growth of the indigenous publishing industry and by examining the continuously expanding range of books in the classical and modern languages through which Indian commercial publishers responded to, and stimulated, market demand. It is time, then, to turn to a publisher who, with his business talent and cultural vision, exercised a decisive influence on the diffusion of the printed word in Hindi and Urdu. The following chapters will narrate his story and that of a publishing house which left its mark on the literary field of nineteenth-century India like no other institution of its kind.

---

natives', in 1869 Kempson advocated a special grant of assistance to town libraries. *PGNWP&Oudh. General Dept.*, 13 March 1869: 5.

2
A Life in Print: Munshi Naval Kishore (1836–1895)

In 1884 the American Methodist Bishop John F. Hurst, on a tour through India, happened to visit the NKP. While Hurst was greatly impressed by Munshi Naval Kishore's multifarious activities in the promotion of religious, especially Islamic, literature, he also perceived them as antagonistic to Christian missionary efforts and accordingly viewed the publisher with some reservation. To Hurst, Naval Kishore was the embodiment of the shrewd oriental trader turned modern print tycoon. His portrait of the publisher is remarkable for being informed by a fundamental cultural misunderstanding:

> He [Naval Kishore] is a Mohammedan, and makes no secret of it. But with the publisher's instinct he keeps his religion in the background. He never puts his faith at the top of his bill-heads. He is a broad man—broad in everything except Christianity, and it is not likely that the Gospel has a more vigorous hater in the whole Gangetic Valley than this wily man. But he is no bigoted professional. Bitter hater as he is of Hinduism and of all the numerous non-Muhammedan faiths, he seems as ready to publish books for the promotion of Brahminism and of its rival faith, Buddhism, as to issue apologies and text-books in behalf of Islam. (Hurst 1887: 353)

The modern researcher will hardly commit the same blunder as this ill-informed American visitor. Yet it remains a difficult endeavour to reconstruct a person's life mainly on the basis of secondary sources and with few personal documents as corroborating evidence. This is especially true for someone like Munshi Naval Kishore, who had already become a celebrity, and thus an object of myth during his lifetime. No comprehensive biography in English or, for that matter, in any other European language has been written on the Lucknow publisher. Existing biographical accounts in Hindi and Urdu invariably go back to a number of nineteenth-century sources, all of them tainted by a highly stylized portrait and glorification of his person. The first and most important of these sources, a Brajbhasha verse biography entitled *Jīvancaritra* (*1895), was composed shortly after Naval Kishore's death by Pandit Bandidin Dikshit, an NKP employee and author of several devotional works in Hindi. Around the same time, a short account of the publisher's life by Ramji Das Bhargava, another press employee and presumably a relative of Naval Kishore, was published in the *Oudh Review*, a literary magazine issued from the press.[1] In 1903 there followed *Jīvancaritar*, an Urdu biography by the Lucknow Kayastha Lalji Munshi, a prolific author and long-standing associate of Naval Kishore's firm. Lalji's account draws heavily on Dikshit's biography and is largely identical in content but for a few supplementary anecdotes.

More panegyric than biography in the classical sense, both the Brajbhasha biography and, to a lesser extent, its Urdu prose version are characterized by their eulogistic style, large-scale omissions, and a pervasive insouciance with regard to chronology. They not only give a very limited picture of Naval Kishore's life, but also contain numerous inaccuracies and factual errors which have been perpetuated in modern biographical accounts. These can be found, for example, in the special commemorative numbers of the journals *Nayā Daur* (Urdu) and *Uttar Prades̍* (Hindi), published in the early 1980s.[2] While the contributions in both magazines, particularly the *Nayā Daur* issue, provide much valuable information on Naval Kishore, they also suffer from the problems inherent in the commemorative genre—notably an eagerness to pay tribute to the publisher and extol his achievements—which clearly go to the detriment of critical examination and scholarly accuracy. This also appears to be a major flaw in the only comprehensive modern biography of Naval Kishore, an Urdu work entitled *Savāniḥ-e Munshī Navalkishor* (1995) by Amir Hasan Nurani. Nurani served as honorary secretary to the publishing house from 1949 to 1964. His study combines a biographical sketch of Naval Kishore with an account of the history of the firm; it includes an exhaustive list of NKP publications in Urdu, Persian, and Arabic.[3] While offering an insider's view, it abounds in inaccurate statements

[1] The article is reprinted in S.Q. Khan 1980: 185–9 and Nurani 1982: 52–61.

[2] *Nayā Daur* 1980; *Uttar Prades̍* 1981.

[3] This monograph is based on an earlier, less detailed biographical sketch. See Nurani 1982.

and unsubstantiated claims. For all its shortcomings, Nurani's account constitutes the most thorough investigation into the publisher's life to date. It appears all the more relevant in light of the fact that Indian scholarship during the past two decades has failed to produce any substantial or original research on the subcontinent's erstwhile largest publishing emporium. A recent conference volume, resulting from a seminar held at Lucknow University in 1998 (Zamani 2000), gives ample proof of the current lack of scholarly interest by its largely repetitive character and conspicuous absence of fresh insights.

The rewriting of Naval Kishore's biography calls then for a critical distinction between myth and reality. It will be attempted here on the basis of the aforementioned sources, as well as hitherto unexploited British records, other English-language material, and a few personal documents authored by the publisher himself. An important caveat relates to certain aspects of the publisher's life which, in retrospect, may have assumed significance different from the time of their occurrence. Caution must be exercised, for instance, with regard to painting a stereotypical portrait of Naval Kishore as a 'great symbol of Hindu–Muslim unity' or a herald of 'national integration'. Latter-day biographers have readily succumbed to this temptation which, admittedly, seems justified by hindsight. Yet it remains doubtful whether such epithets would have come naturally to Naval Kishore's contemporaries. Without wanting to overstate the case of the shared Hindu–Muslim elite culture, nineteenth-century Lucknow—and Avadh for that matter—enjoyed strong cross-communal alliances. As Francis Robinson has shown, the dominant factor in local politics tended to be an Urdu-speaking elite connection based on landed interest, which remained so strong that even in the 1890s communal matters were of little consequence (Robinson 1974). Hence, perhaps more than in any other North Indian urban centre at the time, the cultural and literary climate prevailing in Lucknow was shaped by an urban intelligentsia that would still identify itself in terms of a larger composite culture rather than being preoccupied by the distinction between Hindus and Muslims. It was only later in life when, under the impact of emerging Indian nationalism, Naval Kishore became involved in national politics, that he was first compelled to perceive his public role in communal categories.

Equally, in looking into the motives of Naval Kishore's involvement in philanthropy, education, and literary patronage, this book refrains from interpreting it solely as a function of his altruistic concerns and reformist ideas. No doubt such motives existed, for Naval Kishore was a publisher with a cultural vision and a social mission. However, he was also, as has been conveniently overlooked by many, a shrewd entrepreneur and businessman who, in order to succeed in the increasingly competitive market of commercial publishing, had to build multiple networks and deploy his social alliances in the name of business interests, too.

2.1 Family Background, Education, and Apprenticeship

Naval Kishore was born into a wealthy family of Hindu service gentry, whose genealogy can be traced back to the fourteenth century.[4] During the Mughal reign several of his ancestors had entered imperial service and risen to the position of influential *jāgīrdār*s. His great-grandfather Indra Singh was a military commander in the army of the Maratha confederation, who fought in the famous battle of Panipat in 1761. His grandfather, Pandit Balmukund, held the post of treasurer of Agra in the service of Shah Alam II. In 1792 Balmukund received *jāgīr*s in the region of Agra, Mathura, and Aligarh. It was here, in the small town of Sasni in Aligarh district, that Naval Kishore's father, Pandit Yamuna Prasad, settled and lived as an affluent *zamīndār*.[5] Some sources also mention him as a trader, without, however, specifying the kind of trade he was engaged in.

Surprisingly, earlier biographers have rather casually bypassed the issue of the family's caste affiliation, identifying them variably as Kayasthas, Dhusars, or Bhargava Brahmins, but without according the matter any further attention. In actual fact, far from representing a straightforward issue, the question of what caste Naval Kishore belonged to poses some difficulties that merit closer attention. In its complexity it reflects the fluid nature and flexibility of *jāti* and *varṇa* norms prevailing during the first half of the century, while also illustrating the emergence of caste consciousness and a more homogeneous 'caste society' in the second half.[6] His story is in short that of a Dhusar turned Bhargava, involving a

[4] See, e.g., Z. al-Hasan 1980; Nurjahan 1980; Nurani 1995: 22–4; *Uttar Pradeś* 1981: 28.

[5] The town of Sasni lies in *taḥṣil* Hathras in Aligarh District. The family is said to have settled in the village of Bastoi, sometimes wrongly referred to as Naval Kishore's birthplace. Since there exists no place by the name of Bastoi in Hathras, I take it to be a misreading of Basgoi. Cf. *Census of India 1891. District Census Statistics NWP&Oudh. Aligarh District,* 1895: 10.

[6] For a comprehensive treatment of these developments, see S. Bayly 1999.

shift in *varṇa* affiliation from Kshatriya to Brahmin. While many of the actual forces at work in the process remain obscure, an attempt will be made here to trace this development in its successive stages.

What renders the issue of Naval Kishore's caste even more complicated is a widely prevailing notion that he was born in a family of North Indian Kayasthas. While Nurani (Nurani 1995: 20) and with him several Western scholars seem to unquestioningly accept this notion, I have not come across any conclusive evidence in support of it. There is a conspicuous absence of references to Naval Kishore's caste in contemporary sources pre-dating the 1880s, with the single exception of an entry on the title page of the first Sanskrit book published from the NKP, a *Bhāgavata Purāṇa* edition of 1869, which expressly refers to Naval Kishore as being 'born in a family of Kshatriyas' (*kṣatriyakule jātaḥ*). It can be assumed with some certainty that the publication, being an important one, went through Naval Kishore's own hands and that the statement found his implicit consent, reflecting the family's self-perception as Kshatriyas. From this it could indeed be inferred that he was a Kshatriya Kayastha, as many Upper Indian Kayasthas had begun claiming Kshatriya status at the time.[7] Yet Kayasthas were by no means the only ones to claim Kshatriya descent: various merchant castes also did so. As Kuar Lachman Singh noted in his *Historical and Statistical Memoir of Zila Bulandshahar* in 1874: 'The Banias are now considered pure Vaisya, although the majority of them claim their descent from Kshattri progenitors' (Singh 1874: 167). Nor does the fact that Naval Kishore maintained close links with the Lucknow Kayastha community automatically make him a Kayastha. In the 1870s several important pamphlets on Kayastha caste history and the controversial issue of the community's *varṇa* affiliation were printed at his press. Significantly, not one of these texts identifies the publisher as a Kayastha. Furthermore, if Naval Kishore's Kayastha affiliation were true, it is surprising that there is not a single reference to his subcaste in either private or official records. In view of the fact that North Indian Kayasthas generally identified themselves by one of their twelve subdivisions, this silence in contemporary documents seems odd indeed. British records of the time make no mention of Naval Kishore's caste, while extant late nineteenth-century biographies fail to provide any conclusive evidence on the question, for they are works commissioned at a later point in time when Naval Kishore's identity as a Bhargava Brahmin was already consolidated.

[7] See Carroll 1978: 233–50.

It is only from the 1880s that we are on firmer ground. From that time various documents can be found which expressly identify Naval Kishore as a member of the Dhusar (*ḍhūsar*, also: *ḍhūṃsar*), and subsequently, Bhargava caste. The Dhusars of the NWP present an interesting, hitherto little-studied instance of an upwardly-mobile North Indian merchant caste. They were a traditional trading caste whose homeland lay in the region of Gurgaon in Haryana (then Punjab), with Rewari as their main religious centre. From there the community migrated to the towns of the NWP where, much like the Agarvals, they entered into trade with the colonial rulers. This migration seems to have taken place in the early decades of the nineteenth century, leading to high concentrations of Dhusars in the towns and trading centres of the north-west: Kanpur, Mathura, Farrukhabad, Fatehpur, Jaunpur, Hamirpur, and Lucknow.[8] Reverend M.A. Sherring, in his *Hindu Tribes and Castes as Represented in Benares* (1872), remarks that 'Their occupation, like that of the majority of Vaisyas, is trade and commerce; some take to the profession of soldiers. Under Mahomedan rule the caste was in a flourishing condition' (Sherring [1872] 1974: 293). A quarter century later, the ethnographer William Crooke described the Dhusars as a 'rising, ambitious, thriving class, excellent clerks and men of business' (Crooke [1896] 1974: 303). The Mathura Dhusars, especially, were known for their great wealth and influence.

Excellence in penmanship was a distinctive feature of the Dhusar community.[9] Their scribal tradition and a shared history in clerical and service employment put them in close proximity with the Kayasthas, a circumstance that may explain why Naval Kishore is often taken to be a Kayastha. His family background perfectly corresponds to the following description of the Dhusars given by India's eminent anthropological scholar Jogendra Nath Bhattacharya:

> The Dhunsars are found chiefly in the Gangetic Doab, between Delhi on the west and Mirzapore on the east. There are many big landholders among

[8] The 1865 provincial Census counted a total of 4239 members of the 'Dhoosur' community. *Census of the NWP 1865,* vol. I: *General Report and Appendices*, Allahabad 1867, app. B: 22–3. The 'Dhusar Baniahs' of Sahranpur district were said to have come from Rewari about 1840 (Elliott 1859: 284). See also *Census of India*, 1891, vol. XVIII: *The NWP&Oudh*, pt III, Allahabad 1894.

[9] By contrast, the Dhusar-Bhargavas did not take to Western education. The 1891 Census, in its tables showing 'Education by caste and religion' lists only 77 out of a total of 6557 male adults as having received an English education. Literacy among female caste members was almost nil.

> them. They take their name from Dhusi, a flat-topped hill, near Rewari, in Gurgaon. They are all Vishnuvites, and there are no Jains among them. They do not devote themselves entirely to trade: In fact their chief profession is penmanship, and they combine in themselves the office aptitude of the Kayasth, with the Baniya's capacity for mercantile business. Under Mahomedan rule, they occasionally filled many high offices of State. Under the present régime a good many of them hold such appointments in the public service as are open to the natives of this country now. (Bhattacharya [1896] 1968: 169–70)[10]

The Dhusars are a prime example of an upwardly mobile trading caste for whom the colonial market economy meant growing prosperity and local influence. Their newly-achieved affluence, in combination with their importance in Mughal and, subsequently, colonial service enabled them to claim Brahminical descent. Tracing their genealogy to the mythical *ṛsi* Bhṛgu, they adopted the name Bhargava, thus positioning themselves in the fold of the ancient Brahminical clan of the Bhṛgus or Bhargavas, 'descendants of Bhṛgu'.[11] This process of social mobility was initiated in the 1870s, a time of heightened caste and *varṇa* consciousness, demonstrated by the example of Kayasthas, Kashmiri Brahmins, and various other communities. At first the Dhusars' claim to Brahminical status did not go uncontested by other Brahmin castes. In 1874 Kuar Lachman Singh reports that—

> This clan was always reckoned in the Bania division . . . [b]ut now they lay claim to a place in the Brahmanical list. They have made out several stories in support of the claim, but none of them is admitted by true Brahmans. Having failed in inducing the other castes to call them Brahmans, they have adopted a new name for their caste, viz. Bhargava, or descendants of Brigu [*sic*] . . .' (Singh 1874: 169)

[10] Bhattacharya evidently drew on the heavily biased account in the British Settlement Report, which identified the Dhusars as 'mostly hard landlords and wealthy men' and described them as combining 'the office aptitude of the Kayasth with the keen scent for money making and the flinty hard-heartedness to a debtor characteristic of a Banya' (cited in Crooke 1974: 302).

[11] In ancient Sanskrit literature the Bhṛgus come to prominence in the *Mahābhārata*, a major repository of Bhargava mythology and genealogy. V.S. Sukthankar was the first to discuss the formative influence of the Bhargavas upon the development of the surviving redaction of the great epic, a process for which he coined the term 'Bhṛguization' (Sukthankar 1936). His views have been discussed by R.P. Goldman in his seminal study of the Bhṛgus and Bhargava mythology in the *Mahābhārata* (Goldman 1977).

Merely two decades later the community's Bhargava affiliation was widely accepted. Crooke, writing in 1896, states: 'Their pretensions to Brahmanical origin are admitted by Brahmans themselves, and they are now usually known as Bhārgava or "descendants of Bhrigu" . . . In the hills they appear to be in some places Banyas and in others Brahmans' (Crooke [1896] 1974: 301). Evidence for the caste's transitory status during the period 1870–1900 is also afforded by the British Census reports. Whereas the 1865 and 1872 Census of the NWP still classified the Dhusars as *vaishyas* or *baniās*, both the Punjab Census of 1883 and the NWP Census of 1891 had extrapolated the 'Dhusar-Bhargavas' from the list of *baniā* castes, listing them as a separate category instead.[12] At an individual level the process is paralleled in Naval Kishore's transition from Dhusar to Bhargava, as evinced in the title pages of several NKP Hindi and Sanskrit publications of the 1880s: while up to the early 1880s the publisher is usually eulogized as an 'adornment of the Dhusar lineage' (*ḍhū(ṃ)sar-vamśāvataṃs*), from around 1883 the corresponding entry reads 'adornment of the Bhargava lineage' (*bhārgava-vamśāvataṃs*).[13]

Following a typical pattern of nineteenth-century caste formation, the new caste status was consolidated by the establishment in 1889 of a national caste association, the Akhil Bharatiya Bhargava Sabha or All India Bhargava Conference. As will be shown below, Naval Kishore played a key role in this process.[14] The community established its headquarters in Mathura; several smaller Bhargava Sabhas began operating in Agra, Sahranpur, and Jaipur. Of these, the Jaipur Bhargava

[12] Due to the similarity in names, in the 1872 Census the British data collectors committed a serious blunder by mixing up the Dhusars with the low-caste community of the 'Dusar' or 'Dúsádd' (*dusāṛh*). The resulting statistics were grossly incorrect. D. Ibbetson in the 1883 Punjab Census noted about the Dhusars: 'They are of Brahminical origin, as is admitted by the Brahmans themselves, and it is possible that some of them may have recorded themselves as Brahmans in the schedules. Indeed, I find 1600 Dhusar Brahmans returned . . . but whether these are the same men as the Dhunsars of Rewari, I cannot say . . . They are almost exclusively clerks or merchants, though, like the Khattris, some of them have risen to eminence in the army, and the Court.'

[13] See, e.g., the NKP Hindi translations of the *Liṅga-* and *Bhaviṣyapurāṇa* (1881), which identify Naval Kishore as a Dhusar. Moreover, the former title refers to him as Munshi Naval Kishore Varma. The earliest references to his Bhargava caste affiliation can be found on the title pages of the *Caurāsī bārtta* (1883) and the NKP Hindi prose version of the *Mahābhārat* (1886).

[14] For a general discussion of caste consciousness and the emergence of caste associations in the late nineteenth century, see Carroll 1978: 233–50.

Sabha appears to have been the oldest and most vibrant—it is recorded to have launched an Urdu monthly called *Rūdād-e Bhārgava Sabhā* as early as 1882.[15] Later it maintained a caste journal in Hindi, *Bhārgava Patrikā*. The Jaipur Sabha was also instrumental in supplying British ethnographers with the caste's own account of its history, which highlighted the historical importance of Bhargavas as family priests and ministers to Hindu kings.[16] In its 1970 special issue on Munshi Naval Kishore, *Bhārgava Patrikā* provides a detailed family pedigree, identifying him as belonging to the Bhargava Sharma lineage, Cyavan sub-lineage, Gaur Brahmin sub-branch, and Dhusar Bhargava Brahman division of the sub-branch. According to this account, the religious affiliation of the family was that of Sanatana Dharmis (Bhargava 1970: [24]).

Like the majority of north-western trading castes, the Dhusars were Vaishnavas. Their ascent to Brahminical status was accompanied by a strict adherence to orthodox and dharmic regulations. This process of 'Sanskritization' was described by E.T. Atkinson in his *Himalayan Gazetteer* (1882) for the Dhusars of the hill regions,[17] and corroborated by Crooke for the community living in the plains: 'They regulate their lives by the most orthodox rules of Hinduism and are particularly careful in the observance of Hindu ceremonies' (Crooke [1896] 1974: 302–3). The Sanskritization of the Dhusars also entailed the construction of a textual tradition along Sanskritic lines, of which the *Dhūsī mahātmya* (1901), composed by one Mathuraprasad Bhargava, provides a typical example. Naval Kishore was to make his own distinctive contribution to the promotion of the community's literary heritage in seeing the works of the eighteenth-century Dhusar *sant* poet Charandas into print.

Naval Kishore's family boasted a tradition of Hindu scholarship, his

[15] *RPIR* 1882: 188.

[16] Traditions within the caste regarding its origins and pedigree vary. For the dominant tradition, which traces the caste back to Bhṛgu's son Chivan (Skrt. Cyavana), see Kishori Lal, 'Essay to be read before the Annual Bhargava Conference regarding the origin of the name of Bhargava and Nautor', Jaipur 1916 (OIOC, VT 3890a, in Urdu).

[17] 'The practices of both Brahman and Baniya Dhusars are the same, and in one point both differ from ordinary Hindus. They take their food before *puja* or morning prayer, whilst ordinarily all perform their *puja* first and then eat. Of late years, however, they have begun to adopt the more orthodox custom. They do not eat animal or other prohibited food, nor do they drink spirits. They worship the orthodox deities and consider Brahma, Siva and Vishnu as one god under different forms. The Brahman Dhusar marries with his caste fellows, and the Baniya Dhusars with Baniya Dhusars, avoiding always the same *gotra* or a family having the same favourite deity' (Atkinson [1882] 1973: 443).

grandfather and father were known as Sanskrit pandits. The young Naval Kishore, too, was trained in the Sanskrit scriptures and was sometimes addressed as Pandit Naval Kishore before he came to be generally known as Munshi Naval Kishore. Yet Vaishnavism and Hindu scholastic traditions form only one aspect of the broad cultural milieu in which the future publisher was born and raised. As members of the landed service gentry who had performed clerical and military functions for the Mughal empire and its successor states, his family was deeply steeped in Indo-Persian culture and had embraced Muslim courtly etiquette. In combining Hindu learning with Indo-Persian scholastic and literary traditions and a Persianized lifestyle, they epitomize the composite culture of the Indo-Gangetic belt, for which the Urdu language has coined the term '*gaṅgā-jamnī*'.[18] Naval Kishore was a product of this shared cultural tradition, his subsequent life and career clearly mirroring the composite cultural landscape in which he grew up.

Childhood, Education, and Apprenticeship

Naval Kishore was born on 3 January 1836 (*pauṣ pūrṇimā*, vs 1892) in the village of Rirha near Mathura, home of his maternal grandparents. He was the second of five sons of Pandit Yamuna Prashad and Yashoda Devi. Rirha, a village no longer inhabited which today forms part of the town of Baldeo in Sadabad *taḥṣil*,[19] was part of the ancestral *zamīndārī* and the place where Naval Kishore's ancestors had settled prior to the family's migration to Sasni in Aligarh district. According to the testimony of Dr Ranjit Bhargava, the genealogical records of the family which bear Naval Kishore's name are still kept by local priests in Baldeo.[20] These findings refute all other claims regarding the controversial issue of Naval Kishore's birthplace, notably that Rirha is identical with Rahera, a place near the town of Sahar in the erstwhile Mughal *sarkār* of the same name.[21]

[18] For a discussion of the historical dimension and specific features of North Indian composite culture, see, e.g., Khan 1987 and Alam 1999.

[19] Previously, Baldeo belonged to Mahaban *taḥṣil*. Its population in 1891 was 534, of which 130 were Baniyas. *Census of India 1891. District Census Statistics NWP&Oudh. Muttra District*, 1893: 21. For the religious significance of Baldeo, see Growse 1883: 292.

[20] Private communication, March 1998.

[21] Z. al-Hasan 1980; Nurani 1995: 22-4. Al-Hasan claims that Sahar was home to an eminent family of Dhusar-Bhargavas, who received *jāgīr*s and the hereditary title of 'Munshi' on account of their high office and great learning. He presumes this family, which lived in the haveli of one Udhailal Dhusar, to be Naval Kishore's

The young boy spent his early childhood at his grandparents' home in Rirha. At the age of six he was called to his parental home in Sasni for his primary education. Not surprisingly, the biographical sources in Brajbhasha and Urdu differ significantly as to the nature of this education: while Dikshit speaks of an instruction imparted by Hindu pandits, Lalji Munshi and all subsequent Urdu sources state that Naval Kishore visited the local *maktab*, that is, the primary village school in which elementary reading and writing in Persian and Urdu were taught. These statements are, as T.R. Metcalf has shown through the example of the Avadh *taʿalluqdār*s, not at all contradictory (Metcalf 1979: 358–61). We may safely assume that Naval Kishore received his religious instruction from Hindu pandits at home, while he was simultaneously taught Persian, Urdu, and presumably also some Arabic at the village *maktab*.

Naval Kishore was a studious and intelligent child. Consequently, in a decision that was to enhance the composite character of his education even further, his father enrolled him at Agra College. It must be pointed out here that the unanimous claim of Naval Kishore's biographers that his admission to Agra College took place as early as 1845 is incorrect. While his name is absent from the college lists of scholarships and prizes between 1845 and 1852, it appears for the first time in an official British record of 1852–3, containing a list of twenty-eight 'Youths from a distance who have, during the past year, come to Agra for the sole purpose of being educated'. Next to his name and place of origin, the entry lists the exact date of Naval Kishore's admission to the college as 1 May 1852.[22]

Since most of its records were destroyed during the 1857 uprising, the history of Agra College is much less well researched than that of its famous sister institutions, the Benares Sanskrit College and Delhi College. Established in 1823 on the basis of an endowment by an affluent Hindu Pandit, Agra College functioned as the third major governmental Anglo-Oriental College in North India. Although it was open to students of all denominations, its student body was predominantly Hindu, with over two-thirds of its pupils receiving government or private scholarships.[23] Perhaps more so than other colonial institutions, Agra College

---

ancestors. Due to frequent droughts in the area, they left the place and settled in Sasni.

[22] *GRPI. NWP*, 1852–3: 6.

[23] The 'Hindu character' of Agra College was emphasized much later in the context of Hindu nationalist agitation. The government's plans to close the college on the grounds of irrentability and divert its funds to the Mohammadan Anglo-Oriental

placed a strong emphasis on catering to the educational needs of the commercial and professional classes in the NWP, its objective being 'to diffuse more widely than Native Schools the possession of useful knowledge, to give a command of the language of ordinary life, and of official business—to teach, principally, Hindee and Persian, with the native mode of keeping accounts (Leelavattee), and to have instruction in Sanscrit and Arabic.'[24] By 'useful knowledge' was meant the teaching of geography, astronomy, and mathematics according to the European system, subjects introduced in due course in 1827.[25] It was through a combination of oriental learning and modern European sciences that the students of Agra College were to be rendered fit for state employment or commercial life. The College Principal J. Middleton, in true utilitarian spirit, endeavoured 'to raise up a class of men who are well qualified to take their part in the practical duties of life.' To this purpose, he noted, the sciences were particularly, though by no means exclusively, studied: 'Mathematics and natural philosophy are the branches of learning in which the pupils attain the highest proficiency, though their acquaintance with English literature is also considerable.'[26] A look at the syllabus of the English Department corroborates his statement: the students of Agra College were trained in Milton, Shakespeare, Bacon, and Pope.

Following the introduction of English classes in 1831, a separate Department of English was established at the college in 1835. This measure resulted in a significant drop in student enrolment in the oriental languages.[27] By the time Naval Kishore joined the college in 1852, 272

College in Aligarh met with fierce protest, as borne out by a 'Statement made at a Public Meeting . . . against the abolition of the Agra College by the citizens of Agra', which was submitted to the Education Commission of 1882. It claimed that 'the establishment of the present college was due solely to Hindu influences, for the grants made to Pandit Ganga Dhar came from a most orthodox Principality of Hindu chiefs, *viz*., from the Peshwa. Ganga Dhar himself was a Brahmin of the first water, and after his death the Government too thought it proper to employ the money of a Brahmin on purposes wholly and solely Braminical [*sic*], *viz*., the study of the Vedas. Though one now cannot hear the chanting of Vedic prayers in the ample hall of the Agra College, though one now cannot meet with students of the Vedas in the college precincts, but still this fact can never be ignored nor its value lessened that the college is still essentially a Hindu institution.' *AECR* 1884: 413.

[24] *Selections from Educational Records*, vol. 1, 1859–1871, Delhi 1960: 240.

[25] *Selections from Educational Records*, 1781–1839, Calcutta 1920: 186.

[26] *General Report on the State of Popular Education in the Bengal Presidency*, for 1847–1848.

[27] *Selections from Educational Records*, pt I, 1781–1839: 95.

out of a total of 311 students on the college rolls were studying English.[28] As these figures indicate, by mid century there was a marked demand for Western education and English-language skills. Admittedly, Agra College was slow to receive the same kind of large-scale acceptance that British educational institutions were enjoying among the elite classes in Lower Bengal and elsewhere. Naval Kishore belonged to a small minority of approximately 2000 pupils enrolled in the British colleges and Anglo-Vernacular schools of the NWP at the time.[29] Yet his father's decision to send his bright young son to Agra College is indicative of a remarkable shift in attitudes among the affluent service gentry in the NWP. Much had changed since the times when W. Adam had noted the lack of encouragement, in his 1835 report, of the study of English in this part of India.

Naval Kishore was enrolled in the Oriental Department of Agra College as one of seventy students who learnt Persian in combination with English. While nothing is known about his performance in English, he excelled in Persian and was rewarded a Junior Persian scholarship of Rs 6 in 1853 and 1854.[30] It would seem, however, that the general standard of the Persian classes left much to be desired. As an official report noted, the lower Persian class contained no less than seven divisions, making it impossible for teachers to monitor students' progress, while the textbooks were 'sadly jumbled up together'. The report concluded: 'The Persian Mouluvees have been evidently left to themselves, and in all such cases, the elementary knowledge of Persian can be as well acquired in the bazar schools, as in the Government College.'[31] Complaints about the 'entire want of discipline' in the junior Persian class, particularly, had already been raised in a previous report. With regard to Naval Kishore's veteran Persian teacher, Muhammad Rahim, who had joined Agra College as early as 1824, mention was made of 'the great age of the Moonshee, who has not apparently sufficient energy left, either to teach his pupils effectively, or to control them'.[32]

It is generally claimed that during his college days Naval Kishore developed a keen interest in literature and journalism, which apparently led him to contribute articles to a local Urdu paper called *Safir-e Āgra*.

[28] *GRPI. NWP*, 1852–3: 10.

[29] Robinson 1974: 34 discusses the limited appeal of government schools in the NWP.

[30] *GRPI. NWP,* 1853–4: 24.

[31] *GRPI. NWP*, 1854–5: 42–3.

[32] *GRPI. NWP*, 1852–1853: 16.

While the first part of this claim may be true, the second is almost certainly incorrect, for there is no evidence of the existence of *Safīr-e Āgra* prior to 1856. By contrast, it is attested that a journal by the same name was launched by Naval Kishore in January 1856, that is, some time after his college days.[33] Much of the confusion regarding Naval Kishore's first journalistic endeavours seems to stem from an equivocal line in Dikshit's biography that runs to the effect that Naval Kishore received a government grant in reward of the outstanding quality of his contributions as editor of *Safīr-e Āgra*.[34] It seems that Dikshit, in an understandable attempt to attribute an early aptitude for journalism to the subject of his biography, mistook the college scholarship for a grant given to Naval Kishore in his capacity as editor.

Naval Kishore never graduated from Agra College. In being a 'school dropout' he conforms to a commonly-found pattern among the new professional class of journalist-editors and publishers.[35] Despite leaving Agra College prematurely, he remained attached to the institution all his life. In 1882 he became a member of the Local Board of Trustees that took over the financial management of the college, and also helped finance a boarding house. At this critical juncture in the college's history, he contributed largely to its finances, thus helping the institution to survive.[36]

The year 1854 marked a decisive turn in Naval Kishore's life: he left Agra to take up employment in the famous Koh-e Nur Press of Lahore. Established in 1849 by Munshi Harsukh Rai (1816–90), a Kayastha from Sikandarabad, the Koh-e Nur Press had quickly risen to fame through its paper *Koh-e Nūr*, the first regular Urdu newspaper in the

[33] Khurshid 1963: 124–6. There is no mention of *Safīr-e Āgra* in Siddiqi's work on pre-1857 Urdu journalism (Siddiqi 1962). Sabiri in his standard work on Urdu journalism states that *Safīr-e-Āgra* was first published on 19 January 1856, with Naval Kishore serving as its editor *(mohtamīm)* (Sabiri 1953 [i]: 500). In his later study of 1973 he seems to have succumbed to the popular version, for, contradicting his earlier statement, he claims that Naval Kishore developed a liking for journalism and began writing for *Safīr-e Āgra* at the age of 15. His articles were well received and he consequently abandoned his education at Agra College (Sabiri 1973: 321).

[34] The verse reads: '*Patr Safīr Āgra nām/svayam pracār kīn matidhām/jāni deś unnati parinām// Ati udār sarkār lakhi budhi vidyā parvīn/śrīmannavalkiśor ko niyat vazīfā kīn*' (Dikshit 1895: 6). Abrar makes a dubious claim that he saw articles written by Naval Kishore during his college days (Abrar 1980: 39).

[35] M.K. Ranade in his 1864 *Report on Vernacular Literature* notes the high number of school dropouts among Marathi authors and publishers (cited in Naregal 2001: 185).

[36] *PGNWP&Oudh. Educational Dept.*, November 1891: 34.

Punjab. Apparently, the young Naval Kishore was brought to the notice of Harsukh Rai by the latter's brother Makkhan Lal Rai, a subjudge of Agra and family acquaintance. On his brother's recommendation, Harsukh Rai called Naval Kishore to Lahore to offer him employment in his rapidly expanding business.

Naval Kishore could hardly have chosen a better place for his apprenticeship. On the basis of *Koh-e Nūr*, Munshi Harsukh Rai's press was prospering. *Koh-e Nūr* marked the beginning of serious Urdu journalism in the Punjab. It was first published on 14 January 1850, a few months after the British annexation of the province, and enjoyed the support of the Punjab Administration Board. In fact, it was on the invitation of the colonial authorities that Harsukh Rai, who had previously served as editor of *Jām-e Jamshed* in Meerut, had moved to Lahore to start his own Urdu paper.[37] Initially a mere news magazine that contained abstracts from the *Government Gazette*, rules, acts, and other government news, *Koh-e Nūr* soon broadened its range of contents (Sheo Narain 1916: 51–2). By the time Naval Kishore joined the Koh-e Nur Press in 1854, it had grown into the most popular and influential Urdu newspaper in the Punjab. Its circulation amounted to 349 subscribers, surpassing that of all other papers in the province.[38] The paper was considered to be 'produced and conducted on principles advocated by the Government' (Khan 1991: 246); its loyalty and supportive stance were duly rewarded by government patronage. At the same time, *Koh-e Nūr* was popular with the native elite and enjoyed the patronage of the rulers of Kashmir and Patiala.[39]

During his time at the Koh-e Nur Press, Naval Kishore not only became acquainted with the various aspects of printing, publishing, and newspaper editing, but also advanced from an apprentice's position to that of one of Harsukh Rai's leading employees. In the process, Naval Kishore became Munshi Naval Kishore. There is some controversy regarding his exact position at the press, the sources variously referring to him as

[37] Harsukh Rai rose to a position of eminence in colonial Lahore. He was a member of the Municipal Committee and of the Anjuman-e Panjab. Besides *Koh-e Nūr*, he launched the literary monthly *Khurshīd-e Panjāb* (1856) and became the proprietor of *Toḥfa-e Kashmīr* (1877), the first Urdu paper in Kashmir. Details in Siddiqi 1962: 126-7; 212–17; Sabiri 1953 [i]: 371–422; Bool Chand 1933: 30.

[38] Out of these 349 subscribers, 162 were Hindus, 121 Muslims, and 40 Europeans. The number of books published by the press in the same year amounted to 15 titles. *SRGNWP*, vol. IV, pt XXIV, 1856, art. X: 'Note on the Native Presses'.

[39] Davis 1983: 84. *Koh-e-Nūr* survived until 1904. For further details, see Khurshid 1964: 55–64; Khan 1991: 243–79.

apprentice, editorial assistant, or editor of *Koh-e Nūr*. This is apparently due to the fact that Naval Kishore, after an initial two years at Harsukh Rai's printing press, temporarily left Lahore and returned to Agra, where on 19 January 1856 he launched his own Urdu paper under the name of *Safīr-e Āgra*. This is borne out by a notice published in *Koh-e Nūr* of 25 March 1856, which was itself reprinted from *Riyāẓ-e Nūr* of Multan (Khan 1990: 286).[40] Since no copies of the short-lived *Safīr-e Āgra* have survived, our knowledge about the paper is limited to the bare facts that it was a weekly of twelve pages, sold at a subscription rate of Rs 12 per annum (Sabiri 1953 [i]: 500). What prompted Naval Kishore to leave the Koh-e Nur Press is not known. Presumably, he simply wished to start his own business. There is an unsubstantiated claim that he left Lahore due to growing tension between him and Harsukh Rai (Eʿjazi 1980: 55). In the light of subsequent events, however, this seems unlikely.

While Naval Kishore was busy establishing himself in Agra, the Koh-e Nur Press faced a serious crisis when, in March 1856, Harsukh Rai was arrested for adultery and sentenced to three years in prison.[41] A sneering commentary in the *Lahore Chronicle* of 12 March 1856 suggests that by this time he was no longer in official favour, and that the harsh sentence was politically motivated:

> The sentence has also . . . given the most lively satisfaction to all classes of the native community, by whom Harsook Rai was alike feared and detested. His habit of levying black mail on respectable native officials, under threat of exposing their alleged misdeeds, was a source of intolerable oppression to the community, and large revenue to himself. Many circumstances conspired towards the success of his nefarious system. In the earlier part of his career he contrived to deceive most of our European officials as to his real character. He consequently holds "Testimonials", such as any native gentleman would be proud of, from the most distinguished of our functionaries, including Sir Henry and Sir John Lawrence. Under the sanction of these great names he has contrived for years to carry on an infamous traffic in reputations; while the very fact that his principal partner in business was Bunnoo Lall, the head shereistadar of the Chief Commissioner's office, has helped, in the eyes of the timid natives, to place him beyond the reach of the Law. We even hear that since his imprisonment, Hursook Rae has been heard to boast that Bunnoo Lall would get him out of Jail in ten days,

[40] In outlining these events I follow the interpretation offered by Khan (1990: 286–7).

[41] Harsukh Rai's 'crime' involved a Kashmiri Muslim woman. For details, see the *Lahore Chronicle*, 8 March 1856: 156.

> or at any rate as soon as the Chief Commissioner should return to Lahore—a boast which we doubt not Sir John Lawrence will feel it his duty to 'make a note of'.

Meanwhile, the Koh-e Nur Press was run by Munshi Hira Lal.[42] The predicament of the firm worsened when Munshi Divancand, the rival proprietor-editor of *Cashma-e Faiẓ* in Sialkot, shrewdly exploited the situation to launch his own new paper, *Khurshīd-e ʿālim*. *Koh-e Nūr* complained in an editorial that Divancand had purposely sent copies of his 'third-rate, non-sensical and mindless newspaper' to all its subscribers, encouraging them to abandon *Koh-e Nūr* and buy *Khurshīd-e ʿālim* instead.[43]

Apparently, it was at this critical juncture that Naval Kishore stepped in as an intermediary and managed to settle the feud between the two adversaries. He may have also been instrumental in procuring the bail of Rs 200 to effect Harsukh Rai's release from prison.[44] Out of gratitude, Harsukh Rai offered him the post of manager of the Koh-e Nur Press at a monthly salary of Rs 15 (Singh 1986: 65). Naval Kishore consequently abandoned his own project and returned to Lahore. This must have been by September 1857, for he figures as manager of the Koh-e Nur Press on the title page of a special supplement of *Koh-e Nūr* published on the occasion of the fall of Delhi on 21 September 1857 (Bool Chand 1932: 32). During the following months he played a major role in running the press and in ensuring that *Koh-e Nūr* remained one of the few Indian newspapers in the Punjab that continued throughout the Mutiny. By the end of 1857 it still boasted 257 subscribers (Khurshid 1963: 180).

During his years at the Koh-e Nur Press, Naval Kishore not only conceived the idea of setting up on his own, he also acquired the necessary technical and entrepreneurial skills to do so. More importantly, he was given the opportunity to make himself known to the British authorities as a loyal supporter of the colonial regime during the critical days of the 1857 uprising. This, as we shall see, would prove to be a crucial asset in his future projects. It is not known exactly when Naval Kishore left the Koh-e Nur Press for good. In late 1857 or early 1858 he temporarily returned to Agra, from where he proceeded to Lucknow to start a new chapter in his life and career.

[42] *Koh-e Nūr*, 11 March 1856, cited in Khurshid 1964: 56.

[43] Khan 1991: 271; Sabiri 1973: 244–5.

[44] He was reportedly released on 10 August 1857 (19 zi'l hijja 1273 AH), Sabiri 1973: 232–3.

2.2 Setting up Business in Lucknow

At twenty-two years of age, Naval Kishore settled in Lucknow to set up shop on his own. On 23 November 1858 he opened a small printing press with the official approval of Sir Robert Montgomery, Chief Commissioner of Oudh, and under the special patronage of Colonel Saunders A. Abbott, Commissioner and Superintendent of the Lucknow division. It is likely that Naval Kishore moved to Lucknow at the very instance of Montgomery or Abbott, both of whom had been posted in the Punjab before taking up office in Lucknow: Montgomery had held the post of Judicial Commissioner of the Punjab prior to his transfer from Lahore to Lucknow in April 1858. Colonel Saunders Abbott was transferred from Hoshiarpur in the same month.[45] In a document of 1886, Naval Kishore professes to have come to Lucknow 'under the patronage of Sir Robert Montgomery, the Chief Commissioner of Oudh and Colonel Abbott, Commissioner of Lucknow' and goes on to say that 'These gentlemen extended, in consideration of my loyalty and of what I had done in the Punjab for the British Government, their patronage to my newly-established Press and favoured me with the printing of all English and Vernacular documents connected with their Establishments.'[46]

Lucknow was then a city of some 500,000 inhabitants (Taban 1995: 724–6).[47] Even though it was severely affected by the 1857 uprising, to an aspiring young printer-journalist it presented much better opportunities than Agra. The city's rise to political and cultural prominence dates back to 1775, when Nawab Asaf ud-Daula shifted the capital of Avadh from Faizabad to Lucknow. Under the nawabs of Avadh, Lucknow flourished. It developed into a large and prosperous metropolis and became the scene of a vigorous commercial, intellectual, and literary life.[48] The munificent patronage of the nawabs attracted artisans and artists, poets and

[45] Naval Kishore's lasting gratitude towards Abbott is attested in his *Tavārīkh-e nādir al-ʿasr* (Navalkishor [1863] 1990), the only work authored by the publisher himself. It combines a short account of Abbott's life and administration with a topographical sketch of Lucknow, its rulers and localities.

[46] 'Statement of the Newul Kishore Press', see below, Chapter 4.

[47] Estimates vary greatly, ranging from 300,000 (Thornton 1857) to up to 1,000,000 inhabitants. Taban's estimate is based on figures reproduced from a contemporary local newspaper.

[48] Perhaps more than any other North Indian city, Lucknow has captured the imagination and received the continuous attention of travellers, scholars, and other observers. The last three decades have seen an increasing production of academic literature on the city. For the period of the nawabi, see, e.g., Barnett 1980; Llewellyn-Jones 1985; Fisher 1987; Kidwai 1993; Mohan 1997. For the post-Mutiny period,

scholars from all over India and beyond, making Lucknow the splendid new centre of Indo-Persian courtly culture and Urdu poetry. The repeated ransacking of the Mughal capital of Delhi by both Central Asian and indigenous invaders further enhanced the city's attraction, accounting for a large-scale migration of poets and scholars to the safe haven in the east.[49] Among those who left Delhi to take refuge in Lucknow were some of the greatest figures in eighteenth-century Urdu poetry, Mir and Sauda, as well as some eminent younger poets such as Insha and Mushafi.

Lucknow's importance as a religious centre and seat of Islamic scholarship pre-dated the rise of the Mughal successor state of Avadh to political power. From the early eighteenth century the learned men of Farangi Mahall, a religious seminary run by a family of famous Sunni scholars and mystics, had turned Lucknow into the foremost centre of Islamic learning in India. Attracting scholars and students from all over India and the wider Islamic world, Farangi Mahall played a vital part in the revival and consolidation of the rationalist tradition in Islamic sciences *(maᶜqūlāt)*. The influential curriculum developed by its leading *ᶜālim* Nizamuddin Ahmad, named *Dars-e Nizāmiyyā* after him, remained the dominant system of Indian Islamic education up to the late nineteenth century.[50] Yet the religious importance of Lucknow was not confined to its role as the major seat of Sunni scholarship and religiosity. As Juan Cole has outlined in a compelling study, the nawabs of Avadh made Shiᶜa Islam a powerful and central force in state politics and administration (Cole 1989). Under their patronage, Shiᶜa Islam was firmly institutionalized in the state apparatus, leading to the consolidation of 'a powerful and self-confident Shiᶜite culture in constant interaction with the Shiᶜa heartlands in Iraq and Iran' (Robinson 2001: 24). The climax of this evolution was the introduction of a formal Shiᶜa judicial system and the establishment of a royal *madrasah* in the 1840s.

Lucknow suffered enormously from the British annexation of Avadh and the effects of the 1857 uprising. However, it had not yet lost its role as an eminent intellectual, literary, and religious centre when Naval Kishore moved to the city in 1858. While the legendary decline of the

---

see, e.g., Oldenburg 1989 [1984]; Hasan 1990; Graff 1997; Joshi 2001. For the city's importance as a religious centre see Cole 1989; Malik 1997; Robinson 2001.

[49] For the exodus of poets from Delhi to Lucknow and the city's new role as the centre of Urdu literature, see Naim/Petievich 1997.

[50] For the history and importance of Farangi Mahall and an analysis of the *Dars-e Nizami*, see the seminal studies by Francis Robinson (Robinson 1984, 1987, 1993; reissued together in Robinson 2001) and by Jamal Malik (Malik 1997).

city had already set in and was most strongly felt in the economic sphere, Lucknow retained its fame as the epitome of refined Perso-Islamic civilization and was to remain 'the capital of Hindustani high culture' (Robinson 1997: 199) for some time to come.[51] When, in the wake of the 'Mutiny', Mirza Asadullah Khan Ghalib cast an envious look at the eastern metropolis, it contained all the nostalgia for a Delhi that was no more. Now the role of preserving Urdu culture had to be assigned to Lucknow: 'Nowadays, the people of Dihlī are either Hindus or common workers or men in khaki or Panjabis or Gorās [i.e. Europeans]. Which of these do you intend as the speakers of praiseworthy language?' lamented the famous Delhi poet. 'Lakhna'u life is a different story: there, the population has not been replaced. While the princedom is no more, people of all sorts of skills and accomplishment still live there' (Rahbar 1987: 132–3).

For Naval Kishore, the vacuum created in the central spheres of public and economic life in the immediate aftermath of 1857 turned out to be of advantage in several respects: with most of the earlier presses of the city destroyed or forced to close down, competition in the printing business was virtually eliminated, while real estate and housing could be acquired cheaply, given the right talent for speculation. The city, moreover, offered a vast human potential of highly skilled artisans, scholars, and men of literature who were without a job and easily available for employment. Another crucial factor favouring Naval Kishore's projects was Lucknow's return to political importance and its newly acquired role as the capital and administrative centre of the Avadh provincial government.[52] In the process of reconsolidating power and re-establishing social order in the city, the British heavily relied on the co-operation of the indigenous elites who had to be incorporated into the new administrative set-up or encouraged in other ways. In implementing the three imperatives of 'safety, sanitation, and loyalty' (Oldenburg 1989: xv) such collaboration was vital. To enlist the services of a loyal and trustworthy Indian printer

[51] As A. Azmi notes: 'Immediately after the annexation in 1856 the total industries were crippled either by the abolition of duties on the imported articles or by legislation and enhanced duty. The local artisans suffered severely due to the cessation of demand and were thrown out of job. They either migrated or became day labourers. Much of what remained of crafts and commerce was completely ruined during the Mutiny and the subsequent repressive policy of the British Government. Taking a very conservative view, at least 15% to 20% of the trading and manufacturing class must have either perished or migrated or became day labourers' (Azmi 1970: 169–70).

[52] For a detailed account see Oldenburg 1989.

was a matter of paramount importance. These circumstances help to explain the official support lent to Nawal Kishore at the time he set up his enterprise. The decisive prerequisite for British patronage, however, was the fact that he had given ample proof of his loyalty while editor at the Koh-e Nur Press during the tumultuous times of 1857.

Private Matters

'The Creator bestowed upon him the beauty of Venus and the qualities of Jupiter. He is himself the conjunction of two auspicious stars' (Russell/ Islam 1994: 293). These are the words used by Mirza Ghalib to describe his junior contemporary. Ghalib's poetic appraisal is fully substantiated by the few surviving photographic portraits of Munshi Naval Kishore. They depict a well-built and handsome man whose impressive stature was further enhanced by his elegant attire in the Lakhnavi style (Fig. 1). In the absence of private papers, little is known about the publisher's domestic life, his outlook and opinions in matters of family, worldly affairs and religious issues. As noted earlier, Naval Kishore was raised in a milieu of orthodox Vaishnavism. No information, however, is available as to his private religious practice. In 1850, aged fourteen, he was married to Sarasvati Devi (d. 1901), the daughter of a wealthy *zamīndār* from Rirha. Out of the marriage came three daughters, one of whom died before reaching adulthood. A long-awaited son was born to the couple in 1862, but he also died in infancy. Since the union produced no further male offspring, in 1872 Naval Kishore adopted his nephew Prag Narayan, the son of his younger brother Ramsevak, who was to become his heir and successor. Curiously, Prag Narayan was not brought up by Sarasvati Devi but by a Muslim woman whom Naval Kishore seems to have taken as his second wife. Nothing is known about the background of this woman, who was generally addressed as Begum Sahib and ran a separate household in the Man Singh Haveli in Lucknow's Rakabganj quarter. Apparently, the Hindu publisher's marriage to a Muslim woman did not compromise his social standing. It did, however, create some disturbance at the time of Prag Narayan's own marriage when some people, assuming him to be Begum Sahib's natural son, objected to his getting married to a Hindu girl (Nurani 1995: 33).

Like many Indian pioneers of print, Naval Kishore was a self-made man. When he arrived in Lucknow in 1858, he was virtually empty-handed. Endowed with a rare enterprising spirit and supported by British patronage, over the next thirty-seven years he single-mindedly devoted

Fig. 1: Munshi Naval Kishore (1836–95)

himself to building up a publishing house of unparalleled dimensions. Naval Kishore's business operations, along with the history of the growth of the NKP, will be dealt with in the following chapters. In order to understand how a single individual could build up from scratch what was to become the largest printing and publishing concern in South Asia, however, it is vital to first take a closer look at the various public roles and spheres of influence of northern India's foremost commercial printer-publisher. As will be shown below, the print capitalist Naval Kishore not only solidified his business by seeking alliances with various influential sections of post-1857 colonial society in Lucknow and beyond, but also assumed the role of publisher in a fashion that combined entrepreneurship with traditional notions of patronage. Engagement in philanthropy and social reform, an educator's mission, and political ambitions are the various facets of a public life that command closer attention.

2.3 The Public Life of an Indian Publisher

Given the absence of personal documents and the paucity of information on Munshi Naval Kishore's private life, his views and opinions, values, and motivations must be inferred from his public appearance, that is from the multifarious socio-cultural, reformist, and political activities he became engaged in following his rise to prominence in Lucknow society. Naval Kishore came to Lucknow as an outsider who had no connections with the city's traditional elites. His assimilation into the urban professional class and rise to the position of one of the city's leading notables provides an interesting example of new hybrid elite formation.[53] It also illustrates new mechanisms of social ascent afforded by the colonial public sphere in the post-1857 period. Undoubtedly, the economic power wielded by the publisher and the prosperity that came with the growth of his firm were crucial factors in his social ascent. However, colonial society also provided other mechanisms to rise socially, which became particularly important for the aspiring new middle class of government officials, urban professionals, businessmen, and publicists. The most efficient among these mechanisms, spanning both colonial and indigenous arenas of the public domain, were philanthropy and the patronage of charitable, educational, and religious institutions. It would be naive to interpret the publisher's engagement with charity merely as a disinterested monetary contribution to the good cause, as has been the

[53] For new elite formation in Lucknow, see Oldenburg 1989: 199–238.

general trend in biographical writing on him. Rather, it was a 'social investment' in the sense highlighted by C.A. Bayly in his seminal work on the North Indian merchant class (Bayly 1992). In probing the operations of the merchant family firm, Bayly clearly established the importance of the 'social dimension' of business life.[54] Drawing on Bayly, Douglas E. Haynes, in an essay on the relevance of gift-giving in nineteenth-century India, has argued that studying the philanthropic activities of South Asian commercial magnates significantly enhances our understanding of their social and political motivations (Haynes 1987). Rich merchants' engagement with philanthropy typically followed traditional Indian patterns of donation (*dāna*), particularly to religious institutions, educational charities, schools, and hospitals, while drawing at the same time on modern concepts of civic welfare and educated citizenship.

Against this backdrop, the extent to which Naval Kishore deliberately utilized philanthropy and patronage to maintain and enhance his social position needs to be analysed more thoroughly. Naval Kishore was the proverbial benefactor of widows and heathens who gave largely to all kinds of social and charitable causes. Without wanting to call into question the genuineness of his altruistic commitment and charitable intentions, these investments must be viewed as more than just munificent acts in the cause of society and social uplift. For one thing, philanthropy, in as much as it assumed modern forms of *public* civic engagement, was a prime means of securing the good will of the colonial rulers. As Sanjay Sharma has argued in his study of famine relief in the early nineteenth century, the colonial state clearly favoured institutionalized forms of charity—aimed at public projects such as schools, libraries, and hospitals, and organized along the lines of committees and voluntary associations—over established patterns of indigenous charity, which were often deemed to be lacking in public spirit (Sharma 2001: 192). That Naval Kishore was acutely aware of this becomes evident at a later stage in his career, when he would regularly invoke his dual role of large-scale employer and social benefactor in order to pressurize the colonial authorities (see Chapter 4).

The publisher's philanthropic activities and his liberal patronage to a large number of institutions formed part of a wider strategy of establishing networks of social alliances with both the colonial government and various groups within the indigenous mercantile and social elite. In promoting a climate of mutual trust between individuals and social groupings, such social networks were of prime importance to his business enterprise.

[54] See especially Chapter 10, 'The Merchant Family'.

Naval Kishore followed an established practice among commercial magnates when he began to assidiously build a network of alliances that was to serve his commercial and non-commercial interests alike.

Conquering the Public Sphere: Posts and Patronage

Wealth based on landholding and commerce, influence wielded in local society as an entrepreneur and publicist, and close ties maintained with the British authorities were the three pillars that sustained Naval Kishore's ascent in colonial Lucknow. They also elevated him into the category of *raʾīs* or 'urban magnate'. The urban *raʾīs*, as defined by Bayly, was an agent of 'informal political authority' who characteristically exercised his patronage and control through a network of 'cross-caste and cross-community connexions' and was consequently sought out by the British in his function as a local intermediary.[55] These same attributes also qualified Naval Kishore as what Francis Robinson has aptly termed the 'inevitable municipal board man' (Robinson 1973: 74–5). A new figure in post-1857 urban society, the Indian municipal commissioner was typically a commercial or professional man of substance who maintained a relationship of mutual interest with the government and who frequently used the municipal commissionership as a means of consolidating his local influence and as a stepping stone to a future career in politics.[56] Naval Kishore, as will be shown presently, was a case in point. In 1875 he was nominated as a member of the Lucknow Municipal Committee, a position which he held for the next eighteen years as a representative of the Ganeshganj ward.[57] The personal prestige and influence that came with this position on the municipal board were enhanced by several

[55] Bayly 1971: 290. Bayly defines the social category of *raʾīs* as 'magnates distinguished by their degree of control over resources and groups in the urban political system, and also by the degree of their influence with the local authorities who controlled the inflow of wealth into town society and to some extent confirmed its statuses' (ibid.: 293). *Raʾīs*es, by implication, were neither a caste nor a class but 'a category of political power whose main characteristics were ability to mediate with higher authority and to control webs of patronage beneath' (ibid.).

[56] Robinson greatly stresses the prestige and influence that came with a municipal commissionership (Robinson 1973: 73–4). His assessment has been challenged by Oldenburg, who finds him confusing 'opportunities to make money with real political power' (Oldenburg 1989: 85).

[57] The Lucknow Municipal Committee was established in 1862. In 1864 it comprised nineteen elected and six ex-officio members. It was a precursor of the Municipal

other honorary positions. While implying official recognition of his services to society, they served to tie him further to the colonial administration's interests. In 1881 he was made an Honorary Assistant Commissioner, and in the following year an Honorary Magistrate. He sat on the Oudh-Rohilkhand Railway Board, was an Honorary Inspector of Jails, and an Honorary Manager of the Government Printing Press at Allahabad.

Naval Kishore's appointment to these various posts was preceded and accompanied by continuous acts of patronage to public institutions. In his active support of social welfare schemes, educational projects, and local infrastructural measures he corresponded to the British ideal of an enlightened and cooperative member of the indigenous elite. His liberality and progressive outlook situated him within an envisaged class of local elite citizens who were to constitute 'the pillars of the new urban society' (Oldenburg 1989: xvii) and act as reliable intermediaries for the British in public arenas.

One of the chosen fields of charitable activity for the rich mercantile and professional classes in colonial India was what David Arnold has described as 'medical philanthropy' (Arnold 1993: 270). An opportunity to engage in this kind of highly valorized philanthropic work presented itself to Naval Kishore's contemporaries in the early 1880s with the establishment of the Lady Dufferin Fund. Created by and named after the vicereine, Lady Hariot Dufferin, the fund was designed with the express purpose of providing medical aid to Indian women, and of training native nurses and female doctors, particularly in obstetrics. In its wake, Lady Dufferin Hospitals were established in a number of urban centres. As an active local committee member and benefactor of the fund, Naval Kishore used his paper *Avadh Akhbār* to publish fund-raising appeals in support of the planned Lucknow hospital. He also sponsored an entire wing of the new hospital building with a large donation of Rs 15,000.

Such munificence was bound to favourably impress even the most senior officials. Lieutenant Governor Sir Auckland-Colvin, in outlining the fund's success in a public speech, made explicit mention of the large sums provided by 'the liberality of Munshi Newal Kishore', adding that this liberality was 'eminently characteristic of him'.[58] Of far greater consequence than medical philanthropy, however, was Naval Kishore's

---

Board which came into existence under the operation of the Local Self Government Act in 1884. *OAR,*1863–4: 69. See also Oldenburg 1989: 75–95.

[58] *Selections from Speeches of the Lieutenant-Governors of the NWP, 1867–1891*, 1890: 153.

sustained involvement in the educational sector. In Lucknow, he gave large donations of books to local institutions such as the Canning College and the Lucknow Museum. His financial assistance to Agra College has already been mentioned. Various other institutions of colonial higher education received his support. In the 1880s he helped revive Bareilly College by joining a fund for the promotion of collegiate education in Bareilly, and later became a member of its Board of Trustees, together with Deputy Collector Raja Jai Kishen Das, C.S.I., and other prominent citizens.[59] In 1887 he was appointed a Fellow of the University of Allahabad, having financed a new library building and presented the institution with a large donation of books.

The establishment of the Lucknow Jubilee High School in the same year was largely the result of the publisher's efforts. At the time, only two Anglo-Vernacular schools were operating in Lucknow. That both were run by missionaries was a matter of considerable concern to the colonial authorities. As the Avadh DPI observed, the absence of a secular Anglo-Vernacular school, subject to government control and inspection, in India's fourth-largest city was hardly acceptable. 'This state of things is, I believe, without a parallel in any Province or Presidency within the Empire', he pointed out.[60] Following several abortive attempts, the scheme to establish a government school only materialized in 1885 when Naval Kishore came forward with concrete proposals for an endowment and monthly subscriptions in support of a new school. He was supported in his efforts by his influential fellow citizen Rai Bahadur Brij Bhukan Lal, registrar at the Judicial Commissioner's Office, Honorary Magistrate, and Secretary to the Trustees of the Husainabad Endowment.[61] The two men had been associated with one another for a long time and had cooperated in various arenas such as the Municipal Committee and the Jalsah-e Tahzib, Lucknow's first voluntary association, about which more will be said later. When nothing came of Naval Kishore's initial proposals, on 26 April 1886 he again addressed the authorities, reiterating his offer of an endowment of Rs 15,000 and promising an additional monthly stipend of Rs 50. He also recommended a *nuzūl* building known as the Malka Jahan ki baradari or Agha Mir ki deorhi as a suitable site to house the new school. The building, a former residence of Nawab Ghaziuddin's

[59] *PGNWP&Oudh. Educational Dept.*, June 1885: 3.

[60] *PGNWP&Oudh. Educational Dept.*, March 1887: 3.

[61] Brij Bhukan Lal (b.1820) belonged to a family of Kayasthas. In 1882 he received the title of Rai Bahadur in recognition of his 'long and faithful services' as Registrar of the Judicial Commissioner's Court (*Manual of Titles* 1889: 114).

Prime Minister Agha Mir, was well known to Naval Kishore since it had previously housed his printing presses.[62] On the basis of his endowment and a further contribution of Rs 7500 by Brij Bhukan Lal, the Educational Department was able to secure the building and progress with its plans to set up a school. Naval Kishore busied himself with raising further capital from the local gentry. The institution, which was to impart primary and secondary education in English and the regional languages to students 'irrespective of race or creed', was finally opened in 1887 and named Lucknow Jubilee High School, its opening coinciding with Queen Victoria's Jubilee. The two principal Indian donors were made lifetime members of its Board of Trustees.

Education became a mission and a lifelong concern for Naval Kishore. As is evident from his activities both in publishing and in the wider public domain, the spread of education among his contemporaries meant to him a dual engagement, with the promotion of advanced scholarship on the one hand, and the dissemination of knowledge among the Indian masses on the other. His concept of knowledge, being non-elitist and democratic, was also non-exclusive and all-encompassing, according importance to both Indian and Western thought, and to Hindu and Islamic scholastic traditions. The wide range of private and official educational schemes and institutions that he supported through a combination of scholarships, book donations and pecuniary assistance point to an essentially humanist vision that transcended the narrow boundaries of communal affiliation.

Naval Kishore's patronage of several eminent Islamic institutions corroborates this point. The same man who founded a traditional Sanskrit *pāṭhśālā* on the banks of the river Gomti in Lucknow made the preservation of India's Islamic literary heritage one of his primary concerns. In keeping with this objective, Naval Kishore was eager to aid one of the most prestigious institutions of Islamic learning in northern India, the Dar ul-ʿulum at Deoband.[63] His donations of numerous standard works of Islamic literature were a welcome asset to the seminary's library and

[62] *PGNWP&Oudh. Educational Dept.*, March 1887: 4.

[63] Metcalf 1982: 104. By contrast, little is known about the interaction between Naval Kishore and Farangi Mahall. At least one Farangi Mahall scholar served at the NKP, while a number of important works produced by the learned men of Farangi Mahall and published by Naval Kishore suggest a more or less regular cooperation. One prominent example is the commentary of Rumi's *Masnavī-e maʿnavī* (*1873) by Maulana ʿAbdul ʿAli Bahr al-ʿUlum, of which Naval Kishore obtained the copyright from Farangi Mahall.

were gratefully acknowledged by the Deobandi ʿulama. This is evinced in the school's yearly reports. While the second annual report of 1867–8 lamented the dearth of Arabic textbooks and difficulty in procuring them, subsequent reports expressed their warm gratitude to Munshi Naval Kishore, who 'despite the great distance' had initiated a continuous supply of books free of charge.[64] The eminent Deobandi teacher Manazir Ahsan Gilani would later emphasize the momentous impact of these donations. It has to be understood, writes Gilani, 'that for a long time it was with the help of the books donated by this one non-Muslim that the teachers and students at the Dar al-ʿulum at Deoband fulfilled their religious and scholarly requirements, understood the Qurʾan and solved the linguistic problems of Hadith'.[65]

For all his support of an institution that represented orthodox Islamic learning, Naval Kishore openly sided with the modernist cause of Sir Sayyid Ahmad Khan (1817–98) and the Muslim reformist movement. The relationship between the two men was a close, longstanding, and eventually turbulent one. It dates back to at least the year 1864, when Sayyid Ahmad Khan founded the Scientific Society at Ghazipur, the largest and most influential among early voluntary associations in northern India.[66] Naval Kishore joined the society as a subscribing member on 15 September 1864 and promptly began supporting it with book donations. In 1868 Sayyid Ahmad Khan had his *Aḥkām-e ṭaʿām-e ahl-e kitāb* (Fig. 2), a treatise on the permissibility of interdining with Christians, published from the NKP Kanpur. More publishing collaborations followed, among them reprints of Sayyid Ahmad's early critical edition of *Āʾīn-e Akbarī* (Institutes of Akbar, *1869) and of his widely acclaimed topographical work on Delhi *Ās̤ār aṣ-ṣanādīd* (Vestiges of the Nobles, *1876).[67] Naval Kishore was clearly an admirer of the great Muslim reformer, and in the early 1870s actively supported the latter's controversial reformist journal *Tahẕīb al-Ak͟hlāq* through the columns of his own paper *Avadh Ak͟hbār* (see Chapter 6). Therefore, when Sayyid Ahmad Khan campaigned for the establishment of the Mohammadan Anglo-Oriental College in Aligarh in the 1870s, he was able to count on the publisher's liberal support. The educational and ideological objectives of the college, its reconciliation of traditional Islamic teaching with the

[64] *Rūdād-e salānah* 1284 h, cited in S.T. Khan 1980: 173.

[65] Cited in ʿAli 1980: 93 (my translation from the original Urdu).

[66] Details on the society in Lelyveld 1996: 77–80.

[67] The NKP edition of *Ās̤ār aṣ-ṣanādīd* was a reprint of the first edition of 1847.

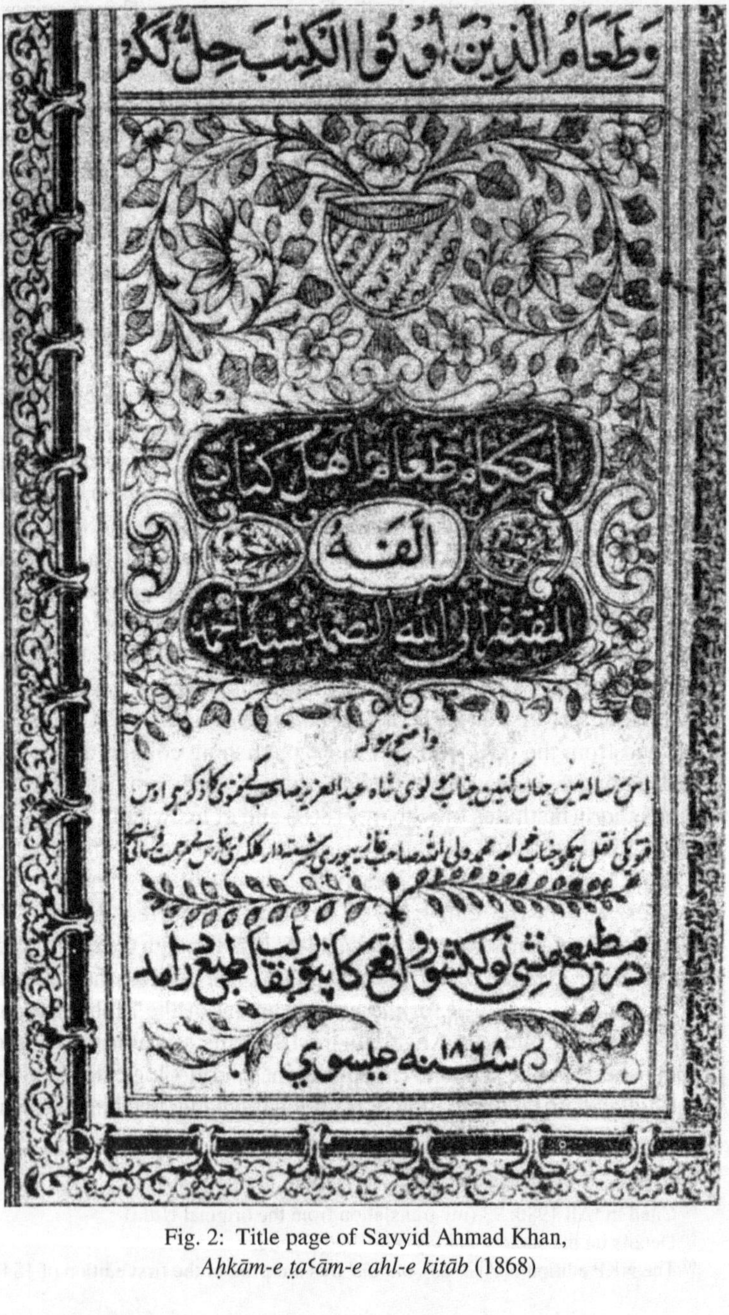

Fig. 2: Title page of Sayyid Ahmad Khan,
Aḥkām-e ṭaʿām-e ahl-e kitāb (1868)

secular rationalism of Western science in a reformist agenda, closely corresponded to Naval Kishore's ideas of how to reform education and lead Indian Muslims on the road to progress. Consequently, fund-raising appeals were published in *Avadh Akhbār*, while Sayyid Ahmad Khan's speeches soliciting support to the college were publicized in printed pamphlets.[68] Naval Kishore made a personal donation of Rs 10,000 to the college funds and contributed books worth Rs 20,000. In the 1880s the two men would again collaborate and finally part ways in the anti-Congress movement.

As mentioned earlier, one of the new measures arising from the colonial state's educational agenda in the post-1857 period was the establishment of public libraries. The scheme was enthusiastically endorsed by the Indian intelligentsia who adopted it as a project of their own. Public libraries, though generally supported by government grants, depended heavily on Indian sponsorship for their upkeep and the supply of books. Not surprisingly, publishers like Naval Kishore volunteered to furbish these new institutions of an emerging middle-class reading culture. The public libraries patronized by his firm spanned a wide geographical region, including not only the libraries of Lucknow, Meerut, Faizabad, Bareilly, and Barabanki, but also the Lyall Library in Aligarh, the Punjab Public Library (Charles Aitchison Memorial Library) in Lahore, and the Lansdowne Library in Calcutta. Several libraries in the princely states of Jammu and Kashmir, Jaipur, and Patiala were also supplied with NKP books. It is a fortunate circumstance that Naval Kishore's largesse was not limited to India. The Indian Institute Library of the Bodleian Library in Oxford received a donation of approximately 2000 bound volumes at the time of its foundation by Sir Monier Monier-Williams in 1884. Today, this well-preserved collection reckons among the largest collections of nineteenth-century NKP books outside India and is probably only outdone in size by the holdings of the British Library.[69]

Educational patronage of such scope and variety not only served as a means to consolidate Naval Kishore's position within indigenous

[68] Two such pamphlets are listed in the QLP Oudh, namely, 'A lecture delivered by Sayyid Ahmad Khan at Lahore, regarding the proposed Mahommadan University' (*1874); and 'Rules regarding the foundation and management of the proposed Mahommadan University' (*1874).

[69] See Sir Monier-Williams's inauguration speech of 14 October 1884, 'How can the University of Oxford best fulfil its duty towards India?', *Oxford and Cambridge Undergraduates' Journal*, 16 October 1884. Another large collection of NKP books outside India can be found at Tokyo University.

circles: like philanthropy it also presented him with an opportunity to ingratiate himself with the colonial authorities. His continuous support of colonial schemes and institutions undoubtedly did much to strengthen an already thriving business relationship with the British and served to enhance further the amount of official patronage accorded to his firm. The implications of colonial patronage for the NKP's commercial history and the nature of the business collaboration with the British will be discussed in detail in Chapter 4. At present, we are more immediately concerned with the impact of Naval Kishore's own acts of philanthropy and patronage on his social ascent in colonial society.

From the mid-1870s British acknowledgement of Munshi Naval Kishore's position among the foremost members of the Lucknow urban elite is manifested in a large number of invitations to official functions and social gatherings organized by senior representatives of the colonial state.[70] Some of these invitations—to the Chapter of the Order of the Star of India in 1876, to the Viceregal *darbār* in Lahore in November 1880, and to the Viceroy's Levee in November 1885—were in fact 'press tickets', extended to Naval Kishore in his capacity as proprietor of the leading Urdu daily in the provinces. At the same time, he gained entry into the more limited circle of Indian elite members whose presence was requested at social events of a more exclusive kind. These events included an 'evening fête' at the Lahore Shalimar gardens hosted by Sir Robert Henry Davies, Lieutenant Governor of the Punjab, during the visit of His Royal Highness the Prince of Wales to India in 1875–6, a garden party given by Richard Temple, Lieutenant Governor of Bengal, on the same occasion, and an evening party given by Lieutenant Governor Lord Lyall to meet the Viceroy and Countess of Dufferin in 1885. The publisher's admittance into this restricted sphere of formal social interaction between the colonial state and the Indian elite is significant, for it testifies to his status as an established community leader. As it turned out, it was precisely the influence Naval Kishore wielded in local society, rather than his achievements in the field of literature and learning, that ultimately accounted for the British decision to bestow an official title upon him.

Naval Kishore had to wait a long time before his services to society were officially recognized by the government. He received a foretaste of such recognition in January 1877 when, on the occasion of the Imperial Assemblage at Delhi, he was among the first Indians to receive

[70] I am grateful to Dr Ranjit Bhargava for kindly putting at my disposal some twenty such original invitation cards dating mainly from the 1880s.

the first class *Kaisar-e-Hind* medal.[71] However, it took eleven more years, several appeals in the Urdu-language press,[72] and the personal intervention of Lieutenant Governor Sir Alfred Lyall before he was honoured with an imperial title. Lyall, who was acutely aware of Naval Kishore's far-reaching influence within the Indian community, took a personal interest in having a title bestowed on the publisher and recommended him for the *Companion of the Order of the Indian Empire*. When his initial recommendation failed to produce the desired results, Lyall wrote to the Viceroy's Private Secretary, Sir Donald Mackenzie Wallace, to reiterate his request. His letter of 19 October 1887 deserves to be quoted in full, for it clearly reveals Lyall's ulterior motives in advocating the expediency of the measure:

> My dear Mackenzie Wallace,
>
> You may remember that when I submitted the list of persons recommended for honours in commemoration of Her Majesty's Jubilee, Munshi Newul Kishore of Lucknow was one of those recommended for the C.I.E. I subsequently learnt, with some regret, that the honour would not be conferred on him; and I write again on the subject before leaving India, because I think it possible that some of the reasons upon which he was recommended may not have been fully apprehended. Newul Kishore holds rather a special position in these Provinces; he is a man of wealth; he is the proprietor of a large business, and he owns the leading native newspaper (vernacular) in Upper India. His energy and activity have placed him in relation with various classes and interests throughout this part of the country and the adjoining Native States, to a degree which has acquired him much influence, and which keeps him widely acquainted with all that goes on. I am told that he also carries a large book trade with Afghanistan; and it is certain that he shows much enterprize as a publisher in various departments. In short, he is a man who might be very useful, both from his connection with native journalism and book-printing, and from the extensive means that he possesses of keeping himself and others informed of the state of feeling and opinion on any questions that concern the native community. He is by no means unwilling to find himself on good terms with the Government; and his intelligence and sagacity make it quite worth while to keep up communications with him. I myself have no doubt whatever as to the expediency of encouraging him, and attaching him more or less to the interests of our administration. At any rate I believe it would be a mistake to let him discover

[71] For a classic account of the Imperial Assemblage and its impact, see Cohn 1983.

[72] See, e.g., the comments in the *Aḥsan al-Akhbār*, *Āgra Akhbār*, and *Tūtī-e Hind* (Meerut), SVN 1880: 178; 1886: 828 and 1888: 36–7.

that the Government does not think that he merits any special consideration. He would be much gratified if the C.I.E. were given to him; and as I think his position in the Provinces is such that the honour might be fitly and wisely bestowed upon him, I shall be very glad if an opportunity occurs of again sending up his name.
His Excellency the Viceroy may possibly be not less disposed to consider favourable the recommendation, as it is the last of this kind which I am making before quitting the Lieutenant-Governorship.

Believe me,

Sincerely yours
(sd.) A.C. Lyall[73]

This time, Lyall's pressing request met with a favourable reply. Consequently, on 2 January 1888 the honorary title of 'Companion of the Order of the Indian Empire' (C.I.E.) was conferred on Naval Kishore. The bestowal of the prestigious title onto a representative of the Indian newspaper and publishing trade was widely acclaimed in the Urdu press. Most papers in a self-congratulatory manner chose to interpret it as a long-overdue tribute to the Indian-language press rather than just a personal honour to the Lucknow publisher. A marked exception was the satirical journal *Avadh Punch*, an old-time rival of *Avadh Akhbār*, which sardonically greeted the new 'Companion of the Order of the Indian Empire' as a 'Sycophant of the Empire'.[74]

Thus far we have looked at Naval Kishore's interactions in an arena of the public sphere that was dominated and controlled by the colonial state, namely the domain of local self-government, of honorary positions and official social functions organized by the British. Juxtaposed to it and frequently overlapping was the vibrant indigenous public sphere shaped by vernacular newspapers, caste associations, literary and social reform societies, and other voluntary bodies. As will be shown below, Naval Kishore moved easily between these two frequently interacting public worlds.

Caste Connections

Munshi Naval Kishore's lifetime coincided with a period of rapid modernization in Indian society. Its implications were felt in all spheres of

[73] The Viceregal Papers of the Marquess of Dufferin and Ava, OIOC, Neg 4367, vol. 52: 342–3.

[74] SVN 1888: 36–7 and 498.

life, including religion. In the process of negotiating, reformulating, and asserting religious identity, the modernizing Hindu nation rediscovered the institution of caste with its concomitant moral and dharmic implications. As Susan Bayly has argued, the new consciousness of caste and its formalized expression of caste associations in the latter half of the nineteenth century was more than just a reaction to colonial schemes of classifying Indian society along hierarchical lines (S. Bayly 1999). Rather, Indian thinkers and social reformers came to view caste as a tool in the social and cultural regeneration of India, investing it with the new meaning of 'a bond of moral community at the national level' (ibid.: 166). Underlying this 'idealised corporation view', as Bayly calls it, was the notion that caste was vested with moral messages. Hence the emphasis that newly-emerging caste assocations placed on social service and reformist activities. Agendas of community uplift had a clearly patriotic thrust and would ultimately entail the uplift of the Indian nation at large. In the modern public arena, caste affiliation came to be portrayed as 'an expression of citizenship and spiritually informed nationality which had the potential to fulfil and regenerate the modern Hindu.' Caste associations in this configuration functioned as 'enlightened citizenries' (ibid.: 173; 166).

Naval Kishore's efforts in formulating a corporate caste identity and supporting the interests of his caste community must be viewed against this backdrop. If his engagement with caste issues was in many ways typical of his times, it also provides a salient example of how the new men of print utilized their position to publicize and foster community interests (Bayly 1996a: 345). Pre-dating Naval Kishore's active involvement in the formation of the Bhargava caste association in the 1880s was his marked interest in the concerns of the Kayastha community. In the 1870s he, on various occasions, lent his support to the eminent Lucknow Kayastha leader Munshi Kali Prasad, a pleader at the Judicial Commissioner's Court. In 1872 Kali Prasad established the Lucknow Kayastha Dharm Sabha and simultaneously launched an Urdu bimonthly called *Kāyastha Samācār*.[75] When, in the following year, he set up the Kayastha Pathshala in Allahabad, Naval Kishore came forward as a patron of the institution. A 1882 record of the Kayastha Pathshala draws attention to his generous contribution to the school library, noting that the library owed its existence chiefly to the Lucknow publisher, 'who

[75] Details in Carroll 1975. For the *Kāyastha Samācār* see Carroll 1973 and Sabiri 1953 [ii]: 445–6.

had generously made a gift of such works as have been printed in his press, and who had promised to give to the library such books as may be printed in his press hereafter.'[76] Furthermore, he funded three out of the six scholarships attached to the school.[77]

Given my earlier attempt to show that Naval Kishore himself was not a Kayastha, it is significant that none of the sources originating from within the community identify him as a caste member. Why then should he actively support a caste community that was not his own? We have already seen that his patronage extended to a large variety of social and educational schemes and institutions. It will be argued here that he had a vested interest in lending special support to the Kayastha community, his own enterprise relying so heavily on the expertise of the large number of Kayasthas employed as translators, compositors, and scribes. There were strong professional and personal ties: for example, the head Persian translator in the NKP's Department of Translation, Munshi Gokul Parshad, was a Kayastha who also happened to be the first editor of *Kāyastha Samācār*. Also, the publisher's assocation with the Kayastha leader Kali Prasad seems to have been a close and personal one. In the 1870s the NKP issued several tracts in Urdu, Hindi, and Sanskrit that dealt with the controversial issue of the Kayasthas' origin and *varṇa* status.[78] Foremost among them was Kali Prasad's *Kāyasthavarṇanirṇay* (*1875), a predecessor to his better known English *Kayastha Ethnology* (Kali Prasad 1877).[79] This treatise, in which he painstakingly tried to prove the Kshatriya origin of North Indian Kayasthas, became a key text in formulating a distinct community identity. Printed at the Lucknow American Methodist Printing Press, it was distributed by the NKP, which acted as agent for the *Kāyastha Samācār*'s Allahabad office. The 1879 NKP catalogue contained a separate list of the office's publications.

In the 1880s Naval Kishore's focus visibly shifted from the Kayastha to the Dhusar-Bhargava community. As outlined earlier, in the last decades of the nineteenth century the Dhusars underwent a process of social mobility in which their new identity as Bhargava Brahmins was

[76] *AECR* 1884: 377.

[77] Ibid.

[78] E.g., *Kāyastha dharm darpaṇ* (*1870), an Urdu tract by Pandit Ramcaran Sharma, and the Sanskrit *Kāyastha-kula-bhāskara* (*1873) by the same author.

[79] *The Kayastha Ethnology: being an inquiry into the origin of the Chitraguptavansi and Candrasenavansi Kayasthas* (Lucknow: American Methodist Mission Press 1877). For the impact of this text and the controversy over the Kayasthas' caste status, see Carroll 1975.

formulated and consolidated. More than a mere witness to this process, Naval Kishore took a leading part in it. He acted as one of the founder-members of the community's first nation-wide caste organization, the Akhil Bharatiya Bhargava Sabha or 'All India Bhargava Conference', established in Mathura in 1889. Reporting on the inaugural meeting held on 31 December 1889 'under the auspices of the members of the Dhusar community', *Hindustānī* noted:

> Among others, Munshi Newal Kishore, C.I.E of Lucknow, Munshi Girdhar Lal, Vakil, Agra, and Lalas Sita Ram and Jagan Prasad, Honorary Magistrates, Muttra, were present, and Seth Lachnam [*sic*] Das, C.I.E., presided. The meeting resolved to establish a school from public subscription. Munshi Newal Kishore will contribute Rs 25 a month . . .[80]

As this passage suggests, the nascent association brought together urban professionals and commercial *ra'īs*es of considerable financial means and public influence. In Seth Lachman Das, a member of a powerful merchant and banking family of Mathura, it had found an eminent patron. Education, social reform, and support of caste interests were the main targets on the association's early agenda. The fact that the second Bhargava Conference was held at Naval Kishore's private Lucknow residence in December 1890 points to his prominent position in the early days of the caste association. On this particular occasion various social issues, particularly the controversial Age of Consent Bill, were discussed. A resolution was passed, advising caste members not to have their sons married before the age of sixteen. The proceedings of the conference were subsequently publicized in *Avadh Akhbār*, by then the most widely read Urdu daily in North India.[81] The third Bhargava Conference took place at Mathura in December 1892. Again, an illustrious congregation assembled: Munshi Naval Kishore and the Agra pleader Munshi Girdhar Lal, the association's secretary, presided over the sessions. Among the prominent dignitaries present were Seth Lachman Das, this time joined by Lala Mangilal, the head manager of his banking business,[82] and Raja Jai Kishen Das, Deputy Collector of Morabadad and an eminent former Hindu spokesman of the Aligarh movement. On the members' request,

[80] *Hindustānī*, 12 January 1890, SVN 1890: 37.

[81] SVN 1891: 47. The event here is referred to as the 'Annual meeting of the Bhargava Social Conference'.

[82] The Mathura Seths became converts to Vaishnavism around 1860. For their family history, see Growse 1883: 14–15.

Seth Lachman Das agreed to oversee and financially support the caste association's newly established Sanskrit *pāṭhśālā* which was to impart education to both boys and girls. Raja Jai Kishen Das promised a monthly grant to the institution.[83]

Naval Kishore consolidated his prominent position within the caste association by giving ample financial support to its educational and social reform schemes. On the occasion of his adopted son Prag Narayan's marriage he donated Rs 8,000 to the Bhargava Sabha, followed later by an even larger sum of Rs 15,000. In 1891 he gave Rs 1000 to the Vidhva Kosh Bhargava Sabha, a charitable fund established in Agra for the support of Hindu widows. The Bhargava Boarding House in Agra received a generous donation of Rs 20,000 at the time of its foundation in 1890, followed by a permanent annual grant of Rs 1500. It seems that in his munificence Naval Kishore was continuously outdoing other community members, to the extent that it actually caused some embarrassment. This is suggested by the association's report of 1891–2, which remarked on the financing of the Bhargava Boarding House:

> No further necessary payments had to be made for the building. However, to support the students Munshi Naval Kishore, C.I.E., has bestowed a certain sum and has kindly agreed to bestow the same sum this year. But to put such a burden on a single individual and have all one's hopes depend on a single gentleman means to discourage the spirit of brotherhood, generosity and munificence of the community. We must all make an effort to fulfil the promises we made and complete this task of our community and our association according to our capacity.[84]

The establishment of the Bhargava Sabha consolidated the identity and public influence of the community and gave its interests a common thrust. For men like Seth Lachman Das and Naval Kishore it had the additional benefit of bringing them into personal contact with other influential men of trade and commerce, thus providing a forum for the corporate interests of Hindu entrepreneurship.

It is worth noting that apart from a temple in Rewari and a Shiva temple reportedly built by him in the Civil Lines of Kanpur,[85] extant sources

[83] *Karravāī cahāram jalsa-e ʿām Bhārgava sabhā*, Agra 1893: 36. The document lists the members of the Sabha's managing committee, most of them public servants and lawyers.

[84] Ibid.: 10.

[85] See the website of the Bhargava community at http:/www.bhargava.indiainformation.com.

provide no evidence of Naval Kishore engaging in religious patronage. Unlike other commercial magnates who would liberally contribute to the building of temples or patronize religious festivals and bodies (Bayly 1971: 298), he seems to have taken only a limited interest in investing in religious charity. As suggested earlier, his public engagement transcended narrow boundaries of caste and religious community to focus on wider issues of education, social reform, and the spread of knowledge and progressive thought among his contemporaries. An ideal forum to help promote these causes presented itself to him in the many voluntary and civic associations that evolved as a constitutive feature of urban public life in colonial India from the 1860s.

Voluntary Associations and Civic Engagement

Reflecting the formation of a new political and literary public sphere, the 1860s saw the rise of an 'associational culture',[86] which found its immediate expression in a proliferation of debating clubs, scientific institutes, and literary or reformist societies. With its focus on education, literature and social reform, this new form of organized indigenous agency grew out of the need of the educated Indian elite to debate the implications of colonial rule and participate in the process of Indian modernization. Embedded in, and representative of, the nascent public sphere, the new associational culture was informed by notions of enlightened and active citizenship.[87] While emulating the discursive forms of Western liberalism, it also drew inspiration from age-old Hindu concepts such as *sevā* ('service') and *dāna* ('gift-giving'), investing them with new meanings of 'service to society' and 'associational philanthropy' (Watt 2006: 65–96). For men like Naval Kishore the new voluntary associations fulfilled various functions: they not only allowed for participation in the East–West encounter at the cultural, literary, and scientific level, but also provided a forum in which to debate public affairs and become actively engaged in 'modern' forms of philanthropy. More importantly, they formed the nucleus of future political representation by providing an institutional framework for the urban elite's self-styled role as spokesmen of indigenous society, and as intermediaries between the colonial state and the Indian masses. Associations, in Anil Seal's pointed formulation, 'brought nineteenth-century India across the threshold of modern politics'

[86] For the concept of 'associational culture', see Harris 1993; Watt 2005.

[87] For the colonial citizen as an educational ideal, see Kumar 1991: 23–46.

(Seal 1968: 194). Implied in this political trajectory was the intelligentsia's use of the associational sphere to postulate its own hegemonic claims.[88]

We have already noted Naval Kishore's subscription to Sayyid Ahmad Khan's Scientific Society in 1864. Four years later, he acted as one of the founder-members of Lucknow's first literary and reformist society, the Jalsah-e Tahzib ('Assembly of Refinement/Culture') or 'Lucknow Reform Club', as it was rather insipidly dubbed in English. Established in 1868 by a group of eminent Hindu and Muslim citizens, the Jalsah-e Tahzib represented a cross-section of Lucknow's upcoming middle-class and professional elite, consisting largely of government servants, men in the legal profession, doctors, and publicists. In an illustration of the intimate nexus existing between the culture of association and new forms of communication and knowledge transfer made available by print, a large section of its members were journalists, newspaper editors, and publishers. It is significant that, at the level of caste, the assocation drew its membership from the city's traditional elites—Kayasthas, Kashmiri Brahmins, and sections of the Muslim aristocracy. The Jalsah was founded partly in response to the establishment of the Avadh *taʿalluqdār*s' British Indian Association in 1861 and with a view to counterbalancing the influence that the rural elite had begun to exert in the urban public sphere of post-'Mutiny' Lucknow. Yet what really brought its members together across traditional boundaries of caste and religious community was the hybrid urban elite's shared vision of their new role in society: while these men commanded considerable influence in their respective communities, their avenues of political participation were still extremely circumscribed and usually limited to a seat on the Municipal Committee. As a collective cross-communal project, the Jalsah provided an institutional basis to the common aspirations of Lucknow's functional elite. Even as they had to confine their activities to the cultural and social domain, the Jalsah's members nourished political aspirations. The association soon counted high British officials among its patrons but prided itself in maintaining an essentially Indian identity.[89] Patriotism, openness to reforms, an educational mission and a self-conscious assertion of Urdu culture were implicit elements of its self-image.

[88] For an elaboration of these points, see, e.g., Seal 1968: 194–244; Robinson 1974: 85–7, Lelyveld 1996: 77–82; Naregal 2001: 232–52.

[89] I have given a detailed account of the Jalsah's foundation, membership, early activities and self-perception in a separate paper; see Stark 2001. For an insightful documentation of the society's early years based on primary sources, see also Siddiqi 1956.

The Jalsah's early years were marked by a high degree of activity. Like other civic associations it engaged in intellectual debate, social reform and education, and particularly espoused the cause of female education. Public lectures were organized on a wide range of subjects relating to history, education, law, social reform and the progress in science and technology. Representing the city's Urdu-speaking elite, the Jalsah also acted as a body of 'cultural entrepreneurs' (Joshi 2001: 2); it propagated the use of Urdu not just as a refined literary idiom but as a language fit for modern scientific and political discourse. In 1869, largely as a result of its efforts, the first public library was set up in Lucknow. State and private agency worked together in furnishing the institution, which was put under the Jalsah's management. The library received a great boost when it was selected as an official deposit library for the province in the early 1870s. Naval Kishore, who from 1869 served as one of the Jalsah's directors, not only acted as a liberal donor of books and capital to the library, but also took charge of the Jalsah's 'public relations'. He printed its journal *Risāla-e Jalsah-e Tahẕīb* (succeded by *Muraqqaᶜ-e Tahẕīb*) and widely publicized the society's affairs through his paper *Avadh Akhbār*. When in 1870 Mir Aulad ᶜAli, professor at Trinity College, Dublin, came to Lucknow to deliver a lecture on the 'Customs and Manners of the English', he advanced the speaker's travel expenses and later published the lecture in pamphlet form. While the Jalsah clearly benefited from his support, to Naval Kishore, it provided an ideal arena in which to consolidate his position in local society.

As I have argued elsewhere, the Jalsah, though outwardly a literary and reform society, carried from the outset the seeds of nationalist thought and claims to political representation. Its self-perception as a body representing public opinion and its self-styled role as an intermediary between the government and its Indian subjects is already manifest in its bye-laws of 1868 (Stark 2001: 57–8). The establishment in 1877 of a second civic society in Lucknow, the Rifah-e ᶜAm or 'Public Welfare Association', was a logical extension of these claims. Its membership overlapped with the Jalsah, its outlook, however, was decidedly more political. The Rifah-e ᶜAm focused on issues of national importance and aimed to operate on a supra-regional level. Claiming to represent 'all classes of the native community', it soon became the centre of political activity in the city (Joshi 2001: 30). The two societies merged in the 1880s. Naval Kishore played a leading part in the Rifah-e ᶜAm's affairs. In 1886 he organized a public meeting to receive the illustrious Marathi social reformer Behramji Malabari on his campaign through North India to raise the 'Age of Consent'. During the meeting, he himself gave a speech in favour of the abolition of child marriage (Baijnath 1886: 12–16).

Naval Kishore's patronage of indigenous societies was not limited to Lucknow but extended to a wider network of associations in the region. In 1865 Garcin de Tassy noted his membership in the 'Society of Agra for the propagation of useful knowledge' (*LLH* 1865: 278). The reference is presumably to the Satya Sabha, a precursor of the Anjuman-e Agra, the principal society for the propagation of Western knowledge and culture in the city after 1870. In 1877 Naval Kishore became actively involved in a committee for the reduction of marriage expenses among Indians. Together with Munshi Pyarelal, the president of the Anjuman-e Hind, he organized several meetings at Lahore and Lucknow, the proceedings of which were subsequently brought to public notice in *Avadh Akhbār* (*LLH* 1877: 66–7). Of more specific interest, since it links him to the Hindi agitation of the 1870s, is his role in the establishment of the Bharat Barshia National Association of Aligarh. This learned society was founded in 1878 by several eminent citizens, among them Raja Jai Kishen Das, C.S.I, and Raja Tikam Singh of Mursan, with the purpose of promoting education and literature in European and Indian languages. It was instrumental in setting up Aligarh's first public library, the Lyall Library. The institution was established through public funds. With a contribution of Rs 5000 Naval Kishore headed the list of donors.[90] Other activities on the society's agenda included the promotion of female education and the translation of scientific works, both western and oriental, into Hindi (Nevill 1909: 87). To this end, a subcommittee called Bhasha Sambarddhini Sabha or 'Society for the Enhancement of Hindi' was established. The Bharat Barshia National Association later figured among the organizations that submitted pro-Hindi memorials to the Education Commission of 1882. The publisher's association with it will be outlined in greater detail in Chapter 7.[91]

In operating through a network of associations, Naval Kishore found himself in constant interaction with other eminent contemporaries—Sayyid Ahmad Khan, Raja Jai Kishen Das, Pandit Shri Kishen, Raja Shiva Prasad, and many others. In their simultaneous and flexible engagements in a variety of philanthropic, literary, social reform, and political bodies, these members of the Indian intelligentsia represented a new type of 'public man' reminiscent of Ernest Gellner's 'modular

[90] SVN 1885: 733.

[91] *Report on Administration for the NWP&Oudh*, for the year ending 31 March 1893: 306.

man', a constitutive feature in his conceptualization of modern Civil Society (Gellner 1994: 97–102). To the modular man, the emerging culture of association provided new modes of combining into 'specific-purpose, *ad hoc*, limited association' and of testing the effectiveness of 'highly specific, unsanctified, instrumental, revocable links or bonds' (ibid.: 100).

There is yet another facet to Naval Kishore's rise as a 'public man': in the process of consolidating his social position he aimed high and sought to establish close relations with influential contemporaries, be it Indian sovereigns and dignitaries, or senior colonial officials. One of the Indian nobles he counted among his associates and benefactors was the ruler of Rampur, Nawab Kalb-e ᶜAli Khan (r. 1865–86), an eminent patron of literature and the arts. As a letter written by Mirza Ghalib to Hargopal 'Tufta' in November 1865 informs us, on the occasion of his second daughter's marriage, Naval Kishore approached the nawab for financial support, which was amply granted (Russell/Islam 1994: 327). That he returned the favour by serving as an inofficial adviser to the Rampur court (M.H. Khan 1980) may be the kind of story cherished by biographers rather than historical fact. Relations, at all events, were close and cordial, as borne out by the publisher's frequent sojourns at Rampur, and the fair number of works produced at Rampur that figured on the NKP's list. Other Indian rulers with whom Naval Kishore was closely associated included the Maharaja of Jammu and Kashmir, the Maharaja of Patiala, and the Raja of Jaipur, Savai Ram Singh II (r. 1834–80). The latter held Naval Kishore in such esteem that he offered him a high ministerial post in the Jaipur state. Judging it wiser to maintain his independence and remain in the business line, the publisher humbly declined.

Equally, Naval Kishore hardly let an occasion pass when it came to honouring eminent representatives of the colonial state, be it through publications produced at his press (see Chapter 5) or through the support of commemorative schemes and committees. One typical instance is the 'Muir Memorial Committee', founded in 1876 at the instigation of the Maharaja of Benares and headed by Sayyid Ahmad Khan, Raja Jai Kishen Das, Raja Shiva Prasad and others. The committee proposed to set up a memorial statue for the late Lieutenant Governor Sir William Muir at Allahabad. With a donation of Rs 250 Naval Kishore headed the list of donors of non-aristocratic origin.[92] In 1890 he joined a committee set up in Lucknow to establish a memorial of 'public utility' for the late

[92] *Aligarh Institute Gazette* of 28 July 1876: 447–502.

Inspector-General of Police, Mr McConaghey, and publicized the cause in *Avadh Akhbār*. In the following year he chaired a public meeting held at Kaiserbagh to commemorate the death of Chief Commissioner J.W. Quinton and other European officers killed during the British annexation of Manipur.[93]

In view of such overt demonstrations of loyalty, how did Naval Kishore perceive British rule and its political, cultural and social ramifications? There is evidence to suggest that his attitude was not free from the typical ambiguities and paradoxes that Sudhir Chandra has depicted as a salient characteristic of educated consciousness in colonial India (Chandra 1992). Like many intellectuals of his generation, Naval Kishore experienced no apparent contradiction in combining loyalty towards the British empire with patriotic concerns, and faith in the benefits of Western civilization with a strong sense of pride in India's rich cultural and literary heritage. In trying to assess his personal attitude one has to look beyond the exigencies of a close and long-standing business relationship with the British. As Chandra suggests, it is important to acknowledge the 'divergence between belief and practice' (ibid.: 32) in Indian intellectual consciousness at that time. For one thing, there were the pragmatic aspects of loyalism. The businessman Naval Kishore had a vested interest in maintaining good and stable relations with the British, his principal and most powerful client; the newspaper-proprietor Naval Kishore aimed for British recognition without wanting to risk alienating the predominantly Indian readership of his paper; the philanthropist and educator in him was always ready to support the government in matters close to his heart, that is, education and social reform. However, it would be wrong to believe that Naval Kishore's commercial interests and his self-styled role as an intermediary between the government and the Indian public automatically made for an uncritical and servile attitude towards colonial rule. His political adversaries, as we will see, were always ready to attribute such motives to him. In actual fact, however, his loyalty drew on a much more complex set of factors and beliefs.

Some of the ambiguities underlying Naval Kishore's views on colonial rule can be gleaned from the evidence he gave before the Public Service Commission in December 1886. The commission had been appointed in response to growing public discontent over the underrepresentation of Indians in the Indian Civil Service. One principal issue of controversy

[93] *Avadh Akhbār*, 13 September 1890, SVN 1890: 452; *Avadh Akhbār*, 13 May 1891, SVN 1891: 330.

was the holding of simultaneous examinations in India and England for British and Indian candidates, a measure vehemently opposed by spokesmen of educated opinion in the NWP&Oudh.[94] When questioned on the issue, Naval Kishore pleaded for equal employment opportunities for British and Indian civil servants, while readily conceding that British civil servants should be paid higher salaries. When asked about the difficulties that overseas travel entailed for orthodox Hindus, he argued that in the name of progress, traditional notions of impurity must gradually disappear. At the same time, he was evidently concerned with the threat that going abroad posed to Indian identity, having witnessed the cultural alienation and offensive emulation of Western behaviour of many a 'foreign-returned' compatriot. In the odd stenographic style of the protocol, Naval Kishore's description of a typical 'England-returned' officer reads as follows: 'He neither likes Indian people nor their mode of living, neither would he like to take off his shoes while eating food; he would like to have English boots on and to dine at table; and he does not like Indian wives; therefore I want to put a stop to going to England.'[95] The description seems almost too cliché-ridden to be taken at face value. Indeed, two decades earlier, the publisher had not been opposed to foreign travel at all, but through his paper *Avadh Akhbār* had offered information on the subject (*LLH* 1867: 355). Naval Kishore's statement before the Public Service Commission merely provides a glimpse of his ambivalent views concerning some aspects of colonial rule. A better understanding of his attitude towards the wider political and social implications of the British presence in India can be gathered from his engagement in the anti-Congress movement.

2.4 The Publisher as Politician: Naval Kishore and the Anti-Congress Movement

Munshi Naval Kishore's political aspirations, as has been shown above, remained for a long time confined to Lucknow and the arena of ordinary local politics. This was to change when the Indian nationalist movement gained momentum in the early 1880s. There is a persisting myth, perpetuated by biographers and other commentators, that Naval Kishore was a fervent nationalist who represented Lucknow during the first session of the National Congress held at Bombay in 1885. This could not be

[94] See Robinson 1974: 114; 118.

[95] *Proceedings of the Public Service Commission*, vol. II. *NWP& Oudh*, 1887: 69–70.

further from the truth. In actual fact, the Lucknow delegate was Munshi Ganga Prasad Varma, the proprietor of the rival Urdu paper *Hindustānī* and another prominent figure in the Lucknow publishing trade. Naval Kishore, much to the contrary, joined the opposition against the Congress no sooner than it emerged in the NWP&Oudh under the leadership of Sir Sayyid Ahmad Khan. Gathered in the United Indian Patriotic Association, the anti-Congress forces set out to demonstrate to the government and public in Britain that the National Congress, far from being representative of Indian opinion, was a seditious organization.[96]

Although there is no shortage of documentary evidence to show that Naval Kishore was among the foremost members of the anti-Congress movement in the province, his role has not been sufficiently acknowledged. That he was indeed a person to be reckoned with among the anti-Congressmen is documented in various contemporary sources. A poignant example is a poem appearing in Balkrishna Bhatt's journal *Hindī Pradīp* of July 1888. In one of its verses, it singled out the three leading opponents of the Congress—Sayyid Ahmad Khan, Raja Shiva Prasad of Benares, and Munshi Naval Kishore—accusing them of being interested in personal gain only. The verse freely translates as follows:

> *They got together for at all costs the Sabha had to be stopped,*[97]
> *the Sayyid came running, the Raja came running,*
> *came running the Bania Munshi Kishore,*
> *hurriedly a brother came running, to amass wealth and riches galore.*[98]

C.A. Bayly has characterized the anti-Congress league as a precarious coalition of interests, explaining the 'uneasy alliance' between Sir Sayyid, Raja Shiva Prasad, and Naval Kishore as 'an attempt to build up support among a functional group, the upper landowners, old service communities, and commercial magnates' (Bayly 1975: 143). Naval Kishore, who

[96] This objective was clearly laid out in a pamphlet entitled *Showing the Seditious Character of the Indian National Congress and the Opinions held by Eminent Natives of India Who are Opposed to the Movement*, edited by Theodore Beck for the Association in 1888. Besides an introduction and statement by Beck, it contained anti-Congress statements by the Raja of Bhinga, the Maharaja of Benares, Munshi Imtiaz ᶜAli, Sayyid Husain Bilgrami (on behalf of the Nizam of Hyderabad), Sayyid Ahmad Khan and Chaudri Nusrat ᶜAli.

[97] 'Sabha' here refers to the Indian National Congress.

[98] '*Mel hon cāhat duniyā meṁ kavanhu yatan sabhā ruk jāya*
saiyad dauṛe rājā dauṛe dauṛe munśī banij kiśor
caṭṭpaṭṭh ek bhatṛhu dauṛe dhan cintāmaṇī lehu baṭor.'
(cited in Singh 1991: 58, my translation).

combined the functions of urban *raʾīs* and wealthy landholder and whose association with Sir Sayyid went back a long way, seemed destined to act as an intermediary between the Muslim leader and the Avadh *taʿalluqdārs*. In December 1887 Sayyid Ahmad Khan opened his campaign against the National Congress with a speech delivered before the Muslim Educational Congress at Lucknow. In its wake a local anti-Congress committtee was set up at Lucknow by Munshi Imtiaz ʿAli, Legal Advisor to the Avadh *taʿalluqdārs*, Nawab Mirza Mehdi ʿAli Khan, Pandit Shri Kishen, Naval Kishore, and others. When in August 1888 Sayyid Ahmad tried to bring together the anti-Congress forces in the United Indian Patriotic Association, Naval Kishore was eager to offer his support. His intervention came at a critical juncture in Hindu–Muslim relations within the anti-Congress movement, for Sir Sayyid had recently alienated the Hindu *taʿalluqdārs* by derogatorily styling the Congress a 'Hindu institution'. In September 1888 Naval Kishore called on Sayyid Ahmad Khan in Nainital to inform him about the ill feelings that his remarks had generated and to discuss how the cooperation of the Avadh *taʿalluqdārs* in the United Indian Patriotic Association could best be secured.[99] The consultation resulted in an agreement that a general meeting of the Avadh aristocracy should be convened by the *taʿalluqdārs*' British Indian Association.[100]

The meeting duly took place in Lucknow on 22 November 1888. It was an apparent success. However, the very next day a serious controversy arose between Sayyid Ahmad Khan and the other anti-Congress leaders over two issues: the first concerned a resolution, based on a proposal by Raja Shiva Prasad, that two separate associations under Hindu and Muslim leadership should immediately be formed in Lucknow and Aligarh, with the Raja of Bhinga and Sayyid Ahmad Khan as respective presidents and secretaries. The United Indian Patriotic Association was

[99] See Naval Kishore's letter to the editor, *The Pioneer*, 1 December 1888: 6. Strangely enough, it appears that Naval Kishore was never a formal member of the United Indian Patriotic Association. His name is not included in the list of donors and members of the Association published in *The Pioneer* of 4 December 1888. More curiously still, Muhammad (1972: 245–6) reproduces a letter of Sir Sayyid, dated 8 August 1888 and published in *The Pioneer* of 10 August 1888, in which Naval Kishore is listed as an official contact of the United Indian Patriotic Associaton in Lucknow. On verifying the original source, I was surprised to find that the letter in *The Pioneer* does *not* contain his name.

[100] For the proceedings of the meeting, see *The Pioneer* of 24 November 1888: 5. The article is reprinted in Muhammad 1978 (3): 938–42.

to merge into a new general association named 'Indian Loyal Association' ('Anjuman-e Khairkhahan-e Mulk-e Hind'). The second bone of contention was a petition drawn up by the Maharaja of Benares urging the government to take legal action against the National Congress on grounds of its 'seditious' character.[101] Sayyid Ahmad Khan, who had agreed to both resolutions, must have had second thoughts, for on 26 November he published a letter in *The Pioneer*, in which he categorically denied the change of name of the United Indian Patriotic Association, his acceptance of the post of secretary to the Aligarh branch of the proposed Indian Loyal Association, and his support for the anti-Congress petition.[102] To the other anti-Congress leaders this meant a gross and deliberate misinterpretation of the meeting's proceedings. Raja Shiva Prasad angrily refuted Sir Sayyid's statement in *The Pioneer* of 30 November 1888. Naval Kishore followed suit and in the issue of 1 December sided with the Raja, expressing his outrage at Sayyid Ahmad Khan's behaviour

> because of the proof it affords that, having once put his hand to the plough of evidently earnest effort to sink sectarian differences and race antagonism in one united effort by the two great communities of these Provinces to combat the political danger which now threatens the best interests of the people of the country, he has allowed self-interest and personal considerations to carry him away into an abandonment of a worthy scheme—a grand national movement. . . . Sir Syed Ahmed has forgotten that the very alphabet of a great reformer's lesson is that at all times and under all temptations he shall, in his public acts, rise superior to the suspicion of self-interest. Far be it from me to attempt to depreciate the work done by Sir Syed Ahmed and his Patriotic Association. He and it have done right good service; yet I am in hopes that the wider and grander scheme, which has for the present fallen through, will in the not very distant future be an accomplished fact, all the more successful because of its recent misadventure. Nor do I desire to raise a controversy. I address you only because Sir Syed Ahmed has somewhat misrepresented our proceedings and attempted to throw reproach upon Hindu willingness for amalgamation with Mahomedans in the struggle against the Congress movement—a willingness for which I am in a great measure responsible; for it was I, when Sir Syed Ahmed appealed to Hindus to join the Patriotic Association, who interviewed him and discussed a scheme whereby Hindus and Mahomedans would be enabled to make a united and harmonious effort to roll back the wave of sedition spreading over the country.[103]

[101] Ibid.

[102] The letter is reprinted in full in Muhammad 1972: 247–9.

[103] *The Pioneer*, 1 December 1888: 6.

Naval Kishore felt personally let down, for he went on to give a detailed account of both his private consultation with Sir Sayyid at Nainital and the proceedings of the Lucknow meeting, contradicting Sir Sayyid's statements in each instance. In his disappointment, he accused the Muslim leader of having sacrificed Hindu–Muslim unity in the anti-Congress movement for selfish motives:

> He told us that he had made a great name for himself and the Indian Patriotic Association, and that he and his association were strong enough to work without the aid of the Hindu and Mahomedan Associations of Oudh, and he would not allow the identity of the *Patriotic Association* to be lost in the untried *Indian Loyal Association*; and having split hairs over the change of name, he sat down and in our presence wrote his resignation of the Presidentship of the Aligarh Branch of the Indian Loyal Association which he had accepted on the previous day. The fact of the matter is that Sir Syed Ahmed having slept over the proceedings at the meeting had a vision portraying the possibility of his being considered not quite such an important personage as a member of the general council of the new association as he would be as a sole director of the Patriotic Association, and he has unfortunately allowed his dread of a possible small loss of power to influence him in upsetting a scheme which would have worked immense good to the people of both communities.[104]

Naval Kishore's insistence on the issue of Hindu–Muslim unity indicates how strongly he resented Sir Sayyid's introduction of a communal element in a cause that demanded solidarity and joint action. Given the mutually reverential and cordial relations that the two men had enjoyed thus far, the acrimonious overtones of his letter are startling and can only be taken as an indication of the extent to which he felt personally betrayed. Nonetheless, Naval Kishore quickly jumped at the occasion to pose as the spokesman of the new Indian Loyal Association and reiterate its message of Hindu–Muslim solidarity. He concluded his letter with a defiant message:

> Much as the members of the Indian Loyal Association regret Sir Syed Ahmed's desertion from its ranks, they are not dismayed at the prospect before them. He has been the one disturbing element in the excellent spirit displayed in last week's effort to unite Hindus and Mahomedans in these Provinces for the fight against the trouble which threatens the well-being of the people and the peace of the country. But we still have many influential Mahomedans, and if they and our Hindu brethren will work cordially and manfully, our new association promises the brightest results. We shall, I

[104] Ibid.

> hope, build up an enduring monument, and if encouraged by our success Sir Syed Ahmed and his following ever care to join us, we shall give them a cordial welcome.[105]

This was a far cry from his earlier respect for Sir Sayyid. Whether in the wake of this altercation the relationship between the two men was ever the same remains doubtful. The petition demanding the suppression of the Congress as a seditious movement was signed in January 1889; while it included Naval Kishore's signature, Sayyid Ahmad Khan's name was absent.[106]

The events of November 1888 clearly exposed the fragile nature of the United Indian Patriotic Association, which did not survive much longer. They also show that Naval Kishore did not hesitate to abandon his long-standing alliance with Sayyid Ahmad Khan and his solidarity with the Muslim cause when he saw the larger aims of the anti-Congress movement put in jeopardy. In light of this, his motivation in supporting the United Indian Patriotic Association demands some elaboration. Surely, an organized anti-Congress association provided him with an opportunity to protect his own interests, which were to a large extent commercial in nature and directed at maintaining a mutually beneficial collaboration with the British. The colonial government had for decades been his most important customer and business partner, and moreover a perennial source of patronage that guaranteed the firm's survival. To preserve the status quo was of prime interest to the businessman Naval Kishore; any radical political change could result in instability and withdrawal of support, putting the very existence of the publishing house at risk. However, the above-cited letter also suggests that the economic factor alone is too simple an explanation and that Naval Kishore's opposition to the Congress drew on a more complex set of motives. First and foremost, it rested on the belief that the progress of the Indian nation could only be achieved under British rule. His vehement reaction to the accusations brought forth by the Congress leader Allan Octavian Hume in *The Pioneer* in November 1888 provides further corroboration of this. Targeting prominent anti-Congressmen, Hume had made some disparaging remarks about Naval Kishore's social standing and trustworthiness and had insinuated that the true motive of his involvement in anti-Congress politics was the fear of losing privileges and British contracts. Greatly angered by these accusations, Naval Kishore responded

[105] Ibid.

[106] *Hindustān*, 12 January 1889, cited in Singh 1991: 65.

in kind, accusing Hume of being 'impatient of contradiction, vulgarly abusive of all those who disagree with him, and unreasonably dogmatic'. He then clarified his position:

> I am at a loss to understand to what I am to attribute Mr. Hume's selection of me as one of the leaders of the Opposition, in the Congress matter. I certainly yield to no one in earnest desire and determined effort to promote the advancement of the true interests of my country and countrymen, *though not by Congress tactics*; but I am a humble worker in the cause of India's regeneration, and though for more than a quarter of century that has been the purpose of my life, both in private effort, and through my newspaper, yet I have been content to co-operate with and not lead in what is known as the Anti-Congress movement. Not that I am by any means half-hearted in the struggle. On the contrary, I am in as deadly earnest against the Congress as Mr. Hume is for it, and so long as God gives me life, my time, my talents, and my means, such as they are, will be devoted to the Anti-Congress cause. But I have always maintained that the leaders of the Opposition movement should be men of position, wealth and influence, and I still hold to that view. But if I am surprised at the honour Mr. Hume has done me, I know that I am in good company, and I am flattered by the compliment. According to his own showing I am and have been an unknown nobody, and yet he has given me prominent place among the good men and true who are engaged in leading the people to a true understanding of the pit-falls of the Congress agitation—influential men who are doing their level "best to frustrate methods and expose proposals which are fraught with danger to the peace and security of the Indian peoples". Better to be damned in such company, and by such a master of scurrilous abuse as the "prophet, priest and apostle" of the Congress-wallahs has proved himself, than to be found on the side of the self-constituted patriots who seem determined, if the authorities will only allow them a little more latitude, *to force disaster and ruin upon the noble work of progress, advancement and freedom, which the British Government has pledged itself to establish in India, and which during the past thirty years it has honestly endeavoured to redeem.*[107] (emphasis added)

The letter, while not devoid of self-fashioning, testifies to Naval Kishore's conviction that colonial rule was the sole guarantor of peace, stability, and progress in India. The Congress to him was an association of sedition-mongers who, by instigating revolt in India's easily influenced illiterate masses, were far from working for the good of the common people and the progress of the nation. The government's lenient attitude towards the Congress, he warned, could have disastrous consequences:

[107] *The Pioneer*, 21 November 1888: 7.

> unless the Government steps in, and that quickly, and adopts measures for the suppression of the seditious talk and writing of the old, disappointed place-hunters and the young hair-brained political adventurers who form the backbone of the Congress agitation, it must be prepared to cope with a convulsion of the country, compared to which the great Mutiny will have been child's play. It is so easy to awaken discontent and to fan the flame that it must come about that the more ignorant of the people, led away by the constant abuse of Government, its measures and its officials, which the Congress-wallahs indulge in so barefacedly, and goaded on by long-drawn and oft-repeated teachings of the wrong, the injustice and tyranny under which they exist—it must come about that they will be driven into giving vent to their worked-up passions. And while a just and severe punishment will fall upon them, and Indian progress be thrown back half a century, those who instigated them and were mainly responsible for their ignorant outburst, will be safe from harm. Down in Bengal there may be no harm in preaching sedition to the agricultural population for Bengal has never been known to have produced a fighting man. But in the United Provinces and in the Punjab, our most warlike races are to be found among the rural peasantry, and it would be no difficult matter to play upon their ignorant but brave natures . . . I warn the Government in all solemn earnestness that so surely as it declines to take effectual measures to extinguish the Congress propaganda, so surely will the loyalty of the masses be estranged from it. The people are being instigated not to pay the "unrighteous" demands made upon them in the way of taxes; they are told that if they demand this and that concession, in a body, they will get them; they are taunted with their poverty, and are mockingly told that they deserve their fate so long as they are content to remain "dumb, driven cattle". What must all this tend to when easily excited natures are worked upon? The ignorant people misconstrue the placid indifference of the authorities to a fear to interfere with the power of the Congress-wallahs. The Government may know and understand the impotency of these agitators, but the masses may be led to believe in their tall talk—and then what must be the result? (ibid.: 7–8)

The arguments contained in the letter not only show Naval Kishore reiterating colonial stereotypes about 'martial races', they also place him in the category of Indian loyalists who called for political moderation, being convinced that India was not ready for self-government and could only advance under colonial rule. Such elite loyalism, as Bayly has argued, cannot be interpreted simply as 'expediency, greed or sycophancy', but drew 'on genuine political ideas' (Bayly 1998: 122). Naval Kishore's arguments are characteristic of elite paternalism, as evident from his stereotypical representation of the Indian masses as 'benighted', ignorant, and devoid of agency.

Loyalism and a paternalistic attitude also shaped his opinion on the question of democratic rule in India. Emotions ran high when, in 1889–90, Bradlaugh's Indian Councils Bill was discussed. In opposing the introduction of the elective principle on the Legislative Council, Naval Kishore and Sayyid Ahmad Khan found themselves joining ranks again. During an anti-Congress meeting held at the publisher's Lucknow residence on 30 April 1890 a resolution against the Bradlaugh Bill was passed and a memorial in favour of a nomination system adopted instead.[108] Two months later, Naval Kishore ventured to explain his position in a public speech during an anti-Congress rally held at Kanpur. Predictably, this made him a prime target for the pro-Congress papers. *Siṃha Sahāy* (Amritsar) asserted that 'Raja Shiva Pershad and Munshi Newal Kishore . . . are no longer looked upon as Hindus',[109] while *Hindustānī* commented that 'The memorials got up by Sir Sayyid Ahmad Khan and Munshi Nawal Kishore present the strange spectacle of intelligent men declaring themselves unfit for the grant of any privileges to them by Government.'[110] *Hindustān* (Kalakankar) made a caustic remark that Naval Kishore, 'far from being an orator, cannot speak properly', and went on to comment in an equally sarcastic vein: 'Munshi Newal Kishore, in commenting upon the proposal of the Congress regarding the introduction of the elective principle, declared that natives were not yet fit for the exercise of such a right, but that when they became fit for it, Englishmen would voluntarily retire from this country! This is loyalty indeed! The Anti-Congressionists say that when they are fit for the right of election they will expel the English!'[111]

Naval Kishore's attitude provides a typical example of the 'classic liberal-gradualist answer of the majority being as yet unprepared for full political status' (Naregal 2001: 245–6) prevalent among parts of the educated elite. Criticism of his political views was especially harsh in Lucknow. Always eager to attack the rival publisher and his paper, the Lucknow pro-Congress papers *Hindūstānī* and *Avadh Punch* had no interest in probing the deeper motives of his opposition to the Congress. Naval Kishore tried in vain to fight off allegations, constantly reiterated in these papers, that he acted out of a situation of economic dependence and was motivated only by self-interest. He was quoted saying that he

108 The proceedings of this meeting were published in *Avadh Akhbār*, 5 May 1890.

109 *Siṃha Sahāy*, 9 July 1890, SVNP 1890: 265.

110 *Hindustānī*, 11 May 1890, SVN 1890: 308–9.

111 *Hindustān*, 4 July 1890, SVN 1890: 429–30. The speech was published in *Avadh Akhbār*, 10 July 1890. The issue was not available to me.

would lose government printing contracts worth two lakhs of rupees if he joined the Congress; it was alleged that Lieutenant Governor Sir Auckland Colvin had personally talked him into opposing the Congress.[112] As will be shown in Chapter 6, much of the criticism was directed at *Avadh Akhbār*. The government's liberal patronage of the paper was taken as a clear indication of its servility and incapability of representing national interests.

It is difficult to dissociate political opposition from professional rivalry in the routine attacks against Naval Kishore and his paper. From the moment the publisher entered the arena of local politics through his seat in the Municipal Committee—thereby acquiring a position that was bound to profit his business relations with the British—the rival Lucknow press had begun to keep a suspicious eye on his official and unofficial dealings with the colonial administration. That such suspicion was not altogether unfounded is borne out by an incident in January 1892 involving William Young, the NWP&Oudh Judicial Commissioner. On the eve of his retirement, Young had hastily issued an order to the provincial civil courts to the effect that, in future, all petition-writers working at the courts were to exclusively use forms of plaint, etc., printed at the NKP. The measure threatened to diminish the already meagre income of the petition-writers who used to obtain cheap forms from local presses. The matter was rendered particularly delicate by the fact that Naval Kishore had organized a farewell party in honour of Young and had assisted the British official in winding up his household. Not surprisingly, there was an outcry in the local press. *Hindustānī* lost no time in publicly denouncing Young's order as a case of blatant favouritism. In an article headed 'The Massacre of the Poor', it sardonically remarked: 'When Munshi Newal Kishore was busy in selling Mr. Young's house furniture and other things and was getting up an address for presentation to him, no one thought that the Munshi would be soon and richly rewarded for his services.'[113]

The attack on Naval Kishore was part of an exchange of blows that had been going on for same time between him and Ganga Prasad Varma, both in the Municipal Committee and in their respective papers *Avadh Akhbār* and *Hindustānī*. Naval Kishore soon found an occasion to retaliate. During the municipal elections in Ganeshganj in March 1892, he appeared as chief canvasser for the anti-Congress candidate, Babu Shri Ram.[114]

[112] *Hindustān*, 12 January 1889 and 15 July 1888, cited in Singh 1991: 65 and 103.

[113] *Hindustānī* of 17 February 1892, SVN 1892: 60.

[114] Babu Shri Ram, a Kayastha *taʿalluqdār* from Faizabad, was a lawyer at the Judicial Commissioner's Court and Vice-president of the Municipal Board.

As such, he presented an application to the city magistrate, accusing Ganga Prasad Varma and his Congress candidate, Pandit Bishan Narayan Dar, of having defamed the Municipal Board in an election manifesto published in *Hindustānī*.[115] When the application was rejected, Naval Kishore again appealed to the city magistrate, charging Varma with an offence against the Press Regulation Act—Varma had failed to state the name of his press on the printed copies of the said manifesto. This time Varma was found guilty and ordered to pay a fine of Rs 100. 'What public service Munshi Naval Kishore has done by bringing a contemporary into trouble may be best known to himself and his fellow-slaves of the Deputy Commissioner', sneered Varma's *Hindustānī*.[116] While the fine was later reduced to the symbolic sum of Rs 5, Naval Kishore's rancorous behaviour towards a fellow Indian publisher did not go down well with the Urdu press. 'Munshi Nawal Kishore, C.I.E, who poses as a friend to the Government and the country, should be ashamed of his cowardly and malicious conduct', commented *Najm al-Akhbār* of Etawah on 12 May 1892.[117] 'It is true that the Hindustani is always ready to expose him, but he was not justified in seeking to revenge himself in the way he did.' The battle between the two men, however, was far from over. When, in 1893, the Lucknow Municipal Board elected its delegate to the Provincial Legislative Council, Naval Kishore again supported Babu Shri Ram against the Congress candidate. When Babu Shri Ram won by a majority of one, Congressmen contested the election results and accused Naval Kishore and his candidate of having won the election by pressurizing the delegate in question (Singh 1991: 144–5).

Naval Kishore's involvement in opposing the Congress continued unabated until death cut short his political ambitions. He died on 19 February 1895 from what appears to have been sudden heart-failure.[118] Mourned by Hindus and Muslims alike, and accompanied by a large

[115] Pandit Bishan Narayan Dar, an eminent member of Lucknow's Kashmiri Brahmin community, was a well-known lawyer and one of the foremost Congress leaders in Avadh.

[116] *Hindustānī*, 27 April 1892, SVN 1892: 154.

[117] SVN 1892: 92, 114, 177.

[118] *The Pioneer*, 21 February 1895, reported the cause of his death as 'heart-disease'. *The Tribune*, 27 February 1895, carried a detailed account on its frontpage: 'The death of Munshi Newal Kishore was quite sudden and he had not to suffer the agonies and pains of death. He was all right on Monday and was engaged in his work till late at night. He felt some heaviness and preferred to fast during the night. He had a disturbed sleep. At about 4 A.M. he passed a stool whereafter he could with difficulty walk to his bed. For fifteen minutes he felt pain in the chest. The Doctor of the

procession, his remains were taken to Allahabad by a special train, where the funeral rites were performed on the banks of the Ganges.[119] Upon his death, his outstanding contribution to India's cultural renaissance and the revival of Indian literature was widely acknowledged. However, his involvement in national politics during the later years of his life remained controversial and did not sit comfortably with the tide of nationalist sentiment that had begun to sweep the country. The *Hindoo Patriot* of Calcutta was typical in commenting that 'The Munshi belonged to the old school but whatever his politics might be, as a man he was such that it was impossible to know him and not to respect him.'[120] Yet the most striking expression of the extent to which Naval Kishore's venture into politics would cast its shadow over a lifetime's achievement in the literary-cultural domain is the tongue-in-cheek and thoroughly ambivalent obituary published in the Lahore *Tribune* of 23 February 1895:

> Munshi Newal Kishore, who died at Lucknow was a successful man in life if success is to be measured by the accumulation of wealth. He was undoubtedly a man of resource and enterprise and the founder of a fortune which is estimated at from 15 to 20 lakhs. But it was as a politician, as an opponent of the Indian National Congress and one of the founders of the Indian Patriotic Association that came from nowhere and went from whence it came that Munshi Newal Kishore became known to the public. Nothing need be said in disparagement of his memory, especially as there is a good deal to admire in his character and to recommend his example to his countrymen. Of course in such success as Munshi Newal Kishore there must be selfishness, but that is not the only secret of wealth. Ill-gotten wealth is not a thing to be envied, but when wealth is come by in the main honestly, as was the case with Munshi Newal Kishore, the qualities at the bottom of such a character are worthy of study. Patience, perseverance, courage and great elasticity of spirit are necessary to the success of an enterprise and to the accumulation of such a fortune. To establish such a large press which becomes the centre of so much literary activity is a great achievement in itself, of which full credit should be given to Munshi Newal Kishore. In all enterprise, all trade and business an unselfish man cannot prosper because there is no mercy in competition and every man must fight for his own hand. [. . .] But when one comes to politics and other matters in which there is room for the development of unselfishness a successful man

Hazratgunj Dispensary was called but before he could prescribe medicine the Munshi breathed his last.'

[119] *The Tribune*, 23 February 1895.

[120] *The Hindoo Patriot*, 22 February 1895.

of business, whose life has been devoted to the accumulation of wealth and also to advancement in the favour of the authorities, feels like fish out of water. Munshi Newal Kishore made a mistake when he drifted towards politics, but who shall judge him uncharitably? Let us all admire what was admirable in him.

3
An Indian Success Story: The House of Naval Kishore

The House of Naval Kishore provides the kind of fascinating success story that enlivens the history of the book. It is a story imbued with the spirit of modernization and pioneering entrepreneurship so eminently characteristic of indigenous agency in the early phases of Indian industrialization. This chapter traces the commercial history of the NKP. It sketches the process by which the firm developed from humble beginnings into an industrial enterprise of unprecedented proportions. Seeking to outline the dimensions of industrial book production and the mechanisms underlying it, the first four sections address aspects of the NKP's internal organization, technology, marketing strategies, and distribution networks. The final section will turn to author-publisher relations, an underresearched aspect of Indian literary and literate culture.

As noted earlier, in writing the business history of the NKP one is faced with the formidable difficulty that no business records, account books, or commercial correspondence of India's erstwhile largest printing and publishing firm have been preserved. This state of affairs is by no means specific to the NKP, but forms a characteristic difficulty in studying the Indian publishing trade. However, in the case of the NKP the absence of records appears to be a rather recent phenomenon. The late A.H. Nurani, in his various monographs on the NKP published from 1982 to 1995, still had some archival material at his disposal. A. Zamani affirms the existence of sixteen different kinds of publisher's ledgers used at the NKP.[1] However, she may not actually have seen any of these records,

[1] I.e. (1) Booksellers' Ledger; (2) Balance of Lost and Found Books; (3) Books under Inspection and/or Ready for Printing; (4) Account-book; (5) Various Book Notifications; (6) Occasional Survey; (7) Books Eaten by White Ants; (8) Miscellaneous Publication Book; (9) Day Book; (10) Expenses; (11) Despatch of Books;

for the only internal source she quotes from is a document of 1889. Mohamad Tavakoli-Targhi, who visited the press in 1992, claims to have rescued over 1000 document fragments—including registers of published books, lists of workers, land deeds, and scholarly correspondence which were 'carelessly dumped in a heap to be later sold as fertilizer' (Tavakoli-Targhi 1993: 18)—and to have classified and stored them. I did not have access to these records. As a result, while making use of the scarce information contained in NKP books and the publisher's catalogue, the following account is largely based on secondary sources originating outside the publishing house. It draws on a variety of nineteenth-century and later documents, but relies particularly heavily on British administrative records which provide the most comprehensive empirical data on the firm's output, printing expenses, sales, etc. While aiming to give a coherent picture, my narrative cannot claim to be exhaustive.

3.1 The Early Years (1858–1865)

When Munshi Naval Kishore arrived in Lucknow in 1858, equipped with an Indian-made hand press and a few lithographic stones, he encountered a vacuum: local competition in the printing business had been virtually wiped out by the events of 1857. The opening of his printing shop in November 1858 marked a turning point in the history of print in Lucknow. As the first Indian to newly open a press in post-Mutiny Lucknow, he heralded a new era of the mass-produced book. He not only set printing in Arabic, Persian, and Urdu on a sound commercial footing, but also established himself as the city's first publisher of Hindi and Sanskrit books. The way in which Naval Kishore reshaped local print culture has been highlighted by Sharar:

> When the monarchy collapsed, Munshi Newal Kishore opened his press. Although its printing could not compare in elegance with that of the Mustafai Press, it was run on such sound commercial lines that it produced a greater quantity of Persian and Arabic books than any other press would have had the courage to attempt. The fact is that the interest taken in the printing press in Lucknow was such that it needed an energetic and ambitious man

---

(12) Warehouse Memorandum; (13) Lithographic Office; (14) Typographic Office; (15) Survey of Pillaged Books in the Warehouse; (16) Internal Affairs and Queries. See Zamani 1980.

> like Munshi Newal Kishore to take full advantage of it. Eventually the Newal Kishore press gained such pre-eminence that it revived all Eastern literatures and Lucknow acquired great distinction in this field. Lucknow benefited in that it was able to meet all the literary demands of Central Asia, including those of Kashgar, Bukhara, Afghanistan and Persia. (Sharar 1975: 107–8)

Upon his arrival in Lucknow, Naval Kishore rented a small place in a neighbourhood known as Agha Mir ki Deorhi in Wazirganj, where he set up a humble printing shop. In the typical manner of early Urdu presses it was named Matbaᶜ-e Avadh Akhbar or 'Avadh Akhbar Press' after the Urdu journal simultaneously launched from it. Originally a lithographic press, the printing shop was equipped within its first year with type presses at the instance of the local colonial authorities. Naval Kishore was fortunate to have found a patron in Colonel Saunders A. Abbott, the commissioner and superintendent of the Lucknow Division from 1858 to 1863. Abbott not only arranged for machinery and equipment to be sent from Calcutta, but also patronized the young printer-journalist by giving him a number of printing contracts. Since Naval Kishore had started off with very little capital of his own, this kind of official support was essential to the growth of his enterprise. Following several contracts for textbook printing, he received a particularly lucrative official commission when, in 1861, he was authorized 'to print and sell on his own account' *Jāmiᶜ al-favā'id* (*1861), a compilation of conversion tables and tables of weight measures 'for use of putwaries, ameens, zemindars & others in Oude'. Yet the commission that was to permanently change the fortunes of the press was still to come: in the same year, and presumably also at the behest of Abbott, the NKP received a contract to print the Urdu translation of the newly enacted Indian Penal Code, *Taᶜzīrāt-e Hind*.[2] Deputy Inspector Nazir Ahmad, the principal translator, personally came to Lucknow to oversee the printing. The Urdu Penal Code was issued in 1861 in 30,000 copies, sold at Rs 3 each. While entailing a considerable profit for the publisher, the successful execution of this important commission also marked a major breakthrough in Naval Kishore's business relations with the British. From this point onwards he came to be officially recognized as a first-rank publisher. Charles Wingfield, the Avadh Chief Commissioner, referred to the NKP as the most excellent press in the province, which dealt with all orders to one's entire satisfaction (S.Q. Khan 1980: 186).

[2] A Hindi version followed in 1868.

Apparently British patronage was not the only means of support for the young printer-publisher during the first years. According to Nurani, initial financial assistance also came from an altogether different source, namely the reputed Islamic scholar Maulana Ahsan Kakorvi who at the time held a high government post at Barabanki.[3] On Maulana Ahsan's advice Naval Kishore started issuing popular religious tracts and excerpts from the Qur'an. When the Maulana later declined the repayment of his loan, Naval Kishore reciprocated the favour extended to him by publishing the scholar's work *Aḥvāl al-anbiyā*.

Religious tracts, prayer books, and individual chapters of the Qurʾan on the one hand, legal forms, registers, and school textbooks commissioned by the British on the other, formed the main output that sustained the printing press during its early years. The second pillar of the NKP was its prospering Urdu newspaper *Avadh Akhbār* (see Chapter 6). Within a couple of years, printing and publishing was no longer confined to texts in English, Arabic, Persian, and Urdu, but also extended to Hindi and, subsequently, Sanskrit works. If the NKP was the first press in Lucknow to take up printing in the languages associated with Hindu culture, it did not remain so for long. Other presses to publish the occasional Sanskrit or Hindi texts were the Samar-e Hind Press of Pandit Baijnath, the Gulzar-e Hind Press of Pandit Bihari Lal (est. 1864), and the Prakash-e Hind Press of Kalicaran.[4] Yet none of these small presses ever engaged in Hindi printing on a larger commercial scale.

The early years of the NKP coincided with a period of general economic growth, brought on by the assumption of direct government by the British crown. The overall technological and infrastructural progress in the 1860s favoured the growth of the young enterprise in several important ways: while Naval Kishore initially had to import machinery and raw materials from Calcutta at very high expense, the procurement of

[3] Nurani 1995: 30. Maulana Ahsan Kakorvi 'Ahsan' (*c.* 1833–91) belonged to a family of ʿulama of Kakori, a country town (*qaṣbah*) in the vicinity of Lucknow which produced a number of eminent Muslim scholars and officials (Malik 1997: 265–8). He was the younger brother of the distinguished *naʿt*-poet Muhsin Kakorvi and himself an author of several scholastic works. He held various government offices including the post of chief judge (*ṣadr al-ṣudūr*), and after his retirement served as minister in the princely state of Bhopal. I am grateful to Professor Jamal Malik, Erfurt, for this information.

[4] There also exists a small number of early Nagari imprints issued from local Muslim-owned presses, e.g. the Gulshan-e Kashmir Press, the ʿAziz al-Matabaʿ, and the Safir-e Hatmam Press (1867). *OAR*, 1869–70, app. 'Statistics of instruction: literary and scientific': cxlix–xlix.

equipment and the diffusion of books were soon facilitated and rendered less expensive by the rapid improvement of transport and communication. The expansion of the postal service and, particularly, the extension of the railway line that reached Lucknow in 1862 were essential to these developments.

If not quite the proverbial one-man enterprise, the NKP started off with only a small handful of employees. The earliest surviving document which gives us some idea of the staff, internal organization, and production capacity of the press in its first years is an article appearing in the *Avadh Akhbār* of 8 January 1862, in which Naval Kishore reviewed the annual progress of his firm.[5] Having gratefully acknowledged the support of his British benefactors Colonel Abbott and Henry Stuart Reid, the new DPI in the NWP, the publisher proudly stated that 'books worth thousands of rupees' had been issued from his press during the past year. Printing in English and in the Oriental languages was undertaken separately in the Typographic and Lithographic Departments. The superintendent of the former was an Englishman by the name of Walter Williams. Next to him the firm's Typographic Department employed at least five other Europeans, among them the head accountant. Their names as given in *Avadh Akhbār* do not correspond to those appearing in the *New Calcutta Directory*, which in 1862–3 for the first time listed the 'Newal Kishore Printing Press' in its 'Mofussil' section.[6] The entry in the 1862 directory gives T.L. Allemand as manager and R. Smith as printer, whereas the corresponding 1863 entry identifies R. Craven as manager and T.H. Williams as printer.[7]

From the very outset, the staff included members of the different religious communities. In contrast to the Typographic Department, which was run by Englishmen, the Lithographic Department was entirely under Indian supervision. Most of the Muslims and Hindus on its managing staff hailed from distinguished Lucknow families. Among them were several men with prior experience in the printing trade: the superintendent (*dārogha*) of the lithographic presses was Shaikh Nisar ᶜAli, the veteran ex-proprietor of Lucknow's eminent Murtazawi Press which had gained distinction in Arabic and Persian printing during the time of the nawabs. With his vast experience in printing and publishing, this septuagenerian

[5] For a reprint of this article, see Bilali 1980: 70–2 and Nurani 1995: 36–9.

[6] The Urdu spelling makes it difficult to read the names correctly. I read them as Mr R. Smith, Mr Gladis, Mr Gomes, Mr Alexander and—surprisingly in this male-dominated space—Miss Poole.

[7] *New Calcutta Directory* (pt 5) 1862: 192 and 1863: 205.

was a great asset to Naval Kishore. Munshi Shiv Parshad, who had initially been hired as a scribe for *Avadh Akhbār*, was appointed the first manager of the Lithographic Department. He later rose to become the general manager of the NKP, a position in which he faithfully served the firm until his death in the late 1890s. It appears that for some time he was also associated with the editorship of *Avadh Akhbār*.[8] Shiv Parshad was a poet of Urdu who wrote under the pen name 'Wahbi' and has a *Kulliyāt-e Wahbī* (*1880) to his credit, a work that has often been wrongly ascribed to his namesake Raja Shiva Prasad of Benares.[9] The head proofreader (*muṣaḥḥiḥ*) in the Lithographic Department was Maulvi Muhammad Hadi ᶜAli 'Ashk' (d. 1865), a renowned Islamic scholar, poet, and master calligrapher who had previously served at the Muhammadi Press of Haji Harmain Sharifain. Other noteworthy figures on the early staff were Mir Hashmat ᶜAli, master calligrapher and stone-corrector (*muṣleh-e saṅg*); Shaikh Amir ᶜAli, illustrator (*naqāsh*); and Munshi ᶜAli Muhammad Khan, printer in the Lithographic Department. Munshi Amirullah 'Taslim', Munshi Ashraf ᶜAli 'Ashraf', Munshi Govind Parshad 'Fiza', Munshi Jvalaparshad, Munshi Imdad Husain, Hafiz ᶜAli Bakhsh, Lala Pyarelal and Lala Jankiparshad were the first among an impressive range of master calligraphers who were to render service to the NKP (see Chapter 5).

The Lithographic Department witnessed a rapid growth. By the fourth year of its existence, it already operated twenty-five hand presses and employed around 300 pressmen and workers. By this time, Naval Kishore's rapidly expanding printing shop had run short of space. To accommodate the growing number of hand presses it had to be relocated twice, first to Golaganj, then to Rakabganj. Here, Naval Kishore rented a large building known as Ajodhya Kothi, formerly in the possession of Maharaja Mansingh. These shifts of premises took place in the early 1860s. Around the same time, further presses were installed in a place formerly known as the *maktabkhāna* (school-house) of Suleiman Qadar, a building located between Lalbagh and Kaisarbagh (Nurani 1995: 36). The acquisition of these new buildings marked the beginning of a prolonged phase of expansion, during which the firm was to extend both its

[8] The SVN somewhat incorrectly lists him as the 'publisher' of *Avadh Akhbār* from 1883 onward to at least 1897.

[9] The first to confound Munshi Shiv Parshad 'Wahbi' with Raja Shiva Prasad was Garcin de Tassy (see *HLHH* III: 268 and 273). The French scholar's error has been perpetuated in most Urdu texts and has led a number of contemporary critics to associate Raja Shiva Prasad with the editorship of *Avadh Akhbār*.

physical presence and business operations far beyond the narrow confines of Lucknow.

3.2 The Phase of Expansion (1865–1892)

By the mid-1860s the NKP had risen to the position of largest privately owned printing and publishing firm in North India. After 1869 the provincial government, in its annual administration reports, rarely failed to emphasize the firm's high reputation, superior workmanship, and leading position among the approximately thirty printing presses operating in the province of Avadh. The NKP's third and final shift to Hazratganj, the modern and fashionable market area in the Civil Lines of Lucknow, took place in 1870. More than just another change of location, this shift signified an actual as well as symbolic move into the heart of colonial power in the province. The very fact that Naval Kishore had been allotted land for purchase in Hazratganj, a privilege generally accorded only to influential *taᶜalluqdārs*, suggests his growing influence with the colonial authorities. The new location of the printing works testified to the NKP's prominent status while visibly marking its close association with the British administration.

Naval Kishore settled in Kothi ᶜInayat Sultan, which formed part of a handsome old building known as Begum Kothi. Built by Nawab Amjad ᶜAli Shah as a palace for his queen in 1844, Begum Kothi had been the site of severe fighting during the 1857 uprising. Some parts of Begum Kothi were later transformed into the General Post Office (Hay 1994: 87–8). At the same time, the publisher acquired prime real estate for the erection of further buildings on the premises, among them a building that today houses the Central Bank. Veena Oldenburg supplies us with the interesting detail that, on constructing his private residence, Naval Kishore submitted plans in 1869 for both a native-style dwelling and an English-style bungalow to the British authorities. In keeping with the colonial architecture of Hazratganj, the native-style house plan was rejected and the bungalow plans approved (Oldenburg 1989: 124). Soon afterwards, he also bought Mubarak Manzil, a building forming part of the Moti Mahal complex built by Nawab Ghaziuddin Haidar.

With sufficiently more space available now, lithographic and type printing was undertaken in two separate establishments located in these different buildings. By far the larger establishment was the Matbaᶜ-e Avadh Akhbar or 'Avadh Akhbar Press' in Kothi ᶜInayat Sultan, adjacent to the General Post Office. It was here that most of the lithographic work was undertaken, including the printing of *Avadh Akhbār* and other Urdu journals. The daily output of the press in 1870 was reported to be 12,000 *juz*, that is, 192,000 printed pages. Kothi ᶜInayat Sultan also served as organizational headquarters to the firm, dealing with all incoming orders and business correspondence. The second establishment, the Matbaᶜ-e Navalkishor or 'Naval Kishore Press' in its narrower sense, was a continuation of the earlier Typographic Department. Situated in Mubarak Manzil, it employed around 150 people and concentrated on typesetting, while occasionally executing some lithographic work as well.[10] It is important to note that this distinction of names was not maintained in later times, with Naval Kishore Press more and more becoming an umbrella term to refer to the House of Naval Kishore. The publisher's imprint variously appeared as Avadh Akhbar Press, Naval Kishore Press (*Navalkiśor kā chāpākhānā*; *Navalkiśor kā yantrālaya*) or Naval Kishore Lithographic Press (*Navalkiśor kā śilāyantra*).

A decade after its opening, the NKP was doing brisk business. In 1869 Naval Kishore reported a credit balance of Rs 250,000.[11] The rapidly growing market demand for printed matter, increased production, and concomitant expansion of the sales and distribution network called for a sophisticated organizational structure. In order to assure smooth and efficient running, the administration of the expanding firm was divided among thirteen different departments. Their various tasks are listed in Table 3.0 below.

The shift of offices to Hazratganj in 1870 entailed several important additions to the printing firm. First, a type foundry was installed in which English, Urdu, and Nagari types were cast. The type foundry was at once a means of asserting greater autonomy and a profitable sideline: its types not only supplied the NKP's own needs but were also offered for sale (Hurst 1887: 355). Second, a large warehouse was set up for the storage of paper and books. The third important new addition to the business was the 'Naval Kishore Book Depot', which served as a retail site and sales agency in Lucknow itself. It formally consolidated the important transition from mere 'Printers' to 'Printers, Publishers, and Booksellers', which had already been initiated through the establishment of various sales agencies outside Lucknow in the mid-1860s (see below).

John F. Hurst, the American visitor to the press in 1884, gives the following description of the Hazratganj premises:

[10] *Avadh Akhbār*, 19 April 1870, cited in Siddiqi 1980: 50.
[11] Ibid.: 51.

TABLE 3.0

Organizational Structure of the NKP

Department	Tasks
1. Lithographic Press	Lithography of books in Arabic, Persian, Urdu, Hindi, and Sanskrit
2. Lithographic Press Office	Bookbinding and stitching
3. Type Press Office	Binding and stitching of type-set books in English, Hindi and Sanskrit
4. Department of Copying and Calligraphy	Copying of manuscripts and books, preparation of drafts for lithography
5. Department of Composition	Composition, compilation, and translation of books; preparation of textbooks, proof-reading, and editing
6. Marketing and Advertising Department	Acquisition of orders from private customers and booksellers; preparation and distribution of book catalogues
7. Sales Department/Book Depot	Direct sale of books to wholesalers, retailers, and private customers
8. Dispatch Department	Packing and dispatch of books
9. Records and Registry Department	Registration of books printed and sold, fixing of book prices
10. Proofreading and Publication Department	Selection of manuscripts suitable for printing; proofreading and correction of drafts; publication of book catalogues, advertisements
11. Correspondence Department	Orders and correspondence
12. Accountancy Department	Accountancy
13. Maintenance Department	Maintenance of buildings

SOURCE: Nurani 1995: 46-8.

> The buildings are numerous, but low, mostly of one story, after the native fashion, and exceedingly plain. Many of them are mere sheds, where the work is done in full view of others on the premises. The roofs are of brick tiling. These buildings cover a vast space, which is divided into many alleys and nondescript passageways, running at all angles with each other, and describing such curves as one can find in the denser parts of Luebeck or Nuremberg. I entered the premises by a long lane running at right angles from the main street. No one in passing along the street would suspect, unless he should turn into the lane, the number of men hard at work at the

> farther end, or the wonderful magnitude of their operations. . . . The huts have no wooden floors. Mother Earth is the common resting-place. The men and boys in great numbers sit on the earthen floor in all possible positions, and carry on their work. They set type, read proof and bind the sheets while sitting squat on the ground. (Hurst 1887: 353)

Another significant consequence of the rapid increase in the firm's business volume and the persisting problem of limited space was that Naval Kishore started to employ a large number of subcontractors to carry out printing work for his press. This innovative scheme of subcontracting was to greatly encourage indigenous enterprise in the local printing trade. The system worked in such a way that the publisher gave permission to experienced and trusted pressmen to shift a hand press to their private home and operate it from there, instead of on the firm's premises. The condition laid down by him was that the pressmen would only receive half of their daily remuneration in cash, the other half being used as instalments to pay for the hand press until it became their own. 'As a result hand presses were established in every muhalla of Lucknow and everyone gave some name to his press', asserts Nurani. 'All these presses worked for the Naval Kishore Press and, if need arise, also took on work from the outside' (Nurani 1995: 45). One of the presses reportedly set up in this way was the Nami Press of Maulvi Qutbuddin (est. *c.* 1874), which subsequently rose to become one of the foremost printing establishments in the city.

A special and seemingly different case of a subcontracted printer was that of the Mumbai al-ᶜUlum Press at Mathura. Set up in 1860 and operated jointly by two brothers, Lala Kanhaiyalal Bhargava and Vamshidhar Bhargava, this press for some time monopolized early Hindi and Sanskrit printing in the western pilgrimage town. Contacts between the NKP and the Mumbai al-ᶜUlum Press date back to at least 1868, when Vamshidhar Bhargava commissioned the NKP Kanpur branch with the printing of an illustrated pilgrimage manual entitled *Banyātrā* (Forest journey). A first edition of the manual had already been issued by Vamshidhar in 1865. It was the first imprint from Mathura that the French Orientalist Garcin de Tassy ever came across, causing him to express his astonishment over the existence of a printing press in 'this sacred town which of late has been reduced to some sort of village' (*LLH* 1866: 315). Presumably *Banyātrā* sold so well that the Bhargava brothers wanted to market it on a larger scale. Their press may not have had the necessary capacity to do so, which would explain why the commission went to the NKP. The situation was reversed in the early 1880s, when the NKP issued various commissions to the Mambaʿ al-ʿUlum Press to lithograph Sanskrit and Hindi works. The reasons for this can only be speculated upon: they may have had to do with the fact that the Mathura press had excellent Nagari scribes at its disposal (Fig. 3).[12] However, following Kanhaiyalal's death in 1883, the Mambaʿ al-ʿUlum Press was not doing well. It only sent in five titles for official registration in 1885, while the following year's report contains one last entry of the press with a single work.[13] In view of this, Naval Kishore's commissions may equally well have been a form of support extended to a caste-fellow in times of financial need.

The steady growth of the NKP was accompanied by a well-planned strategy of geographical expansion. Its beginning was marked by the opening of a large new printing press in Kanpur on 1 September 1865.[14] Located 90 km south-east of Lucknow, Kanpur was an obvious choice: as a military station and distribution point for country produce and European imports the town was rapidly developing into one of the most important industrial centres in northern India.[15] As C.A. Bayly has shown, there was a considerable influx of monied capital from Avadh into Kanpur. Conditions prevailing in the town after 1860 particularly favoured the growth of 'a fringe of enterprises which lay somewhere between the old business world or trade in luxuries and agricultural produce and the world of the pen-pusher and government servant. Printing, bookselling, the commission agency for land sales—all these brought the professional man and the *mahajan* together' (Bayly 1992: 447–8). Since Kanpur was rapidly eclipsing Lucknow as a trading centre, it was imperative for an entrepreneur like Naval Kishore to establish his presence there. The long-term adverse effects of the rise of Kanpur on the Lucknow trade have been described by William Hoey, who noted in 1880: 'The damage done to Lucknow by Cawnpore is chiefly by the diverting of wholesale business from Lucknow to Cawnpore. The present cheapest and most direct route between Lucknow and Calcutta is via Cawnpore. Hence

[12] Among these lithographed titles were Gokulnath's *Caurāsī barttā* ([2]1883) and *Vacanāmṛt* (1883), the Sanskrit *Rūpāvalī* (1883), and *Hīr Rāñjhā kūh* (1884). With the exception of the last work, all were written by the same scribe, one Pandit Keshavdas.

[13] *RPIR* 1885: 45; 1886: 61. For more details on the Mambaʿ al-ʿUlum Press, see Krishnacarya 1966: 45–6; Singh 1986: 70, and Khan 1990: 350.

[14] This is the date given by Khan 1990: 238.

[15] For a detailed account of the industrialization of Kanpur and its role as a new financial centre, see Bayly 1992: 439–48.

Fig. 3: Title page of
Hīr rānjhā kūh, Mambaᶜ al-ᶜUlum Press (1884)

Lucknow retailers of imported goods, cloth and iron for instance, and retailers from all places beyond Lucknow buy in the Cawnpore market' (Hoey 1880: 30).

Naval Kishore's Kanpur press was situated on the banks of the Ganga near Sarsaiya Ghat. Under the joint management of Maulvi Muhammad Ismaʿil and Munshi Lalta Prashad, it rapidly developed into the NKP's largest and most important branch. No business records from Kanpur have survived. British records first mention the press in 1867–8 under the name of 'Cawnpore Gazette Press', after the journal it initially issued. The same sources report an output of nineteen book titles totalling 22,700 printed copies for the year 1867–8. By 1870 the press employed up to 200 workmen and turned out 8000 *juz,* equalling 128,000 printed pages, a day.[16] Throughout the 1870s its production capacity much exceeded that of the mother firm in Lucknow. While later its output was substantially reduced, the Kanpur press remained the NKP's most important branch and continued to operate until around 1949.

The five years following the opening of the Kanpur press in 1865 were a period of intense expansion, during which Naval Kishore sought to establish himself as a bookseller and distributor over a much wider geographical region: first, a printing press was set up in the eastern town of Gorakhpur and put under the supervision of Maulvi Mahbub Ahmad. This seems an odd choice, for though Gorakhpur, located approximately 250 km east of Lucknow, may have enjoyed some local importance for trading agricultural produce, it was otherwise a remote and educationally backward town, which would only develop into a flourishing trade centre with the coming of the railway line twenty years later. For Naval Kishore to set up a printing press in a place that, prior to 1866, was not even served by the Imperial Post can hardly have been a commercial decision.[17] Rather, it may be explained in the context of colonial efforts to enhance education in the region. Around the same time, the NKP opened several branch agencies (*koṭhīs*) that functioned as sales and distribution sites in the trading places of Lahore, Delhi, Faizabad, and Muzaffarpur (Bihar). The Delhi agency was located in a building known as Kothi Ajanti in the busy market area of Dariba Kalan. It was run by Shaikh Nisar ʿAli, the former superintendent at the Lucknow press. With the establishment of a further branch agency and bookshop in the eastern town of Patna

[16] *SRGNWP,* 1868. 'Publications registered at the Curator's Depot': 225; *Avadh Akhbār,* 19 April 1870, cited in Siddiqi 1980: 50.

[17] In 1866 the Imperial Post opened a postal line between Benares and Gorakhpur which was served by runners.

(Azimabad), the firm made an important foray into the vast eastern Indian market. During the eighteenth century Patna had risen to prominence as a stronghold of Persian and Urdu literary culture in Bihar. The NKP Patna branch catered specifically to traders from Purnea, Chittagong, and Dacca, who apparently were particularly keen on buying books in Urdu. As the *Avadh Akhbār* of 19 April 1870 proudly announced, the Delhi and Patna agencies kept books worth Rs 50,000 in stock for sale (cited in Siddiqi 1980: 50).

The establishment of a branch office in Bombay in 1871, while further expanding the range of the NKP's domestic trade, marked an important step in the firm's international trade with the Middle Eastern and European market. The Bombay branch was managed by Mir Ibn Hasan, a trusted and experienced former supervisor of the Lithographic Department at the Lucknow press. Ibn Hasan also served as the Bombay correspondent of *Avadh Akhbār*. The new agency immediately turned into a busy trading spot and was frequented by foreign traders from various countries. As DPI Colin Browning reported in 1871:

> To this Depôt resort traders from Persia, Muscat, Baghdad and Arabia. The Kuran meets with a ready sale. Merchants from Java in May and June 1871, are said to have bought large numbers of the Kuran. Munshi Nawal Kishor had an interview with the Persian envoy at Bombay in 1871, and hopes through his influence to open a trade with Persia. Dictionaries are in request. There is some trade with Leipzig and with London through Messr Trubner [*sic*] and Co. 20 000 copies of the Kuran are reported to have been sold during the year. Before the war with France and Prussia, a few books were occasionally purchased by French gentlemen, with whom Munshi Nawal Kishore corresponded.[18]

In the same year Naval Kishore was invited by the Raja of Patiala to open a printing press in the princely state with the express purpose of launching a newspaper. Before long, a typographic press was set up in Patiala. It assumed operations in September 1871 under its first director Munshi Raunaq ᶜAli, formerly an editor of *Avadh Akhbār*, who had been especially delegated from Lucknow for the task. Within a month, he launched the *Paṭiālā Akhbār,* the first official organ in the state.[19] Set up for official and informational purposes, the Patiala branch only produced a small number of books. The NKP catalogue of 1879 lists a mere three

[18] *RPE Oudh,* 1871–2: 174.

[19] *LLH* 1874: 79. Raunaq ᶜAli died in 1876 and was succeeded by Sayyid Muhammad ᶜAli. See Khan 1990: 124–5.

titles, among them a historiographical work entitled *Tārīkh-e Gorakhpūr* (History of Gorakhpur, *1872).

The Punjab had for a long time been a coveted market for Naval Kishore. As mentioned earlier, he was already operating a sales agency in Lahore in the mid-1860s. Yet it was not before 1883 that he was able to open a full-fledged printing press in the place of his formative years in printing and journalism.[20] Situated in the Mochee Gate area, the Lahore press was furnished with the latest innovation in printing technology, a steam press. It was run by Maulvi Mahbub Ahmad, who had previously been in charge of the Gorakhpur press. Official sources suggest that the Lahore establishment largely survived on government contracts, for its output in printed titles during the first years was minimal. Subsequently, it also specialized in printing religious tracts in Arabic, mostly individual chapters from the Qurʾan. These tracts were produced in large print runs of up to 10,000 copies, and offered to the public at the low price of one anna. Next to producing books and pamphlets in Arabic, Persian and Urdu, the Lahore press also started to issue Punjabi literature written in the Gurmukhi script. Alongside popular Punjabi epics, its publications included various eminent works of the Sikh religion such as *Bālā janam sākhī* (*1890), *Poṭhī das granthī* (*1892) and *Gurūgranth* (*1893).[21] Among its Hindi publications in Gurmukhi script, an annotated edition of Tulsidas's *Rāmāyaṇ* (*1890) and a Hindi *Bhagavad Gītā* (*1891) are worth mentioning. However, perhaps the most famous book to be issued from the NKP Lahore press in 1883 was an Urdu title, namely the second revised and enlarged edition of Muhammad Husain Azad's immensely influential masterpiece of Urdu literary criticism *Āb-e ḥayāt* (Water of life).[22] After Naval Kishore's death in 1895, the Lahore press continued to operate under various names (Naval Kishore Steam Press; Naval Kishore Gas Printing Works; Kashi Ram Press Ltd) until at least 1939.[23]

The last step in the NKP's expansion consisted of the opening of a press in the princely state of Kapurthala in 1892. It was managed by

[20] There is no mention of the establishment in the list of licensed printing presses contained in the *Gazetteer of the Lahore District* 1883–4 (Lahore: Punjab Government 1883–4: 189). *Thacker's Directory* carries a first entry of the Lahore press in 1887.

[21] *Catalogue of Books Registered in the Punjab under Act XXV of 1867*, 1885–95 (OIOC; SV 412).

[22] The first edition of *Āb-e ḥayāt* was published from Lahore's Victoria Press in 1880. For a translation and discussion of the work, see Azad 2001.

[23] *Thacker's Indian Directory* 1895–1939. Kashi Ram apparently held the post of manager of the Lahore NKP.

Ganeshi Lal, presumably a nephew of Naval Kishore, who received a monthly stipend of Rs 100 from the Maharaja of Kapurthala for his services (Barrier/Wallace 1970: 66).

Despite the large investments implied in the establishment and maintenance of the various new printing works, Naval Kishore did not neglect the mother firm in Lucknow. In the late 1880s the Lucknow press underwent modernization. While visiting the firm in 1884, John F. Hurst had expressed his surprise at the absence of power-presses and marvelled at the large number of English-made presses 'still of primitive contrivance' (Hurst 1887: 354) he had encountered instead. Hurst's visit came too early, for just then the NKP was on the verge of a momentous leap into modern printing technology. Around 1885 several modern power-presses were ordered from England. By 1891 twenty steam-powered presses were operating at the Lucknow press under European supervision.[24]

Despite its enormous expansion, the House of Naval Kishore, in the manner of most Indian commercial enterprises, was conducted as a family business. The employment of Ganeshi Lal and other relatives in leading positions suggests as much. In addition to being in charge of the Kapurthala press, Ganeshi Lal served as superintendent of the Avadh Akhbar Press and as personal assistant to Naval Kishore. He also represented the NKP as 'bookseller, publisher and general agent'.[25] Other relatives employed in supervising positions were Manoharlal Bhargava, the superintendent of the printing department and manager of the book depôt, and Ramji Das Bhargava, editor of the *Oudh Review*. Naval Kishore's adopted son Prag Narayan Bhargava was personally trained by him to become the future head of the firm.

As has been noted, the various branches and agencies of the NKP gained prime importance as trading points for the new commercial commodity that the printed book had become on the Indian and foreign market. The firm's export trade formed a particularly important and profitable aspect of business since it catered to a vast market of Islamic countries that were yet to develop a full-fledged printing industry of their own. The Lucknow and Kanpur printing presses were frequented by traders from Kashmir, Bukhara, Yarkand, and Afghanistan who, after selling their goods in India, stopped over on the way back to their respective countries

[24] *PGNWP&Oudh. Educational Dept.*, December 1891: 10. Until recently, an old electric press of G. Mann & Co. Makers Ltd, Leeds, was still in use at the Raja Ram Kumar Book Depot.

[25] *Thacker's Indian Directory* 1890–5.

to purchase large numbers of Arabic and Persian books, especially editions of the Qur᾽an and other religious works. According to Naval Kishore, half the books exported to Bukhara and Afghanistan in this manner hailed from his press.[26] The reputation enjoyed by the NKP beyond the borders of India, particularly in Afghanistan and Iran, is attested by two frequently retold anecdotes: the first relates to the visit to India in 1885 of the Amir of Afghanistan, Shah ᶜAbdul Rahman. During a *darbār* held in his honour in Ludhiana, Shah ᶜAbdul Rahman, in the presence of the Viceroy Lord Dufferin and an assembly of Indian notables reportedly honoured Naval Kishore when he refused to accept the publisher's traditional present and, instead, presented him with an expensive shawl, given as a token to an 'emperor of learning'. Similarly, the Shah of Iran, on the occasion of a speech delivered before an assembly of Calcutta publishers in 1888, allegedly stated that he came to India with the express purpose of meeting two people: the viceroy and Munshi Naval Kishore (Sabiri 1953 [ii]: 117).

According to some sources, the NKP also maintained an agency in London. Its history, however, remains obscure. Since none of the sources furnish any details on it, the existence of an NKP overseas agency in the metropolis seems doubtful.[27] In fact, it may simply be a misnomer for the firm's existing trading connections with London. These involved transactions with the famous firm of Nicholas Trübner (1817-84), the Heidelberg-born bookseller and publisher who was known in the London book trade as 'the prince of oriental publishers' (Howsam 1998: 141). Trübner had set up business in Paternoster Row in 1851; in 1889 his firm merged with Kegan Paul's, a major player in the Indian colonial market.[28] It was through the firm of this 'intermediary between Europe and the East' that NKP imprints from around 1867 reached the metropolis. The flow of oriental books imported from Lucknow is amply documented in *Trübner's American and Oriental Literary Record* (1865–91).

From the outset, the NKP strove to develop a dual profile as a general and scholarly publishing house. Its range of publications grew fast, expanding continuously in scope and size and including both 'high' literary and commercial genres. In the absence of business records, no data is available for the first decade of the firm's existence. Garcin de Tassy refers in 1867 to an NKP catalogue which already listed almost

[26] *RPE Oudh*, 1871–2: 174.

[27] Nurani 1995: 74. After 1895, further branches were established in Ajmer and Jabalpur.

[28] Details in Joshi 2002: 108.

600 titles (*LLH* 1867: 378). Starting from 1868, the first official recordings of NKP publications can be found in the government's *Quarterly List of Publications*,[29] which after 1875 were supplemented by the yearly *Reports on Publications Issued and Registered.* On the basis of these sources Table 3.1 tries to give an overview of the firm's growing turnover by listing yearly numbers of registered NKP titles and relating them to the total of books registered in the NWP&Oudh.

Because of the unreliability of the data (discussed in Chapter 1), Table 3.1 displays great fluctuation. Especially during the first years of

TABLE 3.1

NKP Publishing Figures: Registered Titles per Year, 1868-95

Year	No. of titles registered from NKP Lucknow	No. of titles registered from NKP Kanpur	Total NKP	% of NKP titles of all publications registered in the NWP&Oudh
1868	?	19 (3rd quarter only)		
1874	?	(no books registered)		
1876	40	82	122	19
1877	322	353	675	75
1878	*124	*142	266	26
1879	*82	*145	227	42
1880	**63	**74	**137	33
1881	*173	*195	368	36
1882	*392	*202	594	50
1883	–	–	–	–
1884	141	50	191	25
1885	222	163	385	30
1886	207	165	372	25
1887	161	52	213	20
1888	265	128	393	29
1889	259	115	374	24
1891	73	54	127	13
1892	55	38	93	10
1893	69	64	133	12
1894	87	13	100	7
1895	35	43	78	6

*'Mainly from the NKP'. **no books registered from the NKP during the last quarter of the year. SOURCES: QLP *Oudh*; *RPIR et al.*

[29] Assembled in the *Catalogue of Books Registered under Act XXV of 1867—Oudh 1868–1875* (OIOC; SV 412). I am grateful to Graham Shaw for directing my attention to this catalogue.

registration, the data was often incomplete. However, it suggests that the decade following 1877 was the high-water mark of production and that after 1890 a visible decline set in. The zenith was reached in the years 1877 and 1882, when Naval Kishore's publishing house commanded a seventy-five and fifty per cent share, respectively, of all titles registered in the provinces.

Put in absolute terms, NKP production figures look equally impressive: during the financial year 1872–3, production reached a total of 104,025 printed volumes, valued at Rs 41,806. That the large majority of books were British commissions testifies to the pervasiveness of educational publishing at the time: 98,000 volumes, priced at Rs 13,901, had been ordered by the Oudh Education Department alone.[30] During the following year, production figures leapt to a total of 399,271 volumes, showing a fourfold increase.[31] In 1876 there was a noticeable decline, the total going down to 265,355 volumes, of which 104,000 were commissioned by the Education Department. The latter figures are significant since they demonstrate that within a relatively short period of time non-educational literature had immensely gained in importance. Non-educational titles in this year accounted for more than sixty per cent of the NKP's total production. Among these a high proportion of 74,000 copies were first editions (as against 86,750 reprints), a fact that further testifies to a thriving marketplace. The ratio between Urdu and Hindi titles issued from the NKP will be discussed in Chapter 7. For now, it is important to note that, while Urdu books continued to outnumber those in Hindi/Nagari, Hindi publications continuously gained in importance. Suffice it to say at this point that by the early 1870s the Lucknow press had established itself as a strong presence in the Hindi literary marketplace, defying a popular notion which associates the Hindi book trade with places like Benares and Allahabad only.

Throughout his career in publishing, Naval Kishore displayed an indefatigable zeal in seeking out additional sources of income. The year 1894 saw his last effort to diversify with the establishment of the Lucknow Iron Works. The factory presumably grew out of the NKP's type foundry. It was situated in Wingfield Manzil and operated by an average daily number of ninety workmen. From the outset it did brisk business, sustained mostly by government contracts.[32]

[30] *OAR*, 1872–3: 123.
[31] *OAR*, 1873–4: 96.
[32] *PGNWP&Oudh. General Administration Dept.*, June 1895: 27.

In the course of the NKP's expansion the number of people employed by the firm rose steadily. Between 1870 and 1876, over 700 press hands were working at the Lucknow presses alone.[33] By 1880 the number of workmen and employees had gone up to over 900, turning Naval Kishore into the single-largest Indian employer in the NWP&Oudh.[34] The average wages his printers received at that time ranged from 8 to 12 annas per day. Lithographers earned slightly less, with a daily 6 annas to 1 rupee.[35] All in all, a monthly sum of Rs 15,000 had to be spent on wages and salaries (S.Q. Khan 1980: 188).

With the introduction of steam power in the 1890s, the NKP came to qualify as a factory under the Indian Factories Act of 1891. It was the only Indian-owned printing press in the NWP&Oudh to fall under this category, the other three firms being the British-run Methodist Publishing House (Lucknow), the Oudh and Rohilkhand Railway Press (Lucknow) and the Allahabad Government Press. Not surprisingly, the introduction of steam power entailed a reduction in the NKP's workforce. By 1895 the average daily number of 'operatives employed' at the Lucknow printing works had gone down to 287 male adults and 45 male children.[36] Labour conditions for these children had been considerably improved by the Factory Act of 1881, the first important measure of factory legislation in India. While the act did not regulate the working hours of adults, it was explicitly directed at Indian child labour, giving statutory protection to working children for whom a minimum age of seven was prescribed. The working hours of children aged between the ages of seven and twelve were limited to nine per day and child workers were also entitled to four holidays per month.[37] In keeping with the 1881 Factory Act and the amended 1891 Indian Factories Act, the NKP was regulated by midday stoppage. Sunday was a general holiday. The press was also subject to four official inspections per year, including one by the British Medical Officer. Prior to the enactment of these state regulations, little is known about the lot of the NKP's workforce. In the absence of a publisher's

[33] *RPIR* 1876: 42. *Avadh Akhbār*, 16 August 1870, cited in Haidari 1980: 25.

[34] See 'Statement of the Newul Kishore Press' below, Chapter 4. The high number of 1200 workers and employees, given by Haidar and others for 1884, must refer to all the printing works and branches of the press.

[35] *Gazetteer of the Province of Oudh* II, 1985: 393.

[36] *PGNWP&Oudh. General Administration Dept.*, June 1895. 'Annual statement on the Working of the Factory Act in the Lucknow District for the year 1894': 27.

[37] For an overview of early labour legislation, see Mukhtar 1930: 11–50; Das 1941: 49–54.

archive, it is extremely difficult to assess labour conditions at the firm before the introduction of colonial factory legislation. Contemporary reports on Indian factory labour unanimously deplore the disgraceful, oppressive, and unsanitary labour conditions prevailing in Indian factories at the time. However, there is some evidence to suggest that Naval Kishore took the social responsibility coming with his position as a large-scale employer seriously. The various social security schemes he is reported to have introduced for his workers and employees included pension schemes for retired persons and allowances for the dependants of deceased employees. Apparently he was also concerned about sanitary provisions and employed several allopathic doctors, *ḥakīms* and *vaidyas* to look after his workforce (Sabiri 1953 [ii]: 115).

3.3 Printing Books: Traditional Craftsmanship and Modern Technology

As noted earlier, a decisive factor in the rapid spread of lithography in India was the fact that it was a comparatively inexpensive technology. The material required was limestone, nitric acid for preparing the stone, a special kind of greasy ink, and paper.[38] While in European lithography from about 1830 stone started to be replaced by zinc plates, Indian printers continued to use stone as the printing surface throughout the nineteenth century. Hence, large numbers of stones continued to be imported from Europe, especially Germany. Lithographic stones and other printing equipment were widely advertised in English and vernacular newspapers. An advertisement in the *Lahore Chronicle* of 30 August 1856, for example, not only offered transfer paper, lithographic writing ink, chalks, and sponges, but also boasted of the 'best German lithographic stones', which were said to be carefully selected and of the very highest quality. Importing stones from Europe, however, was expensive and time-consuming. Consequently, many Indian printer-publishers turned to the cheaper alternative and began using local stone. As early as 1826, a suitable limestone had been discovered at Kurnool in the Bellary district of Madras Presidency which, after a period of experimenting, yielded good results.[39]

Despite the high cost involved, Naval Kishore preferred to use stones of foreign origin. In 1872 he made a purchase of 616 new lithographic

[38] For an excellent introduction to the various printing techniques used through the ages, see Griffiths 1996.

[39] Shaw 1998: 108–10. For details on the physical appearance and operating mechanisms of early lithographic hand presses, see Twyman 1967; Szrajber 1997.

stones, involving a considerable expense of Rs 18,000.[40] The Reverend Hurst on his visit to the press in 1884 noted that the engraving stone hailed from Germany, that it was 'precisely the same as that used by the Leipsic engravers', and was 'constantly imported in large quantities' (Hurst 1887: 354). From the financial point of view, the cost of importing good-quality foreign stone was justified by the fact that each lithographic stone yielded a large number of impressions and could also be reused for new impressions, once its surface had been ground down. As a result, the firm was faced with a steady increase of lithographic stones that already bore inscriptions and had to be stored for further use. Apparently, by 1895 their number had grown to a huge total of 21,000 (S. Q. Khan 1980: 188). The resulting problem of space was tackled by a special storage system. Storing the stones was a delicate operation, which Naval Kishore took care to personally supervise.

The preparation of the lithographic stones underwent little change during the course of the century: the stone was first washed with diluted nitric acid and then rubbed with gum arabic to prevent further grease from adhering to it. Two principal techniques of lithography were common: one was to directly inscribe on the stone surface with greasy ink and in a laterally inverted script. This method required the expertise of specially trained calligraphers. The other, by far more common, technique was described as transfer. Here, the text was first copied with a greasy medium unto a special type of transfer paper. The paper copy was then transferred unto the stone surface by placing the paper face downwards on the stone and moistening it until the soluble layer dissolved and left the greasy drawing on the stone.[41] In either case, the actual printing was done on flat-bed scraper presses worked by hand. It is to William Hoey, officiating city magistrate and license tax officer in Lucknow from 1878, that we owe a rare account of the technical procedure of lithography and its attendant expenses, as observed in a small Lucknow printing shop in 1880. It deserves to be quoted in full:

> Sāligrām, whose printing press is in Subhānnagar, is now printing a book called *'Khāliq Bārī'* of 16 pages on white Serampore paper (20x26). 16 pages or 8 leaves make what is called a juz. One sheet of the paper in use suffices for 2 juz and one ream of this paper which costs Rs. 6 consists of 20 dastas (quires) of 25 sheets each. The press-man cuts each sheet into 4 pieces, and one sheet gives 2 juz. One quarter of a sheet can be printed

[40] *OAR*, 1872–3: 123.

[41] Details in Griffiths 1996: 102–3.

> from one stone at a time. Four copies, that is four stones, are required to print one juz. The copy writer who writes up the sheets which are transferred to stone receives 4 a[nna]s per copy or one rupee per juz. The copy is written on French paper and the materials with which the paper is prepared for copy-writing are applied by the printer, *usārā* (gamboge), arrowroot, and *nishāsta* (starch). One sheet of French paper suffices for writing 2 pages and the cost is 1 an[na] 3 pies per dasta (quire). If bought by the ream it is only one rupee per ream. The materials used to prepare the paper come to Rs. 1–9 per ream. A whole ream prepared costs Rs. 2–9. A copy when transferred to stone will give a thousand, nay, an almost unlimited number of impressions. Two sheets of French paper are necessary for one stone for printing this book. One side only of a paper is printed in a day, and one impression is called 'tao'. A thousand tāus is the daily average for a press. Four labourers are employed in a press; one press-man, one pechkash, one isfanjia (sponge man), and one rulia (a lad who applies the ink roller to the stone). The press-man receives 3 a[nna]s; pechkash 2 a[nna]s; isfanjia 2 a[nna]s and rulia 1 an[na] per diem. The press-man damps the paper for the press and cuts the sheets. When the sheets have been printed off the daftari who works by contract, folds and stitches the book. He receives 6 a[nna]s per thousand. The cost of printer's ink is about 6 a[nna]s per thousand impressions for one stone, and miscellaneous expenses for oil and cloths for each press are only one anna per diem. The proprietor of the press sells this book at 3 pies per copy wholesale price to retail book-sellers, who retail at two paisa.
>
> A calculation from above data will show that an edition of 1000 copies costs Rs. 11–2 and sells for Rs. 15–10, that is an edition of 1000 copies of a vernacular work printed in this size, which happens to be that most current, brings the printer Rs. 4 per juz.
>
> The more usual practise for printers to have a large business is to sell their publications to wholesale book-sellers who supply retailers at 40 juz the rupee and retailers vend at 32 juz the rupee. These are the prevailing prices for books printed on Serampore paper of the size 22x29, 20x26, and 18x22, and this system of sale is called *ajza qīmat*. Registered books and school books printed by authority are sold at what is termed *pukhtā qīmat* or a fixed prize. (Hoey 1880: 82–3)

Hoey's detailed account of the printing of *Khāliq bārī*, a standard and frequently reprinted Persian vocabulary, invites a comparison with the NKP. While the technical procedure hardly differed from the above description, the size of operations at the NKP was infinitely larger, with approximately 350 hand presses in use at the time (Nurani 1972: 74). The NKP's own fifteenth edition of *Khāliq bārī*, issued in 1875 in a print run of 1250 copies, was identical in size and number of pages with the text produced at the Shaligram Press. Since textbook prices were fixed, it was sold at the same retail price of 2 paisa per copy. A price comparison with an earlier NKP edition of 1869 indicates how the overall reduction in printing costs impacted on price rates: within the short time span of six years the sales price of *Khāliq bārī* had gone down by fifty per cent from 1 anna to half an anna (that is, 2 paisa).

Prices, of course, also depended on the size of the edition. The number of copies of non-educational NKP titles in Hindi and Urdu displays great variation. First editions usually ranged from 275 to 1250 copies, depending on the kind of publication and, in case of commissions, on the kind of agreement the firm had entered into with the author or person commissioning the manuscript. In keeping first editions comparatively small, Naval Kishore exercised the caution that was necessary to stay afloat in the commercial market. From the publisher's point of view, the greatest risk was involved in promoting texts of contemporary poetry, fiction, or learned treatises—especially, but by no means exclusively, in the case of unknown authors. Such texts were generally issued in much smaller print runs than the staple fare of the commercial book trade—religious texts, prayer books, astrological manuals, folk tales, etc. By far the highest print runs, of course, were for school textbooks commissioned by the British authorities, about which more will be said in the next chapter. Here, first editions generally ranged from 550 to 5500 copies. Reprints of widely used textbooks, such as Raja Shiva Prasad's standard geography, *Jām-e Jahānnumā* (Hindi: *Bhūgol vṛtānt*), could easily command print runs of 10,000 or 20,000 copies at a time.

Apart from the print run, there were other obvious factors determining the price of a non-educational title, such as the book's format and number of pages, the quality of paper and binding, whether or not the book included illustrations. A standard means of making books of substantial size accessible to the readership was to break them up into individually sold volumes and parts. The sizes most frequently used for Persian, Urdu, and Hindi books were foolscap, royal octavo, and royal quarto. Bindings of NKP books exhibit great variety, ranging from thin paper covers or cardboards to expensive leather bindings, often in half-morocco. As in the wholesale book trade in Britain, the prevailing practice was to buy books as unbound sheets rather than as sewn and bound finished products.

The Paper Problem

Highlighting the importance of paper to the development of the periodical and book publishing industry in Victorian England, S. Bennett has pointed to the centrality of paper in shaping modern urban culture: 'Paper was to the urban revolution what iron was to the industrial revolution. The output of paper marked the advance of urbanism just as surely as the output of iron marked the advance of industry' (Bennett 1990: 166–8). Paper was fundamental to commercial mass printing. To printer-publishers in the subcontinent, it was also the most problematic of the various raw materials. Right from the beginning of Indian-language printing in the eighteenth century, its supply posed a major and perennial problem. As Graham Shaw notes:

> Perhaps no other problem of material vexed the eighteenth-century Calcutta printer as much as that of paper. Two kinds were commonly in use: Indian hand-made paper, usually referred to as Patna paper after one of the chief centres of manufacture, and which Carey's biographer George Smith characterized as "a dingy, porous, rough substance", and imported "Europe paper", higher in quality but also in price. Quite frequently the same work would be printed on both types of paper, the European paper version adding between a quarter and a half to the selling price. (Shaw 1981: 35)

After 1800 the leading supplier of Indian-made paper to the printing presses in eastern and northern India was the paper-mill of the Serampore Mission Press. After an initial period of trials and setbacks, it achieved remarkable results in improving the quality of manufactured paper.[42] Yet the Serampore mill was scarcely able to keep pace with the rapidly growing demand of a flourishing domestic print industry. As a result, Indian-made paper remained in short supply throughout large parts of the nineteenth century.[43]

The slow growth of the Indian paper industry may in part be explained by an ordinance passed under Charles Wood in the 1850s to the effect that the entire supply of paper used for government printing was to be met by paper imported from England. Introduced to maintain quality standards and presumably to ensure the durability of official documents, the measure backfired. The resulting situation was described by W.H. Lowe, a British official put in charge of setting up the Allahabad Government Press in 1858. He noted the total undependability of the Calcutta market: '[W]hatever can be procured is generally inferior in quality and exorbitant in price. The reason of this is that all the large presses in India import their own paper and materials and never resort to the dealers except in case of emergency.'[44] Yet these circumstances fail to offer an

[42] Details in Khan 1999: 224–8.

[43] For the indigenous paper industry in various Indian regions, see Liotard 1883; Bhattacharyya 1988; Mehta 1991.

[44] *Home Dept. Public Branch*, October 1858, no. 297: 6.

explanation as to why European investment in the Indian paper industry remained confined to Bengal and why, despite the progress in infrastructure and transport, it never extended to the north-west. Until the late 1870s both official and commercial printing presses in the vast region of northern India were forced to buy their paper from the mills in and around Calcutta or import it from Europe. In either case, prices were often prohibitive.[45] At the NKP, both Serampore paper and high-quality paper from England, Germany, or France was used for printing. The expenses for foreign 'white' (*safed*) paper as compared to the Indian-made paper of light brownish colour (generally called *bādāmī*) were considerable. With his keen sense of business, Naval Kishore soon realized that in the absence of a paper mill in North India the paper trade was a promising field to venture into. Consequently, from around 1870 he began to trade in paper. The *Avadh Akhbār* of 19 April 1870 carried the following announcement: 'The press proprietor, in addition to dealing in books, deals in all kinds of paper. In particular, each month large supplies of paper are ordered directly from German [*sic*], London and France.'[46] To the publisher this step not only meant making a virtue of necessity, but also constituted a welcome opportunity to diversify.

Importing paper for resale in the domestic market was not without its risks, as can easily be gathered from the large sums involved in the transactions: in 1871 Naval Kishore purchased paper worth Rs 140,000 from England, while in the following year paper worth Rs 105,000 was acquired through the Calcutta-based German firm of Ullmann, Hirschhorn & Co. as well as through the merchant house of George Henderson & Co. The firm of Henderson was closely associated with the newly established paper mill at Bally near Calcutta, a large industrial enterprise under British ownership and management.[47] The risks and, at the same time, alluring promise of profit implied in the paper trade are the theme of a frequently retold anecdote in Naval Kishore's biography: on one occasion, during an auction in Calcutta, the publisher, with calculated daring, acquired an entire shipload of seemingly spoilt paper. When it later turned out that the paper was of much better quality than expected, he was able to resell it at a high profit.

Despite the investment in foreign paper, the publishing house continued to use Indian-made paper in large quantities. This is suggested by a complaint raised in a British report of 1872 to the effect that the paper

[45] For paper manufacturing in Lucknow, see Hoey 1880: 127–9.

[46] *Avadh Akhbār*, 19 April 1870, cited in Siddiqi 1980: 51 and Lalji Munshi 1903: 6–7.

[47] *RPE Oudh*, 1871–2: 175; *RPE Oudh*, 1872–3: 120. Bhattacharyya 1988: 87.

used at the NKP was 'always coarse'.[48] It is also borne out by the NKP's 1879 catalogue, which featured various types of paper distinguished by colour and quality: books were printed on white (*safed*), henna-coloured (*ḥinnāʾī*), dove-coloured (*fā<u>kh</u>ta*) or, more rarely, light blue (*ābī*) paper. The different qualities comprised 'fine, superior' (*ʿumda*), 'glossy' (*ciknā*) and 'thick' (*gunda*) paper. Often the same title was made available in various paper qualities.

The difficult situation pertaining to paper only changed in the late 1870s, when the colonial government introduced special measures to promote the growth of the indigenous paper industry and to support the establishment of new paper mills. In seizing the occasion to his advantage, Naval Kishore once again displayed remarkable entrepreneurial foresight: he was instrumental in establishing the first paper mill in the NWP&Oudh. To this end, he founded a company of shareholders in 1879. Support for the project came from the affluent class of the Avadh *taʿalluqdār*s, who supplied much of the original capital (Metcalf 1979: 278). The capital of the company was fixed at Rs 600,000, divided into 6000 shares. Set up in 1879, the Lucknow Paper Mills, or Upper India Paper Mill Co. Ltd,[49] started operating in 1880. Despite the initial flow of local capital, the company went through some teething trouble when, following an order of a plant and machinery from England, it incurred high debts. When the shareholders became suspicious and began to sell their shares at a loss, Naval Kishore was reportedly forced to step in and clear the debts from his own pocket (Sabiri 1953 [ii]: 118).

These events may provide the backdrop to a petition addressed to the government in June 1880 by the secretary of the paper mill, Babu Kaliprasad. The petition asked for official patronage, insinuating that the company founders' confidence that such patronage would be afforded to them 'formed the most powerful incentive to their launching out in a project involving the outlay and risk of such a large capital.'[50] As the paper mill's largest proprietor, Naval Kishore maintained a tight grip over its affairs. For a number of years he served as its honorary manager and also sat on its board of directors. His ties with the management of the paper mill were cemented even further when he arranged the marriage of his adopted son Prag Narayan to the daughter of one of the mill's high officials (Nurani 1995: 33). A notice published in the *Delhi Punch* (Lahore)

[48] *PGNWP&Oudh. General Dept.*, June 1872: 35.

[49] The name was later changed to Upper India Couper Mill Co. Ltd.

[50] *Home Dept. Public Branch*, July 1880, no. 24–5 (B).

of 21 February 1883 suggests that the management of the Lucknow paper mill was subject to a fair amount of nepotism. It portrays Naval Kishore's involvement in setting up and running the mill in a generally unfavourable light:

> A correspondent of the *Delhi Punch* . . . makes some complaints about the Paper mill company of Lucknow. The writer stated that, when the establishment of the mill was projected, Munshi Nawal Kishor, the proprietor of the *Oudh Akhbar*, repeatedly published articles in that paper holding out prospects of a dividend at 40 per cent. These high hopes induced even many poor people to invest their small capital in the speculation. Now the manager of the mill has declared a dividend at 8 annas per cent for three months. It appears that the men employed at the mill are all relatives of the manager of the mill, and are overpaid. The Government should take the projectors to task for deceiving the public by publishing false prospectuses, and compel them to buy the shares of poorer shareholders at par, to save them from loss, or it should itself purchase the whole business at cost price.[51]

It is not known whether this appeal had any effect. Its allegations in any case seem curious in light of the fact that by 1883 the paper mill was already in a flourishing state. It had received a great boost in 1881 when the government, in a shift from its earlier policy, issued an order to the effect that country-made paper should, as far as possible, be used in all government offices (Liotard 1883: 1). With 340 employees and a yearly turnout of nearly Rs 390,000 in 1882, the paper mill was counted among Lucknow's largest industrial enterprises.[52] It not only became the main supplier of paper to the printing presses in the NWP&Oudh, but also started catering to the Punjab. The paper produced at Lucknow was considered to be of good quality, while remaining inexpensive. While it did not quite match the standards of foreign paper, it was well suited to Indian needs. One foreign observer described it as 'very tough, though not pleasing to the eye or agreeable to the touch' (Hurst 1887: 354).

The low-cost factor was of vital interest to the colonial administration, particularly with regard to its textbook-printing scheme. One of the Lucknow mill's largest customers, the Punjab Educational Department reported in 1883:

> Every effort has been made to reduce the price of our vernacular books, and this has been done by two means: 1st by adopting the new style in printing books; and 2nd, by the use of country-made paper from the Upper India

[51] *Delhi Punch*, 21 February 1883, SVN 1883: 191.

[52] *RA NWP&Oudh*, for the year ending 31 March 1883: 141.

> Paper Mills Company of Lucknow. This paper is called Bādāmi, or half bleached, and, though inferior to the English printing paper in appearance, it is substantial and cheap, and cheapness is a great consideration with native students, especially those of vernacular schools. The price of English printing paper is about 5 annas per pound, including cost of transit to Lahore while that of the paper from the Upper India Mills is about 3 annas per pound.[53]

The prime objective of cheapness, if paramount at the time, was to show its adverse effects in the long run: the paper produced at the Lucknow paper mill shares the self-destructive quality characteristic of much industrially manufactured paper in the nineteenth century (Bennett 1990). Whether imported or Indian-made, the paper used for book printing at the NKP was generally highly acidic with the invariable consequence that NKP imprints have been subject to a slow but steady deterioration.

Old Traditions, New Technology, and Quality Standards

The introduction of modern technology, the mechanization of the production process and the imperatives of cheapness and rapidity prevailing in industrial mass printing had fundamentally altered the process of book production. At the same time, commercial publishing did not represent a total rupture with traditional practices of book making and notions of what constituted a fine imprint. At the House of Naval Kishore, tradition prevailed in many respects. The firm's concern with fine books and superior craftsmanship is particularly evident in the way in which texts continued to be carefully prepared for lithographic printing by its scribes and master calligraphers, of whom more will be said in Chapter 5. It is most visibly reflected in the physical appearance of NKP lithographed books. As has been noted before, for large parts of its Arabic and Persian publications, as also many of its Urdu titles, the Lucknow publishing house adopted the distinctive style of formatting lithographic books that had been developed by the early Lucknow printers during the 1840s and 1850s. While this style drew heavily on the manuscript tradition, it was in time further adapted for commercial printing. The result was a standard format and title page layout that was different from the style prevalent, for example, in Bombay. To the trained eye NKP books are easily distinguishable from those produced by any other lithographic press in India.

[53] *Rept. on Popular Education in the Punjab and its Dependencies*, 1882–3: 122–3.

A characteristic feature borrowed from the manuscript tradition was the *'unwān* or superscription. In NKP books it usually appeared as a small and simple drawing on the reverse of the heavily ornamented title page.[54] Glosses were found on the margins, in small handwriting; marginal commentaries were written in slant. As Olga Scheglova notes: 'An important achievement of Munshī Nawal Kishor was to fit very large works such as Khwāndamīr's *Rawḍat al-ṣafā* or Arabic and Persian dictionaries into a single volume. He did this with the aid of thin paper, small handwriting and lithographic artistry' (Scheglova 1999: 18). Scheglova identifies a distinct 'Naval Kishore style', to which she attributes a far-reaching impact: 'For several decades, this style attained in India the status of an accepted canon. It also exerted a significant influence on the graphic design of books produced by Central Asian lithographers' (ibid.: 15). The Naval Kishore style provided a model to publishers in places like Lahore, Delhi, and Kanpur, who would in turn introduce their own variations.

The concern with tradition was also manifest in the production of a special category of printed texts, the sacred scriptures. Even while subjecting the scriptures to the profane process of mass production, the NKP remained sensitive to the meaning of the written text as a sacred item and the weight it carried as an object of reverence. The printing of the Qur'an, in particular, was carried out in accordance with the sacred status of the text and implied a meticulous observance of Islamic precepts: all those involved in the preparation of copies and the printing of the Qur'an—a task which, significantly, was performed exclusively by Muslim employees—had to take a ritual bath before embarking on their work. Smoking or chewing *pān* (betel leaf) was strictly forbidden in the rooms where copies of the Qur'an were being prepared or printing was under way. Unlike other used stones, old lithographic stones bearing the words of the Qur'an were not destroyed but buried (Hasan 1981: 11). Similar measures ensuring ritual purity and a reverential handling of the sacred scriptures were adopted for printing the most revered texts of the Hindu and Sikh religion, *viz.* the *Bhagavad Gītā* and the *Gurū Granth Sāhib*.

The notion of quality was important to Naval Kishore, who took pride in introducing high standards in commercial publishing. Good workmanship and careful editing were equally important prerequisites in building up his firm's reputation. Great care was taken to ensure that the printing was neat, the calligraphy fine and pleasing to the eye, and that

[54] See Scheglova 1999 for a detailed description of the title pages of NKP Persian books.

the transmission of texts from manuscript copies was accurate and correct. Readers of NKP books were expressly told that the work they had purchased had been corrected and edited by expert proofreaders. Statements to the effect that the text had undergone careful revision by the firm's maulvis or pandits regularly featured on the title pages. The edition of Keshavdas's *Kavipriyā saṭīk* (*1886), for example, named a team of seven pandits who had been involved in proofreading and correcting the text. Another typical notice, found in a Hindi rendering of Madhava's *Śaṅkara-digvijaya* (Shankara's Conquest of the Regions, *1870), a popular hagiographical account on the life of the great philosopher Shankaracarya, stressed the fine quality of the edition:

> This work has been printed at the Naval Kishore Press by order of Pandit Debiprasad, Deputy Collector in Ghazipur district. Since this excellent work has not been previously translated into any vernacular language and in view of its fine paper, beautiful calligraphy and neatness, the price is not high. For the sake of widely diffusing this new work and for the convenience of the purchaser, the price has been fixed very low, that is at Rs 2, 8 annas, exclusive of mail charges. Those who are interested are kindly requested to send an advance payment or letter to the afore-said pandit or to the press. The book will then be despatched to you.

Throughout the years the NKP managed to maintain a generally high standard for its publications. Yet there were occasions when notions of accuracy and fine presswork had to be sacrificed to commercial demands. The sheer size of printing undertaken at the firm and the imperative of cheapness could not but leave its mark on some of the publications, especially in the textbook sector. While nothing much could be done if the calligraphy lacked neatness or the printing turned out bad, in case of faulty composition or sloppy editing, lists of errata (*ghalatnāma/ṣahīhnāma*, *śuddhpatr*) were sometimes inserted.

3.4 Marketing Books: Strategies of Advertising and Diffusion

> My father's uncle, Maulvi Ahmad, was very fond of travel and trade at a time when people were frightened of leaving their homes. He went as an agent for Haji Harmain Sharifain from Lucknow as far as Rawalpindi, taking thousands of books with him in bullock carts and other similar conveyances. He used to say that in those days books were very rare. On seeing books printed in Lucknow, people would open their eyes wide and be drawn to them like moths to a candle. They were so eager that at whatever

> town or village Maulvi Ahmad arrived, his coming was known beforehand and his arrival was attended by great pomp and ceremony. When he came to a village, he was surrounded by people, a crowd would collect and any book he offered, at whatever price, was willingly accepted and reverently placed on the brow of the purchaser. (Sharar 1979: 107)

Whether the air of romance attributed to the spread of the printed word in Sharar's recollections was still prevailing in the era of commercial publishing is a difficult question to answer. The organization of the book trade in Indian languages constitutes one of the least explored areas in the early history of print in the subcontinent. The operating mechanisms and level of interaction amongst the various agents who formed the links in the distribution chain from publisher to bookseller to reader are yet to be explored in the Indian context. Beyond the obvious facts that publishers either relied on their own sales agencies or else sold to wholesale booksellers and retailers who, in turn, marketed books to individual buyers, our knowledge of the distribution channels of the printed book is still insufficient. Little, for example, is known about the social identity and range of activities of the South Asian counterpart of the European colporteur. This itinerant hawker, or 'bookwallah' as he was dubbed by British expatriates, played a key role in spreading printed literature to the vast internal market of small town and rural India.[55] As early as 1822, a resident of Murshidabad wrote to *The Friend of India* that he was glad to perceive 'that everyday the natives are increasing in their sales of native books: there are now in and near the city of Moorshedabaad no less than four walking booksellers that I know of. In speaking to one last week, he informed me, that upon an average he sold to the amount of 30 Rupees per month.' Characteristically, the same observer could not refrain from adding that 'The books sold by these, of course, are great trash, but I suppose a press has never yet been introduced among a people without some alloy.'[56] A second, and rather more picturesque, account given by an Englishwoman in the 1830s corroborates the existence of a special group of itinerant hawkers engaged in the sale of English books to British expatriates and English-educated Indians:

> To book-hunters especially, a very interesting character is to be found in British India in the shape of the book-wallah or book-hawker—a sort of

[55] Bayly 1996a: 219. For early soldiers', East India Company, factory and circulating libraries catering to the Europeans in India, see Lockyer 1977. For European firms investing in the colonial market, see Joshi 2002.

[56] *Friend of India*, vol. 5, 1822: 86, cited in Ghosh 1998: 177.

> literary pedlar who wanders about from town to town and from station to station with much patience, and an apparent love of books and periodicals which such glorious old book-worms as our Roscoe and Charles Land would have greatly admired. Without this dispensor of heavy and light literature in our splendid Eastern dominion, we may doubt if India would be as secure as it is. Through the travels of the book-hawker, many antidotes to poisonous writings are administered; educated natives purchase English philosophical treatises, mathematical works, magazines—all with equal exposure; the poorer Hindu or Mahomedan, with Lord William Bentinck's famous remark ringing in his ear—'Education is the first want, education the second, education the third want of India!'—dives into the box or bundle (to the astonishment of the patient coolie or native porter who carries it) for a grammer [*sic*] or spelling-book; while the *burra sahib*, his wife and daughter [. . .] startle at the sonorous voice exclaiming from the door, or beside the refreshing *kus-kus* tatties,—'Book-hawker, Sir!' (cited in Ohdedar 1966: 120-1)

Missionaries and Christian book societies had begun building up their own networks of colporteurs at an early point in time. By the 1870s colportage accounted for half of the regional-language circulation of the British and Foreign Bible Society. Interestingly, missionary colportage was an unpopular job and positions were difficult to fill, as reported the 1874 Conference on Urdu and Hindi Christian Literature in Allahabad (Davis 1983: 26). Indian printer-publishers followed the missionary example and adopted colportage for disseminating their books. Our knowledge, however, is largely confined to Bengal: among early Calcutta printers and booksellers, Gangakishore Bhattacarya led the way in employing hawkers as early as 1816. By 1857 over 200 hawkers were said to be working for the Calcutta presses. Many of them hailed from an agricultural background, working as colporteurs for part of the year only and cultivating their fields during the rainy season. Once again, Long is a valuable source of information on the effectiveness of the colportage system:

> These men may be seen going through the native part of Calcutta and the adjacent towns with a pyramid of books on their heads. They buy the books themselves at wholesome price, and often sell them at a distance at double the price which brings them in probably 6 or 8 Rupees monthly, though we know of one man who realizes by book hawking more than 100 Rupees monthly . . . The Natives find the best advertisement for a Bengali book is a *living agent* who shows *the book itself.* Various valuable Bengali works have been printed, which have rotted on a Book-seller's shelves simply

> because the agency of hawkers was not brought into action. (Long 1859: xiv)

Long's observation on the advantages of colportage over sale in stores and sales depositories is corroborated in the 1857 report of the Vernacular Literature Society of Calcutta. According to this report, few books were sold at the society's depot, whereas encouraging results were achieved through door-to-door selling by hawkers. Interestingly, the Vernacular Literature Society employed several female hawkers who gained direct access to the secluded domestic sphere of respectable Bengali women and reportedly sold books in large numbers.[57] The response to this most direct kind of marketing was vivid, testifying to an urgent demand: when unable to pay for books in cash, people often exchanged them for manuscripts (Ghosh 1998: 181).

Compared to Bengal, we still make do with the sketchiest sense of the colportage system in the early Hindi and Urdu book trade. No doubt, North Indian publishers and booksellers followed their Bengali confreres in resorting to the agency of hawkers for disseminating printed matter in the small town and rural market. Local fairs assumed prime importance in this context. In 1884 the Methodist missionary B.H. Badley gave the following description of bookstalls set up during the annual *mela* in Tulsipur, a small town in eastern Gonda district:

> The book shops are generally small, and not very attractive. They consist chiefly of native publications, printed in pamphlet form on yellow paper, and seldom bound. A few are school-books, but most are filled with stories of gods and goddesses, and illustrated by rude cuts drawn by Hindustani artists. The books are spread out upon the ground on a piece of cloth, and are generally carried from place to place in bundles, not in boxes. (Badley 1884: 148–9)

Even for large-scale commercial publishers like Naval Kishore, colportage was still the most effective means of reaching a wider readership outside the urban centres. John Hurst noted in 1884:

> The practical way by which the native publisher, like Kishore, gets his publications before the public and secures a large sale is by the system of colportage. The drummers circulate through the country very industriously, and know just where to go in order to secure the largest and best patronage. They are very quiet in their methods. What successful book agent the world

[57] Vernacular Literature Society, Report from February 1856 to March 1857, Calcutta 1857, cited in Khan 1999: 380.

over does not know that too much talking is likely to spoil a sale? (Hurst 1887: 356)

Other sales structures existed for the urban market. As we have seen, Naval Kishore took the step from 'Printers and Publishers' to 'Booksellers' early on, by setting up his own sales agencies (*koṭhī*). At the same time, he increasingly resorted to the agency of professional booksellers, whose operations covered a wide geographical region.

In this context, a publisher's notice inserted in the 1865 NKP edition of Malik Muhammad Jaysi's *Padmāvat* (reproduced in translation below) assumes particular importance. It not only contains one of the first copyright notices found in an NKP book, but also supplies some rare information on early sales sites. From it we learn that, by 1865, Naval Kishore was already maintaining *koṭhī*s in Faizabad, Muzaffarpur, Delhi, and Lahore, while also relying on an extensive distribution network beyond these locations. This network involved several fellow printer-publishers, whom Naval Kishore commissioned as sales agents for his firm. The system seems to have worked in a reciprocal way for, as will be shown, the NKP in its turn marketed books for a number of presses in Lucknow and beyond. Obviously, effective marketing and competition were not mutually exclusive.

A substantial item in the cost of publishing was advertising. From the early days of commercial publishing in India, the most conventional means of advertising books was the newspaper advertisement. This format was not only a sure means of reaching a large number of readers and prospective buyers; for the many printer-publishers who ran their own paper it also had the additional benefit of minimizing advertising costs. Naval Kishore regularly announced new and forthcoming publications in *Avadh Akhbār*, including both his own and other publishers' titles. Such announcements were also crucial in soliciting advance subscriptions and inviting the patronage of the wealthy for expensive publications.

A second effective means of advertising were the books themselves. In using the book as an advertising medium, readers who might not be reached by any other means could be directly addressed. NKP books usually included selected or complete lists of titles available in a given language; at a later stage they often also contained blurbs for other topic-related titles. Accompanying these lists were special notices instructing the reader on how to order books from the press.

Given the sophisticated organization of the NKP, where several departments dealt exclusively with marketing and distribution, it is no

Announcement

On account of it being a new version[58] and a first edition and in accordance with Act XX of 18[4]7,[59] an entry of this book has been made in the Government Registry Book. Without permission by the undersigned proprietor of the press no one shall attempt to publish it.

The Undersigned

Naval Kishore, Press Proprietor

This book can be purchased by customers at the locations listed below:

Address & Location	Name of Town	Address & Location	Name of Town
Maulvi ᶜAli Yar Khan and Maulvi Hidayat Yar Khan	Bareilly	Munshi Naval Kishore Press	Lucknow
Hafiz Muhammad Amir, *koṭhī* Munshi Naval Kishore Press	Faizabad	Munshi Naval Kishore Press	Kanpur
Maulvi Mahbub Ahmad, manager, Munshi Naval Kishore Press	Gorakhpur	Nizami Press	*ditto*
Maulvi Ishfaq Rasul	*ditto*	Mirza Muhammad ᶜAli Beg	Agra
Maulvi ᶜAbdul Qadir Sarai Pachchim Darvaza	Patna	Muhammad Machu Khan, manager Ilahi Press	*ditto*
Maulvi ᶜAbdul Hamid, *gomashta*, Nizami Press	*ditto*	Nisar ᶜAli, superintendent, *koṭhī* Munshi Naval Kishore Press	Delhi
Koṭhī Munshi Naval Kishore bookshop, Maulvi Nazim ᶜAli Khan	Muzaffarpur	Maulvi ᶜAbdullah, *koṭhī* Munshi Naval Kishore Press	Lahore
Muhammad Bashir	Monghyr	Maulvi ᶜAli Yar Khan and Maulvi Hidayat Yar Khan	Muradabad
Maulvi Vilayat Husain, *muhalla* Amratala	Calcutta		

[58] I.e. an Urdu version of a Hindi reworking of the text by Maulvi ᶜAli Hasan.

[59] Due to a copyist's mistake, the original Urdu text gives a wrong date, notably 1817. The reference, however, is clearly to the Indian Copyright Act (XX of 1847).

surprise that a publisher of Naval Kishore's means was constantly concerned with developing more effective marketing strategies. Indeed, he was among the first Indian publishers to bring out his own book list (*fihrist-e kutub*). Regularly compiled by skilled calligraphers, this catalogue was distributed to wholesale traders, retailers, and, on request, to private customers, as well.[60] An important means of addressing both professionals of the book trade and the general reading public on a supra-regional level, the catalogue not only gave an overview of the firm's publications but also included additional information of mercantile and general nature. It was, for one, a means of soliciting manuscripts. Readers and writers were invited to bring to the notice of the press any literary composition or compilation deemed worthy of publication, whether old or new. Invoking India's great cultural diversity, the 1874 catalogue encouraged readers from different parts of the country to 'enlighten the publishing house on the state of the arts and sciences in their region of origin' (*Fihrist* 1874: 4–5). Furthermore, readers were informed that provisions for the translation of books into Hindi and Urdu had been made at several NKP branches, and applications were invited from competent individuals for the post of translators from English, Arabic, Persian, and Sanskrit. Authors wanting their works printed for non-commercial purposes were offered full coverage of the costs involved in printing and distribution against the payment of what was termed 'a contributory sum'. By contrast, authors of scientific, scholarly, or legal works designed for textbook use were asked to transfer their copyright to the NKP. Further agreements would be reached once the book was accepted by the [Textbook?] 'Committee'. In the name of preserving and diffusing useful knowledge, the firm made a special request to bibliophiles, asking them to notify the NKP of the contents of their private libraries and submit old and rare manuscripts for publication. In return, they were promised complimentary copies of the printed volume and the safe return of their manuscripts (*Fihrist* 1879: 3). This seems to have been little incentive for collectors to part with their prized possessions, and indeed most of the time such transactions involved substantial payment on the publisher's part.

A comparison between the NKP's 1874 and 1879 catalogues indicates the rapid expansion and diversification of its programme within a

[60] Two such catalogues, of 1874 and 1879, are preserved in the OIOC (*Fihrist* 1874, 1879).

relatively short time span. With more than a hundred different categories, the 1879 classified catalogue gives us an accurate idea of the wide variety of fictional and non-fictional literature in various languages produced by the firm.

Also included in the 1879 catalogue was a list of book dealers from whom NKP titles could be purchased. Reproduced in Table 3.2 below, it reflects the expansion of the firm's sales network to various parts of India and even to the metropolis. The House of Naval Kishore, in its turn, acted as a distributing agent for several smaller printing firms of Lucknow, Kanpur, Delhi, and Meerut. This is borne out by a substantial number of non-NKP titles included in the catalogue.

The 1879 catalogue also contained on its front pages various notifications in which conditions for the printing and purchase of books, terms of payment, modes of dispatch, etc., were laid down. Preceding them was the publisher's solemn declaration that he did not look to personal profit but was intent on the promotion of the arts and sciences among literate audiences. In keeping with this objective, book prices were kept at a minimum and only the lowest rates had been entered in the catalogue.

Since fixed prices obtained for educational books, they were excluded from discounts or commissions. For most other titles, retailing agents were offered standard commissions ranging from ten per cent for orders worth up to Rs 50 to twenty per cent for orders exceeding Rs 100. Interestingly, a special incentive was given to promote the sale of books in Sanskrit and Hindi. Purchasers who bought Sanskrit and Hindi books worth Rs 100 in cash received additional books worth Rs 25 free of charge. Different conditions obtained for wholesale traders, who were given discounts for bulk orders. These were generally subject to negotiation. The system was known as *ajzā qīmat* or 'price by sheet' (*juz*, pl. *ajzā*), since discounts were fixed according to the number of unbound sheets bought (1 sheet = 2 *juz*).

While wholesale traders usually acquired books directly from the NKP's various sales agencies, retailers and private customers often lived too far away from the big towns to frequent these sites. Large numbers of books were ordered by correspondence and dispatched by book post or rail. Distribution thus heavily relied on the colonial postal and transport system, whose role in the functioning and expansion of the commercial book trade can hardly be overstated. According to an estimate given by Naval Kishore in 1870, the average number of communications

NKP Classified Catalogue of 1879

Legal Publications

Urdu
Nagari
Kaithi script
Urdu; Kaithi Mahajani script
English

Books of the Education Department

Urdu
Persian
Arabic
Sanskrit
Nagari and Kaithi
English

Books in Arabic

Qur'an in book form and in miniature editions
Selections from the Qur'an
Exegesis
Hadith
Jurisprudence
Principles of jurisprudence
Rhetoric
Theology
Inheritance law
Miscellaneous religious works
Lexicography
History
Ethics
Medicine
Philosophy
Literature
Rhetoric
Logic
Religious disputation
Grammar and syntax

Books in Persian

Exegesis
Hadith
Jurisprudence
Theology
Miscellaneous religious works
Religious disputes Sunni and Shiʿa
Ethics and Sufism
Rare collections of scholarly works
Geomancy
Kulliyāt, dīvān, qaṣā'id
Taẕkirah
Didactic tales in prose and verse
Lexicography
Medicine
Medical dictionaries
Biographies of saints and prophets
Histories of emperors
Persian grammar
Turkish grammar
Prosody and rhyme
Textbooks/primers
Hindu religion

Books in Urdu

Textbooks/primers
Grammar and syntax
Prosody and rhyme
Calligraphy
Letter-writing
Arithmetic and geometry
Logic
Histories of prophets
History of kings etc.
Human medicine
Veterinary medicine
Medical dictionaries
General dictionaries
Female education
Ethics and Sufism
Kulliyāt, dīvān
Maṡnavī
Wāsokht
Taẕkirah
Rare collections
Music
Astrology
Tales (prose and verse)

Books on Islam (Urdu)

Exegesis
Hadith
Sunni jurisprudence
Shiʿa jurisprudence
Miscellaneous religious works

Books on Hindu Religion

(Urdu)
Publications of the Office of the Kayasth Samacar, Allahabad

Books in Hindi

(in Nagari script)
Epics
Purāṇas
Vedanta
Poetry
Music
Tales, etc.
Medicine
Astrology
Miscellaneous
Textbooks/primers

Books in Sanskrit

Grammar, Dharmshastra, etc.
Astrology
(Sanskrit with Urdu transl.)
(Sanskrit with Hindi transl.)

Books in English

Textbooks/primers
History
Tales/Narrative
Dictionaries
Miscellaneous

Various Maps

Maps of India
Maps of Arabia and the Near East
Asia, Africa, America
Avadh, small and large
Maps of the Turco-Russian war, etc.

TABLE 3.2
The NKP's Sales Network in 1879

	City	Name of Bookdealer	Location
1.	Calcutta	Shaikh Vilayat Husain, bookdealer	Sundaryapati
2.	Calcutta	Maulvi Muhammad Kamil, bookdealer	Taltala Bazar
3.	Calcutta	Miyam Ahmadullah, bookdealer	Wellesley Street No. 9, near Madrasa ᶜAliya
4.	Calcutta	Shaikh Nasiruddin, bookdealer	Wellesley Street No. 84, Rahmani Press
5.	Calcutta	Miyam Rahmatullah, bookdealer	Dharmtala Daftaripati
6.	Patna	Maulvi ᶜAbdul Ghaffur, bookdealer	Korth [?]
7.	Bombay	Qazi Fateh Muhammad and Qazi Salih Muhammad Brothers	
8.	Bombay	The late Haji Muhammad Ibrahim, bookdealer	Bhendi Bazar
9.	Bombay	Mullah Nuruddin, bookdealer	Bhendi Bazar
10.	Allahabad	Headmaster Kayasth Pathshala	Bahadurganj
11.	Kanpur	The Manager, Naval Kishore Press	Sarsaiya Ghat
12.	Kanpur	Nizami Press	Patkapur
13.	Moradabad	Maulvi Haji Hidayat Yar Khan, bookdealer	Chauk Bazar
14.	Bareilly	Maulvi Haji ᶜAli Yar Khan, bookdealer	Katra Manrai
15.	Delhi	Agent, Naval Kishore Press Bookshop	Dariba Kalan
16.	Lahore	Miyam Chiraghuddin, bookdealer	Kashmiri Bazar
17.	Patiala	Agent, Naval Kishore Press	
18.	London	Trubner Company [*sic*]	Ludgate Hill

addressed to the NKP each year was an astounding 25,000 letters.[61] In light of this it is no coincidence that the firm's Lucknow warehouse and head office were situated adjacent to the General Post Office.[62]

Payment for book orders was strictly in advance. It was effected in cash, by money order, bill of exchange, or cheque. Smaller amounts could also be paid in stamps. Customers were urged to insure and register their cash payments if remitted by mail. They were also asked to abstain from sending telegrams or unstamped letters to the NKP. All

[61] *Avadh Akhbār*, 19 April 1870, cited in Siddiqi 1980: 50.

[62] Urdu sources generally claim that the post office was established with the express purpose of meeting the NKP's needs.

communications were to include postal stamps for the firm's reply. Given the surge of letters that reached the firm each year, it proclaimed itself unable to cover the expenses involved in postage. Equally, all dispatch costs were to be met by the customer.

In including various advertisements for stationary and general merchandise, the 1879 list reveals the full extent and diversity of the NKP's trading activities. As a bookseller, Naval Kishore was also a stationer dealing in pens and ink; his firm sold cloth for bookbinding in various colours and different kinds of paper imported from London's famous John Dickinson Company and the German firm of Ullmann, Hirschhorn & Co. Lithographic stones imported from England and types of Nagari founts were advertised alongside popular patent medicines (*Fihrist* 1879: 122–3). The NKP had been appointed sole distributor for the 'celebrated medicines' of one Dr De Roos, which were extensively advertised in *Avadh Akhbār* and sold exclusively on the premises of the press. More surprisingly, Naval Kishore also acted as a broker for several Lucknow-based general merchants. Advertised in the 1879 catalogue was a great variety of general merchandise, including household ware, perfume, drapery, and haberdashery. All these items could be ordered through the NKP's Lucknow agents against remittance of advance payment in cash and a brokerage fee. With brokerage rates ranging from 1 anna per rupee for small orders of less than Rs 100 to half an anna per rupee for orders valued at Rs 250 to 1000, and to a standard two per cent for bulk orders exceeding Rs 1000, the publisher had opened up another attractive sideline for himself (*Fihrist* 1879: 3).

By the 1880s the firm apparently boasted a substantial clientele of European customers. According to the testimony of John Hurst, in the mid-1880s Munshi Naval Kishore issued a comprehensive English version of his catalogue, which listed almost 2500 titles on more than eighty-eight pages and was supplemented by an alphabetical index of another twenty pages. Hurst presumed it to be 'the first time Kishore has given full publicity to the Anglo-Indian world of the issues from his press' (Hurst 1887: 354). While I could not trace this English catalogue, its existence raises the question of the extent of British expatriate and metropolitan consumption of oriental literature.

Diversity was key to commercial publishing. Consistent with its other marketing practices, the NKP tried to induce readers to buy books through a variegated selection of titles that would appeal to individual preferences. Religious classics were issued in various formats, suiting the financial means and intellectual demands of an increasingly heterogeneous readership. The Holy Qur'an, for example, was made available in as many as

19 different editions, meant to suit every pocket and every degree of theological sophistication. A Hindi classic such as the *Rāmāyaṇ* of Tulsidas was offered in plain and illustrated, hardcover (*kitābnumā*) and paperback (*patranumā*) editions, with or without annotations. The firm's abridged and illustrated pocket *Rāmāyāṇ* as well as its 1882 edition in 'very large letters', designed especially 'for children and the elderly', were proudly advertised as the only editions of their kind. A publisher's notice in the large-letter *Rāmāyaṇ* extolled the efforts of its calligrapher Pandit Murlidhar, a Gujarati Brahmin of Agra, who was said to have spent several years of intense labour in copying out the text in large and pleasant letters, 'so that the aged devotees of Hari, too, could read it without difficulty.' To be able to react to the variegated demands of the marketplace had indeed become the hallmark of a successful publisher.

3.5 Author–Publisher Relations

The four great figures in the creation of the nineteenth-century Urdu novel—Nazir Ahmad, Ratan Nath 'Sarshar', ʿAbdul Halim Sharar, and Mirza Hadi Rusva—were each in one way or the other connected with the House of Naval Kishore. Nazir Ahmad published his masterpiece *Mirāt al-ʿarūs* with the NKP. Ratan Nath 'Sarshar' served in the firm's Trans-lation Department and as an editor of *Avadh Akhbār*, in which his novel *Fasāna-e Āzād* was first serialized to wide popular acclaim. ʿAbdul Halim Sharar also served on the paper's editorial board. Rusva, in 1899, immortalized the NKP in his celebrated tale of a Lucknow courtesan, *Umraʾo Jān Adā.*

As noted earlier, in the absence of publisher's records frustratingly little is known about Naval Kishore's dealings with writers, the agreements he entered into with contemporary authors, and the terms of their contracts. Information on this fundamental aspect of the publisher's activities is largely confined to some particularly famous cases and only comes piecemeal. For the time being, it cannot even be said what kind of author–publisher contract was most commonly in use at the House of Naval Kishore. If metropolitan models are a measure to go by, the general practice among authors and publishers in the latter half of the nineteenth century was to enter into one of the following forms of agreement:

(a) Outright sale of copyright to the publisher for an agreed amount
(b) Assignment of copyright for one edition or for a specified period, after which it reverted to the author
(c) Profit-sharing, usually in the form of a half-profit arrangement
(d) Payment of royalty to author on sales
(e) Publication at author's expense and risk. (Allen 1897: 17)

The last form, which implied the least risk for the publisher—not even royalties were payable and the author bore all expenses— was usually limited to new authors, whose commercial value was unpredictable. Outright sale of copyright was one of the simplest forms of contract: in England it had remained the most common form throughout the eighteenth century and well into the nineteenth (Patten 1978: 22).[63] In the absence of original contracts, our principal source of information for the period up to 1880 is a list of NKP copyrights included in the firm's 1879 book catalogue (Table 3.3). It contains 125 titles, plus an extra 25 copyrights of textbooks. Since however, the list is incomplete, the actual number of copyrights acquired by the firm over time must have been higher. Over one-third of the copyrights related to the firm's own translations, which usually involved high expenses and had to be properly safeguarded against piracy. A good proportion of original works registered in Naval Kishore's name were by authors employed by the NKP, others were by minor authors. By contrast, but for a few exceptions, famous names in contemporary Urdu or Hindi literature are conspicuously absent from the list. This may be taken as an indication that established authors of repute were reluctant to part with their copyrights and instead opted for some other form of contract. It is significant that, by this time, Naval Kishore had the collected poetry (*kulliyāt, dīvān*) of over fifty Urdu poets on his list, including some famous contemporary names such as Ghalib, Bahadur Shah 'Zafar', and ʿAbdul Ghafur Khan 'Nassakh'. Yet the NKP only owned four copyrights, namely that of the divans of Nassakh and of three minor Lucknow poets, Amir, Wasti, and ʿAshiq.

Perhaps the earliest known instance of an eminent Urdu literary figure ceding his copyright to the NKP is that of Mirza Rajab ʿAli Beg 'Surur' (1787–1867), the author of the famous prose romance *Fasāna-e ʿajāʾib* (A Tale of Wonders) and himself a native of Lucknow. Sometime in the 1860s, during what must have been one of his many episodes of financial distress, Rajab ʿAli Beg sold the copyright of his collected letters *Inshā-e Surūr* and of *Fasāna-e ʿajāʾib*, by then a decidedly popular work, to Naval Kishore. A second prominent name is that of the poet, literary critic and *tazkirah* writer ʿAbdul Ghafur Khan 'Nassakh' (1834–89), a leading representative of the Bengali Muslim intelligentsia, who is sometimes called the doyen of Urdu poetry in Bengal. Precisely why Nassakh chose to publish with Naval Kishore and sell him the copyright of his collected Urdu poetry is not known, but can certainly be taken as an

[63] See ibid.: 22–7 for other common forms of contracts.

TABLE 3.3

Copyrights Owned by the NKP in 1879[64]

No.	Title of Copyrighted Work	Author/Translator
1	*Sharḥ-e Taᶜzīrāt-e Hind*	Sayyid Ghulam Haidar
2	*Makhzan al-naẓāʾir*	Maulvi ᶜAbdul Qayyum
3	*Amān al-lughāt*	Maulvi M. Aman al-Haq
4	*Tafsīr-e Qādirī*, Urdu trs. of *Tafsīr-e Ḥusainī*	Maulvi Fakhruddin, trs.
5	*Majmūᶜah-e aurād mustanadah Muḥashshā-e khāristān*	Mullah Majruddin Khani
6	*Sharḥ-e Maṣnavī-e Maulāna-e Rūm*	ᶜAbdul ᶜAli Muhammad 'Bahr al-ᶜUlum'
7	*Ḥāshia-e kitāb-e Iᶜjāz-e khusravī*	
8	*Inshā-e asrār-e frīmesan*	
9	*Maṭlaᶜ al-ᶜulūm va Makhzan al-funūn*	Wajid ᶜAli Khan
10	*Sharḥ-e Kulliyāt-e khāqānī*	Muhammad Sadiq ᶜAli
11	*Maṣnavī Sumbulistān*	
12	*Farhang-e Sikandarnāma*	Mir Ibn Hasan
13	*Inshā-e Ṣafdarī*	Mufti Ghulam Safdar
Urdu Titles		
14	*Naẓm-e parvīn*	Debi Parshad
15	*Inshā-e Surūr*	Rajab ᶜAli Beg 'Surur'
16	*Shams al-ẓuḥā*	
17	*Futūḥāt-e Wāqidī*, Urdu trs.	Maulvi Basharat ᶜAli Khan and Sayyid Mehdi Husain, trs.
18	*Taẕkirat al-khulafā manẓūm*, verse trs. of *Futūḥāt-e Wāqidī*	Hakim Amanat ᶜAli, trs.
19	*Annals and Antiquities of Rajasthan*, Urdu trs.	Pandit Ajodhya Parshad and Pandit Kanhaiyalal, trs.
20	*Ṣaulat-e Afghānī*	Haji Muhammad Zardar Khan
21	*Futūḥāt-e Hind*	ᶜInayat Husain
22	*Tārīkh-e ṭilism-e Hind*	Totaram 'Shayan', trs.
23	*Tārīkh-e ᶜahdnāmajāt va iqrārnāmajāt*, Urdu trs.	Pandit Kanhaiyalal, trs.
24	Government Gazetteers, 7 vols	

[64] Not including copyrights of school textbooks.

TABLE 3.3 (*contd.*)

No.	Title of Copyrighted Work	Author/Translator
25	*Tārīkh-e Bonapārt Napolyan*, Urdu trs.	
26	*Tārīkh-e baghāvat-e Hind*, Urdu trs.	Pandit Kanhaiyalal, trs.
27	*Muqaddama-e kamīshan Baroda*, Urdu and Hindi trs.	Pandit Pyarelal, trs.
28	*Tārīkh-e rājparsastī*	Debi Parshad, trs.
29	*Mirāt al-salāṭīn*, Urdu trs. of *Siyar al-mutaʾakhkhirīn*	Gokul Parshad, trs.
30	*Mukhtaṣar-e Sair-e gulshan-e Hind*	Baburam, *raʾīs* of Kanpur
31	*Bahāristān* also called *Gulzārshāhī*	Ghulam Sarvar Lahori
32	*Kārnāma navāʾın*	Debi Parshad
33	*Wāqīʿāt-e panj-hazār sālah*	Radhelal, *raʾīs* of Mohan
34	*Makhzan-e ḥikmat*	Ghulam Sarvar Lahori
35	*Tārīkh-e makhzan-e Panjāb*	Ghulam Sarvar Lahori
36	*Sarod-e ghaibī*	Sayyid Muhammad ʿAli Choya
37	*Ilāj al-ghurabā*, Urdu trs.	Ghulam Imam
38	*Ṭibb-e Akbar*, Urdu trs.	Hakim Muhammad Husain Nanautawi, trs.
39	*Qarābādīn-e Shifāʾī*, Urdu trs.	Hakim Muhammad Hadi Husain Khan, trs.
40	*Qarābādīn-e Zakāʾī*, Urdu trs.	Hakim Muhammad Hadi Husain Khan, trs.
41	*Mujarrabāt-e Akbarī*, Urdu trs.	Hakim Vajid ʿAli Mohani, trs.
42	*Muʿālajāt-e Iḥsānī*	Hakim Ihsan ʿAli
43	*Murrakkabāt-e Iḥsānī*	Hakim Ihsan ʿAli
44	*Ilāj-e Iḥsānī*	Hakim Ihsan ʿAli
45	*Maqālāt-e Iḥsānī*	Hakim Ihsan ʿAli
46	*ʿIlāj al-amrāẓ*	Hakim Muhammad Hadi Husain Khan, trs.
47	*Iksīr al-qulūb*, Urdu trs. of *Mufarriḥ al-qulūb*	Hakim Muhammad Nur Karim, trs.
48	*Kīmiyā-e ʿanāṣirī*, Urdu trs. of *Qārabādīn-e Qādirī*	Hakim Muhammad Nur Karim, trs
49	*Majmaʿ al-baḥrain ṭibb-e yūnānī va angrezī*	Hakim Muhammad Haidar Khan
50	*Zakhīrah-e khvarāzmshāhī*, Urdu trs.	Hakim Muhammad Hadi Husain Khan, trs.
51	*Amritsāgar*, Urdu trs.	Pandit Pyarelal, trs.
52	*Makhzan al-adviyah*, Urdu trs.	Hakim Muhammad Nur Karim, trs.
53	*Lughāt-e Sarvarī*	Ghulam Sarvar Lahori

TABLE 3.3 (*contd.*)

No.	Title of Copyrighted Work	Author/Translator
54	*Arbaᶜ-e ᶜanāṣir*	Muhammad Nasir ᶜAli
55	*Qiṣṣa-e gulāb camelī*	Raja Shiva Prasad
56	*Nikāt-e Iḥsānī*	Hakim Ihsan ᶜAli
57	*Tahẕīb-e Iḥsānī*	Hakim Ihsan ᶜAli
58	*Akhlāq-e Sarvarī*	Ghulam Sarvar Lahori
59	*Rahbar-e rāh-e ḥaqq*	Muhammad Zardar Khan
60	*Kulliyāt-e Nassākh*	ᶜAbdul Ghafur Khan 'Nassakh'
61	*Dīvān-e Amīr*	Amir Ahmad 'Amir'
62	*Dīvān-e Wāsṭī*	Sayyid Fazl Rasul Khan 'Wasti'
63	*Divān-e ᶜĀshiq*	Pandit Kanhaiyalal 'Ashiq'
64	*Maṡnavī Saᶜdain*	Anvar Husain 'Taslim'
65	*Maṡnavī Mirāt al-mashriqain*	Hakim ᶜInayat Husain Dehlavi
66	*Majmūᶜah-e wāsokhthā*	(collection of *wāsokht*)
67	*Sarāpā-e sukhan*	Sayyid Muhsin ᶜAli (comp.)
68	*Taẕkirah-e Gulshan naghma-e ᶜandalīb*	Hakim Qutbuddin Khan Dehlavi
69	*ᶜAjāʾib al-makhlūqāt*, Urdu trs.	Gokul Parshad, trs.
70	*Maṭlaᶜ al-ᶜulūm va Makhzan al-funūn*, Urdu trs.	Zain al-ᶜAbidin, trs.
71	*Maṭlaᶜ al-majāʾib*, Urdu trs. of *Maᶜlūmāt al-ᶜāfāq*	Mehdi ᶜAli Khan, trs.
72	*Ḥirz-e Sulaimānī*	Khvaja Ashraf ᶜAli
73	*Nāfaᶜ-e khalāʾiq*	Muhammad Zardar Khan
74	*Ṭilism-e ruḥanī*	Maulvi Husain Ahmad
75	*Indarjāl*, Urdu trs.	Lala Svamidayal, trs.
76	*Qānūn-e sitār*	Sayyid Safdar Husain Khan
77	*Ghuncah-e rāg*	Nizam ud Daula Navab Muhammad Mardan ᶜAli Khan
78	*Alif-Laila*, Urdu trs.	Totaram 'Shayan', trs.
79	*Alif-Laila manẓūm*	Totaram 'Shayan'
80	*Fasāna-e ᶜajāʾib*	Rajab ᶜAli Beg 'Surur'
81	*Sarosh-e Sukhan*	Sayyid Fakhruddin Husain 'Sukhan'
82	*Ṭilism-e ḥairat*	Maulvi Hamid ᶜAli Shevan
83	*Ṭilism-e faṣāḥat*	Muhammad Husain Jah
84	*Waqāʾi-e rājkumār*, Urdu trs. of *Durgeshnandinī*	Kumvar Jagat Singh, trs.
85	*Fasāna-e maᶜqūl*	Sayyid Ghulam Haidar Khan

TABLE 3.3 (*contd.*)

No.	Title of Copyrighted Work	Author/Translator
86	*Āʾīn-e ʿuqūl*	Sayyid Ghulam Haidar Khan
87	*Jāda-e taskhīr*	Navab Muhammad Haidar ʿAli Khan
88	*Jogannāma*	Batin Akbarabadi
89	*Qiṣṣa maqtūl jafā*	Muhammad Amiruddin
90	*Sikandarnāma*, Urdu trs.	Maulvi Haidar ʿAli Khan Bilgrami, trs.
91	*Nāla-e Manẓūr manẓūm*	Maulvi Sayyid Manzur Ahmad
92	*Maṣnavī bāgh-e ʿāshiq*	Pandit Kanhaiyalal 'Ashiq'
93	*Iksīr-e hidāyat*, Urdu trs. of *Kīmiyā-e saʿādat*	Fakhruddin 'Fakhr', trs.
94	*Durr-e mukhtār*, Urdu trs.	Muhammad Khurram ʿAli and Muhammad Ahsan Nanautawi, trs.
95	*Kanz al-daqāʾiq*, Urdu trs.	Muhammad Sujan Khan, trs.
96	*Davāzdah majlis*	Maulvi Vahiduddin Muhammad Rizvi
97	*Asrār-e Karbalā*	Muhammad Zahiruddin Bilgrami
98	*Mazāq al-ʿārifin*, Urdu trs. of *Iḥyā ʿulūm al-dīn*	Maulvi Basharat ʿAli Khan, trs.
99	*Sirāj al-sālikīn*, Urdu trs. of *Minhāj al-ʿābidīn*	Maulvi Munir, trs.
100	*Guldasta-e karāmat*	Ghulam Sarvar Lahori
101	*Minhāj al-nubūwat*, Urdu trs. of *Mādārij al-nubūwat*	Khvaja ʿAbdul Majid, trs.
102	*Tazkirat al-shuʿarā manẓūm*	
103	*Asrār-e ghaflat*	Muhammad Zahiruddin Bilgrami
104	*Qānūn-e Shaikh bū ʿAli Sinā*, Urdu trs.	Ghulam Hasnain 'Allamah Kinturi, trs.
105	*Sharḥ-e qānūn-e muʿāhada*, Urdu trs. of Act IX of 1872	Muhammad ʿAbdul Qayyum Khan, trs.
106	*Sukhsāgar*, Urdu trs.	Makkhanlal
107	*Bhāgvat manẓūm-e Khushtar Lakhnavī*	Jagannath Sahai 'Khushtar'
108	*Rāmāyan manẓūm-e Khushtar*	Jagannath Sahai 'Khushtar'
109	*Mahābhārat manẓūm*	Totaram 'Shayan'
110	*Rāmāyan manẓūm*	Shankardayal 'Farhat'
111	*Premsāgar*, Urdu trs.	Lala Svamidayal, trs.
112	*Bhaktamāl*	Raja Pratap Singh
113	*Bahār-e Bindrāban*	Acarya Bindraban
114	*Samar-e bahār-e Bindrāban*	Acarya Bindraban
115	*Gyānsāgar*	Girdhari Lal Sahranpuri
116	*Kāyasthdharmdarpan*	Ramcaran

TABLE 3.3 (*contd.*)

No.	Title of Copyrighted Work	Author/Translator
117	*Yogavāsiṣṭha*, Hindi trs.	Pandit Kanhaiyalal, trs.
118	*Hātim Ṭāi*, Hindi trs.	Jivanram Jat, trs.
119	*Alif Laila*, Hindi trs.	Pandit Pyarelal, trs.
120	*Amṛtsāgar*, Hindi trs.	Pandit Kalicaran, trs.
121	*Amarkoś*, Hindi trs.	Mahesh Datt Shukla, trs.
122	*Vratārk*, Hindi trs.	Mahesh Datt Shukla, trs.
123	*Dāstān-e Amīr Hamza*, Hindi trs.	Pandit Kalicaran, trs.
124	*Strī darpan*	Madhav Prasad
125	*Fasāna-e ʿajāʾib*, Hindi trs.	Pandit Ramratan Vajpeyi, trs.

SOURCE: *Fihrist* 1879.

indication of the publisher's widespread reputation in Urdu literature which reached as far as Bengal. The two men knew each other personally: Nassakh, a Deputy Magistrate in the British administrative service, had met Naval Kishore during a visit to Lucknow in 1867.[65] The most important work included in the *Kulliyāt-e Nassākh* (*1874) was *Sukhan-e shuʿarā* (Discourse of the Poets), a large anthology of almost 900 poets, compiled by the poet over a period of twelve years and completed in 1864–5. The publication in 1874 of this understudied work was a considerable step forward in establishing the canon of contemporary Urdu poets. Garcin de Tassy deemed it of such importance that he reprinted the full list of poets in an appendix to his *Discours* of 1876.[66]

Perhaps one of the best sources on author–publisher relations in nineteenth-century Urdu literature, which also offers some insight into what could go wrong in seeing a work into print, is the extensive correspondence of Mirza Asadullah Khan Ghalib (1797–1869). While most of the original correspondence between Naval Kishore and Ghalib is lost, the poet's letters to other correspondents allow us to reconstruct at least some aspects of their relationship. Even if Ghalib's case is special, involving as it did the most prominent of contemporary Urdu poets, some generalizations may be drawn from it regarding the way in which Naval Kishore interacted with his authors.

By the time Ghalib and Naval Kishore established personal contact in the early 1860s, the great poet had undergone various troublesome

[65] Nassakh mentions his acquaintance with the publisher in his autobiography, *Khudnavisht savāniḥ-e ḥayāt-e Nassākh* (Abdus Subhan 1986: 96).

[66] For a discussion of important Urdu *tazkirahs* of the nineteenth century, see Pritchett 2003.

experiences in his dealings with editors and publishers, which had left him wary. The publication of his Persian prose work *Panj āhang* had been disappointing. Of the two printed versions, Ghalib found one 'defective' and the other abounding in mistakes. As he complained to a friend: 'The copyist made "corrections" in my prose of which only my heart can tell. Were I to tell you that no line is free of mistakes, I should be pitching it too high. But I can say without exaggeration that no page is free of mistakes' (Russell/Islam 1994: 266). The ensuing publication of his Urdu divan turned out to be even more vexing, involving a series of mishaps. Initially, Ghalib had somewhat rashly entrusted the manuscript to a nondescript publisher of Meerut and had experienced great difficulty in retrieving it.[67] Having wrested the divan 'from the hands of that unjust usurper', he decided to commit it to the press of his friend Munshi Shivnarayan at Agra, but for some reason changed his mind and instead gave it to the Delhi-based Ahmadi Press—a mistake he was soon to regret.

Meanwhile, in early 1860 Naval Kishore approached Ghalib regarding publication of his collected Persian works. While the publisher's initial letter has not survived, it is significant to note that it was he who took the initiative in contacting the poet, and not vice versa. Ghalib replied on 18 July 1860, in a letter written in Persian, indicating that his three published Persian prose works—*Panj āhang*, *Mihr-e nīmrūz*, and *Dastanbū*—were available for reprint. He also promised to supply the publisher with a few recently composed Persian *ghazal*s. As a subsequent letter to Nawab Ziyauddin Ahmad Khan reveals, Naval Kishore's suggestion had put the poet in a spot, for he was not in possession of a single manuscript of his Persian poems and had to urge his correspondent to part with his copy, so that it could be forwarded to the publisher. Throughout 1861, negotiations for having the Persian verse printed were under way. What may have finally convinced Ghalib to turn away from his previous publishers and entrust the Persian *Kulliyāt* to the upcoming Lucknow publisher was his dismay at receiving an utterly defective volume of his Urdu divan, newly released from the Ahmadi Press in August 1861. Ghalib was appalled and seems to have instantly regretted not having entrusted his divan, too, to the NKP. 'Alas!' he wrote to a friend. 'When the Lucknow press prints a man's diwan, it raises him to heaven. The

[67] On 11 June 1860 Ghalib wrote to a friend: 'That fellow who asked me for my *Dīvān* is not even an acquaintance. . . . He is not a human being but a ghost, a demon! Nasty and foul! . . . So, I am now asking him to return my *Dīvān*. He refuses to give it back. I hope to God that I can retrieve it. You too pray' (Rahbar 1987: 237).

calligraphy is so good that every word shines radiant! May Delhi and its water and its press be accursed!'[68] Meanwhile, he considered his ties with Naval Kishore close and amicable enough to commend his unemployed *shāgird* Mir Ghulam Hasnain 'Qadr' Bilgrami to the publisher. Armed with Ghalib's letter of introduction, Qadr Bilgrami set out for Lucknow and was promptly given employment in the firm's editorial office. (He was to remain with the NKP for some time, despite his repeated complaints to Ghalib about his low salary.)

By the beginning of 1862, the manuscript of Ghalib's collected Persian verse was lying with the NKP. Moreover, the poet had decided to entrust the firm with the publication of his *Qāṭiᶜ-e Burhān*, a sharply worded critique of the Persian dictionary *Burhān-e qāṭiᶜ*, which was to spark off a fierce controversy on publication (see Chapter 5). For a young publisher like Naval Kishore it was a matter of great prestige to have a literary figure of Ghalib's standing on his list. The announcement of the two forthcoming titles was given due prominence on the front-page of *Avadh Akhbār* of 1 January 1862. Advance subscriptions for the *Kulliyāt* were called for, offering readers a special subscription rate of Rs 3, *as* 4, as against the later sales price of Rs 5.[69] *Qāṭiᶜ-e Burhān* was released in March 1862. 'The printing of *Qāte i Burhan* is finished, and I have received one copy which is the author's right', Ghalib informed his friend ᶜAlaʾi on 19 June 1862. 'Other volumes I have ordered as a customer and the order is with the publishers. But they can't be sent until I've paid for them. I am trying to raise the money. If I manage it, I'll send it off' (Russell/Islam 1994: 272). The order referred to by Ghalib involved fifty copies of the *Qāṭiᶜ-e Burhān* which he meant to distribute among his friends and well-wishers. The money seems to have come forward soon afterwards, for in the same month Ghalib made it known that the 'entire stock of the bound copies of *Qāṭiᶜ-e Burhān*' was now in his possession and that he had purchased it according to the terms of his contract (Rahbar 1987: 252).

Things went less smoothly with the Persian *Kulliyāt* which, although announced at the beginning of the year, was not forthcoming. On 5 May 1862 Ghalib wrote to Qadr Bilgrami to enquire about the status of printing and raise a number of questions concerning the insertion of the customary odes and chronograms. Apparently Ghalib had been requested to compose

[68] For a full wording of the letter in which Ghalib complains bitterly about the sloppiness of both copyist and publisher, see Russell/Islam 1994: 259.

[69] The announcement for *Kulliyāt* was in Urdu, that of *Qāṭiᶜ-e Burhān* in Persian. Both are reprinted in Naqwi 1980: 116–17.

the customary chronogram indicating the date of printing of his *Kulliyāt*, for in a subsequent letter to Qadr Bilgrami he refused to comply, maintaining that it could be done by 'the people at the press'. From Qadr Bilgrami's reply he learnt that the printing of the *Kulliyāt* had been postponed: the book's calligrapher had gone on leave and, to make matters worse, its proofreader Maulvi Hadi ᶜAli had been taken seriously ill. Ghalib was particularly impatient to see his collected Persian verse in print, since his own health at the time was rapidly deteriorating. He expressed his growing anxiety in June 1862: 'I cannot see the printing of the collected verse being finished during my life-time' (Russell/Islam 1994: 272). With the *Kulliyāt*'s publication delayed by another year, his patience was put to the test. The volume was at last ready in June 1863.

It was only in December 1863, when Naval Kishore called on Ghalib during a visit to Delhi, that the two men came face to face for the first time. The meeting left a vivid impression on Ghalib, who seems to have been quite taken by the good looks and agreeable manners of his junior contemporary. Moreover, negotiations with the publisher had turned out in Ghalib's favour. On 3 December 1863 he reported to ᶜAlaʾi:

> My kind and considerate benefactor, that man of kindness incarnate, Munshi Naval Kishor came by the mail. He met me, and your uncle, and your cousin Shihab ud Din Khan. The Creator bestowed upon him the beauty of Venus and the qualities of Jupiter. He is himself the conjunction of two auspicious stars. I hadn't said anything to you, and accepted that ten copies of [my Persian] collected verse cost fifty rupees. But now when I mentioned it to him he agreed to accept the price that had originally been advertised in the newspaper—three rupees, four annas per copy. At this rate ten copies come to thirty-two rupees, eight annas, and thirty-two rupees, eight annas is what you are to pay. In all, sixty-five rupees will have to be sent to the *Avadh Akhbar* Press. I shall be ordering on the 10th or 11th of December—this month. I'll give the thirty-two rupees eight annas to Ali Husain Khan, or I'll send it to Lucknow—whichever you say (Russell/Islam 1994: 293–4).

The passage suggests that Ghalib had sold the copyright of his *Kulliyāt* to the NKP. As we have seen, however, there is no mention of it in the list of copyright works included in the 1879 catalogue.

Naval Kishore published two more works by Ghalib during the poet's lifetime, notably a small booklet entitled *Duᶜā-e subah maᶜ tarjuma-e naṣr va tarjuma-e manẓūm* (*1867), containing Urdu prose and verse renderings of the Islamic morning prayer, and the *Kulliyāt-e naṣr-e Ghālib* (*1868), in which Ghalib's Persian prose works were for the first time assembled in one volume.[70] Further titles followed after the poet's death, including reprints of his collected letters, *ʿŪd-e Hindī* (*1874), and the aforementioned Urdu *Dīvān* (*1877). The latter was reprinted from the Nizami Press edition, which again raises the question of copyright.

Among Ghalib's pupils, a poet who followed his great master in choosing to publish with the NKP was Nawab Mardan ʿAli Khan 'Raʿna' (d. 1879), a *raʾīs* of Muradabad. Raʿna, who also used the pen name 'Nizam', was a prolific poet and historian in Persian and Urdu. Up to 1858 he was employed in the Punjab Revenue Department. He became associated with the NKP in the early 1860s as a frequent contributor to *Avadh Akhbār*. In 1867 he went to Marwar, where he rose to the position of prime minister and became a key figure in cultivating Persian and Urdu literature in the princely state. Naval Kishore published most of his works, including *Ghuncah-e rāg* (*1863), *Navā-e gharīb* (*1863), *Ẓabṭ-e ʿishq* (*1864), and *Muhr-e nubūwat* (*1872). A volume of his collected poetry, *Kulliyāt-e Niẓām*, followed in 1875.[71] On occasion, Mardan ʿAli Khan supplied the publisher with rare manuscripts from his private library, the most famous being a manuscript of the *Dīvān* of Shah Wali Allah Gujarati (1667–1707/8), of which a lithographed edition was published from Lucknow in 1878.

How little is known about author–publisher contracts and the publishing history of even the most famous works of nineteenth-century Urdu literature is exemplified by the case of Maulvi Nazir Ahmad (1831–1912). Nazir Ahmad's association with the house of Naval Kishore dates back to the year 1861, when he was sent to Lucknow to oversee the printing of his Urdu translation of the Indian Penal Code. As Deputy Inspector of Schools, he remained closely associated with the press during the following years. Naval Kishore at the time issued several of his minor writings, including a translation of a British official's account of the 1857 uprising entitled *Muṣāʾib-e ghadr* (The Tribulations of the Rebellion, *1863), which Nazir Ahmad had undertaken at the instance of his superior in the education department, Shiva Prasad (Russell 1992: 114). In later years, the author apparently felt quite embarrassed about his involvement in publicizing this particular work, for he never mentioned it in his writings. Left to him, *Muṣāʾib-e ghadr* probably would not have seen a second edition. However, the copyright of the text lay with Naval Kishore, who

[70] The 1868 lithographed edition comprised 212 pages and was printed in 275 copies. An enlarged version of 422 pages was issued in 1100 copies in 1871.

[71] Raʿna also authored a local history entitled *Tārīkh-e Mārwār*. Further details in Sh. A. Khan 1981: 59; *Avadh Akhbār*, 19 April 1870, cited in Nurani 1995: 54.

can hardly be blamed for trying to cash in on the author's fame when he brought out a second edition in 1896 (Siddiqi 1971: 209).

The year 1869 saw the publication of Nazir Ahmad's famous didactic tale *Mirāt al-ʿarūs* (The Bride's Mirror) for which he received a prize of Rs 1000 under the Allahabad Government Gazette Notification. *Mirāt al-ʿarūs* has rightly been called the first bestseller in Urdu fiction. Three years after its release, it had already sold in almost 10,000 copies.[72] By 1888 the novel had been translated into various languages and had sold over 100,000 copies.[73] When *Mirāt al-ʿarūs* was first brought to official notice in 1869, the government at once ordered 2000 copies with a view to including it in the school syllabus. The author was permitted to retain the copyright 'and make suitable arrangements on his own part for printing it' (Ahmad 2001: 203). Whether it was by Nazir Ahmad's own choice or by order of the educational authorities that the printing commission went to Naval Kishore, cannot be said. *Mirāt al-ʿarūs* was first released in December 1869 in a lithographed edition. The print run was 3100 copies, priced at twelve annas each. The 1879 NKP catalogue carried an entry to the effect that the title had been registered by its author, which however does not reveal anything about the precise terms of the agreement reached between author and publisher. Evidence suggests that Nazir Ahmad may have either sold the copyright to the firm or given it on lease, for the NKP continued to reprint the text, issuing a seventh edition of 15,000 copies in 1894. This, in turn, would mean that other editions of *Mirāt al-ʿarūs* such as the one issued from the Qaisari Press of Bareilly in 1880 were pirated. Indeed, it may safely be assumed that due to their enormous popularity *Mirāt al-ʿarūs* as well as Nazir Ahmad's subsequent novels were subject to large-scale piracy.

For the printing of these subsequent works Nazir Ahmad did not remain with the NKP. Meanwhile transferred to Kanpur, he gave the contract for *Banāt an-naʿsh* (The Daughters of the Bier, 1872), the sequel to *Mirāt al-ʿarūs*, to the local Nizami Press. Two years later his masterpiece *Taubat an-Naṣūḥ* (The Repentance of Nasuh) was issued from the Mufid-e ʿAm Press at Agra in a first lithographed edition of 1600 copies.[74] The existence of simultaneous reprints of *Taubat an-Naṣūḥ* from the Nizami Press and the Mufid-e ʿAm Press in 1879, both bearing copyright notices,

[72] *Banāt an-naʿsh* (Agra: Mufid-e ʿAm Press 1879), preface.

[73] Russell 1992: 265. Further details in ibid.: 92–4 and Naim 1984. See also the afterword by Pritchett in Ahmad 2001: 204–21.

[74] *RPIR* 1875: 82.

suggest that the author had ceded his copyright to the government, which then divided the printing work among various presses. However, by the time the fourth edition of *Taubat an-Naṣūḥ* came out in 1882 (2000 copies), Naval Kishore had acquired the copyright of the text. This is borne out by a publisher's notice included in the twelfth NKP edition of 1914, to the effect that the fourth and all subsequent editions of the novel had been issued from the NKP with the author's permission.[75]

From 1877 to 1884 Nazir Ahmad served in the princely state of Hyderabad. Upon his return to Delhi in 1884, he resumed his writing and in the following year completed *Muḥṣināt*: *Fasāna-e Mubtala* (The Story of Mubtala, literally 'an afflicted person'), in which he dealt with the evils of polygamy. For its publication he returned to Naval Kishore, who issued an appallingly slovenly edition of 600 copies in 1887. Finding both the calligraphy and printing defective, Nazir Ahmad did not renew the contract, but decided to publish a fresh edition under his own supervision. By this time he seems to have been thoroughly exasperated by the various badly executed editions of his work, for in 1889 he decided to abandon his earlier publishers and enter into an exclusive contract with the Delhi-based Ansari Press. Whether the author's discontent stemmed from licensed editions or from cheap pirated copies of his work remains open. It also remains a mystery how, despite the existing copyright contract with the NKP, an edition of *Taubat an-Naṣūḥ* could be issued from the Ansari Press in 1889 with the author's consent. In its preface Nazir Ahmad made the following statement:

> For some time I have been observing with much gratitude and joy that all classes of readers appreciate my books much more than is their due. At the same time I am deeply afflicted by the fact that the faults in composition, the badly executed calligraphy, the poor quality of the paper and the faulty printing have generated general discontent. It was for lack of opportunity, nay out of carelessness, that I have not paid attention to this before. Now I have made up my mind that I will no longer allow my books to be spoilt. Therefore after amendment and revision I have started to have all my books registered afresh and published through the good offices of the Ansari Press of Maulvi Talattuf Husain Sahib in Delhi. According to my wishes Maulvi Talattuf Husain Sahib has entered into a special agreement with Muhammad Nazir Husain Sahib, bookseller, that no person whosoever and under no circumstances shall attempt to print my books or have them

[75] *Taubat an-Naṣūḥ*, 12th ed. (Lucknow: NKP 1914), publisher's notice. Cited in Khan 1979: 311.

> printed, otherwise he will be liable to pay both damages and a fine. And whosoever wants to deal in [my] books should deal with Muhammad Nazir Husain, bookseller, Greater Dariba, Delhi.[76]

Authors, as Nazir Ahmad's case shows, were flexible in choosing their publishers, and prompt in dismissing them. Unlike today, few authors at the time identified with a particular firm. The most pressing questions, however, are left unanswered: who made the profit from Nazir Ahmad's books which sold in tens of thousands? How much of the share went to the publisher, and how much to the author?

Next to Nazir Ahmad, the only other famous author of modern prose fiction on Naval Kishore's list was Pandit Ratan Nath Dar, poetically surnamed 'Sarshar' (1846–1902). Sarshar belonged to a family of Kashmiri Brahmins of Lucknow. He joined the press as editor of *Avadh Akhbār* in 1878, Naval Kishore having successfully lured him away from the rival *Avadh Punch.* Soon afterwards, Sarshar's famous novel *Fasāna-e Āzād* (Azad's tale) was serialized in *Avadh Akhbār* to wide popular acclaim. He resigned from his job as editor in 1880 but remained attached to the NKP into the 1890s. His association with the House of Naval Kishore, with whom he published several more novels, will be outlined in more detail in Chapter 6.

Even for a publisher of Naval Kishore's standing, negotiations with authors were not always successful. When he approached Lucknow's celebrated *marṣiya* poet Mir Babar ᶜAli Anis (1802–74) with the suggestion of publishing his collected poetry, his request was declined. Although the two men were personally acquainted and Anis might have materially profited from seeing his elegies promoted by a reputed local publishing house, he refused for some reason to consign his compositions to print. Only a few *marṣiya*s appeared in *Avadh Akhbār*. It was only after the poet's death in 1874 that Naval Kishore could proceed with his project. He lost no time in assigning the task of collecting whatever *marṣiya*s by Anis could be found to Maulvi Tasadduq Husain, who had recently joined his team of editors. The task was not an easy one, for the poet's manuscripts were scattered in the homes and private collections of Urdu literati in Lucknow and beyond. Tasadduq Husain's painstaking efforts resulted in a printed collection of 118 elegies entitled *Marṣiyahā-e Mīr Anīs* (*1877). Had it not been for the publisher's perseverance, many of them would have been lost to posterity. By contrast, it required

[76] Cited in Khan 1979: 312–13. Strangely, the accompanying signature of Nazir Ahmad bears the date 1873, which must be a misprint.

no effort on Naval Kishore's part to acquire the collection of Lucknow's second great *marṣiya* poet, Mirza Salamat ʿAli Dabir (1803–75). Following Dabir's death, his son Mirza Muhammad 'Auj' personally took his father's manuscripts to the publisher. The collection, including 78 *marṣiya*s in two volumes, duly appeared in 1876.[77]

Among less known authors, Mufti Ghulam Sarvar of Lahore formed a long-standing alliance with the NKP. A descendant of the great Sufi Shaikh Bahaʾuddin Zakaria of Multan, Ghulam Sarvar was a highly reputed scholar and a prolific author of religious, historiographical, and lexicographical works in Persian and Urdu. His connections with the NKP can be traced back to 1875, when he offered the copyright of his dictionary *Lughāt-e Sarvarī* (also known as *Zubdat al-lughāt*) to Naval Kishore. Once the deal was done, the publisher sent for corrected proofs from his Lahore agency and had the work published in March 1877. At this time, author and publisher seem to have entered into an exclusive contract. Over the following years Ghulam Sarvar published a large number of works with Naval Kishore, including three historiographical titles (*Tārīkh-e makhzan-e Panjāb*, *Bahāristān-e tārīkh*, and the Persian *Ganjīnah-e Sarvarī*, all *1877), various collections of religious poetry (*Naʿt-e Sarvarī*, *1878; *Guldasta-e karāmat*, *1880 and *Tuḥfat-e Sarvarī*, *1881), and two works on ethics (*Akhlāq-e Sarvarī* and *Gulshan-e Sarvarī*; *1878). Fifteen years later, Ghulam Sarvar still remained loyal to the NKP and commissioned the firm with the publication of his second lexicographical work *Jāmiʿ al-lughāt-e Urdū* (*1892), an advanced dictionary containing idioms from science and medicine.[78]

While over time Naval Kishore built up a reputation as a major publisher in Hindi, prominent contemporary Hindi authors are conspicuously absent from his list. The reasons for this may lie in competition and copyright laws, as will be discussed in Chapter 7. The educationist Raja Shiva Prasad of Benares stands out as the only renowned figure in Hindi writing who published several works with Naval Kishore. Shiva Prasad was a long-time associate of the NKP, having closely collaborated with it while Inspector of Schools in the 1860s and 1870s. The two men also shared common political views and worked side by side in the anti-Congress movement. It is no surprise then that in the 1880s Shiva Prasad chose to cede the copyright of most of his Hindi and Urdu works, including

[77] See *LLH* 1876: 25 for a reproduction of the publication notice carried in *Avadh Akhbār* of 7 April 1876.

[78] According to the *RPIR* of 1878, he also edited the Urdu journal *Makhzan-e Panjāb* (*Punjab Gazetteer*). *DIPL*: 206; Storey 1953: 1043.

his most widely-selling textbooks, to his 'friend' Naval Kishore. Later in life he also consigned his Urdu autobiography *Savāniḥ-eʿumrī* to the Lucknow publisher, who printed it in 300 copies in 1894.

3.6 The Naval Kishore Press After 1895

Upon his death in February 1895, Munshi Naval Kishore left a flourishing enterprise and a huge fortune to his adopted son and designated heir Munshi Prag Narayan Bhargava (1872–1916). Under Prag Narayan's management the firm continued to prosper for some time. Yet, as the twentieth century progressed, it became clear that the heyday of North India's largest publishing house was over. Drastic reductions in British patronage, lower public demand for Persian and Urdu literature, increased competition in the publishing trade and adverse political circumstances combined to bring about its slow but steady decline.

When Munshi Prag Narayan assumed charge of the family business, he was well prepared to do so: following his education at the Jubilee High School, at Agra College, and the Lucknow Canning College, he had been apprenticed at the NKP and risen to the post of superintendent. Prag Narayan profited socially and economically from the fact that Naval Kishore had substantially augmented the ancestral property by investing large amounts of his profits in landed property acquired from various *taʿalluqdārs* (Metcalf 1979: 274). Apart from the ancestral *zamīndārī* in Aligarh District, Prag Narayan held estates in the districts of Gonda, Barabanki, Unao, Kanpur, and Hamirpur.[79] As a large landed proprietor he was admitted into the ranks of the Avadh *taʿalluqdārs*. He gained membership of the British Indian Association and for some time served as its joint secretary. His successful assimilation into the traditional landed elite allowed him to seek marriage alliances for his children in this hitherto hermetic social group.[80] His case illustrates a typical pattern among Hindustani commercial classes, who over time shifted their social and political bases from an urban *raʾīs* background to landowning and *zamīndārī* associations (Bayly 1971: 296).

[79] H.R. Nevill in his *Aligarh Gazetteer* reports: 'The Bhargava family of Sasni holds six *mahals* in the Sikandra Rao *taḥṣil* and five in Hathras, paying in all Rs 3,264: while to the same caste belongs Munshi Prag Narayan, Rai Bahadur of Lucknow, the son of the celebrated publisher Newal Kishore, who owns a property of one whole village and six *mahals* in *taḥṣil* Sikandra Rao, with an area of 4657 acres and a revenue demand of Rs 9,529' (Nevill 1909: 115).

[80] For the rise of Lucknow's urban notables to the status of *taʿalluqdārs*, see Oldenburg 1989: 230–6.

Under Prag Narayan and his relative Manoharlal Bhargava, superintendent of the press, the NKP continued to do brisk business. By 1902 three new book depôts had been opened in Jabalpur, Nagpur, and Raipur. Between 1907 and 1911 the publishing house won several prizes at international exhibitions in Calcutta, Paris, and Brussels (Bhargava 1981: 31). In addition to *Avadh Akhbār*, in 1901 Prag Narayan launched *Avadh Samācār*, a Hindi weekly that was curiously announced as being 'especially suited to agriculturists, tradesmen and females of India.'[81] Among his many publishing ventures, two biographical compilations deserve special notice since they remain of undiminished interest to modern-day scholars of South Asia: *Ṣaḥīfa-e zarīn* (*1902), a two-volume compilation in Urdu published on the occasion of the Coronation *darbār*, which contains over 2000 biographical entries and 500 pictures of Indian chiefs and princes, and its English counterpart entitled *Who's who in India. Containing Lives and Portraits of Ruling Chiefs, Nobles, Titled Personages and Other Eminent Indians* (*1911).[82] J.R. McLane has underlined the importance of these collective biographies as prime examples of the growing interaction, overlapping interests, and mutual favouring among landholders and urban professionals (McLane 1977: 201–2). The inclusion of Indian nationalists and urban professionals such as Prag Narayan himself in the category of 'titled personages and other eminent Indians' vividly testifies to changing perceptions within Indian elite society.

Endowed with the same enterprising spirit as Naval Kishore, Prag Narayan not only invested in the modernization of the publishing house but also sought to diversify and open new sources of income.[83] With the

[81] *Thacker's Indian Directory* 1902.

[82] The following biographical sketch largely relies on the information contained in this work, as well as a short account given in *Uttar Pradeś* 1980: 29–9.

[83] The *Cyclopedia of India* (1908: 362) contains the following description: 'The works, godowns, etc. occupy a very considerable area at Hazratganj, and no expense has been spared in equipping them with the latest printing and steam machinery. They do a very extensive business, giving employment to about 500 men. The works are specially equipped for printing in all the vernaculars of India, and experts are retained who can handle any of the local languages, Arabic, Persian, Urdu, Sanskrit, Hindi, Mahratti, Urya, Punjabi, etc. besides English. In consequence, work flows in from all parts of India, as well as from foreign countries, such as Persia. . . . The press do their own typecasting, having modern machinery for the purpose of casting type in various languages. They also do electro-typing and stereotyping, and all processes necessary for their work. Lithography is a speciality. They also print all descriptions of educational works at prices which place them within reach of the very poorest . . .'.

establishment of the 'Newal Kishore Emporium and Fire Arms Depot' and the 'Newal Kishore Ice Factory' in Kanpur, he built up a mostly family-run commercial empire which provided employment to over 1500 people.[84] Managed by his younger brother Govind Prasad Bhargava, an engineering graduate, the Lucknow Iron Works grew into a thriving business of 300 employees that largely performed government contract work. Prag Narayan further extended his influence in commercial circles as a member of the Upper India Chamber of Commerce, director of the Upper India Paper Mills Company, and president of the U.P. Chamber of Commerce. He also successfully entered the banking business, acting simultaneously as the director of the Bhargava Commercial Bank in Jabalpur and the Bharat National Bank in Delhi, and as treasurer to the Delhi and London Bank. In recognition of his public services, he was conferred the title of Rai Bahadur in 1909. His rise in the world of trade and commerce was accompanied by a political career that followed the regular paths: as a member of the Lucknow Municipal Board he was elected to the Legislative Council of the United Provinces in 1912. Subsequently, he was made a Member of the Imperial War Council and of the Imperial Legislative Council of India.

As a trustee of Agra College and in various other offices Prag Narayan continued his father's involvement in charitable and educational causes. However, it seems that he was especially generous in his support to institutions representative of Hindu culture. For example, he gave a large grant of Rs 10,000 to the Benares Hindu University (Sundaram 1936: 635) and set up a trust for the restoration of ancient Hindu temples.

Following Prag Narayan's death, his son Bishan Narayan (1898–1931) assumed charge of the family business. Bishan Narayan is best remembered for the services he rendered to Hindi literature through the famous Hindi literary magazine *Mādhurī*, launched in 1922. Its first editor was his nephew, the enterprising Dularelal Bhargava. Under Dularelal Bhargava and a number of other illustrious figures—Rup Narayan Pandey, Krishna Bihari Mishra, and Premchand—*Mādhurī* became a greatly influential institution in the Hindi literature of the 1920s

[84] Ibid.: 363. *Thacker's Indian Directory* of 1917 further testifies to the family character of the firm: 'Newal Kishore Press, booksellers, printers, publishers, statnrs., bankers, imptrs. of printing and ice machines, &c.: Propr. Hon. Rai Bahdr. M. Prag Narain Bhargava. Pte secy B. Umrao Lal Shrivastava. Persnl. Asst. B. Mukut Behari Lal Bhargava, B.A. Supt. printing dept. B. Manohar Lal Bhargava, B.A. Mangr., book dept. & Newal Kishore emporium B. Mohan Lal Bhargava. Agt. Banking bch. M. Jugul Kishore. Supdt. "Oudh Akhbar" B. Mukat Bihari Lal Bhargava, B.A.' (p. 276).

and 1930s.[85] As Orsini has shown, its attractive presentation and openness to a variety of themes, styles, and opinions distinguished *Mādhurī* from other contemporary journals, making it 'the foremost forum in Hindi for literary discussion' (Orsini 2002: 57). Yet, despite the journal's wide popularity, Bishan Narayan never recouped the large investment that *Mādhurī* meant for him, but is said to have incurred a financial loss of almost Rs 20,000 in sustaining it.

Soon after Bishan Narayan left the family business to his two sons, Munshi Ram Kumar Bhargava (1915–71) and Munshi Tej Kumar Bhargava (1919–87), conflicts began to emerge in the family. As a result, the management of the firm had to be entrusted to a Court of Wards under the aegis of the British collector of Lucknow. By this time the publishing house was already running at a loss, and the threat of retrenchment of employees and salary cuts had divided the staff into opposing factions. One of those immediately affected by the situation was Premchand, who has left us a vivid account of the tensions gripping the firm.[86]

The establishment of a new branch in Ajmer in 1938 could not conceal the fact that the NKP's days were numbered: in 1947 Partition brought with it the loss of the Pakistan market, while the Uttar Pradesh Zamindari Abolition Act of 1950 severely affected the family fortunes. The mortal blow to the House of Naval Kishore came in the same year, when, following a rift between the two brothers, the firm was divided into two separate enterprises, renamed Ram Kumar Book Depot and Tej Kumar

[85] Himself a poet of Brajbhasha, Dularelal Bhargava initiated a revival of Brajbhasha poetry through *Mādhurī*. Around 1927 he started his own literary publishing house, the Ganga Pustak Mala (Orsini 2002: 75–6; 388). Premchand's association with *Mādhurī* lasted from February 1927 to October 1931. During that time he not only served as editor of *Mādhurī* but also worked in the NKP book depot, preparing textbooks and children's books (Madan Gopal 1964: 261–5; Amrit Rai 1990: 224–33, 266).

[86] On 11 September 1931 Premchand wrote to Dayanarayan Nigam: 'There is a new development here. Manager X, who is the leader of the group hostile to me, has got a new supporter in one Y, who has been taken on as a canvasser. Ever since his appointment, Y has been trying to dominate the affairs of the business house. Taking me for his enemy from the very first day, he has been trying to get me thrown out. A move for economy was already afoot. He has now thought of getting the entire editorial staff dismissed, and securing books written in the name of responsible and influential persons, preferably members of the (textbook selection) committee. These stupid people here do not realise that what they pay me can be easily realised from a single book that I write. In fact, they haven't yet paid me even half of what they have earned from books written by me, and also that the royalties which they have to offer to the influential ones are very high' (cited in Madan Gopal 1964: 330).

Book Depot. Both continued to function separately until recently. The Tej Kumar Book Depot kept up the NKP's venerable tradition of publishing religious and literary classics in inexpensive editions. Moreover, it reprinted a substantial number of approximately ninety Hindi and eighty-five Urdu works first published during the days of Naval Kishore.

External and internal factors thus combined to bring about the slow but steady decline in the firm's fortunes in the course of the twentieth century. The process is clearly reflected in the NKP's production figures: of the estimated total of 12,000 titles issued from the publishing house during its lifespan of almost a century, about 5000 were published during Naval Kishore's lifetime, 3000 during the time of Prag Narayan, and 2000 each during the time of Bishan Narayan and his two sons. These figures only serve to highlight the outstanding individual achievement of the firm's founder-proprietor.

4

The Colonial Factor: Patronage, Collaboration, and Money Matters

As noted in the previous chapters, British patronage was one of the main factors accounting for the NKP's rapid growth and expansion. Without wanting to downplay Munshi Naval Kishore's own achievement as an entrepreneur, it is hardly overstating the case to say that colonial patronage significantly distinguished the history of the NKP from that of other Indian publishers. In this chapter, the business relationship between the NKP and the colonial authorities, along with the circumstances attending colonial patronage, will be analysed in greater detail. The picture that emerges illustrates the complex transactional relations between Indian private entrepreneurship and state authority, depicting at once an intense and extremely successful business collaboration and a sustained dispute over market shares and profits, as well as agency and control in the publishing market.

Some of the locally determined factors underlying the initial support extended to Naval Kishore when he set up his press in 1858 have already been outlined. The patronage by individual British officials, however, also needs to be situated within the context of government policy towards the Indian-language press and print media in the wake of the 1857 uprising. Undoubtedly, the events of 1857 had greatly enhanced British suspicion of the 'native' press and demonstrated the urgency of bringing it under closer scrutiny. At the same time, there was an acute need to establish closer relations with the vernacular press so that in future more effective use could be made of this indispensable means of gaining access to the public. A powerful medium in disseminating information and generating public opinion, the press had to be carefully encouraged. The transfer of power from Company to Crown in 1858 brought with it an attempt to restore public confidence, first signalled in Queen Victoria's proclamation of non-interference in 'native' customs and beliefs. The 'renewed emphasis on caution and conciliation' (Metcalf 1990: 95) translated into a selective application of liberal principles; it was reflected in press legislation. Governor General Lord Canning initiated a policy of simultaneous control and encouragement, in which surveillance and patronage were carefully weighed against each other. Official patronage, especially on the part of the Education Department, came to serve as a potent means of rewarding and controlling editors and publishers.[1]

Viewed against this backdrop, the NKP's collaboration with the colonial administration displays all the characteristics of a symbiotic relationship: at the time of setting up business, Naval Kishore relied heavily on British patronage in the various forms of a license grant, technological and material support, and printing contracts. The Avadh provincial authorities, on the other hand, had a vested interest in securing the collaboration of a loyal representative of the Indian-language press in the politically sensitive post-Mutiny days. An editor–publisher of proven loyalty such as Naval Kishore was an asset to be co-opted and duly instrumentalized in the process of reconsolidating power and counteracting anti-colonial sentiment. At the pragmatic, political, and ideological level, the establishment of the NKP was a welcome opportunity for the new rulers at Lucknow. Moreover, it saved them from having to invest in their own printing works, an important financial consideration given the fact that plans were already under way to establish a large government press at Allahabad, at an estimated monthly operating cost of no less than Rs 8800.[2]

There may have also been considerations of safety and greater public acceptance in opting to rely on a 'native' publisher. The objective, clearly, was to convert Naval Kishore's printing press into an instrument of colonial rule, to be deployed in the diffusion of information and the spread of 'useful' knowledge in the Indian languages. Implied in this was the printing of legal acts and government notifications and, equally important, the production and dissemination of educational material in Persian, Urdu, and Hindi. The colonial administration soon became the NKP's major client; official commissions constituted the single most important source of income and provided a strong financial backbone

[1] Bayly 1996a: 340–1; Barns 1940: 249–62; Sharma 1996: 42–5.

[2] See W.H. Lowe's 'Proposition for the future establishment of a Government Press', *Home Dept., G.G.S. Public*, October 1858: no. 297 (NAI).

for the Lucknow publishing house. If this placed Munshi Naval Kishore in a precarious position of economic and moral dependence, the profits gained from British printing contracts became a crucial factor in subsidizing the oriental publications for which his firm achieved its unique reputation in India and beyond. The impact of this constant flow of capital, which sustained the press over the years, cannot be overstated. It is important to understand that publishing in the oriental languages, on the scale and diversity undertaken at the NKP, would not have been possible but for the profits derived from job printing for the colonial government.[3] There is a distinct irony to the fact that one of the first books to bear the imprint of Naval Kishore is not a classic of oriental literature but an English treatise, issued in July 1859, which, fittingly enough, is entitled *Our Finances*. Its author, George Campbell was Judicial and Financial Commissioner of Avadh and future Lieutenant Governor of Bengal.[4]

The NKP's business collaboration with the colonial authorities extended to various administrative departments which regularly, or on specific occasions, commissioned items for print, initially in both English and the Indian languages, and later, after the opening of the Allahabad Government Press, mainly in Hindi and Urdu. Once the NKP had established a reputation for itself, printing orders no longer remained confined to the regional authorities but also began coming in from the higher administrative departments of the Government of India in Calcutta. In 1874, for example, Naval Kishore forwarded a bill for Rs 1000 to the Foreign Secretary.[5] The bulk of such printing commissions reflected the mundane side of a booming bureaucratic apparatus, consisting of legal and revenue forms, registers, acts and ordinances, and a variety of government documents in Urdu and Hindi. Occasionally, there were lucrative commissions for printing in English, as for instance in the case of Census returns.

The superior workmanship and reliability of the NKP, the continuous flow of old and new books on religion, literature, the arts and sciences emanating from the press, and Naval Kishore's sustained efforts in translating Arabic and Persian classics into the modern languages met with increasing British recognition and, in turn, patronage. The Oudh Administration Report of 1871–2 approvingly noted that 'The spread of vernacular and oriental classics is much aided by the establishment of Munshi Nawal

[3] According to Ranjit Bhargava, the NKP book depot, which sold mostly non-educational publications, always ran at a loss. Private communication, March 1998.

[4] A copy of this work is preserved in the OIOC.

[5] *Procs. of the Chief Commissioner of Oudh in the General Dept. (Home)*, March 1874, no. 559.

Kishore, whose books find their way all over India and are even exported to Bokhara, Persia, Arabia and Afghanistan'.[6] The 1875 report concurred, stating that 'The press of Munshi Nawal Kishore continues to hold the first place in Oudh. All large and valuable publications, classical and vernacular, are the outcome of this press.'[7] In 1877 the Secretary to Government found Naval Kishore standing 'far ahead in the number and value of his publications' among Lucknow and Kanpur publishers.[8]

A decisive factor in the success of the business co-operation with the British were the reasonable rates that Naval Kishore was able to offer. His services not only tended to be cheaper than those of most of his Indian competitors, but at times even put the government's own printing presses on the spot. In March 1874, following a comparison of prevailing rates, the Superintendent of the Lucknow Central Jail Press found himself faced with the official query of whether his press would be able to supply vernacular forms at NKP rates. The reply, on this one occasion, was in the affirmative.[9]

On the face of it, business transactions between the NKP and the colonial authorities appear to be an example of a highly successful collaboration between state and private agency, in which a feeling of mutual benefit prevailed. On closer investigation, however, it becomes apparent that relations were by no means free from conflict. As will be shown below, the business relationship between the commercial publisher and the colonial state involved constant negotiation which could easily turn into open confrontation. The issues at stake were money and profit margins, the extent and limits of patronage, but also fundamental questions of agency and control over the publishing market. The latter was especially pronounced in the domain of textbook publishing, where state and private agency both collaborated and competed.

4.1 Textualizing Mass Education: The Textbook Venture

The spread of formal education and the colonial state's increased engagement with the primary and secondary sectors resulted in the urgent need for written instructional material in Indian regional languages. While

[6] *OAR*, 1871–2: 118.

[7] *RPIR, NWP&Oudh*, 1875: 106.

[8] *RPIR, NWP&Oudh*, 1877: 119.

[9] *Procs. of the Chief Commissioner of Oudh in the General Dept. (Home)*, March 1874, no. 32.

traditional forms of Indian education centred around the teacher, colonial education was firmly built on textuality, and from the outset gave prime importance to the printed textbook. In Krishna Kumar's apt formulation, the prescribed textbook became 'a sacred icon of required knowledge'; it was treated as 'the de facto curriculum, rather than as an aid' (Kumar 1991: 64). Under colonial aegis, textbooks came to constitute the most widely produced and distributed category of printed matter in the modern Indian languages. In business relations between the NKP and the colonial administration, textbook production in Hindi, Urdu, and the classical languages assumed central importance, accounting for an intense collaboration throughout the century. If not always profitable from the publisher's point of view, it represents an important aspect of Naval Kishore's involvement in official printing, for it had a direct bearing on linguistic standardization and the formation of readerships in Hindi and Urdu. The ideological implications of colonial textbook production have been dealt with elsewhere and are not of prime concern in the present context.[10] Instead we will focus on economic aspects and the ways in which the colonial government, in its massive programme of introducing a new educational tool among the masses, employed a double strategy: securing the help of private Indian enterprise, and, at the same time, jealously guarding its control over the textbook sector.

A brief overview of the history of the printed textbook in India may be helpful here: the production of textbooks in Indian regional languages had first been undertaken by, and for some time remained the sole domain of, Christian missionaries. As noted earlier, the Serampore Mission Press and the Baptist Mission Press in Calcutta were the most active pioneers in the field. The establishment of the Calcutta School Book Society in 1817 constituted a landmark in the history of early schoolbook production, it being one of the first combined efforts of Europeans and Indians in the promotion of education.[11] Significantly, it insisted on secular knowledge and pointedly excluded all religious texts. Similar schoolbook and education societies were set up in Bombay (1816/1821), Madras (1820), Benares (1820), and Agra (1833). Supported by the Sikandara Orphan Press, the Agra School Book Society assumed prime importance

[10] For textbook ideology, see e.g., Kumar 1991: 64–70; Bayly 1998: 77–8, Powell 1999; Stark 2000; Naregal 2001: 55–78; Stark 2004a.

[11] The early history of the Bengali and Hindi textbook is relatively well documented. See Laird 1967 on the missionary contribution and Basak 1959 on the Calcutta School Book Society. For Hindi textbooks, see Vedalankar 1969: 113–65; Dalmia 1997: 169–74.

for the NWP. As Naregal has pointed out, these early schoolbook and educational societies were important in establishing 'structures of ideological mediation' between the colonial state and the Indian educated elite. More than just producing an impressive number of educational texts, they provided a 'minimal collaborative space for the construction of colonial ideology' (Naregal 2001: 66–7).

The age of the mass-produced textbook in Hindi and Urdu dawned in the 1840s and 1850s. The Vernacular Education Despatch of 1854 formally institutionalized state education, instigating a process described as the 'vernacularization' of Indian education. In its wake, educational departments were established in the various provinces; they assumed charge of all aspects of education, including textbook production. Prior to 1854 the NWP had already been the site of far-reaching official efforts in the field of education which would later earn them credit for being 'the pioneers of the policy of extending primary education among the masses' (*ECR* 1882: 41). Besides the opening of *halkabandī* and vernacular model schools, the pioneering measures of Lieutenant Governor James Thomason also included the levy of a local rate for educational purposes and the introduction of a series of elementary textbooks in Hindi and Urdu meant to address the dire need for suitable reading material for use in the new schools.[12] Circulated under the name of Ram Saran Das Series, the Hindi titles remained in use for decades. They served as linguistic models for the emerging Hindi prose style and played an important role in standardizing the language (Dalmia 1997: 172–4). Yet, contrary to the intention of Thomason's scheme, they remained largely confined to government schools and were seldom put to use in traditional indigenous schools. This was partly owing to the fact that many private schools run by Indians continued to insist on imparting classical training in Sanskrit and Persian and did not teach Hindi or Urdu. Others catered only to specific castes or professional groups and had no use for Hindi and the Nagari script, using Kaithi and Mahajani instead. As John Nesfield noted in a somewhat sweeping statement in 1882, the 'vernacular' was not studied 'in any of the indigenous schools' in Avadh:

> Pupils taught in the Kaithi and Mahajani schools can neither read a Nagri book nor write in the Nagri character. Those taught in Sanscrit schools cannot avoid learning the Nagri character, because Sanscrit books are written in Nagri; but they never study a modern Hindi book or practise Hindi com-

[12] Vedalankar 1969: 149–53. By 1851, 78 textbooks had been lithographed, for which see ibid.: 236–44.

> position. Those taught in the Persian schools are never set to read an Urdu author or to write an Urdu letter. The first aim of Primary schools should be to teach pupils to read and write their own Vernacular; but this is what the Indigenous schools studiously avoid.[13]

Moreover, indigenous schools continued to emphasize oral transmission and learning by rote. If writing was involved, it usually meant that students would copy out texts onto slates. As Nesfield remarked, the sole reason why most pupils in the Sanskrit *pāṭhśālās* mastered the Nagari script fairly well was that in the absence of textbooks they were compelled 'to be constantly copying out some Sanscrit text'.[14]

While failing to make a more profound impact in traditional schools, the printed textbook became an essential feature of state education. Textbook production accounted for a large portion of the work undertaken at the government presses. Brought to a temporary standstill by the 1857 uprising, printing at the Agra Government Press resumed with vigour in December 1857. By the end of 1858, 64 different titles were ready for use in schools. Print runs ranged from 250 to 100,000 copies and aggregated over 500,000 copies in total.[15] Yet it quickly became apparent that the colonial state alone could not cope with the awesome task of providing the Indian masses with this new educational tool. Private enterprise had to be enlisted. As we have seen, Naval Kishore was among the first Indian printer-publishers whose collaboration was sought. Henry Stuart Reid, first DPI in the NWP Educational Department (est. 1855), favoured his enterprise with contracts for textbook printing. A second supporter emerged in the person of Babu Shiva Prasad, Joint Inspector of Schools in the Benares Circle from 1856. Among the earliest textbooks printed at the NKP were a number of widely used Urdu works composed by this eminent champion of primary education. The first was Shiva Prasad's four-volume geography of the world, *Jām-e jahān numā* (*1858–9, Fig. 4), which remained the standard geography textbook in Urdu-medium schools for decades. With its publication date of 1858–9 it must be one of the first substantial books ever printed at the NKP. A second edition of 5000 copies followed in 1860, priced between six and ten annas per volume. Editions of the abridged version of the geography, *Choṭā jām-e jahān numā*, and of Shiva Prasad's Urdu rendering of *Sandford and*

[13] 'Indigenous schools in Oudh and North-West Provinces', *Calcutta Review* 75, 1882: 305–6.

[14] Ibid.: 304.

[15] *Rept. on the State of Popular Education NWP*, 1856–7 and 1857–8: 38.

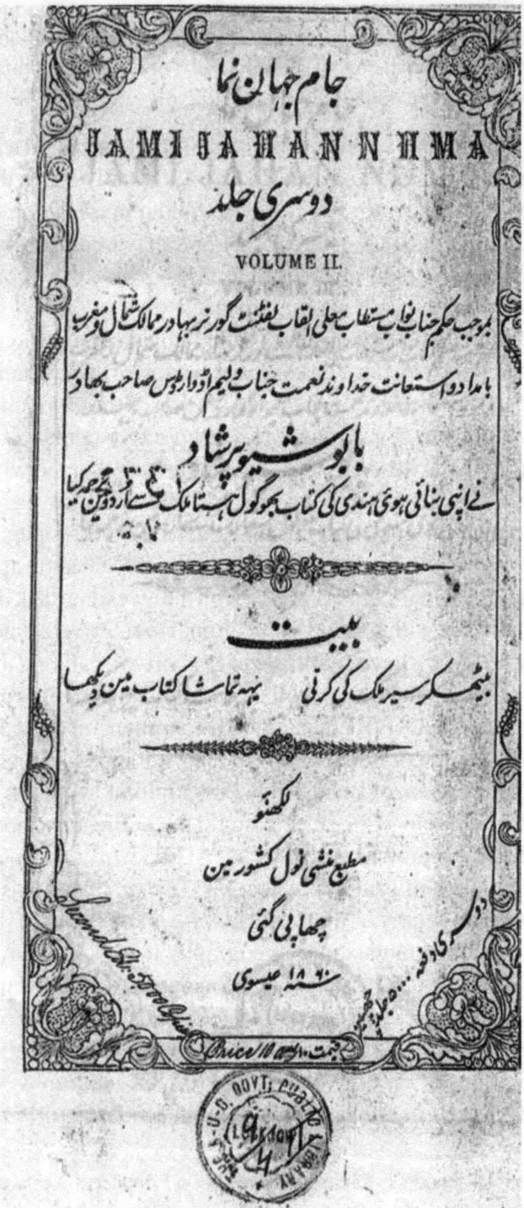

جام جہان نما

JAMI JAHAN NUMA

دوسری جلد

VOLUME II.

بموجب حکم جناب نواب مستطاب معلی القاب لفٹنٹ گورنر بہادر ممالک شمال و مغربی

بامداد و استعانت خداوند نعمت جناب ولیم اڈوارڈ بس صاحب بہادر

بابو شیو پرشاد

نے اپنی بنائی ہوئی ہندی کی کتاب بھوگول ہستاملک سے اردو مین ترجمہ کیا

بیت

بیٹھکر سیر ملک کی کرنی   یہہ تماشا کتاب مین دیکھا

لکھنو

مطبع منشی نول کشور مین

چھاپی گئی

سنہ ۱۸۶۰ عیسوی

Fig. 4: Title page of *Jām-e jahān numā* (^{2}1860)

Merton, a didactic tale by Thomas Day, were produced in the same year. Since the demand for such textbook classics remained continuously high, printing contracts were particularly lucrative.

Textbooks also constituted the earliest specimens of Hindi typesetting at the NKP, testifying to the fact that Hindi printing at the press was introduced at the instance of the British authorities. Most of the early Hindi textbooks issued from the press were reprints of the Agra textbook series. They included *Paṭvāriyoṁ ke hisāb kī pustak Hindī bhāṣā meṁ* (*1860) and Sukhlal's *Kitāb jantrī* (*1861), two books on village accountancy; Reid's *Sūrajpur kī kahānī* (*1862), an instructive prose tale for villagers; and Shrilal's *Jñān cālīsī* (*1862, Fig. 5), a collection of forty instructional maxims.[16] Printed in large type-set editions of 3000 to 5000 copies, these booklets were priced at one anna per copy, and were thus readily affordable.

Business relations with Reid's successor, M. Kempson, who was appointed DPI in 1861, started off on a less promising note. Whatever agreements Naval Kishore had come to with Reid, it would seem that he was interpreting them far too liberally. In March 1863 Kempson issued a set of regulations for Deputy Inspectors which contained a special paragraph to the effect that, without direct orders from the Inspector, Deputy Inspectors were not to purchase books for school use from any source other than the curator's depot in Allahabad. This rule, he explained, was rendered necessary 'by the wholesale piracy of Educational works printed by the Government on the part of a Lucknow printer, one Newal Kishore'.[17]

Following the establishment of a separate Educational Department in Avadh in 1864, the focus of the NKP's commercial relations in the textbook sector naturally shifted back to Lucknow. Since the production of textbooks in Hindi and Urdu was a pressing issue, the Oudh Educational Department dispensed with the expensive and time-consuming task of setting up its own printing works; instead it granted the NKP monopoly rights to print and publish educational books.[18] In return, Naval Kishore promised to permanently keep a sufficient supply of books in stock, in order to meet the demand of the department at any time. More importantly, he also took upon himself the entire financial risk implied in surplus production, outdated editions, and unsaleable stock due to curricula changes.

[16] First published in Agra 1851 and 1852, respectively.

[17] *Rept. on the Progress of Popular Education NWP*, 1862–3, app. C, 20 A.

[18] *RPE Oudh*, 1869–70: 113.

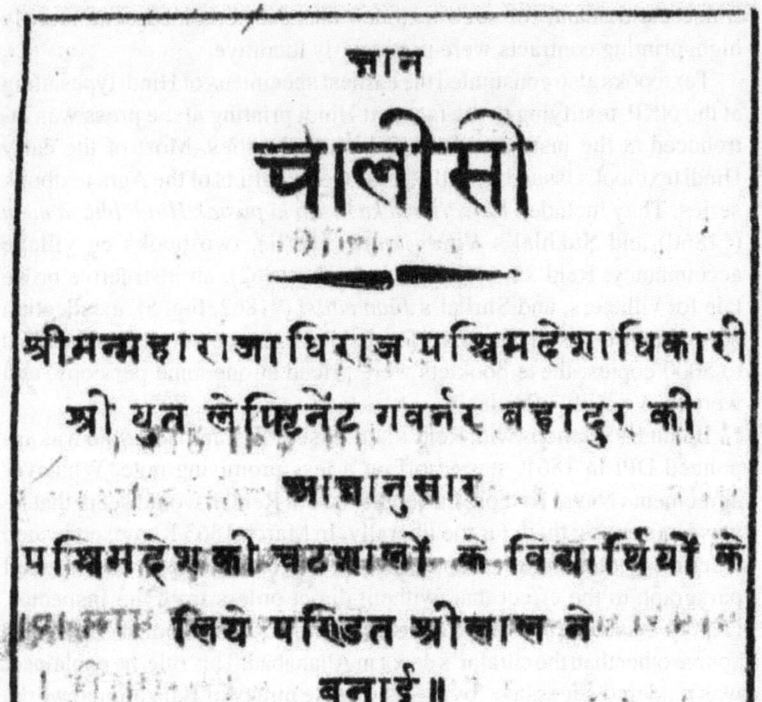

ज्ञान

चालीसी

श्रीमन्महाराजाधिराज पश्चिमदेशाधिकारी
श्री युत लेफ्टिनेंट गवर्नर बहादुर की
आज्ञानुसार
पश्चिमदेश की पाठशालों के विद्यार्थियों के
लिये पण्डित श्रीलाल ने
बनाई॥

लखनऊ
मुंशी नवलकिशोर के प्रेस में छापी गई
सन् १८६२ ई०

Printed 2000 Copies, price 1 Anna per copy.
२००० जिल्द छपीं कीमत फी जिल्द –)

Fig. 5: Title page of *Jñān cālīsī* (1862)

The considerable financial risk implied in this agreement is borne out by the sales figures of 1869: in this year, the value of books purchased by the government from the NKP, and the value of the actual sales effected, showed a large deficit of Rs 3390.[19] Nonetheless, the publisher profited from the arrangement. Over time, his interaction with the state authorities intensified to such an extent that Avadh officials came to consider the NKP an integral part of their educational apparatus. At the same time, there was no doubt as to who remained in control of textbook production. As one haughty official put it: 'The Nawal Kishore Press, though it is owned and managed by a private person, may be considered the Press of the Educational Department.'[20]

As a result of this intense collaboration, textbook production in Avadh almost doubled within a short time span of six years. Its full dimension is reflected in Table 4.0, which lists the number of books sold by the Oudh Educational Department and the money effected from sales.

The collaboration between the NKP and the Oudh Educational Department also extended to the distribution of textbooks. The Educational Department had its own book depot, which was divided into two sections—one for English and one for vernacular publications. Each section consisted of a central depot in Lucknow and twelve branch depots in the provincial districts. Naval Kishore acted as manager of the central vernacular depot in Lucknow, and, by special agreement, was also put in charge of the English depot.[21] In this capacity he assumed sole responsibility for the distribution of textbooks to the branch depots. These

TABLE 4.0

Textbook Production in Avadh: Books Sold by the Oudh Educational Department, 1865-71

Year	No. of books sold	Value of books sold (Rs)
1865–6	32,520	4, 988
1866–7	39,162	5,885
1867–8	54,154	9,013
1868–9	50,542	9,570
1869–70	55,542	12,607
1870–1	60,623	10,183

SOURCE: *RPE Oudh*, 1868-71

[19] *RPE Oudh*, 1870–1: 133.

[20] *OAR*, 1873–4: 96.

[21] *RPE Oudh*, 1871–2: 172.

supervision of Deputy Inspectors who, acting as his agents, were responsible for textbook distribution to village schools. On account of this monopoly, Naval Kishore did not receive the sales commission of ten per cent usually given to inspectors in charge of the branch depots. The arrangement, however, held other advantages for him, since it allowed him not only to sell the bulk of the textbooks produced at his press to the Educational Department, but also to engage in selling textbooks on his own account. In 1872 educational books to the value of Rs 19,769 were purchased by the government, of which Rs 12,205 worth of books were sold. These figures only refered to the transactions of the government book depots and did not represent the sales effected by Naval Kishore to 'persons not in the Educational Department'.

Given this mutually favourable configuration, textbook production and distribution in Avadh was extremely efficient. How well it was organized becomes evident in view of the problems faced by the NWP provincial government at the time: here, due to the lack of an efficient distribution system, the rural population was observed to experience 'very great difficulties' in obtaining books. To make textbooks more accessible, plans were under way to open book stores under the charge of schoolmasters, rather than leaving distribution to the Deputy Inspectors in the district headquarters alone. Interestingly, in trying to provide better facilities for the supply of books in rural areas, the authorities were reluctant to rely on the agency of Indian booksellers. Underlying this reluctance were both economic considerations and a general attitude of mistrust towards 'native' agency, a seemingly characteristic feature of M. Kempson's tenure as DPI. As one report contended, 'The scheme would be expensive; it would be necessary to pay the book vendors fixed salaries, and the account keeping would be intricate and troublesome.'[22]

The price of textbooks was settled by the DPI, usually in consultation with Naval Kishore. The low rates and favourable conditions offered by the publisher were of vital interest to the British. Given that only a small minority of Indians was able to afford elementary education for its children, the production of inexpensive textbook material was a crucial prerequisite in the scheme of mass primary education. In 1872 DPI Colin Browning noted with great satisfaction that, in joining hands with a local publisher, textbook prices in Avadh had been reduced to a minimum:

> This department owing to the enterprise of Munshi Nawal Kishore is exceedingly well managed at very trifling cost. The lithographic and printing charges obtaining at Bombay, Allahabad and Lahore are known, and the price is

[22] *Report on the Progress of Education in the NWP*, 1871–2: 104.

> fixed at a lower rate than any that rule there. Munshi Nawal Kishore's works are marvels of cheapness, and care is taken that all educational works should be correctly and clearly lithographed.[23]

The collaboration between private and state agency was, therefore, not only profitable to both parties involved, but ultimately benefited North Indian students and the general public at large. With their textbooks being less expensive than those issued by any other Educational Department in India, the Avadh authorities had every reason to pride themselves in the outcome of this joint effort:

> Owing to the establishment of so large a press school books are mostly very cheap. In our primary village school course for Urdu–Persian students 16 books are used costing Rs 2-10-6 or as the course extends over 4 years the annual cost is Rs 0-10-7 to each student. The total cost of primary school books in Bengal is Rs 2-12-6. The total cost of books for a Hindi scholar at a primary school is Rs 2-11 or the annual cost is about Rs 0-10-9. In the Middle Class Urdu school course the cost of books is Rs 6-9-0 and in the Hindi Middle School Course the price is Rs 5-6. So the annual cost of books for a pupil educated in Urdu and Persian up to the middle class standard is Rs 1-1-6 and for a Hindi student is 0-13-5.[24]

In terms of the number of titles, the textbooks issued from the NKP by 1870 already exceeded 200 different works in Hindi and Urdu.[25] The demand was high, not just in the NWP&Oudh but also in Bengal and Bihar. Occasionally, textbooks produced in Avadh were also despatched to the Central Provinces, which still lacked an Urdu press capable of coping with large official commisions.[26]

Around that time, Naval Kishore approached the Punjab Government to obtain permission to print regional-language textbooks for use in Punjab schools. His plans to conquer the Punjab market with cheap texts, however, came at an inopportune moment, for the Punjab DPI W.R.M. Holroyd had recently embarked on an ambitious campaign to improve the Educational Press at Lahore. Holroyd's endeavour was not only to make the government book depot self-sufficient, but also 'to render the Educational Press at Lahore superior to any other Lithographic Press at present existing in Northern India.'[27] Seeing the success of his project

[23] *RPE Oudh*, 1871–2: 172.

[24] *RPE Oudh*, 1872–3: 121.

[25] *Avadh Akhbār*, of 19 April 1870, cit. in Nurani 1995: 55.

[26] *RPE Oudh*, 1872–3: 121.

[27] Letter from Holroyd to Secretary of Govt., Lahore, 10 December 1868, *PG. Punjab. Educational Dept.*, January 1869: 26.

threatened by a commercial publisher's initiative, he was naturally anxious to defend what he considered his own territory. In the process, he went as far as soliciting official sanction to prosecute Naval Kishore 'should he print certain educational works, the copyright of which has been registered.'[28] Naval Kishore was issued an official warning that in case of copyright infringement he would be liable to legal action. The government's stern refusal to cede textbook copyrights to an Indian printer was not well received by the local press. Pointing to the valuable services that Naval Kishore had rendered to Indian literature, the *Rohilkhaṇḍ Akhbār* of 12 November 1870 applauded his initiative and criticized the Punjab Government 'for not complying with the Munshi's reasonable request'.[29] The wider backdrop to this critique was the growing dissatisfaction with the government's refusal to give more job work to private enterprises, the rejection of Naval Kishore appearing to be a typical instance of this prejudice. Apparently, the authorities did not relent: criticism of the government's reluctance to cease its monopoly on educational printing continued to be voiced in the Punjab press.[30] It was only in the 1880s that a shift in policy resulted in greater official encouragement for private enterprise. Naval Kishore must have quickly jumped at the opportunity to assert his presence in the Punjab market, for by 1884 he is reported to have entered into contracts 'for supplying books in the Indian tongues to schools in large portions of the Punjab' (Hurst 1887: 353). Eventually, however, the Punjab Government opted in support of local enterprise and in 1887 gave an exclusive contract for printing and distributing textbooks and maps issued under the authority of the Educational Department to the Lahore-based Mufid-e ᶜAm Press of Munshi Gulab Singh.[31] Understandably, Naval Kishore was not willing to easily relinquish his share of textbook printing in the Punjab. When, in 1891, new contracts for government printing work were offered, he again appeared as one of the bidders. At this point the alarmed Punjab presses were called into joint action. If their rates were lower than those offered by Naval Kishore, they argued, there was no reason why the contract should be given to a resident of another province.[32] Their protest was heeded: educational printing was made over to a local contractor. Reportedly, the result was a rise in textbook prices.[33]

[28] *PG. Punjab. Educational Dept.*, July 1870, B No. 5.
[29] SVN 1870: 443–4.
[30] *Koh-i Nūr* n.d. and *Mufid-e ᶜĀm*, 15 July 1874, SVN 1874: 2 and 293.
[31] *Cyclopedia of India*, vol. 2: 324.
[32] *Akhbār-e ᶜĀm*, 21 August 1891, SVNP 1891: 299.
[33] *Sirmur Gazette*, 29 February 1892, SVNP 1892: 62.

Shifting our attention back to Avadh, the arrangements with the Educational Department remained in force, more or less undisturbed, until 1877. Official acknowledgement of the NKP's valuable collaboration in the textbook venture was poignantly summed up in the 1877 provincial *Gazetteer*, which asserted that the cause of education was much enhanced by the private enterprise of Naval Kishore, 'whose busy press disseminates, even beyond the utmost limits of the empire, a cheap, abundant, and useful literature, and is of greater public benefit and importance than many State institutions' (*Gazetteer* 1877: lxi). Soon afterwards, the amalgamation of the NWP&Oudh ushered in significant changes for the firm. It not only initiated a slow withdrawal of government patronage, but also a curtailment of Naval Kishore's monopoly in textbook publishing.

Following the amalgamation of the provinces, Naval Kishore faced a new situation that was markedly different from the privileged position he had enjoyed in Avadh. For one, the NWP provincial government ran its own government press in Allahabad, which monopolized the production of textbooks whose copyright belonged to the government. That Naval Kishore obtained the privilege to print and publish new or revised editions of these copyright works speaks volumes for his negotiating skills. In doing so, he was forced to accept lower rates than previously offered to him in Avadh.[34] Despite this initial financial setback, over time he was able to regain some of his previous status as 'official' textbook publisher. In the wake of the amalgamation, the English book depot in Lucknow was abolished in 1880. However, the authorities had a vested interest in maintaining the city's vernacular depot. It was regarded as 'a great convenience', even more so since Naval Kishore had 'always dealt liberally' with it.[35] Under his experienced management the depot was indeed running strong. In the following years it effected record sales, with the number of books sold rising steadily: from 78,000 in 1882 to 135,679 in 1883 and 141,681 in 1884.[36]

The publisher's cooperation with the state authorities reached new heights in 1886 when, following considerations to make over government printing to commercial agency and distribute more work to Indian-owned presses, the provincial government decided to close down its educational

[34] Books for which the copyright did not lie with the government were purchased directly from their authors or publishers and then distributed by the Government Book Depot or the NKP. *AECR* 1884: 108.

[35] *RPE NWP&Oudh*, for the year ending 31 March 1880: 61.

[36] The latter figure included maps and slates. *RPE NWP&Oudh*, for the year ending 31 March 1883; and for the year ending 31 March 1884: 132.

book depot at the Allahabad Government Press. Among the tenders invited for the purchase of stocks, Naval Kishore's offer was given preference. Consequently, in March 1886, the entire stock of educational works—amounting to a huge total of approximately 500,000 volumes—was sold to him and transferred to Lucknow. The implications of this transaction were momentous: the duties of the British curator were from now on confined to the storage of official publications, while the registration of books, and the control of public libraries, the responsibility of production, distribution, and sale of departmental vernacular textbooks in the provinces was made over entirely to the House of Naval Kishore.[37] In negotiating the deal, Naval Kishore had obviously hoped to expand his monopoly, for he stipulated that no educational work must thereafter be published by the Educational Department at the Allahabad Government Press or elsewhere. Not surprisingly, his demand was rejected outright. Moreover, the authorities deemed it necessary to explicitly remind him that no monopoly was being conferred on him for the sale of any books that, 'with the expressed or implied assent' of the Educational Department, had up to this point been purchased for use in government schools from other private firms.[38]

If, in taking over the book depot, Naval Kishore's intention had been to cement and further expand his monopoly, the transaction soon turned into an immense financial liability. Besides the actual purchase price of Rs 24,000, it entailed further investments exceeding Rs 100,000 for a new building in Hazratganj, new lithographic and steam printing presses, as well as the astounding number of 10,000 lithographic stones. Moreover, the Allahabad book depot had scarcely been purchased when a series of curriculum alterations threatened severe financial losses. When the publisher saw his hopes of what he loftily described as 'doing a service to the Government and country' thwarted, he embarked on a crusade for the expansion of his monopoly. In the process he became embroiled in a fierce controversy over copyrights.

4.2 Copyright Controversies

At the time of selling the educational book depot to Naval Kishore, the provincial government decided to advertise its textbook copyrights (of which there were ten) for sale to private enterprise. The publisher immediately intervened, requesting that no sale of copyrights be effected until

[37] *NWP&Oudh Administration Rept.*, for the year ending 31 March 1886: 49.
[38] *PGNWP&Oudh. General Dept.*, January 1887: 26.

the large stock of books he had just purchased was entirely exhausted. Consequently, it was agreed upon that the government would hold on to its copyrights for another five years. One financial risk successfully averted, Naval Kishore set about tackling the vexing problem of curricula changes. In at least one instance he managed to influence official decisions on textbook selection by successfully defending his commercial interests: in November 1889 he was informed by John Nesfield, then Inspector of Schools in Avadh, that he should no longer print copies of the *Jughrāfiya-e Hind shomālī* and *Jughrāfiya-e duniya,* two standard Geography textbooks used in primary and secondary schools, since they were to be replaced by Hill's textbook on Geography. Naval Kishore replied that he still had over 4000 copies of the said titles in stock and requested their continuation in the Avadh schools 'for some more time' in order to prevent heavy losses.[39] Nesfield complied and issued a notice to all Deputy Inspectors that as soon as Hill's Geography had been sold off, they could revert to the former books. This was a indeed a special personal favour, for, as Nesfield cared to inform the publisher, he had acted without official authorization.

Encouraged by, but seemingly not content with the privilege accorded to him, Naval Kishore soon afterwards addressed Nesfield again in order to reiterate his fears concerning the introduction of new textbooks. Following the amalgamation of the NWP&Oudh, he stated, frequent changes had occurred in the curricula, each resulting in a loss of thousands of rupees to his press. He was particularly concerned about the introduction into the syllabus of books whose copyright did not belong to government. Most were authored by officers of the NWP Educational Department. These officers, he asserted, 'have made it a trade, and a very profitable one too, of writing vernacular books for the schools in their own control, and get them printed and published by their own authority and under the protection of authority conferred on them in virtue of their office.'[40] As a result, most of the books he had taken over from the government depot had been superseded and had become unsaleable. The accompanying loss was so heavy that the depot risked being closed.[41]

The list of proposals that Naval Kishore came up with to remedy his predicament presented a thinly disguised attempt to extend the monopoly

[39] Letter to Inspector of Schools, 2nd Circle, NWP&Oudh. *PGNWP&Oudh*, September 1890: 3.

[40] Ibid.: 5.

[41] Ibid.: 5–8.

he had thus far enjoyed in Avadh to the entire United Provinces. His proposal, in particular, that the copyright of *all* educational books should be secured by government, and that authors should be given an honorarium in compensation, implied the hope that the exclusive right of printing and publishing such titles would automatically go to the NKP. In putting forward his arguments, the publisher took great care to act the role of a disinterested advocate of the people and loyal supporter of the colonial scheme of mass education. To this effect, he not only insisted that a continuous and cheap supply of textbooks could best be assured by one single large firm, but also posed as a moral guardian of official textbook production:

> The resolution of the Government of India published last year laid particular stress upon the moral training of our children, but what in reality may be called morality is in the majority of cases conspicuous by its absence in the vernacular books introduced in our schools. Books forming the curriculum of the Indian schools, especially those taught in the lower classes, the students of which are of an impressionable age, treat of those familiar objects not unknown even to those small boys, but conveying no moral or lesson in them. And it is admitted by all thoughtful persons that generally slur and void of morality tone [*sic*] of the great mass of the indigenous literature forms a serious barrier to the moral and intellectual progress of the Native community.[42]

In February 1890 Naval Kishore brought his correspondence with Nesfield to the notice of the DPI of the NWP&Oudh, again urging the extension of his monopoly. The DPI then consulted Nesfield, who not only strongly recommended the continuance of the monopoly Naval Kishore enjoyed in Avadh, but also advocated its extension to the NWP. There were 'obvious advantages' in having one central depot and publisher for the entire United Provinces. Nesfield supported the publisher's proposal that authors should be given an honorarium instead of copyright and also denounced the malpractice that, in sharp contrast to Avadh, educational officers in the NWP were allowed to publish, sell and appraise their own textbooks. The prices of these were often exorbitantly high, and certainly far in excess of those charged by Naval Kishore. Moreover, seeing the profits that could be made from textbook publishing, educational officers in Avadh had begun to claim the same privileges as enjoyed by their colleagues in the NWP. The practice, thus, needed to be curtailed.[43]

[42] Ibid.: 7.

[43] Letter to DPI, NWP&Oudh, 21 April 1890, ibid.: 11–13.

In his ensuing report to government, the DPI concurred with Nesfield's views and advised that the copyright of textbooks should generally be obtained by government, and that only those authors whose books were officially sanctioned for curricula use should be permitted an honorarium. However, he cautioned, the scope of educational printing in the NWP was too large and too much of a responsibility to be undertaken by a single firm only. Consequently, it was agreed that, in order to distribute the work more equally, and at the same time ensure an efficient and cheap supply of textbooks, tenders were to be invited from several competent printing firms.[44]

As a result of these deliberations, on 16 September 1890 the provincial government issued a momentous order to the effect that no new textbook could be introduced into the curriculum of which the copyright had not previously been secured by government. In other words, all new textbooks used in NWP&Oudh schools would henceforth become government property. However, in order for new books to be produced and sold at the lowest possible price, printing tenders were to be called for. This ruling, as the Secretary to Government explained to an alarmed Naval Kishore, applied only to *new* textbooks introduced into the curriculum; it was not the government's intention to disturb arrangements regarding books previously in use.[45]

In requiring that printing tenders be called for, the September 1890 ruling supported the principle of competition and entailed a redistribution of official printing commissions to the various printing firms in the provinces. In the process the NKP's workmanship and rates came under closer scrutiny. During its meetings in April and October 1891, the Vernacular Textbook Committee reported cases of overcharging on the part of Naval Kishore and advocated that printing should be given to other presses, notably to Munshi Gulab Singh's Mufid-e ᶜAm Press in Lahore, whose workmanship was judged 'decidedly superior' to that of the NKP. The Lahore firm, moreover, promised 'much greater probability that the quality of workmanship and paper and the price to be charged for each book that is sold will be adhered to.'[46] Following the committee's recommendations, in March 1892 DPI White ordered that contracts for printing Urdu textbooks in the NWP would in future be given to the Mufid-e ᶜAm Press, while Hindi textbooks would be printed by the Methodist Publishing House in Lucknow. Predictably, Naval Kishore interpreted the order

[44] Ibid.: 13–14.

[45] *PGNWP&Oudh. Educational Dept.*, December 1891: 13.

[46] *PGNWP&Oudh. Educational Dept.*, July 1892: 16.

as a serious encroachment upon his 'customary rights'. He immediately complained to the provincial government, insinuating that his tenders had not been fairly considered and that, moreover, the DPI's decision was against the September 1890 ruling.[47] In rejecting his 'rightful claims' to the printing for the NWP, the authorities had 'altogether lost sight' of the work done by him for the past thirty years in connection with the Oudh Educational Department.[48] For lack of valid arguments against his rival publishers he resorted to polemic: 'One should have naturally thought that in the selection of publishers, regard would be given to the encouragement of local industry and the benefit of persons of the province, in preference to total strangers and persons of speculation whose sole object is to enrich themselves without doing anything for the country . . .'[49] His second point, regarding the printing of Hindi textbooks, seemed more valid: why should government give a contract to the Methodist Publishing House, which was owned by a religious body, and whose sole object was 'the propagation and spread of certain religious doctrines and principles?'[50]

In a move that can be seen as characteristic of his negotiations with the state authorities, Naval Kishore also played the 'social card', invoking the large body of almost 1000 workmen to whom his firm provided employment. These workers were allegedly 'quite unfit for Government or any other service and . . . in the event of the NKP being deprived of Government patronage and support, would be thrown out of employment and reduced to a state of misery and privation in these hard times.'[51] To what extent this profession of humanitarianism was genuine rather than just a pressure tactic is difficult to say.

At government level there was confusion over whether the contracts that DPI White had given to other publishers concerned new textbooks only and thus did not interfere with the September 1890 ruling. Once again Nesfield, who in the meantime had succeeded White as officiating DPI, was consulted. By that time his attitude towards Naval Kishore's firm had taken a dramatic and surprising turn. Not only was he no longer supportive of the NKP, he openly voiced his hostility towards Naval Kishore. In his report to government, Nesfield declared the publisher's

[47] Letter to Secretary to Govt., NWP&Oudh, 9 April 1892, *PGNWP&Oudh, Educational Dept.*, July 1892: 9–10.

[48] Ibid.

[49] Ibid.

[50] Ibid.

[51] Ibid.

complaint to be wholly untenable and groundless, since the monopoly he enjoyed in Avadh, and in Avadh *only*, was in no way encroached upon.[52] In all other divisions of the United Provinces the Educational Department was at perfect liberty to employ new contractors for work, as had recently been done by White. Nesfield seized the opportunity to bring a number of charges against the NKP, and openly accused Naval Kishore of malpractices such as overcharging and violation of copyright. To this effect he included the testimonies of various booksellers and authors who had allegedly been dealt with unfairly by the Lucknow publisher. On the given grounds, he finally, and in a complete reversal of his former stance, urged that Naval Kishore's monopoly in Avadh be discontinued:

> In fact it was high time that the Educational Department in the Oudh districts turned over a new leaf in the matter of village schoolbooks. Munshi Newal Kishore has enjoyed this monopoly for some 30 years, and I think that on the whole he has profited by it more than the schools have done. The books affected by his monopoly are old and in many respects out of date. Deputy Inspectors and teachers are tired of them. There is a want of new blood . . . Better books and better printing can be got elsewhere. Moreover, it is time that the department should be released from the risk of bad paper and almost illegible printing in which (contrary to contract) his books are sometimes issued, and from the risks to which the poor village schoolboys are exposed of being charged unauthorized prices in order to enrich one of the wealthiest publishing firms in Upper India.[53]

Despite the serious nature of the charges, the Lieutenant Governor ruled in favour of the NKP. In June 1892 he ordered that the firm's monopoly for Avadh be continued for another seven years, encompassing 'all school text-books for Oudh, whether text-books already in use or text-books selected from time to time by the Text-book Committee'.[54] It would seem that Naval Kishore was at this point reaping the fruits of over three decades of loyal collaboration: as was especially emphasized, the Lieutenant Governor was not prepared to assent to 'the proscription in this manner of a local press which, whatever may be its defects, has in the past done good service . . . and has given to Oudh the first example of an industrial enterprise on a large scale.'[55] By contrast, with regard to the NWP, the

[52] Letter to Secretary to Govt., NWP & Oudh, 16 June 1892, ibid.: 12–15.

[53] Ibid.: 14.

[54] Letter to DPI, NWP & Oudh, 30 June 1892, ibid.: 16–18.

[55] Ibid.: 17.

DPI was authorized to place contracts for 'any existing text-books or any new text-books' with any firm that made the most advantageous tender to government. These orders were to be regarded 'by the Department as final and by Naval Kishore as fully and exhaustively disposing of any claims which his press may have to special consideration on account of its past connection with the Educational Department.'[56]

It soon became clear that the vague expression 'all school text-books for Oudh' was open to widely differing interpretations. While British officials presented Naval Kishore with a list of ten titles, notably those whose copyright lay with government and which had earlier been conferred unto the Mufid-e ʿAm Press,[57] the publisher chose to take the expression literally, interpreting it as his exclusive right to print *all* textbooks used in Avadh. Accordingly he voiced his protest. By this time Nesfield was truly exasperated with what he perceived as Naval Kishore's rapacity, and threatened him with legal consequences:

> Munshi Newal Kishore, C.I.E., is not a novice in matters of trade; and he must be well aware that he cannot under the imaginary shelter of a Government order take unlawful possession of the property of others, and that he will be involved in a lawsuit or a series of lawsuits if he prints any book or books the copyright of which is private property . . .
>
> Munshi Newal Kishore has been repeatedly informed by me of late years that private authors have a perfect right to select their own printers and publishers, and that no pressure could or would be put upon them to employ his press for his special enrichment or benefit in preference to any other. His claim to compel authors to use his press and no other for the printing and publication of educational books is one of the most rapacious and extraordinary demands ever put forth by a publisher living under a civilised Government.[58]

The controversy over copyrights had turned into a fierce personal confrontation between the two men, as indicated by the increasingly exacerbated tone of their correspondence. Indignant at Nesfield's disparaging remarks, Naval Kishore retorted in the same vein: he not only insisted on his interpretation of matters, but in order to underpin his argument cited the example of educational officers of rank—Raja Shiva

[56] Ibid.: 18.

[57] i.e., in Urdu: *Mufīd al-mubtadī*; *Taʿlīm al-mubtadī*, *Arithmetic in Urdu*; *Mufīd al-Inshā*; *Khilqat al-bayān*; in Hindi: *Varṇa prakāśikā*; *Kaithī varṇamālā*, *Bāl śikṣā*, *Arithmetic in Hindi*, *Patra hitaiśiṇī* and *Sṛṣṭī kā varṇan*.

[58] Letter to Inspector of Schools, 2nd circle, Lucknow, 20 August 1892, *PGNWP&Oudh. Educational Dept.*, June 1893: 96.

Prasad, M. Kempson, Nazir Ahmad—who had willingly ceded their copyrights to government for public good, while others kept their copyrights, thus 'making themselves rich at the expense of poor students'. To illustrate his point, he inserted an exhaustive list of textbooks which, as he alleged, had recently been introduced into the curriculum in open contravention of the 1890 ruling, since their copyright was never secured by government, but still lay with the authors, all of them educational officers. That the list was headed by a large number of titles authored by none other than Nesfield himself amounted to an open declaration of war.[59] Naval Kishore further defended himself against the charges brought forth by Nesfield. He also thought it expedient to bring the matter before the provincial government, requesting clarification as to the exact extent of his monopoly.[60]

As a result, government asked Nesfield for an explanation, especially with regard to Naval Kishore's allegations concerning the textbooks 'unlawfully' introduced. Nesfield was only too glad to reiterate his accusations against Naval Kishore, whom he found behaving 'as if he was a licensed monopolist of the Dark Ages, entitled to trample upon private enterprise and crush the efforts of rival printers and publishers more honest than himself.'[61] He also cast serious doubts on the publisher's veracity and accused him of a deliberate attempt to deceive the government through a series of false allegations. Nesfield painstakingly set out to prove that each and every one of the ten textbooks on his list had been introduced into the curriculum prior to the September ruling. Finally, he reiterated his demand that the NKP's monopoly be cancelled and indicated that he would be able to prove from his long acquaintance with the House of Naval Kishore that 'the good services in the past for which he claims to be rewarded are something worse than mythical'.[62]

This time Nesfield's letter did not fail to make an impact. In November 1892 Naval Kishore received a final communication from the government in which the extent of his monopoly was laid down in unequivocal terms: the monopoly was limited to the Avadh region and extended only to textbooks hitherto printed by him as well as to those new textbooks introduced by the Avadh textbook committee for which the copyright was secured by government in accordance with the September 1890 ruling. The publisher's claim that he should also be given the right to print schoolbooks

[59] Letter to Offg. DPI, 12 September 1892, ibid.: 97–100.

[60] Letter to Secretary of Govt., 29 September 1892, ibid.: 93–4.

[61] Letter to Secretary of Govt., 31 October 1892, ibid.: 104.

[62] Ibid.: 107.

already in use in Avadh but hitherto printed by other firms was rejected as 'wholly inadmissible'. The government seized the opportunity to severely reprimand Naval Kishore, stating that they would have expected of him 'the propriety of resting content with the very favourable concession made to [him]' and exacting that he at once withdraw the charges made against the Educational Department should he wish his privileges to continue.[63]

Naval Kishore had to all appearances lost the battle and been humbled in the process. For Nesfield, however, the affair was not yet over. Three months later he submitted a long report to government in which he addressed the issue of copyright and authorship in principal. His objective was to expose the practice prevalent in Avadh, i.e. that textbook copyrights should belong exclusively to government, as impracticable and nonsensical.[64] Having proved that government itself had on several occasions infringed the rules laid down in the order of September 1890, he pointed out that no such rules existed in any other province of India, that they were in fact the outcome of 'the rapacious instincts of Munshi Newal Kishore' and should therefore be cancelled. Bound by its own ruling, the Educational Department had forsaken its freedom of choice and action, since it could no longer introduce into the curriculum any book whose copyright belonged to some author or publisher: such a state of things, Nesfield maintained, was 'intolerable', for it placed the department 'in a worse position than any other Educational Department in India or in any other part of the world except perhaps in autocratic Russia.'[65] Moreover, the 1890 ruling had an adverse effect on literary activity: the prospect that no schoolbook could be prepared without the DPI's written authorization and that copyright had to be yielded to government was bound to discourage authorship, since it deprived an author of the 'legitimate fruit of his own labours and skill.' In conclusion, Nesfield asserted that 'No really valuable book will ever be written under these conditions. In point of fact no such book *has been* written since these rules were issued.'[66] The order, therefore, ought to be repealed.

While the government's immediate reaction to Nesfield's queries is not known, there is evidence to suggest that his advice was heeded. In 1893 a new Provincial Textbook Committee was formed. One of its tasks, as stipulated in an appendix to its constitution, was to ascertain

[63] Letter to Proprietor, NKP, 17 November 1892, ibid.: 108.

[64] Letter to Secretary of Govt., 6 February 1893, ibid.: 109–15.

[65] Ibid.: 111.

[66] Ibid.: 112.

whether a textbook author was willing to assign the right and risks of publication to government or whether he preferred to publish at his own risk. Authors were thus free to choose but still needed official approval in order for their books to be introduced to the school curriculum. The government on the other hand, reserved itself the right to remove 'at any time and without notice' any textbook introduced under these rules from the official curriculum and declared itself not liable to pay compensation for any financial loss resulting from such removal.[67]

While all this was going on, Naval Kishore had acquired the copyrights of several bestselling textbooks, including twenty standard works by Raja Shiva Prasad (*Jām-e jahān numā*; *Qiṣṣa-e Sanḍfarḍ-o-Marṭan*; *Itihās timir nāśak*, etc.) and the widely used history textbook *Waqiᶜāt-e Hind* by Karimuddin. At a later stage he ceded the copyright of *Wāqiᶜāt-e Hind* to the government. This act of generosity was duly acknowledged in a later edition of the book, which informs us that the proprietor of the NKP was 'deserving of high credit', since he had 'without renumeration, actuated solely by the idea of the public good' handed over the copyright to government.[68]

The controversy over textbook copyrights has been described at some length to highlight the strongly competitive nature of the textbook market and the various conflicting interests involved in it. Rather than just exemplifying Naval Kishore's toughness in trade bargaining, it provides a good illustration of the amount of negotiation it took for a commercial printer-publisher to obtain and maintain his share of government patronage. Accounting for the largest portion of the Indian publishing sector, educational printing remained a highly contested arena throughout the nineteenth and well into the twentieth century.[69] Control over the textbook market not only carried larger implications of cultural hegemony and ideological domination, determining what kind of knowledge was propagated and by whom; economically speaking, it also meant control over a rapidly expanding and profitable business. The colonial state found itself facing an obvious dilemma: while it relied on Indian collaboration and had to encourage indigenous enterprise through patronage, it also had a vested interest in securing its own share in the flourishing and lucrative textbook publishing market. For the average Indian commercial publisher, on the other hand, the stakes were even higher: to be given or denied a share in textbook printing could decide the viability of an

[67] *PGNWP&Oudh. Educational Dept.*, December 1894: 63.

[68] Editorial notice, 1897, *Wāqiᶜāt-e Hind*, Bombay 1900, *preface.*

[69] For the early twentieth century, see Orsini 2002: 95–7.

enterprise. As we have seen, in trying to get their share of the pie Indian printer-publishers not only faced stiff competition from one another, they also had to vie with the interests of the government and individual colonial officials. In such a situation, it took an adamant and shrewd negotiator like Naval Kishore to succeed.

4.3 Money Matters

As noted in the previous section, the amalgamation of the NWP&Oudh in 1877 constituted a watershed in the commercial relations between the NKP and the colonial administration. It affected not only textbook production but also all other areas of collaboration. Previously, the Lucknow publishing house had enjoyed a privileged and barely contested position: personal contacts and direct interaction on the spot had ensured a smooth and highly effective collaboration with the Avadh administration, while also encouraging a kind of semi-official favouritism on the part of local officials. The amalgamation of the provinces not only brought Naval Kishore in contact with a more remote, impersonal, and tightly controlled administration, it also entailed new policies regarding the distribution of government patronage among Indian presses. Moreover, the fact that the Government of the amalgamated provinces operated its own Government Press in Allahabad, called for a fundamental redefinition of the NKP's role in official publishing. In his initial assessment of the new situation, M. Kempson, by then DPI of the United Provinces, gave a favourable résumé:

> The absorption of the publishing trade at Cawnpore and Lucknow is remarkable. It is chiefly due to the enterprize of Munshi Newal Kishore of Lucknow who, following the example of the kings of Oudh, before the annexation, has opened a branch press at Cawnpore, which is more conveniently situated for the resort of book merchants from Upper and Central and Western India. Nearly one-half of the publications at Cawnpore and Lucknow together are from his presses; and his only important rival is the old Nizami Press at Cawnpore, which is famous for the excellency of its lithography. The increasing cheapness and excellence of Newal Kishore's work is gradually absorbing the public patronage. I have already noticed one beautiful specimen of the lithographic art from his establishment. The demand for inexpensive books, however, necessitates the use of inferior sorts of paper and inferior calligraphy in the majority of instances. M. Newal Kishore's position as an employer of labour is unique in the Province, and I am glad to add that he is a liberal and considerate master. His

services to the Education Department in Oudh have been invaluable and I wish to see them still further utilized in the North-Western Provinces.[70]

However, with Allahabad as the new seat of government, Naval Kishore found himself confronted by a number of new decision-makers who were not personally acquainted with him and who soon came to regard the former, often semi-official, business agreements between the NKP and the Avadh administrators with growing suspicion. Foremost among them was Colonel A. Dodd, Superintendent of the Allahabad Government Press, who had been put in charge of carrying out the amalgamation of the government presses. His first assessment of the NKP's future status was decidedly more reserved than Kempson's:

> I have, as a rule, plenty of work to occupy my vernacular press in Allahabad, and am not anxious to add to it for the present. Munshi Nawal Kishor has apparently been encouraged by the Oudh authorities to procure machinery and materials on the strength of Government patronage. I would recommend that present arrangements be allowed to stand—at any rate, experimentally—for two years, provided that the work executed gives satisfaction, and that the sale of charges does not exceed that sanctioned for his press. I have provided Rs 14,000 in my revised budget under 'job work' to meet bills on his account.[71]

Such words did not augur well for the NKP's future. Naval Kishore received a foretaste of the changing climate when his attempt to introduce higher rates for government subscriptions of *Avadh Akhbār* failed. Likewise, a petition to the new government in which he asked for financial support to maintain his press in Kanpur, was declined.[72] It appears, however, that it did not take him long to overcome these initial setbacks and form new alliances, for by the early 1880s we find the NKP enjoying the lion's share of official British patronage to commmercial and private presses in the amalgamated provinces. As indicated in Table 4.1, the firm received at the time over two-thirds of all official printing orders.

The only other chief beneficiary of state patronage was the Pioneer Press in Allahabad, with which in 1889-90 the NKP shared commissions

[70] *RPIR* 1877: 117.

[71] *PGNWP&Oudh. General Dept.*, May 1877: 23.

[72] *PGNWP&Oudh. General Dept.*, June 1877, App. B, no. 218; and October 1877, no. B, 124. The reasons for this application, which appears strange in view of the firm's overall growth, are unknown. They may be related to the changed administrative setup or to the effects of the devastating drought and famine of 1876–80 on the general economy.

TABLE 4.1
Offical Patronage Accorded to Presses in the NWP&Oudh

	1880-1		1881-2		1882-3	
	Rs	%	Rs	%	Rs	%
NKP	14,244	61.9	37,836	88.2	22,851	78.7
Other presses	8,781	38.1	5,034	11.8	6,186	21.3
Total	23,025	100	42,870	100	29,037	100

SOURCE: PGNWP&Oudh. General Dept., May 1886: 16.

of almost Rs 56,000, that is over 84 per cent of the total sum. Two years later, there was a slight reduction in patronage to the two presses, with the ratio dropping to 78 per cent or a total of Rs 68,964. The remainder of the work was distributed among seventeen smaller presses, each receiving between Rs 200 and Rs 1000. The gulf was indeed huge and prone to incite resentment.[73]

These figures were brought to official attention in the context of a sustained controversy between the NKP and the colonial administration. It was occasioned by an official enquiry into the working of the Allahabad Government Press and Book Depot, particularly its account and pay systems. The officer in charge of the enquiry was W.H. Dobbie of the Accounts Department. In April 1885 Dobbie submitted his report in which he heavily criticized the unequal distribution of government patronage and the blatant favouring of Naval Kishore's firm by the Government Press, demanding a revision of prevailing arrangements. Referring to an earlier arrangement that secured a yearly supply of work worth Rs 26,000 to the NKP, Dobbie stated:

> It is evident (1) that the distribution of the patronage of the Government has been very unequally made, Munshi Newal Kishore having been awarded by far the greatest amount; (2) that prior to January, 1882, there are no orders that so large a share of that patronage should be given to Munshi Newal Kishore; (3) that subsequent to that date, although there is no sanction of Government to 80 per cent. of their patronage being given to him, yet there is a sanction to the lion's share of that patronage being so given, the percentage varying with the provisions made in the budget; and (4) that in 1883-84 the limit sanctioned by Government to which work might be given to him was exceeded.[74]

[73] *PGNWP&Oudh. General Dept.*, July 1890: 4; October 1892: 3.

[74] *PGNWP&Oudh. General Dept.*, May 1886: 17.

Dobbie further criticized the 'excessively high' rates granted to the NKP which, according to his estimate, exceeded the prevailing government rates by nearly double. While the rates for work done by private presses were generally fixed in accordance with the rates of the Government Press, and had in the course of time undergone a reduction of 60 per cent, those accorded to the NKP still remained at a level that had been fixed as early as 1874. There was no official sanction for this. Moreover, Naval Kishore was found to be making undue profit by supplying the paper required for government printing himself and charging the British very high rates for it. Dobbie summed up his report with an impressive calculation to the effect that, by granting the NKP special rates, the government had incurred a loss of Rs 19,000 during the year 1883–4 alone. In conclusion, he emphasized the necessity of keeping a better check on Munshi Naval Kishore's bills.[75]

Following the report, Colonel Dodd received official orders to submit an explanation as to the special rates paid to Naval Kishore and the arrangements regarding the supply and rates of paper.[76] Not surprisingly, Dodd had a vested interest in repudiating the charges which impugned his authority and cast doubts on the way he was running the Allahabad Government Press. In a statement of September 1885 he justified the special patronage accorded to the NKP:

> Apart from the frequently expressed wish of the Government that Munshi Newal Kishore's claims to liberal patronage should be steadily borne in mind, all the circumstances connected with the maintenance of his press and the Munshi's own services to the State establish his title to a far larger share of official favour than need be awarded to other private institutions in the province. Roughly I should say the numerical strength of his establishment equals the aggregate of nearly all the other presses in the North-West and Oudh. He employs close to 900 men at a monthly cost of over Rs 6000 in salaries and Rs 4000 in contingent expenditure, in addition to pensionary allowances to some 50 former employees. Of his own personal services in the cause of education and enlightenment I need not enlarge. The translation and sale at his own risk of important official and semi-official publications, his munificent contributions to the several literary societies in India and England, and other voluntary works, valuable and costly, are well known to the Government. For my own part, considering his resources, and his enterprising labours, official and private, I would advocate an extension, rather than any withdrawal, of the present patronage accorded to his press. Munshi Newal Kishore was certainly a loser by the amalgamation of the

[75] Ibid.: 18–19.

[76] Letter from Chief Secretary of Govt., 28 May 1885, ibid.: 38.

> two provinces, so that any undue favouritism I may be accused of having shown him of late would seem more than justified by the action of the Oudh authorities in years gone by.[77]

As for the preferential rates accorded to the NKP, Dodd pointed out that they had been fixed earlier by the Avadh authorities and that he saw no reason to intervene, particularly since it had been the professed desire of Lieutenant Governor Sir George Couper that the NKP's privileges be continued after the amalgamation. Moreover, the rates were justified by the fact that they included the cost of paper as well as by the special conditions that Naval Kishore offered the British in that he held himself financially responsible 'for all risks of a too large edition and all the expense of reprints to meet supplementary demands, as well as the storage and distribution of the forms.'[78] Lastly, Dodd defended Naval Kishore against the accusation of charging exaggerated rates for paper.

Despite Dodd's advocacy of the NKP's case, the special rates hitherto accorded to the firm were withdrawn by a government order of 15 January 1886. Although Naval Kishore's claim to special patronage was duly acknowledged, it seemed expedient, against the backdrop of mounting public pressure, that in future his firm be placed 'on the same footing' as other presses in the provinces. The publisher reacted to the decision on 8 June 1886 with a letter of complaint to the Chief Secretary to Government, in which he emphasized the distinct status of his enterprise and explained why he considered himself entitled to special privileges:

> Sir,
>
> Some little time ago I received from the Superintendent Government Press an extract from an order of Government, anent revision of rates of work done for Government in our Press. With reference thereto I beg to state that the principle set forth in it by the local Government of recognizing the claims of all the presses alike is highly praise-worthy and no objection can be raised by any party to it. But the case of my Press is a special one which is evident from the statement submitted herewith. This special favour has been shown to me since the establishment of the Press in 1858 and up to date it has been continued. I am still in hopes that the local Government will not be so unkind as to withdraw the privilege extended to me, not only during my life time, but also during that of my heirs, when it takes into consideration the system and policy adopted by the Press and by myself similar to what the Government does in the case of loyal Zemindars.

[77] Ibid.: 45.
[78] Ibid.: 46.

Regarding the Superintendent's order for submission of tender for work, I most respectfully beg to say that such a course takes away from me all the privileges I have been enjoying during the last 28 years. I beg to remind you of a circumstance, which happened at the time of amalgamation of the two Provinces in 1877. I had the honour of accompanying Colonel Dodd to Government House, when if my memory does not fail me (and I think he also recollects), Sir George Couper was pleased to explain both in English and Hindustani that the privileges which I had been enjoying under the kind patronage of the Oudh Government should also be extended to me after the amalgamation. I am highly thankful for having been allowed to enjoy the same privileges. In 1882 I complained to the Government of not receiving work continually and when the matter was referred to Colonel Dodd, he was pleased to draw out a scheme which was approved of by Government, promising me about Rs 26,000 worth of work every year, a promise which was kept up to about the 31st January last.

Regarding the rates, I beg to state that with the exception of the Judicial and Revenue Forms, printed especially for Oudh and for which special rates were sanctioned 17 years ago, a time when the rates of the other presses were very high, my rates were comparatively cheaper and I think it is only proper that the same rates be continued. I suffered loss at that time, and taking this into consideration, they should not be reduced, though paper may have become somewhat cheaper than before. This is included in the promised work of the value of Rs 26,000. The remaining portion of the whole work is rated by the Superintendent, Government Press. The benefits arising from the special rates are expended in giving pensions to superannuated hands of the Press and donations in the shape of money and books. But if the rates for these two Forms are reduced, I shall be under the painful necessity, either of putting a stop to the pensions, &. c., or of making reductions in my establishment on a large scale, and the effect will tell hard on the people of Oudh, so many of whom are employed. And if in the face of this reasonable but humble representation, the Government is bent on reducing the rates, I beg the favour of having timely notice of their decision, that I may arrange accordingly with my large establishment.

In conclusion, I beg to draw your attention to the statement I append hereto and request you to be kind enough to submit the same to His Honour the Lieutenant Governor and Chief Commissioner for his favourable consideration.

[. . .]

Newul Kishore[79]

The letter has been quoted in full because it affords a good illustration of the strategies employed by Naval Kishore in his dealings with the British

[79] Original autograph letter, UPSA, File no. 288.

authorities. Thinly disguised beneath an outwardly deferential attitude was the self-assertive stance of a large entrepreneur who was acutely aware of the influence he commanded in both economic and public life. His status as the single-largest Indian employer in the provinces put Naval Kishore in a powerful position *vis-à-vis* the government. The way he exploited this circumstance to exert pressure on the state authorities is reminiscent of many a modern-day industrialist. His allusion to the adverse effects that a reduction in rates would have on the social fabric of the province was a barely concealed threat.

The letter's argument was underpinned by the accompanying 'Statement of the Newul Kishore Press'. Composed by Naval Kishore himself, this rare and elaborate document provides an eyewitness account of the history, publishing policy, and achievements of the NKP while also revealing a good deal about the publisher's self-image. It attests to his self-perception as a leading representative of the indigenous elite, who in his steadfast loyalism and commitment to the cause of social welfare and education considered himself an indispensable collaborator of the British in the common agenda of 'uplifting' the Indian masses. As a unique first-hand testimony from inside the publishing house the 'Statement' deserves to be reproduced here in its entirety:

Statement of the Newul Kishore Press

I established this Press in 1858, when the Province of Oudh was a scene of general, if not universal rebellion, and when peace had yet to be restored. The Province was virtually in the possession of armed rebels and warlike preparations on the part of the British Government were in progress to crush their rebellious spirit. I came here under the patronage of Sir Robert Montgomery, the Chief Commissioner of Oudh and Colonel Abbott, Commissioner of Lucknow. These gentlemen extended, in consideration of my loyalty and of what I had done in the Punjab for the British Government, their patronage to my newly-established Press and favored me with the printing of all English and Vernacular documents connected with their Establishments. My Press was then the first of its kind in the Province, and as Railways were not then in existence, I had to incur a great deal of expense and trouble in having the materials needed, to make it a success, fetched from Calcutta.

2. In 1867, although the Government Press was opened for the publication of the Government Gazette, the flourishing condition of my Press attracted towards it and almost monopolized the Vernacular printing of the different Departments of the Publice Service; and consequently the Press received sufficient work to keep it in good working order.

3. Under the auspices of the Local Authorities, the policy pursued was that of translating and publishing the standard works of the well-known ancient authors of the country, the object being to prevent the effacement of their names. This policy received special encouragement from the officers of various grades employed in the Province, and nearly all the money earned was devoted to the great work associated with it. About 2000 works of various celebrated authors have been, in pursuance of this standing policy of the Press, printed and published, and no less than 500 different books of the most useful kind have been translated from Sanskrit, Arabic, Persian, English and Nagri into the Vernacular and printed for the benefit of all classes of our country men. The Press has moreover laid out a good deal of capital in publishing new books and compilations of authors of fame and in this way it has subserved the cause of education and progress and rendered thereby material help to the Government.
4. This liberal policy has always been steadily kept in view by the Press; nearly Rs 10,000 are annually expended in work of this sort *viz*, that of compiling and publishing new works of a useful stamp. Manuscripts of books of new authors and translations are pouring in from all quarters and as soon as those on the table are disposed of, fresh ones come in and demand fresh outlay and labour.
5. The Government has expended hundreds of thousands of rupees on procuring copies of valuable Sanskrit, Arabic and Persian works. Even in Oudh, a large sum is annually set apart by Government for the Asiatic Society of Calcutta to help in the publications of books of ancient authors. The work which that Society has done with the liberal assistance of the Imperial and Local Governments in 100 years, has been done in this Press to a very great extent during the entire period of its existence.
6. A reference to the list of books prepared according to Act XXV of 1867 will show that, of the newly published books of a scientific character, which have emanated from all the Presses in Oudh, and the N.-W.-Provinces and the Panjab, the majority by far have been issued from this Press. Its claim therefore to Government patronage, is decidedly more valid than that of any other Press.
7. The Newul Kishore Press has, in consequence of its attempts to further the work connected with the Department of Public Instruction, been a loser. Since 1864, the prices of School books have been reduced to such an extent, that the aforesaid Department has on the whole been a gainer. The prices of Vernacular Books in other Provinces are four or five times the amounts the Department of Public Instruction in Oudh is called upon to pay.
8. The accounts of the Press show that in supplying books to students at cheap rates, it has rendered assistance to the Department of Public Instruction to nearly two lacs of rupees. The book department connected

with the Press sustains great losses, when books are struck out of Public Instruction curricula, as well as on account of varieties of accidents, such as books being eaten up by white-ants, &c., &c. The existence of our book department is a source of very great saving to Government, as it is not obliged to organize a department of its own to execute orders from Schools and to keep accounts by means of a paid establishment, as the entire responsibility of such an organization has been assumed by us.

9. In the Oudh Educational Reports honorable mention is always made of the Press, the utility of which together with the assistance rendered to the cause of Public Instruction, has thus been again and again brought to the notice of the Local Government.
10. Again the works printed on this Press have been, by special arrangements, sent in large numbers to foreign cities, such as Bokhara, Yarkand, Cabul &c., as well as to northern Persia and Europe. And in this way the peace enjoyed by India under a benevolent Government and the great improvements that are being effected under its auspices are noised abroad and the prestige of the British name is raised in foreign lands.
11. The great officers of Government and residents of Oudh and the North Western Provinces can bear testimony to the fact that scientific works and productions of ancient authors which were at one time not available, have been brought within reach of the poorest of Students.
12. It is also worthy of consideration that in consequence of our reduced prices and the amount of work rapidly and at the same time neatly done, a general reduction of rates is being realized and thus a saving to Government is being ensured. For instance, the Government used to expend about two lacs of rupees for Patwari and Settlement Forms. When Mr Buck was the Director of the Department of Agriculture and Commerce, the foundation was laid at my suggestion of a permanent reduction of rates of printing, the consequence of which has been an annual saving of more than a lac of rupees to the land-holders. And the Government, moreover, incurs no loss as it formerly used to do. If arrangements for the printing of these forms were made with the Government Press, an establishment consisting of highly paid officers would have been a necessity and considerable expenditure would have been incurred. But this has been saved by our Press doing the work cheaply, and being content with small profits.
13. Owing to the annexation of Oudh, the people of Lucknow were thrown into great distress, which has been mitigated by the charitable institution, the foundation of which was laid in 1863. Government contributes Rs 15, 000 annually to its funds. This general distress has been to a very limited extent alleviated by the employment it [i.e. the NKP] has given to hundreds of persons. Its present establishment consists of 900 persons, who but for its existence might have been without employment.

It is to be noted that some expense is always incurred in giving our hands the preparatory training without which they can be of no service to us. It is a well-known fact that in Government and Railway Presses in different parts of the country, thousands of persons are working who learnt their duties in this Press; and though we have been losers, the public has gained. Through the little assistance accorded to the Press by Government, general distress in Lucknow has thus been to a small extent mitigated.

14. Over and above trying to improve the country in the ways indicated, the following steps have been taken towards introducing improvements.

i.—Great assistance has been given towards founding and maintaining the Lucknow Reform Club (*Jalsa Tahzib*) in the shape of money and books; and thus a great step has been taken towards the spread of useful knowledge and civilization in these parts of the country.

ii.—Libraries have been organized in large cities and towns in different parts of the country in honor of Government officers of distinguished merit and marked benevolence; and books worth thousands of rupees have been presented to these Libraries. In this way also the cause of education and civilization has been subserved.

(1.) Muir College, Allahabad, in the name of Sir William Muir.
(2.) Kayastha Pathshala, Allahabad.
(3.) Canning College, Lucknow in the name of Sir George Couper.
(4.) Carmichael Library, Benares,
One set in the name of Mr Carmichael.
One set in the name of Mr Kempson.
(5.) Public Library, Barielly [*sic*], in the name of Sir John Inglis.
(6.) Public Library, Fyzabad, in the name of General J. Reid.
(7.) Bhargav National Association, Muthra.
(8.) Library Jummoo, Cashmere, in memory of Maharaja Ranbir Singh.
(9.) Library Jeypore, in memory of Maharaja Ram Singh.
(10.) Library Patiala, in memory of Maharaja Mahendra Singh.
(11.) Punjab Public Library, in the name of Sir Charles Aitchison.
(12.) Indian Institute, Oxford University, Oxford, in the name of Mr Sparks.

iii.—The Press has done much to encourage the art of *Khoosh Nawisi* (Caligraphy) [*sic*] *Naqqashi* (Drawing), as well as the study of Arabic and Sanskrit; and it has moreover employed lots of trained men for these purposes.

iv.—Omitting minor items of assistance, the Press has made the following grants of money and books:—

(a.)—The sum of Rs 15,000 has been promised and therefore may be considered as given to the Lucknow Municipal Committee for the establishment of a School.

(b.)—Rs 15,000 to the National Association called the Bhargav Sabha.
(c.)—Rs 1000 to the Bareilly College.
(d.)—Rs 1000 to the Kayasth Pathshala.
(e.)—Besides these grants, twenty-five scholarships from Rs 2 to Rs 15 per mensem, have been promised for the benefit of poor students, and a lump sum has been promised for the benefit of poor students in the Agra College specially.
(f.)—The Press moreover allows its superannuated servants and families of those who did good service and are now dead, pensions amounting to Rs 3000 a year.

15. This Press issued an English Newspaper in 1859,[80] with the sole view of assisting Government; but it was discontinued when there was no necessity for its existence. It has however maintained up to date a first class Vernacular Daily, called the "Oudh Akhbar", to discuss all political questions and to keep the people informed of all administrative affairs, social improvements, &c. This Journal has furthered the cause of education and loyalty by original articles as well as by translations of select Speeches in Parliament, &c., &c.

The Oudh Akhbar has been confessedly a power in these Provinces and its voice has been invariably raised in behalf of measures, political and social, fitted to do good to the country, and no paper has done more to promote loyalty among the people of the country than the Oudh Akhbar. For instance, it helped materially by its articles, &c., in the organization of the Canning College, and it received through Col. Bradford, the thanks of the Government for its articles in behalf of the great Delhi assemblage for the purpose of recognizing Her Majesty's assumption of the title of the "EMPRESS OF INDIA." The Oudh Akhbar had about a hundred articles in behalf of the amalgamation scheme, and the difficulties thrown in its way by the opponents of the scheme are well-known to Col. Erskine and Mr Woodburn. The Oudh Akhbar did much good during the Afghan War in 1878–9, in interpreting the real motives of Government and removing misunderstandings. During the Egyptian War with Arabi Pasha and also in the Soudan affair, it did its best to promote loyalty among the excitable portion of our Mahomedan fellow-subjects. It also raised its voice in favour of Government in 1885, when war with Russia seemed imminent. It is needless to specify the various ways in which the Oudh Akhbar has been trying to benefit the people and to promote loyalty amongst them.

16. Through the influence of this paper and the public confidence inspired by it, the Paper Mills of Lucknow were established and the benefit the country has derived is incalculable. These Mills have reduced the price

[80] I presume this to be the *Oudh Gazette*.

of paper 50 per cent., and effected a saving of nearly 25 lacs of rupees annually to Government. The proprietor of this Press had the honor of establishing the Mills and conducting their business for five years and a half as their Honorary Manager, and of making the scheme a success by incurring personal losses.

17. The Press has obtained Medals and Certificates for its valuable assistance during the time of the Exhibitions.

Newul Kishore[81]

The 'Statement' combined a self-assertive and unequivocal claim to patronage and special privileges with an impressive enlisting of arguments underpinning the indispensability of the services that Naval Kishore had rendered and continued to render to the government and the Indian public in his various public roles of publisher, newspaper proprietor, industrialist, employer, and social benefactor. It left no doubt as to his influence within indigenous society and stressed his function as a mediator between the government and the public in political and social matters. In proudly enumerating Naval Kishore's multifarious achievements in publishing, and in cleverly combining a list of his past contributions to social and educational charity with the promise of future benefits, it insinuated that all former achievements were put in jeopardy by the proposed measures. Moreover, these measures clearly included an element of social injustice on the part of the British authorities. The gist of the statement was that, instead of cutting down privileges, the government ought to be grateful to Naval Kishore and accordingly continue favouring his enterprise.

As it turned out, Naval Kishore's well-crafted Statement was of little avail. The colonial authorities were unwilling to go back on their decision to reduce the NKP's rates, asserting that the 'special reasons' that had hitherto justified the granting of higher rates 'no longer existed', and that 'it was neither necessary nor expedient that they should be continued'.[82] However, they did recognize the need for a compromise and proposed to compensate for the publisher's loss by assigning him a greater amount of work. Subsequently, the fixed allowance of work was raised to Rs 30,000 a year.[83] This was achieved by according the NKP the right to print and distribute police forms. That Naval Kishore stubbornly chose to ignore the newly fixed rates and for some months kept on submitting

[81] UPSA, File No. 288.

[82] *PGNWP&Oudh. General Dept.*, April 1887, File No. 288.

[83] *PGNWP&Oudh. General Dept.*, December 1888, File No. 288.

bills at the old rates was generously overlooked. However, officials were acutely aware that to accord him any further privileges was sure to entail a public outcry, cautioning that 'the large share of patronage already given to his press has excited the comment and remonstrances of other presses.'[84]

A new bone of contention presented itself in 1888 when Colonel Dodd, who had continuously objected to the decision to raise the NKP's share of work to Rs 30,000, decided that Naval Kishore should henceforth only be allowed machine rates for hand work, thus hoping to bring down the payments made to the NKP to the former Rs 26,000. The same work, Dodd argued, could be done by machine at the Allahabad Government Press. By this time, the perennial struggle over rates and Naval Kishore's insistence on defending his privileges was wearing out the patience of even senior officials. 'This case is a continual source of vexation', lamented Chief Secretary W.C. Benett.[85]

There was more to come. In July 1890 Naval Kishore again appealed to the government. Still not satisfied with the fact that the majority of official vernacular forms were printed at his press, he requested that the remainder also be bestowed upon him.[86] The offer he made in return, notably to produce all Urdu forms by lithography instead of type-printing, provides some interesting insight into the limited acceptance of type-set texts among the contemporary Urdu readership. It was 'only with difficulty', Naval Kishore asserted, that the people could read Urdu printing type throughout the province. He therefore intended 'to get all vernacular work printed in good lithography.'[87] His proposal to charge all lithographic work at type-printing rates ten per cent lower than those prevailing at the Government Press would amount to a great financial saving to the British. The letter closed on a defiant note, with Naval Kishore once again alluding to the endangered existence of his firm and appealing to the British to fulfill their 'obligations' towards the NKP:

> It is as well here to point out that this Press has suffered a great loss in the trade of Oriental Books exported beyond the Western frontier on account of a tax imposed by the Amir of Kabul, while the internal supply of the Oriental literature is now considerably diminished on account of the very extensive spread of English education; besides under the present

[84] *PGNWP&Oudh. General Dept.,* March 1891, Notes and Orders [p.1].

[85] Ibid.: 3.

[86] Letter by Naval Kishore, 18 July 1890. *PGNWP&Oudh. General Dept.,* March 1891: 1.

[87] Ibid.

> circumstances the educational text books are supplied by their respective authors (though at a much higher rate than the prices of the publications of this Press), the arrangement of publishing and supplying of which was hitherto under the control of the Book Depôt.
>
> Therefore there is no remedy but to ask the Local Government to save from ruin a firm in which about one thousand persons are working in every grade and position, and by the favour and help now asked for this Press hopes to publish the remaining works of the Oriental Science hitherto nowhere published.
>
> This Press has been printing official work for the last 33 years with great promptness, and has ever been ready to execute the orders of the Government, therefore it has established some claims for favour at the hands of the Government.[88]

Naval Kishore's claim that his firm was close to ruin was nothing but exaggeration to the colonial authorities. His proposal was declined outright. What motivated the government's decision were no longer financial considerations alone but also mounting public pressure. Giving in to Naval Kishore's demands would have provoked large-scale resentment among contending printer-publishers who had grown increasingly jealous of the NKP's privileges. 'There will certainly be a howl raised if Naval Kishore gets what he wants—the monopoly of vernacular printing',[89] the financial secretary warned. His fears were not unfounded: several years later, following the Bengal Government's decision to shift printing work from the government press to Indian-owned presses in the districts, *Najm al-Hind* (Jaunpur) still urged the NWP&Oudh Government to follow suit and 'also encourage any other Press but the *one* at Lucknow'.[90]

As the previous sections have shown, in matters of finance Naval Kishore was not a person to give in easily. In March 1894 we again find him appealing to the British authorities, this time with the complaint that the agreement to give him work worth Rs 30,000 had not been kept. Worse than that, his firm was facing a new and serious threat on account of the plans of the new Superintendent of Government Press, Frank Luker, to charge only machine rates for lithographic work done on hand-presses. Naval Kishore warned that this might force him to close the press, which had been working for so many years 'with credit and satisfaction to public and Govt.'.[91] Luker's plans were based on the fact that,

[88] Ibid.

[89] *PGNWP&Oudh. General Dept.*, March 1891, Notes and Orders: 5.

[90] *Najm al-Hind*, 16 September 1894, SVN 1894: 397.

[91] Handwritten (autograph?) letter, 2 March 1894, UPSA, File No. 866c.

meanwhile, five lithographic steam presses had been installed at the NKP, which allowed for a substantial increase in production while greatly reducing manufacturing costs. This, to him, more than justified a reduction in rates. Moreover, he was of the opinion that the settled amount of Rs 30,000 included the cost of paper, for which Naval Kishore allegedly charged the British at a rate that was 6.25 per cent higher than that of the government paper suppliers. Luker accused Naval Kishore outright of using paper of a lower weight and quality than stated in his bills to government. Overcharging was attempted in nearly every bill, and so great had his distrust of the press become that he had requested that all completed work be sent to the Government Central Press for inspection and delivery.[92]

There must have been some truth to these repeated allegations. Significantly, at this point, Naval Kishore for the first time relented and accepted the terms imposed on him by government. Barely a month after launching his complaint, he agreed to accept the new rates and also announced that he would gladly forgo the liberal rate of 6.5 per cent above the Government Press rates for paper 'so as to avoid all chances of dispute in this matter'. In accepting machine rates, Naval Kishore pointed out, he was forced to replace more and more handpresses by printing machines, meaning an extra investment estimated at Rs 50,000. In return, he asked for a comparatively moderate sum of 'not less than Rs 20,000 worth of printing work' to be allotted to the NKP. This sum to him constituted the absolute minimum, not only to make operations profitable but to guarantee some degree of job security for his workforce. Otherwise, there was a risk that a large number of workmen 'who as a rule live from hand to mouth' would be out of work for a considerable part of the year.[93]

The government's immediate reaction to this letter is not known, since unfortunately at this critical juncture the documents stop. The NKP continued to receive government patronage right into the twentieth century, albeit at a substantially reduced rate. A memorial submitted to the Lieutenant Governor of the United Provinces by Naval Kishore's heir and successor Prag Narayan in 1904 indicates that official patronage had reached its height in 1889–90, with an approximate value of printing work amounting to Rs 40,000. By 1895–6 this amount had undergone a drastic reduction, coming to Rs 14,200. In 1904 government patronage

[92] Letter to Secretary to Govt., NWP&Oudh, 9 May 1894, *PGNWP&Oudh. General Dept.*, May 1894, UPSA, File No. 866c.

[93] Handwritten (autograph?) letter to W.H.L. Imfrey, 2 April 1894, UPSA, File No. 866c.

did not exceed a meager Rs 2,100.[94] It was at this point that Prag Narayan, faced with the prospect of having to dismiss a large number of workmen, appealed to the government for more work. The received printing commissions, he argued, could hardly meet the requirements 'of so large an establishment as the demand for vernacular books is diminishing day by day.'[95] While the validity of this argument remains debatable, the golden days of government patronage were clearly over.

[94] Memorial submitted to J.J. de la Touche, Lieutenant-Governor of the United Provinces, UPSA, File No. 866c.

[95] Ibid.

5

Calligraphers, Scholars, and Translators: The Publishing House as an Intellectual Space

> *'Munshi Sahib, . . . I thought you were in Qanungos' Muhalla, Sikandarabad, and in fact you are sitting smoking the long-stemmed Lucknow hookah at the Avadh Akhbar Press in Raja Man Singh Mansion in Lucknow, and talking to Munshi Newal Kishor.'*
>
> —Ghalib to Hargopal 'Tufta', 12 February 1865

The British annexation of Avadh in 1856 and the cataclysmic events of 1857 severely affected cultural and commercial life in Lucknow. To the large number of poets and musicians, artisans, calligraphers and scholars who had been attracted to Lucknow by the legendary generosity of the Avadh court, the end of the *navābī* meant the loss of both a means of subsistence and a distinct cultural centre. In the aftermath of the 'Mutiny', the newly emerging commercial presses at Lucknow not only provided a means of livelihood to many, they also helped to fill the cultural lacuna by opening up a new institutional space for literary and intellectual pursuits. At a time when traditional structures of court patronage were rapidly disintegrating, presses came to constitute a new type of semi-public intellectual arena, which served as a discursive forum to members of different knowledge communities. The NKP is an excellent, if extraordinary, example of how a publishing house, notwithstanding its commercial aims, evolved into a vibrant intellectual microcosm where maulvis and pandits worked side by side in translating old texts and generating new ones, where *mushāʿira*s were held, and where the urban literati would gather to engage in literary and cultural debate.

Unlike today's commercial book industry, nineteenth-century printing and publishing houses had not yet witnessed the division of text composition, printing, and publishing from one another. Readers, editors, and translators worked in close physical proximity to printing presses, while authors frequented the premises of the publishing house and often maintained personal links with their publisher. As in premodern Europe, writers and intellectuals in nineteenth-century India were on much closer terms with print shops and the people involved in printing than is the case today (Eisenstein 1980:18). In a direct reflection of this, the NKP's printing works, warehouse, editorial office, and bookshop were located adjacent to one another. In its dual function of commercial enterprise and intellectual meeting place, the House of Naval Kishore is indeed reminiscent of Eisenstein's description of early European print shops:

> As pioneers in new manufacturing and marketing techniques, early printers shared something in common with other urban entrepreneurs; but as pioneers in advertising and publicity, in agitation and propaganda, in lexicography and bibliography they must be placed in a class by themselves. Their shops were different from those run by earlier manuscript bookdealers and lay stationers, because they contained new machines and mechanics trained to operate them. At the same time, the new workshops also differed from those run by other contemporary manufacturers because they served as gathering places for scholars, artists and literati; as sanctuaries for foreign translators, emigrés, and refugees; as institutions of advanced learning, and as focal points for every kind of cultural and intellectual interchange. (Eisenstein 1980: 23)

On observing the amount of literary activity and press work conducted on the NKP's premises in 1884, the American missionary John Hurst was instantly reminded of the famous Imprimerie Catholique in Paris. The only parallel to the NKP he had ever seen, noted an impressed Hurst, was the Abbé Migne's establishment in Paris, 'where even the editors of the complete editions of the Fathers prepared all their matter beneath the same roof under which the compositors did their work, the pressmen completed it, and the packers sent off the great folios into every land' (Hurst 1887: 354).[1]

The South Asian context provides another interesting point of comparison. A *kār<u>kh</u>āna* or 'factory' in the modern sense of the word, the NKP shared many of the characteristics of the traditional *kār<u>kh</u>āna* or 'workshop' of the Mughal period, with its departmental structure, meticulous method of keeping records, and wide array of artisans, artists, and culture specialists situated at the core of book production—calligraphers, stone-correctors, illustrators, bookbinders, translators, and

[1] The Benedictine priest Jacques Paul Migne (1800–75) rose to fame for singlehandedly publishing the entire corpus of the Greek and Latin Fathers from his Imprimerie Catholique.

scholar-editors. Naval Kishore, in his self-perception as a patron of literature and learning, consciously drew on the model of the *kārkhāna,* which he strove to perpetuate, albeit in a modern commercial setting. While post-Mutiny Lucknow and its surrounding *qaṣbah*s undoubtedly abounded in skilled artisans and learned men looking for work, he must be credited with attracting some of the most distinguished talent of the day to his press. 'No other press in India was fortunate to have such a large number of *ḥāfiẓ* [scholars who have memorized the Qurʾan], learned scholars, historians, writers and poets, as were gathered simultaneously at this press in Lucknow', writes Nazir Kakorvi (Kakorvi 1939: 184).

In this refashioned modern *kārkhāna*, traditional learning and craftsmanship were held in high esteem. Naval Kishore was acutely aware that his firm's reputation relied and thrived on the expertise of the large number of culture specialists employed by him. The NKP's outstanding achievement in the promotion of oriental literature and learning was as much due to its founder-proprietor's vision and entrepreneurial skills as to the many individual contributions of calligraphers, scholar-translators, and literati working at the press. Preservers of knowledge as much as innovators, these men applied their talent and expertise to the collection, correction, and editing of old texts, as also to the composition of a host of original writings and translations. Due to their multifarious efforts, the NKP's role in promoting literature was original and creative; it was at no time limited to commercial mass production alone. In depicting the House of Naval Kishore as an intellectual and literary arena, this chapter will take a closer look at the NKP's engagement in scholarly and literary publishing. Some light will be shed on the social background and contribution of the men employed at or associated with the press who, if not poets or prose writers in their own right, are conspicuously absent from literary histories. Many of them belonged to traditional artisan and knowledge communities and were living embodiments of the transition from scribal to print culture.

5.1 The Department of Copying and Calligraphy

Commercial printing in nineteenth-century India, to the extent that it relied on the technique of lithography, required a large number of calligraphers (*khushnavīs, khaṭṭāt*) and scribes (*kātib*). Calligraphy traditionally held a high and privileged position in Islam; it was the most revered form of Islamic art and considered one of the few vocational activities suitable for the ʿulama. As a major centre of Islamic learning and the site of the *navābī* court and administration, Lucknow boasted an eminent tradition of master calligraphers.[2] About 700 calligraphers alone are said to have been employed in the nawabs' *Bait al-inshā* or 'Department of Letters'. The transition from manuscript to print culture, however, coinciding with the end of the *navābī* and the 1857 uprising, dealt a severe blow to their art and made employment at a printing press or *madrasah* one of the few alternatives to a life in dire straits. Even the greatest artists were forced to exercise their skills for commercial purposes, a fact much bemoaned by Sharar:

> Now there are katibs, clerks, not calligraphers. If one or two well-known penmen have remained, they are forced to earn their living by kitabat, the copying out of documents and manuscripts, which is actually inimical to the art of calligraphy. . . . Earlier calligraphists thought that getting involved in writing a manuscript was beneath their dignity as it would be impossible for anyone who wrote out a whole book to maintain throughout the principles and standards of calligraphy. (Sharar 1975: 103–4)

Forced to eke out a living, the calligraphers could do little but compromise. This situation was by no means confined to Lucknow. As Metcalf notes, in 1873 the ʿulama at the Deoband *madrasah* reacted to the changing situation by employing a skilled calligrapher 'to train students for work at the increasingly important lithographic presses' (Metcalf 1982: 103). Undoubtedly, the lithographic presses were the chief beneficiaries of what may be perceived as the plight of the calligraphers. Like other Lucknow presses, the NKP benefited greatly from the city's expertise in penmanship. By enlisting the services of the finest artists, it soon gained a reputation for the excellent calligraphy of its texts. 'When the Lucknow press prints a man's diwan it raises him to heaven. The calligraphy is so good that every word shines radiant!' wrote an enthusiastic Ghalib in 1861.[3]

Yet this configuration was also advantageous to the calligraphic profession in post-*navābī* Lucknow. In providing employment to several generations of masters and pupils, firms like the NKP played a vital role in keeping their tradition alive. By 1872 Naval Kishore alone gave employment to sixty-eight scribes and calligraphers, including some highly

[2] Qureshi a.o. 1986: 82. For the tradition of Lucknow calligraphers, see Sharar 1975: 102–8, and Danish Lakhnavi 1996: 262–4. For calligraphy in the Islamic world, see Schimmel 1984.

[3] Letter to Majruh, 8 August 1861, Russell/Islam 1994: 259.

distinguished artists and scholars.[4] While some calligraphers wrote in both *naskh* and *nastaᶜlīq*, others specialized in one particular style only. Since Lucknow calligraphers did not sign their names in books, little is known about the artists to whom early lithographed books owe so much of their distinct physical appearance and character. Whatever information we have on the NKP's calligraphers is owed largely to A.H. Nurani, who in a 1994 monograph collected biographical details on forty-nine individuals.

One of the first master calligraphers to join the NKP in 1859 was Munshi Amirullah 'Taslim' (1820–1911), a pupil of the noted Lucknow calligrapher ᶜAbdul Hai Sandelvi. Born in Faizabad district, Taslim had served as a soldier in the army of Muhammad ᶜAli Shah and worked as a scribe for the Mustafaʾi Press. On opening his printing shop, Naval Kishore employed him at a monthly salary of Rs 20. Because of his knowledge of Arabic and Persian, Taslim was assigned the task of proof-reading. He also temporarily joined the editorship of *Avadh Akhbār*. Taslim was not only an excellent calligrapher (one of his masterpieces being the 1862 edition of Ghalib's *Qāṭiᶜ-e burhān*), but also an able Urdu poet of the Delhi school. His poetic mentor, Muhammad Asghar ᶜAli Khan 'Nasim' Dehlavi (1794–1864), a *shāgird* of Momin, was also associated with the NKP for some time.[5] The NKP published an early collection of Taslim's poetic work entitled *Kulliyāt-e Amīruʾllāh Taslīm* (also known as *Naẓm-e arjmand*, *1872) as well as his *Maṡnavī Nālah-e Taslīm* (*1872). In 1875 Taslim shifted to Rampur where he rose to a position of eminence among the poets of the Rampur court. From there he published numerous romances, collections of poetry, and a history of the Rampur State entitled *Tārīkh-e badīᶜ*.[6]

Second only in fame to Taslim was the Lucknow master calligrapher Maulvi Hadi ᶜAli (d. 1865). Hadi ᶜAli was a distinguished Islamic scholar and a poet of Persian and Urdu who wrote under the pen name 'Ashk'. He was considered an expert in the art of composing chronograms (*tārīkhgoī*).[7] His career provides an excellent example of how calligraphy shifted from a context of traditional Islamic art and scholarship to the commercial domain: born in a scholarly family in the *qaṣbah* of Bijnor, Maulvi Hadi ᶜAli had been educated at Farangi Mahall and trained in

[4] *RPE Oudh,* 1872: 120.

[5] For 'Nasim' Dehlavi, see Siddiqi 1991: 175–86.

[6] For Taslim, see Saxena 1990: 196–8; Bailey 1932: 76–7; Siddiqi 1991: 433–9; and ᶜAbdul Hai 1923: 441–53. For Taslim's poetry, see Beg 1955: 474–86.

[7] Nurani 1994: 96–100; Sabiri 1953: 277; *TUH*: 549. For a witty anecdote illustrating the excellence of Maulvi Hadi ᶜAli's penmanship, see Sharar 1975: 105–6.

calligraphy by Hafiz Muhammad Ibrahim. Together with his poetic mentor Nawab Fateh ud-Daulah (Mirza Muhammad Riza) 'Barq', he spent some time at the court-in-exile of Wajid ᶜAli Shah in Matia Burj and also worked as a scribe and proofreader for Haji Harmain Sharifain's Muhammadi Press. Upon joining Naval Kishore's print shop in 1859 he was appointed the first formal editor of *Avadh Akhbār* and soon became head proofreader in the Lithographic Department. In this position he continued to work as a calligrapher, while also writing and editing various commentaries on religious works. Hadi ᶜAli not only excelled in *nastaᶜlīq* but was considered to have no equal in the writing of *naskh* and the design of Tughras (Sharar 1975: 104). An expert in both large and miniature scripts, he won special distinction for his calligraphy of the Qur'an. He did not live to see the publication of his masterpiece, a widely acclaimed large-letter edition of the Qurʾan, which took him five years to prepare. It was published posthumously as *Qurʾān sharīf jalī qalam* (*1868) with the Persian commentary *Baḥr al-ᶜulūm al-islāmīya* in its margins. *Avadh Akhbār* extolled the edition as a specimen 'of exquisite handwriting, prepared with such beauty and excellence as has never been seen to the present day. This Qurʾan is the legacy of the late Maulvi Hadi ᶜAli, whose calligraphy has no equal in the whole of Hindustan. By studying it, women and children will easily learn the Qurʾan.'[8] Naval Kishore also relied on Hadi ᶜAli's skills as an editor, entrusting him with some important Persian publications such as Ghalib's collected Persian verse, *Kulliyāt-e naẓm-e fārsī* (*1863), and the *Dīvān-e Ḥāfiẓ* (*1866). By 1869 his edition of Hafiz had made it onto the list of Trübner & Co., where it was offered to Western readers 'at such a price as will make it accessible to all students' (i.e. 7 *sh.*, 8 *d.*).[9]

One of the most accomplished of Hadi ᶜAli's pupils was Munshi Muhammad Shamsuddin Lakhnavi (1831–1921), known as 'Iᶜjaz raqam' or 'Miraculous Pen'. He is credited with having invented a new style of *nastaᶜlīq* which became popular in Afghanistan and Iran. He authored several widely used instructional tracts on calligraphy and trained many young calligraphers at the NKP and the Madrasah ᶜAliya Furqaniya.[10] The handsome monthly salary of Rs 50 he received indicates his superior status among NKP calligraphers. One of the most splendid specimens

[8] *Avadh Akhbār*, 19 April 1870, cit. in Nurani 1995: 54.

[9] *Trübner's American and Oriental Literary Record*, no. 49, 16 September 1869: 550.

[10] I.e. *Iᶜjāz raqam*, *Tanvīr al-Shams*, *Kāpībuk-e khushkhaṭī*, *Muraqqaᶜ-e nigārīn* and *Guldasta-e riyāḥīn*. *Tanvīr al-Shams* has been reprinted several times by the Uttar Pradesh Urdu Akademi.

of his artistry is an illustrated large-letter edition of Saᶜdi's *Gulistān* (1886); his calligraphy of the *Būstān* (*1877) was extolled as 'a gem of lithographic elegance' by a British observer.[11]

Embedded in a highly refined aesthetic tradition and invested with sacred meaning, the copying of the Qurᵓan required particular expertise and could only be entrusted to the most accomplished artists. In addition to Maulvi Hadi ᶜAli, two master calligraphers were hired for the purpose. The first was Hadi ᶜAli's pupil Maulvi Hamid ᶜAli, known as 'Murassaᶜ raqam' ('Precious Pen'). A descendant of the venerated Lucknow saint Hazrat Muhammad ᶜAli Shah, Hamid ᶜAli was a scholar of Arabic and Persian who taught calligraphy at the local Madrasah ᶜAliya Furqaniya. Next to several fine editions of the Qur'an, he copied a host of Arabic and Persian texts for the NKP (Nurani 1994: 74–5). The second newly hired master of Qurᵓan calligraphy was the scholar and poet Munshi Ashraf ᶜAli 'Ashraf', surnamed 'Javahir raqam' ('Jewelled Pen'). Ashraf ᶜAli belonged to Lucknow and had received his training from Amirullah Taslim. An expert in the writing of *naskh*, he prepared at least five different editions of the Qurᵓan, among them a large-letter edition that included ᶜAbdul Qadir's Urdu translation (*1872).[12] Another noteworthy accomplishment was his calligraphy of Shaikh Abuᵓl Faiz Faizi's voluminous Qurᵓan commentary, *Sawāṭiᶜ al-ilhām* (*1888), an extraordinary work to which we shall return later.

Maulvi Muhammad Ismaᶜil, a scholar of Arabic and Persian and an expert in *nastaᶜlīq*, was in charge of supervising the scribes and calligraphers at the NKP's lithographic department. In this position he was responsible for the compilation of the firm's catalogues and also oversaw the preparation of lithographic drafts in Nagari script. On the opening of the NKP's Kanpur press in 1865, he was promoted to the position of branch manager (Nurani 1994: 64).

By employing several experts in 'mirror' or reverse writing (*maᶜkūsnigārī*) and stone correction (*iṣlāḥ-e sang*), the NKP contributed to the survival of a rare and waning calligraphic art. In reverse writing, the calligrapher writes on the stone's surface in inverse script, which then appears the right way round in print.[13] According to Sharar, this rare art

[11] *RPIR* 1877: 115.

[12] Nurani 1994: 64–6; *HLHH* I: 245.

[13] The technique is not to be confounded with the Arabic calligraphic art of *muthannā* ('facing each other') where a text is worked into a pattern in which one half is a mirror image of the other.

was invented in Lucknow.[14] Foremost among the masters of reverse writing was Mir Hashmat ᶜAli, who learnt his craft whilst working at the Nawab's Royal Press before 1857. He joined the NKP in its early years, to remain with the firm until his death. A laudatory poem composed in 1870 by Mohsin ᶜAli Khan 'Saqi' bears witness to his exemplary artistry:

Vah ustād hai Mīr Hashmat ᶜAlī	A great master is he—Mir Hashmat ᶜAli
Ke patthar pe likheṁ khafī o jalī	He writes on stone both fine and bold
Kahūṁ kyā patthar banāte haiṁ vah	Ineffable—the stones he engraves
To qudrat khudā kī dikhāte haiṁ vah	Reflect the Divine power of God
Chape sāf-sīdhā jo ulthā likheṁ	What he writes in reverse is printed clear and correct
Na kahie karāmat to phir kyā kaheṁ?[15]	If not a miracle, what else can you call it?

The second master of mirror-writing and stone-correction was Munshi Sayyid ᶜAli Husain, a pupil of Shamsuddin, who excelled in *naskh*, *nastaᶜlīq*, and *shikasta*. One of his admirers was ᶜAbdul Halim Sharar, who would later employ him as a calligrapher for his journal *Dilgudāz* (Sharar 1975: 108). Further experts in mirror-writing were Ghulam Muhammad Khan and Maulvi Mahbub Ahmad—the latter became supervisor of the lithographic department in the early 1870s.

In the transition from scribal to print culture, calligraphy provided an important visual link between the lithographed book and the manuscript. Even though calligraphic hands would over time become adapted to the exigencies of commercial printing, and connoisseurs would much bemoan the decline of the calligraphic art, the fact that lithographed books were handwritten remained crucial to their cultural acceptance. Publishers were well aware that exquisite handwriting could decide over the sale of a printed book, particularly when it came to cherished religious and literary classics. This also applied to another typical feature of manuscripts, the insertion of commentaries and glosses. As in the manuscript,

[14] Sharar 1975: 108. According to Ulrich Marzolph, an expert in Iranian lithography, the technique was not used in Iran. Private communication, November 2001. Reverse writing is of course known in various calligraphic cultures from Europe to Korea.

[15] Cited in Nurani 1995: 41. I am grateful to Huma Dar for assisting me in the translation of this verse.

they appeared in fine writing in the margins of the book and were usually written at a pronounced slant.

The manuscript tradition also served as a model for lithographic illustration.[16] Title pages of printed books were embellished with decorative borders and drawings of floral ornaments, while narrative texts were often illustrated. Steeped in the Persian tradition, the early Lucknow printers had developed a particularly ornate style of title page decoration. 'The first impression on seeing a Lucknow lithographed title page of the small folio size . . . is a feeling of extreme heaviness—entirely too much decoration within the available compass', writes Diehl. 'But looking more carefully at the detail, and holding the object at some distance, the effect is that of a Persian carpet, with its many themes and variations always regular and always neat' (Diehl 1973: 121). Although in the age of commercial printing title page drawings and illustrations were no longer as elaborate and refined as in the manuscript days, they still speak of aesthetic endeavours and artistic skill (Fig. 6). Woodcut illustrations were often inserted in commercially produced texts of the epic, romance, and fictional genres to enhance their attraction. To this purpose, Naval Kishore enlisted the services of a family of distinguished illustrators (*naqāsh*) and drawers (*muṣawwir)*, notably Munshi Amir ᶜAli, his son Vazir ᶜAli, and his brother Qasim ᶜAli. Specimens of their artistry were exhibited at the Colonial and Indian Exhibition in London in 1886. Perhaps Qasim ᶜAli's finest accomplishment was his illustration of Saᶜdi's *Gulistān* (Figs 7 and 8) produced in the same year. His art was held in such high esteem that Naval Kishore granted him monopoly rights on further editions of the *Gulistān* (Scheglova 1999: 21).

The Hindu calligraphers employed at the press were almost exclusively recruited from the two principal scribal and clerical castes in Avadh, the Kayasthas and the Kashmiri Brahmins. Both communities ranked among the traditional elites in the province; Kayasthas, in particular, had held high positions in the administration of the nawabs.[17] Not surprisingly, then, many of the firm's Hindu scribes and calligraphers belonged to distinguished local families. Most were occupied in copying Persian and Urdu books, while others prepared drafts in the Nagari script. Naval Kishore's apparent difficulties in finding skilled Nagari scribes

[16] For a magisterial study of lithographic illustration in Persia, see Marzolph 2001.

[17] Details in Fisher 1987: 52–7; 68–70. According to Fisher, no less than forty-five prominent administrators in *navābī* Avadh were Kayasthas. For the Kashmiri Pandits of Avadh, see Sender 1988, esp. pp. 47–58.

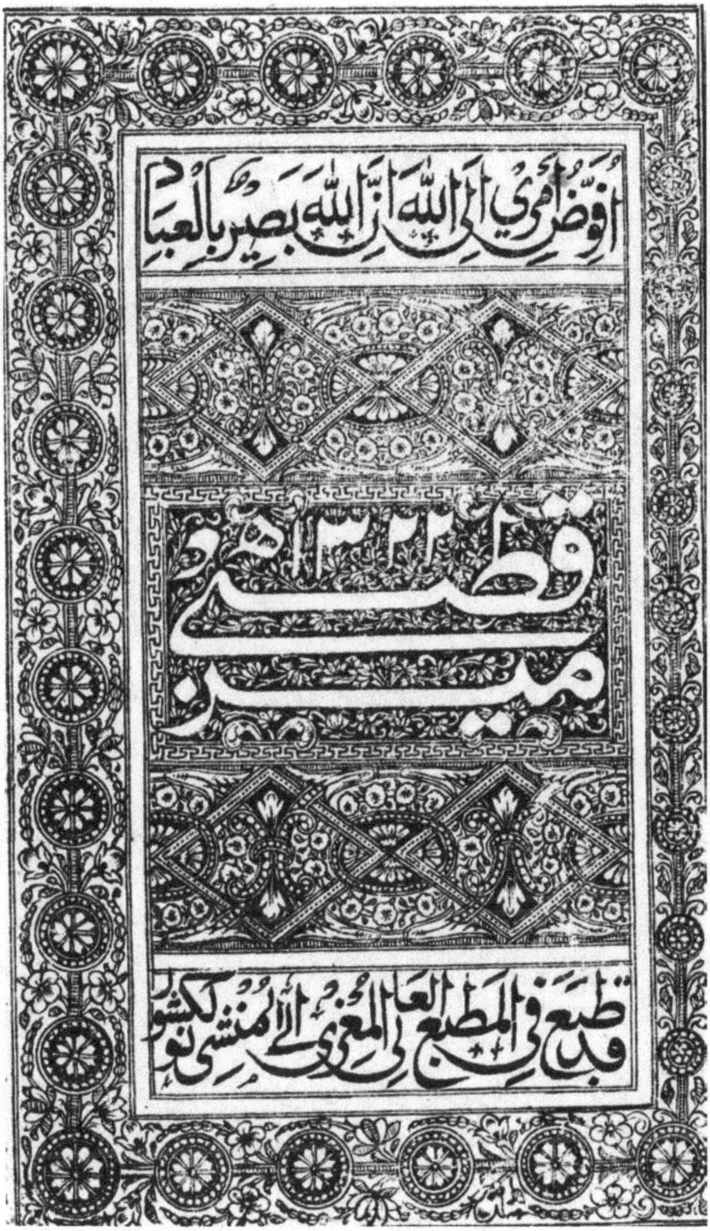

Fig. 6: Specimen of NKP title page calligraphy

موسی علیه السلام

همان درویش برهنه در حالت گرفتاری

شعر گربه مسکین اگر پر داشتی	تخم گنجشک از جهان برداشتی
هیچکس را اگر خود نگذاشتی	این دو شاخ گاو گر خر داشتی
شعر عاجز باشد که دست قدرت یابد	برخیزد و دست عاجزان برتابد

ولو بسط الله الرزق لعباده لبغوا فی الارض شعر

ماذا اخاضک یا مغرور فی الخطر	حتی هلکت فلیت النمل لم یطر نظم
سفله چو جاه آمد و سیم و زرش	سیلی خواهد بضرورت سرش
آن نشنیدی که فلاطون چه گفت	مور همان به که نباشد پرش

حکمت پدر را عسل بسیارست ولیکن پسر گرمی دارست فرد

آنکس که توانگرت نمیگرداند	او مصلحت تو از تو بهتر داند

حکایت ۱۶ - اعرابی را دیدم در حلقهٔ جوهریان بصره که حکایت میکرد که وقتی در بیابان راه گم کرده بودم و از زاد معنی چیزی با من نمانده دل بر هلاک نهاده

Fig. 7: *Gulistān bā taṣvīr* (1886)

انصاف دادم که من او را بهمت و جوانمردی بیش از خود دیدم
حاتم طائی
خارکش
حکایت ۱۵ - موسی علیه السلام درویشی را دید از برهنگی بریگ اندر شده گفت ای موسی
دعا کن تا خدای عزوجل مرا کفافی دهد که از بیطاقتی بجان آمده ام موسی دعا کرد و برفت
موسی علیه السلام
پس از چند روزی که باز آمد مر او را دید گرفتار و خلقی انبوه بروی گرد آمده گفت این چه
حالتست گفتند خمر خورده و عربده کرده و کسی را کشته اکنون بقصاص فرموده اند

Fig. 7 (*contd.*)

باب پنجم ۱۵۹ گلستان با تصویر

وگر بچشم ارادت نگه کند در دیو | فرشته اش بنماید بچشم محبوبی

مثنوی هر که سلطان مرید او باشد | گر همه بد کند نکو باشد

وانکه را پادشه بیندازد | کسش از خیل خانه ننوازد

حکایت ۲- گویند خواجهٔ را بندهٔ نادر الحسن بود و باوی بسبیل مودت و دیانت نظری داشت با یکی از دوستان گفت دریغ این بندهٔ من با حسن و شمائلی که دارد اگر زبان درازی و بی ادبی نبودی چه خوش بودی گفت ای برادر چون اقرار دوستی کردی توقع خدمت مدار که چون عاشقی و معشوقی در میان آمد مالکی و مملوکی برخاست قطعه

خواجه با بندهٔ پری رخسار | چون در آید ببازی و خنده

چه عجب کو چو خواجه حکم کند | وین کشد بار ناز چون بنده

بیت غلام آبکش باید و خشت زن | بود بندهٔ نازنین مشت زن

Fig. 8: *Gulistān bā taṣvīr* (1886)

۱۵۸
باب پنجم
گلستان باتصویر
قرآن خوان ناخوش آواز
باب پنجم در عشق و جوانی
حکایت ۱- حسن میمندی را گفتند سلطان محمود چندین بندهٔ صاحب جمال دارد
که هر یکی بدیع جهانی اند چگونه افتادست که با هیچ کدام از ایشان میلی و محبتی ندارد
چنانکه با ایاز با آنکه زیادت حسنی ندارد گفت هر چه در دل فرو آید در دیده نکو نماید
بندگان صاحب جمال
بندهٔ بدیع الجمال
ایاز
سلطان محمود
حسن میمندی
قطعه کسی بدیدهٔ انکار گر نگاه کند
نشان صورت یوسف دهد بناخوبی

Fig. 8 (*contd.*)

are a significant illustration of the continuing prevalence of the Persian scribal tradition in Avadh.[18]

A notable figure among the Kayasthas working at the NKP was the Urdu poet Munshi Govind Parshad 'Fiza', a pupil of Mendu Lal 'Zar' Lakhnavi. His poetic compositions include a divan, a *Maṣnavī Gulzār-e Fiẓā*, and an oft-reprinted Urdu verse rendering of Saᶜdi's *Būstān.*[19] Govind Parshad had joined the press as a copyist of Persian, Urdu, and Hindi works. One of his calligraphic masterpieces is the first NKP edition of Rajab ᶜAli Beg Surur's *Fasāna-e ᶜajāʾib*, produced some time in the 1860s. Two lesser known Lucknow poets on the permanent staff were Munshi Tilakram 'Hosh' and Munshi Khairati Lal 'Shigufta', the latter a pupil of Nasim Dehlavi. Both had been trained in calligraphy by Amirullah Taslim. Special mention must be made of Munshi Debi Parshad 'Sihr' Badauni (b. 1840), whose position as Deputy Inspector of Schools in the Aligarh District had brought him in close contact with the NKP. Upon his dishonourable dismissal from public service in 1875, he joined the press and was put in charge of the textbook publishing section. Debi Parshad was a prolific writer of textbooks and the author of two popular instructional manuals on calligraphy entitled *Naẓm-e parvīn* (1868) and *Arzhang-e Cīn* (*1868).[20] His poetic work was published in his *Dīvān-e Siḥr-e sāmirī* (1893).

As this brief overview has shown, the NKP's foremost calligraphers, if not scholars in their own right, were well-trained men firmly grounded in the literary tradition who often engaged in writing poetry themselves. Their tasks at the press were rarely confined to the copying of texts alone. Master calligraphers performed a variety of duties, including proofreading and emendation, editing, and translation. Many of them served in the Department of Composition and Translation, the creative heart of the publishing house.

5.2 The Department of Composition and Translation

'The only building in Kishore's house through which I was conducted that had a second story was the literary workshop. Here, by a not over-secure stairway, leading up from the outside, I found a group

[18] *RPE Oudh*, 1872: 120.

[19] *Būstān mutarjim manẓūm* (Kanpur *1878).

[20] Apparently, Debi Parshad was dismissed for some major offence. His complaint against the dismissal was rejected, as was his petition for a pension grant, official opinion being that his punishment was 'fully deserved' (*PGNWP&Oudh. Educational*

> *of quiet, grave and steady workers. They were the editors and revisers. They, like all Indians, sat upon the floor, and I must confess that they were the most dignified squatters whom it has ever been my privilege to meet.'*
>
> —John F. Hurst, 1887

The perhaps most distinguishing feature in the NKP's institutional setting was its Department of Composition and Translation (*Shuᶜba-e taṣnīf va tarjuma*), itself a novelty in Indian commercial publishing.[21] This literary workshop constituted the creative centre of the modern *kārkhāna*; it was a vibrant intellectual arena at the interface of tradition and modernity. Next to translation, the department's operations included manuscript edition, proofreading and emendation, the preparation of textbooks, and the compilation of lexicographical works. Its dual focus on text editing and translation is an authentic reflection of the way in which Naval Kishore interpreted his function as a publisher: it illustrates both his antiquarian interest in the recovery and preservation of India's literary heritage and his engagement with Indian modernity through the diffusion of 'useful' knowledge and the translation of works old and new into the modern languages. This dual concern with the promotion of traditional and modern learning in the name of Indian progress was neither new nor unusual. Sayyid Ahmad Khan's Scientific Society (est. 1864), for example, expressed a similar concern in its bye-laws, its chief objective being, firstly, to 'translate into such languages as may be in common use among the people those works on arts and sciences, which being in English or other European languages are not intelligible to the Natives', and, secondly, 'to search for and publish rare and valuable oriental works . . .' (Muhammad 1978.1: 4). The Scientific Society maintained a policy of religious neutrality and expressly forbade the translation of religious works. In sharp contrast, religious texts assumed central importance in Naval Kishore's scheme of promoting the classical literary heritage in Arabic, Persian, and Sanskrit among contemporary literate audiences. It was clearly not in the interest of a commercial publisher to exclude the most widely consumed form of literature from his list.

A cursory look at the British Museum's standard catalogues by A.J. Arberry (Arberry 1937), C.A. Storey (Storey 1927–77) and A.G. Ellis

---

Dept., August 1875, no. 24 (B); June 1878, no. 6; July 1878, no. 3). His textbooks include *Miᶜyār al-imlā* (Kanpur: Nizami Press 1867/68; NKP 1876), *Khulāṣat al-manṭiq* (1871), *Muḥīt al-masāḥat*, and *Mirāt al-ᶜālam*.

[21] See A. al-Hasan 1980: 74–80.

(Ellis 1894–1901) will testify to the immense number of Arabic and Persian works that the NKP saw through the press in a laborious process that involved careful transcription, verification, and emendation, often on the basis of various manuscript copies. The firm's initiative in seeing a wide range of Arabic and Persian works into print, including both canonized and little-known authors of both foreign and Indian origin, is all the more remarkable in that it involved considerable expense and was rarely profitable. In the process, substantial numbers of rare works designed for an exclusive scholarly readership were rescued from oblivion. Evidently, Naval Kishore was not satisfied with being a large general publisher but sought to become one of the foremost scholarly publishers in India. In his efforts to make important works of classical scholastic literature accessible to the reading public, he looked to the past contributions of Indian pioneers of print as well as colonial institutions. A considerable number of NKP publications were reprints of works published earlier in the century from Calcutta and other centres of print. At the same time, Naval Kishore began to systematically explore the vast storehouse of manuscripts that was India. In his antiquarian pursuits he placed himself on a par with British Orientalists and kept a close watch on the activities of the Asiatic Society of Bengal. This is suggested by a substantial number of Indo-Persian texts issued almost simultaneously from the NKP and from the Asiatic Society in its prestigious Bibliotheca Indica series (see below).[22] It is also evident from the self-assertive manner in which he, at one point, compared his efforts to those of the Asiatic Society, leaving no doubt that his initiative in preserving India's literary heritage could well vie with officially sponsored Orientalist undertakings: 'Even in Oudh, a large sum is annually set apart by Government for the Asiatic Society of Calcutta to help in the publications of books of ancient authors', Naval Kishore pointed out to the British authorities. 'The work which that Society has done with the liberal assistance of the Imperial and Local Government in 100 years, has been

[22] The project of the Bibliotheca Indica series was started in 1847–8 at the Court of Directors' request with a view to publishing 'the literature of the Hindus', especially Vedic texts, and translations thereof. Publication of the Old Series began in 1849, a New Series followed in 1860. Given its initial focus on Arabic texts, the series in the 1850s came under heavy criticism from H.H. Wilson, the Asiatic Society's agent in England, who found it becoming 'more of a *Bibliotheca Arabica*, than a *Bibliotheca Indica*, inconsistent with the intention of the *Bibliotheca Indica*, which was to furnish scholars with books to read, not to provide students with the means of learning to read them' (Chaudhuri 1956: xi).

done by this press to a very great extent during the entire period of its existence.'[23]

Much of the NKP's lasting fame in the field of oriental book publishing rests on its editions of Islamic, Persian, and Indo-Persian literature. The large body of Arabic and Persian titles on religion, philosophy, law, historiography, medicine, sciences, grammar, lexicography, and belles lettres issued from the press during the period 1858 to 1895 deserves separate study and cannot be analysed here. What concerns us in the present context are the firm's efforts in making this corpus of knowledge accessible to the contemporary readership through translation. The 1860s saw the beginnings of a sustained scheme of translating classical works into the modern languages. A collective undertaking that involved the labour of a large number of scholar-translators, it remains unparalleled in Indian publishing.

Translation was integral to the colonial encounter. Through its activities the House of Naval Kishore participated in the great translation venture that marked the nineteenth century. Translation from the English was germane to negotiating the terms of colonial modernity in India, while translation from the classical oriental languages was central to the dissemination of Indian religious and scientific knowledge and, ultimately, helped reassert Indian cultural identity in the face of colonial hegemonic claims. The mediation of ancient and modern knowledge through translation had received much initial stimulus from the pioneering efforts of Orientalists, Christian missionaries, and British scholar-administrators—all pursuing their own agendas. By the second half of the century, translation was no longer confined to the initiative of prominent educational institutions such as Fort William College, the Calcutta School Book Society, or the Vernacular Translation Society (est. 1844) of Delhi College, but had turned into a widespread concern among learned individuals and indigenous voluntary associations.[24] Emulating the model of the Aligarh Scientific Society, a proliferation of literary and reformist societies put translation on their agendas.

It was only natural, then, that a large scholarly publisher should wish to make his own contribution to India's intellectual progress. In making the production of translations a substantial part of its operations, the House of Naval Kishore assigned itself a no less active role in the grand

[23] See 'Statement of the Newul Kishore Press', above, ch. 4.

[24] For the Vernacular Translation Society and its publications, see ʿAbdul Haq 1945: 119–45 and Minault 1999; 2003.

task of disseminating general and scientific knowledge than did other institutions and bodies at the time. However, rather than making the translation of Western works his prime focus, Naval Kishore set out to promote oriental literature and Eastern knowledge traditions. The task at hand was to render classical and standard Islamic and Hindu works accessible to an audience of modern readers who no longer had a sound command of the classical languages.

Considerable financial and human effort was invested in what was an intense and sustained intellectual engagement with the past. By 1886 Naval Kishore could pride himself on having produced 'for the benefit of all classes of our countrymen' Urdu translations of 'no less than 500 different books of the most useful kind'.[25] This body of translated works constituted a significant contribution to the consolidation of Urdu, not only as a religious idiom but also as a new language of academic, scientific and political discourse. More than just a reflection of the growing acceptance of Urdu, it helped enhance the new status of the language in the public sphere. If literary and cultural historians of Urdu have associated the NKP with the 'revival of all Eastern literatures' (Sharar 1975: 107–8) and referred to its foundation as 'the most important event in the history of vernacular presses' (Saksena 1990: 268), it is largely on account of its unparalleled output of translations.

What is obscured by the above reference to the '500 Urdu translations' is the fact that the activities of the NKP's Translation Department covered much wider cultural ground in also extending to the Sanskrit and Hindi literary traditions and, to a somewhat lesser extent, to works of English literature and learning. NKP translations and modern-language adaptations created a textual bridge between the past and the present, Muslim and Hindu traditions, and Western and Indian knowledge. Representative of various intellectual contexts and their attendant theological, academic, and epistemological discourses, they fall into the following principal categories:

(1) translations of Arabic and Persian texts into Urdu
(2) translations of Sanskrit texts into Urdu and/or Hindi
(3) translations or transliterations of Urdu texts into Hindi
(4) translations or transliterations of Hindi texts into Urdu
(5) translations or adaptations of English texts into Urdu

Manuscript editions and, to an even greater extent, translations, were complex undertakings fraught with linguistic, religious, cultural, and

[25] See 'Statement of the Newul Kishore Press', above, p. 256.

often political implications. Indian publishers operated in a multireligious and multilingual context, which required the skills of erudite experts of different denomination, linguistic background, and varying specialization. In order to ensure a high standard for his publications, Naval Kishore not only relied on his own permanent staff of translators but enlisted the services of reputed intellectuals from outside the firm. These external collaborators were usually hired on a temporary basis and paid on contract. Extant sources do not always allow us to make a clear distinction between translators with fixed employment and those who were only loosely associated with the press and worked on commission. Representatives of both categories will be introduced below.

Preserving the Islamic Heritage: The NKP and its ʿUlama

For Indian Islam, the spread of print in the nineteenth century resulted in a period of intense publication and translation activity. Along with the printing presses run by ʿulama or Islamic institutions in places like Delhi, Aligarh, Bareilly, Deoband or Lucknow, the NKP assumed a leading role in the preservation and dissemination of Islamic textual knowledge. Previously, large parts of Islamic scholastic literature had been available only in manuscript form. Even those works of which printed editions did exist—produced early on by Fort William College, the Asiatic Society of Bengal, and pioneering Indian presses—came in limited numbers and were hard to get hold of. If not the scarcity of copies, it was high prices that put these early editions beyond the reach of the average Indian scholar or student. Naval Kishore was acutely aware of this predicament. The financial aspect therefore became a chief concern in his endeavours to make classic Islamic texts accessible to a larger audience of literate Muslims in India and beyond. His efforts at popularizing the printed book were directed at two different audiences: the general public and the 'ulama. This point is best illustrated by what may be regarded as the basic core of NKP Islamic publications, the more than seventeen different editions and approximately fifty commentaries of the Qurʾan (Siddiqi 1981: 17). Naval Kishore, a Hindu, made his mark in the history of Qurʾan publishing: he was presumably the world's first publisher to issue a finely lithographed Qurʾan at the sensational price of Rs 1, 8 *as.* in 1868.[26] This indeed was the first time that the holy book was rendered

[26] The 544-page edition in royal octavo was published from Kanpur. Its calligrapher was Maulvi Hamid ʿAli. Prices of Qurʾan editions at the time ranged from three to five rupees. By 1876, 19,000 copies of the 'Cawnpore edition' had been issued, its

accessible to a genuine mass audience. The low price had a strong symbolic ring to it, inviting Muslims of moderate means to acquire their own copy of the Qurʾan. In the same year the firm issued one of the first Qurʾan commentaries in Urdu, the versified *Zād al-ākhirat* by Maulvi Muhammad ʿAbdus Salam Badaʾuni. Clearly, the aim was to cater as much to the common man's desire to grace his home with a copy of the Holy Qurʾan as to the specific religious and intellectual pursuits of Islamic scholars.

As noted earlier, the NKP's outstanding role in Islamic publishing was largely based on the expertise of the numerous Islamic scholars employed or associated with the press. It would go beyond the scope of this study to fully assess their contribution to the intellectual renaissance of Indian Islam. While this topic still awaits study by an expert in the field, it must suffice here to give an overview of the scope and diversity of their activities through the example of a few prominent figures. In what seems a fitting reflection of the scholarly talent gathered at the House of Naval Kishore, Rahman ʿAli's standard collective biography of Indian Islamic scholars, *Tazkirah-e ʿulamā-e Hind*, was first published by the NKP in 1894.

The way in which the publishing house engaged with Islamic scholasticism can best be illustrated by the example of a celebrated work, *Iḥyāʾ ʿulūm al-dīn* (Revival of the Religious Sciences), by the great theologian and philosopher Iman Abu Hamid al-Ghazali (1058–1111). One of the most widely read works after the Qurʾan, *Iḥyāʾ ʿulūm al-dīn* has continued to exert immense influence in the Muslim world. In India, too, it was a standard piece of ethical reading and the subject of much comment and study. It formed the turning point in the spiritual life of an influential *ʿālim* such as Maulana ʿAbdul Bari of Farangi Mahall, who after studying the text was drawn away from the rational sciences towards mysticism (Robinson 2001: 82). Yet it was not the Arabic *Iḥyāʾ* to which the text owed its widespread popularity in India, but al-Ghazali's own simplified Persian synopsis entitled *Kīmiyā-e saʿādat* (The Alchemy of Happiness). Naval Kishore played a key role in the dissemination of al-Ghazali's masterpiece: not only did he make the Arabic and Persian texts widely available in book form, he also supplied the first Urdu translations of both.

---

price being further reduced to 13 1/2 annas. By this time, inexpensive editions of the Qurʾan were flooding the market. British reports list an edition of 4400 copies brought out from Meerut and sold at 12 annas (*RPIR* 1876: 25).

In 1862 the NKP published its first edition of *Kīmiyā-e saʿādat*, prepared by Maulvi Hadi ʿAli 'Ashk'. It was only the second time that the text had been circulated in print; an earlier edition of uncertain date had previously been published at Calcutta. The Arabic *Iḥyāʾ al-ʿulūm* followed in 1864 (1281 ah), being the second edition after the Cairo *editio princeps* of 1278 ah, and the first printed on Indian soil. Its editor Muhammad Muzhir had prepared the text from a collation of several manuscripts and the Cairo edition. Around the same time, Naval Kishore commissioned Maulana Fakhruddin Ahmad Qadri 'Fakhr' Lakhnavi (d. 1892) with an Urdu translation of the *Kīmiyā-e saʿādat*. Fakhruddin was a scion of Farangi Mahall who was renowned for his rhetorical skills. He joined the NKP as a proofreader and translator and was for some time associated with the editorship of *Avadh Akhbār* (see Chapter 6). Published under the title *Iksīr-e hidāyat* (The Elixir of Guidance, *1866), his translation of the *Kīmiyā-e saʿādat* was of a distinctly popular character. Written in a pleasant and lucid style, it came to be viewed as a text especially suited to the moral instruction of Muslim women and was to figure in several standard works on female education, notably Altaf Husain Hali's *Majālīs an-nisā* and Ashraf ʿAli Thanawi's *Bihishtī Zewar* (Minault 1998: 46; B. Metcalf 1990: 378). It may have also been the version on which Claud Field based his first abridged English translation of *Kīmiyā-e saʿādat*, published from London in 1909 in the 'Wisdom of the East' series. While at the NKP, Fakhruddin contributed a second widely acclaimed translation in the form of *Tafsīr-e Qādrī* (*1879–80), an Urdu rendering of *Tafsīr-e Ḥusainī*, a commentary on the Qurʾan by the fifteenth-century Persian moral philosopher Husain Vaʿiz Kashifi. With its lucid and simple style, the commentary was to head the list of books deemed suitable for women in Thanawi's *Bihishtī Zewar* (B. Metcalf 1990: 376). In sharp contrast to the popular character of Fakhruddin's texts, the ensuing translation of the Arabic *Iḥyāʾ ʿulūm al-dīn* clearly addressed an elite audience of learned scholars. The translation was done by Maulvi Basharat ʿAli Khan; it was published with the Arabic original as *Maẕāq al-ʿārifīn* (Relish of the Wise, *1875) in four volumes of over 3000 pages.

Nurani makes the ill-informed claim that Maulana Muhammad Ahsan Nanautawi (d. 1895), an eminent representative of the Dar ul-ʿulum of Deoband and Arabic teacher at Bareilly College, assisted the NKP for some time in proofreading and editing Arabic texts. In actual fact, rather than enlisting the Maulana's services, the NKP seems to have obtained permission to reprint several works that had been published previously from his own press, the Matbaᶜ-e Siddiqi in Bareilly.[27] As these reprints indicate, Naval Kishore maintained close and friendly ties with the Deobandi ᶜulama. In 1876 he reprinted *Ghāyat al-auṭār*, Maulana Khurram ᶜAli's Urdu translation of Haskafi's authoritative Arabic law book *Durr al-mukhtār*, which had first come out from Bareilly in 1872.[28] The reprint of over 2800 pages was appreciatively received by Indian scholars of Islamic law and British administrators alike. DPI White judged it 'a very useful work, and one which if translated into English would be of material help to our law-courts.'[29]

Inspired in the sixteenth century by Shaikh ᶜAbdul Haq Dehlavi (1551–1642) and much enhanced in the eighteenth century by Shah Waliullah (1703–62), the study of Hadith (traditional sayings of the Prophet), continued to hold great importance for contemporary Indian Islam. Naval Kishore published most of the standard collections of Hadith in Arabic and Persian. His 1869 edition of *Irshād al-sārī*, a famous Arabic commentary on al-Bukhari by Ahmad Qastalani (d. 1517), was a landmark in Hadith publishing. A reprint of the Bulaq edition of 1868, the ten-volume edition of 3833 pages sold at Rs 52. Other editions included the widely used *Mishkāt al-Maṣābīh,* a collection arranged by al-Tibrizi in 1336 on the basis of al-Baghawi's *Maṣābīh al-sunna*, and its equally popular Persian translation cum commentary by Shaikh ᶜAbdul Haq Dehlavi, *Ashiᶜat al-lamaᶜāt*, issued in a fine edition of over 2300 pages in 1872–3. There was an obvious demand for the *Mishkāt* and its translation: a standard work in traditional Sunni education, it was the only text of Hadith prescribed in the Farangi Mahall's *Dars-e Niẓāmī* curriculum.[30] Several Hadith compilations were issued in Urdu translation. By far the most important was *Maẓāhir-e ḥaqq* (*1870–3), a comprehensive translation cum commentary of the *Mishkāt*. With its high-flown style and Arabicized language this scholarly work had little appeal for the layman but was popular among students of Islam. Its author Maulana Muhammad Qutbuddin Khan Dehlavi (1804–72) was a noted scholar of Hadith and Islamic jurisprudence who spent part of his adult life in Mecca and Medina.[31] Naval Kishore published most of

[27] The Matbaᶜ-e Siddiqi was established in 1862. For further details on Muhammad Ahsan, see Metcalf 1992: 242–4.

[28] The greater part of the work was done by Maulana Khurram ᶜAli. After his death in 1855, Muhammad Ahsan finished the translation.

[29] *PGNWP. General Dept.* May 1888: 1.

[30] Malik 1997: 525; Robinson 2001: 49.

[31] Born in Delhi, Navab Qutbuddin Khan Bahadur Dehlavi was a pupil of the famous Hadith scholar Shah Muhammad Ishaq, himself a grandson of Shah ᶜAbdul

Qutbuddin's prolific oeuvre; the contacts between author and publisher, however, remain obscure. Other Hadith collections in Urdu included a translation of *Mashāriq al-anvār* entitled *Tuḥfat al-akhyār* by Maulana Khurram ᶜAli, and *Shamīm al-riyāẓ* by Qazi Fazil bin ᶜIyaz. Maulana Fazl Ahmad Ansari, a scholar associated with the NKP Lahore, translated al-Tirmizi in his two-volume *Jāmiᶜ-e Tirmīẓī maᶜ tarjuma-e Urdū* (*1891–4).

In the late 1880s the NKP's staff of Islamic scholars was joined by Maulana Sayyid Amir ᶜAli Malihabadi (1858–1919), who would soon rise to fame as a leading authority in Qurʾanic exegesis and Islamic jurisprudence. Prior to his appointments as head teacher at the Madrasah ᶜAliyah in Calcutta and the Nadwat al-ᶜUlama in Lucknow, Maulana Amir ᶜAli served at the publishing house for some time. Upon joining the NKP on a monthly salary of Rs 50, he was assigned a special project: the *editio princeps* of the *Sawāṭiᶜ al-ilhām* (Brilliant Lights of Inspiration, *1888). This celebrated commentary on the Qur'an by Shaikh Abuʾl Faiz Faizi, the great scholar and Poet Laureate at Akbar's court, is remarkable in that it does not make use of dotted letters. In his preface to the edition, Amir ᶜAli adhered to the same principle. His second project involved the first Urdu translation of *Fatāwā-e ᶜĀlamgīrī* (*1890), an exhaustive and authoritative survey of Hanafi jurisprudence compiled during the time of Aurangzeb. Previously, Naval Kishore had reprinted the original Arabic text, *Al-Fatāwī al-ᶜĀlamgīrīyat* (*1875), from the Calcutta edition of 1828–35. In 1885 two volumes had been translated into Urdu and published in monthly instalments by Maulana Ihteshamuddin Muradabadi.[32] Completed in four volumes in 1890, Amir ᶜAli's Urdu version was a substantial work of 4660 pages, priced at Rs 20. Next, Amir ᶜAli finished *ᶜAin al-hidāyah* (*1896), a voluminous Urdu commentary of al-Marghinani's *al-Hidāya*, a twelfth-century standard work of Islamic law that formed part of the traditional Islamic curriculum. His most outstanding achievement, however, is the Urdu translation of *Tafsīr Mawāhib al-raḥmān* (also known as *Jāmiᶜ al-bayān*), a vast commentary on the Qurʾan compiled from various Arabic sources. Naval Kishore did not live to see this important work make it through the press. Issued in 1896–1902 in 30 volumes of over 8500 pages, it remains the

ᶜAziz. *Maẓāhir-e ḥaqq* was a reworking in the form of a commentary of Shah Muhammad Ishaq's own Urdu translation of the *Mishkāt al-Maṣābīh,* prepared by Qutbuddin at the former's instance (*TUH*: 392; Rizvi 1980: 71).

32 Maulana Ihteshamuddin was also a noted commentator of the Qurʾan. His voluminous Urdu commentary was called *Tafsīr-e Iksīr-e ᶜaẓam* (*1895).

most comprehensive commentary on the Qur'an ever written in Urdu and is a hallmark of Islamic publishing in the subcontinent.

While representing only a small proportion of Islamic works issued in Urdu translation, the foregoing examples indicate the NKP's wide-ranging engagement with the Islamic textual tradition. Next to editions and commentaries of the Qur'an, it covered a variety of textual genres relevant to religious education and contemporary debate on theological and scholastic issues. In encompassing works of both *manqūlāt*, the 'transmitted' or 'revealed sciences' (including jurisprudence, principles of law, hadith, and Qur'anic exegesis), and *maʿqūlāt*, the 'rational sciences' (including logic, theology, philosophy, and mathematics), of Shiʿa and Sunni theology and of Sufi mysticism, the firm's list reflected contesting scholastic traditions within Islamic thought.[33] Significantly, some of the above-named titles reappear in the 1895 first-hand account by an Islamic scholar which Barbara Metcalf cites in her magisterial study of the Deoband seminary. The passage deserves to be reproduced in full here, for it vividly testifies to the profound impact of commercial print culture on Indian Islamic education and scholarship:

> Now God has been gracious by providing books. Books which one could not see in dreams or conceive of in imagination are now sold for cowries. . . . The [*Fatawa-yi*] *ʿAlamgiri* used to be unavailable. The government published it in Calcutta before the Mutiny, but it sold for 90 rupees. Similarly, the *Tafsir-i Kabir* sold for 300. The king had a copy of it and when Shah ʿAbduʾl-ʿAziz needed it, he borrowed it from him. No one even knew the *Fathuʾl-Bari*, for in all of Delhi there were only parts of it, scattered among three places. There were only eighteen copies of Bukhari, and of these, generous people had divided copies into parts and distributed them among students so that they could study them. When I studied Tirmizi from Miyan Sahib [. . .] three of us shared one copy; and we three lived in different sections of the city. . . . One of us would study it for a few hours, then another would carry it off. . . . No one had a chance to study a whole book. A copy of the *Hidayat* was divided among students: one would start it from one place, another from another. . . . Because of reading incompletely and out of order, [the study of] every book was deficient. If a person had even a faulty copy of a book, that was considered a great blessing and he was held to be very wealthy. (Metcalf 1982: 205–6)

Moving away from strictly Islamic literature, the following sections will take a closer look at two textual disciplines that were paramount in reflecting contemporary epistemological and cultural concerns: medicine and

[33] For an extensive discussion of the contesting claims and discourses of followers of the traditional and the rational sciences, see Malik 1997.

historiography. An integral part of Indian and especially Indo-Persian intellectual traditions, the two disciplines figured prominently in the new interface of indigenous and Western knowledge systems generated by the colonial encounter. The large number of medical and historical works on the NKP list not only reflect this interface, they also illustrate the variegated Indian response to the hegemonic claims of colonial science and the British appropriation of the Indian past. In promoting these genres, the publishing house reacted to a discursive encounter between contesting knowledge traditions in the two areas where it was most significant and intense.

5.3 Medicine and History for Lay and Scholarly Readers

Revitalizing Indigenous Medicine

From the outset, Naval Kishore made the publication of medical texts, primarily of works of the Greco-Arab Unani (*yūnānī*) system prevalent in the Islamic world, an important area of specialization. The number of ancient and contemporary medical treatises, materia medica, and pharmacopoeias issued from his press in the original Arabic and Persian or in Urdu translation is estimated at over 130 titles (Siddiqi 1981: 15).[34] Such emphasis on medical publications was a corollary to the revival of the classical medical tradition within Indian Islam, itself a result of the interaction between Western and indigenous medicine.

The encounter between Indian and Western medicine has generally been portrayed as part of a wider process in which Indian knowledge was transformed into colonial knowledge and subjected to the latter's empiricist trajectories. The early generation of British physicians and Orientalist scholars had professed a keen interest in the textual sources of Unani and Ayurvedic medicine. 'British physicians', writes David Arnold, 'were engaged in a typically Orientalist exercise, widening the bounds of Western knowledge by interrogating Oriental texts and "native informants"' (Arnold 2000: 66).[35] Colonial interest in indigenous medical knowledge, particularly its more 'sophisticated' textual tradition, was

[34] Most of the Persian works are listed in Storey 1971.

[35] 'The practical utility of discovering Indian drugs and incorporating them into the Western system of medicine was thus the primary official motivation behind the investigation of Indian medical texts, but it would be a mistake to imagine that material advantage was the only incentive. The growing tendency (mainly, but not exclusively, within the medical profession itself) to see medicine as a demonstration of the superiority of the civilization of the West over that of the East also had a

partly a consequence of setbacks in fighting cholera, plague and other epidemic diseases, which 'not only challenged attempts to establish the superiority of Western medicine but also emphasized the physical frailty and political vulnerability of colonial rule' (ibid.: 198).[36] By mid-century, British interest in Indian medicine had somewhat diminished and given way to a growing belief in the superiority of Western medical science. Indigenous scholars and practitioners responded to these hegemonic claims in a variety of ways. Championed by Hakim Ajmal Khan (1836–1927) of Delhi and Hakim ᶜAbdul ᶜAziz (1855–1911) of Lucknow, Muslim professionals both engaged with, and resisted, colonial medicine. Hakim ᶜAbdul ᶜAziz proposed a reformed Unani medicine as a commonly acceptable national substitute for the colonizing drives of state medicine (Alavi 2003; 2005). In 1870 he set up a clinic to teach a reformed and standardized form of the Unani system. The revived interest in Unani medicine could also be seen elsewhere: in 1875 Shaikh Imamuddin Ahmad launched a monthly medical periodical in Urdu entitled *Āʾīna-e Ṭibābat* (Mirror of Physic) from Agra.[37] In 1889 the first official school of Unani medicine, the Tibbi Madrasah, was opened in Delhi. Several years later, the ᶜulama at the Deoband *madrasah* institutionalized Unani medicine in their curriculum in what was part of the larger Islamic revival generated from the seminary (Metcalf 1982: 103, 349). By the end of the century Unani medicine had come to hold a privileged role in the reaffirmation of Muslim identity since it proved 'the continuing validity of Islamic values in a changing context' (Vanzan 2000: 3).

Yet the revival of Unani medicine also followed a different trajectory. There was a shift in emphasis from the mastery of the theory to the practice of Unani (Alavi 2005), which went hand in hand with a new concern to simplify medical knowledge and render it accessible to the general public (Kumar 1997: 177). Medical texts were no longer intended to be

---

powerful effect on the way Indian medicine was perceived and its relationship with Western medicine was understood. Medicine was one of the fields of inquiry through which Oriental scholarship sought to represent and capture the essence of Indian (especially Hindu) civilization, just as through their topographical exercises medical writers sought to define the nature of India's physical environment' (Arnold 1993: 44).

[36] For further illustrations of the interest of European physicians in 'native' knowledge and their interaction with Indian specialists, see Bayly 1996a: 264–81. For the Indian reaction to Western medicine, see Kumar 1997 and Alavi 2003.

[37] QLP, NWP, 2nd quarter, 1876.

consumed by professional specialists alone. An increasing number of Urdu original tracts and translations addressed the new audience of lay readers. A manual like *Zubdat al-ḥikmat* (Compendium of Wisdom, *1869), by Hakim Sayyid Muhammad Qamar ᶜAli of Mathura, was clearly designed for household use, giving instructions on how to employ items of daily life (*rozmarra cīzeṁ*) in the treatment of disease. The laicization of Unani medicine also extended into other genres: writers of educative fiction like Nazir Ahmad introduced a basic knowledge of medicine and hygiene as part of good housekeeping and mothering. Maulana Ashraf ᶜAli Thanawi, in his classic of female education *Bihishtī Zewar*, devoted a whole chapter to Unani medicine and health care (Vanzan 2003).

Printed texts were central to these various manifestations of the revived interest in medicine. If the intense production of medical literature by the NKP reflected the general revival of Unani medicine, it also had to do with the firm's location in Lucknow, a stronghold of the medical profession. Headed by its famous ᶜAzizi family of Hakims, from the late eighteenth century Lucknow had been home to some of India's greatest Unani physicians. As Sharar with his usual hyperbole tells us, 'the science progressed to such a degree that there were few quarters . . . which did not contain a celebrated family of professional physicians. Apart from those existing in the hundreds of quarters of the city itself, thousands of clinics had been set up in neighbouring villages and small towns. All the famous physicians practising at the courts or in the towns of India had come from Lucknow or its neighbourhood' (Sharar 1975: 97).[38] Having published the great Persian classics of Unani, in the early 1870s Naval Kishore began to produce Urdu translations of popular medical texts. This was the time when Hakim ᶜAbdul ᶜAziz, in an effort to standardize and institutionalize education in Unani medicine, opened his clinic and school in Lucknow. As Seema Alavi has shown, the Hakim enlisted the support of the NKP and the Nami Press in getting medical texts printed and supplied at reasonable rates (Alavi 2005). Underlying this collective effort at popularizing Unani knowledge in Urdu was a new self-assertiveness *vis-à-vis* colonial medicine. Naval Kishore's *Avadh A<u>kh</u>bār* provided a forum for a lively debate on Unani versus English medicine (ibid.: 118). In July 1875, for example, a correspondent of the *Aligarh Institute Gazette* reported on a 'very sensible' article on indigenous

[38] As Bayly points out, 'Praising a town for the learning of its hakims was an aspect of eulogy from ancient Baghdad through to modern cities like Delhi' (Bayly 1996a: 266).

medical practice recently published in *Avadh Akhbār*, which made a strong case for the continuing usefulness of the Muslim and Hindu medical systems. These were said to enjoy widespread acceptance in spite of the 'sheer neglect and cold treatment' they met with on the part of India's present rulers.[39]

NKP medical publications spanned across space and time, from the early Greek, Arabic, and Persian classics to the great physicians of the Mughal period and the works of modern authors writing in Persian or Urdu. While most titles were standard works used in the traditional Unani curriculum and in general practice, the publisher's list also included some rare and specialized works that had not been circulated in print before and were eagerly received by medical specialists.[40] The sales aspect of medical literature must not be overlooked: in being in constant demand by a large class of professional practitioners and those interested in medicine, standard medical texts were profitable publications.

In his scheme to popularize the key texts of Indo-Persian medicine, Naval Kishore first turned to the works of Muhammad Akbar Arzani (d. 1722), the celebrated Sufi physician of Aurangzeb's court. In 1867 Arzani's *Mujarrabāt-e Akbarī*, a formulary of compound remedies, was released in Hakim Wajid ᶜAli Muhani's Urdu translation. It marked the beginning of an intense and prolonged effort to acquaint the Urdu readership with the glorious past of Unani medicine in India. Soon afterwards, Naval Kishore acquired the copyright of an Urdu translation of Arzani's *Ṭibb-e Akbar* by Hakim Muhammad Husain Nanautawi. The text, revised and edited by the Hakim's brother Muhammad Yaᶜkub, came out in 1870. Around the same time Hakim Muhammad Nur Karim Daryabadi (d. 1878?), a reputed local physician and author of *Shifā al-amrāẓ*, was commissioned to render into Urdu two of Arzani's hitherto

[39] *Aligarh Institute Gazette*, 16 July 1875.

[40] E.g., Muhammad Akbar Arzani, *Ṭibb-e Akbar* (1860–3), *Mufarriḥ al-qulūb* (1865), *Mīzān al-ṭibb* (1870), *Mujarrabāt-e Akbarī* (1871), and *Qarābādīn-e Qādirī* (1875); Mushrif Husain, *Tuḥfat al-aṭibbā* (1868); Mansur Ahmad, *Kifāyah-e Manṣūrī* (1869); Ibn Sina, *Tuḥfat al-ᶜāshiqīn* (1870); ᶜAbdul Haqq b. Shah Abī 'l-Hasan Mungiri, *Ilāj al-abdān* (1871); Hakim ᶜAlawi Khan Shirazi, *Muṭibb-e ᶜAlawī Khān* (1872); Shaikh Rahim Allah Ansari, *Fatāwā-e ṭibb* (1872); Amanullah 'Amanī' Husaini, *Umm al-ᶜilāj* (1873); Yusufi, *Ṭibb-e Yūsufī va Sittah-e zarūrīyah* (1874); Muhammad Husain Khan b. Muhammad Hadi Khan, *Makhzan al-adwiyah* (1874; on its margin Mir M. Mumin, b. Zaman Husaini Tunakabuni, *Tuḥfat al-muᶜminīn*); Muhammad Sadiq ᶜAli Khan, *Zād-e gharīb* (1874); Hakim Ihsan Ali, *Tahzīb-e Ihsānī* (1875); Nuruddin Muhammad ᶜAbdullah Shirazi, *Alfāz al-adwiyah* [*sic*], followed by *Anīs al-muᶜālijīn* (1881); Mahmud Jaghmini, *Qānūnchah* (1883).

untranslated works. The first was *Mufarriḥ al-qulūb*, a Persian commentary on Mahmud ibn ᶜUmar al-Jaghmini's *Qānūnchah,* itself a popular epitome of Avicenna's *Canon of Medicine*. It was published as *Iksīr al-qulūb* (*1870). The second was Arzani's *Qarābādīn-e Qādirī*, an elaborate pharmacopoeia, issued in Urdu as *Kīmiyā-e ᶜanāsirī* (*1870). Previously, Nur Karim had translated the *Makhzan al-adwiyah* (The Storehouse of Medicaments, *1865?), a widely used eighteenth-century compendium on simple and compound medicaments by Muhammad Husain Khan Shirazi.[41] His translation became one of the standard medical dictionaries in Urdu.

Hakim Nur Karim was one of several reputed Unani physicians from Lucknow and its environs who assisted the publishing house in its translations of Arabic and Persian medical texts. Another was Hakim Ghulam Hasanain ᶜAllamah Kinturi (1831–1918), a distinguished scholar and pharmacologist.[42] At the behest of Naval Kishore, he prepared the first full-length Urdu translation of the most celebrated of Unani classics, Ibn Sina's (Avicenna's) *Kitāb al-Qānūn fi al-ṭibb* or *Canon of Medicine*. In the reformed curriculum devised by Hakim ᶜAbdul ᶜAziz, Ibn Sina's encyclopaedic work held central importance. The Urdu version came out in five volumes in 1871–2. Following *al-Qānūn*, Ghulam Hasanain translated al-Jaghmini's *Qānūnchah* (*1889) and *Kāmil al-ṣināᶜah al-ṭibbīyah* (Complete Book of the Medical Art, *1889), a systematic tenth-century work by ᶜAli ibn al-ᶜAbbas al-Majusi that had been the standard before Avicenna. His fourth important contribution was *Mulakhkhaṣ-e Fuṣūl-e Buqrāṭī* (*1872?), a translation into Persian of the *Aphorisms* of Hippocrates and Galen's commentary.

A third and particularly prolific translator associated with the NKP was Hakim Muhammad Hadi Husain Khan Muradabadi, author of a Persian medical catechism entitled *Kanz al-asrār* (*1871). His Urdu translations of standard Persian works include the following titles: (1) *Qarābādīn-e Shifāʾī* (*1870), a sixteenth-century pharmacopoeia by Muzaffar Shifaʾi Kashani; (2) *Qarābādīn-e Zakāʾī* (*1871), an eighteenth-century work by Hakim Zakaullah Khan; (3) *Zakhīrah-e khvārazm-shāhī* (*1878), a comprehensive twelfth-century medical encyclopaedia by Ismaᶜil ibn Hasan al-Jurjani, said to be the most important systematic

[41] Muhammad Husain ibn Muhammad Hadi al-ᶜAqili al-ᶜAlavi al-Khurasani al-Shirazi, known as Muhammad Husain Khan (fl. 1771), was the great-nephew of the famous Persian physician ᶜAlavi Khan Shirazi. His *Makhzan al-adwiyah* is a verbatim reproduction of the alphabetical pharmacopoeia in the latter's *Jamiᶜ al-javāmiᶜ*.

[42] *DIPL*: 198-9; Storey 1971: 194.

thesaurus of medical science in Persian; (4) *Kifāyah-e Manṣūrī* (1890), a fifteenth-century medical handbook by Mansur; (5) *Qarābādīn-e Kabīr* (1890), a treatise on compound medicaments by Muhammad Husain Khan (b. Muhammad Hadi Khan) Shirazi; and (6) *ʿIlāj al-amrāẓ* by Muhammad Sharif ʿAli Khan of Delhi. Directed at a more general readership was his Urdu rendering of *Zād-e gharīb* (*1885), a contemporary Persian medical handbook for travellers by Sadiq ʿAli Khan of Delhi.[43]

The NKP's sustained efforts in making Unani classics widely available in print did not go unnoticed by the British authorities. The 1880 edition of *Makhzan al-adwiyah*, for instance, was approvingly acknowledged as 'one of the series of old elaborate standard works of the Greek system of medicine, hitherto unpublished and scarcely procurable, which are being printed by Munshi Naval Kishore'.[44] Scholarly interest and acute concerns about public health combined in attracting government patronage for such publications. In the intensified interaction between Western and indigenous medical systems, pharmacopoeia and medical treatises had indeed come to serve as 'a textual window between Europe and Asia'(Bayly 1996a: 266).

As will be shown in Chapter 7, the NKP's specialization in medical texts was not confined to Unani works but also extended to Ayurvedic medicine. Once the firm began to produce books in Hindi and Sanskrit, Ayurvedic works appeared as a distinct category on its list. In sharp contrast to the creative interface that Unani and Ayurvedic medicine had enjoyed well into the eighteenth century (Arnold 2000: 4), the translation of medical classics followed clear cultural demarcations and allowed for little interchange between the two systems: Unani works were generally rendered into Urdu, and Ayurvedic works into Hindi. Significantly, the only exception to this pattern were the firm's two medical bestsellers, both of recent origin: the first was the Persian *ʿIlāj al-ghurabā* (Aid to the Poor), a popular medical treatise compiled by Hakim Ghulam Imam around 1847. Its Urdu translation, *Tashīl al-shifā* (*1865) by Hakim Asghar ʿAli Khan, was highly acclaimed and had gone through seven

[43] See Alavi 2005: 104–7 for a discussion of *Zakhīrah-e Khvārazm-shāhī*. Further translations of standard medical texts published include: *Maʿāljāt-e Sadīdī* and *Kulliyāt-e Sadīdī* by Sadid al-Din al-Kazaruni (d. 1357) (trs. by Hakim Sayyid ʿAbid Husain); *Bahr-e muhīṭ* (trs. by Hakim Asghar Husain Farrukhabadi), *Makhzan-e Sulaimānī* (trs. by Hakim ʿAbdul Ghariz), and *Al-Jawhar al-nafīs fī sharḥ urjūzat*, being an edition of al-Baghdadi's fifteenth-century Arabic commentary on Ibn Sina's didactic poem 'On Medicine' with an Urdu trs. by Maulvi ʿAbdul ʿAziz Batalwi.

[44] *RPIR* 1880: 133.

editions by 1881. Such was its popular appeal that Naval Kishore deemed it expedient to invest in a Hindi translation. Prepared by Pandit Pyarelal in 1882, *Ilāj al-gurabbā bhāṣā arthāt dīn jan cikitsā* was equally well received and frequently reprinted. In a similar fashion, the first Urdu translation in 1878 of *Amṛtsāgar* (Ocean of Nectar), a medical bestseller on the NKP Hindi list, was the result of a market-oriented decision on the publisher's part.

What about translations of Western medicine? The relationship between Western colonial and indigenous medicine has often been portrayed as antagonistic. As Mark Harrison notes, there was 'a widespread distrust of Western medicine stemming from its association with an alien regime' (Harrison 1994: 19). State medical intervention, as in the case of coercive smallpox vaccination, was strongly resented (Arnold 1988). Yet over time colonial public health policy and the movement for sanitation did make some inroads into indigenous society. According to Deepak Kumar, they generated a heightened awareness of health issues among educated Indians and entailed a demand for 'greater availability of Western medicine' (Kumar 1997: 177). There is, however, little indication of this at the textual level. Judging by the market, it was only towards the close of the century that Western medical knowledge had begun to gain enough public acceptance to make the translation of English medical treatises commercially viable. Naval Kishore only invested in two such translations; the first was the *Sanitary Primer* (*1886) by J.M. Cuningham, the Government of India's Sanitary Commissioner, the second Samuel Osborn's widely used *Ambulance Letters, First Aid to the Injured* (1885), issued as *'Ilāj bar maḥall* in 1896. If the publisher showed no apparent interest in promoting works of allopathic medicine, he certainly did not hesitate to promote western-style pills and patent medicines.

Engaging with the Past: Works of Indo-Muslim Historiography

Much recent scholarship has sought to explore the way in which colonialism engaged with and appropriated Indian history. The study of the Indian past through its historiographic textual sources was a major imperative in British efforts to secure information about the country; it was key to establishing and maintaining colonial rule in India. As Bernhard S. Cohn has argued, among the different 'investigative modalities' devised by the British to rule India, the 'historiographic modality' was the most complex and pervasive mode of probing India's past and civilization: 'Knowledge of the history and practices of Indian states was seen as the most valuable form of knowledge on which to build the colonial state' (Cohn 1997: 5). Academic debate has centred on the variegated Indian response to the hegemonic claims of colonial historiography, as formulated in the works of James Mill, Mountstuart Elphinstone, James Tod, John C. Marshman, and Henry M. Elliot's and John Dowson's monumental *History of India as Told by its Own Historians* (1867–77). Implied in the debate is a strong refutation of the colonialist notion of an Indian 'lack of historical consciousness'. While the existence of historical sensibilities has been traced back to premodern India,[45] it has been argued that the rationalist principles of modern European historiography were readily embraced by sections of the Indian intelligentsia; over time they would exert a formative influence on the development of historiography as a modern academic discipline in India. At the same time, the appropriation of India's past by colonial historiography was vigorously contested and resisted. Faced with the bias and distortions of colonial history writing, educated Indians engaged in developing an agenda for an alternative and authentic indigenous historiography of their own (Guha 1988). In Bengal, English-educated authors of textbooks were the first to openly contest the colonialist interpretation of Indian history (Chatterjee 1993: 76–94), long before the great spokesman of the Bengali intelligentsia, Bankimchandra Chattopadhyaya, launched his famous nationalist appeal in 1880, urging his compatriots to join together and write 'their own history' (Guha 1988: [1]) Meanwhile, in North India eminent Muslim reformers like Sir Sayyid Ahmad Khan and Maulana Shibli Nomani became the chief advocates of a new Islamic historiography, responding to the challenges of both colonialist and incipient Hindu nationalist historiography.[46]

The various ways in which Indians engaged with and simultaneously resisted the dominant discourse of colonial historiography and its 'hegemonic texts' underscore the existence of an already vibrant indigenous debate. Historians like C.A. Bayly have strongly argued against

[45] See, especially, Narayana Rao, Shulman, and Subrahmanyam 2001. Among the increasing number of studies describing the Indian contestation of colonial historiography and the formation of an indigenous nationalist historiography, see, e.g., Sen 1973; Chatterjee 1993; 1995; Guha 1988; 1997; Kaviraj 1995; and Ludden 1996.

[46] The promotion of Islamic historiography remained a concern of Muslim reformers into the twentieth century. It was a professed aim of the Lucknow Nadwat al-ʿulama's journal *Al-Nadwa,* launched in 1902 with a view to fostering Muslim self-confidence and counteracting the ill-informed and prejudiced portrayal of Islam in official school textbooks. Details in Malik 1997: 438–9; 465–6.

an understanding of indigenous historical consciousness that dates the beginning of modern Indian historiography to the needs of the modern, that is colonial state. A 'self-consciously modern history', contends Bayly, had already begun with the attempt of the post-Mughal elite to adjust to the rise of Hindus and the British (Bayly 1996: 84). His argument that historical memory was paramount in shaping the identity of this elite is corroborated by much textual evidence. The collective concern with the past manifested itself in a variety of literary forms, some of which were vigorously dismissed by colonialist historiography as irrational and lacking factual accuracy. Its most overt expression was the proliferation of historical and topographical writing in Persian and Urdu chronicles, generally denoted as *tārīkh*. Other manifestations were the *tazkirah*, or collective biography, and the Persian/Urdu lyrical genre known as *shahr āshob* ('city destruction'), that is poems lamenting the decline of Mughal civilization and fallen state of present society, which were infused with a strong sense of collective loss.[47] Within the Hindu tradition, historical memory was contained in the *Purāṇa*s and in genealogical texts known as *vaṃśāvalī* and *khyāt*, written in Sanskrit and the regional languages. Up to the early nineteenth century Puranic history remained 'a valid form of retelling the political history of Bhāratavarṣa' (Chatterjee 1993: 79).

These different genres, supplemented by an increasing number of latterday *tārīkh* writing in Urdu, were widely consumed by Indian readers. On the NKP list, historical writing in Persian and Urdu was classified under the subheadings of '*Tazkirah*', 'Biographies of Saints and Prophets', 'Histories of Prophets', and 'Histories of Kings and Emperors', forming a distinct category alongside the obvious history textbooks prescribed in colonial education. By contrast, among Sanskrit and Hindi titles, there was no special category for 'historical works', which still belonged within the traditional forms of '*itihās*', that is the great epics, and the *Purāṇa*s. Leaving aside textbooks such as Shiva Prasad's *Itihās timir nāśak* (History as the Dispeller of Darkness, 1864–73), in Hindi commercial publishing there was still little sign of the abandonment of Puranic history in favour of a rational historiography as described by Chatterjee for Bengal (Chatterjee 1993: 76–115).[48]

[47] Ibid.: 196–9. For specimens of early historiographical writing in Urdu, see J.A. Khan 1994 and 1995; for *shahr āshob*, see Petievich 1990; for a disccusion of the changing nature of the genre, see Pritchett 1984 and Naim 1984.

[48] As an institutionalized form of colonial historiography widely used in schools, official history textbooks provided an obvious target for indigenous criticism. This

In this climate of heightened historical consciousness and increased activity in historiographical writing, it comes as no surprise that history titles should constitute an important part of an Indian publisher's list. What is more remarkable is the pioneering spirit and untiring zeal displayed by Naval Kishore in recovering a variety of medieval Persian sources hitherto unpublished or existing in rare early-nineteenth-century editions only. His strategy in promoting works of Indo-Persian historiography was the same as previously encountered in the case of medical texts: firstly, to make the Persian classics widely accessible, and secondly to have them translated into Urdu to meet the growing demand for historical knowledge among the vernacular readership.

At first Naval Kishore turned to the same sources that nineteenth-century colonialist historiography had increasingly come to rely upon, that is, the works of the great medieval Indo-Muslim historians.[49] Whether or not he did so at British instigation is difficult to say in hindsight. He was certainly aware of British historians' work. The beginning of the NKP's engagement with Indo-Persian historiography in the mid-1860s was marked by the reprints of two famous works that had, early on, attracted Orientalist attention. The first was *Tārīkh-e Firishta*, a general history of India down to the year 1612, written by Muhammad Qasim Hindushah (commonly called Firishta) during the reigns of Akbar and Jahangir. As early as 1768, select portions of the text were available in an English translation by Alexander Dow, who relied heavily on Firishta in compiling his *History of Hindostan* (1768–72). The complete text was translated by John Briggs in his *History of the Rise of Mahomedan Power in India* in 1829. Soon afterwards, the first editions of the original Persian

---

particularly regarded textbooks authored by Indians who, themselves products of the colonial education system, perpetrated the biases of colonial historiography. Shiva Prasad's *Itihās timir nāśak*, the first history of India written in Hindi, is a famous case in point. It was widely disseminated in M. Kempson's English translation, *A History of Hindustan* (1866), and the author's own Urdu version *Āʾīna-e tārīkh numā* (1867–74). An open appraisal of the benefits of British rule which had rescued India from the 'darkness of centuries of Muslim despotism', the book came under heavy criticism for its vehemently anti-Muslim stance. Hindus, on the other hand, attacked it for its anti-Brahminical invectives. It was eventually replaced by W.W. Hunter's *Brief History of the Indian Peoples*. Its reintroduction into the curriculum in 1890 provoked fierce criticism in the media. See SVN 1890: 267 and 370; Powell 1999; Dalmia 1997: 330–2.

[49] For the shift in Orientalist interest from ancient to medieval Indian history and the indebtedness of nineteenth-century colonial historians to Indo-Muslim historiographers, see Hardy 1960: 1–3.

text were issued from Bombay and Poona in 1831–2. However, over thirty years went by before *Tārīkh-e Firishta* was reissued from Lucknow in 1864. Prepared by Munshi Kaliparshad, the NKP's two-volume lithographed edition was sold at the reasonable price of Rs 4, *as* 8. As befitted the momentous occasion, Naval Kishore presented Sayyid Ahmad Khan's Scientific Society with a complimentary copy.

The second work was *Siyar al-muta'akhkhirīn* (Overview of the Modern Age, *1866), a history of India in the eighteenth century written by Ghulam Husain Khan Tabataba'i around 1783. With its lucid critique of British Company rule in Bengal and Bihar, this text presents an important example of the early indigenous discourse on colonial rule in India.[50] Its publishing history much resembles that of *Tārīkh-e Firishta*: like Firishta, *Siyar al-muta'akhkhirīn* was first circulated in print in an English translation prepared in 1789. The *editio princeps* of the Persian text was printed at Calcutta in 1832. Again, the text had been unavailable for more than thirty years when, in the 1860s, Naval Kishore decided to invest in a reprint.

In his scheme of promoting the key texts of Indo-Persian historiography, Naval Kishore looked closely to the activities of the Asiatic Society of Bengal. The near simultaneous release of a number of important works suggests that he even entered into some sort of tacit competition with the Asiatic Society. One particularly notable instance of his successfully pre-empting British Orientalist efforts is Abul Fazl's celebrated *Akbarnāma*, the most influential historical work of medieval India. The publication of *Akbarnāma* from the NKP in 1866–7 was a momentous event: it was the first time that this important text appeared in print. The three-volume lithograph edition of over 1800 pages was sponsored by the Maharaja of Patiala. Its small print run of 275 copies and high price of Rs 50 (low compared to the £12, *s.* 12 it would later be advertised for in Trübner's Catalogue!) suggest a deluxe edition; so does a rather disparaging comment in Elliot and Dowson's *History of India*: 'It is a handsome and costly work, and it is greatly to be regretted that its literary value is by no means commensurate with the money expended upon it' (Elliot/Dowson 1875: 8–9). It is important to note that, subsequently, *Akbarnāma* was sold to the general public at a substantially reduced price of Rs 20 (*Fihrist* 1879).

The NKP *Akbarnāma* preceded the Bibliotheca Indica edition (1873–86) by several years. Yet Naval Kishore hardly found time to contemplate his achievement. In 1867, assisted by a sumptuous government grant of

[50] For an analysis and discussion of the text, see Khan 2000.

Rs 5000, the Asiatic Society commenced its critical edition of Abul Fazl's *Āʾīn-e Akbarī* (Institutes of Akbar). Soon after the first fascicles had appeared in the Bibliotheca Indica series, Naval Kishore launched a reprint of Sayyid Ahmad Khan's early critical edition of *Āʾīn*, previously issued in an incomplete version only. Complete in three volumes, the NKP edition of 1869 was 'copiously illustrated and produced with impressive thoroughness and clarity' (Lelyveld 1996: 73).[51] At Rs 30 it was only marginally more expensive than the Calcutta edition of 1877, which sold at Rs 27, *as.* 8. More of this seemingly 'competitive' publishing followed: shortly after the Asiatic Society had begun its edition of ʿAbdul Qadir Badaʾuni's *Muntakhab al-Tavārīkh* (1864–9), Naval Kishore brought out his own edition in 1868.[52] H. Blochmann, in an introductory article on Badaʾuni appearing in the *Journal of the Asiatic Society* in 1869, commended it as being 'a very fair edition' (Blochmann 1869: 144).[53] In terms of price, too, the NKP text compared favourably with the Calcutta edition. At Rs 9, *as.* 6, the three-volume Calcutta edition was priced almost twice as high as the NKP edition, which sold at Rs 5.

Conversely, in the case of *Iqbālnāma-e Jahāngirī*, the Bibliotheca Indica edition preceded the 1870 NKP edition by five years. Composed by Nawab Muʿtamad Khan (also known as Muhammad Sharif), a high officer at Jahangir's court, *Iqbālnāma* was famous for its third part, which was based on the Emperor's own memoirs and covered his entire reign in the form of annals. Several years later, the NKP was again a step ahead of the Asiatic Society when it brought out the first lithographed edition of *Ṭabaqāt-e Akbarī* (*1875), a general history of India from the beginning of Muslim rule to the 38th year of Akbar's reign. Composed

[51] According to his biographer Altaf Husain Hali, Sayyid Ahmad Khan had first been approached with the request of preparing a critical edition of *Āʾīn-e Akbarī* by Haji Qutbuddin, a rich Delhi merchant, who also promised a lavish remuneration of Rs 1600. Sayyid Ahmad declined, but after his transfer to Bijnor returned to the idea of editing the text. A first incomplete edition was published from Delhi in 1856 (Hali 1966: 102). It seems that the 1869 NKP edition of the *Āʾīn* was issued in two different versions. Arberry's catalogue lists an illustrated text of 1205 pages, whereas the edition mentioned in the 1879 NKP catalogue, 'complete with illustrations and maps', is said to comprise 1342 pages (*Fihrist* 1879: 66).

[52] Badaʾuni's general history of India from the Muslim conquest to the reign of Akbar forms an important contrast to Abul Fazl's chronicles. It is not to be confused with *Muntakhab al-tavārīkh* (*1860) by Javahirlal Akbarabadi, an abridged Urdu translation of *Makhzan al-tavārīkh*. Its author, a hakim and newspaper editor of Agra, translated a number of Persian historical works into Urdu (*HLHH* II: 91).

[53] Blochmann gives the date of 1864 for the NKP edition of *Muntakhab al-tavārīkh*.

towards the close of the sixteenth century by Khwaja Nizamuddin Ahmad, the work served as a model for later writers of Mughal history. It was not until the year 1911 that the Persian text, together with an English translation, was taken up for publication in the Bibliotheca Indica series. Its editor B. De, in addition to three manuscript copies, relied heavily on the NKP edition.

While this completes the list of works published from both the Asiatic Society and the NKP, it does not exhaust the Lucknow publisher's repertoire of Persian historiographical titles.[54] In 1871 Naval Kishore issued *Jāmiᶜ al-tavārīkh*, a contemporary world history by Faqir Muhammad. Other works of importance followed, among them *Tavārīkh-e Ṭabarī* (*1874), an abridged Persian translation of Tabari's universal history, and *Rauẓat al-ṣafā* (Garden of Purity, *1874), a celebrated fifteenth-century work by Mir Khwand. Despite its enormous prestige—'There is no Oriental work that stands higher in public estimation than the *Rauzat al-safā*' (Elliot/Dowson 1872: 129)—*Rauẓat* had only been printed once in the 1840s in Bombay. Again, Naval Kishore was the first to reprint it. The lithographed edition of over 1500 pages (3 vols) sold at Rs 12.

Despite several flaws and imperfections, Naval Kishore's editions of Persian historiography achieved a certain standing as authoritative sources. While they may not have matched the standards of modern critical editing, they were certainly consulted by British Orientalists. Frequent references to the 'Lucknow edition' of Firishta, Badaʾuni or Abul Fazl suggest as much. In the case of the NKP *Akbarnāma*, Orientalist usage of the text was accompanied by harsh criticism. Dowson noted the abundance of 'gross and obvious errors' and the want of entire passages (Elliot/Dowson 1875: 9); H. Blochmann dismissed it as 'worse than the worst possible MS.' (Blochmann 1872: 52). Likewise, the Bibliotheca Indica editors of *Akbarnāma*, who consulted the NKP text alongside various manuscripts, heavily criticized its shortcomings. It was only later that H. Beveridge, the English translator of *Akbarnāma,* gave a more impartial assessment of the respective achievements of the Bibliotheca Indica and NKP editions:

> The Bibliotheca Indica edition is by no means so good as it might have been, for the learned native editors were destitute of geographical or historical knowledge. Hence they have often made mistakes in the names of

[54] A work of Arabic historiography also deserves mention here: In 1870, the NKP issued *Futūḥ al-shām* (also called *Maghāzī al-Rasūl*), a history of the Syrian conquest ascribed to al-Waqidi. It was first edited by W. Nassau Lees for the Bibliotheca Indica in 1858–62.

> persons and places. They have also no explanatory notes. In their preface they are severe upon the Lucknow edition. No doubt that edition has many faults, but it was the first in the field, and it is on the whole a creditable monument of the enterprise of the publisher, Munshi Newal Kishor, and of the liberality of the Maharajah of Patiala.[55]

Naval Kishore's growing reputation in the field of Persian history publishing also attracted the patronage of British officials. William Young, Judicial Commissioner of Avadh and a member of the Asiatic Society, chose to commission the Lucknow publisher with the edition of his English translation of *Tauqīᶜāt-e kisrawīyah* (*1892), a sixth-century work on early Persian history and geography attributed to King Khusrau Anushirwan. The Persian text, itself a translation from the Arabic, had already been published by the NKP in 1870. The English translation posed a challenge to the firm's editorial office, for it was the first time that a Roman transliteration from Persian had to be prepared. Young was clearly satisfied with the result: in the preface to his work he profusedly thanked Naval Kishore 'for the hearty aid he has given me throughout and that moreover in a matter not within his ordinary scope as a printer and publisher.'[56]

From the 1870s onwards, the preoccupation with the past was also reflected in a spate of works on regional and local history written in Urdu.[57] In 1876 Naval Kishore issued *Ṣaulat-e Afghanī*, a substantial work of over 700 pages by Muhammad Zardar Khan, which provided a historical account of the Afghan people and its clans. A British reviewer considered it 'well worthy of the study of those who are interested in frontier politics.'[58] Not surprisingly, in promoting contemporary historiographical writing the NKP placed a certain emphasis on the history of Avadh. Its most important publications on local history were *Qaiṣar al-tavārīkh* (*1879) and *Savāniḥāt-e salāṭīn-e Avadh* (*1879) by Kamaluddin

[55] *The Akbar Nāmā of Abu-l-Fazl*, trs. from the Persian by H. Beveridge, reprint Delhi 1993, [Preface].

[56] *The Wisdom of Naushirwan 'The Just', King of Iran, commonly called Tauqiyat i Kisrawiya* (*1892): viii.

[57] Incidentally, one of the earliest historical works on the NKP Urdu list was *Tārīkh-e mamālik-e Cīn* (*1864), a history of China authored by the Indo-British poet James Cochrane, poetically surnamed 'Karkaran'. Cochrane, a former translator at the High Court of Bengal, was a lawyer at the Allahabad High Court (Saksena 1941: 145–6).

[58] *RPIR* 1877: 113.

Haidar, the foremost chronicler of *navābī* Avadh.[59] In a telling indication of his pronounced interest in history, Naval Kishore himself chose to enter the fray of writers with a work of history. His *Tārīkh-e nādir al-ʿaṣr* (A Unique Chronicle, *1863) combined a brief account of the administration of his patron, Colonel Saunders Abbott, with a sketch of the local history and topography of Lucknow. In calling his account a *tārīkh*, the publisher consciously placed himself in the tradition of local historians.

Naval Kishore's objective of enhancing historical knowledge by making the principal works of Mughal historiography available in Urdu translation tallied with colonial efforts. Hence, it is often difficult to determine whether specific translations were undertaken at his own initiative or prepared under the aegis of the British authorities. The total of original and translated historiographical works in Urdu on the NKP list easily surpasses fifty titles. Included in it are a number of translations of European works, which will be dealt with separately below. Among the firm's first history texts in Urdu translation, proudly announced in the *Avadh Akhbār* of 31 October 1865, was *Tārīkh-e Rum*, a history of Greece translated from the Arabic by Muhammad Qudratullah Khan (*LLH* 1865: 317). Another translation of an Arabic classic followed in the form of *Futūḥāt-e Wāqidī* (*1870–4), a history of the Islamic conquests ascribed to al-Waqidi. The bulk of translations, however, related to the above-named works of Indo-Persian historiography. By 1874 Urdu versions of *Tavārīkh-e Ṭabarī*, *Jāmiʿ al-tavārīkh*, *Tārīkh e Firishta*, *Muntakhab al-tavārīkh* and *Siyar al-mutaʾakhkhirīn* were ready. It is important to note that most of these texts had not been translated before. Various translators were involved in the effort: Maulana Ihteshamuddin, a scholar of Muradabad who had previously assisted the NKP in translating *Fatāwā-e ʿĀlamgīrī*, translated *Tavārīkh-e ʿAbd al-Qādir Badaʾunī* (*1874). The translation of *Siyar al-mutaʿakhkhirīn* was entrusted to Munshi Gokul Parshad, a Srivastava Kayastha of Kanpur. Published in three volumes as *Mirāt as-salāṭīn* (*1874), it earned him steady employment in the NKP's translation department. Gokul Parshad also composed poetry under the pen name 'Raza'. He was in many ways typical of the firm's

[59] Later published jointly as *Tavārīkh-e Avadh* (*1896; 1907). Other histories of Avadh include Ghulam Ahmad, *ʿImād al-saʿādat* (*1864, in Persian); Totaram 'Shayan', *Tārīkh-e Sitāra-e Hind* (*1871) and *Ṭilism-e Hind* (*1874); Radhelal, *Tārīkh-e farmān ravayān-e Avadh* (*1878); and Durgaprasad, *Būstān-e Avadh* (*1892). For an overview of historiographical writing in Avadh, see Husain Akbarpuri 1991.

bilingual Persian-Urdu translators, who were equally well versed in both languages.

5.4 A Transition in Print: From Persian to Urdu

The nineteenth century witnessed the gradual replacement of Persian by Urdu, both in its official role of court and administrative language, and as a medium of poetry and of journalistic, scientific, and fictional prose. The new public role of Urdu and its growing prestige as the new lingua franca of northern India entailed the slow but steady decline of Persian. While Persian literature continued to be held in high esteem among the educated classes, and there was still a considerable market for books in Persian, by the end of the century the transition from Persian to Urdu had led to a quantitative reversal in the number of Persian and Urdu books produced in North India. It had also led to a proliferation of translations and bilingual formats.

In a reflection of the cultural continuum that Persian and Urdu presented, Naval Kishore, like most North Indian commercial publishers, produced books in both Persian and Urdu from the very beginning. The large number of Persian works continuously emanating from his press mirrors the still vigorous tradition of Persian scholarship and its continuing importance in Indian intellectual culture, while also reflecting the literary tastes of educated Indians. Naval Kishore catered to prevailing interests through a wide range of inexpensive reprints of Persian religious and literary classics. Yet he was seemingly not satisfied with doing so, for he also sought to assume a more prominent role in Persian publishing, acting as a custodian and preserver of the rich tradition of Persian and Indo-Persian literature in the subcontinent. To this end, he produced an unparalleled range of scientific, historiographical, legal, lexicographical, and medical titles, including a substantial number of works lithographed for the first time and circulated in India even before they appeared in print in the Middle East. Others, as has been shown, were reprints of rare editions published early in the century and no longer available. It would go beyond the scope of this study to give a comprehensive overview of the vast array of both popular and scholarly editions of Persian literature issued from the NKP. Instead, we shall continue to concentrate on the publisher's grand cultural project: the promotion of Persian and the Indo-Persian literary heritage through Urdu translation.

For a long time the House of Naval Kishore followed a 'dual language' policy, according equal status to the literatures of northern India's old and new lingua franca and promoting them side by side. It was only at the end of the nineteenth century that the dwindling position of Persian in the public sphere and the attendant decline in the demand for Persian books became visible in NKP publication figures, when the ratio between Persian and Urdu publications shifted noticeably in favour of Urdu.[60] It would be wrong to attribute this shift to a deliberate departure from the earlier policy or an intentional relinquishing of Persian on the publisher's part. On the contrary, the NKP continued to remain a supplier of high-class editions of Persian works well into the twentieth century.[61] It played a decisive role in upholding the position of Lucknow as the main stronghold of Persian publishing in the United Provinces. The city still accounted for 41,000 copies of Persian books in 1900 and over 10,000 in 1914 (King 1994: 41).

On the NKP list, the linguistic transition from Persian to Urdu found its immediate expression in a host of formats designed to facilitate comprehension, that is translations, popular reworkings, and commentaries on Persian texts, as well as annotated and bilingual editions. While encompassing a variety of genres, the majority of such titles pertained to the canonical texts of the Persian intellectual tradition, including epics and poetry, history, *akhlāq* (a genre of ethical literature encompassing both politics and ethics), and *inshā* (the art of composition and letter-writing). A typical publication in the latter category was *Inshā-e Safdarī* (*1872), a collection of Persian model letters with Urdu versions by Ghulam Safdar. Like other publishers, Naval Kishore reprinted popular works like *Gulistān-e mutarjam* (*1867), an edition of Saᶜdi with interlinear Urdu translation and marginal notes.[62] However, the demand for Urdu versions was such that he decided to also invest in producing his own translations and commentaries.

In the book trade, as elsewhere, the transition from Persian to Urdu was gradual. Its living embodiments inside the publishing house were

[60] This tallies with King's observation that the overall number of Persian publications in the NWP&Oudh only fell precipitously around the turn of the century (King 1994: 41).

[61] An impression of the quantity and continuously wide range of Persian titles can be gathered from the NKP's catalogues of 1929 and 1941.

[62] This title was first published from the Sultan al-Matabiᶜ of Lahore in 1850.

the large numbers of bilingual Munshis engaged in proofreading, editing, and translating Persian texts into Urdu. Some of them were poets in their own right. Like their archetypal representative Mirza Ghalib, these men belonged to a generation of north Indian literati who were fluent in Persian and deeply steeped in its literary traditions; at the same time, they increasingly took to Urdu for private and social communication and began to adopt the modern language for their own literary compositions.

The first prominent figure on the NKP's team of Persian translators was the Urdu poet Totaram 'Shayan' Lakhnavi (d. 1879). He belonged to an eminent family of Srivastava Kayasthas of Ayodhya; his grandfather Mansukhrai and father Atmaram had been important courtiers of the Avadh nawabs. Fate ordained that Totaram should live in much humbler circumstances: in the early 1860s he joined the NKP as an editor-translator. Totaram was a versatile author whose poetical works include *Wāsokht-e Shāyān* (*1869) and *Farhang-e ʿishq* (*1868). He also established himself among local historians with two brief histories of Avadh entitled *Tārīkh-e Sitāra-e Hind* (*1871) and *Ṭilism-e Hind* (*1874).[63] His fame, however, rests largely on his work as a translator. At the behest of Naval Kishore he prepared Urdu translations of several great Persian texts, starting with *Mahābhārat manẓūm*, a verse rendering of the Persian *Mahābhārat* prepared at Akbar's court by Abul Fazl, ʿAbdul Qadir Badaʾuni, and others, itself a celebrated example of the splendid tradition of translation at the Mughal court. Totaram's abridged Urdu version appeared in 1862; the edition was richly illustrated with woodcuts. In the same year, he completed a verse rendering of the Hamzah romance known as *Ṭilism-e Shāyān* (*1862). With its 30,000 lines this version of *Dāstān-e Amīr Ḥamzah* is one of the longest Urdu *maṣnavī*s ever written in North India (Pritchett 1991: 23–4). It was also the first step in the NKP's sustained efforts towards popularizing the *dāstān* genre (see below). Totaram's second translation was of another classic of oriental literature, *Alf Laila* or *Arabian Nights* (*1867). Two existing previous Urdu versions of the *Arabian Nights*, prepared by Munshi Shamsuddin Ahmad Shirvani and Munshi ʿAbdul Karim for the use of Fort St George College and Fort William College, were meant for European learners of Urdu and written in a simple prose style.[64] By contrast, Totaram's version of 1867 was the first Urdu prose rendering designed specifically for a

[63] *HLHH* III: 122–3. For further details on his life and works, see Husain Akbarpuri 1991: 222–8.

[64] Shamsuddin Ahmad Shirvani, *Ḥikāyat al-jalīlah* (Madras 1836); ʿAbdul Karim's translation (Kanpur 1847) was apparently based on Edward Foster's English version of the *Arabian Nights*.

readership of Indian connoisseurs. Comprising over 1000 pages, his *Hazār Dāstān* was much closer to the original text in retaining the arrangement of the narrative into nights and adopting a highly metaphorical and ornate style replete with Persian and Arabic idiom. While for that very reason the translation did not find favour with the British Orientalist James Blumhardt, it was well acclaimed by the Urdu readership.[65]

Significantly, Naval Kishore did not leave it at that. Given the popular demand for poetry, the prose version of the *Arabian Nights* needed to be complemented by a verse rendering. The task was assigned to Muhammad Asghar ᶜAli Khan 'Nasim' Dehlavi (1794–1864), a poet of repute employed at the NKP. On completing the first volume Nasim apparently fell out with the publisher, who found his progress too slow. The translation was handed over to Totaram, who undertook the second and third volumes; the last two volumes were translated by Shadi Lal 'Chaman'. Complete in 1244 pages, *Alf Lailā nau manẓūm* (*1861–8) was widely advertised in the columns of *Avadh Akhbār* and various other newspapers. The publication notice in *Mufarrah al-Qulub*, a Persian paper of Karachi that regularly carried announcements of NKP titles, is worth quoting, for it nicely illustrates the emphatic and flowery rhetoric of book advertising at the time:

> Alf Lailah Versified
>
> Scarce, exceptional and select are the people in this age whose natures have experienced Pain, whose hearts are familiar with Love, who are fond of the sweet pleasures of Poesy and take interest in listening to tales and fables. True it is that consciousness comes by learning of the conditions of the Past; the curtain of Ignorance is thus removed from the mind and

[65] Blumhardt wrote: 'The translation is virtually in prose, but it abounds in snatches of poetry, songs and couplets taken from the writings of Persian poets, and here and there a verse-rendering of bits of the story. This translation, though substantially agreeing in the main with that of ᶜAbd al-Karim, yet differs widely from it in the treatment. It is full of flowery metaphors and is written in a rich, ornate style full of Persian and Arabic words and idioms, which renders it far less easy to understand than the simple language of ᶜAbd al-Karim. Some passages have been considerably enlarged and sometimes contain quite different reading from that of ᶜAbd al-Karim with occasional additional matter. In other places descriptions have been much curtailed so that although the thread of the story may be the same in both translations, it is hard to believe that the two translators worked from the same version. Unfortunately Totaram Shayan makes no mention at Ali [*sic*] the source whence he made his translation whether English or Arabic. This translation reached its fourth edition in 1883, and has been published with the addition of several badly executed full-page illustrations evidently taken from English prints.' Burton 1887: [n.p.].

heart. Is it ever possible for the Men of Insight to be satiated with the Sight of books? Are men of wisdom ever too contented with tales and stories? There are stories, creations of poets, but this story of a thousand and one nights is pleasantly provocative of Love. Where else can anyone get a more interesting story? To the lovers, every night of this attractive Laila brings the delights of the night of meeting with the beloved. Every morning of this attractive Salma is an exegesis of the Surah 'wa-alshams'. First it was printed and liked in the Arabic tongue. Then it was translated into English: the high and the low liked it. Next, it was put into Urdu prose which was praised by everyone . . . Wits and men of insight prefer the verse form of 'mathnavi'. Therefore, this humble man, Naval Kishore, the owner of Matbaʾ *Avadh Akhbar*, asked the poets associated with the Matbaʾ to raise an edifice of poetry in such a way as to make this attractive Mistress . . . beautified by verse. First of all . . . Janab Mirza Asghar Ali Khan tried his hand at it. The stories of the first two hundred and fifty nights were versified . . . The next five hundred nights were put into verse form by Munshi Tota Ram 'Shayan'. He had already made his mark by translating *Mahabharat* and *Dastan-e-Amir-Hamza* into Urdu verse. The remaining story of the last two hundred and fifty nights were put into poetic form by Munshi Shadi Lal Chaman, the disciple of the late Mirza Nasim. (cited in Khan 1991: 292–3).

No history of the NKP would be complete without describing the firm's singular role in the preservation and promotion of the traditional Persian and Urdu prose narrative known as *qiṣṣa* and *dāstān.*[66] In the case of the *dāstān*, the transition from Persian to Urdu antedated an even more significant transition from orality to written texts. There is no other literary genre in which the NKP's role at the interface between the oral and the written has been so well explored as in the case of the *qiṣṣa* and *dāstān*. Frances Pritchett (Pritchett 1985; 1991) has documented in great detail how, on a single publisher's initiative, a hitherto oral tradition was complemented by a written one, which through its printed texts ultimately outlasted the former: 'In the long run, Naval Kishor turned out to be a more important patron of the Urdu dastan than any prince or aristocrat: he was responsible for creating and preserving most of the texts which today provide our only real access to the tradition' (Pritchett 1991: 29).

Persian *qiṣṣa*s and *dāstān*s were well-established and popular genres in India by the beginning of the Mughal period, particularly in the form

[66] Whereas in Persian the terms *qiṣṣa* and *dāstān* describe the same romance genre, in Urdu they came to be differentiated on the basis of length, *dāstāns* being, as Frances Pritchett puts it, 'long qissas' and *qiṣṣas* 'short dastans' (Pritchett 1985: 4).

of *Dāstān-e Amīr Ḥamzah*, a vast cycle of romances about the life of Hamzah, the uncle of the Prophet and legendary champion of Islam. Transmitted orally, the *dāstān* developed its own Indo-Persian tradition and subsequently established itself as a genre in Urdu literature. By the latter half of the nineteenth century the narration of Urdu *dāstāns* by professional storytellers (*dāstān-go*) enjoyed enormous popularity. Lucknow became the single most important centre in the cultivation of oral *dāstān* telling.[67] It comes then as no surprise that the most consequential undertaking in fixing the popular genre in print should be initiated by an enterprising local publisher such as Naval Kishore. Significantly, his pivotal role in promoting the *dāstān* in print was not limited to Urdu but also extended to the popularization of *qiṣṣa* and *dāstān* texts in Hindi (see Chapter 7).

Qiṣṣas and *dāstans* were first printed at Fort William College. Next to the well-known *qiṣṣa*s of *Cahār darvesh* (*Bāgh o bahār*), *Gul-e bakāvalī*, *Ḥātim Tāʾī*, and so forth, in 1801 the college also published one of the earliest written versions of *Dāstān-e Amīr Ḥamzah*, composed by Khalil ʿAli Khan Ashk. More than half a century later, the history of *dāstān* publishing shifted to Lucknow. Having issued a reprint of Ashk's text in 1869, Naval Kishore soon deemed it expedient to replace it with an improved and 'updated' version that would appeal to the changed literary tastes of the contemporary Urdu readership. The task was entrusted to Maulvi Hafiz ʿAbdullah Bilgrami, a teacher at the Arabic school of Kanpur. Working on an earlier version by Ghalib Lakhnavi, Bilgrami delivered a much improved and revised text which was free of archaisms and written in 'a grandiose and highly ornate language' (Farooqi 2001: 169).[68] The title page of this *Dāstān-e Amīr Ḥamzah Ṣāḥibqirān* (*1871), as translated by Pritchett, offers some interesting publication details:

[67] 'For ordinary people, there were almost daily public performances by dastangos in Chauk, starting "when the lamps were lit". And for the elite, there were private sessions—even for ladies. Upper-class women kept their own female dastan-gos and storytellers, who were treated with real respect. Story-telling sessions often went on and on in the early evening "until the dining cloth was spread"' (Pritchett 1991: 15). See also Sharar 1975: 91–4 for a graphic account of *dāstān* cultivation in Lucknow.

[68] Bilgrami's *Dāstān* was first translated into English by Pritchett on the basis of its revised and expurgated eleventh edition of 1969 (Pritchett 1991). Pritchett's choice of source came under heavy criticism by M. Farooqi who supplied a new translation of the text in the *AUS* on the basis of Bilgrami's original 1871 version (Farooqi 2000).

> Although [the Ashk version], because of its appeal to great and small, has been printed in thousands of copies in Calcutta, Bombay, and Delhi, and at the *Avadh Akhbār* Press, it has always been disliked by purists for its archaic idioms and convoluted style. With the greatest effort and energy Maulvi Ḥāfiẓ ᶜAbdullah Ṣāḥib, teacher at the Arabic school (*madrasah*) of Kanpur, has made modern additions and alterations and corrections in the language and idioms, at the desire of the Master of the Press. And under the supervision of the employees of the press of Munshī Naval Kishor, situated in Lucknow, in the month of November 1871 AD, at the special request of Janāb Maulvī ᶜAbdul ᶜAzīz Ṣāḥib Bookseller of Lucknow, who has generously promised before publication to buy a great number of copies, with the greatest haste it has undergone publication. (Pritchett 1991: 29)

Bilgrami's modernized version was, in turn, revised by the NKP emendator Tasadduq Husain Rizvi, who was in charge of the fifth edition of 1887. Variously revised and simplified over the years, it continued to sell extremely well and was kept in print at the Tej Kumar Press until the 1990s.

The publication of the Bilgrami version was only the beginning of the NKP's sustained efforts in preserving the Urdu *dāstān*, which culminated in the firm's celebrated edition of the complete Amir Hamzah cycle. In 1881 Naval Kishore hired the most reputed *dāstān-go*s of Lucknow, notably Shaikh Tassaduq Husain, Munshi Ahmad Husain Qamar, and Munshi Muhammad Husain Jah, who recited their stories in the presence of scribes or else wrote them down themselves. The outcome of this singular collective effort was a monumental 46-volume edition of *Dāstān-e Amīr Ḥamzah,* issued from the press between 1883 and 1917. The first seven volumes to be completed in 1883–93 were *Ṭilism-e Hoshrubā* (The Stunning Enchantment), the fifth book of the *Dāstān*, which came to enjoy immense popularity in its own right. Since Muhammad Husain Jah fell out with Naval Kishore at an early stage of the venture, most volumes were edited by Tassaduq Husain and Ahmad Husain Qamar. *Dāstān-e Amīr Ḥamzah* represents a unique achievement in the history of Urdu publishing. Ironically, it also marked the end of *dāstān* writing in Urdu, for the traditional narrative genre was soon to be replaced by the modern novel. The NKP edition of the *dāstān* remained, as Pritchett has so aptly put it, 'both its crowning glory and its *coup de grâce*' (Pritchett 1985: 6).

Reverting our attention back to the late 1860s, the project of translating the Persian classics into Urdu started in earnest in 1868–9, with two different renderings of Firdausi's great epic *Shāhnāmah.* One was prepared by Munshi Fida ᶜAli 'Aish', an Urdu poet employed at the press, the other by Munshi Gokul Parshad 'Raza', who has already been introduced as the translator of *Siyar al-mutaᵓakhkhirīn.*[69] As the NKP's new Persian head translator, Gokul Parshad contributed an Urdu reworking of Nizami's *Sikandarnāmah* entitled *Kārnāma-e Sikandarī* (Chronicle of Alexander the Great, *1873).[70] He also translated two rare Persian texts that commanded high prestige in learned circles: *Nūr-e ᶜain* (Light of the Eye, *1872), a translation of Dara Shikoh's famous metaphysical discussion of Sufism and Vedanta known as *Majmaᶜ al-baḥrain* (The Meeting-Place of the Two Oceans); and *ᶜAjāᵓib al-makhlūqāt* (The Wonders of Nature, *1877), itself a Persian version of Qazwini's Arabic cosmography. Gokul Parshad's Urdu translation sold so well that in 1886 it was complemented by a Hindi version entitled *Adbhut sṛṣti caritra*.

Gokul Parshad was also one of the many Indian translators of Jalal al-Din Rumi's *Maṣnavī-e maᶜnavī*, a celebrated work of Sufi mysticism that commanded immense popularity and was the focus of much study in India. The range of NKP editions, translations, and Persian as well as Urdu commentaries on Rumi's mystical poem provide a good example of how the same text was offered in various formats to appeal to different audiences: for the sophisticated scholastic reader and learned mystic the most important publication by far was the NKP's three-volume edition (1873) of the Arabic commentary of the *Maṣnavī* by the famous Farangi Mahall scholar ᶜAbdul ᶜAli Bahr al-ᶜUlum. ᶜAbdul ᶜAli interpreted Rumi in the light of the teachings of Ibn ᶜArabi; his study became a Sufi classic and an important point of reference in the development of nineteenth-century Indian Sufism (Robinson 2001: 24, 82). Readers not classically trained could choose between two different Urdu translations by Gokul Parshad and Ghulam Haidar; or else resort to *Laṭāᵓif al-lughāt* (*1877) and *Laṭāᵓif-e maᶜnavī* (*1877), a dictionary of expressions and commentary by ᶜAbdul Latif; *Pīrāhan-e Yūsufī* (*1889), a translation-cum-commentary by Muhammad Yusuf ᶜAli Shah; and *Būstān-e maᶜrifat*

[69] Gokul Parshad had come to Lucknow from Kanpur in search of a living. After a temporary job in the Education Department he was facing unemployment and was about to return to his native place when Naval Kishore offered him employment at his firm (*Mirāt al-ṣalatīn*, *1874, translator's preface).

[70] The translation was submitted under the Allahabad Government Prize Notification but returned as 'unworthy of notice' (*PGNWP. Educational Dept.*, Oct 1873, No. 23 B). By contrast, Garcin de Tassy applauded Naval Kishore's initiative in the translation (*LLH* 1873: 21).

(*1894–5), a voluminous Urdu commentary by ᶜAbdul Majid Khan of Pilibhit.

Like translations, Urdu commentaries of the Persian classics were in high demand. In 1876 Naval Kishore commissioned Maulana Sayyid Muhammad Sadiq ᶜAli Rizvi to prepare a commentary on the collected verse of Hafiz. In 1882 there followed *Guldasta-e khayāl*, a commentary on Saᶜdi's *Gulistān* by Maulvi Sayyid Razak Bakhsh of Jaunpur. Meanwhile, the firm had enlisted the services of another experienced Persian-Urdu translator, Maulana Abul Hasan Faridabadi. Abul Hasan, who combined a background in Islamic scholarship with excellent English skills, had worked for the Education Department and also served as official translator to the Avadh *taᶜalluqdār*s' British Indian Association (Anjuman-e Hind). His *Minhāj al-sālikīn* (*1871), an Urdu translation of the celebrated Persian *Yogavāsiṣṭha* composed under Dara Shikoh, was widely acclaimed. In the 1880s the Maulana prepared a series of translations of standard Persian commentaries on the panegyric poems by ᶜUrfi, Jami, and Badr-e Chach for the press. He also rendered *Riyāẓ-e riẓvān*, a famous commentary on Saᶜdi's *Gulistān,* into Urdu.[71] As will be shown later, his skills were also sought in a special undertaking of cultural translation—that of English works into Urdu.

Mediating between the vanishing world of Persian and the new vernacular cultures, these bilingual scholars and munshis worked side by side and, occasionally, in close interaction with another group of cultural intermediaries serving the publishing house: its Hindu pandits.

5.5 Sanskrit Shastric Texts for the Modern Reader

Although the province of Avadh was a treasure trove of Sanskrit manuscripts (Nesfield/Deviprasad 1874–93), no significant contribution to Sanskrit publishing emerged from Lucknow until the late 1860s, when the NKP began to systematically engage in the publication and translation of Sanskrit texts. Naval Kishore deserves credit for being the first publisher in the city to promote Sanskrit works on a commercial scale.[72]

[71] *Tarjuma-e Urdū-e sharḥ-e Yūsuf Zulaikhā* (*1890), *Tarjuma-e sharḥ-e qasāʾid-e Badr-e Cāc* (*1889), *Sharḥ-e mutarjim qasāʾid-e ᶜUrfī* (*1887), *Tarjuma-e Urdū Riyāẓ-e riẓvān sharḥ-e gulistān* (*1884).

[72] The only other Lucknow press to occasionally bring out Sanskrit texts was the Samar-e Hind Press of Pandit Baijnath. One of its earliest publications was the *Yajurveda Saṃhitā* (1869).

Since nineteenth-century Lucknow is hardly associated with Sanskrit cultural production, his contribution to the revival of the Sanskrit heritage and the promotion of Hindu shastric texts in the modern languages has escaped scholarly attention altogether. Even if largely reproductive in nature, this contribution deserves to be noticed, for it was substantial and did not lag behind similar efforts undertaken at the main centres of Sanskrit publishing.[73]

Naval Kishore's approach to the Sanskrit canon was in keeping with the firm's overall policy of popularizing religious classics among a wide section of the contemporary readership. His target audience was the general reader rather than the Sanskrit scholar, whose needs were increasingly met by specialized Sanskrit publishers in the metropolises of Bombay and Calcutta, as also the nearby Hindu pilgrimage towns of Benares and Allahabad. Naval Kishore had no ambition to compete with their vast and variegated output of Sanskrit scholastic and scientific literature. His objective clearly was to promote the classics in inexpensive editions, while simultaneously producing a body of standard works in translation that were easily accessible in terms of both cost and content.[74] At the time, notions of what constituted the canon of Sanskrit literature, both sacred and profane, were by no means uniform. While we have a fair picture of those Sanskrit scriptures regarded as authoritative by eminent contemporary Hindu reformers and nationalists,[75] it is no less interesting to take a look at the texts selected for publication and translation, that is, in other words, considered representative of the 'perpetual' Hindu tradition, by a commercial publisher. The publisher's choice was based on market demand, itself indicative of a common consensus of what constituted the Sanskrit tradition for the majority of the Hindu literate public. Rather than reflecting sectarian or scholarly interests, it featured a much more 'popular' canon of Hindu texts.

By the time Naval Kishore turned his attention to the Sanskrit literary heritage, there was considerable activity in translating Sanskrit texts into the modern languages.[76] His own engagement in promoting Sanskrit

[73] See Appendix V for a list of NKP Sanskrit publications.

[74] Consequently, there are no overlappings between NKP Sanskrit titles and the scholarly publications contained in the Benares Sanskrit Series, published from 1880 by the pandits of the Benares Sanskrit College.

[75] See, e.g., Killingley 1981 (for Rammohan Roy); Llevelyn 1993: 157–215 (for Dayananda Sarasvati); King 1977 (for Bankim Chandra Chatterjee); Dalmia 1995: 176–209 (for Bharatendu Harishchandra).

[76] See Das 1991:108–9; 178–9; *Hindī sāhitya kā bṛhat itihās*, vol. 8, 312–13.

works in Hindi cannot be viewed in isolation from the pervasive cultural process that Vasudha Dalmia has described as the 'nationalization of Hindu traditions' (Dalmia 1997). Instigated by Hindu nationalism and revivalism, this complex process involved the construction of a cultural and ideological configuration in which Hindi, the proclaimed national language of the modern Hindu nation, was linked with its Sanskrit, pre-Muslim past, perceived as the glorious and untainted Golden Age of Hindu civilization. As Dalmia has shown, the 'historicization of Hindi' took place as much at the linguistic level—that is by way of the deliberate Sanskritization of the language and insistence on its Aryan pedigree—as through the construction of its literary tradition. In the retrospective canonical search for the 'true' corpus of Hindi literature and the attendant creation of a national literature, the proponents of the new Hindu cultural consciousness looked beyond medieval Hindi texts to the classical models of Sanskrit literature. Underpinning the narrative of continuity from Sanskrit to Hindi, Sanskrit texts in translation came to form an essential textual link between the present and the past; once easily accessible in mass-printed editions and an idiom intelligible to the common people, they formed one of the key elements in the construction of the religio-cultural identity of the new Hindu nation.

Providing a good illustration of this linguistic-ideological bridging, a standard format adopted by commercial publishers was the bilingual edition, in which the Sanskrit text was accompanied by a modern-language translation, commentary, or simple prose paraphrase. Needless to say, the bilingual format was not exclusively motivated by Hindu revivalist considerations; it was also a pragmatic reaction to the noticeable decline in Sanskrit knowledge. In his analysis of publishing patterns in the NWP&Oudh, King points to the disproportionately high increase of such dual-language works, which multiplied 'at a greater rate than any other language or language combination' (King 1994: 41). That a large proportion of Sanskrit–Hindi and Hindi–Sanskrit titles were school textbooks explains their significant statistical impact: 7200 copies of bilingual works were issued from Lucknow in 1884, as opposed to 2000 from Allahabad and 1500 only from Benares. By 1900 the figures had risen to over 14,000 for Lucknow, compared to 6000 in Allahabad and 2750 in Benares (King 1994: 43).

It is no coincidence that the NKP's expansion into the field of Sanskrit publishing was inaugurated with the publication of one of the most revered Hindu scriptures, the *Bhāgavata Purāṇa*, in 1868–70. Sponsored by the Raja of Patiala, the two-volume edition of nearly 1300 pages included the standard commentary by Shridhara Svamin. It was issued in a run of 1375 copies and sold at the rather high price of Rs 15. The *Bhāgavata Purāṇa* not only provided the religious auspiciousness befitting the start of a venture into Sanskrit publishing, but, as a key text of Vaishnavism, it also set the tone for much future publishing of Hindu religious texts at the press. An edition of the *Bhagavad Gītā* with the Hindi commentary by Harivamsh Lal followed in 1875. It was supplemented in 1888 by *Śrīmadbhagavadgītānavalbhāṣya*, which assembled the standard commentaries by Shankara, Anandagiri, and Shridhara, and also contained a translation of Shankara's commentary in 'easy national language' (*saral deśbhāṣā*), composed at the publisher's instance by Pandit Umadatt Tripathi of Farrukhabad.[77] As stated in the publisher's notice, Naval Kishore had spared no expense in having the new commentary produced specifically for 'those who only knew Hindi (*bhāṣā*)'.

Prior to launching its Sanskrit *Bhāgavata Puraṇa*, the NKP had already made a momentous contribution to the diffusion of this most widely cherished scripture of Krishna devotionalism with its reprint of *Sukhsāgar* (Ocean of Bliss, *1866). Composed in 1846–7 by Makkhanlal, a Panjabi

Fig. 9: Title page of the *Daśamaskandha, Bhāgavata Purāṇa* (1885)

[77] I follow Dalmia in translating '*deśbhāṣā*', lit. 'language of the region/country', as 'national language' (cf. Dalmia 1997: 192). In the early nationalist rhetoric of the nineteenth century, *deśbhāṣā* was indeed the common precursor of the later current term '*rāṣṭrabhāṣā*', which, however, carried much stronger Hindu nationalist connotations.

Khatri settled in Benares, *Sukhsāgar* appears to be the earliest Hindi prose translation of the complete *Bhāgavata Purāṇa*. The text was first released in 1854; no copies of this edition have survived. It was only with the 1866 NKP edition of *Sukhsāgar* that the *Bhāgavata Purāṇa* was for the first time made available to Hindi readers in its entirety. The publication found a prominent sponsor in Maharaja Mansingh of Ayodhya, who may have also been the channel through which the NKP acquired the copyright of the text. *Sukhsāgar* was clearly designed for the pious lay reader and was not overly concerned with the theological intricacies of the text. Written in remarkably simple and fluent narrative prose, it became a perennial favourite with Hindi readers. The text owed much of its popularity to the fact that it was particularly well suited for a female readership and for being read to children.[78]

From the early 1870s Naval Kishore began to produce his own translations and commentaries of Sanskrit texts. In the absence of programmatic statements it is difficult to determine to what extent he was motivated by commercial considerations or whether Hindu revivalist and nationalist ideology played any part in his decisions. Garcin de Tassy in his lecture of 1873 posited a direct connection between the NKP's translations of the 'Puranas and Vedas' and the concerted effort at promoting the shastras by several learned societies of Mirzapur, Benares, Patiala, and Lucknow at the instance of one Pandit Indra Prakash. The pandit, according to the French scholar, had argued the necessity of translating not only works of the arts and sciences, but also religious scriptures, into Hindi, so that 'the name of the Hindu nation remain on the pages of history' (*LLH* 1873: 60–1). Such considerations notwithstanding, the sales aspect certainly played a substantial part in the selection of titles, for the corpus of NKP Sanskrit works in translation consisted almost exclusively of titles with a reasonably assured market potential. Besides the classics of shastric literature, it included works of traditional Hindu medicine and astrology, two textual categories that served the practical needs of the large professional groups of medical practitioners and astrologers, while also being increasingly consumed by lay readers. In sharp contrast, Sanskrit philosophical, poetic, and scientific works that appealed to a select audience of scholars and literary connoisseurs only, rarely made it onto the Lucknow publisher's list. The market demand for such titles was too limited, their publication better left to those who specialized in Sanskrit literature. Similarly, Sanskrit texts of the poetic (*kāvya*) or dramatic

[78] For an analysis of the text and its impact, see Stark 2007.

(*nāṭya*) genre, which did not lend themselves easily to translation, scarcely figured in NKP catalogues. Exceptions to the rule were almost certainly instigated by pragmatic reasons, as demonstrated by the translations of Kalidasa's *Kumārasambhava* and Magha's epic *Śiśupālabadha* in the early 1890s. What prompted the translation of these texts was their incorporation into the syllabus of the Calcutta University Examination. They are a typical example of a publisher providing comprehension aids to a student readership with an increasingly defective knowledge of the classical language. As the NKP translator Pandit Kalicaran asserted in the preface to the Hindi *Śiśupālabadha*, 'by reading [this work] those with little knowledge of Sanskrit as well as those gentlemen connoisseurs of poetry who are fluent in the Khari Boli of Delhi and Agra will easily be able to understand the purport of the *ślokas*. It is hoped that this book will also be of great assistance to students undergoing university examinations, for there will be no necessity to consult any other commentary in order to understand the implied meaning [of the *ślokas*].'[79] In his preface to the Hindi *Kumārasambhava*, Kalicaran went even further in reassuring students, claiming that they would get 'much help' from the translation and would not even have to read the Sanskrit original: 'By studying this one book alone they will be able to pass their exams.' Surely an attractive proposition!

Another factor underlying the selection of Sanskrit texts for translation was private patronage (Table 5.0). Substantial numbers of works were commissioned by connoisseurs of Sanskrit from among the affluent urban intelligentsia or the ranks of the Avadh *taᶜalluqdār*s, who increasingly served as patrons of Hindu culture. Some sponsors had a personal interest in seeing a particular text into print: when Raja Shiva Prasad sponsored the publication of *Gītāgovindādarś* (*1875), a Hindi translation of Jayadeva's famous twelfth-century lyrical poem, he wished to publicize a work that had originally been commissioned by his great-grandfather Raja Dalcand, one of the Jagat Seths of Murshidabad. The Lucknow advocate and Kayastha leader Munshi Kali Prasad patronized an extraordinary publication in the form of the Persian version of the *Mitākṣarā* (*1879), a standard text of Hindu law, and also sponsored the translation into Hindi of *Śukranīti* (*1881), a 'Mirror for Princes' and standard work in the science of Hindu political ethics (*nīti*) by Shukra. What was true for *taᶜalluqdār*s and other private patrons also applied to the publisher. If, from a commercial point of view, translations from

[79] *Śiśupālabādha* (*1891), *bhūmikā*.

TABLE 5.0
Some Private Patrons of Sanskrit Texts in Translation

Title of Work	Date of Publication	Patron
Sukhsāgar	1866	Maharaja Mansingh of Ayodhya
Śrimad Bhāgavat saṭīk (text with Hindi comm.)	1869–70	Maharaja Mohindar Singh of Patiala
Devībhāgavata (text with Hindi comm.)	1870?	Raja Madhav Singh of Amethi
Mahābhāratdarpaṇ (reprint)	1874	Raja Madhav Singh of Amethi
Gītāgovindādarś (text with Hindi trsl.)	1875	Raja Shiva Prasad of Benares
Sānkhyatattvakaumudī (text with Hindi comm.)	1880	Raja Madhav Singh of Amethi
Śukranīti bhāṣā	1881	Munshi Kali Prasad, advocate

Sanskrit into Hindi or Urdu were not always profitable, they were certainly an avenue for Naval Kishore to accumulate cultural capital as a patron of Hindu literature. Title pages of NKP shastric texts routinely eulogized him as a 'munificent well-wisher of Hindu culture and religion' and emphasized the publisher's readiness to incur large personal expense in seeing a particular text or translation into print.

Private patronage was also crucial to a major publishing venture of the early 1870s: the reprint of the *Mahābhāratdarpaṇ* (Mirror of the *Mahābhārat*, *1874). This earliest comprehensive translation of the Hindu epic into Brajbhasha verse had been initiated in the 1820s under the aegis of the Maharaja of Benares. The first publication of the text along with its supplement—*Harivaṃśadarpaṇ*, from the Calcutta Shastra Prakash Press in 1829–30—had constituted a landmark in early Hindi publishing. Garcin de Tassy hailed it as one of the most important Hindi works to have appeared in print and commended the translation for its elegance and exactitude (*HLHH* I: 499–500). When, over forty years later, Naval Kishore embarked on the awesome task of reissuing *Mahābhāratdarpaṇ* he did so at the instance, and with the financial assistance, of Raja Madhav Singh of Amethi, a prominent patron of Hindu culture among the Avadh *taʿalluqdārs*.[80] Apparently, by that time, copies of the Calcutta edition had become so rare 'that they could not be procured

[80] See Metcalf 1979: 352n. Madhav Singh also engaged in writing himself. His *Rāg Prakāś*, a musicological treatise, was published by the NKP in 1870.

even if one was willing to spend fifty rupees'. The new edition, thoroughly revised by the NKP's head pandits Pyarelal and Ramratan Vajpeyi, was ready in 1874. With over 6000 pages in four volumes, it was a monumental scholarly achievement. Each volume was supplemented by an elaborate index, permitting a more systematic use by readers. Reasonably priced at Rs 12, the edition was a runaway success and was swiftly sold out ('*grāhakoṁ ne hāthoṁ hāth liyā*', as the more graphic Hindi has it). The British publication report acknowledged it as the most important event in Hindi publishing during the year 1874.[81] Second and third editions followed in 1883 and 1891. Observing the swift sale of the *Mahābhāratdarpaṇ,* in 1881 Naval Kishore invested in another well known but hitherto unprinted Brajbhasha adaptation of the epic, composed in *doha* and *caupāī* verses by Sabalsingh Chauhan towards the end of the seventeenth century. For reasons not known, this edition remained incomplete.

The great success of the Brajbhasha *Mahābhāratdarpaṇ* encouraged Naval Kishore to engage in another herculean venture, the translation of the *Mahābhārata* into modern Khari Boli prose. By the 1880s the time was certainly ripe for such a project. Indeed, he was not the first to popularize the great Hindu epic in Hindi. Previous efforts highlight the increased use and acceptance of Hindi prose in the context of epic and religious literature: in 1872 the Agra publisher Jvala Parshad Bhargava had launched two monthly series consisting of portions of the epic, with a Hindi and Urdu translation, respectively. The Urdu series, *Ma<u>kh</u>zan-e Mahābhārat*, was priced at Rs 1 per monthly copy; the Hindi version, *Saddharmāmṛt vārṣiṇī*, was slightly cheaper at 8 *as*. Each enjoyed a circulation of 250 copies. In 1875 the first comprehensive Hindi prose *Mahābhārat*, by Krishna Chandra Dharmadhikari of Benares, had been issued in a three-volume edition from Calcutta. The existence of this widely publicized work, which even appeared in Trübner's Oriental Catalogue, raises the question of why Naval Kishore thought it expedient to invest in his own Hindi *Mahābhārat* in 1886. Was Krishna Chandra's translation out of print? Was it too expensive or was its style too difficult? The NKP's own translation was composed in 'pure' Hindi, sanitized of any vocabulary of Arabic or Persian origin. At the same time, the language was kept fluent, avoiding heavy Sanskritization and excessive ornation.[82] Begun by Pandit Kunjbihari Lal and completed by his uncle Pandit Kalicaran, it constituted an unprecedented effort on both the translators'

[81] *RPIR* 1874: 34.

[82] *Hindī sāhitya koś*, vol. II, 437; Caturvedi 1981: 5.

and the publisher's part, involving the collective labour of the NKP's Hindu scholar-translators.[83] A team of more than eight pandits was constantly engaged in proofreading. If the prose *Mahābhārat* was a major event in early Hindi publishing, the financial risk involved in the publication was considerable. The four-volume edition comprised an unprecedented 7284 pages. To make it affordable for the general readership, the volumes were further divided into individually sold parts corresponding to the eighteen books (*parvva*s) of the epic. Moreover, Naval Kishore, with his customary caution, limited the first edition to 600 copies. In order to prevent piracy, he also took care to have the copyright registered.

Before continuing this account, some remarks on the Hindu scholars associated with the NKP's Department of Composition and Translation seem in order. Not surprisingly, their identities and range of activities are less well recorded than those of their Muslim counterparts. While the number of pandits on the publisher's permanent staff was comparatively small, Naval Kishore had recourse to a wide circle of scholars in Lucknow and beyond who regularly assisted the NKP in its Sanskrit editions and translations. These external translators of Brahmin or Kayastha background were mostly employed in the educational sector, constituting a further link between the publishing house and the colonial administration. Like Naval Kishore himself, many of his Hindu scholar-translators exemplified the composite culture of the upper Gangetic region—firmly rooted in their own Hindu culture, they used Urdu for their social communication and were conversant with the Persian literary tradition. Their linguistic versatility made them a special asset to the publishing house.

The firm's head pandit, Pyarelal Ruggu, son of Bhavani Prasad Sharma Suri, is a case in point. Born in a Kashmiri Pandit family of Lucknow, Pyarelal was well-versed in Persian, Sanskrit, Hindi, and Urdu. Upon joining the NKP in the early 1870s, he became involved in a great variety of editing and translation projects, some of which have already been noted. He deserves special credit for preparing the first modern Hindi translation of *Yogavāsiṣṭha* (*1877), a famous soteriological text of disputed date in which Vedanta philosophy found a popular exposition. Traditionally attributed to Valmiki, *Yogavāsiṣṭha* had in the course of its

[83] Kunjbihari Lal, the translator of the first seven books, was the son of Mohanlal and grandson of Gokulcandra. Kalicaran was Gokulcandra's son, hence his uncle. He translated all other books, with the exception of the *Udyogparvv*, which was translated by Maheshdatt Shukla.

history been accepted as a standard canonical text of Hindu scholarship and continued to be of central importance to the living traditions of monistic advaita. It was transmitted in various recensions and had seen several translations into Persian during the Mughal period.[84] Yet by the 1870s there existed no Hindi translation of the text but for an eighteenth-century version in archaic language by Ram Prasad Niranjani, a priest attached to the Patiala court. Pyarelal revised the text and purged it of its Panjabi element, making it suitable for contemporary Hindi readers.[85] The modernized version became so popular that in 1890 it was supplemented by an Urdu translation, *Tarjuma-e Jogbāsisht*. Pandit Pyarelal also contributed to the firm's *Purāṇa* series with an Urdu prose rendering of *Devībhāgavata* (*1874) and a *Śivapurāṇa* (*1886) in Hindi. His various translations from Urdu into Hindi and vice versa will be examined in Chapter 7.

Perhaps the most prolific among the NKP's external Sanskrit translators was Pandit Kalicaran Sharma, mentioned above as the translator of the Hindi prose *Mahābhārat*, *Kumārasambhava*, and *Śiśupālabadha*. Kalicaran, a Gaur Brahmin from Pipalmandi near Agra, was a Sanskrit teacher at the Lucknow Canning College.[86] He further contributed a Hindi version of *Bhāva Prakāś* (*1894), a famous medical encyclopaedia, and was also engaged in preparing modern Hindi versions of Brajbhasha texts.

The reprint of *Mahābhāratdarpaṇ* and the ensuing Hindi prose *Mahābhārat* were not the only large projects started by Naval Kishore in the mid-1870s. Inspired by the success of *Sukhsāgar*, which had quickly become one of the NKP's best-selling Hindi titles, in 1875 he set out to produce an entire series of Hindi *Purāṇas*. Though frequently condemned by European Orientalists and vehemently rejected by eminent Hindu reformers—above all by the Arya Samaj leader Svami Dayanand Sarasvati—the popular appeal of the *Purāṇas* was unabated.[87] As is well known,

[84] For details on the text, see, e.g., Mainkar 1977 and Slaje 1994.

[85] Issued from Bombay in 1865, Ram Prasad's early version showed 'appreciable Panjabi admixture and some marginal Brajbhāṣā features' (McGregor 1984: 214). Another Hindi translation in Urdu script by Shyam Lal was printed at Kanpur in 1868. The British report deemed it 'unintelligible to persons who are acquainted with the Court Urdu only' (*PGNWP. General Dept.*, March 1869: 3).

[86] Pandit Kalicaran is most probably not identical with his namesake, the translator of the Hindi *Dāstān-e Amīr Hamzā*.

[87] See his attack on the *Bhāgavata Purāṇa* in his early pamphlet *Bhāgavata khaṇḍaṇ* (Refutation of the Bhāgavata, 1866) and his wholesale condemnation of the *Purāṇas* in his principal opus *Satyārthaprakāśa*.

Lalluji's *Premsāgar,* a Hindi version of the celebrated tenth chapter of the *Bhāgavata Purāṇa*, was one of the most widely consumed Hindi texts in the nineteenth century.[88] Naval Kishore would hardly have invested in an entire series of *Purāṇa*s in translation had there not been a demand by the market. The scheme seemed especially promising since several *Purāṇas* had not been translated before. That Naval Kishore expected swift sales is suggested by the fact that the first title in the series, an abridged translation of the *Devībhāgavata* (*1876), was issued in a high print run of 1300 copies. The choice of the *Devībhāgavata* (Fig. 10) is an interesting one, for its status among the major *Purāṇas* was contested and had formed the subject of a prolonged controversy among pandits in the 1840s (Bayly 1996a: 241). What prompted Naval Kishore to inaugurate his *Purāṇa* series with this controversial text? Perhaps it was simply the fact that he was in possession of a rare Sanskrit manuscript of the text, including a commentary by Nilkanth Shashtri. It had been presented to him by Raja Madhav Singh of Amethi, who had already sponsored the publication of the Sanskrit original in 1870.

The Hindi *Devībhāgavata* was prepared by Pandit Maheshdatt Shukla, one of the firm's regular external translators. Shukla, who is also known as the author of a Hindi poetical anthology entitled *Kāvyasaṅgrah* (*1874), belonged to Dhanauli in Barabanki district and worked as a teacher at the Ayodhya Sanskrit *pāṭhśālā*. Next to several titles of the *Purāṇa* series, he translated Amarsingh's classic vocabulary of Sanskrit nouns *Amarakośa* (*1875) for the press. His most voluminous contribution, however, remains his Hindi rendering of the Valmiki *Rāmāyaṇa*, issued in seven volumes in 1882–3. The second scholar involved in the *Purāṇa* project was Pandit Durgaprasad Sharma, a Kashmiri Brahmin whose father had been chief astrologer to the Maharaja of Kashmir and who was himself attached to the court of Maharaja Ram Singh of Jaipur. This circumstance and the fact that the Hindi *Devībhāgavata* was dedicated to the maharaja, strongly suggest Ram Singh's patronage of the *Purāṇa* series.

Published between 1876 and 1884, the NKP *Purāṇa* series came to include Hindi versions of the *Bhaviṣya-*, *Devībhāgavata-*, *Garuḍa-*, *Liṅga-*, *Skanda-*, *Varāha-*, and *Viṣṇupurāṇa*. It constituted a major step towards the popularization of Puranic literature in Hindi, while also visibly reflecting the new status accorded to Hindi as the cultural link language of Hindu India: on some of the title pages, Hindi was for the first time

[88] For an overview of *Purāṇa* literature and list of modern-language versions, see Rocher 1986.

Fig. 10: Title page of *Devībhāgavata bhāṣā* (3rd ed. 1882)

denoted as '*ārya bhāṣā*', echoing the new cultural consciousness propagated by the Arya Samaj and Hindu revivalism.[89] In his preface to *Liṅgapurāṇa*, Durgaprasad underscored the necessity of translating the

[89] One of the first occurences of the term '*ārya bhāṣā*' can be found in the constitution of the Arya Samaj of 10 April 1875, which in rule no. 5 stated that 'The principal Samaj shall possess various Vedic works in Sanskrit and Aryabhasa (Hindi) . . .' (Rai 1967: 40).

Purāṇas into Hindi. His statement provides a characteristic example of how Hindi was now taken to perform an essential role in upholding Hindu dharma and fostering Hindu culture:

> In the present time the Aryans generally are no longer familiar with Sanskrit. Hence, they cannot study the *Purāṇas,* etc., and do not know the *varṇāśrama* dharma. When the knowledge of dharma is wanting, how can there be righteous conduct? Without righteous conduct they have become devoid of longevity, intelligence, strength, majesty, energy, knowledge, wealth, vigour, offspring, fame, etc., and are becoming more so by the day. Seeing his fellow Aryans in this pitiable condition, and knowing that wise and righteous conduct is the root of the attainment of all objects of human existence, and that a thorough study of the *Purāṇas*, epics, etc., is the root of knowing dharma, but also realizing that the Aryans are generally unfamiliar with Sanskrit, the wise and knowledgeable eminent well-wisher of *Bhāratvarṣ*, who is intent on the prosperity of the Aryans, the very capable ornament of the Dhusar caste, the honourable Munshi Naval Kishore, editor of *Avadh Akhbār*, has expressed his desire that all *Purāṇas* be translated into *ārya bhāṣā*, so that all Aryans can easily understand their meaning and by realizing the essential nature of true dharma abstain from bad conduct and engage in virtuous actions. With this purpose in mind the Munshi Sahib has respectfully entrusted us with the task.[90]

Predictably, and at the same time ironically, neither the invocation of puranic texts as sources of 'true Arya dharma' nor the Hindu nationalist rhetoric and reference to Hindi as *'ārya bhāṣā'* sufficed to prevent the Arya Samaj from taking objection to the NKP's *Purāṇa* series. In what seems a poignant reflection of the lasting popularity of the series, as late as 1899 the leading Arya Samaj journal *Saddharm Pracārak* deemed it necessary to publicly denounce it as obscene and especially endangering the virtue of female readers. 'If . . . the Hindus wish to see members of their society tread the path of virtue and morality, they should lose no time in discarding these books', the *Saddharm Pracārak* warned. 'Otherwise, the day is not distant, when under the pernocious teachings of the *Puranas* the little morality the Hindu females now possess will vanish.'[91]

The great success of the *Purāṇa* series encouraged Naval Kishore to engage in another ambitious venture and launch a series of *Upaniṣad*s

[90] *Śrī Liṅgapurāṇa kā bhāṣā meṁ anuvād*, trs. by Durgaprasad Sharma (*1881), *bhūmikā*.

[91] *Saddharm Pracārak*, 5 May 1899, SVN 1899: 142.

with Hindi translation. Unlike the *Purāṇa*s, the status of the *Upaniṣad*s as essential and authoritative texts of Hinduism was largely uncontested. Earlier on, Devendranath Tagore had called on his compatriots to turn away from the *Purāṇa*s 'which were all divisive, toward the Vedas, i.e. the upaniṣads, in order again to unite all Hindus into one religion' (Rocher 1986: 9). For the *Upaniṣad* series Naval Kishore reverted to an extant collection of texts prepared by Pandit Yamunashankar Pancoli, a Nagar Brahmin from Kolakhya and author of various philosophical works.[92] This collection included Hindi versions of the *Aitareya-, Atharvavedīya-, Chāndogya-, Īśa-, Kaṭhvallī-, Kena-, Māṇḍūkya-, Muṇḍaka-* and *Praśna-upaniṣad*. The titles were thoroughly revised by the NKP's pandits and reissued in the early 1880s, each containing the Sanskrit original along with Yamunashankar's Hindi paraphrase in 'simple national language' ('*saral deśbhāṣā*').

The insistence on '*saral deśbhāṣā*' is significant. In a deliberate departure from the linguistic agenda of Hindu revivalism and nationalism, most NKP translations eschewed the highly Sanskritized style of Khari Boli favoured by many proponents of the Hindi movement. NKP texts neither tried to emulate the model translations of Kalidasa by Raja Lakshman Singh, a chief advocate of Sanskritized pure ('*śuddh*') Hindi, nor discarded the Sanskrit element altogether in favour of an overly Persianized style.[93] Instead, they opted for a middle ground. The chief imperative was to produce modern-language versions in an idiom that would appeal to a broad spectrum of contemporary readers by being at once easily intelligible and aesthetically pleasing. References to the language being 'simple' (*saral*) were as much a recurring feature on NKP title pages as was the claim to the translations being 'beneficial to all' (*sarvopakārak*). The propagation of the classical Hindu heritage and the greatness of the Sanskrit literary tradition notwithstanding, at the level of language the Lucknow publishing house maintained its own distinct policy.

By and large, NKP translations of Sanskrit religious classics fulfilled both the linguistic and material criteria for a truly 'popular' kind of religious literature, composed in an idiom that could be understood by the common people, and circulated in large and inexpensive editions. At

[92] E.g., *Vijñanlahrī* (*1883), *Avatārsiddhi* (?) and *Rāmāyaṇ adhyātma vicār* (*1887). Yamunashankar's *Śrīrāmgītā* (*1883) is a Hindi translation of part of the *Adhyātma Rāmāyaṇa* (Spiritual Rāmāyaṇ, c. 1500?).

[93] Ayodhya Prasad Khatri in his work *Khaṛī bolī kā padya* (1887) distinguished five different styles of Khaṛī bolī. Details in King 1994: 30.

a time of vigorous efforts to revive, reform, and nationalize the Hindu religion, they assumed an important function in the 'democratization of religious knowledge' (Dalmia 1997: 225).

Besides religious texts, Naval Kishore published a series of standard Hindu works on sacred law and ethics, which assumed significance in the ongoing discussion revolving around the reformulation of Hindu dharma. At the publisher's behest, Pandit Durgaprasad prepared a Hindi translation of *Mitākṣarā*, a celebrated twelfth-century commentary on *Yājñavalkya smṛti* by Vijnaneshvara. First translated into English by T.B. Colebrooke in 1810, *Mitākṣarā* had been used as a textbook on Hindu inheritance law in NWP schools and colleges since the 1840s.[94] The Hindi translation, which was sponsored by Maharaja Sajjansingh of Udaipur, took fifteen years and finally came out in 1888 (Dalmia 1997: 355). In the 1880s Naval Kishore also acquired exclusive copyright of *Mānavdharmsār* (Essence of Manu's laws), a popular abridged Hindi version of the *Manu smṛti* by Raja Shiva Prasad. Following its first edition from the Benares Medical Hall Press in 1857, *Mānavdharmsār* had been adopted as a textbook and variously reprinted. It did not remain confined to school use for long, but was widely consumed and came to serve the need of new dharma *sabhās* in presenting basic tenets of Hindu dharma in an easily intelligible fashion. This usage was well in keeping with the author's intentions. 'It is a matter of regret that our country men, though called Hindus, know not their own *Institutes of Manu*. So that all they do is contrary to them', wrote Shiva Prasad, bemoaning the decline of righteous conduct among his Hindu compatriots. His express purpose in supplying a Hindi version of *Manu smṛti* was not simply to make the text generally accessible to those with little knowledge of Sanskrit, but to enlighten his countrymen on its contemporary relevance, 'So that it become apparent to them what the original dharma of the Hindus is. And the nature of the actions of those who now call themselves Hindus.'[95]

Yet Hindi was not the only language used in popularizing classic Hindu texts among contemporary readers. With an estimated total of 124 titles (Siddiqi 1981: 16), translations and renderings into Urdu formed an equally important aspect of the NKP's promotion of the Sanskrit legacy. Sanskrit-Urdu translations basically extended to the same textual

[94] An earlier Hindi translation had been prepared by Pandit Dayashankar of Agra College and published under the authority of the General Committee of Public Instruction. Sponsored by the Lucknow Kayasth leader Munshi Kali Prasad, a Persian translation of the text by Lal Bihari Saksena was issued from the NKP in 1879.

[95] Trs. by Dalmia 1997: 355, cited from the reprint Lucknow 1926: 1–2.

categories as outlined above, that is the epics and *Purāṇa*s, works of Hindu dharma and ethics, ritual and prayer books. Only a few Urdu renderings—the *Bhagavad Gītā* by Shyamsundarlal (*1881), the Valmiki *Rāmāyaṇa* by Parameshvar Dayal (*1884),[96] and *Lālcandrikā* (*1886), a translation of Chanakya's *Nītiśāstra* by Lal Singh—appear to have been direct translations from the Sanskrit. Most works were translations or transliterations into Persian characters, prepared from extant Brajbhasha or Hindi versions, which in the process underwent a certain amount of linguistic modification.[97]

Naval Kishore was the first to widely promote the *Purāṇa*s in Urdu. Like the Hindi series, the NKP's Urdu *Purāṇa*s enjoyed widespread popularity among Urdu-speaking Hindus, one of their most prominent readers being the young Munshi Premchand (Amrit Rai 1991: 18). To what extent educated Hindus relied on Urdu even in a Sanskritic literary context is exemplified by the first Urdu *Purāṇa* to appear on the NKP list in 1871, a translation of the *Śivapurāṇa* by Shivsingh Sengar. To Sengar, better known as the author of the famous Hindi anthology *Śivsiṃh saroj* (see Chapter 7), it was nothing out of the ordinary to translate the text into both Urdu and Hindi. At the time, Naval Kishore only published the Urdu version (it was retranslated into Hindi much later).[98]

Not surprisingly, the successful format of the bilingual edition was adopted for Sanskrit-Urdu, too. Texts widely used in Hindu ritual practice such as *Mahimnastotra* (*1879), a famous panegyric hymn to Shiva, and *Vratārk* (*1877), a seventeenth-century treatise on votive rites by Shankar Bhatt, were published in dual-language editions.[99] In addition, the firm offered as a special feature trilingual editions, which next to the original Sanskrit text included translations or commentaries in both Hindi and Urdu. *Viṣṇusahasranāma saṭīk* (*1879), a standard prayer book used in

[96] Prepared at the instance of Deputy Collector Pandit Debi Parshad.

[97] For other genres see, for instance, *Sakuntalā nāṭak*, trs. from a Hindi version into Urdu by Kazim ᶜAli Jawan (*1875).

[98] The genesis of Sengar's translation of the *Śivapurāṇa* is also of some interest in that it throws light on the difficulties experienced by author-translators in locating manuscript copies. For ten long years, Sengar had tried in vain to get hold of a complete copy ('*koī pūrī pustak*') of the text and had ended up with a collection of ten different manuscripts, none of which appeared suited for translation. It was only in 1869 that he acquired a decent manuscript from a Hindu scholar of Rai Bareli who, in turn, had procured the text from South India.

[99] The Urdu *Vratārk*, a transliteration of a simultaneously issued Hindi version, was prepared by the NKP translator Pandit Maheshdatt Tripathi, a Brahman from Nandapur (Sultanpur district).

Vaishnava ritual, was printed in two columns, containing the Sanskrit original and a Hindi commentary on one side and an Urdu transliteration of both parts on the other. Underlying such publications were pragmatic and economic considerations: to have one text for Nagari and Urdu readers was the cheapest solution for the publisher. Arguably, the texts were also meant to acquaint Urdu readers with the increasingly important Nagari script—how else should one interpret the fact that the text portion was preceded by a table showing the Hindi and Urdu alphabets? Four more works were edited in similar fashion: the two most revered scriptures on sacred Hindu law, *Manu smṛti* (*1871) and *Yājñavalkya smṛti* (*1880), *Mārkaṇḍeyapurāṇa saṭīk* (*1884), and *Mithilāmāhātmya saṭīk* (*1884).[100] The polyglot formula certainly worked well: by 1889 the trilingual *Manu smṛti* had gone through five editions.

As will be shown later, another form of popularizing the Sanskrit heritage through the medium of Urdu was to promote contemporary Hindu poets of Urdu, who produced a great number of verse renderings of the epics, *Purāṇa*s and other religious classics. Among NKP staff members, the translator and later biographer of Naval Kishore, Lala Lalji Munshi—a Kayastha belonging to Kakori—provided a series of Urdu works on Hindu religious themes, including a collection of puranic tales, *Majmūʿah-e ṣifāt-e insānī* (*1874), an Urdu *Gayā māhātmya* (*1876), and a translation of *Bhāminīvilās,* a seventeenth-century collection of allegorical and erotic verse by Jagannath, entitled *Z̲akh̲īrah-e saʿādat* (*1875).

To understand both the pragmatic and ideological implications of this body of Sanskrit texts in Urdu, one has to bear in mind that, during the period under review, an influential section of educated North Indian Hindus, notably Kayasthas, Kashmiri Brahmins and Khatris, were not familiar with the Nagari script, nor felt any strong religio-cultural affiliation with it.[101] The NKP continued to cater to this substantial clientele throughout the nineteenth century. However, against the backdrop of the Hindi–Urdu controversy, the firm's sustained engagement in promoting Sanskrit classics in Urdu cannot merely be viewed in commercial terms, but also has wider significance. One of the most far-reaching consequences of the debate over Hindi and Urdu was the dichotomization of the

[100] The transliteration of the *Yājñavalkya smṛti* was based on an earlier Hindi translation (Lahore: Mitra Vilas Press 1871) by Pandit Guruprasad of Lahore University College.

[101] As King has pointed out, the Hindu community was divided in another respect, too, i.e. the competition between Nagari and Kaithi, a variant script used by a number of Hindu business and trading castes (King 1994: 65–75).

two languages and scripts by way of an exclusive ideological identification with Hindu and Muslim culture, respectively.[102] The NKP's promotion of Sanskrit works in Urdu was, in part, an attempt to counteract this process. Needless to say, the circulation of Hindu religious texts in Urdu or Urdu-script versions had a long tradition and was nothing out of the ordinary in the 1860s and 1870s, when the language controversy first gained momentum. However, the fact that the NKP continued to assiduously produce such titles well into the 1890s implied a clear statement against the essentializing equation of language with religious community. While the firm's policy with regard to Hindi and Urdu will be discussed in Chapter 7, it should be pointed out here that the Lucknow publishing house put a clear emphasis on assimilation rather than differentiation. Underlying its policy was the desire to perpetuate the shared and composite culture that had shaped North Indian intellectual traditions for centuries.

In this context, one of Naval Kishore's cherished projects assumes distinct significance, notably his efforts in recovering some of the celebrated translations and adaptations of Sanskrit classics into Persian that had been prepared during the Mughal period. Some of these works had never been consigned to print. In 1863 Naval Kishore issued a famous Persian verse translation of the *Bhagavad Gītā*, composed at the behest of the Mughal emperor Akbar by his Poet Laureate Abuʾl Faiz Faizi. Two verse renderings of the *Bhāgavata Purāṇa* and the Valmiki *Rāmāyaṇa* by Amanat Rai Dehlavi, entitled *Bhāgavat manẓūm fārsī* (*1868) and *Rāmāyan manẓūm fārsī* (^{2}1872), followed. Next, the publisher edited *Nargistān* (*1875), a Persian verse translation of the *Rāmāyaṇ* composed under Aurangzeb by Chandarman 'Bedil', and the *Rāmāyaṇ-e Amarparkāsh* (*1877) by Amarsingh. Both works were for the first time circulated in print.[103] The Persian version of the Sanskrit allegorical drama *Prabodhcandrodaya* by Banvali, a poet in Dara Shikoh's service, came out in 1877. The series was completed by a four-volume collection entitled *Majmūʿah-e Vedānt sār* (Collection of the Essence of Vedanta, *1877), which assembled abridged Persian renderings of the *Yogavāsiṣṭha*, *Bhagavad Gītā* and *Bhāgavata Purāṇa*. In the heated atmosphere of the late 1860s and 1870s, to rescue these textual witnesses to a great tradition of cross-cultural and interreligious dialogue from oblivion was to make a powerful cultural statement.

[102] This process of differentiation has received much scholarly attention. See, e.g., Amrit Rai 1884; King 1994; Dalmia 1997.

[103] Wrongly attributed in the NKP catalogue to ʿAbdul Qadir 'Bedil'.

5.6 Selective Encounters with the West: Translating English Works

The colonial encounter and the growing prestige of English education had generated an interest in Western thought and knowledge among educated Indians, which led to an intense translation activity. By the mid-nineteenth century, the task of disseminating Western knowledge through Indian languages was no longer left to missionary and colonial agency or to eminent educational institutions alone. Indian learned associations, private scholars, and commercial publishers increasingly engaged in the translation of English works. In the commercial market, the rapidly rising popularity of works of Western fiction made their translation a viable proposition for publishers.

Whether undertaken under colonial aegis or as independent projects by members of the new bilingual elites, translation in the colonial context was rarely a simple linguistic transfer. In cutting across cultural divides, it was invested with ideological and political meaning.[104] As cultural translation, it was a creative process that implied selection, assimilation, or rejection at every stage of the venture. Translation, therefore, constituted a 'transaction' in the sense proposed by Harish Trivedi and others with respect to the cultural encounter at large. The literary and cultural exchange between India and the West was not a unidirectional imposition of dominance. Rather, it was an 'interactive, dialogic, two-way process . . . involving complex negotiation and exchange' (Trivedi 1993: 1).

In looking at NKP translations of Western works, it is important to distinguish between two categories of texts: those that were government commissions, hence a by-product of the firm's collaboration with the colonial administration, and those that originated in an independent decision on the publisher's, patron's, or translator's part, each coming with its own specific intentions. In the first category we find translations of official documents or government reports pertaining to the legal, revenue, or administrative sector, which were considered of particular relevance to the Indian audience. The *Report on the Trade and Products of the North-Western Provinces* by Sir Robert H. Davies, of which Naval

[104] Naregal discusses colonial translation as a hegemonic project '*endemic* to the construction of colonial discourse', which, while pretending that the English and vernacular publics could be endowed with 'symmetrical expressive and cognitive repertoires', actually placed Indian languages in a relation of subordination *vis-à-vis* English (Naregal 2001: 102–4).

Kishore issued an Urdu version in 1871, is a typical example.[105] Of greater interest—because reflecting a deliberate selection on the publisher's part—is the second category. Here, translations of historiographical and political works assumed prominence. As outlined in Chapter 2, Naval Kishore patronized several learned societies devoted to the promotion of Western knowledge in the modern Indian languages. His association with the Aligarh Scientific Society, in particular, may have provided the initial impetus for him to produce his own translations of English works. The Society aimed to render 'those works on arts and sciences, which being in English or other European languages are not intelligible to the Natives' into Indian languages; from the outset it focused on historiographical writing.[106] Rollin's *Ancient History of Egypt*, his *Ancient History of Greece*, and Elphinstone's *History of India* were among the first texts to be taken up for translation (Muhammad 1978 [1]: 147–8). On at least one occasion, notably the publication of the Urdu translation of the *Life of Napoleon Buonaparte* (1835), the Society enlisted Naval Kishore's services as a printer. The book was issued in 1871 as *Sarguzasht Napoliyan Bonāpārṭ shahanshāh-e farāns*. The Education Department bought one hundred copies for distribution as a prize book and rewarded its translator Muhammad Mushtaq Husain with Rs 100.[107]

If Naval Kishore was inspired by the Scientific Society's work, he was not to be outdone by it. Before long he was able to boast his own collection of Western works in Urdu translation. Though small in number, it included some important titles. By far the most consequential was the first Urdu translation of James Tod's influential *Annals and Antiquities of Rajasthan* (Fig. 11). The project was initiated in 1871 on the suggestion of Nawab Muhammad Mardan ʿAli Khan 'Raʿna', a longstanding associate of Naval Kishore who had risen to the position of chief minister in the princely state of Marwar. Since its first publication in 1829–32, Tod's *Rajasthan* had been widely acclaimed in colonial India, where it had a marked impact on both British and indigenous public debate. With its glorification of Rajput valour and 'Romantic pan-Indian nationalism' (Peabody 1996), it became a key text in the process of national identity formation and was eagerly appropriated by the Indian nationalist movement. The quasi-canonical status it enjoyed among Indians is borne out by the name it was generally referred to: '*Ṭaḍnāma*'. Tod's *Rajasthan* inspired several Bengali novelists and was the first book to receive a

105 *Rapaṭ darbāb tijārat paidāvārī mumālik vāqaʿ sarhad śomāl maghrabī* (*1871).

106 'Bye-Laws of the Scientific Society', cited in Husain 1966: 16.

107 *PGNWP. Education Dept.*, October–November 1873, no. 19 (B).

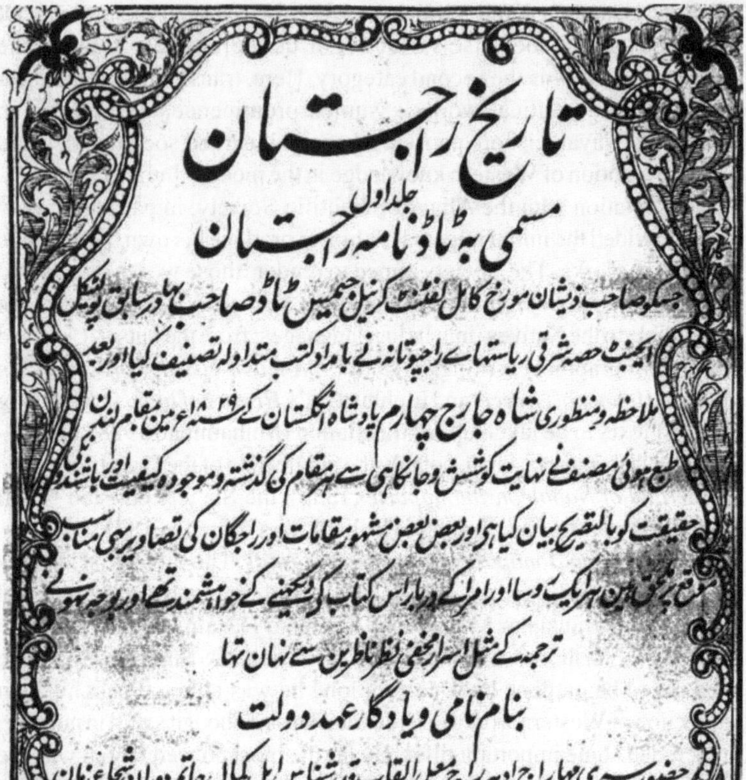

تاریخ راجستان

جلد اول

مسمی بہ ٹاڈ نامہ راجستان

جسکو صاحب ذیشان مورخ کامل لفٹنٹ کرنیل جیمیس ٹاڈ صاحب بہادر سابق پولٹیکل
ایجنٹ حصہ شرقی ریاستہاے راجپوتانہ نے بامداد کتب متداولہ تصنیف کیا اور بعد
ملاحظہ و منظوری شاہ جارج چہارم پادشاہ انگلستان کے ۱۸۲۹ء مین بمقام لندن
طبع ہوئی مصنف نے نہایت کوشش و جانکاہی سے ہر مقام کی گذشتہ و موجودہ کیفیت اور باشندونکی
حقیقت کو بالتصریح بیان کیا ہی اور بعض بعض مشہور مقامات اور راجگان کی تصاویر بھی مناسب
موقع پر کھینچی ہین ہر ایک رئیس اور امرا کے دربار اس کتاب کے دیکھنے کے خواہشمند تھے اور بوجہ نہونے
ترجمہ کے مثل اسرار مخفی نظر ناظرین سے نہان تہا

بنام نامی و یادگار عہد دولت

حضور سری مہاراج ادہراج معلی القاب قدرشناس اہل کمال حاتم دوران شجاع زمان
عالی مرتبت مہارانا سجن سنگہ بہادر والی اودے پور

و بیادگار شکر گزاری

صاحب والا شان ستطاب معظم و مکرم کرنیل چارلس ہربرٹ صاحب بہادر پولٹیکل ایجنٹ میواڑ
و ادای سپاس مشورہ فرمائی
نظام الدولہ نواب محمد مردان علیخان بہادر تخت قائم جنگ سابق دیوان مارواڑ

بمطبع نامی گرامی منشی نول کشور مین بمقام لکہنو بحسن و زیبائش طبع ہوئی
ماہ جنوری ۱۸۷۷ء

Fig. 11: Title page of *Tārīkh-e Rājistān* (1877)

raving review in *Harischandra's Magazine* in 1873.[108] It was also of specific importance to Hindi literary history, for the author's glorification of the epic poet Chand marked a decisive step in the construction of an early canon for Hindi (Dalmia 1997: 194).

To provide the first translation of Tod in an Indian language was therefore a significant undertaking. In order to ensure a high-quality translation, Naval Kishore commissioned two veteran translators: the preparation of the first volume was assigned to Pandit Ajodhya Parshad, the translator of Davies's *Trade Report* and other works. The second volume was prepared by Pandit Kanhaiyalal, the estate manager of Raja Madhav Singh of Amethi, and former translator in the Chief Commissioner's Office. Naval Kishore was well acquainted with Kanhaiyalal's skills, having acquired the copyright of two of his earlier translations, notably *Tārīkh-e baghāvat-e Hind* (*1861), an account of the 1857 uprising compiled from English sources, and *ʿAhd nāmajāt va iqrār nāmajāt* (*1866), a voluminous collection of treaties concluded by the East India Company and the British Government with different Indian states and principalities. Kanhaiyalal also figured on the NKP list as an Urdu poet in his own right. He wrote under the pen name 'ʿAshiq' and has a *Dīvān-e ʿĀshiq* (*1877) and a local history called *Tārīkh-e rāj-e riyāsat-e gaṛh Ameṭhī* (*1882) to his credit.

Completed in 1877, the Urdu *Tārīkh-e Rājistān* comprised almost 2000 pages, including maps and illustrations. It was issued in a two-volume deluxe edition on high-quality glossy white paper. Heavily priced at Rs 50, it clearly targeted the Indian gentry and nobility. There seems to have been no dearth of advance subscriptions. Having examined the translation, and finding it 'accurate and idiomatic', DPI Kempson noted: 'The enterprize of the great publisher of Upper India, and his judgement in the selection of this work are commendable. I understand that the Native Chiefs of western India are much interested in the issue of this publication.'[109] The joint dedication to Maharana Sajjansingh of Udaipur

[108] Mukherjee 1994: 44–5; Dalmia 1997: 329. Peabody 1996 challenges Inden's analysis of Tod as an 'essentializing' Orientalist text.

[109] *RPIR* 1877: 113. Much later, Dvarkaparshad 'Ufuq' Lakhnavi (1864–1913), a poet and prose writer of Urdu and Persian associated with the NKP, prepared another Urdu translation of Tod, published in twelve volumes as *Ṭāḍ Rājistān* from Lahore in 1909. Ufuq belonged to a learned Kayastha family of Lucknow. His elder brother, Ramsahaʾe 'Tamanna' (1854–1932), was a prolific poet and local historian. His younger brother, Mataparshad 'Nizam', also worked for the NKP. Ufuq himself joined the press in the 1880s as an assistant editor of *Avadh Akhbār*. In 1888 he

and Charles Herbert, the Political Agent of Mewar, suggests the patronage of these two influential figures. Naval Kishore also took a personal interest in the translation. As he explained in his editorial preface, his maternal grandfather Rai Bindravan had served as head clerk (*mīr munshī*) to James Tod. The release of the translation was nicely stage-managed and implied a symbolic tribute to colonial rule: the book was launched on 1 January 1877, the day that Queen Victoria was proclaimed Empress of India at the first Imperial Durbar in Delhi.

A second translation of immediate political relevance followed in the mid-1880s, when Naval Kishore decided to bring out Donald Mackenzie Wallace's highly successful *Russia* (1877) in Urdu. With memories of the Turko-Russian war still fresh, and Russian expansionism continuing to pose a threat on the north-western borders of the Indian empire, he anticipated a wide Indian interest in a book whose author, moreover, occupied the high position of Private Secretary to the Viceroy and Governor General of India.[110] In his long preface (in English), Naval Kishore eulogized Wallace's first-hand account as a work of great authenticity, written by an author who possessed 'a personal knowledge of the subject . . . having lived as he did among all classes of the Russian community low as well as high'. The book was recommended to all those 'desirous of knowing what Russia and the Russians are like: . . . for no other book will give an equally true insight into the administration of the Empire, the social condition of the people, and the iron hand with which the Muscovite Government rules the country.'[111] Involved in the Urdu translation were two prominent contemporaries, one Indian, the other British: the main translator was Pandit Ratan Nath Dar 'Sarshar', the famous Urdu prose writer and former editor of *Avadh A<u>kh</u>bār,* whose long-standing association with the NKP will be examined in more detail in the next chapter. For the proofreading of Sarshar's translation Naval Kishore enlisted the British scholar and Member of the Royal Asiatic Society William Hoey, stationed in Lucknow as city magistrate and license tax officer. To rely on an Englishman, however learned, to go over the work of one of the foremost prose writers in Urdu was not exactly a wise choice. Indeed,

launched his own Urdu paper, *Nazm A<u>kh</u>bār*, but returned to the NKP in 1895 as a translator and editor. Next to works of Western fiction, he translated R.F. Burton's English *Alif laila* into Urdu. The translation, however, remained unpublished (Nurani 1995: 141).

[110] For this perceived threat, see e.g. the contemporary pamphlet by Charles Marvin, *Russia's Power of Attacking India* (London 1885).

[111] *Tārī<u>kh</u>-e Rūsiya* (*1887), Preface.

Hoey committed several linguistic blunders in correcting Sarshar's Urdu (Saksena 1941: 47–8). *Tārīkh-e Rūsiya* was completed in 1887. It was sold to the nobility and gentry at Rs 50 a copy and to the general public at Rs 10.[112] Wallace gratefully acknowledged the book's release in a letter to the publisher, expressing his hope that '[it] may be a success and that I may have the pleasure of seeing my child dressed not only in Urdu costume but also in that of other vernacular languages.'[113] It would seem that official patronage was at work in granting his wish—within two years the NKP *Tārīkh-e Rūsiya* was followed by versions in Bengali, Hindi, Panjabi, and Persian.[114]

The market response to translations of English works was not always as enthusiastic as in the case of the above-named titles, especially if the works selected for translation were more suited to ingratiate Naval Kishore with the colonial authorities than cater for the interests of Indian readers. This is borne out by a series of works-in-translation commemorating the life of senior officials of the Indian Empire. Again, it is difficult to determine whether these publications were initiated and financed by the publisher, individual patrons, or the government. Some projects, such as the Urdu translation of R. Bosworth Smith's *Life of Lord Lawrence* (*1886), were joint ventures. Sponsored by Naval Kishore at the suggestion of A.J. Lawrence, the late John Lawrence's nephew, the translation was done by the NKP translator Sayyid Zavvar Husain and revised by Raja Shiva Prasad.[115] It was dedicated to the Viceroy and Governor General Lord Dufferin. The translation illustrates the considerable financial risk incurred by the publisher in producing such titles, for it involved a large expenditure of Rs 3000 for copyright fees payable to its British author. A subscription notice was published in *Avadh Akhbār* inviting the Indian nobility to sponsor the publication with subscriptions of Rs 100 each. Foremost among those who responded was the Maharaja of Kashmir, who alone subscribed to ten copies.[116] Moreover, Naval Kishore personally went on a 'promotion tour' of the Punjab to ensure the patronage of Punjabi notables. He carried two letters of introduction

[112] *Avadh Akhbār*, 30 July 1887, SVN 1887: 472.

[113] Autograph letter, 27 June 1885. Private papers in the custody of Dr Ranjit Bhargava.

[114] *RPIR* 1887: 51; *RPIR* 1889: 52. The Persian translation was prepared by Maulana Abul Hasan Faridabadi, probably from the Urdu version.

[115] *Swanah* [*sic*]*-i-umri Lord Lawrence or Urdu translation of the Life of Lord Lawrence* (*1886), title page.

[116] SVN 1886: 850.

written by A.J. Lawrence, who warmly recommended the project to the addressees, one an unnamed maharajah, the other a senior government official at Lahore, urging them to assist the publisher in introducing the translation to 'the Punjab nobility and gentry'.[117] Yet Naval Kishore had obviously misjudged the book's appeal. In his preface to the edition, A.J. Lawrence noted:

> As yet there has been little or no response to the advertisements of the more elaborate addition [*sic*] of the Life. The Munshi must therefore look to the masses for that support, which the classes have failed to afford him. But book buying is not an Indian custom. The non-existence of books worth buying, the general poverty, and the habits of the richer classes account for this. The Munshi is however actuated more by the desire of making known to his countrymen what manner of man the late John Lawrence was than by the hope of gain. His wellwishers, and those who think that his efforts deserve encouragement will join me in hoping that he may not fail of material reward.

The alleged lack of interest on the publisher's part should not be taken at face value, for the tepid public response must have been compensated by the government patronage that such publications were bound to attract. Even if he did not recoup his investment on this occasion, Naval Kishore was far from being discouraged and had the *Life of Lord Lawrence* followed by more translations in the same vein. In 1887 he launched *Kalām al-mulūk mulūk al-kalām,* a collection of the speeches of Sir Alfred C. Lyall, Lieutenant Governor of the NWP and Chief Commissioner of Avadh. Compiled 'to commemorate the distinguished services rendered to the country by his Honor', the volume paid overt homage to British rule. The same purpose was served by the publication in 1888 of *Maktūbāt-e Lārḍ Ḍafrin* and *Savāniḥ-e ʿumr-e Lārḍ Ḍafrin*, being a translation of the *Letters from High Latitudes* (1857), and a biography of the Marquis of Dufferin and Ava, Viceroy of India from 1884 to 1888. The first work was translated by Pandit Ratan Nath Sarshar, the second by Maulana Abul Hasan Faridabadi. Naval Kishore himself wrote a laudatory preface to the biography, in which he asserted that 'Lord Dufferin's administration of India can only be reviewed in panegyric', for 'the great hopes that were entertained of Lord Dufferin's rule in India have been more than realized.' The series was rounded off by *Kārnāma-e Colvin* (*1893), a brief account of the administration and selection of the speeches of

[117] Autograph letters, 25 November 1883; Private papers in the custody of Dr Ranjit Bhargava.

Sir Auckland Colvin, Lieutenant Governor of the NWP&Oudh from 1887 to 1892. From a commercial point of view, such publications were almost certainly unprofitable. While targeting a select elite of the politically minded or those actively involved in colonial politics and administration, they held no attraction for the general readership—indeed, none of them saw a second edition.

From the 1880s the range of titles selected for translation expanded slowly, suggesting a more diversified interest in European thought on the part of the readership. In 1881 Naval Kishore invested in a translation of John P. Brown's *The Dervishes, or Oriental Spiritualism* (1868), a pioneering study on Sufi orders published by Trübner & Co., from whom he obtained the copyright. The translation, entitled *Kashshāf-e asrār al-mashā'ikh* (Revelations of the Secrets of the Dervishes, *1881), supplemented the great number of works on Sufism and the Sufi literary tradition in India that Naval Kishore had seen into print over the years.[118] Several years later, he took up John Stuart Mill's classic *Principles of Political Economy* (1848) for translation. From the outset, Mill's work had been accorded considerable importance in colonial society. A first attempt to translate Mill into Urdu had been made by Wazir ʿAli for the Vernacular Translation Society of Delhi College in the 1850s.[119] It was not well received, with a member of the British evaluation committee judging it 'a wretched piece of Oordoo'.[120] Next, it was Sayyid Ahmad Khan who emphasized the need for the Indian public to become acquainted with the science of political economy and urged that Mill's *Political Economy* be among the first texts to be translated by the Scientific Society. He was dissuaded by British members of the society's directing council, who judged the work too voluminous, too complicated, and generally unsuited for an Indian audience (Muhammad 1978.1: 16–22). While the society settled for N.W. Sender's *Political Economy*, the task of publicizing Mill in Urdu fell to the NKP. *Muʿallim al-siyāsat* (Instructor of Governance) was completed in 1890. Addressing an elite audience of the educated and politically conscious, Mill's translator Maulana Abul Hasan Faridabadi reiterated Sayyid Ahmad Khan's arguments regarding the importance of the text in his preface. In a typical articulation of indigenous concern, he argued that the availability of modern scientific knowledge in Indian languages was a basic prerequisite for national progress:

[118] The publisher's outstanding role in the promotion of Sufi literature still awaits study.

[119] For the translation of Mill into Marathi, see Naregal 2001: 120.

[120] *SRGNWP*, 1855: 480.

> I am helpless with regard to those gentlemen among our respected readers who apart from poetry, romances, etc. or religious writings do not take an interest in any other sort of subject. But usually those gentlemen who have a habit of reading newspapers and are fond of reading books, who understand or try to understand the mood of our times and who want to be conversant with the social and political situation, that is with the social structure and political organization of the gifted, spirited and mighty nation on whom the Almighty has bestowed the reins of power over the Indian Empire, will find this treatise extremely interesting and profitable. And, to tell the truth, in the present time this book is really a boon, because from casting a discriminating look at its contents it will become apparent what the political ideas and opinions of our Indian patriots and well-wishers of the country are, and to what extent they are applicable. Apart from this, it is also imperative that the translation of such a rare book in this extraordinary science be included in our language. Because it is due to the want of such scientific books that our language is not counted among the world's important scientific languages: as long as there are no modern sciences in our mother tongue how can the sciences in our country progress?[121]

The 1880s also saw the first translations of Western fictional literature, even though it was not before the close of the century that the NKP would respond to the rapidly growing demand for entertaining fiction on a larger scale. Perhaps the earliest title of European fiction on its list was *Ek rūsī zāmīndār kā qissā* (Story of a Russian Landlord, *1880), translated from an English version of the French novel by Henry Greville.[122] The novel's translator Henry Fanthome was a figure of some interest on the NKP's staff of translators. Born in a well-known family of poets of Indo-French origin, Fanthome had an excellent command of Persian and Urdu and composed poetry in both languages. He joined the publishing house in the early 1870s to become head translator of *Avadh Akhbār*.[123]

Not surprisingly, the first translations of English literature appearing on the NKP list related to the plays of William Shakespeare, the most admired and frequently translated of English authors.[124] In 1890 Naval

[121] *Muʿallim al-siyāsat*, trs. by Abul Hasan Faridabadi (*1890): 5 (Preface).

[122] Pseudonym of Alice Durand. The English version previously appeared in the Lahore *Civil and Military Gazette*.

[123] While at the NKP, Fanthome also prepared a revised and enlarged edition of the romanized *English and Hindustani Dictionary* (*1872), a work designed for the use of English students. For further details, see Saxena 1941: 179 and 185.

[124] For the reception of and contrasting attitudes towards Shakespeare in colonial India, see Trivedi 1993: 10–28. According to Trivedi, since the 1870s over 70 full-length translations and adaptations and over 100 abridgements and narrative renderings had been undertaken into Hindi alone (ibid.: 16).

Kishore commissioned Maulvi Muhammad Ahsanullah to translate Charles Lamb's *Tales from Shakespeare* (1886), an immensily popular compilation of easy prose adaptions from Shakespeare. The Urdu *Tales* came out in a small series entitled *Afsāna-e dilpaẕīr* (Pleasant Stories, *1890), including renderings of *The Winter's Tale*, *Cymbeline*, *Macbeth*, *Pericles*, *Romeo and Juliet*, and *The Two Gentlemen of Verona*. Soon afterwards, Naval Kishore began to bring out the first translations of Victorian entertainment novels, which by the end of the century had come to constitute a favourite leisure-time reading in India. In doing so, he hoped to give a boost to Urdu prose fiction. As a contemporary editor put it, 'The chain of progress in Urdu literature which has been set in motion by the translation of English novels must not be stopped' (cited in Oesterheld 2004: 209). However, it was not until the turn of the century, that is after the period under review here, that the novels of G.W.M. Reynolds and other popular British fiction writers appeared on the NKP list on a larger scale.[125]

5.7 Coping with Multilinguality: Dictionaries and Vocabularies

In dealing simultaneously with texts in various languages, both Indian and foreign, classical and modern, the editors and translators at the House of Naval Kishore daily faced the complexity of India's linguistic heterogeneity—unlike most of their compatriots, however, they were in the privileged position of having direct access to lexicons, grammars, and other linguistic tools. From the outset, Naval Kishore specialized in works of lexicography. In making the provision of lexicons and dictionaries a pronounced focus on his agenda, he not only responded to the specific exigencies created by the polyglot setting of nineteenth-century India, but also strove to uphold a long and eminent tradition of indigenous lexicography in the subcontinent.

The multilingual situation generated various requirements that, from the late eighteenth century, forced British scholar-officials into action and entailed an increased activity in the field of lexicography. To the colonial rulers, knowledge of the classical and spoken Indian languages was 'the prerequisite form of knowledge for all others' (Cohn 1997: 4).

[125] For a list of modern fiction titles in Urdu, see Nurani 1995: 306–9. The NKP catalogue of 1929 includes, among others, Urdu translations of Reynold's *Faust: A Romance of the Secret Tribunals*; *Leila, Star of Mingrelia*; *The Seamstress*; *Rye House Plot*; *Pope Joan, the female pontiff*; *The Necromancer*; *Rosa Lambert*; *Margaret*; and *Wagner, the Wehr-wolf*.

As Cohn has outlined in a seminal essay on the 'languages of command' (Cohn 1997), the colonial state's need to familiarize itself with India's spoken idioms—in order to effectively rule over the country and command an army of Indian soldiers—constituted a major impetus for lexicographical production in Persian and Hindustani (Urdu).[126] At the same time, colonialism advanced English as the language of power and prestige, introducing far-reaching changes in existing language hierarchies. Employment in higher public service came to presuppose a knowledge of English. Educated Indians needed to familiarize themselves with it, should they wish their social and economic aspirations to materialize.[127] Following the English Education Act of 1835, the classical languages of Arabic, Persian, and Sanskrit lost official support. Regarded as dysfunctional by the colonial rulers, they found themselves relegated to the sphere of religion, literary culture, and traditional scholarship. This process was much enhanced by the replacement of Persian by Urdu as official language in the NWP in 1837, and by the Education Despatch of 1854, which entailed an institutional cutback in education in the classical languages. While Arabic, the language of the Qurʾan and Islamic law, and Sanskrit, the repository of Hindu culture, remained sources of cultural pride for Indians, by the 1870s they had became marginalized subjects in state institutions and were no longer mastered by students (Rahman 2002: 88). Their importance as markers of cultural and religious identity lasted somewhat longer in indigenous higher education, but was also in decline. Urdu and, at a later stage Hindi, assumed a steadily more important function and prestige in the public domain. Hindi, for all its claims to serve as the new national language, was still in the process of being codified and standardized.[128]

In this situation of linguistic transition and contest, where classical languages competed with modern ones, Indian languages with English, and Urdu with its new rival Hindi, language remained a highly political and ideologically charged issue. The multifaceted problem of language

[126] For an overview of early Hindustani/Hindi dictionaries compiled by British scholars, see Dalmia 1997: 186–91.

[127] For the linguistic qualifications required for various kinds of public service appointments after 1877, see King 1994: 88–116. Naregal 2001 offers a challenging discussion of the tensions and contradictions implied in the colonial project of creating bilingual elites.

[128] See Dalmia 1997: 181–91. Closely intertwined with the lexicographical project was the codification of the modern languages through grammars, for which see ibid. For a detailed study on the evolution of Hindi and Hindustani grammars, see Bhatia 1987.

affected individuals and knowledge communities at many different levels. Over time, new linguistic requirements in educational, administrative, and other public contexts generated transformations in the linguistic competence of an entire section of Indian society. At the most pragmatic level, they entailed a growing need for lexicographical tools.

After mid-century the new colonial engagement in vernacular education created an urgent demand for practical dictionaries and teaching aids for students' use. As a result, lexicographical production underwent significant changes: from being sophisticated repositories of linguistic knowledge, refined taste, and correct poetic usage, lexicographical works were gradually transformed into easy-to-use reference works for students and those speakers of Urdu and Hindi who were no longer conversant with the classical languages. The perennial lament of British educators regarding the dearth of suitable textbook material makes us forget that the demand for lexicographical aids was not only felt in public instruction but also in other educational contexts. Indian Islamic scholars, for example, often faced the problem of gaining access to the standard Arabic and Persian lexicons due to the rarity and costliness of printed copies.

Given the strong traditional nexus between publishing houses and lexicographical production, it comes as no surprise that North India's foremost general and scholarly publisher should offer a broad and diverse range of dictionaries to the literate public. The NKP's shifting focus in dictionary publishing provides a good illustration of the transformations taking place in the field of lexicography as a result of shifts in both educational policy and linguistic competence: the firm's initial focus was on the great scholastic tradition of lexicography in the classical languages, as evident from a series of standard works of ancient and medieval Arabic and Persian lexicography. Some of these were rare works, circulated in print for the first time; others were reprinted after a long period. At a later stage the firm reacted to the growing public importance of the modern languages. It not only began to reprint a wide range of existing lexicographical works in Hindi and Urdu, but also invested in the production of its own dictionaries.[129]

Even by the 1860s, printed dictionaries were still rare and costly. With its Arabic and Persian dictionaries the NKP responded to an urgent demand among indigenous scholars. Naval Kishore deserves special credit for issuing the first mass-printed editions of two of the most important monolingual Arabic dictionaries, *al-Qāmūs* (*1872) and *Asās al-balāgha* (*1893). *Al-Qāmūs* was a standard work of Arabic idioms

[129] For an overview of NKP lexicographical production, see ʿAli 1980.

and figures of speech compiled by Muhammad Ibn Yaᶜqub al-Firuzabadi during the early fifteenth century. The text was first printed at Fort William College in 1817, and reprinted at Bombay in 1855. Both the Calcutta and Bombay edition remained confined to a small number of Orientalists and well-to-do Indian scholars. It was only in its 1872 NKP reprint that *al-Qāmūs* became widely accessible to Indian scholars and students of Arabic. Reasonably priced at Rs 5, *as.* 10, the two-volume edition was eagerly received.[130] Owing their first printed copy of *al-Qāmūs* to a gift by Munshi Naval Kishore, the ᶜulama at the Deoband seminary warmly congratulated the publisher on his initiative in issuing a dictionary 'so much in want that every *madrasa* and every student remains in need of it.'[131] The second important publication in Arabic lexicography followed two decades later in the form of Maulvi ᶜAbid Husain Lakhnavi's edition of *Asās al-balāgha*, a twelfth-century thesaurus by Mahmud Ibn ᶜUmar al-Zamakhshari, which was largely concerned with the language of rhetoric. It had first been printed in Cairo in 1882. In making this important work accessible to an Indian audience, the 1893 NKP edition was a milestone in Arabic book publishing in the subcontinent.

The continuing importance of Arabic in Indo-Islamic scholarship could also be seen in the demand for bilingual Arabic-Persian dictionaries. Naval Kishore's perhaps first lexicographical publication, undertaken as early as 1859, was a reprint of a work of precisely this kind, the celebrated *Muntakhab al-lughāt-e Shāhjahānī* (commonly known as *Rashīdī-e ᶜarabī*). Compiled during the reign of Shahjahan by ᶜAbdul Rashid Tatawi, it had first been published at Fort William College in 1808 and had seen several editions since then.[132] The second work was *aṣ-Ṣurāh māᶜ farhang-e qarāh* (*1872), a thirteenth-century abridged version by Abul Fazl Muhammad bin ᶜUmar Qurashi of al-Jauhari's famous Arabic dictionary, to which a later Persian glossary was added in the margins.[133]

Spanning the medieval and modern periods, the NKP's contribution to Persian lexicography was equally impressive. With a wide range of dictionaries and vocabularies, the firm paid tribute to and reinforced India's traditional role as 'the home of Persian lexicography'.[134] Among its various publications the following five works deserve special mention:

130 The Bombay edition of *al-Qāmūs* sold for a high £3 *s*.3 in Trübner's Catalogue of 1868.

131 *Rūdād-e salānah* 1289 ah, cited in Sh. Khan 1980: 173.

132 E.g. Calcutta 1816; Lucknow 1835 and 1845.

133 Previously edited from Calcutta (1812–15).

134 See Tauer 1968 for an overview of Persian lexicography in India.

(1) *Ghiyāṣ al-lughāt* (*1863–4), a nineteenth-century dictionary by Maulvi Ghiyasuddin Rampuri which enjoyed great popularity in both India and Iran. The NKP edition in its margin included *Chirāgh-e hidāyat*, an eighteenth-century work by the great Indian lexicographer and poet Sirajuddin ᶜAli Khan 'Arzu', which dealt with words and figures of speech of post-classical poets not mentioned in earlier dictionaries. (2) *Burhān-e qāṭiᶜ* (*1871), one of the most widely used Persian dictionaries in India. It was compiled during the mid-seventeenth century by Muhammad Husain Tabrizi Burhan in the Deccan, and had first been issued in print by T. Roebuck in 1818. (3) *Farhang-e Jahāngirī* (*1876), a dictionary and synopsis of Persian grammar compiled by the Persian scholar Mir Jamaluddin Husain Inju during the reigns of Akbar and Jahangir. The NKP edition of Muhammad Sadiq ᶜAli Ghalib was the first time this work appeared in print. (4) The monumental *Bahār-e ᶜajam* (*1879), compiled over a period of twenty years by Lala Tekcand 'Bahar' and completed in 1739. It was edited by Maulvi Hadi ᶜAli from an autograph copy by Lala Tekcand. (5) *Haft qulzum* (*1879), a dictionary and grammar in seven volumes compiled by Qabul Muhammad, a courtier of Nawab Ghaziuddin, and first printed in Lucknow at the Nawab's Royal Press in 1822. Naval Kishore reportedly got hold of a copy of this rare work from the Madrasah ᶜAliyah in Calcutta (ᶜAli 1980: 94).[135]

At a time when the notion of 'pure' Persian and its 'proper' usage were vividly discussed, and different literary styles competed with one another, dictionaries became the object of linguistic debate.[136] When, in 1861, the NKP published Mirza Ghalib's *Qāṭiᶜ-e burhān* (The Chopper of the Argument), a harsh critique of Tabrizi's above cited *Burhān-e qāṭiᶜ* (The Cutting Argument), a fierce controversy arose in learned circles. Ghalib, the foremost among contemporary Indian poets of Persian, had listed numerous inaccuracies and errors of derivation in Tabrizi. More importantly, he rejected Tabrizi's work for its many 'Indianisms'. No sooner had *Qāṭiᶜ-e burhān* come out than passionate rejoinders appeared in defence of Tabrizi, an authoritative source to many. Ghalib and his supporters, among them his friend and later biographer Altaf Husain 'Hali', responded in kind. Having produced nearly a dozen

[135] Other Persian dictionaries listed in the 1879 catalogue are *Lughāt al-mubtadī* (*1871) and *Kashf al-lughāt* (1876).

[136] S.R. Faruqi has addressed the question why, from the late eighteenth century, Indian Persian began to be held in low esteem and the Persian usage of Iranian authors was privileged over Indian Persian, which in turn had its repercussions on Urdu. See Faruqi 1998.

refutations and counter-refutations, the affair culminated in a case of libel instigated by Ghalib against one of his antagonists.[137] Hali chose to dismiss the uproar caused by Ghalib's critique as 'a blind acceptance of tradition' (Russell/Islam 1994: 358) on the part of the conservative element among poets and scholars. His explanation failed to acknowledge that the indignant response to Ghalib was in direct retaliation to his calling into question the legitimacy of words and expressions in common use among Indian poets of Persian (Rahbar 1987: 617). To them, Ghalib's rejection of *Burhān-e qāṭiᶜ* amounted to nothing less than a denigration of their own Persian usage as inauthentic and defective.

Hardly prone to excite such intense confrontations over language usage was a different category of lexicographical publications, namely special glossaries of the famous Persian classics. These usually unilingual comprehension aids were in acute demand, as indicated by high print runs and frequent reprints. At first Naval Kishore resorted to older titles such as *Farhang-e Gulistān* (*1869), a concise gloss of difficult Persian words and Arabic quotations in Saᶜdi by Junaid ᶜAbdullah al-Musawi, or *Laṭāʾif al-lughāt* (*1877), a seventeenth-century vocabulary of Sufistic idioms occuring in Rumi's *Mas̤navī-e maᶜnavī* by ᶜAbdul Latif Abbasi. Later, he produced his own small series of modern glossaries. Prepared by Mir Ibn Hasan Maududi, it included *Farhang-e Sikandar-nāmah* (*1879), *Farhang-e Būstān* (*1880), and *Farhang-e Yūsuf va Zulaikhā* (*1882).

As for Urdu, there was little indigenous lexicographical activity before the mid-nineteenth century. One only has to recall the difficulties experienced by John Gilchrist who, when compiling his *Dictionary English and Hindoostanee* in the 1780s, found that his Indian collaborators were neither able to supply him with a dictionary of their language nor understood the pressing need for it. Rather, he was asked 'if it was ever yet known in any country that men had to consult vocabularies and rudiments for their own vernacular speech' (cited in Cohn 1997: 35). Lexicographical production in Urdu remained for some time dominated by the colonial state and its needs. Many early Urdu lexicographers were employed in the state educational sector.

[137] *AUS* 3, 1983: 99–100. For further details, see Lakhanpal 1960: 122–5 and Rahbar 1987: 359–60; 509. Ghalib's wholesale condemnation of Indian lexicographers is evident in the following statement of 1865: 'Native writers of Persian lexicons rely for the most part on conjecture. Whatever strikes them as right, they put down on paper. Now, a lexicon written by Nizami or Saᶜdi or their like would be acceptably authoritative to us. Why should we consider Indian authors of dictionaries as authentic?' (Ibid.: 79–80).

Reflecting the transition from the old to the modern lingua franca, much lexicographical production in Urdu during the second half of the century took the shape of Persian–Urdu dictionaries. Hitherto, the standard vocabulary for beginners of Persian had been *Khāliq bārī*, a rhymed vocabulary of Arabic and Persian words with Urdu meanings, generally ascribed to Amir Khusrau. After 1860 it was supplemented by several new works designed for use in Persian and government schools. The most popular was *Karīm al-lughāt*, a Persian–Urdu dictionary for beginners compiled in 1861 by Maulvi Karimuddin at the instance of the Punjab Educational Department. While these works continued to feature on the NKP list, the firm invested in several new students' dictionaries, including *Nafā'is al-lughāt* (*1869), a dictionary of Urdu words and phrases explained in Persian by Auhaduddin Bilgrami, and two works by Maulvi Muhammad Aman al-Haq entitled *Amān al-lughāt* (*1870) and *Lughāt-e fārsī* (*1874). Naval Kishore acquired the copyright of *Amān al-lughāt* from the author, a teacher at the Lucknow Model School. One would expect that, as the copyright owner, he would have had a vested interest in selling the largest possible number of copies. Yet it seems that he was acutely aware of the shortcomings of both *Amān al-lughāt* and the other Persian–Urdu dictionaries on his list, for shortly afterwards he decided to invest in the production of a new unilingual Urdu dictionary which was to surpass all existing works in quality and scope. The person entrusted with its compilation was Maulvi Tasadduq Husain Rizvi, a scholar from Kintur on the NKP's staff of translators and editors.[138] The new dictionary was ready in 1877. It was named *Lughāt-e Kishorī* in tribute to the publisher. In the preface, Tasadduq Husain heavily criticized earlier lexicographical works, particularly *Karīm al-lughāt*. Scholars and students, he contended, had been complaining for a long time that on account of its conciseness *Karīm al-lughāt* was unable to satisfy their needs—it 'contained too few entries, failed to include metaphors, idioms or technical terms and gave too few explanations of the words listed.'[139] The first Urdu dictionary of its kind, *Lughāt-e Kishorī* professed to remedy these deficiencies and comply with the requirements of modern speakers of Urdu. It lived up to its promise and became so popular with students that is was kept in print at the Tej Kumar Press until recently, seeing its twenty-sixth edition in 1994.

The 1870s saw a spate of new works. Munshi Debi Parshad prepared

[138] This writer is not to be confounded with his namesake, the aforementioned *dāstān-go*.

[139] *Lughāt-e Kishorī* (Lucknow 1994), Preface.

Miʿyār al-imlā (*1876), a treatise on Urdu orthography, with a list of incorrect words in ordinary use, their meaning, and correct modes of spelling. *Arbaʿ-e ʿanāṣir*, a compilation in four columns of Urdu words with their Persian, Arabic, and English equivalents by Muhammad Nasir ʿAli followed in 1878, and the same author's *Lughāt-e Nāṣirī* in 1880. In 1883 the NKP issued *Naṣīr al-lughāt*, a translation into easy Urdu by Muhammad Nasiruddin Ahmad Khan of *Ghiyāṣ al-lughāt*. From Mufti Ghulam Sarvar Lahori, mentioned earlier as one of the Islamic scholars associated with the press, Naval Kishore obtained the copyright of two dictionaries, namely *Zubdat al-lughāt* (also known as *Lughāt-e Sarwarī*, *1877), a student's dictionary of Arabic, Persian, and Turkish words used in Urdu, and the more elaborate *Jāmiʿ al-lughāt-e Urdū* (*1892) which was designed for an advanced readership.

Compared to this proliferation of Urdu titles, Hindi lexicons and dictionaries were slow to appear on the NKP list. The first title produced by Naval Kishore in 1874 was a Hindi translation of *Amarakośa*, a popular early Sanskrit thesaurus, which served as an important model for Hindi lexicography. There followed *Rāmāyaṇśabdārthkoś* (*1875), a special glossary on Tulsidas's *Rāmāyaṇ* by Raghunath Das. The Hindi lexicographical tradition was represented in a joint edition of *Anekārtha* and *Nāmamālā* (*1875), two of the earliest lexicons in the Hindi language composed by the sixteenth-century Vaishnava poet Nanddas. The backdrop to this particular publication was the firm's scheme of promoting works of Hindi poetics and rhetoric started in the 1870s: both *Anekārtha*, a versified glossary of words with their various possible poetic meanings, and *Nāmamālā*, a similarly versified thesaurus of synonyms which drew largely on *Amarakośa*, were scholastic works designed for those poetic connoisseurs of Nanddas's time who did not understand the Sanskrit terms in Brajbhasha poetry (McGregor 2003: 943). They were of little practical use to contemporary Hindi readers.

Indeed, had Naval Kishore wanted to supply the Hindi audience with a modern Hindi–Hindi dictionary, he would not have found an extant work to turn to. Prior to the 1870s the only dictionaries devoted specifically to the Hindi language were bilingual productions designed for 'students of Hindee, both native and European', notably the Reverend M.T. Adam's *Hindi Koṣa or A Dictionary of the Hindee language* (1829), his *Dictionary, English and Hinduwee* (1829), and J.T. Thompson's *Dictionary in Hindee and English* (1846).[140] In the wake of these pioneering efforts by European

[140] Vedalankar 1969: 233; Dalmia 1997: 187. By contrast, Mathuraprasad Mishra's voluminous *Trilingual Dictionary, being a Comprehensive Lexicon in English, Urdu*

lexicographers, an indigenous Hindi lexicography was slow to develop. The first major achievement and simultaneous culmination point in this field was reached only in the twentieth century, in the form of the still unsurpassed *Hindī śabd sāgar* (Ocean of Hindi Words, 1912–27), edited by Shyamsundardas under the aegis of the Nagari Pracharini Sabha.[141] Compared to this momentous scholarly achievement, previous nineteenth-century Hindi lexicons seem minor and insignificant undertakings. Yet, even if for the most part 'commercial rather than literary enterprises' (Bahri 1948: 91), they did exercise an important function of their own, being the first reference works available to the newly educated Hindi readership. In assessing their impact, one has to bear in mind that simultaneous official or missionary productions, such as Reverend J.D. Bate's *Dictionary of the Hindee Language* (Benares: Medical Hall Press, 1875), were unaffordable for the majority of Indian students. This fact was remarked upon by a British reviewer, who, while judging Bate's dictionary 'extremely useful to students of Hindi' and a major improvement on Thompson, criticized its 'rather high price' of Rs 15.[142]

Given the small output of the period, two NKP titles come into prominence. One was the two-volume Sanskrit-Hindi dictionary *Maṅgalkoś* (*1875), the first of its kind. Compiled by Mangalilal, a teacher at Paintepur in Sitapur district, *Maṅgalkoś* was designed for students; in providing Hindi explanations and synonyms of difficult Sanskrit words, it was meant to assist in reading the classics and became a standard work in public schools. It was only in the 1890s that the NKP came out with its first commercially marketed Hindi–Hindi dictionary, *Śrīdhar bhāṣā koś* (*1894). This compilation by Pandit Shridhar Tripathi is one of the more noticeable achievements of the pre-*Hindī śabd sāgar* period: a large lexicon of almost 20,000 entries, it was supplemented by an introduction on grammar and two appendices containing geographical names and short biographical notices of Sanskrit and Hindi poets.

In the course of almost four decades, the NKP adapted its repertoire of lexicographical titles to changing linguistic and educational needs. Its expanding range of dictionaries catered to diverse audiences of advanced

---

and Hindi (1865), the first major work compiled by an Indian, was primarily an English dictionary designed for 'English-reading native students'. Its author was a teacher at Queen's College, Benares.

[141] For a fascinating account of the genesis of the *Hindī śabd sāgar* and an exhaustive survey of earlier Sanskrit and Hindi lexicography, see the introductions by Shyam-sundardas and Karunapathi Tripathi (vol. 1, 1935: 1–32).

[142] *RPIR* 1875: 84.

scholarship, literary connoisseurs, and students of public and indigenous schools. From the initial antiquarian emphasis on the preservation of the great lexicographical tradition of the Orient and, particularly, the subcontinent, the focus shifted to contemporary lexicographical production in the modern languages. With the rapid spread of formal education, the promotion of a new genre of student's dictionaries became paramount. A corollary of the ongoing lexical separation between Hindi and Urdu was the production of easy-to-use dictionaries in both languages. To provide the growing readerships of Hindi and Urdu with such tools was not only a sound commercial investment. For an educationally minded publisher like Naval Kishore it also meant fulfilling his duty in the cause of Indian modernity.

6

Avadh Akhbar: Politics, Public Opinion, and the Promotion of Urdu Literature

The news of every continent is openly published.
The world's news is revealed to the world.
Nothing which happens anywhere is hidden.
All that happens upon the face of the earth is like a mirror.

—Altaf Husain 'Hali', *Musaddas*

In a manner characteristic of nineteenth-century Indian publishing houses, the NKP not only engaged in printing and marketing books but also issued its own 'vernacular' newspaper.[1] The firm's reputation in the literary field and its impact in the colonial public sphere are inextricably linked to its famous Urdu paper *Avadh Akẖbār*. That contemporary sources often refer to Munshi Naval Kishore as the 'Editor' or 'Proprietor of Avadh Akhbar', rather than designate him by his profession of publisher and press proprietor, is a telling reflection of the importance assumed by the paper both within the firm's organization and in the wider public image.

Launched in early 1859, *Avadh Akẖbār* (hereafter *AA*) was Naval Kishore's most lucrative journalistic venture and a great success with the Urdu reading public. At a time when most Urdu papers were short-lived, it remained in circulation up to the year 1950, its lifespan of almost a century—from the Crown's assumption of direct control over India to the first years of Independence—covering a crucial period in the history of colonial India. In 1877 *AA* became the first Urdu daily in northern India. It was to remain the only commercially viable Urdu daily newspaper for a whole decade, until its first serious rival emerged in the form of the

[1] An earlier version of this chapter was published in *AUS* 18.1, 2003: 66–94.

Paisa Akhbār (est. 1887) of Lahore, a paper emulating the concept of the British penny paper.[2] Exemplifying the early phase of commercialization in the Urdu newspaper trade, *AA* was read across a wide geographical region ranging from Delhi to Hyderabad and from Lahore to Calcutta. This chapter traces the history of the paper's first forty years, during which it made a distinct impact on the emerging Urdu public sphere. Outlining the growth, contents, and policy of *AA*, it looks at both economic and human factors in the making of an outstanding success in nineteenth-century Urdu journalism.

Through *AA*, Naval Kishore joined the ranks of eminent Hindu publicists who figure prominently in the history of nineteenth-century Urdu journalism. By the time he launched *AA*, Urdu journalism was already well established. Urdu had received a great boost in 1837 when it replaced Persian as the court language in the NWP. Previously, it had not been a popular language for prose and journalistic writing, a field still occupied by Persian. The earliest ventures in Urdu journalism were not successful, as illustrated by the chequered career of the short-lived *Jām-e jahān numā,* the first Urdu paper issued from Calcutta in 1822. It was only when Urdu was accorded official language status that newspapers and journals began to appear in considerable numbers, the *Dehlī Urdū Akhbār* (est. 1837), *Sayyid al-Akhbār* (est. 1841), and *Khair Khwāh-e Hind* (est. 1837) of Mirzapur counting among the first influential papers. The 1840s and 1850s witnessed a steady increase in Urdu papers and periodicals; they soon became a conspicuous presence in social and political life.[3]

Compared to other urban centres in North India, Urdu journalism started late in Lucknow. This was due to the strict censorship that prevailed in the city following the temporary closure of local presses by Wajid ʿAli Shah in 1849. No sooner had the *navābī* come to an end than at least seven Urdu weeklies were launched in Lucknow in 1856–7 (Khan 1991: 294–355). The two most influential were *Ṭilism-e Lakhnaʾū*, issued from the Muhammadi Press (est. 1856) of Maulvi Muhammad Yaʿqub Ansari

[2] According to Muhammad Sadiq (1995: 616), the *Paisa Akhbār* marked a turning point in Urdu journalism and a dividing line between older and modern journalism in that it initiated the diffentiation between the literary journal and the newspaper as a mere purveyor of news. In actual fact, the matter is hardly that simple, for Urdu newspapers continued to include poetry and fiction in their columns. *AA* is a case in point. For the difficulties in providing a theoretically rigorous distinction between newspaper and literary magazine in the nineteenth century, see Law 2000: xv.

[3] Out of the 19 newspapers in circulation in the NWP in 1848, 11 were in Urdu, 5 in Persian, and 3 in Hindi. 5 of the Urdu papers were owned by Hindus. By 1884–5 there were 25 Urdu as compared to only 2 Hindi papers in Avadh.

of Farangi Mahall, and *Siḥr-e Sāmirī*, issued from Pandit Baijnath's Samar-e Hind Press (est. 1856). Both papers provided intimate details of contemporary life in Lucknow between the annexation and the 1857 uprising; their tone was fairly critical of British policy. Local journalism had only just begun when the 'Mutiny' brought the city's thriving print industry to a complete standstill. The vacuum that Naval Kishore encountered on his arrival in Lucknow in 1858 and the initial absence of local competition in the newspaper trade did much to enhance the growth of *AA* during its early years. The paper's lasting success, however, must be attributed to several other factors.

First, there was British patronage in the form of subscriptions and the overall support extended to the firm. As outlined in Chapter 4, the NKP received the lion's share of official patronage accorded to the presses in the NWP&Oudh. A large proportion of the profits made from government job work was reinvested in Oriental book publishing; some went into sustaining *AA*. The government, moreover, patronized the paper by subscribing to a number of copies which were distributed to schools and colleges in the provinces. If official statistics are a measure to go by, colonial patronage of the paper was not quite as substantial as later voices made it out to be: with 50 out of 820 copies in 1877, 94 out of 732 in 1886, and 94 out of 521 in 1895, government subscriptions hardly ever exceeded 20 per cent of the paper's total circulation (see Table 6.1).[4]

The second success factor was the professional management of the paper. *AA* was one of the first Urdu papers to be run along sound commercial lines. It partly financed itself through advertisements. Compared to British newspapers at the time, which made larger incomes from advertising than from sales (Brown 1985: 16), the proportion of space given to advertisements seems relatively small. A typical issue of *AA* in 1871, for example, comprised sixteen pages of which an average of four would be given to advertising. Over time, however, advertising came to account for an increasingly important part of the paper's revenue. In 1879 the rate obtaining for occasional small advertisements was 2 annas per line and column. Rates for regular commercial advertisements depended on how often an ad was placed in the paper and ranged from Rs 12 for insertion once a month to Rs 60 for insertion six times a month (*Fihrist* 1879:

[4] The circulation of *AA* during the nineteenth century never exceeded 850 copies. It has to be borne in mind, however, that circulation figures at no time reflect actual readership. Newspapers like *AA* were widely recirculated and frequently read out to groups of non-literate people in both private homes and public arenas. See Joshi 2001: 38–9; Stark 2002: 69–70.

4). By that time *AA* carried regular advertisements for branded goods and for patent medicines such as the widely advertised Holloway's pills and ointments or the 'celebrated medicines' of Dr De Roos, of which the publishing house acted as sole distributor. Local firms such as Murray & Co., a large retail company selling wine and general merchandise, and the Shaikh Haji Muhammad Bakhsh Company, a contractor of tents and uniforms, began placing regular full-page ads in the paper. Naval Kishore, of course, also used the paper as a cheap medium to extensively advertise and solicit subscriptions for his publications. In the early days of *AA*, announcements of important books such as Ghalib's Persian *Kulliyāt* would feature prominently on its front page (*AA* of 1 January 1862). Later, such notices were relegated to the interior or back of the paper but still appeared so frequently that in 1876 the Delhi-based *Nuṣrat al-Akhbār* was prompted to accuse *AA* of being totally 'self-interested': 'The editor has been instructed not to write any article beneficial to the public, but only to print reviews of the books [published by] the press.'[5]

The third success factor, to be discussed later, were the various individuals who led the paper. *AA* had the distinction of being headed by a number of eminent editors who were scholars, poets, or prose writers in their own right. This also accounts for the paper's influential role in the promotion of modern Urdu literature, for, in the typical fashion of early Urdu papers, *AA* combined the functions of newspaper and literary journal. It carried poetry, fiction, and essayistic writing and evolved into a forum for literary debate, attracting the contributions of eminent Urdu literati of the day. The press office of *AA*, then, was not only a site where information was generated, it was also a vibrant meeting place for the Urdu literary scene.

6.1 From Weekly to Daily: The Making of an Urdu Newspaper

Either because the study of a commercially produced newspaper does not fall within the purview of modern Urdu scholarship, or because of the scarcity of extant early issues, *AA* has received surprisingly little attention outside the standard works on Urdu journalism.[6] In tracing the

[5] *Nuṣrat al-Akhbār* of 1 August 1876; cit. in Sabiri 1953, ii: 97–8.

[6] A study of *AA* needs to be preceded by a survey of issues available in Indian and foreign libraries. According to Nurani, some files from 1862 and 1870 are preserved in the Aivan-e Ghalib Library, Delhi. The Khuda Bakhsh Oriental Library, Patna, holds issues of *AA* from 1866, 1869, 1870–2, and 1875. The OIOC has in stock almost complete runs of the paper between 1875 and 1884.

early history of the paper, the following discussion will address several inaccurate claims concerning its format, frequency, and editorship.

As with many early Urdu papers, there is some disagreement over the date of first publication: while most authorities on Urdu journalism maintain that the first issue of *AA* did not appear before January 1859, Amir Hasan Nurani asserts that on the closure of the firm's Kanpur branch he chanced upon the inaugural issue of the paper dating from 26 November 1858. Unfortunately, he lent the rare document to an unnamed scholar and could not retrieve it (Nurani 1995: 136). While there is no reason to disbelieve Nurani, later editorial notices appearing in the paper contradict his information and support the 1859 date.[7] Most importantly, the issue of 8 January 1862 was marked as volume 4, no. 2, which clearly indicates the year 1859 for the first volume. This, however, does not altogether preclude the possibility that Naval Kishore did indeed launch a first issue in 1858. Given the many tasks he had to attend to on opening his press, he may at first not have been able to publish his new paper on the intended weekly basis. Regular weekly publication of *AA* only took off a couple of weeks later, starting a fresh count with volume 1 in January 1859.

AA was initially a four-page weekly in the standard format of early Urdu papers, that is, 18 x 22 cm. Its frontispiece was adorned with a drawing of the Chattar Manzil and Farhat Bakhsh palace complex, evoking the erstwhile grandeur of *navābī* Lucknow. It is worth noting that the frontispiece in its layout bears a striking resemblance to that of *The Illustrated London News*, one of the most popular Victorian weeklies at the time (Fig.12).

AA appeared each Wednesday. It was well received and during the following years successfully competed against the rapidly growing number of Urdu papers. By 1864 its size had increased to sixteen pages (*LLH* 1864: 245).[8] Simultaneously, the format was enlarged to 22 x 29 cm. So overwhelming was the success of *AA* that, on opening his Kanpur press in September 1865, Naval Kishore decided to launch a local edition in the form of the *Kānpūr Gazaṭ*. Muhammad Ismaᶜil, the manager of the

[7] An editorial notice in *AA*, 22 December 1871 referred to the paper's lifespan with the words 'This is the thirteenth year of God's divine grace', pointing to 1859. A similar notice in *AA*, 2 January 1874 expressly stated that 'In this factory, in 1859 [a paper] called *Avadh Akhbār* was put into circulation.'

[8] Garcin de Tassy's claim that by 1867 the size of *AA* had further increased to 24 pages (*LLH* 1867: 372) is inaccurate. Regular issues of the paper in 1871 still comprised no more than 16 pages on average.

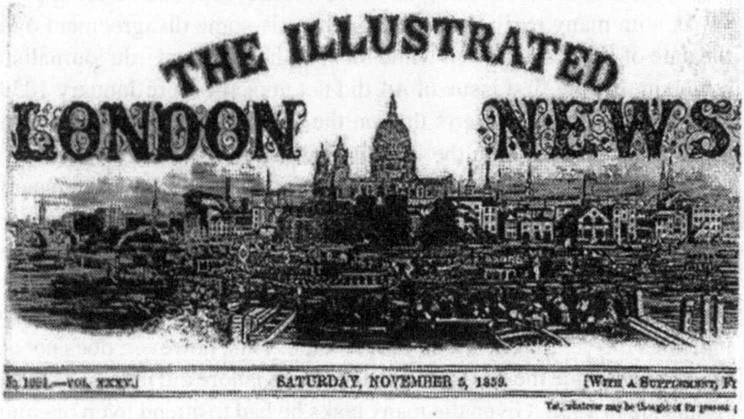

Fig. 12: Title pages of *The Illustrated London News* and *Avadh Akhbār*

Kanpur branch, became its editor. Within two years, however, improvements in communication between Lucknow and Kanpur had rendered the Kanpur edition superfluous—it was discontinued (*LLH* 1867: 373).

The next step in the growth of *AA* illustrates the direct impact of government measures on the still volatile newspaper market. In 1871 the standard postage for newspapers was reduced from one anna to half an anna. With newspaper distribution depending almost entirely on the colonial postal system, postage had from the outset constituted a vital factor in the commercial history of the vernacular press. Nothing much had changed since 1822, when Harihar Datt had solicited the government for free postage, complaining that the circulation of his weekly *Jām-e Jahān Numā* had been 'materially impeded and obstructed even in spite of my best exertions and efforts to extend it.' This, Dutt maintained, was 'in consequence of its being liable to payment of full postage, which has restrained many intending subscribers in the mofussil from patronising the said News Paper' (cited in Nair 1990: 35).

The adverse effects of postage on circulation continued to be a vexing problem for Indian newspaper proprietors. So much so that in March 1869 Naval Kishore initiated a campaign for the reduction of postage for newspapers and periodicals and rallied a group of twenty-five influential newspaper proprietors and editors from all over North India, Calcutta, and Bombay in drawing up a petition to the government. The petition was rejected (Stark 2002: 67–8). Yet the government seems to have had second thoughts, for in 1871 it introduced a 50 per cent reduction in the standard postage. Not surprisingly, the measure had a catalyzing effect on the Urdu newspaper trade. It not only led to a 'striking increase' in the number of new launches, but also benefited well-established papers like *AA* which were able to attract larger numbers of subscribers.[9] From August 1871 *AA* began to appear twice a week, and from May 1875 three times a week. Even after the reduction, postage continued to account for a considerable proportion of readers' expenses: in 1877 the annual cost for ordinary subscribers was Rs 20 excluding and Rs 30 including postage, postage thus comprising a third of the costs. Higher subscription rates of Rs 40 and Rs 50 obtained for the gentry and nobility. One major exception concerned distribution of the paper to large urban centers: if these were directly connected to the railway line and showed over fifty subscribers, postal fees were covered by the press. The provincial

[9] *OAR*, 1871–2: 128. Khurshid 1963: 180. See also S. Ghosh 1998: 73–6 for the impact of postal charges on the circulation of early Bengali papers.

government at the time subscribed to 50 copies charged at ordinary subscription rates: Naval Kishore's attempt to introduce higher rates for government copies was rejected outright.

AA did much to enhance the spread of the newspaper reading habit among the urban and rural gentry and the educated middle class in the NWP&Oudh. The paper typically drew its subscribers from among a cross section of the higher social strata of Muslim nobles, *taʿalluqdārs*, *raʾīses*, urban professionals, and government servants. An idea of its readership can be gathered from the 'List of Receipts' (*rasīd-e zar*) that regularly appeared in the paper, indicating the names of individual subscribers and the fees paid by them. The following list, taken from the issue of 11 April 1875, gives the amounts received in March 1875. As the many different amounts suggest, payment was highly irregular:

His Highness Shahzada-e ʿAlam-o-ʿAlamiyan Sahib-e ʿAli Mirza Mustafa ʿAli Haidar Bahadur, Prince of Avadh	Rs 4–11
His Highness Maharaja-e Rajgan Huzur Sri Maharaja Sahib Bahadur, ruler of Kapurthala	Rs 2–7
His Highness Nawab Muhammad ʿAbd al-Vasih Khan Sahib Bahadur, ruler of Rajgarh	Rs 13–6
His Highness, Mansur al-zaman Nawab Muhammad Sikandar Khan Sahib Bahadur, ruler of Radhanpur	Rs 15–13
ʿAli Janab Huzur Sri Maharaja Anand Rao Nawab Sahib Bahadur, ruler of Dhar	Rs 15
The Hon'ble Kumvar Surat Singh Sahib Bahadur, ruler of Nahan [?]	Rs 20
The Hon'ble Nawab Mumtaz ud-Daula Muhammad Faiz ʿAli Khan Bahadur, C.S.I, Political Agent, Kotah state	Rs 3–4
The Hon'ble Nawab Zulfikar ud-Daula Bahadur, *raʾīs*	Rs 4
The Hon'ble Raja Nilkanth Dahojshah Sahib Bahadur	Rs 30
Raja Shivnath Singh Sahib Bahadur, *raʾīs*	[no amount given]
Babu Devkumar Singh Sahib Bahadur, *taʿalluqdār*	Rs 2–11
ʿAgha ʿAli Khan, Former Governor of Avadh a.k.a ʿAghaʾi Sahib, *raʾīs-e ʿaẓim*	Rs 12
Hazrat Sayyid Muhammad Baqir Sahib Isfahani	Rs 23–4
Munshi Muhammad Shihabuddin Sahib, *mīr munshī*	Rs 22
Munshi Hasan Khan Sahib, prime minister of Sarkar-e ʿAli Raja Muhammad Suleiman Shah Sahib Bahadur	Rs 11–10
Mr Wagentreiber Sahib Bahadur, Government Reporter, The Vernacular Press of Upper India	Rs 23–4

Mr W. Walker, Assam	Rs 10
Mr [?] Davies Sahib Esq. Barrister-at-Law	Rs 2
Sayyid Muhammad Khan Sahib, *raʾīs*	Rs 15
Babu Suraj Kumar Parshad Sahib, *raʾīs*	Rs 23–4
Maulvi Muhammad Nazir ʿAli Khan Sahib, Secretary at the Judge's office	Rs 15
Sayyid Muhammad ʿAli Sahib, court pleader	Rs 10–11
Muhammad Jangbaz Khan Sahib, merchant, Sadr Bazaar	Rs 2
Mirza ʿAbdul Karim Sahib, dealer in books	Rs 20
Muhammad Fateh Khan Sahib, Major, Cavalry	Rs 17–10
Muhammad Asadullah Sahib, court pleader	Rs 0–1
Sayyid Muhammad Sahib, subregistrar	Rs 7–8
Vaman Rao Prabhakar Sahib, Secretary Library	Rs 13
Pandit Krishan Rao Sahib, *taḥṣīldār*	Rs 15
Munshi Kishorilal Sahib Bahadur, *ṣadr amīn*	Rs 15
Mirza Amirullah Sahib	Rs 6
Munshi Durgaparshad Sahib, Superintendent of Jails	Rs 10
Amir Singh Sahib Bahadur, Major, Cavalry	Rs 6–8
ʿAlimuddin Sahib, jailor	Rs 10
Govarn Parshad, police sergeant	Rs 2–12
Pyarelal Sahib, merchant, Sadr Bazaar, Chavni	Rs 11
Pandit Dayanarayan Sahib, *taḥṣīldār*	Rs 10
Divan Lalta Parshad Sahib, Sarkar Bharatpur	Rs 6
Babu Keshab Dip [?] Anandmal, Secretary [?]	Rs 10
Babu Isri Parshad Sahib	Rs 4
Thakur Sahib, *raʾīs*, Milvadah, Ratlam, by means of Munshi Muhammad Nasiruddin Sahib, Superintendent's Office	Rs 23
Lala Narottam Lal Sahib	Rs 6
Maulvi Nadiruddin Sahib, schoolteacher	Rs 23–4
Babu Sher [?] Singh Sahib	Rs 16
Bhavani Din Sahib, Kathiawar	Rs 10
Babu Raghubar Sahai, Deputy Registrar in the Judicial Commissioner's Office	Rs 15
Babu Parameshari das, government servant in the Judicial Commissioner's Office	Rs [?]
Babu Udharsingh Sahib	Rs 6–8
Rai Godar [?] Sahai Sahib	Rs 0–8
Munshi Fida ʿAli Sahib	Rs 5–12

That the formula of *AA* met with wide public approval is also evident from a subscriber's enthusiastic letter to the editor published in the issue of 19 July 1870. In it, the advantages that *AA* was seen to have over other Urdu papers were clearly spelled out:

> Munshi Sahib, your paper is a fountainhead of eloquence and a source of enchantment. Who am I to praise it—'Big words from a little mouth'! Judging from the multitude of news and the acceptance on the part of our contemporaries one could rightly call it 'the mother of newspapers' (*umm al-akhbār*). A great many newspapers are filled with news culled from it, and these newspapers have a fixed number of pages only. [By contrast], your paper offers an unlimited succession of pages—sometimes one finds more than twenty pages and more than three sections in it. Latest news from provinces far and near and useful articles of the most pleasant and excellent kind are inserted, and in a mind-pleasing feast of meaningful poetic oration, it also carries [items on] history, *ghazals*, *qaṣīdas*, etc. News from England reach your paper very fast. In the issue of 28th June, I came across events that had occurred in London on 21st and 22nd June. Even letters from London don't reach within six days, while your paper gives readers information on the sixth day! Even earlier, the arrangement of the writings contained in the paper was always of the most excellent kind. But now the new arrangement as found in the issue of 28th June is particularly pleasing, that is news, letters to the editor, correspondent, etc., local news, selections of rules from the Government Gazette, general and special public notices, and verse compositions of outstanding poets. Each content has been assigned a separate section so that all kinds of enthusiasts will find an assembly of desired writings in one place. If the paper were to introduce a special section giving news of the Education Department, it would gain even further in attractiveness.[10]

Leading educational institutions such as the Dar al-ʿUlum at Deoband received free copies of *AA* from the press, as evident from a profuse note of thanks included in the seminary's annual report of 1877.[11] That the paper also enjoyed growing popularity among those sections of society who could not afford to subscribe to a newspaper regularly is borne out by the quaint testimony of a correspondent of *AA* who, writing from Hoshangabad in 1874, complained of the common malpractice of servants of the post office who were in the habit of opening the covers of the paper

[10] (My translation), *AA*, 19 July 1870, cit. in Haidari 1980: 26.

[11] The report stated: 'Our special thanks are due to Janab Munshi Nawal Kishore, proprietor of *Oudh Akhbar*, and Janab Rao Amar Singh, proprietor of the newspaper, *Safeer-e Badhana*, that despite the fact that both these gentlemen are Hindus, they send—applause and a hundred thousand applause over their generosity and favour—their precious newspapers free of charge to this Madrasah. All the counsellors of this Madrasah thank them from the bottom of their hearts and pray for the good of all of them that Allah Most High bestow progress constantly upon their newspapers and presses and maintain their power and independence' (cit. in Rizvi 1980: 129).

addressed to him. Not only did they read it themselves, they circulated it among their friends, on which account the paper reached him very late.[12]

One eminent subscriber who publicly welcomed the growing influence of *AA* was Sir Sayyid Ahmad Khan. In the opinion of the great Muslim reformer, Naval Kishore was to be credited with having popularized the notion of a news magazine and created widespread public awareness for modern concepts of information among Urdu speakers in the NWP&Oudh (Haidar 1981: 20). In an article published in his own reformist journal, *Tahẕīb al-A<u>kh</u>lāq* (est. 1870), Sir Sayyid expressed his hope to see *AA* expand even further: '*Avadh A<u>kh</u>bār* has been a very respected paper before and nothing can be added to it now. We hope that our contemporary journalists will imitate *Avadh A<u>kh</u>bār*, and as for Munshi Naval Kishore's magnanimity—God's blessings upon him—we hope that his paper will appear on a daily basis in the manner of the large renowned English newspapers. May God let it be so.'[13] The praise and good wishes were mutual, for *AA* openly sympathized with Islamic modernism and the Aligarh movement. It did its best to support *Tahẕīb al-A<u>kh</u>lāq* when, soon after its inception, the paper faced severe opposition from the Muslim orthodoxy. The editor of *AA* at the time, Ghulam Muhammad Khan 'Tapish', was a long-standing supporter of Sir Sayyid. He not only reprinted various articles published in *Tahẕīb al-A<u>kh</u>lāq,* among them Sir Sayyid's review of William Hunter's influential *The Indian Musulmans: are they bound in conscience to rebel against the Queen*? (*AA*, 22 December 1871), but he also adopted a policy of refusing to include in the columns of *AA* any article or letter that took an open stance against the Muslim reformer.[14] As a result of this active support for the controversial reformist journal, *AA* in turn became a target for Sir Sayyid's orthodox opponents. As Ghulam Muhammad Khan informed Sir Sayyid in a confidential letter, on a visit to Kanpur Naval Kishore had been summoned by the Deputy Collector, Maulvi Imdad ʿAli, and severely reprimanded for 'bringing about the ruin of his paper by having employed a Christian editor'. The allusion was to the many articles by Sayyid Ahmad Khan that *AA* used to reprint. Out of consideration for his enterprise in Kanpur, Naval Kishore could not but humbly submit to the scolding. Nonetheless, as the letter went on to report, the Deputy Collector had mounted a diatribe

[12] *AA*, 16 October 1874, SVN 1874: 493.

[13] *Tahẕīb al-A<u>kh</u>lāq*, 1 jamādī alsānī 1288 h, cit. in Khurshid 1963: 180–1.

[14] See Ghulam Muhammad Khan's letter to Sir Sayyid, cit. in Rizvan 1980: 232.

against the editors of both papers. Ghulam Muhammad was eager to assure Sir Sayyid of Naval Kishore's friendship and esteem, but also pointed out that the publisher was operating under many constraints. Finally, he urged Sir Sayyid to occasionally write to the publisher and assure him of his solidarity and their common cause.[15]

Eagerly anticipated by Sayyid Ahmad Khan, the shift of *AA* to a daily paper came in 1877. A special supplement to *AA* announced on 23 May 1877 that starting from 1 June 1877, the paper was to be published on a daily basis, initially for a six-month trial period. The bold venture followed public demand, for readers had for some time expressed a keen desire to receive information on a more regular—daily—basis. Moral and financial support came from prominent citizens such as Lucknow's veteran printer-publisher Maulana Haji Harmain Sharifain, C.S.I, and Deputy Collector Raja Jai Kishen Das, C.S.I., the former secretary of the British Indian Association. Muhammad ʿAbdullah Khan Bahadur of Tonk promised a yearly subscription of Rs 100 in support of the venture. Extolling his generous contribution, the paper hoped that other members of the local aristocracy and affluent classes would follow suit (*AA*, 25 May 1877).

That *AA* could continue as a regular daily even after the six-month trial period is closely linked to the specific historic context, notably the urgent need for news that the Turko-Russian war (1877–8) and the Second Anglo-Afghan war (1878–80) were creating among North Indians, particularly among Muslims.[16] The paper provided extensive coverage of the wars. In the process, it introduced new features such as a special column entitled 'Latest news from the battlefield' (*maidān-e jang kī tāzatarīn khabareṁ*) and inserted maps and illustrations. It is interesting to note that even though *AA* was never an illustrated newspaper, the visual element became increasingly important in its coverage, especially of foreign news. Readers were, among others, regaled with large drawings of the Paris International Exhibition of 1878 (*AA*, 1 Oct 1878), of scenes from a Kabul war camp (*AA*, 28 Feb 1879; Fig. 13), and of a Zulu warrior chief (*AA*, 31 May 1879).

There was another factor in sustaining the publication of *AA* on a

[15] 'Letter from Editor Oudh Akhbar to Syed Ahmad Khan' (undated), cit. in Husain 1966: 210–11. Given *AA*'s unrelenting support of Sayyid Ahmad Khan, it is curious that in 1873–4 the NKP published a number of pamphlets authored by one of his most outspoken critics, Maulvi ʿAli Bakhsh Khan, who wholeheartedly condemned him as a heretic.

[16] For a similar increase in sales of British newspapers provoked by the Turkish crisis, see Brown 1985: 40.

Fig. 13: Scenes from the Second Anglo-Afghan War,
Avadh Akhbār of 28 February 1879

daily basis: following the appointment of Pandit Ratan Nath 'Sarshar' as editor, serialization of his famous Urdu novel *Fasāna-e Āzād* (The Tale of Azad) began in August 1878. It was the first time that serialized fiction was successfully introduced in an Urdu newspaper. A landmark in modern Urdu fiction, *Fasāna-e Āzād* met with an unprecedented public interest which gave a great boost to the paper.[17] The survival of *AA* as a daily, then, rested on a combination of contemporary politics and modern prose fiction. Information and entertainment as the two sustaining factors can hardly be dissociated from one another, for Sarshar cleverly incorporated current political affairs into his fictional narrative: readers of *Fasāna-e Āzād* were made day-to-day witnesses of the hero's journey to Europe and his brave exploits in fighting the Russians on the side of his Turkish fellow-Muslims.

6.2 Contents and Policy

AA was a product of the colonial experience in that it aimed to be a modern, professional news magazine. It emulated British models, its coverage including local, national, and international news. In the name of spreading education and enlightenment among the Urdu reading public, *AA* aimed high, aspiring to be nothing less than the North Indian equivalent of *The Times* of London (*AA*, 1 January 1879). The news section made up the largest portion of the paper, which prided itself in being able to cover 'the whole world'.

How was efficient news coverage achieved and what were the channels of information transfer? It was only three years prior to the inception of *AA* that the opening of the first telegraph lines in India had induced radical changes in the dissemination of news in the subcontinent.[18] No modern news agencies, however, were operating in India before the year 1866, when Reuters started extending its services there.[19] Reuters,

[17] This was rather late as compared to Britain where serial fiction was by no means an invention of the Victorian era but dates back to the eighteenth century. For the history of serialized fiction and instalment publication in Britain, see Law 2000.

[18] The rapid development of the telegraph system has been summed up by David Arnold: 'From a few miles of line in 1851, telegraphs had been extended over 4,250 miles of India and linked forty-six receiving stations by the end of 1856: they ran from Calcutta to Agra and the northwest as well as connecting Bombay, Madras and Ootacamund. By 1865 there were 17,500 miles of telegraph lines, rising to 52,900 miles by the end of the century' (Arnold 2000: 113).

[19] Opened in 1855, the first domestic lines were from Calcutta to Bombay via Agra, from Agra to Peshavar, and from Bombay to Madras. Reuters set up its first

however, was too expensive for the majority of Indian newspaper editors to make use of its services. To ensure a rapid and steady flow of information, Naval Kishore relied on a more traditional system of information distribution and operated his own network of correspondents posted in the major urban centres of India. As a contemporary saying had it, in every district and every princely state one would find correspondents of the colonial government and of Munshi Naval Kishore (Sabiri 1953 [ii]: 112). A substantial portion of the domestic and foreign political news was reprinted from English newspapers, particularly *The Times* (London), *The Pioneer* (Allahabad), and *Friend of India* (Calcutta). News items regarding the Islamic world were culled from Persian and Arabic newspapers. Generating news and information was also turned into a public, collective concern in which the participation of the readership was explicitly invited: those who would regularly supply the paper with 'important, recent, reliable and interesting news items' were promised free copies of *AA* in return.

While introducing new concepts of modern informational culture, *AA* retained some features of the traditional newsletter as described by Michael H. Fisher (Fischer 1993: 79–81). For one, there was the physical appearance of the handwritten and lithographed sheets. The paper retained the term '*akhbārāt*' for various categories of news; it adopted a Persianized vocabulary and cultivated a fairly ornate style. Published in two parts, on Wednesday and Friday, a typical issue of the paper in 1871 combined elements of traditional and modern newswriting in its standard departments. In the following contents overview (Table 6.0) the original Urdu has been retained to show how this intermingling of the traditional and the modern was reflected in the vocabulary used to label the various sections.

By 1878 telegraph news had moved to the front part of the paper, whereas the advertisement and local news section had been relegated to the back. While directly prompted by the wars, this increased emphasis on rapid coverage of domestic and external affairs also formed part of a wider policy shift: *AA* slowly moved away from older conventions of

office in Bombay in 1866. Other offices in Calcutta, Madras, and Karachi followed, supplying the Indian press not only with foreign but also domestic information. The opening of the London-Bombay submarine telegraph cable in June 1870 greatly speeded up the transmission of news from England. Details in G. Storey 1951: 62–8; see also Barns 1940: 311 and Raghavan 1994: 63–4. For traditional systems of information distribution, see Bayly 1996a, esp. chs 1–4.

TABLE 6.0
Avadh Akhbār in 1871

Part One (issued on Wednesday)	Part Two (issued on Friday)
1. General advertisements (*ishtihārāt maʿmūlī*)	1. Lucknow
2. Poetry (*naẓm*)	2. Telegraph news (*akhbārāt tār-barqī*)
3. Correspondence (*khaṭ-kitābat*)	3. Editorial (*aḍīṭoryal*)
4. Proceedings of the Committee, etc. (*maẓāmīn kamīṭī vaghairah*)	4. Correspondent (*kāraspānḍanṭ*)
5. Telegraph news (*akhbārāt tār-barqī*)	5. Translations from the English (*tarjuma angrezī*)
6 Editorial (*aḍīṭoryal*)	6. Reprints from other papers (*manqūlāt*)
7. Correspondent (*kāraspānḍanṭ*)	7. Correspondence (*khaṭ-kitābat*)
8. Translations from English newspapers (*tarjuma angrezī akhbārāt*)	8. Translations from the *Government Gazette* (*Tarjuma gavarnmanṭ gazat urdū*)
9. Miscellanea (*akhbārāt mukhtalif*)	9. Special notifications (*ishtihārāt ghair-maʿmūlī*)
10. Local news/Lucknow (*lokal akhbārāt*)	

assembling and presenting news, towards a new kind of 'efficient' and professional journalism based on Western models.

The local section of the paper, providing information on current affairs in Lucknow, was comparatively small. Next to news items on crimes and spectacular incidents, it regularly featured the timetables of the Oudh Rohilkhand Railway (printed in Urdu and Nagari script), legal notices, and the timings of court sessions.[20] It also covered a wide array of cultural events, including *mushāʿiras*, public lectures and, most importantly, the activities of local civic associations such as the Jalsah-e Tahzib. *Mushāʿiras* organized by the NKP and taking place regularly on its premises received special coverage. The reports on these gatherings, which attracted both well-known and minor Lucknow poets, read like an inventory of local poetic talent. The *AA* of 1 January 1878, for example, carried the following notice:

[20] The railway timetable had become an integral part of suburban newspaper content in London's local papers since the 1840s (Harris 1990: 110). In introducing this feature, *AA* obviously acted on official instructions.

> A special gathering of poets took place on Monday at the Avadh Akhbar Press. The occasion was graced by eminent poets among the noblemen of Lucknow. The pattern-line was '*sac to yah hai ki burā hotā hai acchā honā*' (True it is, indeed, that being good is bad). But since, due to the lack of time, the distinguished poets had only been informed one day in advance, there were very few ghazals that conformed to the pattern-line. Indeed, most did not conform to it. The audience gained extreme delight from the compositions of Janab Nawab Siraj ud Daula Bahadur 'Junun', Janab Mirza Haidar Sahib 'Afsun', Janab Darogha Mir Vajid ᶜAli Sahib 'Taskhir', *raᵓīs* of Lucknow, Janab Munshi Ghazanfar ᶜAli Sahib 'Halim', Mir Afzal ᶜAli Sahib 'Afzal', the sons of Janab Tadbir ud Daula Munshi Muzaffar ᶜAli Khan Bahadur, and other distinguished gentlemen. The honourable proprietor of the press was extremely grateful for the kindness of all these gentlemen.[21]

Besides its variety of news items, the paper contained articles on social and cultural topics, education and literature. In matters of social change, it generally adopted a reformist and progressive stance: for example, it urged the government to take strict measures against female infanticide (*AA*, 19 July 1870) and condemned the 'sinful practice' of polygamy (*AA*, 26 July 1870).[22] It equally condemned *satī* and urged both Hindu and Muslims to advance widow remarriage (*AA*, 21 November 1875). Education needed to be modernized: the *AA* of 11 February 1887 appealed to the Hindu intelligentsia in the provinces to not stay behind in the competition for modern education but establish their own college on the model of the Aligarh Muhammadan Anglo-Oriental College.[23] 'Public welfare' or '*rifah-e ᶜām*' was a frequently invoked key concept in such articles, in the name of which the paper also gave vent to public grievances. Complaints ranged from the want of proper sanitation in Lucknow (*AA*, 15 March 1869) to the introduction of new taxes by the Municipal Committee which, together with the government income-tax, were said 'to have disgusted the people at large, and created a general disaffection and distrust towards the ruling power' (*AA*, 28 June 1870).[24] While such reports professed to give voice to public discontent, they were generally moderate in tone and clearly testify to the paper's self-styled role as an intermediary between the government and the Indian people.

[21] (My translation), cit. in Sabiri 1953, II: 95. For other *mushāᶜiras* and their participants, see Nurani 1995: 201. In the usual fashion, the poetic contributions presented at these gatherings were published in collections entitled *Guldasta*.

[22] SVN 1870: 289.

[23] SVN 1887: 99.

[24] SVN 1869: 126; SVN 1870: 252.

The political outlook of *AA* was characterized by loyalty towards the colonial state and support for its policies. Official British opinion considered the paper to be 'moderate and respected' and early on noted 'the ability' with which it was written.[25] Yet at times this moderate and cautious stance could border on a kind of opportunism that was suspicious even to British eyes. As an official report noted in 1881:

> Of the Oudh papers the best is the Oudh Akhbar. This paper is, however, somewhat timid in tone, and rarely ventures to advocate strongly any important measures till satisfied that they are likely to find favour with Government. Though a consistent and admiring supporter of Lord Lytton's various measures, no sooner did it hear of his resignation than it hastened to advocate those changes in policy which seemed likely would take place under the new Government.[26]

Following the formation of the Indian National Congress in 1885, *AA* became a prime target for the nationalist Urdu press, particularly once its proprietor Naval Kishore had joined ranks with Sayyid Ahmad Khan's United Indian Patriotic Association and assumed a leading position in the anti-Congress movement. As noted earlier, it is difficult to dissociate political opposition from professional rivalry in the bitter attacks on *AA* that various Urdu journals begun to indulge in at the time. The continuously large share of government patronage that Naval Kishore's firm and, with it, *AA* enjoyed was indeed prone to incite jealousy. The rival Urdu press routinely portrayed Naval Kishore as a sycophant of the colonial empire who, in opposing the Congress, was motivated by self-interest and servility alone. *AA* was declared unable to represent national interests. *Avadh Punch* defamed the paper as a money-minded '*baniā akhbār*', while *Hindustān* accused it of consisting chiefly of 'translations of articles abusive of natives' taken from *The Pioneer* and the *Civil and Military Gazette*.[27] Ganga Prasad Varma's *Hindustānī* denounced it along with other anti-Congress papers that allegedly thrived on government patronage:

> The Oudh Akhbar, the Aligarh Institute Gazette and the Kashi Patrika receive large sums of money from the local Government. Indeed, those three vernacular journals chiefly depend on Government aid for their support and would not long survive the stoppage of the subsidies. . . . In return for the

[25] *Home Dept., Public Procs.*, August 1879: 292–303; February 1883: 187–8 (B); *OAR*, 1869–70: 145.

[26] *RA NWP&Oudh*, for the year ending 31 March 1881: 359.

[27] Cit. in Singh 1991: 25; 65.

> subsidies which the newspapers above referred to receive, they blindly support all government measures and proceedings, in utter disregard of the interest of the people. Hence the payment of such subsidies is subversive of the freedom of the press. It is almost needless to say that the people have no confidence in the Oudh Akhbar, the Aligarh Institute Gazette and the Kasi Patrika.[28]

AA in its turn claimed to have public opinion on its side and retorted that the public trusted the colonial government more than it did the seditious Congress and its organs. In lashing out their polemics, the pro-Congress papers deliberately overlooked the deeper motives of Naval Kishore's opposition to the Congress. No doubt, the publisher had to protect his commercial interests and was careful not to endanger business relations with his major customer by publishing anti-British propaganda in his paper. Yet to narrow his motivation down to economic dependence is certainly overstating the case. *AA* was not a loyalist paper by constraint but by choice. It firmly believed in the benefits of colonial rule. Loyalty and support of colonial rule, as understood by the proprietor and editors of *AA*, did not automatically exclude a critique of government. True to its claim of representing public opinion, the paper was on occasion quite capable of articulating dissonant 'native' views. C.A. Bayly has poignantly described its stance as 'covert criticism of British rule in Hindustan along the lines of old patriotism, but in the voice of unalloyed loyalism' (Bayly 1998: 91).

The coverage of the visit to Lucknow of the Prince of Wales in May 1876 provides a characteristic example of this stance. The paper not only published numerous poetic eulogies to the distinguished visitor, in its issue of 28 May it also contained a critical piece entitled 'Can the Indian Subjects be Content with the British Government?' which openly expressed dissatisfaction with an administration that failed to cater to the basic needs of a populace assaulted by poverty and hunger.[29]

AA also liked to pose as a spokesman of the Indian-language press and frequently took up its cause in its columns. The issue of 25 August 1874, for example, carried a complaint about the government's double standards in dealing with the English and Indian-language press, stating that it was 'extremely unjust that, while Government grants special indulgences to editors of English newspapers, and exalts them to high offices

[28] *Hindustānī* of 6 July 1890, SVN 1890: 452. See also the *Siṃha Sahāy* of 28 May 1890, SVNP 1890: 197.

[29] For a summarized reproduction of this article, see *LLH* 1876: 8–12.

in the public service, it should confer no such favours on the editors of vernacular newspapers.'[30] In sharp contrast, an anonymous article entitled 'The English Papers are jealous of our Freedom' (*'Angrezī akhbār hamārī āzādī par khār khāte haiṁ'*) in the issue of 11 April 1875 argued that the vernacular press enjoyed a freedom of expression that was unknown to the English press which, motivated by envy, was therefore provoked into claiming that such freedom was undeserved, premature, and dangerous.[31] Undoubtedly, careful sifting of *AA* will produce further such examples. A detailed assessment of its content, socio-political profile, and public impact remains to be undertaken. Against the backdrop of Naval Kishore's active involvement in national politics, such an investigation will also have to address the intricate question as to what extent the political profile of *AA* was shaped by its proprietor rather than its various editors. In any case, it promises to provide valuable insights into how the leading Urdu daily in North India was walking the tightrope between loyalty to the colonial government and the increasing exigencies of Indian nationalism.

What can be safely said at this point is that from around 1890 *AA*'s circulation was stagnating. By the turn of the century the paper had lost much of its former appeal. According to Balmukund Gupta, editor of the politically trenchant Hindi journal *Bhāratmitra*, this was due to the paper's refusal to engage in nationalist politics. In resisting modernization and refusing to formulate its own distinct 'policy', the veteran journalist opined, *AA* had failed to keep up with the tide of the times. Moreover, despite the paper's monetary resources and its excellent staff, the selection of English news items was 'nonsensical' and their translations into Urdu 'barely intelligible'. Writing in 1905, Gupta concluded: '[*AA*] is exactly the same as it was twenty years ago, and for this very reason it has not established a reputation for itself in the newspaper world during the past twenty years. Most newspaper readers won't even know its name' (Gupta 1994: 262–3). To this critical observer at the beginning of the new century *AA* no longer met the needs of modern journalism, but had become a *'laqīr kā faqīr'* and a *'besūṇḍ kā hāthī'*.[32]

[30] SVN 1874: 355.

[31] Contrary to a curiously misinformed but frequent claim in writings on *AA*, the article was *not* entitled 'Our Freedom'. Nor, for that matter, was it the first instance of Bal Gangadhar Tilak voicing his famous slogan 'Swaraj is my birthright' in an Indian newspaper.

[32] I.e., a 'conventionalist' and an 'elephant without a trunk'. Indeed, the paper did not show any substantial increase in circulation since the 1880s. In 1904 its circulation was still no more than 800 copies (Sharma 1959: 367).

6.3 Promoting Urdu Literature: Editors and Contributors

The self-proclaimed aim of *AA* was to work towards the progress and welfare of India by informing and educating the Indian public through broad news coverage. At the same time, the paper assumed the function of a literary journal. It promoted poetry and prose writing, covered literary events, announced new publications and provided a discursive forum for the Urdu literati. While the paper attracted the contributions of some leading literary figures from outside Lucknow, its role in the promotion of Urdu literature and the consolidation of a modern prose style goes specifically to the credit of several eminent intellectuals among its editors. According to Sabiri, no other Urdu paper of the period boasted such an illustrious range of editors as *AA* (Sabiri 1953, II: 59). While some of them were already well-known figures in the intellectual and literary world when they joined the paper, others used *AA* as a stepping stone in their future careers as publicists and writers.

Although we have a fair picture of the various personalities associated with the editorship of *AA*, to establish a definite chronology of the paper's editors remains problematic. Since there was no formal declaration of the editor on the front cover, and since, according to common practice, editorial pieces generally remained unsigned, their names can only be gleaned from references within the paper or from secondary sources. With many contradicting statements standing in the way, the following account can only be tentative.[33] Also, given the scarcity of extant issues for the period 1859–75, we can do little more than establish the identity of the various intellectuals that *AA* was able to attract. To assess their contributions and the way in which their writings helped to shape the profile of *AA* remains subject to the future availability of source material.

The first issues of *AA* were almost certainly edited by Naval Kishore himself. However, he was soon forced to delegate this time-consuming task to others. In 1859 Maulvi Hadi ᶜAli 'Ashk', who has already been introduced as one of the NKP's foremost scholars and calligraphers, was appointed the first formal editor of *AA*. Due to his failing health Ashk was not able to carry out the demanding job for long, but had to abandon it in 1864.[34] It is not clear who took over after him. According to Garcin de Tassy, Munshi Shiv Parshad, the manager of the NKP, assumed the editorship in 1864. The French scholar, however, may have

[33] The following paragraphs draw largely on Sabiri 1953 (II) and Haidari 1980.

[34] In 1864 the publication of Ghalib's *Kulliyāt,* for which Maulvi Hadi ᶜAli prepared the calligraphy, had to be suspended due to his frail health.

confused the tasks of press manager and editor: he certainly made a rather consequential mistake in confounding Shiv Parshad with his namesake Raja Shiva Prasad of Benares—the eminent educator and textbook author, who, ever since, has been erroneously associated with the editorship of *AA* (*HLHH* 3: 268–73). Munshi Shiv Parshad had originally been hired as a calligrapher for *AA*. By 1862 he had risen to the post of manager of the NKP. He was a poet of Urdu who adopted the *ta<u>kh</u>alluṣ* 'Wahbi' and has a *Kulliyāt-e Wahbī* (*1880) to his credit. Specimens of his verse frequently appeared in *AA*.

According to an editorial notice published in a later issue of *AA*, it was the reputed Farangi Mahall scholar Mufti Fakhruddin Ahmad 'Fakhr' Lakhnavi (d. 1892) who took over the editorship from Maulvi Hadi ᶜAli, presumably in early 1865.[35] His contribution in the NKP's translation department has already been noted. Fakhruddin did not remain editor of *AA* for long. In 1866 he was succeeded by Muhammad Mehdi Husain Khan, the ex-proprietor of the Riyaz-e Nur Press (est. 1851) of Multan and former editor of an Urdu weekly of the same name. It appears that Mehdi Husain Khan had been forced to close his press in 1856, following a sentence of imprisonment of several years. He joined *AA* after his release from jail.[36]

Following Mehdi Husain Khan, in 1867 the post of editor was assumed by Maulvi Raunaq ᶜAli (1846-76), a scholar and poet of Persian and Urdu who wrote under the pen names 'Afsun' and 'Raunaq'. The son of a *taᶜalluqdār* of Barabanki district, Raunaq ᶜAli had come to Lucknow in 1859 to receive his higher education in Islamic learning from Khvaja ᶜAzizuddin Kashmiri and Maulvi Nazir ᶜAli, the Arabic professor at the Mahmudabad *madrasah*. He joined the NKP as a proofreader for *AA* but was soon promoted to the position of editor. Naval Kishore seems to have thought highly of him, for in 1870 he sent him to Patiala to oversee

[35] The notice states: 'In this factory in 1859 [a paper] called *Avadh A<u>kh</u>bār* was put into circulation. It was launched at a time when the government forces were busy exterminating the mutineers. In the beginning its editor was Maulvi Hadi ᶜAli Ashk. Maulana Afzal al-ᶜulama Maulvi Mufti Fakhruddin Fakhr for many days served as the editor. He is the same Maulvi Sahib who published a translation of the *Kimiyā-e saᶜādat* entitled *Iksīr-e hidāyat*. He is also preparing, with perfect eloquence, an Urdu translation of the *Tafsīr Husainī* for the press. Some time later Mehdi Hasan [*sic*], who was formerly a correspondent of the *Riyāz-e Nūr* of Multan, was in charge of the editorship of the paper. In 1870 Maulvi Ghulam Bakhsh [*sic*] Khan Tapish assumed the responsibility of the editorship with great fervour.' (*AA*, 2 January 1874, my translation), cit. in Sabiri 1953, II: 58–9.

[36] Khan 1991: 259–65; Khurshid 1963: 123.

the establishment of a new printing office in the princely state. In October 1871 Raunaq ᶜAli launched the *Paṭiālā A<u>kh</u>bār* at the request of the Maharaja of Patiala. He died in 1876 at the early age of thirty (*LLH* 1876: 136–7).

A new era dawned for *AA* in 1870, when Maulvi Ghulam Muhammad Khan (d. 1904) became its editor. A native of Delhi, he had spent part of his youth in the company of the Nawab of Patauri and subsequently gained experience as a journalist and editor in Meerut and other places. He was also a pupil of Mirza Ghalib and composed poetry in Persian and Urdu under the pen name 'Tapish'. During the eight years of his editorship *AA* thrived.[37] His close and amicable relationship with Naval Kishore, however, took a dramatic turn in September 1876 when, following a serious altercation between the two men, Ghulam Muhammad Khan left the press. Apparently he felt that he was not receiving due recognition for his intellectual exertions and the effort he put into running the paper. The row may have also been sparked off by his editorial policy, for around that time *AA* had come under heavy criticism by *Nuṣrat al-A<u>kh</u>bār* of Delhi, which in its issue of 1 August 1876, wrote:

> [*AA*] has not exercised any good influence on the customs of Lucknow. It has not created unity and harmony between Sunnis and Shiᶜas, nor has it spared the people there from calamity. Perhaps it regards writing on religious matters as contrary to the rule; but at least it is a blessing that there is no special discussion by Mushtari and Zohra.[38] Instead, it covers domestic law suits of Lucknow. Outsiders are flustered by such disputes. What is new about it, compared to all other papers, is that it is very self-interested. It desires no one's welfare. The editor is instructed not to write any article beneficial to the public, but only to print reviews of books [published] by the press.[39]

Whatever the reasons for Ghulam Muhammad leaving *AA*, it was none other than Sir Sayyid Ahmad Khan who personally came to his defence: in an article that appeared in the *Aligarh Institute Gazette* of 29 September 1876 he expressed his deep regret over Ghulam Muhammad's departure and pointed out that Naval Kishore had carelessly let go of one of the most capable editors of his paper, to whom *AA* owed its entire success.[40]

[37] It seems that Munshi Fida Ali ᶜAish was assistant editor at the time. Nurani 1995: 74.

[38] Two famous courtesans and poetesses of Lucknow who took part in some of the literary debates held in *AA*. See Kazim ᶜAli Khan 1986: 138.

[39] (My translation) cit. in Sabiri 1953 [ii]: 97–8.

[40] *Aligarh Institute Gazette* of 29 September 1876.

The article did not fail in its purpose: a week later, the *Aligarh Institute Gazette* was happy to report that Ghulam Muhammad had resumed editorship of *AA*.[41] Yet he did not remain with the paper for much longer, but several months later decided to resign and leave the NKP for good. In March 1877 he informed readers of *AA* that, having devoted his energy to the paper for some eight years and having ruined his health and eyesight in the process, he would quit *AA* and start his own paper, *Mushīr-e Qaisar-e Hind*, instead.[42]

Consequently, a notice was published in *AA* of 27 April 1877 soliciting applications from learned individuals for the post of editor. The necessary qualifications were excellent compository skills in Urdu and a perfect knowledge of Arabic, Persian, and English. There is a rather dubious claim, probably going back to Garcin de Tassy, that, following Tapish, for a short period Maulana Sayyid Amjad ᶜAli 'Ashhari' (b. 1848/49) took charge of the paper. This claim is not substantiated by biographical accounts on Ashhari.[43] Indeed, it would seem strange that this distinguished scholar of Persian and Arabic should give up his high administrative post in the state of Bhopal and shift to Lucknow. In January 1881 Ashhari established his own printing press Amjad al-Matabaᶜ in Bhopal, from where he launched the journal *Dabīr al-Mulk.* A prolific poet and writer, he made an important contribution to historiographical and biographical literature in Urdu.[44]

Mention has already been made of the next and most famous editor of *AA*, Pandit Ratan Nath 'Sarshar' (1846-1902). If *AA* must be credited with having 'launched the career of one of the most important prose fiction writers in Urdu' (Naim/Petievich 1997: 171), it was Sarshar who, in turn, brought about the heyday of the paper's fame. Born in a Kashmiri Brahmin family settled in Lucknow, Sarshar received his education at Canning College and later took up employment as a schoolteacher. He had for some time contributed articles to various journals, particularly to Sayyid Sajjad Husain's satirical *Avadh Punch* (est. 1877), when, on 10 August 1878, Naval Kishore appointed him editor of *AA* (Mookerjee 1992: 57–8). Apparently Sarshar had been introduced to the publisher

[41] *Aligarh Institute Gazette* of 6 October 1876.

[42] Part of Ghulam Muhammad Khan's article has been reproduced by Garcin de Tassy (*LLH* 1877: 40–2). For further details, see also Sabiri 1953 [ii]: 99–104.

[43] See, e.g., Salim Hamid Rizvi, *Urdū adab kī taraqqī meṁ Bhopāl kā hiṣṣa* (Bhopal 1965: 174–6). I am grateful to Claudia Preckel for directing my attention to this work.

[44] Ibid. See, e.g., his biography of Mir Anis, *Ḥayāt-e Anīs* (1904), which he wrote on the suggestion of Shibli Nomani.

by DPI R.T.H. Griffith and employed with a view to counteracting the fierce attacks on *AA* that *Avadh Punch* had begun to indulge in at the time (Saxena 1990: 325). Needless to say, Sarshar's change of sides did little to alleviate the tension between the two papers. On the contrary, the publication of *Fasāna-e Āzād* and the ensuing boost it gave to the circulation of *AA* provoked jealous attacks and criticism from *Avadh Punch*. The result, according to Sadiq, was 'an open war between the two papers, which, after a crescendo of abuse and whacking blows on both sides, resulted in an honourable truce' (Sadiq 1995: 418). This is not quite accurate, for the attacks continued throughout the 1880s: in August 1880 *Avadh Punch* accused *AA* of being an anti-Muslim paper. In 1886 serialization of Sarshar's novel *Sair-e-Kohsār*, a titillating narrative about a young Nawab's illicit affair with a low-caste woman, prompted *Avadh Punch* to publicly urge the government to take legal action against Naval Kishore for publishing a 'very obscene' novel in a paper delivered to countless schools in the province.[45]

Fasāna-e Āzād was published in instalments in *AA* from August 1878 to January 1880. It started out as a series of humorous sketches (*ẓarāfat*) appearing in loose succession from 13 August onwards.[46] With its vivid and humorous portrayal of contemporary social life in Lucknow, it took the reading public by storm and, from January 1879, was published at daily intervals. Later it assumed the form of a special supplement to *AA*, printed on loose sheets of white paper as against the brown paper used for the newspaper (Madan Gopal 1964: 31). While Sarshar's claims to *Fasāna-e Āzād* being a 'modern novel' remain controversial,[47] its publishing pattern marked the breakthrough of a new narrative genre in Urdu—the serialized novel. As the first piece of original fiction in Urdu written expressly for publication in a newspaper, *Fasāna-e Āzād* broke new ground: for one, it was a text conceived in instalments, demanding self-contained units which were sufficiently barbed with suspense to hook the reader to the plot before he was relegated to the next issue of the

[45] *Avadh Punch* of 20 May 1886, SVN 1886: 406.

[46] For the publishing history of *Fasānā-e Āzād*, see Mookerjee 1992: 78–80. As Mookerjee points out, the common notion that the novel was published in *AA* from December 1878 to December 1879 is based on an incorrect statement given in the first edition in book form (1880). The first instalments appeared in the following issues of *AA*: August 13, 28; September 6, 9, 13, 19, 23, 27; October 3, 9, 18; November 7. Publication in daily instalments began in late January 1879.

[47] For a discussion of *Fasāna-e Āzād* under this aspect, see Mookerjee 1992: 87–97; Russell 1992: 87–92; Asaduddin 2001: 84–6.

paper by the inevitable '*bāqī āʾinda* . . .' ('to be continued . . .'). Daily intervals imposed enormous pressure on the writer. The regular doses of opium that Sarshar was allegedly supplied with by the publisher may be a reflection of this. More important than the demands that the new mode of writing put on the author, however, was the new form of reader–writer interaction prompted by serial publication in a paper. Reader reaction to *Fasāna-e Āzād* was vivid, testifying to the existence of a critical literary public eager to discuss the notion of realism in literary fiction. Readers of *AA* sent in letters of criticism or suggestions to which Sarshar readily responded with comments or ad hoc modifications in the plot of his narrative (Mookerjee 1992: 102–33).

As R. Patten has pointed out in the context of the unprecedented success of Charles Dickens's *Pickwick Papers*, serial publication was a chief means of democratizing and enormously expanding the reading and book-buying public in Victorian England (Patten 1978: 45). In India, too, if much later than in Europe, serialized fiction became a staple and important part of literary magazines and periodicals. Its wider impact on the development of modern fiction and the growth of the reading public in North India still awaits study.[48]

Sarshar contributed to the success of *AA* not only with *Fasāna-e Āzād*, but with numerous articles on literary, educational, political, and social themes in which he advocated progressive thought, enlightenment, and modernity along the lines of what was called the 'New Light'. In his first editorial he laid out the editor's tasks as fourfold, notably (1) to serve his countrymen and lead them to prosperity, (2) to teach them to improve their ways, (3) to bring Indian views to the notice of the government, and (4) to 'illuminate with the radiance of the sun of refinement the dark chambers of the heart of those who languish in the pitch darkness of unfathomed ignorance, begging for light' (cited in Mookerjee 1992: 58). Accordingly, under his editorship, increased coverage was given to social reform issues. His editorials reflect a particular concern with education and the status of Indian women. Moreover, in their poignant and sometimes humorous literary style, they gave a new dimension to journalistic prose in Urdu and assumed model character for many later writers.

[48] Other famous early instances of serialization include Bankimchandra's *Anandamath*, published in the monthly *Bangadarshan* (1881–2); the Hindi translation of his *Durgeshnandinī*, serialized in *Kavivacansudhā*; ʿAbdul Halim Sharar's Urdu historical romances, serialized in his *Dilgudāz* in the 1880s and 90s; and, of course, Devkinandan Khatri's *Candrakāntā* (1892), the first best-seller in the history of modern Hindi fiction.

Sarshar could self-mockingly pose as an 'inveterate hemp smoker', who in a fictitious letter to the proprietor of *AA* complained about the outrageous articles against drug-smoking and drinking through which the paper's new editor had driven half of Lucknow's population out of the city. He could equally well address the ailments of society in a more serious manner, never losing sight of his objective of bringing 'New Light' to his compatriots.

Sarshar resigned from the editorship of *AA* on 1 February 1880 but remained attached to the NKP for some time. His novels *Fasāna-e Jadīd* (later published in book form as *Jām-e Sarshār*) and *Sair-e Kohsār* appeared in serial publication as special supplements to *AA* in 1880 and 1886, without, however, enjoying the same kind of success as *Fasāna-e Āzād*. Sponsored by Naval Kishore, Sarshar was able to return to his fascination with *Don Quixote*, which had already inspired *Fasāna-e Āzād*, and complete a long-cherished project of preparing an Urdu version of Cervantes' great picaresque novel. His *Khudāʾī Faujdār* was published from the NKP in 1894 (Mookerjee 1992: 229).

It is difficult to reconstruct the various editors of *AA* after Sarshar, the reason being a shift in the paper's organizational structure: the issue of 11 February 1880 announced that the NKP was to take charge of the paper and that no formal editor would be appointed in future. Instead, a group of 'excellent and experienced persons' would be employed to run the paper.[49] How strictly this policy was adhered to cannot be said. Among those subsequently associated with the editorship were Ghulam Hasnain Qadr Bilgrami (d. 1884), Maulvi Ahmad Hasan 'Shaukat' Merathi, Mirza Hairat Dehlavi and several others who have already been mentioned in connection with the NKP's translation department, such as Munshi Debi Parshad 'Sihr'. By far the most outstanding figure on the editorial staff during the period, however, was ʿAbdul Halim Sharar (1860–1926), the great Urdu essayist and cultural historian of Lucknow. Sharar had spent his childhood in Lucknow and studied at Farangi Mahall. In 1869 he joined his father at the court in exile of Wajid ʿAli Shah in Matia Burj, from where he contributed his first articles to *AA*. When, in 1880, he returned to Lucknow in search of a job, he was promptly employed by Naval Kishore as assistant editor at a monthly salary of Rs 30. With Sharar as editor, *AA* went a step further in according Urdu prose writing a prominent place in its columns, while also giving increased coverage

[49] *AA*, 11 February 1880, cit. in Khurshid 1963: 184–5. This also explains why from 1883 onward the SVN list Munshi Shiv Parshad, the manager of the NKP, as the editor/publisher of *AA*.

to subjects of cultural and social interest. Contributing articles on a great variety of topics, Sharar remained with *AA* until at least 1884, when he went to Hyderabad as a special correspondent of the paper. Soon after, he started his own monthly magazine *Dilgudāz*.[50]

Next to its formal editors, *AA* also attracted the contributions of eminent Urdu literati, not least because it was among the first Urdu papers able to offer remuneration to its contributors. Unfortunately, the sources are silent as to the customary amounts paid. Inviting 'useful, excellent, and interesting articles written in idiomatic and fluid English or Urdu', notices in the paper made a discreet promise of 'adequate compensation' (*kāfī muʿāvaẓa*). The best-known outside contributor in the 1860s was none other than Mirza Ghalib who submitted articles on a number of topical themes, among them a piece on the Afghanistan war (*AA*, 22 April 1862). Ghalib from the outset was a keen reader of *AA*. His correspondence suggests that within the first year of its existence *AA* was circulated and read by the Urdu intelligentsia across a wide geographical region. When, in November 1859, Ghalib's friend and publisher Munshi Shivnarayan 'Aram' forwarded him a copy of *AA* from Agra, Ghalib returned it with the comment that there was no need to waste postage since he already received the paper through his cousin Ziyauddin Khan, a regular subscriber (Russell/Islam 1994: 220). Several months later, in a letter to Munshi Naval Kishore dated 18 July 1860, Ghalib announced his own subscription to *AA* (K.A. Khan 1980: 140). About to enter into a publishing agreement with Ghalib, Naval Kishore did not deem it suitable to ask the venerable poet for payment and began sending him the paper free of charge. In a letter to ʿAlaʾi dated 13 December 1863 Ghalib, who was in continuous financial distress at the time, gratefully acknowledged the savings of Rs 24 that his 'respected friend' Naval Kishore had thus afforded him. 'True', he hastened to add with his customary pride, 'I send forty-eight stamps every year to cover the postage' (Russell/Islam 1994: 295).

Among Ghalib's *shāgirds* who contributed to *AA* we find Ghulam Hasnain Qadr Bilgrami and Nawab Mardan ʿAli Khan 'Raʿna' (d. 1879). The latter, a *raʾīs* of Murabadad, was a regular contributor to the paper in the 1860s and continued to write for it even after his rise to the position

[50] Sharar's famous literary controversy with Pandit Brajnarayan Cakbast over the foremost *maṣnavī*-writer of their times did not, as sometimes claimed, take place in *AA* but in the columns of *Dilgudāz* and *Avadh Punch* in 1905. The NKP, however, published the debate in book form as *Mubāḥaṣa-e Gulzār-e Nasīm yaʿni Maʿraka-e Cakbast va Sharār* (1913).

of Chief Minister in Jodhpur State in 1870. The way in which these representatives of Urdu literature adopted the modern medium of the newspaper to publicly expound their views not only on literary but also social and political affairs, to either engage in a critique of colonialism or to extol the benefits of Western civilization, deserves to be explored in greater detail.[51] *AA* also had a foreign correspondent in London and counted among its regular contributors the eminent Orientalist scholar and linguist Edward Henry Palmer (1840–82). Palmer, a Fellow at St John's College, Cambridge, had an excellent command of Arabic and Persian. He had studied Urdu with Sayyid ʿAbdullah of University College London and was proficient enough in the language to compose original pieces of Urdu poetry. He contributed articles and poems to *AA* from the early 1860s.[52]

Finally—and although it falls outside the time frame of this study—a claim frequently raised in Urdu sources shall be addressed here, since it concerns no less famous a literary figure than the great Hindi and Urdu writer Munshi Premchand. The claim that Premchand was one of the paper's editors in the twentieth century is not supported by any of the standard biographies on him. In 1914 Premchand actually declined an offer to join the editors of *AA*. The busy professionalism reigning in the press office of a daily newspaper did not suit his disposition. As he explained to his friend Dayanarayan Nigam:

> Here, even though I am a slave, I have a lot of freedom, for I have no boss sitting on my head nor am I answerable to anybody. That's why I feel free. And I shudder to think of the daily office routine of ten-to-five, with constant mental exertion, and a paper to be published daily. I don't think I can do it. My literary work here is like a pastime; it would then become a profession. (Amrit Rai 1991: 90)

Premchand, however, did become associated with the NKP much later, when he was appointed editor of the Hindi literary journal *Mādhurī* in

[51] Kazim ʿAli Khan gives a list of issues of *AA* which carry contributions by Ghalib and various of his *shāgirds* or announcements of their works. (K.A. Khan 1980: 136–50).

[52] It is not clear whether Palmer himself was the official correspondent of *AA*. *AA* of 22 August 1871 carried the following statement which (unless a form of self-praise) suggests two different persons: 'The English Correspondent of the 'Oudh Akhbar' had bestowed great praise on the poetry of Mr Edward Palmer . . . He writes that Mr Palmer composes excellent and delectable verses in Qasaid which have extorted praise from the Arabic poets' (cit. in Saxena 1941: 316). For Palmer, see also Arberry1960: 122–59; *LLH* 1864: 245–6.

Table 6.1

Avadh Akhbār: *Circulation, Frequency, Editors*

Year	Circulation/ Government subscriptions	Frequency	Editor
1858		weekly	Munshi Naval Kishore
1859–64		weekly	Maulvi Hadi Ali 'Ashk'
1865–6	*ca.* 400	weekly	Maulvi Fakhruddin 'Fakhr'/ Muhammad Mehdi Husain Khan
1867–9		weekly	Maulvi Raunaq Ali 'Afsos'
1870		weekly	Maulvi Ghulam Muhammad Khan 'Tapish'
1871		weekly/ bi-weekly	Maulvi Ghulam Muhammad Khan Tapish'
1872		bi-weekly	Maulvi Ghulam Muhammad Khan 'Tapish'
1873		bi-weekly	Maulvi Ghulam Muhammad Khan 'Tapish'
1874		bi-weekly	Maulvi Ghulam Muhammad Khan 'Tapish'
1875–6	600	bi-weekly/ thrice-weekly	Maulvi Ghulam Muhammad Khan 'Tapish'
1877	820/50	thrice-weekly/ daily	Maulvi Ghulam Mohammad Khan 'Tapish'
1878	719/50	daily	Maulvi Amjad Ali 'Ashhari'/Pandit Ratan Nath 'Sarshar'
1879	719/50	daily	Pandit Ratan Nath 'Sarshar'
1880	685/?	daily	
1881	715/?	daily	
1882	620/?	daily	
1883	620/90	daily	Editoral board consisting of several persons, including ʿAbdul Halim Sharar (assistant editor from 1880–2), Mirza Hairat Dehlavi, Munshi Shiv Parshad, Maulvi Ahmad Hasan 'Shaukat', Munshi Debi Parshad 'Sihr'
1884	605/94	daily	
1885	605/94	daily	
	732/94		
1886	732/90	daily	
	660/94		
1887	660/94	daily	
	595/94		
1888	595/94		
	690/94	daily	
1889	690/94		
	550/94	daily	
1890	550/94	daily	
1891	540/94	daily	
1892	540/90	daily	
1893	521/87	daily	
	503/92		
1894	503/92	daily	
	521/92		
1895	521/94	daily	

1927. In this position, he may well have contributed occasional pieces to *AA*.

While giving a preliminary overview of the rich material contained in *AA*, this chapter could only hint at some of the issues raised by the study of the most influential and widely-read Urdu newspaper in nineteenth-century colonial India. *AA* merits much closer analysis for it offers a prime example of how, under the impact of colonialism, modern informational culture took shape in the Urdu public sphere, while at the same time the forum for literature and literary discourse expanded into a new medium that was available to the general public across various regions and communities. As pointed out by M. Asaduddin, in engaging in an 'intellectual-cultural-literary encounter' between East and West, periodicals and newspapers like *AA* had a wider bearing on colonial society, in that they became 'a vibrant and contested site for negotiating the terms of colonial modernity' (Asaduddin 2001: 82). Perhaps one of the most fascinating points of investigation in this context is provided by the ongoing dialogue that *AA* kept up with its readers and subscribers. Official patronage notwithstanding, in order to not only survive but flourish in the volatile and highly competitive arena of nineteenth-century Urdu journalism, *AA* was heavily dependent on the goodwill and support of its readers. To exercise its role as a representative and mediator of public opinion, *AA* had to listen closely to their voice.

6.4 Other Journalistic Ventures

The immense success of *AA* and steadily growing demand for information among the Urdu reading public encouraged Naval Kishore to further invest in the newspaper trade. He was quick to recognize the market potential of the newspaper media which, if run on a sound commercial basis, could be turned into a profitable business. Consequently, over the years various Urdu newpapers and journals were launched from the NKP Lucknow and the firm's other printing offices. One of the first was the *Paṭiālā Akhbār,* an Urdu weekly started soon after the opening of the Patiala press in September 1871. As already noted, it was put in charge of the former editor of *AA*, Munshi Raunaq ᶜAli. By a special arrangement between Naval Kishore and the Maharaja of Patiala, the paper contained as a supplement the 'Patiala State Gazette', an official organ put under the supervision of the Patiala Council. By 1880 the circulation of the *Paṭiālā Akhbār* had gone up to 300 copies. The Patiala state subscribed to over 130 copies which were distributed to the local colleges and law courts.[53] Following the example of Patiala, in 1892 the NKP launched the weekly *Kapūrthālā Akhbār* from its Kapurthala branch. It was edited by Sayyid Hamid Husain. Its initial circulation was no more than 75 copies; 50 were taken by the Raja of Kapurthala, the remainder distributed among state officials (Barrier/Wallace 1970: 66).

In January 1895 Naval Kishore ventured into a new field of journalism with the *Oudh Review (Avadh Rīviū)*, a monthly literary magazine in Urdu. Emulating the model of the European 'review', the new periodical was devoted exclusively to cultural topics and to contemporary literature of both Indian and foreign provenance. Its express purpose was to cater to Urdu readers' increased appetite for leisure reading. The programme was spelled out in the inaugural issue: the *Oudh Review* was to include contributions on 'novels, drama, narrative, pleasantries and humour, poetry, biography, scientific and moral essays, events and news of the month, newspaper and book reviews', as well as translations of the works of 'Europe's famous and celebrated novelists'.[54] Starting off with a fairly high circulation of 500 copies, the *Oudh Review* might have turned into another successful project but for the sudden death of Naval Kishore within the first month of publication. For some months the periodical was continued by its editor Ramji Das Bhargava. In September publication was temporarily suspended but resumed after some time. The review survived until at least 1902 (Nurani 1995: 21).[55]

The aforementioned papers were all owned by Naval Kishore. In addition, he was in charge of printing and distributing a number of periodical publications run by government or private institutions. This meant a lucrative additional business for the firm. Among them was the official Urdu organ of the Oudh Educational Department, *Akhbār-e Sarrishtā-e-Taᶜlīm-e Avadh* or *Educational Department Gazette*. Its editor was Pandit Shivnarayan, the untiring secretary of the Jalsah-e Tahzib. Next to providing information on the department's activities, the journal contained news and articles on educational topics as well as short narrative pieces. It was not designed for the general reading public but for the department's staff and teachers: of its total circulation of 720 in 1869, 679 copies were distributed to the schools in the province, 30 went to the journal's contributors, and 6 to private subscribers.[56] After 1873 Naval Kishore also

[53] *LLH* 1874: 79; Barrier/Wallace 1970: 106.

[54] (My translation), cit. in Nurani 1982: 44–5.

[55] Neville in his *Gazetteer* refers to it as 'a well got up monthly magazine with a circulation of 500, owned and edited by Ramji Das, [a] relative of the founder' (Neville 1904: 87).

[56] *Oudh Education Rept.*, 1869–70, No. 402: 69.

took charge of printing the Jalsah-e Tahzib's official organ, *Risālah-e Jalsah-e Tahẕīb*, a periodical on social, educational, and political subjects.[57]

If generally a profitable sideline, in one instance the printing of an external journal turned into a major source of vexation for the publisher. In the early 1870s Naval Kishore was temporarily put in charge of publishing the journals of the Avadh *taʿalluqdār*s' British Indian Association (*Anjuman-e Hind-e Avadh*). The association maintained two weeklies, *Akhbār-e Anjuman-e Hind* (Urdu) and *Lucknow Times* (English), the latter being a successor to *Oudh Gazette*. Both journals had initially been printed at the Lucknow Times Press, owned by Maharaja Man Singh of Mehdona, vice-president of the Anjuman-e Hind. Man Singh's case provides a striking example of the financial risk involved in such amateur engagement with the print media: not only did he incur considerable financial loss in purchasing the press, he apparently spent Rs 100,000 in subsidizing the publication of *Oudh Gazette* (T. Metcalf 1979: 335). The Anjuman-e Hind had agreed to a monthly contribution of Rs 300 in support of the maintenance of the press, on the condition that the appointment and dismissal of its editors were left in its own hands.[58] Following Man Singh's death in September 1870, the Anjuman's members asked Naval Kishore to take charge of the Lucknow Times Press. In concluding the deal, the publisher agreed to carry out printing jobs for the Anjuman amounting to Rs 1000 per annum free of cost. Matters came to a pass when Naval Kishore failed to comply with his obligations. Moreover, he had allowed an article abusive of the *taʿalluqdār*s to be published in the *Lucknow Times* of 5 March 1871. The Anjuman's secretary, Mirza Abbas Beg, decided to take action against him and before long presented Naval Kishore with a bill that claimed the outstanding amount for the promised printing work (Ahmad 1937: 82–3). It is not clear what happened next, but in December of the same year the proprietorship of the Lucknow Times Press was transferred to Mirza Abbas Beg. The new proprietor promptly began to engage in private trade, having agreed to divide the profits 'in the proportion of seven annas in the rupee to Moonshee Nawal Kishore in return for the balance owing to the latter.'[59] Apparently, this share was never paid. Moreover, Mirza Abbas Beg failed to pay back a sum exceeding Rs 2000 which he owed Naval Kishore for purchasing another press and for having three numbers of the *Lucknow Times* printed

[57] *OAR*, 1873–4: 98.

[58] *Akhbār-e Anjumān-e-Hind*, August 1872, SVN 1872: 441.

[59] *Akhbār-e Anjumān-e-Hind*, August 1872, SVN 1872: 442.

at the NKP. With the money not forthcoming, Naval Kishore lodged a suit against Abbas Beg. The Anjuman-e Hind, which as before had continued to pay its monthly contribution of Rs 300 towards the maintenance of the Lucknow Times Press, was set down as a defendant; it protested in vain that it had never had any real connection with the press. While the outcome of the lawsuit is not known, the episode provides another poignant example of Naval Kishore's adamant stance in matters of finance. In this particular instance he was even willing to risk severing his close and longstanding relations with the influential Avadh *taʿalluqdār*s' association.[60]

[60] No details were available for the *Buddhi Prakāś*, a Hindi fortnightly published from the NKP from 1889 to *c.* 1898. Apparently the earliest Hindi magazine to appear in Lucknow was the monthly *Bhārat Dīpikā*, started in 1881. A newspaper called *Dinkar Prakāś* was established around 1883 but did not survive for long (Chandra 1959: 366–7).

7

Hindi Publishing in a Stronghold of Urdu

Concluding a humorously disparaging travel sketch of Lucknow in 1871—a city of filthy lanes, debauched and reactionary Hindu *raʾīs*es, effeminate men, and shrewd prostitutes—Bharatendu Harishchandra listed the localities worth visiting as 'Aminabad, Hazratganj, the traders' shops, Chauk, the printing press of Munshi Naval Kishore, and the photographer's shop of Nawab Mashkur ud Daula'.[1] It was with good reason that the House of Naval Kishore attracted the attention of the great pioneer of modern Hindi literature: at the time it was not only the largest establishment of its kind in the entire subcontinent, but also the single-most important institution in the mass production of low-priced printed books in Hindi.[2]

Epitomizing urban Indo-Muslim culture and the highly refined Persianized style of Urdu poetry, nineteenth-century Lucknow is not a place one would automatically associate with Hindi literature. If, for the contemporary Hindi literary scene flourishing in Benares and Allahabad, Lucknow occupied a somewhat peripheral position, this is even more true for modern scholars of Hindi literature, whose passing references to the city in the nineteenth century are generally confined to Insha Allah Khan and his early linguistic experiment *Rānī Ketkī kī kahānī*.[3] As a result, the NKP's contribution to Hindi publishing, and with it the preservation

[1] Harishchandra 1954: 947. The sketch was originally published in Harishchandra's journal *Kavivacansudhā* (vs 1928).

[2] For an earlier version of this chapter, see Stark 2004b.

[3] The Urdu poet Insha Allah Khan (d. 1817) was for some time associated with the court of Lucknow. Around 1803 he composed *Rānī Ketkī kī kahānī,* also known as *Kahānī ṭheṭh hindī meṁ*, a prose tale written 'in pure Hindi', i.e., an idiom which, while representing the spoken idiom of the genteel, was to contain no Persian or Arabic words. It later came to be acknowledged as one of the first works in standard Hindi.

of the Hindu literary and cultural heritage, has been largely ignored. Dhirendranath Singh was the first to highlight the full scope of this contribution in his study of the Khadgavilas Press of Bankipur: in his survey of early Hindi publishing he singled out the NKP as the only institution to publish a large and varied selection of Hindi books during the period 1858–80 (Singh 1986: 64). This chapter will explore the NKP's activities in promoting and popularizing Hindi literature, both traditional and modern, during a period that marked the early rise of Hindi in the public sphere.[4]

As discussed in Chapter 4, it was at the behest of the colonial authorities that Naval Kishore first took up Hindi printing. When, in 1860, he began to operate several letterpresses for Hindi in his shop, it was with the sole purpose of printing official forms, administrative documents, and textbooks in the 'vernacular'. The earliest extant NKP imprints in Hindi are two textbooks on village accountancy dating from 1860–1. At first, Hindi printing remained essentially confined to educational works; nearly all of the fifteen Hindi titles submitted for official registration in 1869 were for educational purposes rather than for the commercial market.[5] Educational publishing in itself reached astounding proportions: according to King's analysis of publishing patterns, almost 55,000 Hindi books were printed in Lucknow in 1868, accounting for over a quarter of the city's total book production and outnumbering Benares by 45,000 printed volumes (King 1994: 43). While indicating the sheer size of the colonial textbook venture, this remarkable figure tells us little about what was actually bought and read by the nascent Hindi readership. In order to find out about readers' tastes during this early period, one would have to turn to the hitherto largely unexplored area of the bazaar, with its output of 'cheap' tales, religious tracts and prayer books, ritual, astrological and pilgrimage manuals, almanacs, and so on. Due to the ephemeral nature of these products of early print culture, such a study poses enormous difficulties. However, as Krishnacarya's catalogue of early Hindi imprints (Krishnacarya 1966) suggests, 'respectable' publishers, too, relied heavily on the popular bazaar genres in order to stay afloat in the market.

Prior to the 1860s there was not much of a market for printed matter in Hindi beyond the aforementioned genres. Despite the fact that Nagari, including its cursive variant Kaithi, was the script most popularly used

[4] See Appendix III for a chronological list of major NKP Hindi publications.

[5] The distinction between educational and non-educational titles was, of course, rarely clear-cut. Texts such as Tulsidas's *Rāmāyaṇ* or Lalluji Lal's *Premsāgar* would figure in both categories.

(Dalmia 1997: 176), and that Hindi played an important role in primary education, it had not yet been accorded official language status. With the exception of the hill districts of Kumaon and the Saugor and Nerbudda (Narmada) Territories of the NWP, in the colonial public sphere Hindi was largely dysfunctional, since it could not provide an avenue into the highly coveted public service. As King has argued, this anomalous situation was due to the contradictions inherent in British language policy: 'The British educational system fostered a Hindi-speaking elite, served as an agent of social mobilization, and provided a stimulus to the growth of Hindi literature and the use of the Nagari script. The British administrative system, by recognizing only Urdu and the Persian (Urdu) script for official purposes, supported a group—perceived chiefly as Muslims though including many Hindus—opposed to the interests of Hindi advocates' (King 1994: 118). As a result, the use of Hindi as a print language remained largely confined to missionary and educational publishing. The situation was to change dramatically from the 1860s, when official support and a changing cultural climate combined to give a tangible boost to literary activity in Hindi. This activity was in part inspired by the protest against the neglect of Hindi and the attendant demand for its official recognition that had followed the introduction of Urdu as the court and administrative language in the NWP, Bihar, and part of the Central Provinces in 1837. By the 1860s the controversy over the court language had gained momentum, rallying supporters of Hindi and the Nagari script in a plea for greater official use of their language. The proposed scheme of instituting a vernacular university in the NWP led to a public debate on whether this 'vernacular' was to be Urdu or Hindi, further fuelling the rivalry between the two languages. In 1868 the Allahabad Institute made a declaration in favour of Hindi and the Nagari script. In the same year Shiva Prasad published his influential *Memorandum. Court Characters in the Upper Provinces of India*, in which he took up the cause of Hindi and vehemently attacked the government for forcing a 'foreign language', Urdu in Persian characters, upon the 'helpless masses'. The memorandum had strong anti-Muslim overtones; it expressly linked its plea for making Hindi the court character to the restoration of 'Hindu nationality' and revival of Sanskrit culture. Drawing on the myth of the antiquity of Hindi, the language of Hindustan before the Muslim invasion, Shiva Prasad made a case for Hindi to be the legitimate successor of Sanskrit, for it provided the common linguistic bond for the whole of North India.[6]

[6] For a more detailed analysis of the Memorandum, see King 1994: 130–1.

Such formulations helped to strengthen the notion of a separate Hindi identity. Once the Hindi agitation had found a common voice, it also began to receive official support. An important first step was made in 1872 when Hindi was granted official language status in the Central Provinces. In 1880 the Bengal Government ordered the exclusive use of the Nagari or Kaithi script in large parts of Bihar. By contrast, in the NWP&Oudh, the majority of British administrators continued to favour Urdu. Even though Hindi had found an influential supporter in M. Kempson, DPI from 1861 to 1877, it was not before 1900 that it was accorded equal status with Urdu. Its late triumph has been described as an 'inconclusive and largely symbolic victory' (King 1994: 77).[7]

Although official recognition was still some forty years away, from the 1860s Hindi was definitely on the rise. The resulting impetus to printing and publishing was not only visible in 'a dramatic upsurge of Hindi readers and manuals' (McGregor 1974: 74), but also in an increased activity in the literary marketplace. The impact on the market was both quantitative and qualitative: the thus far limited array of printed works in Hindi expanded considerably in size and scope. That the new support of Hindi was 'an aspect of the larger cultural consciousness rather than a direct product of encouragement at official level' (ibid.) is most visibly reflected in a rise in the proportion of non-educational works as compared to those devoted to educational subject matter. A NWP report of 1869 noted an 'abundance' of religious works with around twenty titles, totalling 27,000 copies. Equally important, it also acknowledged for the first time the existence of twenty-eight books of 'light reading', a substantial number. The noticeable increase in Hindi titles was attributed to 'a considerable anxiety on the part of educated Hindus in this part of India, to bring the Hindi language forward as the proper vernacular of the people.'[8]

The nascent Hindi reading public grew increasingly self-conscious in its choice of reading matter: inspired by Hindu revivalist and nationalist sentiment, Hindi readers turned to their religious as well as literary heritage. The new cultural consciousness generated a process of retrospective reflection on what constituted the Hindi literary tradition; over time it led to the first attempts at the formation of a literary canon. Publications such as Raja Lakshman Singh's model translation of Kalidasa's *Śakuntalā*

[7] For an account of government language policy, see King 1994: 53–79.

[8] *PGNWP. General Dept.*, 13 March 1869: [4].

(1863), Shiva Prasad's anthology of Hindi pieces entitled *Guṭkā* (1867), and Harishchandra's journal *Kavivacansudhā* (est. 1868), provided major impulses in a pervasive cultural process in which Hindi and its literature were gradually made into prime symbols of Hindu national identity. Vasudha Dalmia (1997) has brilliantly analyzed the evolution of Hindi as the national language of the Hindus as a threefold process involving first, the dichotomization from Urdu and concomitant assertion of the autonomy of Hindi; second, the standardization of the language by means of grammars, dictionaries, and school textbooks; and third, its historicization, that is the construction of an ancestry and unbroken literary tradition going back to the great Sanskrit past (ibid.: 148). How were these developments reflected in the Hindi publishing market? To what extent did a large commercial publisher like Naval Kishore participate in or even try to actively influence this process?

An astute entrepreneur, Naval Kishore could not but react to the new cultural consciousness and concomitant demand for greater public use of Hindi. The circumstances clearly called for an investment in Hindi publishing. Technically it was a small step, the firm being already in possession of the necessary typographic equipment and know-how to print in Nagari. Consequently, while continuing to print educational material for the British, from the mid-1860s Naval Kishore began to engage in Hindi publishing on his own account. His initial selection of titles was tempered by entrepreneurial caution and clearly reflected a market-oriented approach, limited as it was to works of assuredly high popularity. In making his choices, he looked to the chief presses of Bombay, Agra, and Benares for guidance, as is suggested by a substantial number of low-priced NKP reprints of Hindi works previously published elsewhere. Ultimately, however, Naval Kishore's publishing strategy was geared towards enhancing the market for Hindi through a combination of the tested classics and a selection of previously unpublished works. His approach was at once conservative and innovative; it firmly relied on a varied selection, low pricing, and effective marketing.

What does the NKP's early Hindi list tell us about reading tastes in the late 1860s? What genres were represented, and what kinds of books were most likely bought for religious, instructional, or recreational purposes? Readers were most interested in devotional literature in Brajbhasha and Avadhi, particularly the classics of the great medieval poets Tulsidas and Surdas. Popular prose tales of the *Baitāl paccīsī* kind and pilgrimage guides such as *Avadh yātrā* (Journey Through Avadh) and *Banyātrā*

(Forest Journey), a text describing the traditional circumambulation of Braj, were next in popularity.[9] A further bestselling category, to be discussed later, consisted of medical and astrological manuals. Finally, the NKP, like all major presses, issued its own Hindi almanac.

As the above categories indicate, the time was not yet ripe for new literary genres, which only appeared on commercial publishers' lists after *c*. 1870. The NKP's early Hindi list tallies with McGregor's observation that until the end of the 1860s there occurred little of the hoped-for literary development, with most literary publications being, as before, editions of medieval Brajbhasha verse (McGregor 1974: 74). According to the British publication report of 1865, even a place like Benares produced only a 'very small amount of publishing work': no more than sixteen Hindi and Sanskrit titles were issued from the Benares presses during the latter half of the year, out of which two were almanacs and twelve reprints. The sole new Hindi work was a commentary on Tulsidas's *Rāmāyaṇ*.[10]

Not surprisingly then, the market for non-educational Hindi books at first hardly satisfied Naval Kishore's commercial aspirations. In 1870 we find him complaining that, with the exception of Tulsidas's *Rāmāyaṇ* and Lalluji's *Premsāgar*, Hindi titles were not selling well.[11] The publisher had reason to be impatient, for by that time he had already invested in some twenty-five titles. With the Hindi reading public still in the making, it was imperative to offer incentives for people to read and, as importantly, purchase books. The most promising way to enlarge the audience for printed texts was to draw on a familiar corpus of religious classics. Whether newly edited or issued in cheap reprints, these were crucial in stimulating an interest in other genres as well. Another strategy was to rely on inexpensive mass-produced editions. In the scheme of popularizing Hindi literature, the two criteria of affordability and accessibility were paramount. At the NKP, an 'average' first print run for a non-educational Hindi title ranged from 550 to 1250 copies, while reprints could easily amount to several thousand copies. 550 copies appears to have been the lowest number to make the production of a title commercially viable. With prices generally not exceeding a few annas in the case of small tracts or booklets, and a maximum of two or three rupees for voluminous publications of several hundred pages, the NKP tried to keep Hindi

[9] *Avadh yātrā* was based on the *Padmapurāṇa* and *Skandapurāṇa*. Its compiler Munshi Rai Gursharan Lal was a pleader at the Gorakhpur court.

[10] *Home. Public Branch*. 7 June 1866, nos 18–19: 2.

[11] *RPE Oudh*, 1871: 175.

books within the reach of the average urban reader. Its 1869 typeset edition of the *Rāmcaritmānas,* for example, comprising 600 pages, was sold at Rs 3. The 1870 lithographed *Padmāvat* of 360 pages was sold at Rs 2. The bulk of publications, however, consisted of small booklets in the anna-range, that is chapbooks containing prayers, devotional verse, popular tales, etc.

In the Hindi literary marketplace, the transition from a publishing system dominated by religious literature to a system that put more emphasis on secular titles took place roughly from the 1870s onwards. Having said this, it is important to remember that the distinction between the two categories is hardly clear cut, particularly in the case of large sections of pre-nineteenth-century Hindi poetry. The NKP's expansion into the domain of secular literature after 1870 is suggestive of the larger trend. At this point, Hindi publishing entered a new phase, increasing rapidly in both size and scope. While religious and devotional titles continued to prevail on the publisher's list, the growing secularization of subjects found its reflection in the introduction of new generic categories: rhetoric poetry, drama, and prose fiction. The successive stages of the NKP's shift from the sacred to the secular are outlined in detail below.

7.1 Popularizing the Classics of Hindu Devotional Literature

It is hardly surprising that, when embarking on Hindi publishing, Naval Kishore first turned to the classics of Hindu devotional (*bhakti*) literature and, in doing so, to the most widely cherished devotional text, the great Hindi epic *Rāmcaritmānas* (Holy Lake of Ram's Deeds) by Tulsidas. Since the release of the first printed edition in *c.* 1810 from Calcutta, the *Rāmcaritmānas* or *Rāmāyaṇ Tulsīkṛt*, as it was commonly known, had remained a steady seller. Most Indian commercial publishers relied on it, as testified by more than a hundred printed editions prior to 1890 (Lutgendorf 1994b: 77). Individual chapters of the text, especially *Kiṣkiṇḍa kāṇḍ* and *Sundara kāṇḍ*, were also prescribed as school textbooks, and were hence in high demand. The NKP brought out its first *Rāmcaritmānas* in 1863, in an illustrated lithographed edition. Another edition, sponsored by the Lucknow Pandit Dindayal Tripathi, followed in 1865.[12]

[12] Although written by the same scribe Pandit Murlidhar, a Nagar Brahmin, the two lithographed editions of 1863 and 1865–6 are distinct from one another. A copy of the earlier NKP *Rāmāyaṇa* preserved in the OIOC gives no date on its title page, but bears a stamp of the British Museum dated 8 February 1866. Given the time it took

At this early stage, private literary patronage still played a significant role in financing Hindi publications. Another famous devotional classic, the collection of poetry ascribed to Surdas and known as *Sūrsāgar* (Ocean of Sur, *1864), was printed at the instance, and with the support, of Maharaja Mansingh of Ayodhya, whose role as a literary patron has already been mentioned. By that time the corpus of compositions attributed to Surdas had grown into a large oeuvre of over 2000 poems (Hawley 1984:37). While parts of *Sūrsāgar* had earlier appeared in *Rāg sāgarudbhav rāg kalpadrum* (1843), it was the NKP compilation, prepared by Pandit Kalicaran and Munshi Jamunaprasad, which came to be regarded as the first 'standard' edition of the collected verse of Surdas (Fig. 14).[13] To make it affordable for the general reader, the typeset edition of 770 pages was divided up into eight individually sold parts.[14] In this format, *Sūrsāgar* was well received and by 1882 had gone through five editions.

The NKP's early focus on Tulsidas and Surdas was one of the first attempts by a commercial publisher to provide Hindi readers with the collected works of the great icons of medieval Vaishnava bhakti. The publication of the *Rāmāyaṇ* was followed by further works of Tulsidas, including (1) *Dohāvalī* (*1864), (2) *Hanumān bāhuk* (*1868), (3) *Gītāvalī* (*1870), (4) *Kavitāvalī rāmāyaṇ* (also called *Kavitt rāmāyaṇ*, *1874), and (5) *Vinayapatrikā* (*1876) with the commentary '*Rāmtattvabodhinī*' by Shivprasad Simha. *Sūrsāgar* was supplemented by some of Surdas's minor and hitherto unprinted verse collections: *Cīrharaṇ* (*1868), *Bāṃsurī līlā* (*1868) and *Bisātin līlā* (*1869).

Initially the NKP's corpus of bhakti titles was rather limited in scope. Next to the aforementioned works by Tulsidas and Surdas it included only three additional titles. The first, *Sukhsāgar* (Ocean of Bliss, *1866), Makkhanlal's Hindi prose version of the *Bhāgavatapurāṇa,* has already been discussed in Chapter 5. The second was *Brajvilās* (Enjoyment of Braj, *1866), an eighteenth-century Brajbhasha composition by the Vallabhan poet Brajvasidas (b. 1733), which was explicitly intended as a digest of the *Sūrsāgar*, conveying the life of Krishna 'in a single,

books from India to reach the British Museum, 1863 seems a plausible date of publication.

[13] Krishnacarya lists two earlier editions of *Sūrsāgar*, albeit without any reference to size and content, issued from the Ilahi Press in Delhi and the Mumbai ul-ʿulum Press in Mathura in 1860 (Krishnacarya 1966: 145).

[14] Notably, (1) *Sūrsāgar sarāvalī*, (2) *Rāgkalpadrum nityakīrtan*, (3) *Rāgsāgarodbhav*, (4) and (5) *Rāgkalpadrum* (*Dānlīlā*, *Anurāglīlā*, *Rāslīlā*, *Mānlīlā*), (6) *Prabhujī ko mahātmya*, *Vinayapatrikā*, (7) *Mathurālīlā* and (8) *Bhramargīt*.

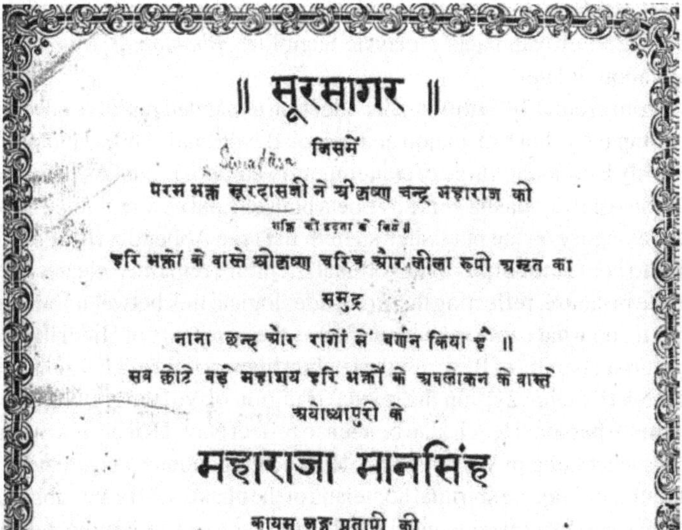
॥ सूरसागर ॥
जिसमें
परम भक्त सूरदासजी ने श्रीकृष्ण चन्द्र महाराज की
भक्ति की दृढ़ता में किये॥
हरि भक्तों के वास्ते श्रीकृष्ण चरित्र और लीला रूपी अमृत का
समुद्र
नाना छन्द और रागों में वर्णन किया है ॥
सब छोटे बड़े महाशय हरि भक्तों के अवलोकन के वास्ते
अयोध्यापुरी के
महाराजा मानसिंह
कायम जङ्ग प्रतापी की
अनुमति से
मुंशी नवलकिशोर ने अपने यंत्रालय में बहुत स्पष्ट शीसे के अक्षरों में
मुंशी जमुनाप्रसाद को संयुक्त करके
पण्डित कालीचरण से अत्यन्त शुद्ध करवाके छपवाया ॥
स्थान
लखनऊ
सन् १८६४ ईसवी व सम्वत् १९२० विक्रमादित्य ।

Fig. 14: Title page of *Sūrsāgar* (1864)

connected narrative rather than so many parts' (Hawley 1984: 58). With its lucid style and popular subject matter, *Brajvilās* already enjoyed the status of a pre-print classic when it was first issued from Lalluji Lal's Sanskrit Press in 1817. The NKP edition was one of several subsequent reprints.[15] The third work, *Bhaktakalpadrum* or *Bhaktamāl* (Garland of Devotees, *1870) by Raja Pratap Singh of Sidhua, was not an original

[15] E.g., Agra 1862; Calcutta 1863.

Hindi text but a prose translation of a popular nineteenth-century Urdu adaptation of Nabhadas's classic hagiology *Bhaktamāl*. More will be said about it later.

From around 1870 this small collection expanded rapidly and came to encompass a host of major and minor devotional works, including a steadily increasing surge of contemporary compositions. As before, collections of Brajbhasha verse by poets both old and new remained a dominant category on the publisher's Hindi list (see Appendix III). For some time to come the corpus of devotional literature remained clearly Vaishnavite in nature, reflecting the strong ideological link between Vaishnava bhakti and what came to be identified as the core texts of Hindi literature by Harishchandra of Benares, the leading literary figure of his generation. The NKP's emphasis on the textual tradition of Vaishnava bhakti may, at a more personal level, also be seen to reflect Naval Kishore's own religious grounding in Vaishnavism. His ancestral home was situated near Mathura in Braj, the spiritual homeland of the bhakti sect of Vallabhacarya (1479–1531). While it would be going too far to make inferences on the publisher's sectarian affiliation, it is interesting to note that, with titles such as *Sūrsagar* and *Brajvilās,* his early selection of devotional works shows a certain predilection for poets associated with the Vallabha *sampradāya*. Indeed, the NKP was to assume a leading role in the dissemination of the key texts of the Vallabha *sampradāya* in the 1880s, when it issued a series of reprints of the sect's most important prose works. These hagiographical *vārtā*s (sectarian accounts) had first been printed in the late 1860s at the Vyaghrapad Press at Beswan (Aligarh district), a small amateur enterprise owned by Thakur Giriprasad Varma.[16] Issued in 1883–4, the NKP reprints included (1) *Caurāsī* [*vaiṣṇavan kī*] *bārttā* (Account of Eighty-four Vaishnavas), the oldest and most popular work within the sect's hagiographical literature; (2) *Vacanāmṛt* (Nectar of Speech), a text ascribed to Gokulnath which holds significance as one of the oldest extended prose texts in Brajbhasha; (3) *Vallabhākhyān* (Account of Vallabha), a seventeenth-century Gujarati text by Gopaldas;

[16] Varma was an enthusiastic champion of the orthodox Hindu tradition. As a British report noted: 'This gentleman has established a press in his village, and busies himself with the publications of editions and Bhasha versions of Sanskrit works. His object is the revival of the old Hindoo religion in its integrity, as he is impressed with the idea of the vicisnouess [sic] and unreality of modern Hindooism, or the creed of the Purans as opposed to that of the Vedas' (*PGNWP. General Dept.*, 19 March 1870: 42).

and (4) *Śrī Govardhannāth kī prākaṭya vārtā* (Account of the Revelation of Shri Govardhannath).[17] While being NKP publications, all four texts were printed at the Mumbai ul-Ulum Press in Mathura, run by Naval Kishore's caste-fellow Kanhaiyalal Bhargava. The NKP also promoted the works of a contemporary Vallabhan poet by the name of Govardhandas Dhusar who, as his name indicates, was another caste-fellow. His compositions *Dohāvalī—do sau bāvan kī nāmāvalī* ([2]1884), *Brajvilās sārāvalī* (*1884) and *Mohanmālā—caurāsī kī nāmāvalī* (?1884) appear to be minor reworkings of the classic *vārtās*, for neither they nor their author find mention in the standard reference works on Hindi literature. While the *vārtās* had long enjoyed canonical status within the Vallabha *sampradāya*, the NKP's mass-produced reprints served to introduce them into the wider Hindi literary market. It is significant that this happened shortly after Bharatendu Harishchandra had begun his efforts to reformulate Vaishnavism and re-establish the Vallabha *sampradāya* in Benares. In his *Uttarārdha-bhaktamāl* (Later-day *Bhaktamāl*), a poem published in *Hariścandracandrikā* in 1876, Bharatendu had drawn heavily on the *Caurāsī Vaiṣṇavan kī vārtā*, highlighting its importance to contemporary readers as a key text of the Vaishnava tradition. Later, in his influential essay '*Vaiṣṇavatā aur bhāratvarṣ*' (Vaishnavism and India, 1884), he propounded a historically coherent and all-inclusive Vaishnavism which he placed at the core of a new Hinduism of national dimensions.[18] The timing of the NKP's editions of major Vallabhan sectarian texts is too obvious not to suggest a connection with this ongoing discourse.

A second sectarian trend mirrored in NKP Hindi religious and devotional literature after 1870 was the proliferation of works originating within the *Rāmrasik* community. The term *rasik* (one who savours *ras*, literally 'juice, essence, flavour') refers to a group of poets devoted to Ram and the twin deity Sita-Ram that emerged in the late sixteenth century. Influenced by Krishnaite theology, they cultivated a devotional attitude in which they identified themselves with the *sakhīs* or female consorts of Sita.[19] The *rasiks* had their roots in Rajasthan, from where they migrated to the most famous sites of Ram bhakti, the pilgrimage

[17] For the relevance and publishing history of these texts, see Tandan 1960 and Barz 1994.

[18] For a discussion of both texts, see Dalmia-Lüderitz 1992.

[19] Further details in Simha 1957; McGregor 1984: 167–71. Lutgendorf 1994a: 310–21.

centre of Chitrakut in Central India and the city of Ayodhya. Here, the community flourished. The body of poetic and poetological works produced by these connoisseur poets generally shows a high degree of accomplishment and poetic skill; in it, poetological and ritual concerns are deeply intertwined. Prominent works include Janaki Prasad's *Rāmnivās-Rāmāyaṇ* (*1889), a reworking of the *Rāmāyaṇ* from a Ramrasik perspective, and *Nṛtyarāghav* (*1892) by Ramsakhe, a native of Jaipur who flourished in the early eighteenth century. These and several other *Rāmrasik* works commercially produced by the NKP point to existing processes of canon formation within the community, while also underscoring the readiness of its leading intellectuals to engage with the new medium of print. Moreover, they suggest a strong connection between the Lucknow publisher and the nearby town of Ayodhya, one of the community's main centres. Ayodhya was home to the reputed *rasik* theologian Yugalananya Sharan 'Hemlata' (1818–76), a prolific author of seventy-four works. Following Yugalananya's death, Naval Kishore acquired the manuscript of his *Pārasbhāg* (*1883), a reworking of al-Ghazali's *Kīmiyā-e saᶜādat* which was allegedly retrieved 'with great effort' and the help of Yugalananya's successor Janaki Var Sharan from the late scholar's private library.[20] The library also seems to have yielded a rare manuscript of the earliest known Hindi commentary on Tulsidas's *Rāmcaritmānas*, composed in 1805 by the Ramanandi sadhu Mahant Ramcharandas (*c.* 1760–1835), another key figure in Ayodhya's flourishing *rasik* community. Naval Kishore acquired the copyright and first published it in 1882.[21] A further prominent *Rāmrasik* exponent on the NKP list was the Raja of Rewa, Vishvanath Singh (1789–1854), a descendant of a line of local rulers famous for their patronage of the arts. Vishvanathsingh was a prolific poet credited with thirty-eight works, and the author of an influential sectarian commentary on Kabir's *Bījak*. We will return to the commentaries of Ramcharandas and Vishvanathsingh later.

Next to a host of works representative of personal devotion to Ram and Krishna, the NKP also invested in a small number of works reflecting the heterodox *sant* tradition. With the publication of *Jñansvarodaya* (Ascent of the Sun of Knowledge, *1874) and, later, *Bhaktisāgar* (Ocean of Devotion, *1895), it was the first to widely publicize the principal works of the eighteenth-century Rajasthani *sant* poet and founder of a sectarian tradition Charandas (1703–82). It was perhaps no coincidence that Naval Kishore chose to put his teachings into print, Charandas

[20] Publisher's notice inserted in Mangaldas, *Jñantaraṅg* (*1889).

[21] QLP, NWP&Oudh, 2nd quarter 1883.

being a Dhusar by caste. To promote his writings meant paying tribute to an illustrious caste member and fostering the sense of a distinct literary tradition within the Dhusar-Bhargava community. Another *sant* poet to be published was Sundardas (1596–1689), a prominent disciple of the Rajasthani sectarian leader Dadu. The 1882 NKP edition of *Sundarvilās* (Pleasure of Sundar, also known as *Sundarkṛt savaiyā)* was the first instance of Sundar's principal verse collection appearing in print. In being 'for the most part corrupt and questionable' (Sharma vs 1993: 17), it reflected an early stage in the accomplished poet's canonization in print.[22]

Expositions and Commentaries

Popularizing the classics of Hindi literature also meant expounding them. Print culture had brought with it the transition gradual from practices of collective oral exposition to silent individual reading, entailing the need for a new type of textual explanation. This was particularly evident in the case of religious texts, which traditionally relied on oral exposition in the form of public readings (*kathā*). Whereas such oral practices centred on the Brahmin priest or learned pandit as the sole exegete of the text, in a private reading situation this interpretive function had to be assumed by the text itself. What was needed were commentaries that would facilitate contemporary readers' understanding of the classics with regard to both their archaic and dialectal language and their subject matter.

Once the NKP had published the classic works of medieval and later Hindi poets, it embarked on the second step in the popularization venture and, in the mid-1870s, launched a series of editions with commentaries. Catering for varied audiences of religious specialists on the one hand, and lay readers on the other, some of these editions included learned commentaries by scholars of authoritative standing while others gave popular expositions or paraphrases in simple Hindi prose. The firm's attempt to appeal to scholarly and lay readers alike is evident in its substantial contribution to the tradition of expounding the *Rāmcaritmānas*.[23] Starting with the publication of *Mānashaṃs bhūṣaṇ* (*1866), a hitherto unprinted commentary by Shukdevlal of Mainpuri, the NKP engaged in a sustained effort to expound the cherished Hindi epic to readers of different intellectual, social, and geographical backgrounds.

[22] For further details on these two sant poets, see Caturvedi vs 2021: 509–11; 718–24. For Sundardas, see also Thiel-Horstmann 1983: 13–18.

[23] For the textual tradition of commentaries, see Krishnacarya 1989.

By 1873 the NKP had turned out over 50,000 copies of the *Rāmāyaṇ*. The pride of the publishing house was its large-letter edition, designed specifically for juvenile and aged readers; nothing like it 'had ever been produced by any press in Hindustan'. Another edition, *Rāmāyaṇ saṭīk*, contained an introduction and commentary by Raghunath Das, one of the foremost contemporary exegetes.[24] The volume introduced significant new features, such as a sixty-page glossary of difficult words, later published separately as *Rāmāyaṇśabdārthkoś* (*1875). Changes had also been made in the textual arrangement: for the first time the different stanzas were clearly separated from each other. While the edition may not measure up to modern standards of critical editing, the great editorial effort that went into it is obvious. According to the publisher's notice, in revising the text the NKP's pandits had consulted a large number of manuscripts in order to eliminate the 'thousands of inaccuracies' contained in earlier editions.[25] A second *Rāmāyaṇ saṭīk* of 1873 contained a different glossary, as well as a section entitled '*Itihās*' which provided explanations on mythology and was also published separately. Frequently reprinted, these NKP editions exemplify a general trend in the publishing history of the epic. As Lutgendorf has shown, the many line-to-line prose glosses, glossaries, and other explanatory features that came to form a standard part of *Rāmcaritmānas* editions after 1870 were designed to serve the needs of 'a literate but geographically and culturally heterogeneous audience which increasingly expected editions to supply them with an interpretive framework with which better to understand the epic' (Lutgendorf 1994a: 78). Naval Kishore was acutely aware of the growing demand for such interpretive tools. Therefore, he did not stop at the various *Mānas* editions, but, in the 1870s, invested in an entire series of modern prose expositions on Tulsidas. The ambitious project was put into the hands of Pandit Baijnath Kurmi, a Nagar Brahmin belonging to Barabanki district. The pandit was a literary connoisseur whose interpretation of Tulsidas relied heavily on poetical and aesthetic theory.[26] Published between 1878 and 1892, the NKP series came to include commentaries on thirteen different works of Tulsidas.[27] The example of Baijnath shows how widely circulated editions like those produced by Naval Kishore could greatly enhance the reputation of individual exegetes and

[24] Raghunath Das's commentary was first published from Benares in 1835.

[25] *Rāmāyaṇ saṭīk* (Lucknow *1873), *vijñapanpatra*.

[26] Lutgendorf 1994a: 158 and 1994b: 68–70.

[27] I.e. (1) *Gītāvalī saṭīk*, with the commentary *Maṇidīpikā*; (2) *Kavitāvalī saṭīk* with the commentary *Ratnadīpikā*; (3) *Tulsī satsaī saṭīk*; (4) *Rāmāyaṇ tulsīkṛt saṭīk* with the commentary *Rāmcaritmānas-bhūṣan*; (5) *Vinayapatrikā saṭīk*; (6) *Barvai rāmāyaṇ*

the influence of their interpretations (Lutgendorf 1994a: 61). Baijnath's commentaries, especially his '*Rāmcaritmānas-bhūṣaṇ*' (*1884), were to accord him a prominent place among contemporary exegetes of Tulsidas. They also attracted the attention of the eminent British linguist G.A. Grierson, who judged them to be among the best available expositions on Tulsidas (Grierson 1889: 46–7). Baijnath subsequently assisted Grierson and the Khadgavilas Press in preparing the first 'critical edition' of the Hindi epic in 1889.

Meanwhile, following the publication of F.S. Growse's highly acclaimed English translation of the *Rāmcaritmānas* in 1880, the NKP made another important contribution to the exegetic history of the text when, in 1882, it issued the first printed edition of '*Rāmānand Lahirī*', the earliest known complete Hindi commentary. It was composed by Mahant Ramcharandas of Ayodhya around 1805. Born in a Brahmin family of Pratapgarh, Ramcharandas had renounced the world and settled in Ayodhya, where he rose to a position of eminence as leader (*mahant*) of his own religious establishment. His daily public lectures (*kathā*) on the *Mānas* were famous and well attended. Resulting from them, '*Rāmānand Lahirī*' was committed to writing over a period of twelve years, with the assistance of a team of twelve pandits. The commentary distinguished itself in its claim to be based on an autograph manuscript by Tulsidas (Lutgendorf 1994a: 140–1). It was issued in seven volumes as *Rāmāyaṇ Tulsīdās kṛt saṭīk* (*1882) in a high print run of 1200 copies, and sold at Rs 7. 'One of the most highly esteemed commentaries' (Grierson 1889: 46), it not only held importance in scholarly circles, but also appealed to a wider readership. The publisher's notice extolled the author's lucid style, advertising the commentary as 'so easily intelligible that even those of little knowledge will understand the full purport of the *Rāmāyaṇ*'. The second edition of 1888 was exhausted within a year. A third edition, issued in both hardcover and paperback form, followed in 1890. If the most highly acclaimed, it did not remain the last commentary on the *Mānas* issued from the NKP, but was followed by '*Mānasdīpikā*' of Ishvar Mishra ([2]1894, Fig. 15).

In responding to a contemporary 'concern with textual authenticity and textual purity' (Lutgendorf 1994a: 77–9), the NKP's various annotated editions and commentaries of the *Rāmcaritmānas* corroborate

---

saṭīk; (7) *Chandāvalī rāmāyaṇ saṭīk*; (8) *Jānakīmaṅgal saṭīk;* (9) *Chappaya rāmāyaṇ saṭīk*; (10) *Kuṇḍaliyārāmāyaṇ saṭīk*; (11) *Vairāgya sandīpanī saṭīk*; (12) *Rāmājñā praśnāvalī saṭīk*; (13) *Hanumān bāhuk saṭīk*. Baijnath Kurmi's poetical and devotional works include *Ṣadṛtuvarṇan* (1887) and *Śrīrāmnāmkalāmaṇi kośmañjuṣā* (1894).

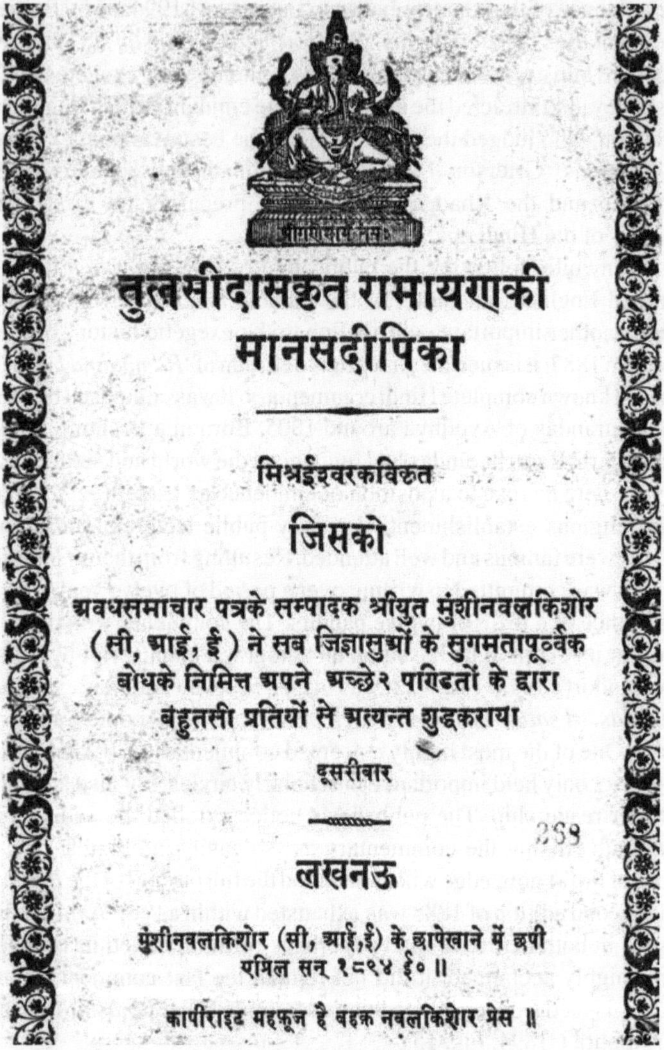

तुलसीदासकृत रामायणकी
मानसदीपिका

मिश्रईश्वरकविकृत

जिसको

अवधसमाचार पत्रके सम्पादक श्रीयुत मुंशीनवलकिशोर
(सी, आई, ई) ने सब जिज्ञासुओं के सुगमतापूर्वक
बोधके निमित्त अपने अच्छे२ पण्डितों के द्वारा
बहुतसी प्रतियों से अत्यन्त शुद्धकराया

दूसरीवार

लखनऊ

मुंशीनवलकिशोर (सी, आई,ई) के छापेखाने में छपी
एप्रिल सन् १८९४ ई० ॥

कापीराइट महफूज है बहक नवलकिशोर प्रेस ॥

Fig. 15: Title page of *Mānasdīpikā* (²1894)

Lutgendorf's argument that indigenous critical engagement preceded and paralleled British Indological interest in the epic, rather than just being a reaction to it. Mass-produced editions were crucial to the indigenous debate on written sources and historic authenticity in that for the first time they made identical textual sources available to a large audience of scholars and laymen dispersed over different geographical regions.

Though they held the most prominent place, the works of Tulsidas formed part only of a wider ensemble of devotional classics that were issued with commentaries, testifying to a demand for interpretation and a growing interest in questions of literary history among Hindi readers. Two titles deserve special mention: the first is the *Bījak* of Kabir, the first authoritative collection of the foremost among medieval North Indian *sant* poets. The *Bijāk* was first issued in 1868 from Pandit Gopinath Pathak's Benares Light Press in a lithographed edition that contained the sectarian commentary by Raja Vishvanath Singh of Rewa. Naval Kishore acquired the copyright of the text and reprinted it in 1883. The NKP typeset edition of 1200 copies much enhanced the circulation of the text, adding to the acceptance of the 'Raja of Rewa edition' as a standard commentary.

The second text was *Bhaktamāl saṭīk* (*1883), an edition of the classic hagiology by Nabhadas with the standard commentary '*Bhaktirasbodhinī*' by Priyadas. Composed in *c.* 1600, Nabhadas's *Bhaktamāl* (Garland of Devotees) was the most widely renowned among hagiographic collections that gave an inventory of Vaishnava poet-saints and devotees. Priyadas's commentary of 1712, as William Pinch has pointed out, was almost always included as a running gloss in manuscript or printed editions, since it added substantial new and interesting hagiographical detail (Pinch 1999: 372).[28] Why would Naval Kishore wait until 1883 to bring out a text of such standing and importance? The answer to this question may lie in the fact that he had already successfully invested in two contemporary adaptations of *Bhaktamāl.* Both were extremely popular and commanded high sales: the first was an Urdu prose version entitled *Bhagat māl* (*1871), composed in 1854 by Tulsiram, a notable Ramanandi scholar of Ambala, who had left his position of *sarrishtedār* at the Delhi Commissionary to settle in Vrindaban. Interestingly, he passed on his interest in *Bhaktamāl* to his nephew Sitaramsharan Bhagvan Prasad, who was to produce the most authoritative commentary of the text, *Śri Bhaktamāl: Tikā, tilak aur nāmāvalī sahit* (Benares 1903–9), in the early twentieth century. Tulsiram's own Urdu rendering had first been printed at the Lahore Koh-e Nur Press in 1854. For the NKP edition of 1871, this first edition was revised, enlarged, and supplemented by a gloss of difficult

[28] An early edition of the *Bhaktamāl* with Priyadas's commentary and an anonymous commentary in modern Hindi was issued from Benares in 1866, another from Bombay in 1876.

words and names in both Nagari and Urdu script. In this new format it was quickly sold out. A second edition followed in 1873. By 1880 the text had been reprinted four times, reflecting the wide interest in Vaishnava hagiology among Urdu-reading Hindus.[29]

Meanwhile, Naval Kishore had also launched *Bhaktakalpadrum* (Wishing Tree of Devotees, also called *Bhaktamāl*, *1870), a Hindi version of Tulsiram's text by Raja Pratap Singh of Sidhua (North Bihar). Pratap Singh's version was originally in Brajbhasha. Prior to publication it had been revised by Pandit Kalicaran, who ended up recreating it in modern standard Hindi. Thus re-fashioned, the Hindi *Bhaktakalpadrum* sold as well as its Urdu counterpart and was frequently reprinted. Much later, when Grierson first introduced *Bhaktamāl* to an English-speaking audience in the 1909 and 1910 issues of the *Journal of the Royal Asiatic Society,* he consulted the NKP edition of *Bhaktakalpadrum.* He judged it 'a useful and convenient work' which, however, had to be used with caution, since 'the original Persian [i.e. Urdu] had not always been read correctly by the author' (Grierson 1909: 608).

7.2 Expanding the Horizons of Poetry

From the mid-1870s a new trend can be perceived in the Lucknow publisher's list of Hindi books: in addition to devotional literature, the court poetry of the late sixteenth, seventeenth, and eighteenth centuries began to be promoted on a large scale. This period, classified by later literary historiography as *rīti kāl* or *rīti* era (*rīti* = method, style), distinguished itself by a proliferation of poetry that is often described by the unfortunate English term 'mannerist'. What it seeks to denote is a more 'secular-oriented' poetry, produced in a court milieu and with the patronage of nobles or kings, which often dealt with erotic (*śṛṅgār*) themes, focused on style and figures of speech and, in addition to the traditional *dohā*, comprised more elaborate metres of *kavitta*, *savaiyā*, etc. The *rīti kāl* was also a period of intense poetological reflection and formulation of poetic theory by scholastic poets, demonstrated by a substantial output of specialized treatises on poetics and rhetoric. The new interest in *rīti* poetry on the part of the commercial publisher indicates a broadening of literary taste among the Hindi readership. If the number of connoisseur readers with interests in secular topics was on the rise, it must be stressed again that

[29] While Tulsiram's was perhaps not the first Urdu version of Nabhadas's hagiology, it was the only one to be widely publicized in print. Earlier Persian renderings include those by Lalla Lalji Das (*c.* 1771) and Lala Gumani Lal (*c.* 1841).

there was no clear-cut division between the devotional and the secular, as the conventional distinction between the bhakti and *rīti* periods adopted by later Hindi literary historiography would suggest.[30] For all its concern with rhetoric and aesthetic formalism, with wordplay and coded language, with the display of poetic virtuosity in the taxonomy of heroes and heroines (*nāyak nāyikā bhed*) and the minute description of their physical attributes, large parts of *rīti* poetry remained imbued with a spiritual message and a deeply devotional attitude.

The NKP's shift of attention towards the *rīti* period can be dated quite precisely to the years 1874–5, which saw the simultaneous publication of several important poetological and rhetorical works. Besides *Rasrāj*, a collection of some 430 verses on a *śṛṅgār* topic by the seventeenth-century poet Matiram Tripathi, the firm issued *Kavikulkalpataru*, a treatise on poetics composed in 1650 by Cintamani Tripathi; *Citracandrikā*, of work on rhetoric by Kashiraj of uncertain date; and *Chandorṇav piṅgal*, a treatise on metrics composed by the Brajbhasha poet Bhikharidas in 1742, said to form 'the most extensive exposition of this subject hitherto made in the vernacular' (McGregor 1984: 189). It also published two popular *rīti* poets who flourished in the nineteenth century, namely Gval Kavi, and Padmakar Bhatt—a poet of Banda who worked for the Rajas of Jaipur and other illustrious patrons. Gval Kavi's *Yamunālahrī* (Wave of the Yamuna), a poem composed in 1861, was a rhetorical reworking of a devotional theme; Padmakar Bhatt's *Gangālahrī* (Wave of the Ganga) and *Jagadvinod* (Pleasure of the World) dealt with *ras* and *nāyikā bhed.* An edition of Bihari's celebrated *Satsaī* (Seven Hundred Verses) followed in 1876. Why Naval Kishore delayed publication of the works of Keshavdas, the great poet of Orccha and foremost exponent of the *rīti* tradition, for several more years is difficult to say. Presumably he was still looking for suitable commentaries to facilitate comprehension of Keshav's technically brilliant but difficult scholastic verse. When *Rasikpriyā* (Companion to Love, *1880), *Rāmcandrikā* (Moonlight of Ram, *1882) and *Kavipriyā* (Companion to Rhetoric, *1886) finally came out in the 1880s, they were supplemented by the commentaries of Sardar Kavi, a prolific poet attached to the Benares court who flourished

[30] Recent scholarship has challenged the validity of the bhakti-*rīti* dichotomy as a chronological development where a period of 'devotional' literature is said to have given way to a 'secular' one. Allison Busch gives an excellent discussion of the issue (Busch 2006). Instead of being used as period markers, she argues, these terms can be applied more meaningfully to specify distinct contexts of production, performance, and audience.

in *c*. 1850–1880. The NKP promoted several other of Sardar Kavi's works, including his commentary on *Dṛṣṭikūṭ* (*1890), a collection of enigmatic couplets ascribed to Surdas, and *Śṛṅgār saṅgrah* (Collection of Erotic Verse, *1888), an anthology of rhetoric poetry compiled in 1848 (discussed later).

The NKP's new focus on *rīti* poetry was not an isolated phenomenon. Before long, Ramkrishna Varma, the proprietor of the reputed Bharat Jivan Press of Benares, issued a widely acknowledged series of fine large-letter editions of *rīti* poets.[31] Other editions by both literary and commercial publishers followed, pointing to the place attained by *rīti* poets in the emerging literary canon of Hindi. Large editions of up to 2400 copies and multiple reprints of *rīti* poetry and poetic theory further indicate a new market demand for poetry of an aesthetic rather than purely devotional kind.[32] By the late 1870s the expanding readership and changing literary taste had created a situation in which religious lyrics were no longer the only commercially viable poetic genre.

Another NKP title of the 1870s is suggestive of the publisher's role in canon formation. In 1874 the NKP brought out a joint edition of *Padmāvatīkhaṇḍ Ālhākhaṇḍ*, two popular folk epics on the life of the great North Indian Hindu king Prithviraj Cauhan. *Padmāvatīkhaṇḍ* celebrates the marriage of Prithviraj with Padmavati, while *Ālhākhaṇḍ* describes the feats of the two warrior heroes Alha and Udal. As orally transmitted folk epics, both texts existed in many different recensions, some of them showing a distinct literary influence. In their subject matter they were closely related to the famous heroic epic *Pṛthvīrāj rāsau* (12th century) by the court bard Chand. That the publishing history of *Padmāvatīkhaṇḍ Ālhākhaṇḍ* should run parallel to that of the *Pṛthvīrāj rāsau* provides an interesting example of how Orientalist and indigenous efforts combined in elevating the epic of *Pṛthvīrāj* to its present canonical status as the first substantial work of Hindi literature. The first step towards the canonization of *Pṛthvīrāj rāsau* was taken by James Tod in his *Annals and Antiquities of Rajasthan* (1829); his appraisal of the *rāsau*

[31] Ramkrishna Varma (1859–1906), a Khatri of humble origin, established the Bharat Jivan Press in 1884 with a second hand-press bought from Calcutta. Patronized by Harishchandra and other local literati, he rose to become one of the leading publishers in Benares. Almost half of the titles published from his press were collections of Brajbhasha poems and songs (Singh 1986: 79–80; Orsini 2004: 119).

[32] The first edition of Keshav's *Rāmcandrikā saṭīk* (*1882), for example, commanded a print run of 1200 copies, the third edition of Motiram's *Rasrāj* (1883) one of 2400 copies.

as a key text of Rajput, and by extension Hindu, valour would later assume great significance in Hindu nationalism. It is important to note that at the time there existed no printed edition of the *rāsau*, while manuscripts, as Garcin de Tassy tells us, were 'very rare and very costly' (*HLHH* I: 385). After Tod, the first to highlight the importance of the epic was F.S. Growse, who published a report and translated an excerpt of it in the *Journal of the Royal Asiatic Society of Bengal* in 1868, urging for a translation of the entire text. Growse only had two manuscripts at his disposal, one from the Agra College Library, the other from the library of the Maharaja of Benares. 'Copies of the poem are exceedingly scarce, and not two seem to agree', he noted (Growse 1868: 119). Applauding the plan of a translation, Garcin de Tassy expressed his philological interest in the text, extolling it as 'a work of inestimable value, not only for history but also for philology because of the particularities of the Hindi dialect in which it is written' (*LLH* 1868: 430–1). Meanwhile, the Asiatic Society had assigned the task of preparing an edition of the complete *Rāsau* to John Beames. Working from different manuscripts, Growse and Beames soon became embroiled in a fierce controversy over translation issues in the pages of the *Journal of the Asiatic Society of Bengal*. Because of the dearth of manuscripts and the linguistic difficulties of the text, Growse was convinced that many years would elapse before a satisfactory edition could be prepared (Growse 1869).

Meanwhile, the headmaster of Agra College, Keshavprasad Dvivedi, who was almost certainly aware of these efforts, prepared an edition of *Padmāvatīkhaṇḍ Ālhākhaṇḍ* on his own account. It was first issued in 500 copies from the local Vidyaratnakar Press in 1871. In his editorial notice Dvivedi pointed out that due to the extreme rarity of manuscript copies the text had not been printed before, and that is was only following a prolonged search that he had managed to procure a copy from Jodhpur, which he then subjected to a thorough linguistic revision. Because of the high expense and editorial labour involved in the publication, he also had the copyright registered in his name.

Back in Calcutta, the Asiatic Society brought out the first fascicle of Beames's edition of *Pṛthvīrāj rāsau* in 1873. This presumably prompted Naval Kishore's interest in the text—as we have seen, he kept a close watch on the Society's publications. Since no manuscript of Chand's epic was available to him, he settled for *Padmāvatīkhaṇḍ Ālhākhaṇḍ*. He must have bought the copyright from Keshavprasad Dvivedi, for the 1874 NKP edition is identical to the 1871 Agra edition. What is surprising, and perhaps an indication of official patronage, is the high NKP print run of 3375 copies. Frequently reprinted, *Padmāvatīkhaṇḍ Ālhākhaṇḍ* remained the most widely consumed among early printed versions of the Prithviraj epic until 1904, when the Nagari Pracharini Sabha published its critical edition of Chand's *Rāsau*.

For Naval Kishore it was only a small step from the promotion of Hindi literary classics to the classical works of Sanskrit literature. In view of the growing demand for Hindi, popularizing the Sanskrit scriptures in vernacular versions clearly seemed a good business proposition. For reasons of the inner logic of this book, the NKP's promotion of Sanskrit texts in Hindi and Urdu translation has already been outlined in Chapter 5. It is important to note that this initiative was not limited to religious literature, but formed part of a wider effort to acquaint modern readers with the Sanskrit scholastic tradition. The publisher's interest in ancient knowledge extended to the textual tradition of two venerated systems of Hindu science which continued to be of practical use in the modern colonial world: Ayurvedic medicine and Hindu astrology.

7.3 Commercializing Hindu Science

Medical Tracts and Manuals

The nascent Hindi readership not only consumed works of poetry and fiction but also a wide range of non-literary texts. A well-selling category of texts that featured continuously on the NKP's list was medical works. Naval Kishore's project of popularizing the principal works of indigenous medicine in their original and in modern translation was not limited to Unani texts in Arabic and Persian, but also included several classics of Ayurveda. The NKP produced an estimated thirty-nine Ayurvedic titles, fifteen of them in Sanskrit and twenty-four in Hindi (Siddiqi 1981: 15). Incorporating most of the standard works of ancient Hindu medicine, this body of texts attests as much to the practical needs of professionals as to a general revival of public interest in Ayurveda. At the same time, it formed part of the contestation of the hegemonic claims of Western medicine by indigenous medical practitioners and scholars. Medicine, David Arnold argues, represented 'the most practical, and therefore most contentious, area of engagement between Hindu and Western science' (Arnold 2000: 176). In the East–West encounter, the textual tradition of Ayurveda assumed paramount importance, for it was 'central to establishing claims for the validity and rationality of Hindu science as a whole' (ibid.).

The revived interest in Ayurvedic medicine was reflected in a growing variety of medical publications: next to a number of selected Ayurvedic classics in Sanskrit, the NKP list featured a substantial proportion of dual-language publications in which the Sanskrit text was supplemented by a modern commentary or translation. Over time, the firm offered more and more medical tracts and treatises in Hindi, some original compositions, others translated from the Sanskrit or other languages.[33] This hitherto largely unacknowledged proliferation of commercially distributed medical works warrants separate study in that it documents not only the revitalization of an ancient science but also a significant shift from 'specialist' to 'public' knowledge effected by print. While continuing to serve medical practitioners as reference works in daily practice, an increasing number of medical publications was designed for private use by laymen, assuming an important new function as household manuals.

Since the target audience of mass-produced medical manuals was no longer the professional group of ayurvedic practitioners alone, the majority of NKP editions of Sanskrit medical texts came in a more popularly accessible format, that is, with a Hindi translation or commentary. In this way specialists could consult the original, while others would profit from the translation. This is not to say that medical specialists were necessarily proficient in Sanskrit and could have done without the Hindi translation, a point to which we will return shortly. The first Hindu medical text published by Naval Kishore in 1868 was *Vaidyajīvan* (A Living for Physicians), an immensely popular sixteenth-century tract in 238 verses by Lolimbaraja. It included a modern Sanskrit commentary by Sukhanandnath.[34] Another edition, supplemented by an abridged Hindi verse translation by Shankaraprasad, followed in 1870. Between 1872 and 1874, Madanpala's *Nighaṇṭu*, a famous compendium of medicaments, and Amarsingh's *Amarvinod,* a standard classical dictionary of medical terms, drugs, and their properties, were issued simultaneously in their Sanskrit original and in editions containing a Hindi translation. Two further authoritative compendia, *Sārṅgadhāra-saṃhitā* (*1874) and *Caraka-saṃhitā* (*1900), were issued with Hindi commentaries. *Mādhav-nidānam* (*1881), the earliest compendium on pathology (*nidāna*) by Madhava, was one of the few medical works that came out in a plain text version only.

[33] The best documentation of Ayurvedic works and their various published versions can be found in G.J. Meulenbeld's herculean *History of Indian Medical Literature* (2000).

[34] *Lolimbadīpikā* was completed in 1863–4.

The revival of Hindu medicine, as Arnold has argued, was also a corollary of nascent Hindu nationalism. By the 1890s public interest in ancient and modern ayurvedic science was certainly widespread enough for Naval Kishore to not only reprint extant texts, but also invest in his own translations. To this end he commissioned Pandit Ravidatt, an ayurvedic practitioner from Rohtak district, with a series of Hindi translations of famous works, including *Nighaṇṭaratnākar* (*1892),[35] *Suṣrutā saṃhitā* (*1891), and *Bhaiṣajya-ratnāvalī* (*1892). In keeping with the NKP's policy to make ayurvedic knowledge accessible to non-specialists, the editions were supplemented by commentaries and glossaries of difficult words. In 1894 there followed a translation by Pandit Kalicaran of *Bhāvaprakāśa*, a famous sixteenth-century medical encyclopaedia by Bhava Mishra of Benares. Its preface offers interesting insights into the linguistic abilities of contemporary ayurvedic practitioners. After the customary appraisal of the work, the Pandit set out to explain why a Hindi translation was much needed. While echoing colonial notions of the degeneration of indigenous medical practice, his statement also expresses a deep concern about the effects that the rapid decline of Sanskrit knowledge had among professional *vaidyas*:

> This precious work is in the Sanskrit language and nowadays, through the effect of time, not even the *vaidyas*, let alone other people, generally know Sanskrit. For this reason these people are not even able to acquire a sound knowledge of all the drugs of medical science by studying this one work. Yet, in order to live decently, they engage in treatments in full knowledge, and when the sick, tormented by their illness and without recourse, come to them for help, the *vaidyas* give them medicine for relief, but usually the effect is to the contrary. Seeing this pitiable state of affairs, by order of . . . Munshi Naval Kishore, Pandit Kalicaran, . . . with the assistance of . . . Vajpeyi Ksamapatiji, has prepared a Hindi translation of this supreme and beneficial medical work called *Bhāvaprakāśa*. In preparing the Hindi version, the aforesaid gentlemen have resorted to many printed and manuscript copies of the *Bhāvaprakāśa*[36] and have also collected, as far as were available, those works cited in it as authoritative, as well as other dictionaries. They have made a great effort in eliminating textual variants, in finding out the names of drugs and in correcting the original copy. Now some gentleman may have doubts as to the purpose of this reissue, since Hindi translations of the text have already come out from Bombay and

[35] First published from the Nirnay Sagar Press of Bombay in 1867 (Meulenbeld 2000, IIb: 388).

[36] The first edition of the Sanskrit *Bhāvaprakāśa* dates from 1875.

other cities. The reason for this effort is that the translations printed so far are, first, very costly and, second, written in a language which is not beneficial to the common people. Therefore, this translation has been undertaken in extremely pleasant, simple and pure Hindi (*atyant manohar saral aur śuddh bhāṣā*) and printed along with the original text.[37]

The underlying objective of such translations—to make Ayurvedic medicine more generally accessible—can also be seen in the proliferation of new medical treatises written in Hindi, which offered a more 'popular' version of Ayurveda to the lay readership. The increasing demand for medical knowledge in Hindi was by no means confined to human medicine; it also extended to a field that has largely remained outside the purview of classic Ayurveda, veterinary medicine. As Bayly notes, the treatment of the diseases of animals was a favourite topic in the emerging Hindi literature of Rajasthan (Bayly 1996a: 266). Most of these texts were a direct result of colonial efforts to introduce basic 'useful' knowledge on the treatment of cattle disease among India's rural population. For example, *Paśucikitsā* (*1875), a work on the treatment of animals, was translated from an Urdu text to be used in rural primary schools in Avadh.[38]

The nature and purport of this new kind of popular medical literature is best exemplified by the earliest and most successful title among NKP Hindi medical publications, a manual on health, diagnosis and treatments entitled *Amṛtsāgar* (Ocean of Nectar, *1864). Composed by or, more probably, at the behest of Maharaja Savai Pratap Singh of Jaipur (r. 1769–1803), *Amṛtsāgar* was first issued in its original Marwari dialect from Agra in 1864. Naval Kishore was quick to realize its market potential and promptly commissioned Pandit Kalicaran with a translation of the text into standard Hindi. The twofold purpose of serving medical specialists and laymen alike was spelled out in the editor's preface, which stated that the text had been translated into the '*kharī bhāṣā* of Delhi and Agra which is known to people from every region', for the benefit of 'everybody, young and old, and especially all the *taᶜalluqdār*s and Pandits of Avadh.'[39] The latter reference was in acknowledgement of the publication's sponsor, Maharaja Mansingh of Ayodhya. The preface also contained the conventional promise that, by studying this one text alone, the reader would acquire knowledge in all areas of diagnosis

[37] *Bhāvaprakāś* (Lucknow ²1904), *bhūmikā*.

[38] In 1875 Ram Narain's Hindi translation of 'Cattle Diseases' was published from Bareilly in a large edition of 4500 copies, to be circulated in the villages of Rajputana (*RPIR* 1875: 84).

[39] *Amṛtsāgar* (*1864), *bhūmikā*.

and treatment of illnesses. Ultimately, he would become his own doctor: *Amṛtsāgar*, the translator-editor asserted, had been written in such a way that 'even someone of little intelligence can comprehend it and be a *vaidya* [an ayurvedic practitioner].' *Amṛtsāgar* was a runaway success; it remained by far the most sought after title among NKP medical publications in Hindi. If its terse and matter-of-fact diagnostics were seldom bound to reassure the reader, the text was certainly commendable for its useful content and lucid, colloquial style. The following is a typical exerpt:

> *Jis rogī ko rātri meṁ garmī aur din meṁ śīt lage aur kaṇṭh meṁ kaf bole vah rogī niscaya marai aur jis rogī kī nāk kā agra bhāg śītal hoy aur uske hāth pair aur hṛday bhī śītal hoy vah rogī bhī niscaya marai.*
>
> The patient who feels hot at night and cold during the day and who has phlegm in his throat will certainly die; and the patient whose tip of the nose is cold and whose hands, feet and heart are also cold, will certainly die, too.

Despite such gloomy prospects *Amṛtsāgar* sold extremely well. Its second edition of 1869 already commanded an exceptionally high print run of 5500 copies, a figure usually found in textbook printing only. Priced at one rupee (reprint of 1876), the 450-page book was readily available. By 1878 *Amṛtsāgar* had gone through four editions. Its great commercial success called for an Urdu translation which was duly prepared by the NKP translator Pandit Pyarelal and published in the same year.

Following *Amṛtsāgar,* the NKP issued a series of Hindi medical works, including *Rāmvinod* (*1874) by Ramcandra, *Vaidyamanotsav* (*1874) by Nainsukh, *Auṣadhisaṅgrah-kalpavallī* (*1875) by Radhakrishna, *Dil lagan* (*1882) by Sitaram, as well as two other works of which the publication date could not be ascertained: *Rasāyan prakāś*, and *Vaidyadarpaṇ,* a work composed in 1827 by Prannath. What all these treatises, whether versified or in prose, had in common was the lofty promise of providing complete and exhaustive coverage of 'all diseases', their diagnostics, and suitable forms of treatment. Medical manuals undauntedly advertised their utility for the non-specialist: self-diagnosis and self-treatment were explicitly encouraged. Widely circulated in print, they became a household commodity. As such, they not only began to contest the traditional place of the indigenous medical practitioner, but also offered a viable alternative to the challenge of colonial medicine and public health care schemes.

Astrological Manuals and Almanacs

Astronomy was another area where colonial and indigenous systems of knowledge engaged with each other in a relationship of contestation, competition, and selective appropriation.[40] The pervasiveness of Hindu astronomy and astrology (*jyotiḥśāstra/jyotiṣa*) in Indian social life extended to the body politic, making the astral sciences a highly political discipline.[41] More important in the present context, *jyotiṣa* had a direct bearing on individual lives in determining auspicious times for life-cycle and other rites, and in regulating day-to-day transactions in both the domestic and professional spheres. Practical needs as much as theoretical debates together created what Bayly has succinctly called 'the public sphere of the sciences of the heavens' (ibid.: 248).

Even though some of the scholastic debates between contemporary adherents of the Ptolemaic, Copernican, Siddhantic, and Puranic systems were staged in print, there was little reflection of them in commercial print culture.[42] Commercial printing instead focused on traditional and applied Hindu astrology. A telling indication of how publishers reacted to the practical needs of both professional and amateur astrologers was the new proliferation of mass-produced tracts and manuals in the three principal categories of electional astrology (*muhūrtta*), horoscopy (*jātaka*), and predictive astrology (*phalita jyotiṣ*). Print catered to the interests of a wide range of practising astronomer-astrologers, from the skilled pandit who was trained in the precise science of the Sanskrit *Siddhānta*s ('Correct doctrines') down to the lowly fortune-teller and practicer of necromancy. Horoscope charts, tracts on palmistry, almanacs, and other ephemera became a staple of the commercial book trade.

In the promotion of Hindu astrological texts, the preferred format was the dual-language edition, combining the Sanskrit original with a Hindi

[40] For an account of British engagement with Indian astronomical traditions, mainly during the early nineteenth century, see Bayly 1996a: 247–64.

[41] Traditionally divided into three categories: *saṃhitā* (omens), *gaṇita* (astronomy), and *horā* (astrology). For a detailed introduction into *jyotiḥśāstra*, see Pingree 1981.

[42] See, e.g., Minkowski 2001. One of the few such texts which enjoyed wide circulation was Omkar Bhatt's *Bhūgolsār* (also known as *Jyotiṣcandrikā*, *c.* 1837), a Hindi commentary on the *Siddhāntaśiromaṇī*, which bore the English subtitle 'A Comparison of the Puranic and Siddhantic Systems of Astronomy with that of Copernicus'. It was adopted by the Agra School Book Society and variously reprinted (ibid.: 85). Naval Kishore reprinted it in 1882.

commentary.[43] Starting from 1874, Naval Kishore brought out a series of standard classics in this format, including (1) *Bṛhaj-jātaka* (*1879), the most authoritative textbook on *jātaka*; (2) its summary *Laghu-jātaka* (*1876) by the great sixth-century astronomer Varahamihira; (3) the same author's *Bṛhat-saṃhitā* (*1884); (4) *Ṣaṭpañcaśikā* (*1876) by Varahamihira's son Prithuyashas; (5) *Pārāśarī* (*1874), a work on divination by Parashara (c. 600/750); (6) *Jātakālaṅkār* (*1879), an early seventeenth-century text by Ganesh, (7) *Śīghrabodh* (*1874), a sixteenth-century text by Kashinath Bhattacharya; (8) *Muhūrttacintāmaṇī* (*1879), a text completed by Rama at Benares in 1600; (9) *Sāmudrika* (*1874), a work on palmistry; and (10) *Lagnacandrikā* (*1882), a much-used treatise on *jātaka* by Kashinath.[44] Single-language Hindi manuals and astrological digests were also in great demand, as borne out by a surge of titles issued from the 1870s onwards.[45]

Not surprisingly, the bestselling printed item in the category of *jyotiṣa* was the ubiquitous almanac (*patrā*; *jantrī*), a seemingly universal feature of written culture. In the transition from manuscript to print almanacs lost none of their popularity. On the contrary, they came to constitute 'by far the most common form of printed literature throughout India' (Bayly 1996a: 263). Eighteenth-century Calcutta printers already relied on their market potential, while by the mid-nineteenth century, low-priced almanacs featured as the single largest category of printed items in Bengali.[46] Large commercial publishers like Naval Kishore prided themselves in annually producing their own 'house' almanac. An almanac could even form the basis of a future publishing house, as is illustrated by the history of the famous Nirnay Sagar Press of Bombay. As the story goes, one day in 1869, Javaji Dadaji, still a mere printer then, was approached by a reputed pandit with the request to lithograph an almanac. He convinced

[43] Titles issued only in Sanskrit include the voluminous *Muhūrttagaṇapatiḥ* (*1875), a seventeenth-century work by Ganapati Raval; *Jātakābharaṇa* (*1879), a popular early sixteenth-century work by Dhundiraja; *Horāmakaranda* (*1879) by Gunakar; and the commentaries *Muhūrtta-cakradīpikā* (*1874) by Ramdayalu and *Muhūrttadīpikā* (*1874) by Ramsevak Trivedi.

[44] The *Bṛhatsaṃhitā* had first been published in the Bibliotheca Indica series in 1864–5. The NKP translation in '*ārya bhāṣā*' was prepared by Pandit Durgaprasad Sharma.

[45] Including *Indrajāl*, *Muhūrtt cakradīpikā*, *Jātakālaṃkār*, *Tulsī śabdārthaprakāś*, *Daivajña-bharaṇ*, *Saṅgrah śiromaṇī*, *Laghu jātak*, *Jātak candrikā*, *Ramal nauratan*, and *Ramalsār praśnāvalī*, a tract on geomancy which dealt with divination by throwing dice.

[46] Shaw 1981: 16–17; Roy 1996: 41.

the pandit that a more beautiful specimen could be produced by typesetting. A proofsheet was printed with new types especially cast for the job. The pandit was so satisfied with the results that Javaji took the decision (Hindi: *nirṇay*) to set up his own letterpress shop in order to print the almanac (Singh 1986: 73).

7.4 New Genres and a New Historical Perspective

The gradual expansion and generic diversification of printed literature in Hindi is most visibly reflected in the NKP's catalogues and publication lists. Up to the early 1880s, the classification of genres in Hindi clearly followed the Sanskritic model, the standard categories being epics and *Purāṇas*, poetry, lexicography, medicine, Vedanta, astrology, etc. (Table 7.0). If this classificatory scheme favoured the notion of historical continuity between the classical and the modern literatures, it proved no longer adequate once new genres began to emerge in Hindi. Additional categories had to be introduced, which, somewhat ironically, at first bore Urdu denominations such as *mutafarriqāt* ('Miscellaneous') or *qiṣṣa vaghairah* ('Tales etc.'), randomly grouping various genres together that no longer fitted the Sanskrit paradigm.

Addressing a Female Readership

Perhaps the most salient feature in the table below is the appearance of a separate category of 'books for women' in an 1889 book list. While this acknowledgement of women as a distinct readership category is significant in itself, the excitement it might generate in the modern researcher is premature, for the reference remains an isolated phenomenon. On NKP lists there was as yet little reflection of the rich body of women's advice literature produced in Hindi from around the 1870s onwards. Throughout the period 1858–95, the number of NKP Hindi books designed specifically for a female audience barely exceeded a dozen titles. All of them were instructional works for use in primary or secondary female education. Such works generally combined moral instruction and practical advice in domestic management and household duties with some basic education in the three 'r's: reading, writing, and arithmetic. They were a direct outcome of the colonial state's engagement in female education in the wake of Charles Wood's Education Despatch of 1854, which had stressed the importance of educating Indian women and demanded that the government give its 'frank and cordial support' to the

TABLE 7.0

Classification of Nagari Publications in NKP Book Lists

	1879	1880	1881	1883	1889
1.	*itihās, purāṇa*	*bhāṣā purāṇa,*	*bhāṣā itihās*	*bhāṣā itihās*	*itihās*
2.		*itihās, koś*	*purāṇa*	*purāṇa*	*purāṇa*
3.		*vaidyak*	*vaidyak*	*vaidyak bhāṣā*	*vaidyak*
4.	*vedānt*	*vedānta ādi*	*vedānt*	*vedānt*	*vedānt*
5.	*kāvya*	*kāvya*	*kāvya*	*kāvya*	*kāvya bhāṣā*
6.	*mūsīqī*	–	*rāg*	*rāg*	*rāg*
7.	*qiṣṣa vaghairah*	–	*qiṣṣa vaghairah*	*qiṣṣa vaghairah*	*kahānī*
8.	*jyotiṣ*	*jyotiṣ*	*jyotiṣ*	*jyotiṣ*	*jyotiṣ*
9.	*mutafarriqāt*	*mutafarriqāt*	*mutafarriqāt*	*mutafarriqāt*	*mutafarriqāt*
10.	*kutub-e sanskrit*	*saṃskṛt purāṇa smṛti vyākaraṇ ityādi*	*saṃskṛt kī pustakeṁ*		*saṃskṛt*
11.	*saṃskṛt maᶜ tarjuma-e bhāshā (nāgarī)*		*saṃskṛt bhāṣā ṭīkā sahit*		*ṭīkā bhāṣā upaniṣad*
12.		*Sarrishtā-e tālīm kī pustakeṁ*			*dārsī*
13.				*nāṭak*	*nāṭak*
14.					*striyoṁ ke lie*
15.	*saṃskṛt maᶜ tarjuma-e urdū*				*saṃskṛt bātarjumā urdū*

cause. However, with their predominantly Indian authors, compilers, and translators, textbooks also provided a site for Indian interpretations of the nature and purport of female eduction.

Composed at the instance of the colonial authorities, the new textbooks for girl students were invariably authored by men, most often by Indian employees of the Educational Department. Next to alphabetical primers and letter-writers such as *Bālābhūṣaṇ* (Girl's Adornment, *1872) and

Striyoṁ kī hitopatrikā (Well-Wishing Letters for Women, *1873), they included a more interesting category of 'female readers' prescribed for secondary education. While providing some insight into the Indian discourse on female literacy and education, these texts are significant in being hybrid products in which Indian notions of womanhood, both traditional and reformist, merged with ideals of Victorian domesticity. Two such works stand out on the NKP's Hindi list: the first is Shiva Prasad's *Vāmāmanrañjan* (Pleasure of Women, 1856), a popular text that served as the standard Hindi reader for generations of schoolgoing girls in northern India. The compilation, the first of its kind in Hindi, was undertaken at the behest of the Benares Commissioner, Henry C. Tucker. Drawing largely on Elizabeth Starling's *Noble Deeds of Woman* (1848), it offered a selection of brief biographies of Indian and Western exemplary women of both mythical and historical origin. *Vāmāmanrañjan* provides perhaps the earliest example of how, under the impact of Victorian notions of gender, textbooks were deployed in redefining Indian women's role in society. Shiva Prasad's attempt to reinterpret the traditional Indian ideal of the *pativratā* (virtuous and dutiful wife) involved a recasting of European women in the image of the *pativratā.* His Western role models, like their Indian sisters, are emblems of virtue, self-sacrifice, and service (*sevā*) who faithfully act out their domestic roles as devoted daughters, wives, and mothers. Yet, and this is what distinguishes this book from others, they are also shown to make an impact in the male-dominated public realm by displaying new qualities of courage, intelligence, resourcefulness, and self-reliance. Such transgression of the boundaries of the domestic was invariably legitimized by *sevā*, in its extended and redefined meaning of service to society and to the nation. As Dalmia and others have shown, such a presentation of new role models in a traditional guise was to become a frequently employed strategy in nineteenth-century writing for women.[47] In promoting a new ideal of 'enlightened domesticity' (Minault 1998b: 202) and simultaneously extending the realm of female agency into the public domain, *Vāmāmanrañjan* accorded women a new social purpose within and beyond the home. In doing so, it prefigured later nationalist reinterpretations of women's role in society.

Equally interesting in its hybrid character was *Lakṣmī-Sarasvatī saṃvād* (Dialogue Between Laksmi and Sarasvati), a female reader

[47] Dalmia 1997: 247–9. See Stark 2004a for a more detailed discussion of *Vāmāmanrañjan.*

authored by the Brahmo Samaj leader and champion of Hindi in the Punjab, Babu Navincandra Roy (1838–90). Composed in 1869 and issued from Lahore in the same year, it began to receive lasting publicity in its NKP reprint of 1881. Further editions followed in 1886 and 1906 (Stark 2000). *Lakṣmī-Sarasvatī saṃvād* was divided into two rather disjointed parts, one imparting conventional moral and domestic instruction, the other 'modern' knowledge in the science of geography. Adopting the traditional form of a *guru–śiṣya* dialogue between Sarasvati, the goddess of learning, and Lakshmi, the goddess of wealth, the text conveyed a strikingly progressive message: women had every right to receive the same kind of knowledge as men. In a cultural climate where female learning was still largely defined by the exigencies of 'domestic serviceability' (Sangari 1999: 147) such a bold claim required special legitimizing strategies. Navincandra effectively underpinned his message in a programmatic preface in which he justified the necessity of female education on religious grounds: since learning was a means to attain higher knowledge and, ultimately, spiritual emancipation, female education could not be limited to imparting basic skills of reading and writing alone but demanded instruction of a much more pervasive kind.

After 1869 the acknowledged and officially patronized model for much instructional writing for women was Nazir Ahmad's Urdu novel *Mirāt al-'arūs* (*1869).[48] While *Vāmāmanrañjan* continued to figure as its counterpart in the Hindi syllabus, several new Hindi books were written in emulation of *Mirāt al-ʿarūs*.[49] Two of them were published by Naval Kishore: *Strīdarpaṇ* (The Mirror of Women, *1875) by Madhavprasad, an Extra Assistant Commissioner in Sultanpur District; and *Nārībodh* (Woman's Intelligence, *1883) by Avinashcandra Vishvas, a work first issued from Ludhiana in 1882. While expressly acknowledging *Mirāt al-'arūs* as their model, both authors adapted their subject matter to a Hindu context and adopted a more Sanskritized style in keeping with their audience of Hindu girls and women.

Next to colonial textbook production, there was no lack of indigenous efforts to create a body of works suitable for female readers. In the 1880s the Aligarh Bhasha Samvarddhini Sabha (Society for the Improvement of Hindi) set out to produce its own women's advice literature. Since Naval Kishore was closely associated with the society he published some of its books. The Sabha's choice was not always endorsed by colo-

[48] Details on the novel in Naim 1984.
[49] See Khalsi 1990; Sangari 1999: 196–278.

nial opinion, as is illustrated by the case of *Bhāryahit* (*1883), a translation of Pye Henry Chavasse's immensely popular Victorian manual on health and hygiene, *Advice to a Wife* (1842).[50] The British DPI dismissed it as 'worse than useless to native women'.[51] Perhaps on account of this criticism, and even though *Bhāryahit* was well received, the Bhasha Samvarddhini Sabha soon decided to invest in a more indigenized textbook. The task was assigned to Sannulal Gupta, a *qānūngo* of Bulandshahar district, who came out with *Strī subodhinī* (The Woman's Easy Instructor) in 1885.[52] A project of encyclopaedic proportions, the voluminous five-volume treatise not only gave guidelines for correct social and religious behaviour, but professed to cover all subjects, maintaining that knowledge of a more pervasive kind would avert women 'from foolishness and evil thoughts'. In emulation of Chavasse, the author accorded special attention to topics like pregnancy, women's health and hygiene, medical care, and the treatment of illnesses of household members. He also took great care to adopt a lucid and colloquial style, dismissing all difficult Sanskrit and Perso-Arabic words and keeping sentences deliberately short and simple.

Given this narrowly confined range of books written for women, did books written *by* women have any chance of entering the commercial market? As critics have pointed out, one reason why we know so little about how and to what extent women engaged in literary composition is that their works seldom made it into print. The reasons were many, ranging from fear of social stigmatization to being denied access to the book trade and lack of patronage. The NKP's list only featured three (two?) works by female authors. The first, *Premratna* (Jewel of Love, *1875), was a collection of devotional poetry authored by Ratnakumvar Devi, the learned grandmother of Raja Shiva Prasad, who saw the work into print. The second, *Satībilās* (Pleasure of a Virtuous Woman, *1880), was a conventional description of the duties of a wife in Brajbhasha verse by Kumvari Viranji, 'wife of Amarsingh of Jaunpur district'. The third and by far most intriguing item was a translation of an anonymously published Urdu work entitled *Qiṣṣa-e aurat mard* (Story of a Woman and a Man, *1882), which professed to offer a depiction of 'the faults of women as

[50] Its full title was *Advice to a Wife on the Management of her own Health and on the Treatment of Some Complaints Incidental to Pregnancy, Labour and Suckling* (12th ed., 1878).

[51] *RPIR* 1883: 85. For a discussion of the book, see Sangari 1999: 320–8.

[52] *Nūtan strī subodhinī*, a revised and updated version of Sannulal Gupta's text edited by L.P. Bhardvaj, was published from the Tejkumar Press in 1995.

imagined by men'. Situating itself in the tradition of popular folk narrative, the text offered a pungent tale of male infidelity and female shrewdness; it was replete with worldly wisdom and openly challenged patriarchal norms. Since such *qiṣṣas* were proscribed for respectable women (Sangari 2004: 242–3), the work was not intended for a female audience, nor was it advertised as such.[53] Indeed, it remains doubtful whether its anonymous author was 'a respectable woman from a distinguished Agarval family of the Jain faith' (*ek agravāl śreṣṭh kul kī kulīn jainmatī strī*), as proclaimed by the book's cover. Was it a ruse to attract a larger readership? British publication records which list one Munshi Ujagar Mall, a *taḥṣīldār* of Sikandara Rao in Aligarh district, as the book's author suggest as much.

What conclusions can be reached from looking at the small body of NKP books 'for women'? There is little to suggest that Naval Kishore made any special efforts to target the emerging market of female readers. In a reflection of what Kumkum Sangari has called a 'patriarchal consensus across religious lines' (Sangari 1999: 187), on the firm's Urdu list, too, books for women were relegated to a small rubric entitled 'Female Education' (which, next to *Mirāt al-ʿarūs*, included only three other titles),[54] while most conventional advice literature for Muslim women was subsumed under the category of religious works. In fact, from the commercial publisher's point of view a distinct 'female' market hardly existed. Undoubtedly, with Hindi being the language of choice in female primary education, the number of literate women was steadily growing. Yet it would seem that, before the turn of the century, the numerical strength of the female readership in Hindi was too small, and the range of literature deemed suitable for women too restricted by patriarchal norms, for it to be commercially exploited. Appearing before the Education Commission in 1882, Shiva Prasad gave an apologetic appraisal of the level of education enjoyed by upper-caste Hindu women, whose learning defied colonial stereotypes of female backwardness. While he claimed to know of 'innumerable instances of women being well versed in reading and writing and keeping accounts in high and well-to-do families',[55]

[53] As Sangari suggests, the very proscription of *qiṣṣa*s for women functioned as 'an invitation to read'. Reading a *qiṣṣa* became 'a desired and often practised transgression' (2004: 243).

[54] Notably, *Hidāyat an-nisvān* by ʿAli Muhammad; *Qavāʾid an-nissā* by Muhammad Zahiruddin Bilgrami (a Nizami Press imprint); and *Qiṣṣa-e gulāb cambelī* by Raja Shiva Prasad.

[55] 'I have already said that Hindi reading and writing is so easy that women learn among themselves. Often Panditanis and Purohitanis (family priestesses or caste

his assessment was heavily influenced by his own background in an elite Jain family with a tradition of female learning. His elitist perspective was a far cry from the continuously low female literacy rates and the disappointing results that more than a quarter century of formal education had yielded in the NWP&Oudh. After a promising start in the period 1854–74, when the number of schoolgoing girls in the NWP had shot up from less than 400 to over 16,500, a change in official policy interrupted further progress. By the 1880s it was clear that formal education had failed to make an impact, with less than one per cent of girls of schoolgoing age receiving formal schooling (*ECR* 1883: 42; lxxv).

Evidently, the NKP's catalogue makes for a poor source of information if one wants to learn about the reading tastes of literate women at the time. Rather than showing us what women read, its small and closely monitored selection of 'books for women' merely reflects prescriptive patriarchal notions of what women ought to read. The reading horizon of literate and, even more so, cultured women was of course much wider. To find out more about their diverse literary tastes one has to probe a variety of largely untapped sources—autobiographies, memoirs, letters, etc.[56] Interestingly, and ironically, when the House of Naval Kishore was first immortalized in Urdu fiction, it was through the figure of a female reader, Mirza Hadi Rusva's celebrated courtesan of Lucknow. An accomplished representative of her trade, Umraʾo Jan Ada is depicted as an avid reader of the Persian classics, among them 'the *Danish Nama Ghyas Mansur* which had just then been published by the Naval Kishore Press' (Ruswa 1993: 150).

Unlike the metropolis with its flourishing market for women's popular fiction and impressive range of female professional writers, the Indian domestic market had not yet created a niche for women's leisure reading but showed a conservative insistence on didactic, religious, and edifying literature.[57] The Hindi periodical press, too, remained aloof from the idea that women might read for pleasure: Harishchandra's *Bālābodhinī* (1874–8), the first woman's journal in Hindi and still a

---

priestesses) also teach when going round occasionally to pay visits'. *AECR* 1884: 323.

[56] See, e.g., Borthwick 1984; Karlekar 1991; Sarkar 1999.

[57] There exists a great deal of writing on Victorian professional women writers. See, e.g, R.C. Terry (Terry 1983: 68–132) on Mrs Oliphant, the 'Queen of Popular Fiction', and on Rhoda Broughton; T. Ransom (Ransom 1999) and A.R. Federico (Federico 2000) on Marie Corelli, a favourite with Indian readers. J. Sutherland analyses a sample of 312 female Victorian writers (Sutherland 1995: 151–64).

largely male-dominated enterprise, was typical of the patronizing male discourse on women in that it imparted various kinds of moral and practical advice, but did not offer a single form of entertaining reading to its prospective female audience (Dalmia 2004: 404–14). It was only in the first decades of the twentieth century that a distinct periodical and fictional literature for and by women emerged in Hindi.[58] In the meantime, a space for female reading was being created in English by the colonial fiction industry (Joshi 2002) and, in its wake, by the new generation of Hindi fiction writers who emerged during the last decades of the century. Work on the early novel in India (Mukherjee 2002) stresses the centrality of women both as characters in and consumers of nineteenth-century novels. This is evident from the large number of narratives that had female names in their titles, starting with Pandit Gauridatt's *Devrānī jeṭhānī kī kahānī* (The Story of Two Sisters-in-Law, 1870). Even as fiction authors, if not always explicitly, began to address a female audience of readers and listeners, anxiety about the corrupting influence of the novel remained.

Drama

As shown in Table 7.0, drama (*nāṭak*) was another new genre that made a late appearance on the publisher's Hindi list. This is hardly surprising in light of the fact that modern Hindi drama was still in its formative phase. In a deliberate departure from older forms of the popular folk stage, Harishchandra of Benares took the lead in formulating a new aesthetics, and redefining the form, content, and ideology of what was to become a national theatre for the Hindus.[59] He not only contributed to the development of modern Hindi drama through a host of plays and theoretical writings, but also actively participated in making the first ever staging of a Hindi play a much publicized and successful event. The performance of *Jānakī maṅgal* (Sita's Marriage), a play written by Sital Prasad Tivari of the Benares Sanskrit College, took place in the newly-founded Benares Theatre in 1868, in the presence of the Maharaja of Benares. Harishchandra and some of his literary friends acted in it.[60] Outside Benares, the growth of the new Hindi drama received little attention at first. Compared to the popularity in print of the *svāng* (*sangīt*) and

[58] See Orsini 2002: 260–308; Talwar 1989.

[59] As Kathryn Hansen has argued (Hansen 1989), Bharatendu's 'invention' of the modern Hindi drama implied an 'articulated, intentioned rejection' of popular folk stage traditions.

[60] Dalmia-Lüderitz 1992; Dalmia 1997: 277–9; 300–14; Shukla vs 2051: 248.

other forms of the folk stage (see below), the limited number and small print runs of Hindi dramas issued from the NKP suggest that modern plays were not yet commercially viable.[61]

As befitted a publisher based in Lucknow, one of the first titles to appear in the category of 'drama' on NKP Hindi and Urdu lists was a verse play closely associated with the *navābī* court culture of Avadh: *Indarsabhā* (Assembly of King Indar). Composed in 1853 by Amanat ᶜAli (1816–59), a poet attached to the court of Wajid ᶜAli Shah, *Indarsabhā* has generally been acknowledged as the first original Urdu drama. Assimilating different forms of Persian romance, Urdu, and Hindi poetry and song, it was popularized across India by Parsi theatre companies and enjoyed a phenomenal success. Kathryn Hansen has traced the process in which the drama moved out of its courtly milieu into the larger public domain, and shifted from stage drama into popularly printed text (and later back to the visual realm of modern cinema: Hansen 2001). Starting from 1869, the NKP circulated *Indarsabhā* in both Amanat's version and an equally popular reworking by Madari Lal. Before long, the two dramas were issued in a joint edition which saw numerous printings and by 1876 had also appeared in Hindi transliteration.

Second in popularity only to *Indarsabhā* were *Gopīchand Bhartarī* (*1874) and *Sangīt Prahlād* (*1882), two frequently reprinted musical dramas by Lakshman Singh. The three titles stand somewhat apart (*Indarsabhā* for its overt syncretism, *Gopīchand Bhartarī* and *Sangīt Prahlād* for their origin in and closeness to the folk stage) from the other dramas on the publisher's list, which clearly reflected the preponderance of the classic Sanskrit tradition in Hindi drama. Not surprisingly, the NKP's first publications in the dramatic genre included two different Hindi adaptations of the Sanskrit *Prabodhcandrodaya nāṭak*, an eleventh-century allegorical drama by Krishna Mishra that had inspired poets throughout the ages and was still an important model for Harishchandra's early plays. The first was a popular rendering in Brajbhasha verse by the eighteenth-century Vallabhan poet Brajvasidas (*1875), the second a modern reworking in simple Khari Boli (*1883) by Atmaram, itself based on a Gurmukhi translation by Anathdas.[62] Sanskritic models continued to be of importance, as is attested by the simultaneous publication

[61] The *svāng* (lit. 'mime') was a musical form of theatre including song and dance. From the 1860s *svāngs* were widely circulated in print in the form of illustrated librettos known as *sangīt*.

[62] Brajvasidas's version was based on a Persian prose rendering composed by Banvalidas 'Wali' in 1662, which was itself based on Nanddas's version of the drama. The NKP published Wali's Persian text in 1877.

in 1891 of two modern Hindi ('*desbhāṣā*') renderings of *Nāgānanda* by Lala Sitaram, and *Hanumān nāṭāk* by Ramanand Caturdas.

Forming part of the NKP's series of *rīti* works, the *editio princeps* of *Ānand Raghunandan nāṭak* (The Joy of Ram, *1881) by Maharaja Vishvanath Singh of Rewa (1789–1854) was an event of some consequence for Hindi literary history. A drama in verse and prose which dealt with the traditional theme of Rama's early life, *Ānand Raghunandan* is regarded as the first original drama in Hindi. Its mixed Brajbhasha language, which included some English phrases, suggests a late date of composition by the mid-nineteenth century (McGregor 1984: 170–1). At the time the text was consigned to print, its status as a 'modern' Hindi drama was by no means uncontested. Harishchandra, while acknowledging *Ānand Raghunandan* as an early specimen of *nāṭak*, found it lacking in the essentials of dramatic poetry and preferred to attribute the beginning of Hindi drama to *Nahuṣ nāṭāk*, a play written by his father Girdhardas in 1858.

The NKP list also reflected the two other main sources of inspiration for contemporary Hindi drama, the Shakespearian and the Bengali drama, in plays such as *Rāmābhiṣek nāṭak* (*1877), a translation of a Bengali play by Manmohan Basu, and *Bhramjālak nāṭak* (*1882), a popular Indianized version of Shakespeare's *Comedy of Errors* by Ratnacand. The author, a future Allahabad High Court Judge, had composed the play in 1868 while studying Shakespeare at Agra College. Finally, in 1891 the NKP issued its only modern Hindi drama in the form of *Mayaṅkmañjari*, a romantic play with nationalist and reformist overtones by Kishorilal Gosvami (1865–1932). Generally, however, the publisher steered clear of nationalist drama and political plays in which anti-colonial sentiment might be expressed.

Towards a National Literature: From Anthology to Literary History

Subsumed under the new heading of 'Miscellaneous' (*mutafarqāt*), literary anthologies were to gain central importance in the evolution of a canon of national literature in Hindi. In assembling basic biographical data about Hindi poets, anthologies paved the way for the subsequent writing of literary history. Hindi literature owes to the NKP not only the publication of Shivsingh Sengar's famous *Śivsiṃh saroj* (Lotus of Shivsingh, *1878), a work generally acknowledged as the first serious attempt at writing literary history in Hindi, but also an impressive variety of old and new anthologies. These compilations provided the starting point for a systematic survey of past and present Hindi authors; they were a crucial precondition for the future creation of a literary canon.

As Peter Hohendahl has shown for early-nineteenth-century Germany, the evolution of the writing of literary history was more than just the production of a particular kind of text. 'The rapid rise of literary history in the early nineteenth century becomes explicable only when we investigate its function', points out Hohendahl. 'Beyond the purported task of describing the evolution of a national literature, its purpose was to secure *literary tradition*' (Hohendahl 1989: 38). In the process, the selection of important authors and the analysis of filiation assumed distinct 'strategic importance'. Notwithstanding the different political and social circumstances, his argument is fully applicable to the Indian context. The beginning of literary historiography in Hindi was marked by Garcin de Tassy's *Histoire de la Littérature Hindouie et Hindoustanie* (3 vols, Paris 1839–47), of which a revised and considerably augmented second edition appeared in 1870–1. The French Orientalist drew largely on Urdu *tazkirahs* (collective biographies) and consciously adopted their format for his own *Histoire*. The result was 'a massive . . . *tazkirah* of sorts' (Pritchett 2003: 881) which showed a marked preponderance of Urdu and Muslim authors. It was only once revivalist and nationalist thought gave rise to a new cultural consciousness that the Hindi literati in their turn began to explore their literary heritage in a more systematic manner. By the mid-nineteenth century the effort to document the Hindi literary tradition manifested itself in an increasing number of poetical anthologies of Brajbhasha verse. Emulating both the *tazkirah* and Sanskritic models, these compilations combined specimens of poets' works with brief biographical accounts. The largest and most important was *Rāg sāgarudbhav rāg kalpadrum* (1843), prepared by Krishnadas Vyas Dev on the model of the Sanskrit *Śabdakalpadrum* (Grierson 1889: 109). It included specimens of the work of over 200 poets. *Ras chandroday* (1863) by Thakur Prasad Tripathi, *Digvijaybhūṣaṇ* (1869) by Gokul Prasad, and various other works followed in the 1860s. By far the most popular anthology was *Sundarī tilak* (1869), a collection of poems by Brajbhasha *śṛṅgār* poets composed exclusively in the *savaiyā*-metre. Compiled by the Benares poets Mannalal Sharma 'Dvij' and Hanuman Kavi at the instance of Harishchandra, it assumed distinct relevance in the early canonization of Hindi poets. *Sundarī tilak* first came out in

1869; a revised and enlarged version issued from Mannalal's Kashi Sanskrit Press followed in 1872.[63] So great was its popularity that it was not only frequently reprinted but also circulated in manuscript form, providing an interesting instance of the continuing vitality of scribal traditions. The handwritten copies, however, were often at variance with the over 420 verses and 70 different poets included in Mannalal's edition of 1872 (Singh 1991: 13). Naval Kishore reprinted *Sundarī tilak* in 1883 and several times after that, assuming a key role in the commercial dissemination of a standardized edition of the text.

Against this backdrop, S.K. Das's assertion that, except for Urdu and Persian compilers of poetic *tazkirahs* 'Indians did not take any interest in the history of literature or biographies of writers' (Das 1991: 174), does not withstand closer examination. Admittedly, Hindi was slow to follow Bengali and other Indian languages that already boasted their first works of literary historiography. Formally, there was little development in Hindi since Kalidas's *Hazārā*, the first 'early modern' anthology dating from the late seventeenth century. However, the compilations produced in the latter half of the nineteenth century not only introduced new contents, they also took on a whole new trajectory in increasingly functioning as a medium for nationalist endeavours to document and fix indigenous tradition and—dismissing India's Muslim past—situate Hindi literature in the context of the classical Sanskrit tradition. In this they prefigured later works of literary historiography that sought to establish a literary canon for the new national language, Hindi. Anthologies, in short, provided the fundamentals and 'raw material' for later canon-making efforts.

While indigenous canonization efforts concentrated on poetry, reflecting the predominance of lyrical genres in the Hindi literary tradition, a different type of anthology emerged under the aegis of colonial education. Constantly in need of 'easy' reading material, British educators turned to prose. Various officially produced 'Selections' contained mostly prose pieces suitable for instructional purposes, and mark a parallel development in the formation of the Hindi literary canon. The oldest such work was William Price's *Hindee and Hindoostanee Selections* (1827). Initially designed for British students of Fort William College, it became a standard work for generations of Indian students

[63] For a critical new edition of *Sundarī tilak*, see Singh 1991. Singh gives a detailed account of the genesis and publication history of the work, in which he convincingly shows that it was not, as often claimed, compiled by Harishchandra.

before it was supplemented by Shiva Prasad's *Guṭkā or Hindi Selections* in 1867.[64]

The transition from traditional anthology to the beginning of modern literary historiography was mirrored in the NKP's publication repertoire. In the same way that religious and sectarian self-reflexivity was encouraged through the promotion of hagiographic key texts—*Bhaktamāla*, *Caurāsī bārttā*, etc.—, the publishing house also reacted to the new historical awareness generated by and among Hindi literati. As Dalmia has pointed out, an important step in the systematic exploration of the evolution of Hindi literature was Harishchandra's essay '*Hindī kavitā*' (Hindi Poetry), published in *Kavivacansudhā* in 1872. In attempting a preliminary sketch of the evolution of Hindi poetry and drama, Harishchandra evaluated this evolution 'according to criteria which were extensions of the traditional' (Dalmia 1997: 274–5). The NKP's promotion of anthologies is clearly linked to such efforts.

By far the most important publication was Shivsingh Sengar's aforementioned *Śivsiṃh saroj* (*1878), a landmark in the early formulation of literary history in Hindi. Sengar, a police inspector of Unnao district with pronounced literary interests, had already published an Urdu translation of the *Śivapurāṇa* with the NKP. In his anthology he was expressly concerned with historic accuracy, wanting to supply 'a detailed account of the lives, date of birth, caste, residence, etc., of past and present poets together with their poetical works' (Sengar [1878] 1966: [1]).[65] Formally, little was new in *Śivsiṃh saroj*, which emulated Kalidas's *Hazārā* in that it purported to be an 'exquisite collection of the biographies of one thousand *bhāṣā* poets with specimens of their poetry'.[66] In presenting his material, Sengar had opted for an alphabetical rather than chronological order, which would have been more suitable to his historic concern.[67] What was new, however, was his methodological approach in collecting and assessing his textual sources. Sengar was conscious of the novelty of his historicist method and eager to point out that his anthology was the

[64] For Price's work, see Dalmia 1997: 274–5. Another such reader was *Gadyapadyasaṅgrah* (*1889) by Ambikaprasad, an assistant inspector of schools in Oudh.

[65] '. . . ab koī granth aisā banānā cāhiye, jismeṁ prācīn aur avārcīn kaviyoṁ ke jīvancaritra, san-saṃvat, jāti, nivāssthān ādi kavitā ke granthoṁ-samet vistār-pūrvak likhe hoṁ'.

[66] In actual fact, the number of poets included in the anthology went from 998 in the first to 1003 in the seventh edition of 1926. 839 specimens of poetry were given.

[67] For a discussion of Sengar's sources, his methodology and flaws, see T.N. Dikhshit's detailed introduction to the 1966 edition (Sengar 1966: 4–40).

first of its kind. Having studied numerous texts in Sanskrit, Arabic, Persian, Hindi, and English, he ended up drawing on fourteen major works, of which he meticulously listed composition dates and gave a description of their content. A closer look at Sengar's sources reveals that in compiling *Śivsiṃh saroj* he had recourse to three works lately published by the NKP, notably (1) Tulsiram's Urdu version of Nabhadas's *Bhaktamāl* (*1871);[68] (2) *Kavitt ratnākar* (*1876), a compilation of forty-two poets by Matadin Mishra; and (3) *Bhāṣākāvya-saṅgrah* (*1875) by Maheshdatt Shukla, which contained specimens of poetry and short biographical sketches of fifty-one Hindi poets. Shukla's anthology had received an award of Rs 100 under the 1868 Allahabad Government Notification and had been adopted as a textbook in government schools.[69] It provided the initial impetus for the compilation of *Śivsiṃh saroj*, for Sengar found it utterly defective.

Included in Sengar's preface was a section entitled 'The Evolution of Hindi Poetry' (*Bhāṣā kāvya kā nirṇay*) which was of special significance to Hindi literary historiography. Sengar posited an uninterrupted poetical tradition, starting from the classical Sanskrit poets up to the modern ones, that covered all of India (Dalmia 1997: 276). The ideological and political implications of this view, if still unformulated by Sengar, were momentous: Hindi literature, as it was presented in *Śivsiṃh saroj*, was a literature of the Hindus, to the large exclusion of Muslims poets. Propounded in an extremely popular anthology (Sengar's work had gone through seven reprints by 1926), this reduction of Hindi literature to Hindu literature served the interests of Hindu nationalism.[70]

Śivsiṃh saroj was to have a lasting impact on the subsequent development of literary historiography in Hindi. It became the principal source for Grierson's *The Modern Vernacular History of Hindustan*, which accordingly showed the same preponderance of Hindu authors. The Mishra brothers drew on it in their influential four-volume anthology *Miśrabandhuvinod* (1913 onward), while Ramchandra Shukla acknowledged Sengar's pioneering position in Hindi literary historiography in his *Hindī sāhitya kā itihās* (1929), the first fully-fledged literary history of Hindi in the Hindi language (Shukla vs 2051: *preface*). By his time, the claim to a distinct Hindu identity of the Hindi literary heritage had become solidified.

[68] Sengar erroneously refers to Tulsiram as Tulsidas.

[69] *RPE Oudh*, 1874: 71.

[70] Following the seventh edition of 1926 the work remained out of print for decades. It was only in 1966 that the Tejkumar Press issued a reprint, edited by Triloki Narayan Dikshit.

Second only in importance to *Śivsiṃh saroj* was the Benares poet Sardar Kavi's *Śṛṅgār saṅgrah* (Collection of Erotic Verse), a work compiled in 1842 and first printed by Naval Kishore in 1888. It contained verses by some 125 poets dealing with rhetoric figures of speech (*alamkār*) and erotic themes. Grierson judged it a 'deservedly popular work on rhetoric' (Grierson 1889: 120) and used the printed edition as a source for his *Modern Vernacular History of Hindustan*.

In their significance for Hindi literary historiography, the aforementioned anthologies have tended to overshadow other, more popular compilations. The NKP issued a series of works that enjoyed great success in the marketplace but subsequently failed to attract the attention of scholars. Among them are the various compilations of *śṛṅgār* poets by Paramanand Suhane—*Nakhśikh hazārā* (*1893), *Pāvas kavitt-ratnākar* (*1893), and *Ṣadṛtu hazārā* (*1894)—as well as the compilations of Brajbhasha lyrics by Hafizullah Khan (b. 1857), a school teacher in Hardoi district. Born in a family of Afghan Muslims, Hafizullah had grown into a lover and zealous collector of bhakti poetry. Published in the 1880s, his collections *Ṣadṛtu kāvya saṅgrah*, *Hazārā*, *Manmohinī*, and, particularly, *Navīn saṅgrah* enjoyed lasting popularity—the latter title had, by 1953, gone through twenty-two editions.

Efforts to identify and establish a canon of leading Hindi poets also extended to the contemporary period. A prominent example is *Sujānsaroj* (Sujan's Lotus, *1896), a late-nineteenth-century anthology which, as its title suggests, was designed as a continuation of *Śivsiṃh saroj*, offering the reader 'poetry and biographical sketches of an assembly of contemporary nineteenth-century poets'.[71] The collection self-consciously positioned itself at the interface of modern literary history and the traditional anthology. Its compiler, Pandit Bakhshram Pandey 'Sujankavi', a scholastic poet of Ballia, envisaged nothing less than to supply an authoritative collection for posterity's sake. As he informed his fellow poets, his hope was that 'in the future this work will take the form of a history (*yah granth itihās rūp ho*) [and] that your names will all be of longstanding existence'. Pandey was evidently concerned with providing a complete and exhaustive overview of contemporary poetic writing. His fifty-three sketches of poets were supplemented by a list of thirty-six further poets on whom he had not been able to procure biographical data, followed by an appeal to the said individuals to promptly forward their biographies to Naval Kishore so that the anthology could be supplemented

[71] Pandit Bakhshram Pandey authored several other works, among them *Rahasyacandrikā*, a collection of verse on the *rāsa*-theme.

by a second volume. At the linguistic level, the underlying nationalist agenda of *Sujānsaroj* translated into a concern with the overpowering effect of Anglicization on the idiom of educated Hindi speakers. Prior to the demise of Hindi's great icon Bharatendu, Pandey warned, 'it did not occur to our brothers to say *practice* instead of *abhyās*.'

Changing Tides: The New Appetite for Fiction

While the NKP's list allows us some insight into ongoing attempts at writing the literary history of Hindi and early canon formation, it provides little information with regard to the most conspicuous trend in late-nineteenth-century Hindi literature: the rise of prose. The publishing house was surprisingly slow to react to the new demand for modern prose fiction and the contemporary audience's growing fascination with the novel. Apart from occasional titles, such as Hindi versions of *Robinson Crusoe* or Rajab ʿAli Beg's early Urdu bestseller *Fasāna-e ʿajāʾib*, modern prose fiction, whether of Western or Indian origin, was not promoted on a large scale until the turn of the century. Given the increased output of popular fiction during the last decades of the century and the immense popularity it came to enjoy, the publisher's delayed response to and hesitant engagement with a textual genre that had an obvious market potential calls for an explanation. Firstly, it must be borne in mind that Naval Kishore was a conservative publisher, who exercised caution with regard to new genres and did not seem overly interested in rushing into the risky field of launching new authors whose commercial value was unpredictable. Given the House's pronounced focus on religious and literary classics, discovering new literary talent was clearly not one of his top priorities. Secondly, as already outlined in Chapter 1, print culture in the second half of the nineteenth century no longer operated outside a legal framework: with the promulgation of the Indian Copyright Act of 1847 and the Press and Registration of Books Act of 1867, intellectual copyright had, at least in theory, become an issue that no publisher of repute could ignore. Even if literary property and copyright were not widespread public notions yet, the law clearly stipulated that contemporary literature, unlike older religious or poetic texts, could not be printed or reprinted without prior authorization from the author. Intimately linked to this was the third factor, namely the increased competition in the publishing trade: by the last decades of the century, Benares, Allahabad, and the smaller country towns boasted a thriving Hindi publishing industry of their own. After 1880 the Khadgavilas Press of Bankipur (Patna) rose to prominence as the first literary publishing house in Hindi and started to attract many of the leading authors of the day. For writers residing in these localities there was no longer any compelling reason to turn to the Lucknow publisher.

It is a telling fact that the NKP published only a single work of Harishchandra's prolific oeuvre, namely a collection of devotional poems and songs entitled *Rāg saṅgrah* (*1881). Of Harishchandra's extended literary coterie the only noteworthy person on the NKP list was Kishorilal Gosvami, also with a single title. Indeed, it would seem that, as far as the market for modern fiction and drama was concerned, the NKP had to concede its leading role in the Hindi book trade to presses that were in more direct contact with the contemporary Hindi literary scene flourishing in Benares and elsewhere. Ironically, the rise of prose fiction, soon the most 'marketable' of literary genres, ushered in the demise of the House of Naval Kishore as a commanding presence in Hindi publishing.

7.5 Against the Divide: Patterns of Hindi and Urdu Publishing

In recent years much debate has focused on the social and political ramifications of the language controversy between Hindi and Urdu, which emerged in the NWP&Oudh in the 1860s.[72] Paul Brass in his *Language, Religion and Politics in North India* (1974) coined the term 'multi-symbol congruence' to describe a process characteristic of nascent nationalism, in which Hindu and Muslim political elites chose religion as a primary symbol of communal differentiation and then strove to make language and other symbols congruent. Drawing on Brass, Christopher King has portrayed the Hindi movement as a corollary of Hindu nationalism, in the course of which the traditional identification of Urdu with both Muslim and Hindu culture was transformed into a new equation identifying Urdu exclusively with Muslims and Hindi with Hindus (King 1994: 15). Given the complex social and linguistic situation created by the competition between Hindi and Urdu during the period under review, Naval Kishore's growing involvement in Hindi publishing cannot be viewed in isolation from the language debate. How did the ongoing differentiation between Hindi and Urdu affect the NKP's publishing policy? Apart from the obvious commercial motives, were there ideological

[72] Several studies have analysed the controversy in the light of Hindu nationalism, Hindu-Muslim politics, and group mobilization. In addition to the early works by the German scholars Jürgen Lütt (Lütt 1970) and Kerrin Dittmer (Dittmer 1972), see, e.g., Das Gupta 1970, Brass 1974, Rahman 1996 and Dalmia 1996.

considerations prompting Naval Kishore's entry into Hindi publishing? Did his own Hindu background influence his professional choices? It will be argued here that Naval Kishore's sustained involvement in the Hindi book trade did not have any adverse effects on the firm's operations in Urdu. The NKP remained largely aloof from ideological partisanship with either of the two languages or scripts. Instead, a clear emphasis was laid on assimilation rather than differentiation. Publishing in both languages became a way of defying the process of cultural dichotomization between Hindus and Muslims. The firm's overall policy, as reflected in many of its publishing projects, aimed at perpetuating the mixed cultural heritage and enhancing the composite element inherent in North Indian intellectual and literary traditions.

Before turning to the patterns of Hindi and Urdu publishing at the House of Naval Kishore, it may be useful to look at the broader picture. As King's analysis of publishing patterns in the NWP&Oudh has shown, during the period 1868-1925 publications in Hindi were continuously gaining advantage over Urdu. By 1868 Hindi-language publications, in absolute numbers, already outnumbered those in Urdu (NWP). By contrast, in Avadh and its capital Lucknow the 'complete hegemony' of Urdu continued for much longer. Here it was not until the third decade of the twentieth century that the proportion of Hindi works finally surpassed that of Urdu (King 1994: 37–45). A major drawback of King's otherwise very useful analysis is that he is interested only in the overall picture and does not attempt to relate the statistical data to the activities of official or privately owned presses in specific locations. His failure to mention, for example, that Allahabad was the seat of the government press, which continuously churned out large numbers of Hindi textbooks for use in formal education, makes his data subject to misinterpretation. Equally, no explanation is given for the high number of Hindi books produced from Lucknow: as outlined in Chapter 4, it was the result of the collaboration of the Education Department and the NKP. This alerts us to a larger methodological problem: in order to correctly assess the dynamics of the marketplace, it is crucial to distinguish between educational and non-educational titles; unfortunately, statistical sources do not always allow us to do so. In 1874, for example, book production in Hindi still showed a marked preponderance of educational over non-educational titles, whereas in Urdu non-educational works of religious or general character by far exceeded educational titles, suggesting very different market and readership configurations.[73] Moreover, since the figures

[73] *RPIR* 1874: 23.

cited by King do not differentiate between reprints and first editions, they make it all but impossible to determine the scope of recent literary activity and new generic trends. Drawing on the same sources as King, Table 7.1 invariably shares some of the shortcomings of his data. Nonetheless, by focusing on the number of registered titles rather than giving absolute numbers of printed volumes, it tries to give a more accurate picture of the parallel growth of Urdu and Hindi publishing in the NWP&Oudh.

TABLE 7.1

Publishing Patterns in the NWP&Oudh:
Number of Registered Titles in Urdu and Hindi, 1868–95

Year	Urdu Titles		Hindi Titles		Remarks
	NWP	Oudh	NWP	Oudh	
1868	146	?	107	?	
1869	57	?	55	?	No books registered in Oudh during the 2nd quarter of the year
1870	81	?	52	?	
1871	88 /*161	?	48/*116	?	*books *and* pamphlets
1872	68	?	33	?	No books registered in Oudh during the 4th quarter of the year; no books registered from Kanpur
1873	83	108	67	27	No books registered from Kanpur
1874	78	134	69	41	No books registered from Kanpur
1875	130	84	86	35	
1876	109	132	117	16	
1877	338		121		
1878	237		100		
1879	206		88		
1880	139		79		incomplete registration
1881	380		218		
1882	489		265		
1883	337		201		
1884	238		227		
1885	491		295		
1886	522		468		
1887	452		262		
1888	558		295		
1889	569		361		
1890	408		213		
1891	301		199		
1892	295		208		
1893	469		306		
1894	623		354		
1895	560		354		

SOURCES: RPIR; *Educational and Home Dept. Reports*.

Perhaps the most striking feature in Table 7.1 is the great fluctuation displayed by the data, which makes it extremely difficult to indicate more specific trends. Neither Urdu nor Hindi titles show regular growth rates but rather follow an up- and-down pattern. Whether this is owing to the unreliability of the data, fluctuations in the market, or to a combination of both, cannot be said. Colonial officials themselves were frequently at a loss in trying to explain these fluctuations, especially in years where incomplete registration could not be held responsible. However, what clearly emerges from the table is the continuing prevalence of Urdu over Hindi titles, even though intermittently, as for example in the year 1884, the number of Hindi titles could approach those of Urdu.

A somewhat less problematic indicator for the increasing importance of Hindi in the public domain is the number of students learning Hindi and Urdu in NWP&Oudh government schools. As Table 7.2 reflects, by 1876 their number was almost equal.

King cites another example documenting the relative strength of Hindi and Urdu in the NWP&Oudh in the 1870s, namely the number of non-official letters circulated through the imperial and district post offices. At 33 per cent, Hindi letters came fairly close to the 40 per cent of letters written in Urdu (King 1994: 46–7). To acknowledge this roughly equal share of Hindi and Urdu in education and literate practice is helpful in understanding the laws of the market, in a discourse that usually centres around the political and ideological implications of the language controversy. In the commercial market it was numbers of potential readers that counted. Hindi had surely become an attractive proposition.

When the language question first gained momentum in 1868, it was

TABLE 7.2

Number of Students Learning Urdu and Hindi in NWP&Oudh Government Schools[74]

	1866–7	1871–2	1873–4	1876–7
Urdu	10,137	25,586	28,233	35,674
Hindi	7,702	18,977	22,353	34,232

SOURCE: *Annual Report of the Administration of Oudh.*

[74] The figures given here do not differentiate between primary and secondary education and may thus obscure different patters existing at both levels, as suggested by King's more elaborate analysis (King 1994: 97–101).

vividly discussed in *Avadh Akhbār*. The paper initially published articles and letters in support of either of the two languages. The issue of 2 February 1868 carried a piece in favour of Urdu reprinted from the *Aligarh Institute Gazette*. The following year, in discussing the question of whether Hindi or Urdu was better suited to be the court language in Avadh, the paper adopted a more cautious stance. It argued that, 'it is difficult to offer a correct opinion on the subject; but that the language which suffers no injury, and can be learned in its correct form, and in which existing evils might be remedied, should be best suited for the purpose. It is known that the Mahomedans were the cause of abolishing the use of the Hindee language, and it now becomes necessary to do what is best suited to the times.'[75] However, with *AA* being a medium of the Urdu-speaking elite, it did not take long before the paper became more outspoken in its defence of Urdu. The introduction of the Nagari script in Bihar in 1876 was decried as a 'calamity' and described as a forceful and nonsensical government measure in utter disregard of the popular usage of the people (*LLH* 1876: 18). While the discussion in *AA* offers some points of interest, it would be wrong to infer that the publishing policy of the NKP followed the same trajectory. Naval Kishore refrained from openly taking sides in the language controversy. Perhaps his only statement on the language issue can be found in an 1876 Hindi translation of *Alf Laila* (*Arabian Nights*). In its preface he wrote:

> When we turn our attention to the Nagari language, we find that the qualities of this script are beyond description, i.e. the writing is so clear that what is being written is being read. For a long time the discussion has been going on whether the language of the government offices should be Urdu or Nagari. In the government offices in Bihar, the Central Provinces and special districts of the Deccan, the national language [*deśbhāṣā*, i.e. Hindi] and the Devanagari script have become current. Therefore many people desire that books of all kinds should be translated into Devanagari. Works written in Hindi by ancient scholars in which there is a large admixture of Sanskrit words are available in abundance, and many of them have also been printed, but as long as books advancing *all* the arts and ideas are not available in Devanagari characters, correspondence in the Nagari script will not be written well. Therefore, since there is a large admixture of Urdu in the idiom of the government offices and in colloquial speech, we thought that it would be excellent for an understanding of the current manner of speech (*bolcāl*) if the tales and stories were in Devanagari. An effort was made to simplify difficult words of Arabic or Persian origin which have come into Urdu, and

[75] *Avadh Akhbār*, 27 January 1869, SVN 1869: 64.

> occasionally such Sanskrit words as are also used in Hindi (*deśbhāṣā*) have been introduced.[76]

Such a statement was clearly determined by its specific context of advertising a popular work of oriental literature among the target audience of Nagari readers. Even though it to some extent adopted the rhetoric of the Hindi movement in calling Hindi *deśbhāṣā* or 'national language', in its pragmatic thrust it should not be interpreted as an ideological positioning in favour of Hindi and against Urdu. It is important to understand that Naval Kishore's increasing involvement in Hindi publishing was not a deliberate departure from Urdu but a reaction to the market. That it never worked to the detriment of Urdu is borne out by sheer numbers. NKP figures correspond to the general trend in book publishing in the NWP&Oudh. As noted earlier, throughout the 1860s Hindi books made up only a small percentage of the NKP's output. For the year 1869–70, official statistics list 9 works in Hindi/Nagari as compared to 70 Urdu works.[77] In the following year there was a slight proportional increase of Hindi works, with 14 Hindi and 68 Urdu titles.[78] The book publishing market at this point was still heavily dominated by Urdu. As Naval Kishore himself asserted: 'Urdu is becoming more and more the current Indian language.'[79]

By the mid-1870s a slow transformation of the market had set in, with Hindi publications steadily gaining in importance. In 1876, 133 Hindi and 241 Urdu titles were issued in the NWP&Oudh, translating into a ratio of 1:1.8.[80] NKP figures for non-educational Hindi and Urdu books 'printed for the public' during that year show a corresponding ratio of 1:1.7. On closer analysis, however, the NKP data reveals two opposing trends: in the category of first editions, Hindi books had begun to outnumber those in Urdu, with 26,350 volumes in Hindi against 20,545 volumes in Urdu. These figures testify to the growing literary activity and increased demand for general reading matter in Hindi. Yet the impression that Hindi might be taking the lead over Urdu is immediately corrected when one looks at second editions produced during the same year. Here an altogether different picture emerges: with 36,500 Urdu as

[76] *Sahasra rajnī caritra* (*1876), *bhūmikā*.
[77] *OAR*, 1869–70: cl–cliv.
[78] *OAR*, 1870–1: ccxix–ccxxv.
[79] *RPE Oudh*, 1871: 175.
[80] *PGNWP. General Dept.*, July 1876: 30.

compared to 7050 Hindi volumes, Urdu books continued largely to surpass those in Hindi.[81]

Rather than indicating a deliberate shift of allegiance from Urdu to Hindi, Naval Kishore's investment in Hindi publishing was first and foremost a commercial decision in reaction to the growth of the readership and rising market demand for Hindi reading matter. While over the years it entailed a proportional decline in the firm's production of Urdu titles, in absolute numbers Urdu always maintained a substantial lead over Hindi publications. In 1894 the NKP list featured 1007 titles in Hindi, as compared to 1441 titles in Urdu (ratio 1: 1.43) (Suzuki/Tanaka 1981: 18). More importantly, throughout the nineteenth century the House of Naval Kishore maintained an outward 'Urdu' identity; well into the twentieth century it continued to edit its catalogues in Urdu, with Hindi titles always relegated to the back pages.

Arguably, this does not altogether preclude the existence of motives other than commercial expediency in Naval Kishore's engagement with Hindi. His interest in Hindi literary culture and tradition, if never exclusive, was genuine and well in keeping with his larger objective to promote knowledge and enlightenment among his compatriots, both Hindu and Muslim, and instil in them a sense of pride in Indian literary traditions. Thus, from the late 1870s we find him extending his patronage to some of the newly-established Hindi associations. Apparently, Naval Kishore felt no contradiction in simultaneously patronizing Urdu-dominated societies such as the Jalsah-e Tahzib and associations that openly favoured Hindi such as the Bharat Varshiya National Association. Established at Aligarh in 1878 with a view to promoting education and literature, the Bharat Varshiya National Association was soon to figure among the various bodies that submitted pro-Hindi memorials to the Education Commission of 1882. Interestingly, even in making a strong plea for Hindi as the 'true vernacular' of the province, the memorialists did not intend to denigrate Urdu or the Indo-Persian cultural heritage. The way in which they introduced themselves to the Commission suggests that notions of a composite culture of learning were still prevalent:

> The Association was established here chiefly through the influence of Munshi Nawalkishore, proprietor of the *Oudh Akhbar*, the only daily Urdu newspaper in these provinces and it is in its contemplation, in consideration of the present state of funds at its disposal, to establish a library consisting

[81] *RPIR* 1876: 41–2.

> of books of literature, history, science, and arts in the English, Urdu, Persian, Sanskrit and Hindi languages, and as Aligarh, through the indefatigable exertion of our venerable countryman the Hon'ble Syed Ahmed Khan promises to be a seat of learning, such a collection of books is calculated to confer immense benefits on the reading public, besides supplying a crying want of a suitable place for holding meetings for educational and social purposes.[82]

The pro-Hindi tendencies crystallized in the Bhasha Samvarddhini Sabha, a body originating in and closely interlinked with the Bharat Varshiya National Association. Its express purpose was to enrich Hindi through the encouragement of 'original composition and free importation of useful matter from the ancient as well as the modern languages of the world'. Its president, Raja Lakshman Singh, was a prominent advocate of the heavily Sanskritized and pure style of Hindi.[83] Since the Allahabad Government Notification of 1868 had failed to make an impact on the development of Hindi literature, the sabha instigated its own prize-awarding scheme, offering up to Rs 200 for translations and original compositions 'on useful subjects such as Indian agriculture, female education, chemistry, Hindi series, &c.'[84] Naval Kishore patronized the society and assisted it in some of its publications. When in 1890 he commissioned Pandit Mihiracand to prepare a Hindi translation of *Manu smṛti*, he did so for two reasons: one was to provide the Hindi reading public with an easily comprehensible version of this key text of Hindu law—previously existing translations were deemed elusive and obstructing comprehension. The second reason, as expressly stated, was to lend support to the Bhasha Samvarddhini Sabha.[85] Again, while indicating Naval Kishore's sympathies with Hindi, such patronage must not be equated with a newly acquired anti-Urdu position on the publisher's part. Rather, it was a natural extension of his multifarious activities in promoting literature and learning.

Unlike some of his contemporaries, Naval Kishore clearly had no interest in becoming entangled in the ideological pitfalls of the increasingly embittered controversy over Hindi and Urdu. Yet, as much as he tried to steer clear of the language debate, in the heated atmosphere of the late nineteenth century such impartiality was not always easy to maintain. The more he gained recognition as an important figure in Hindi publishing,

[82] *AECR* 1884: 416–17.
[83] For further details, see Nevill 1909: 87, and *RA NWP&Oudh*, 1893: 306.
[84] *AECR* 1884: 418.
[85] *Manu smṛti saṭīk* (*1890), *vijñāpanpatra*.

the more he became subject to an ideological 'appropriation' on the part of partisans of the Hindi movement. Undeterred by his reputation as one of the foremost Urdu publishers in North India, and despite the fact that his mother tongue was undoubtedly Urdu (and a very Persianized one at that), proponents of Hindi tried to claim him for their cause. This not only took the form of routine appraisals of the Lucknow publisher as a patron of Hindi literature, but, at a later stage, also involved an attempt to subsume him altogether into the Hindi fold. The most striking expression of this appropriation can be found in the preface to the NKP's Hindi translation of *Kathāsaritsāgar* (*1896), issued in the year following the publisher's death. It informs us that the translation was commissioned and sponsored by Munshi Naval Kishore, 'the foremost well-wisher of the Hindi language . . . for the sake of raising the prestige of *his mother tongue Hindi (apnī mātṛbhāṣā Hindī)*' (emphasis added).

Defying Linguistic and Cultural Dichotomization

Undeterred by, but not oblivious to, the increasing polarization effected by the debate over Hindi and Urdu, Naval Kishore continued to invest in the promotion of literary and non-literary works in both languages. If an ideological trajectory is to be detected at all in a policy that was largely determined by the laws of the market, I would call it 'cultural assimilation through the medium of print'. This policy drew on notions of a shared literary culture and accorded importance to the Urdu language and Indo-Persian literary traditions for Muslims and Hindus alike; it was in keeping with the composite nature of Naval Kishore's upbringing and reflected an intellectual climate still prevalent among large parts of the Lucknow intelligentsia.

In the underlying project of cultural assimilation, it was paramount to counteract the ongoing communal bifurcation of Hindi and Urdu. Even as he avidly seized the possibilities opened up by the emerging market for Hindi books, Naval Kishore sought to bridge the growing linguistic and religio-cultural divide by focusing on the common cultural heritage and shared literary tastes rather than cultural differences among Hindi and Urdu readers. This was done through various categories of texts. We have already noted the publisher's efforts in promoting the classics of Sanskrit literature in Urdu and the NKP's bi- or trilingual editions of Sanskrit shastric texts, with paraphrases in Urdu and/or Hindi. A wide range of translations or transliterations from Hindi into Urdu and, to a lesser extent, from Urdu into Hindi, were deployed to the same end.

The various Hindi-Urdu translations and transliterations generated by the publishing house over the years bear testimony to a policy that was guided by pragmatism rather than linguistic and cultural ideology. The backdrop to much translation activity was indeed a pragmatic one: in promoting Hindi religious and literary classics in Urdu versions, the NKP catered mainly, if by no means exclusively, for the three Hindu communities traditionally associated with Persian and Urdu literary culture, that is Kayasthas, Kashmiri Brahmins, and Khatris. Even outside these influential communities, who favoured Urdu for cultural and economic reasons and did not identify with Hindi/Nagari, there was a large educated class of mostly urban Hindus who used Urdu as their language of communication and were accustomed to reading and writing in the Urdu script. It was with a view to this sizeable audience, sometimes quaintly denominated as 'Persian-reading *bhakta*s' on NKP title pages, that Urdu-script versions or translations of cherished devotional classics such as *Brajvilās*, *Premsāgar*, *Sukhsāgar*, and *Bhramargīt*, were prepared at the press.[86] As late as 1887 Naval Kishore invested in an annotated edition of Tulsidas's *Ramāyāṇ* with an Urdu commentary by Munshi Svamidayal. It was issued in a voluminous 1222-page edition of 1200 copies. The continuous public demand for such texts exposes the exclusive identification of Urdu with Muslims as an ideological construct.

Another important aspect of the project of counteracting the religio-cultural divide was the NKP's patronage of contemporary Hindu poets of Urdu, many of whom wrote on Hindu religious themes. Mention has already been made of Totaram 'Shayan' (d. 1880), a versatile poet employed at the press who next to his poetic oeuvre contributed a number of important translations. Next to him, the NKP promoted several poets of local repute, notably two poets of Kayastha origin, Jagannath Das Sahai 'Khushtar' Lakhnavi (1809–64) and Shankardayal 'Farhat' Lakhnavi (1843–1904), and the Kashmiri Pandit Kanhaiyalal 'ᶜAshiq' (alive in 1877). Minor though these poets may appear to be to the modern observer, they deserve to be noticed as authors of some of the earliest modern Urdu versions of the Hindu epics and *Purāṇa*s, as also a host of original compositions on Hindu religious topics. Khushtar's prolific oeuvre includes one of the first widely acclaimed *Rāmāyaṇ*s in Urdu, written in 1850 in the reign of Wajid ᶜAli Shah. Generally known as

[86] The following publication dates are given in Urdu lists: *Brajvilās* (*1866); *Premsāgar*, trs. by Lala Svamidayal (*1872), *Sukhsāgar* (*1873), and *Bhaunargīt* (*1878). The latter, a word by word transliteration of Surdas's *Bhramargīt*, was prepared by Munshi Natholal, a Dhusar from the *qaṣbah* of Rewari.

Rāmāyan-e Khushtar (*1864, Fig. 16), it assumed a prominent place among Urdu *Rāmāyaṇ*s and became a perennial favourite, as borne out by more than sixteen reprints (Nabhvi 1993: clv). Khushtar's compositions further include Urdu verse renderings of the celebrated tenth chapter of the *Bhāgavata Purāṇa* (*1863), *Kathā Satnarāyan* (Story of Satnarayan, *1875), and *Sudāmā carit* (Story of Sudama, *1877), an extremely popular myth of *Bhāgavata Purāṇa* origin which existed in countless Hindi versions. Khushtar's younger contemporary Munshi Shankardayal 'Farhat', whom Garcin de Tassy described as a 'very distinguished contemporary Urdu writer' (*HLHH* 1: 448), worked as a teacher at the American Mission School in Lucknow. Farhat's verse renderings of Tulsidas's *Rāmāyaṇ*, known as *Rāmāyan-e Farḥat* (*1866), and of Lalluji's *Premsāgar* (*1868) were issued in richly illustrated editions to wide acclaim. His prolific oeuvre further includes Urdu versions in the *maṣnavī* style of *Adbhut Rāmāyaṇ* (*1870), *Ganeṣapurāṇa*, *Śivapurāṇa* (*1874 [1862?]), *Śiva sahasra nāma* (*1875), and *Jānakī bijay* (*1874). Many of the Urdu compositions of these two poets were, in turn, reissued in Nagari versions.

It was only in the 1880s that the first instances of a deliberate effort to produce translations of a more distinct 'Hindi' character can be witnessed. A salient example is that of Malik Muhammad Jaysi's celebrated Avadhi romance *Padmāvat* (1540), a classic of Sufi poetry. *Padmāvat* (*1865) had for some time been circulated in an Urdu-script version, when in 1880 Lala Raghuvar Dayal was assigned the task of preparing a Hindi/Nagari version of the text. By that time the author could draw on a distinct notion of differentiated vocabularies existing for Hindi and Urdu. While opting for a fairly Sanskritized style, he found it necessary to include a colophon of current 'Urdu' synonyms for the Sanskritic Hindi vocabulary he considered 'difficult' (the expression used is '*gūṛh*', i.e. 'abstruse, hidden, secret'). This extensive colophon affords some insight into the kind of linguistic ability expected from the new Hindi readership. Interestingly, most of the Hindi words glossed appear fairly common and not at all '*gūṛh*' to the modern observer. At the time, however, they were considered to belong to a higher speech register, with which the 'common' reader was yet to become familiarized. Here are some examples of the terms glossed ('Urdu' variants in brackets): *kar* (*hāth*), *yaś* (*neknāmī*), *rain* (*rāt*), *dṛṣṭi* (*nazar*), *śaśī* (*cand*), *gagan* (*āsmān*), *mūl* (*jaṛ*), *bhūmi* (*zamīn*), *madhu* (*śarāb*). A similar concern with general comprehensibility can be detected in an entirely different publication, Nabhadas's *Bhaktamāl* (*1883). As mentioned before,

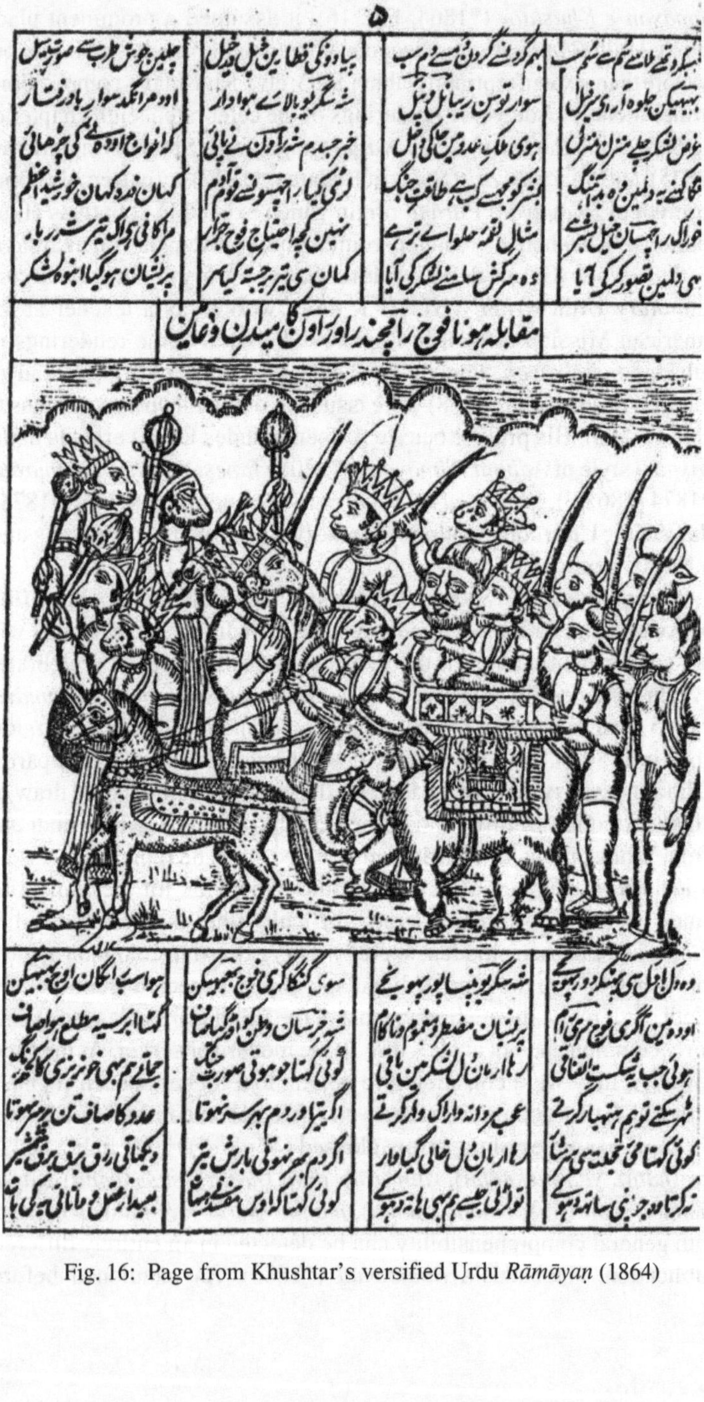

Fig. 16: Page from Khushtar's versified Urdu *Rāmāyaṇ* (1864)

Naval Kishore had popularized the text in Tulsiram's Urdu prose version and Raja Pratap Singh's Hindi translation thereof. When the firm finally invested in the publication of the original *Bhaktamāl*, a text written in terse medieval Brajbhasha verse, it was supplemented with a gloss of difficult Sanskrit and Hindi words.

Thus far we have looked at the translation and promotion of Hindi and Hindu-heritage texts in Urdu. What about the reverse process? Was it a viable commercial proposition for a publisher like Naval Kishore to invest in making texts that belonged to the Urdu literary heritage accessible to the new Hindi reading public? Since the number of literate Hindus who had direct access to Urdu was still considerable, the market for such translations did seem limited. In the case of classical Urdu poetry it was all but non-existent (quite unlike today's growing demand for Urdu poetry in Nagari versions). Hence, Naval Kishore focused on a corpus of popular prose tales and romances which belonged to a joint oral or semi-oral culture and were enjoyed by a wide audience of readers and listeners across communal, regional, and class barriers. That he should do so was not surprising: in a tradition reaching back to Fort William College, tales like *Siṃhāsan battīsī*, *Baitāl paccīsī*, or *Gul-e bakāvalī* were circulated in both Urdu and Nagari script versions right from the time they were first seen into print. In keeping with the comparatively late development of a sizeable Hindi reading public, Urdu-script versions or translations generally preceded those in Nagari. The largest number of Urdu-into-Hindi translations produced at the NKP belonged to the Persian/Urdu narrative genres of *dāstān* and *qiṣṣa* literature. The NKP's pivotal role in fixing the Urdu *dāstān* in print has already been outlined. Largely eclipsed by this momentous achievement are the firm's less spectacular but nonetheless significant efforts in circulating *qiṣṣa* and *dāstān* titles in Hindi. In fact, Naval Kishore was among the first to provide the Nagari readership with printed versions of a number of immensely popular texts.

In 1871 a start was made with *Mohinī caritra* (Fascinating History), a Hindi rendering of Rajab ʿAli Beg Surur's *Fasāna-e ʿajāʾib* (The Story of Wonders), itself a latter-day tale in the *qiṣṣa* tradition composed in elaborate and complex Urdu. While the translation enjoyed wide popularity, Naval Kishore was apparently not satisfied with it, for only four years later he ordered the NKP's managing director Pandit Ramratan Vajpeyi to prepare a new version. *Apūrv kathā* (Extraordinary Tale) came out in 1875. Soon afterwards, Pandit Pyarelal finished his translation of the Urdu *Alf Laila*. Bearing the more suitable Hindi title *Sahasra rajnī* *caritra* (*1876), it appears to be the first comprehensive Hindi version of the *Arabian Nights* circulated in print. Previously, Hindi readers had to content themselves with *Sahasra rātrī saṃkṣep*, an abridged translation from the Bengali by Pandit Badrilal of Benares College, which was published from the Benares Medical Hall Press in 1861. In 1877 the NKP continued its series of *dāstān* and *qiṣṣa* titles with Jivanram Jat's translations of three works belonging to 'the hardy perennials of the qissa genre' (Pritchett 1985: 26): The first, a Hindi version of Mir Amman's *Bāgh o bahār*, was called *Cahār darveś* (The Four Dervishes) after its Persian original but bore the nicely assimilated Hindi subtitle *'Cār yogiyoṁ ke deśāṭan kī citrabicitra kahānī'* (A picturesque tale of the travels of four yogis from one country to another). The second and third were *Hātimtāī kā qissā* by Haidar Bakhsh Haidari, and *Gul o sanaubar* by Nemcand. Once again, it was emphasized that the translations had been executed in 'simple Hindi, that is in a colloquial style from which difficult words have been removed'.[87]

The firm's most noted publication, however, followed in 1879 in the form of *Amīr Hamzā kī dāstān*, the first Hindi version of the celebrated *dāstān* of Amir Hamza. The immense popularity of *Dāstān-e Amīr Hamzā* prompted Naval Kishore to invest in an abridged Hindi version even before he embarked on his huge project to see the complete Urdu *dāstān* into print. As Pandit Kalicaran, the translator of the Hindi *dāstān*, explained in his preface, 'When reading the *qiṣṣa* of Amir Hamza most people felt that it would be of great benefit if this book were translated into Hindi *(devanāgarī bhāṣā)*'. Hence, 'for the benefit of connoisseurs of Nagari' he had been commissioned by Naval Kishore to render the text into 'easy colloquial Hindi (*bolcāl kī saral hindī bhāṣā*)'.[88] The result was a 520-page version in which the Persian vocabulary had been replaced by suitable Sanskritisms and Persian verse forms by Indic *kavitt*, *soraṭhā* and *chaupāī* metres (Pritchett 1991: 23). 'With its assimilation of a highly Islamic content into a self-consciously Sanskritized form', Pritchett notes, *Amīr Hamzā kī dāstān* 'offers a fascinating early glimpse of the development of Hindi' (ibid.). It does not, however, as she also presumes, represent 'a radical departure' in the publisher's repertoire of Hindi books, but rather forms the culmination point in a series of translations of popular Persian/Urdu prose narratives. As has been

[87] '. . . saralbhāṣā arthāt kliṣṭ śabdoṁ ko nikālkar bolcāl kī rīti', *Hātimtāī kā qissā* (Lucknow ²1882), *bhūmikā*.

[88] *Amīr Hamzā kī dāstān* (Lucknow ²1883), *bhūmikā*.

shown, these had been incorporated into the list of Hindi publications right from the early 1870s, marking the departure from a publication repertoire which at first consisted primarily of Hindu religious, poetical, astrological, and medical texts. The *dāstān* and *qiṣṣa* renderings were eagerly received by the Hindi reading public and within a short time went through second and third editions. By the mid-1870s the literary tastes of Nagari readers had broadened considerably, making the publication of Persian and Urdu prose romances in Hindi/Nagari versions a commercially lucrative venture.

This chapter has argued that in studying early commercial print culture in Hindi, our attention needs to shift from the urban centres usually associated with Hindi and its literature to a somewhat unexpected place: the city of Lucknow. It is due to the enterprising spirit and farsightedness of Munshi Naval Kishore that Lucknow, a traditional stronghold of Persian and Urdu print culture, deserves a prominent place on the map of nineteenth-century Hindi publishing as well. As the first large-scale commercial publisher in the history of Hindi, the House of Naval Kishore played a pivotal role in the diffusion of Hindi literature and the expansion of its reading and book-buying public. Supported by colonial patronage and run on sound commercial lines, it was the first to address a prospective mass public of Nagari readers with a steadily expanding range of widely circulated and inexpensive texts, also accessible to readers of more modest means. Beyond its involvement in textbook publishing, the Lucknow publishing house came forth with an unprecedented range of influential publications—many of them originating in its Department of Composition and Translation—which contributed to the consolidation of modern standard Hindi and provided a major impulse for the spread and development of its literature.

Moreover, through the promotion of Sanskrit classics in Hindi translation, the NKP joined in the grand effort to revive Hindu literary tradition and reinforce the historico-cultural nexus with the Hindu past. In some respects, Naval Kishore's efforts in preserving and promoting classical Hindi literature may even be taken to prefigure subsequent collective efforts undertaken by the Nagari Pracharini Sabha of Benares (est. 1893), the leading Hindi organization in the nineteenth century. It would be difficult, however, to read any Hindu nationalist ideology into his involvement in Hindi and Sanskrit literature, for, at the same time, he continued to exercise his role as one of the foremost publishers of Urdu, Persian, and Islamic literature in northern India. The NKP's publishing policy clearly aimed at defying the ongoing dichotomization of Hindi and

Urdu, with its multifaceted translation activities—from Sanskrit into Urdu, from Hindi into Urdu and vice versa—constituting one of the last sustained efforts in propagating the values of a shared and composite Indian culture. It is important to understand that for commercial publishers in nineteenth-century North India to bring out translations or transliterations from Hindi into Urdu and vice versa was nothing extraordinary in itself. What distinguished the House of Naval Kishore was that it produced an unparalleled range of translations, particularly of Hindu religious literature in Urdu, and that this translation activity continued unabated into the 1890s, that is for several decades after the Hindi-Nagari movement first started to propagate an exclusive Hindi-Hindu identity. Against this backdrop, translation assumed a broader cultural significance: it meant counteracting dichotomization through a textual ensemble which not only bridged the linguistic divide but implied a clear statement against the narrow identification of language and script with religious community.

With its host of inexpensive editions of religious and literary classics, popular tales, dramas and songs, medical and astrological manuals, the NKP did much to introduce the Hindi book as a household commodity in North Indian homes. The lasting impact of Naval Kishore's contribution to the popularization of Hindi, and by extension, Hindu-heritage literature, would later be attested by no less famous an observer than Munshi Premchand, who in 1928 noted that 'the number of important books in Hindi and Sanskrit published from this press up to now has not been attained by any other Indian press' and that NKP Hindi books 'have spread to every village and every household' (Dvivedi 1928: 1).

Conclusion

This study has been designed as a contribution to the history of the book in Hindi and Urdu. It argues that from the 1840s and 1850s the field of cultural production in North India underwent far-reaching changes as a result of a process which has been described as the 'commercialization' of print. Based on technological advances and a variety of socio-economic and political transformations wrought by colonialism, commercialization was a major turning point, ushering in a paradigm change and a new phase in the history of print in the subcontinent. It introduced the mass-produced and inexpensive book in Hindi and Urdu and for the first time afforded north Indian literate audiences general access to the products of print culture in their respective modern regional languages. By altering the relationship between participants in literary production and transmission, commercial print culture affected literary practice and the ways in which knowledge was generated, circulated, and preserved. A major objective of this study has been to trace the commodification of the book and the way it made its entry into the homes of an unprecedented number of ordinary people.

Previous research on print culture has tended to concentrate on the role of Christian missionaries and the colonial state in diffusing the printed word in nineteenth-century India. By contrast, this book posits the centrality of the Indian-owned publishing house as a principal agent in the rapidly expanding market of regional-language print. The role of Indian printer-publishers in shaping Hindi and Urdu print culture has often been superficially acknowledged, but has rarely been analysed in greater depth. Through a case study of the foremost north Indian publishing house, *An Empire of Books* has sought to demonstrate how much our understanding of nineteenth-century literary and intellectual culture can profit from such an investigation.

To study the operations and activities of Indian publishers means nothing less than to restore to Indians their agency in shaping literary culture and diffusing knowledge in the colonial setting. By continuing to ignore their contribution, we risk perpetuating a one-sided picture that depicts literary creation and knowledge formation under colonialism as only a hegemonic project on the part of a dominant and oppressive foreign regime. In foregrounding Indian agency, this book has striven to illuminate a process that has been called the 'indigenization of print' (Orsini 2004b). In doing so, it positions itself within an ongoing discourse that interprets the colonial encounter and the creation of knowledge in nineteenth-century India as a transactional and 'dialogic process' (Irschick 1994), in which Indians, despite the asymmetric power configuration in which they found themselves, assumed an active and self-assertive role in engaging with colonial knowledge in a process that involved both assimilation and contestation.

To study the operations of a publishing house is a pertinent approach to this endeavour. An exploration of publishing practice reminds us of the materiality of the book, resituating the production of books in its social and economic contexts. Scholars from various disciplines have dealt extensively with the socio-cultural and political ramifications of the formation and rise to public importance of Hindi and Urdu and their literatures in the nineteenth century, yet, little attempt has been made to examine the material, economic, and organizational-structural aspects of contemporary literary production. This study has drawn on the conceptual frameworks of Bourdieu's field of cultural production and Hohendahl's institution of literature. As sophisticated theories of context, they each allow us to assess the cultural significance of the publishing house in its particular spatial and temporal setting and view its operations within a larger discursive formation of other sub-institutions, both British and Indian, which constituted the literary field in nineteenth-century colonial India.

Combining the functions of industrialist, literary patron, educator, and intellectual stalwart, Indian publishers operated within and also helped shape the public sphere. An investigation into their public lives provides valuable insights into the social and economic networks through which the professionals of the book trade interacted with each other and larger groups of the colonial intelligentsia. Frequently sustained by acts of philanthropy and patronage, such networks were deployed to various ends: to foster commercial interests, enhance social standing, and gather support for political aspirations. Publishers of Munshi Naval Kishore's stature and economic power rose to positions of considerable influence in the colonial public sphere. As has been shown, it was precisely the social authority and influence which the Lucknow publisher wielded in indigenous society that made him a coveted figure in British eyes. Colonial administrators had a vested interest in co-opting Naval Kishore both as a formal collaborator in official printing ventures and as an informal informant who would act as a cultural intermediary and mediate public opinion. The honorary positions he received and the bestowal of an honorific title upon him were less a recognition of the services he rendered to literature and learning than an effective means of tying him to British interests.

As *An Empire of Books* has shown, the imperatives of profitability and increased turnover reigning in the commercial marketplace did not preclude Indian publishers' engagement with the diffusion of specialized knowledge, scholastic texts, and high literary culture. As businessmen, commercial publishers were also cultural entrepreneurs. The advancement of academic, scientific, and general knowledge in Indian languages, the preservation of the classical literary heritage and its popularization by way of translation became equally important issues of concern for them. A print capitalist with a cultural vision and a social mission, Munshi Naval Kishore provides a salient example of how the different functions of general and scholarly publishing could be reconciled in commercial printing. In catering to the specific needs of different indigenous knowledge communities and in responding to their literary and scholastic discourses, publishing houses formed an essential link in a network of institutional spaces through which Indians created and disseminated their own knowledge. In the process, they helped popularize and instil cultural pride in indigenous literary traditions of past and present. Mass-produced standardized texts enhanced the socio-cultural identities of scholastic, sectarian, and caste communities, while also creating new interpretive communities. They enabled readers to participate in 'unified fields of communication' and allowed for cultural interaction on a supra-regional level.

The Naval Kishore Press was by all means an extraordinary institution. To print and publish almost 5000 titles in various languages in a period of less than four decades remains an unparalleled achievement in the history of print in the subcontinent. Yet, as this book has argued, despite the unusual size and scope of its operations, Naval Kishore's firm is representative of the north Indian publishing scene, in that it embodied the energy and spirit of enterprise that permeated the world of print in the nineteenth century. In outlining what a single firm achieved on its own, my objective was not to insist on the quantitative impact alone, but rather to convey an impression of the dynamism and enormous potential inherent in the domestic publishing trade despite its various economic and other limitations. Providing a model to other agents in the publishing field, the success of the Naval Kishore Press rested on three cornerstones:

colonial patronage; a publishing policy that engaged with a wide range of genres, both literary and non-literary, but had at its core the popularization of religious, literary and educational classics in inexpensive and accessible formats; and the maintenance of a commercially run vernacular newspaper, which attracted the collaboration of some of the leading literary talent in contemporary prose and journalistic writing.

The interaction between Indian publishing houses and the colonial state was decidedly more complex and multifaceted than the asymmetrical power configuration of colonialism might suggest at first sight. My investigation into the business relationship between the British administration and the House of Naval Kishore has brought to light some of the tensions and contradictions arising from the state's perception of the domestic publishing trade as a field that had to be simultaneously encouraged and subjected to close monitoring and control. The conflicting aims of state support and state surveillance became manifest in state legislation, censorship practice, and the distribution of patronage. They were especially pronounced in the booming textbook sector, the largest and most important area of regional-language book production in the nineteenth century. Here Indian printer-publishers emerged as both collaborators and economic rivals of the colonial state. We have seen that a substantial proportion of publishing at the House of Naval Kishore was undertaken at the instigation of or in collaboration with the British. The profits made from British commissions were indeed the single most important economic factor in sustaining the operations of the firm. Collaboration in educational and official printing was intense and mutually beneficial, but nonetheless involved constant negotiation. Due to the enormous economic power he wielded, Naval Kishore was in a privileged position *vis-à-vis* government, a position he cleverly exploited. Even then, he was not always successful in his negotiations with the state. Small-scale publishers found it infinitely more difficult to get their share of government patronage.

As the analysis of Naval Kishore's professional and cultural choices has shown, there was much overlap between the colonial state's and his own agendas. This often makes it difficult to determine whether particular publication initiatives were instigated by the British or by the publisher himself. However, as this book has sought to demonstrate throughout, much of the activity going on at his press and, for that matter, in Indian publishing, happened outside the purview of the colonial state and was clearly not associated with the British civilizing mission and its utilitarian program of 'useful literature'. Previous accounts of print culture that have depicted print as a tool of the hegemonic interests of the colonial state and a small indigenous elite of the bilingual upper-caste intelligentsia have added to our understanding of the construction of textual hierarchies and the propagation of elite cultural ideology, but have failed to adequately address Indian engagement with the commercial genres. Commercial publishers catered for a reading public whose needs were not limited to education and information. Nineteenth-century readers also wanted to be diverted and entertained; they sought emotional pleasure and spiritual consolation from their reading. Naval Kishore and his confrères responded to the tastes of the reading public by circulating folk and popular literature, song and prayer books, dramas, mythological stories and, increasingly, entertaining fiction (a wide range of genres that fell outside the categories of 'useful' and 'refined' literature and were therefore dismissed by most British administrator-educators and sections of the Indian elite). In constantly blurring the boundaries between elite and popular literature, commercial print culture calls for a re-evaluation of these categories. 'Respectable' publishers engaged with 'high' and 'low' literature and did not shy away from ministering to the popular tastes.

Indian publishers negotiated a field that cut across caste and class distinctions and communal divisions. One significant conclusion that emerges from this study of a North-Indian publishing house is that in the commercial marketplace delineations of Hindi–Urdu and Hindu–Muslim were much less pronounced and rigid than is suggested by many studies that have analysed precisely the formation of this dichotomy in the nineteenth century. As an intellectual meeting place where Hindu and Muslim scholars and literati found themselves in close physical proximity and constant interaction, the publishing house *qua* institution defied such communal divides. However, the validity of this particular observation needs to be counterchecked against the policies and operations of other publishing firms. While the operations of Naval Kishore have been taken to be representative of much of the activity going on in the Hindi and Urdu print market, it would be inaccurate to posit a uniform trajectory for commercial publishing. True, commercial publishers were subject to the same laws of supply and demand and, indeed, there was much overlap in the books they produced. Yet, within this configuration, their motivations, policies, and ensuing output showed considerable variation. A publisher with an overt Hindu nationalist outlook was bound to pursue a different agenda than Naval Kishore who, with his notion of a shared and composite literary culture, did not privilege Hindu over Muslim traditions in his promotion of Persian and Urdu, Sanskrit and Hindi literature.

Reflecting the sources I drew upon, this book has offered a narrative of an Indian publisher's achievements; only rarely has it told us about his failures. In a publishing career that spanned almost four decades, there must have been many instances of misguided choices, abortive publication ventures, financial crises, unsuccessful negotiations and disputes with authors. To go on from here and direct our attention to the authors' perspective would be a meaningful supplement and, presumably, corrective to the present study. Authors, as we know from countless examples in European book history, generally have very different stories to tell about the making of their books. Ghalib's extensive correspondence provides a glimpse into what this 'counternarrative' might look like, hinting at publishers usurping manuscripts, at editors meddling with texts, at sloppy copyists spoiling them, and at the many vicissitudes encountered by the author in his dealings with the professionals of the book trade.

An Empire of Books also alerts us to some of the methodological difficulties in studying Indian print culture. Historians of the book in India continue to face formidable obstacles regarding both the paucity of source material and the difficulties in accessing it. Much documentary evidence is contained in British official records, which, though immensely rich in information, reflect a colonial preoccupation with statistical enumeration, and in a more or less overt fashion, focus on the category of 'useful' literature. In the absence of publishers' archives, nineteenth-century Indian publishers speak to us mainly through their legacy: the books they produced. These books need to be studied in a new way, both as physical objects and as 'tools for the making of context and content alike', to borrow Adrian Johns's phrase in *The Nature of the Book*. Printed books, as we have seen in the preceding chapters, were collective products. With their title pages, forewords and afterwords, customary chronograms, laudatory poems, publisher's notices and advertisements inserted at the back, books reveal some of the collective effort that went into their making; they may tell us about the motivation of their authors and patrons, and sometimes even indicate their target audience. Nita Kumar's contention about research on indigenous education certainly rings true for the study of Hindi and Urdu print culture: our involvement with the extant data in South Asia is barely beginning (Kumar 2000: 31).

While this book has emphasized the vibrancy of the publishing trade in Hindi and Urdu, it finally leaves us with an unresolved question concerning the power and authority of the printed word in a society marked by widespread illiteracy. I have argued that literacy figures are not an adequate analytical tool to estimate the impact of the printed book in nineteenth-century Indian society. A more promising approach to the complex question of the effects of print seems to be the exploration of readership and consumption practices. To study aspects of production and transmission, as this book has done, is a useful and necessary preliminary step in this project. Conversely, the study of production raises many queries that can only be answered through a study of consumption. Books were put to use in a vast range of different ways, Adrian Johns contends, their consequences being 'as dependent on the practices of the users as on any putatively objective content they may possess' (Johns 1998: 636). While quantitative indicators (the publisher's output, circulation figures, print runs, and the frequency of reprints) have been crucial to the present project, they ultimately did not tell us who read a given NKP book and to what effect. Equally, we may have acknowledged Naval Kishore's multifarious efforts to popularize the printed book and enlarge the audience of readers and book buyers through cheap formats, reprints, and modern translations of cherished classics; the success of such attempts to introduce qualitative changes in the readership, however, cannot be measured in terms of circulation. The history of production, it seems, must remain an incomplete narrative as long as it is not supplemented by a history of reading. If still a distant project, reconciling these two areas of inquiry will be a fruitful and highly consequential enterprise in the study of North Indian intellectual culture. It promises to provide us with a better insight into how the printed book affected not only literary and cultural practice but also peoples' lives.

Appendices

Appendix I

Early Printing Presses at Agra, Lucknow, and Benares (1817–57)

Location	Name of Press	est.	Proprietor/Editor	Paper(s)
Agra	Zubdat al-Akhbar Press	1833	Wajid ʿAli Khan	*Zubdat al-A<u>kh</u>bār* (P)
	Asaʿd al-Akhbar Press	1847	Qamaruddin	*Asaʿd al-A<u>kh</u>bār* (U);
	Nur al-Absar Press	1852	Sadasukh Lal	*Nūr al-Absār* (U); *Buddhi Prakāś* (H)
	Mufīd-e Khalaʾiq Press	1856	Shivnarayan ʻAram'	*Mufīd-e <u>Kh</u>alāʾiq* (U); *Sarvopakārak* (H) *Meʿyār al-Shuʿarā* (U)
	Aftab-e ʿAlamtab Press	1857	Ganesh Lal	*Aftāb-e ʿĀlamtāb* (U); *Sūrajprakāś* (H)
Lucknow*	Sultani Press (Royal Press)	1817	Nawab Ghaziuddin Haidar	
	Muhammadi Press	1837	Muhammad Husain (Haji Harmain Sharifain)	
	Mustafaʾi Press	1839	Muhammad Mustafa Khan	
	Mir Hasan Press (Hasani Press)	1840	Mir Hasan Rizwi	
	Muhammadi Press	1842	Haji Wali Muhammad	
	Haidari Press	1844	Muhammad Uzzaman	
	Jaʿfari Press	1845	Mirza Muhammad Jaʿfari Khan	
	Sangin Press	1845	Nawab Mirza ʿAli Khan? Hafizullah?	

Appendix I (*contd.*)

Appendix I (*contd.*)

Location	Name of Press	est.	Proprietor/Editor	Paper(s)
	Masihayi Press	1845	Masihuzzanab b. Maulvi Nur Muhammad	
	ʿAlavi Press	1846	ʿAli Bakhsh Khan	
	Murtazavi Press	1846	Sheikh Nisar ʿAli	
	Muhammadi Press	1856	Muhammad Yaqub Ansari	*Ṭilism-e Lakhnaʾū* (U)
	Sehr-e Samiri Press	1856	Pandit Baijnath	*Seḥr-e Sāmirī* (U)
Benares	Benares Akhbar Press	1844	Govind Raghunath Thatte	*Banāras Akhbār* (H); *Banāras Gazaṭ* (U)
	Sudhakar Press	1847	Rataneshvar Tiwari	*Sudhākar* (H)
	Bagh o Bahar Press	1847–53	Kedarnath Ghosh and Kaliparshad Banerjee	*Mirāt al-ʿUlūm* (U); *Bāgh o bahār* (U) *Candrodaya* (H); *Candra Uday* (B)
	Gulzar-e Hamesha Bahar Press	1848	Virsingh Khattri	
	Mufid-e Hind Press	1850–53	Harbanslal	*Zāʾirīn-e Hind* (U)
	Kashi Press	1851	Kashidas Mitra	*Kāśī Yātrā Patrikā* (B); *Aftāb-e Hind* (U)

P = *Persian* B = *Bengali* H = *Hindi* U = *Urdu*

*Where dates for Lucknow presses given by Diehl 1973 and Khan 1990 differ, I have opted for the earlier date.

Appendix II

Leading Indian-Owned Presses at Lucknow and Benares (1840–1900)

a. Lucknow

Name of Press	1840–1845	1845–1850	1850–1855	1855–1860	1860–1865	1865–1870	1870–1875	1875–1880	1880–1885	1885–1890	1890 1895	1890–1900
Aftab-e ʿAlimtab							*	*	*			
ʿAlavi Press		*			*	*	*	*			*	
Anjuman-e Hind Press					*	*	*					
Asadi Press						*	*	*				
Asafi Press					*	*	*	*	*	*	*	
Anwar-e Muhammadi							*	*	*	*	*	*
Bhagvandin Press					*	*	*					
Chashma-e Faiz								*	*			
Dabdaba-e Ahmadi									*	*	*	*
Dilpazir Press											*	*
Ganga Prasad Varma and Brothers									*	*	*	*
Gulshan-e Faiz Press											*	
Gulshan-e Muhammadi							*	*				
Hasani Press	*	*										
Husaini Press							*	*				

Appendix II (*contd.*)

Appendix II (*contd.*)

Name of Press	1840–1845	1845–1850	1850–1855	1855–1860	1860–1865	1865–1870	1870–1875	1875–1880	1880–1885	1885–1890	1890 1895	1890–1900
Isna- ʿAshari Press							*	*	*	*	*	*
Islamiya Press										*		
Jaʿfri Press									*	*	*	*
Kanya Kubja Press										*	*	
Karnama Press					*	*	*					
Muhammadi Press	*	*	*	*	*	*	*	*	*			
Murtazawi Press	*	*	*	*	*	*	*	*				
Mustafaʾi Press	*	*	*	*	*	(*shifted to Delhi*)						
Nami Press		*	*	*	*	*	*					
Naval Kishore Press (Avadh Akhbar Press)				*	*	*	*	*	*	*	*	*
Qaumi Press										*	*	*
Rozana-e Akhbar										*	*	
Samar-e Hind Press (Pt. Baijnath's Press)				*	*	*	*					
Sham-e Avadh								*			*	
Shaukat-e Islam										*	*	
Tamannaʾi Press								*	*	*		
Yusufi Press												*

Appendix II (*contd.*)

Appendix II (*contd.*)

b. Benares

Name of Press	1845–1850	1850–1855	1855–1860	1860–1865	1865–1870	1870–1875	1875–1880	1880–1885	1885–1890	1890–1895	1895–1900
Amar Press								*	*	*	*
Benares Press (Kashi Press?)				*		*		*			*
Benares Akhbar Press	*	*	*	*	*						
Benares Light Press (Gopinath Pathak)				*	*	*	*	*	*	*	
Benares Printing Press						*	*	*	*	*	
Bharat Jivan Press								*	*	*	*
Candraprabha Press								*	*	*	*
Divakar Press			*	*	*	*	*				
Ganesh Press		*	*	*	*	*					
Hariprakash Press								*	*	*	*
Jain Prabhakar Press							*	*	*	*	
Kashi Sanskrit Press				*	*	*	*	*			
Kedar Prabhakar Press			*	*	*	*	*	*			
Mufid-e Hind Press		*	*	*	*						
Rajarajeshvari Press									*	*	*
Siddiqi Press; *name changed to* Sayyid al-Matabi									*	*	*
Sudhakar Press	*	*	*								
Timir Nashak Press									*	*	

Appendix III

Select Chronological List of NKP Hindi Publications

Year	Title	Author/Translator	Category	Remarks
1860	*Paṭvāriyoṁ ke hisāb kī pustak*	Ramsharandas	textbook/mensuration	pts. 1–4
1861	*Kitāb jantrī*	Maganlal (trs.)	textbook/mensuration	trs. from the Urdu of Sukhlal
	Jñancālīsī	Shrilal	textbook/moral instruction	
1862	*Sūrajpur kī kahānī*	Shrilal (trs.)	textbook/moral instruction	trs. from the English of H. S. Reid
1863	*Dharmsiṃha kā vṛttānt*	Shrilal (trs.)	textbook/moral instruction	trs. from the English of J. Muir
	Rāmāyaṇ	Tulsidas	epic	
1864	*Bālābodh*	Chotelal Tivari	textbook/primer for girls	
	Premsāgar	Lalluji Lal	textbook/devotional	
	Dohāvalī	Tulsidas	textbook/devotional	
	Sūrsāgar	Surdas	devotional poetry	
	Nityakīrtan	Surdas	devotional poetry	
	Amṛtsāgar	Savai Pratap Singh of Jaipur	medicine	
1865	*Varṇaprakāśikā*	Durgaprasad (trs.)	textbook/primer	transl. of *Mufīd al-mubtadī*
	Rekhāgaṇit	Mohanlal and Vamshidhar (trs.)	textbook/geometry	Euclid's Elements of Geometry

Appendix III (*contd.*)

Appendix III (*contd.*)

Year	Title	Author/Translator	Category	Remarks
	Gaṇitprakāś	Shrilal and Vamshidhar (trs.)	textbook/arithmetic	transl. of *Mubādi al-ḥisāb*
	Hindī bīj gaṇit	Mohanlal (trs.)	textbook/arithmetic	trs. from the English
	Bhāṣācandrodaya	Shrilal	textbook/ grammar	
	Bhūgoltattva	Kalicaran (trs.)	textbook/geography	transl. of *Anīs al-sayyahīn*
	Padārthvidyāsār	Vijayshankar (trs.)	textbook/natural science	transl. of *Risāla-e ʿilm-e tabīʾat*
	Inglistān kā itihās	Harilal (trs.)	textbook/history	transl. of *Tavārīkh-e Inglistān*
1866	*Rāmāyaṇ*	Tulsidas	epic/devotional poetry	
	Sukhsāgar	Makkanlal	Purāṇa	transl. of the *Bhāgavata Purāṇa*
	Brajvilās	Brajvasidas	devotional poetry	
	Dānlīlā	Surdas	devotional poetry	
	Mānashaṃs bhūṣaṇ	Shukdevlal	commentary	commentary on *Rāmcaritmānas*
1867	*Bhāratvarṣīya itihās*	Ramcandra Sen	textbook/history	
1868	*Barṇmālā*	Shiva Prasad	textbook/primer	
	Barṇprakāś	Ramcandra Sen	textbook/primer	
	Patradīpikā	Ramcandra Sen & Kalicaran	textbook/letter-writer	
	Patramālā	Kalicaran	textbook/letter-writer	
	Vidyācakra (Bidyācakra)	Shivnarayan (trs.)	textbook/natural science	transl. of *Dāʾirah-e ʿilm*
	Rāmāyaṇ	Tulsidas	textbook/epic/devotional	first type-set edition
	Cīrharaṇ	Surdas	devotional poetry	

Appendix III (*contd.*)

Appendix III (*contd.*)

Year	Title	Author/Translator	Category	Remarks
	Bāṃsurī līlā	Surdas	devotional poetry	
	Hanumān bāhuk	Tulsidas	devotional poetry	
	Guptgīt	Patitdas of Nawabganj	music/songs	
	Banyātrā	Kanhaiyalal	pilgrimage manual	
1869	*Bhūgol darpaṇ*	Ramprasad & Kalicaran	textbook/geography	
	Bhūgolvarṇan	Ramprasad	textbook/geography	
	Vidyāṅkur	Shrilal (trs.)	textbook/physical science	transl. of *Haqāʾiq al-maujūdāt*
	Sabhā bilās	Lalluji Lal	textbook/poetic anthology	
	Saccī bahādurī	Shiva Prasad (trs.)	textbook/moral instruction	
	Nānārthnavasaṅgrahāvalī	Matadin Shukla	textbook/poetics and rhetoric	
	Bhāratvarṣīya itihās	Maganlal (trs.)	textbook/history	transl. of *Wāqiʿāt-e Hind*
	Kiṣkiṇḍā kāṇḍ	Tulsidas	textbook/epic/devotional	
	Premsāgar	Lalluji Lal	textbook/devotional	first type-set edition
	Bisātin līla	Surdas	devotional poetry	
	Kṛṣṇamālā		devotional poetry	
	Satnām poṭhī = *Viṣṇusahasranāma*		hymns/ritual	
	Ratnāvalī	Ajit Simha	devotional poetry	
	Avadh yātrā	Gursaran Lal	pilgrimage manual	

Appendix III (*contd.*)

Appendix III (*contd.*)

Year	Title	Author/Translator	Category	Remarks
1870	*Bhojprabandhsār*	Vamshidhar (trs.)	textbook/reader	from the Sanskrit of Ballala
	Vikrāmvilās	Bholanath Caube	textbook/reader	metrical version of the *Baitāl paccīsī*
	Kṣetraprakāś	Govind Lal	textbook/mensuration	transl. of *Risāla-e Gobind Lāl*
	Gaṇitkāmadhenu	Ramnarayan	textbook/arithmetic	
	Patrahitaiśiṇī	Sheonarayan (trs.)	textbook/letter-writer	transl. of *Mufīd al-inshā*
	Jagadbhūgol	Ishvari Prasad	textbook/geography	transl. of *Jughrāfiyah-e ʿālam*
	Bhāṣā bhāskar	W. Etherington	textbook/grammar	
	Śabd prakāśikā	Shitalprasad Gupt	textbook/grammar	
	Gītāvalī	Tulsidas	devotional poetry	
	Premprakāś	Gaurishankar Dvivedi		
	Basant dīpikā			
	Siṃhāsan battīsī		tales	
	Mādhavī Śaṅkar digvijay bhāṣā	Madhavanand Bharti (trs.)	biography	from the Sanskrit of Sayanacarya
	Bhaktamāl (Bhaktakalpadrum)	Raja Pratap Simha of Sidhua	hagiology	trs. into modern Hindi by Kalicaran
	Rāg prakāś	Raja Madhav Singh of Amethi	music	
	Vaidya jīvan	Shankarprasad (trs.)	medicine	from the Sanskrit of Lolimbaraja
1871	*Akṣarārambh*	Lakshmi Narayan	textbook/primer	

Appendix III (*contd.*)

Appendix III (*contd.*)

Year	Title	Author/Translator	Category	Remarks
	Bhāṣātattvadīpikā arthāt Hindī bhāṣā vyākaraṇ	Harigopal Upadhyaya	textbook/grammar	
	Śikṣāvalī	Kalicaran (trs.)	textbook/reader	transl. of *Taʿlīm al-mubtadī*
	Padmāvat	Fakhruddin	romance	
1872	*Bālābhūṣaṇ*	Jamna Kumvar	textbook/primer for girls	
	Avadh deśīya bhūgol	Maganlal (trs.)	textbook/geography	transl. of *Jughrāfiya-e Avadh*
	Rekhāgaṇit praśnāvalī	Babu Banke Lal	textbook/arithmetic	
	Nighaṇṭ bhāṣā	Madanpal (trs.)	medicine	transl. of *Madanavinoda*
1873	*Akṣarāvalī*	Sayyid Safdar Ali	textbook/primer	
	Akṣaradīpikā	Shrilal	textbook/primer	
	Rājnīti	Lalluji Lal	textbook/fables	trs. from the *Hitopadeśa*, Hall's edition
	Pahāṛoṁ kī pustak	Gopal Singh	textbook/mathematics	
	Strīyoṁ kī hitopatrikā	Sheonarayan (trs.)	textbook/primer for girls	transl. of *Mufīd an-nisā*
	Brahmasār	Dindās	devotional poetry	
	Rāmāyaṇ saṭīk	Tulsidas	epic/devotional poetry	with the commentary *Mānasdīpikā* by Raghunath Das
	Satsaī	Tulsidas	devotional poetry	
	Hanumān cālīsā		devotional poetry	
	Sudāmācaritra	Narottam	devotional poetry	

Appendix III (*contd.*)

Appendix III (*contd.*)

Year	Title	Author/Translator	Category	Remarks
	Samar Bahārbindrāvan	Rai Bindraban (also Vrindaban)	philosophy	A lecture on the teachings of the Vihar Vrindavan Sect
	Indrajāl (nāgarī)	Vamshidhar (comp.)	astrology/divination and magic	trs. from the Sanskrit
	Kāyasthkulbhāskar	Ramcaran Sharma	caste history	
1874	*Kṣetracandrikā*	Vamshidhar (trs.)	textbook/mensuration	transl. of *Miṣbāh al-masāḥat*
	Līlāvatī (nāgarī)	Rai Chand Nagar	textbook/arithmetic	trs. from the Sanskrit
	Bhāṣākāvyasaṅgrah	Maheshdatt Shukla (comp.)	textbook/poetical anthology	
	Sundar kāṇḍ	Tulsidas	textbook/epic/devotional	from the *Rāmāyaṇ*
	Kavitāvalī rāmāyaṇ	Tulsidas	devotional poetry	
	Gītāvalī	Tulsidas	devotional poetry	revised edition
	Bijay muktāvalī	Chatra Singh	devotional poetry	
	Dohāvalī rāmāyāṇ	Tulsidas	devotional poetry	
	Jugalvilās	Ramsimha Dev	devotional poetry	
	Kṛṣṇabhajanāvalī	Jivan Das	devotional poetry	abr. version of Makkhanlal's *Sukhsāgar*
	Gaṅgālahrī	Padmakar Bhatt	devotional poetry	
	Dohāvalī ratnāvalī	Umapati Tripathi	devotional poetry	
	Dānlīlā aur Nāglīlā	Gangadhar	devotional poetry	
	Janak paccīsī	Mandan	poetry	

Appendix III (*contd.*)

Appendix III (*contd.*)

Year	Title	Author/Translator	Category	Remarks
	Sṛṅgārprakāś	Ramprasad	poetics	
	Jñansvarodaya	Charandas	yoga	
	Lāvnī vā śer Banārsī arthāt marhatī khyāl	Kashigiri Banarsidas	music	
	Jñanmālā	anon.	religion/ethics	
	Gopālsahasranāma		hymns/ritual	
	Ānandāmṛt vārṣiṇī	Anandgiri Svami	religion/Vedanta	
	Gopīcand Bhartarī kā qissā	Lakshman Simha	musical drama	
	Bakāvalī suman = Gul-e bakāvalī	Baijusimha Varma	romance	from the Persian of ʿIzzat Allah
	Śaniścarjī kī kathā	Joravarmal (trs.)	poetry	
	Anekarth aur Nāmamālā	Nanddas	vocabularies	
	Rāmkalevā	Ramnath		
	Baitāl paccīsī (nāgarī)	Surat Kavi (trs.)	tales	
	Śukbahattarī	anon.	tales	from the Sanskrit *Śukasaptatī*
	Brahmasār	Ramnarayan	poetry	
	Padmāvatīkhaṇḍ Ālhakhaṇḍ	Cand Bardoi	epic	from the *Pṛthvīrājrāsau*
	Mahābhāratdarpaṇ	Gokulnath et alia	epic	
	Amarvinod bhāṣā	Amar Singh	medicine	trs. from the Sanskrit
	Rām vinod	Ramchandra	medicine	

Appendix III (*contd.*)

Appendix III (*contd.*)

Year	Title	Author/Translator	Category	Remarks
	Vaidyamanotsav	Nainsukh	medicine	
	Bhāṣā jātakālaṅkār	Lochan Singh (trs.)	astrology	from the Sanskrit
	Muhūrtt cakradīpikā	Ramdayalu	astrology	
	Tulsīśabdārthaprakāś	Gopaldas	astrology	
	Daivajñabharaṇ	Shambunath	astrology	
	Ramalsār praśnāvalī		astrology/geomancy	
1875	*Strīdarpaṇ*	Madhav Prasad	textbook/primer for girls	
	Paśūcikitsa	Magan Lal (trs.)	textbook/veterinology	transl. of *ʿIlāj al-mawāshī*, an Urdu version of J.H.B. Hallen's *Treatment of Cattle Disease*
	Kavikulkalpataru	Cintamani Tripathi	poetics	
	Chandorṇava piṅgal	Bhikhari Das	poetics	
	Chitracandrikā	Kashi Raj	poetics	
	Rasrāj	Motiram	poetics	
	Yamunālahrī	Gvalkavi	devotional poetry	
	Premratna	Bibi Ratan Kumvar	devotional poetry	
	Bhajanāvalī	Jagannath Sahai	devotional poetry	
	Kṛṣṇabāllīlā	Jagannath Sahai	devotional poetry	
	Kṛṣṇasāgar	Jagannath Sahai	devotional poetry	
	Bhairav prakāś	Randhirprasad Simha	devotional poetry	
	Gītagovindādarś	Jayadeva/Raicand Nagar	devotional poetry	Sanskrit text and Hindi version

Appendix III (*contd.*)

Appendix III (*contd.*)

Year	Title	Author/Translator	Category	Remarks
	Bārahmāsā	Baldevprasad	poetry	
	Prabodhcandrodayanāṭak	Brajvasidas (trs.)	drama/philosophy	from the Sanskrit of Krishna Mishra
	Saṅgrah śiromaṇī	Saryu Prasad	astrology	
	Laghu jātak	Manohar Acarya	astrology	
	Kathā Citragupta kī	Jagannath Prasad	caste history (Kayasths)	
	Kāyasth dharm darpaṇ	Ramcaran Sharma	caste history	
	Kāyasthvarṇanirṇay	Kaliprasad	caste history	
	Hindū dharmaśāstra	Kaliprasad	religion/ethics	
	Kalpasūtra bhāṣā	Kavi Raichand (trs.)	religion	trs. from the Sanskrit of Bhadrabahu
	Auṣadhisaṅgrahkalpāvallī	Radhakrishna	medicine	
1876	*Śabdārṇava*	Ramavatar Das	textbook/dictionary	
	Vidyārthī kī pratham pustak	Jaishankar and Maganlal (trs.)	textbook/primer	from the English of J.P. Walker
	Laṅkā kāṇḍ	Tulsidas	textbook/epic/devotional	
	Bhūgol Nāgpūr		textbook/geography	
	Gaṇit kāmdhenu		textbook/arithmetic	
	Kavittvaratnākar	Matadin Mishra (comp.)	textbook/poetical anthology	
	Jagad vinod	Padmakar Bhatt	poetics	
	Bihārī Satsaī	Biharilal	poetry	

Appendix III (*contd.*)

Appendix III (*contd.*)

Year	Title	Author/Translator	Category	Remarks
	Sundarī caritra (= Durgāpāṭh bhāṣā)	Akshar Ananya	devotional poetry/ritual	trs. from the Sanskrit
	Viśrāmsāgar	Raghunath Das 'Ramsanehi'	devotional poetry	
	Vinayapatrikā-rāmtattva bodhinī tilak	Tulsidas	devotional poetry	with a commentary by Shivprakash Simha
	Gaṅgājī kī kathā (= Kathā śrī gaṅgājī)	ascr. to Tulsidas	devotional poetry	
	Sudāmā caritra	Jagannath Prasad	devotional poetry	
	Rāmvilās Rāmāyaṇ	Ramprasad (trs.)	epic	from the Valmiki *Rāmāyaṇa*
	Mārkandeya Purāṇa bhāṣā		Purāṇa	trs. from the Sanskrit
	Paramārthsār	Keval Ram	religion	
	Apūrv kathā	Ramratna (trs.)	prose fiction	transl. of *Fasāna-e Ajā'ib*
	Sahasra rajnī caritra	Pyarelal (trs.)	tales	transl. of *Alif-Laila*
	Indarsabhā (nāgarī)	Amanat ʿAli and Madari Lal	drama	transl. of *Indarsabhā*
	Ṣaṭpañcāsikā saṭīk	Prithvi Datt	astrology	
	Jātak candrikā (nāgarī)	Shambunath	astrology	
	Avadhsamvād		history	
1877	*Kaithī varṇmālā*	Hanuman Prasad	textbook/primer	
	Maṅgalkoś	Mangali Lal	textbook/dictionary	Sanskrit-Hindi dictionary
	Padyasaṅgrah	Hanuman Prasad (comp.)	textbook/poetical reader	

Appendix III (*contd.*)

Appendix III (*contd.*)

Year	Title	Author/Translator	Category	Remarks
	Rādhāṣṭamī vrat kathā	Jagannath Sahai	religion/ritual	
	Nāmāvalī	Jagannath Sahai	devotional poetry	
	Śṛṅgār battīsī	Maharaja Mansingh of Ayodhya	devotional poetry	at the instance of Trilokinath Singh
	Vratārk bhāṣā	Maheshdatt Shukla (trs.)	ritual	from the Sanskrit of Shankara Bhatta
	Rāmābhiṣek nāṭak	Ramgopal Vidyant (trs.)	drama	from the Bengali
	Viśvavinaya	Svami Patitdas		
	Yogavāsiṣṭha bhāṣā	Pyarelal (trs.)	philosophy	from the Sanskrit
1878	*Gītāvalī*	Tulsidas	devotional poetry	with the commentary *Maṇidīpikā* by Baijnath Kurmi
	Bhāṁvargīt	Surdas	devotional poetry	
	Śivsiṁh saroj	Shivsimha Sengar	poetical anthology	
	Vaṃśaprakāś	Ganga Sahay (comp.)	history/genealogy	from the *Vaṃśabhāskara* of Surya Mall
1879	*Hindī kī kitāb No. 2*	Munshi Radha Lal	textbook/reader	also in Kaithi script
	Amīr Hamzā kī dāstān	Kalicaran & Maheshdatt (trs.)	romance	
	Kathā Satyanārāyaṇ	Bhakhtavar Singh (trs.)	devotional poetry	
	Jal jhūlan	Nandkishor Dube	devotional poetry	
1880	*Kaithī patramālā*	Ambikaprasad (trs.)	textbook/letter-writer	transl. of *Maktūb-e Aḥmadī*
	Manmaujcaritra	Caturdas	devotional poetry	

Appendix III (*contd.*)

Appendix III (*contd.*)

Year	Title	Author/Translator	Category	Remarks
	Rasikpriyā	Keshavdas	poetics	with a commentary by Sardar Kavi
	Padmāvat	Raghuvar Dayal	romance	reworking of Jaysi's *Padmāvat*
1881	*Lakṣmī-Sarasvatī saṃvād*	Navincandra Rai	textbook/female reader/ geography	
	Upadeś kathā	W.T. Adam (trs.)	textbook/history	from Stewart's *Historical Anecdotes*
	Bhāṣālaghuvyākaraṇ	Keshavprasad Tripathi (trs.)	textbook/grammar	
	Itihās timir nāśak	Shiva Prasad	textbook/history	
	Hitopatrikā		textbook/letter-writer	
	Bījgaṇit		textbook/mathematics	
	Guṭkā	Shiva Prasad (comp.)	textbook/reader	
	Rāmāyaṇ kā itihās		epic/mythology	
	Rāmāyaṇ Gītāvalī sa Vinayapatrikā	Tulsidas	devotional poetry	
	Kathā Satyanārāyaṇ sa Hanumānbāhuk	Tulsidas	devotional poetry	
	Manoharlahrī		devotional poetry	
	Rāmcaritmānas = Rāmāyaṇ saṭīk	Tulsidas	epic/devotional	with the commentary *Mānashaṃs bhūṣaṇ*
	Mahābhārat	Sabalsimha Chauhan	epic	incomplete edition
	Kṛṣṇapriyā	Mangali Lal (trs.)	Purāṇa	from the *Bhāgavata Purāṇa*

Appendix III (*contd.*)

Appendix III (*contd.*)

Year	Title	Author/Translator	Category	Remarks
	Śukranīti bhāṣā	Maheshdatt Tripathi (trs.)	ethics/political philosophy	trs. from the Sanskrit
	Satsaī saṭīk	Biharilal	poetry	with a commentary by Krishnakavi
	Citracandrikā	Kashiraj Kavi Balvan Simha	poetics	
	Rascandrodaya va rasvṛṣṭi	Udaynath & Shivnath	poetics	
	Qissā Cahārdarveś		tales	
	Qissā Hātimtāī		tales	
	Qissā Gulsanovar		tales	
	Rāvinsan kā itihās		prose fiction	adapt. of Defoe's *Robinson Crusoe*
	Satyanām Bihār Bṛṇḍāvan	Brindaban Acarya	religion/philosophy	
	Bhārtī bhūṣaṇ	Giridhardas Gopalcandra	rhetoric/commentary	commentary on the *Bhāṣābhūṣaṇ* by Jasvant Simha
	Gītārasikā	Hiralal	music?	
	Rāgsaṅgrah	Harishcandra 'Bharatendu'	anthology	
1882	*Bhāṣā vyākaraṇ*	Keshavprasad Tripathi	textbook/grammar	
	Siddhānt saṅgrah bhāṣā		textbook/philosophy	
	Rāmāyaṇ Tulsīkṛt saṭīk	Tulsidas	epic	with a commentary by Mahant Ramcarandas of Ayodhya

Appendix III (*contd.*)

Appendix III (*contd.*)

Year	Title	Author/Translator	Category	Remarks
	Bhaviṣyapurāṇa	Durgaprasad Sharma (trs.)	Purāṇa	
	Liṅgapurāṇa	Durgaprasad Sharma (trs.)	Purāṇa	
	Viṣṇupurāṇa	Durgaprasad Sharma (trs.)	Purāṇa	
	Skandapurāṇa	Durgaprasad Sharma (trs.)	Purāṇa	
	Varāhapurāṇa	Durgaprasad Sharma (trs.)	Purāṇa	
	Kavitāvalī saṭīk	Tulsidas	devotional poetry	with the commentary *Ratnadīpikā* by Baijnath Kurmi
	Rāmcandrikā saṭīk	Keshavdas	devotional poetry	
	Sundarvilās also known as *Sundardās kṛt savaiyā*	Sundardas	devotional poetry	
	Brajvilās sārāvalī	Govardhandas Dhusar	devotional poetry	
	Adbhut Rāmāyaṇ	Lala Lalmani	devotional poetry	
	Bhuvaneś bhūṣaṇ	Trilokinath Simha		
	Vijay muktāvalī	Chatra Kavi	devotional poetry	
	Śaṅkara carit sudhā	Rajaram	hagiography	
	Navīnsaṅgrah	Hafizullah Khan (comp.)	poetical anthology	
	Sangīt Prahlād	Lakshman Simha	musical drama	
	Hanumān nāṭak	Bakhshi Ram	drama	
	Qissā aurat aur mard	anon.	tale	trs. from the Urdu
	Dillagan	Sitaram	medicine	

Appendix III (*contd.*)

Appendix III (*contd.*)

Year	Title	Author/Translator	Category	Remarks
	Ilāj ul gurabā arthāt dīn jan cikitsā	Pyarelal (trs.)	medicine	trs. from the Urdu
	Ramal Nauratna	[Paramsukh Upadhyaya?]	astrology/geomancy	
1883	*Rasāyan prakāś*		textbook/chemistry	
	Pāṭhśālāoṁ kā prabandh	Muhammad Husain	teacher's manual	
	Bījāk Kabīrdās saṭīk	Kabir	devotional poetry	with a commentary by Vishvanath Singh, Raja of Rewah
	Baṃśīlīlā	Shyamlal Vajpeyi	devotional poetry	
	Kuṇḍaliyā	Giridhardas	devotional poetry	
	Brahmaprakāś	Bhagvat Prasad Singh	devotional poetry	
	Pārasbhāg	Yugalananya Sharan 'Hemlata'	religion/philosophy	
	Kaṭhvallī-upaniṣad	Yamunashankar Pancoli (trs.)	Upaniṣad	
	Kena-upaniṣad	Yamunashankar Pancoli (trs.)	Upaniṣad	
	Śrīrāmgītā	Yamunashankar Pancoli (trs.)	epic/philosophy	trs. and commentary of part of the *Adhyātma Rāmāyaṇ*
	Rāmāyaṇ bālmikīya bhāṣā	Maheshdatt Shukla (trs.)	epic	trs. of the Valmiki *Rāmāyaṇa*
	Vijñānlahrī	Yamunashankar Pancoli		
	Avatār siddhī	Yamunashankar Pancoli	religion	
	Satīvilās	Kumvari Viranji	religion/duties of women	
	Vīṇāprakāś	Pyarelal (trs.)	music	transl. of *Qānūn-e sitār*

Appendix III (*contd.*)

Appendix III (*contd.*)

Year	Title	Author/Translator	Category	Remarks
	Prabodhcandrodaya nāṭak	Atmaram	drama/philosophy	from Anathdas's version of the Sanskrit of Krishna Mishra
	Bhaktmāl saṭīk	Nabhadas	hagiology	
	Vacanāmṛt	Gokulnath	hagiology	printed at Mathura
	Vallabhākhyān	Gopaldas	hagiology	printed at Mathura
	Caurāsī bārttā		hagiology	printed at Mathura
1884	*Pahilā jugrāfiyā*		textbook/geography	trs. from the Urdu
	Praśn-upaniṣad	Yamunashankar Pancoli (trs.)	Upaniṣad	
	Hīr rāñjhā Kūh	Bhajanlal	romance	printed at Mathura
	Svapnaprakāś	Nandkishor Dube		
	Mohanmālā caurāsī kī nāmāvalī	Govardhandas Dhusar	hagiology	
	Dohāvalī do sau bāvan kī nāmāvalī	Govardhandas Dhusar	hagiology	
	Ṣaḍṛtu hazārā	Paramanand Suhane (comp.)	anthology	
	Bhagavadgītā bhāṣā	Harivallabh (trs.)	religion/philosophy	
1885	*Kṣetramāp prakrīya*	Zakaullah	textbook/mensuration	
	Tulsīkṛt rāmāyaṇ kī mānaspracārikā	Janakidas	commentary	
	Śṛṅgār sudhākar	Baldev Prasad	poetics	
	Adhyātma rāmāyaṇ	Umadatt (trs.)	epic/philosophy	trs. from the Sanskrit

Appendix III (*contd.*)

Appendix III (*contd.*)

Year	Title	Author/Translator	Category	Remarks
	Vidyāvilāsī va sukhbandhnī nāṭak		drama	
	Bhramjālak nāṭak	Ratnacandra	drama	adapt. of Shakespeare's *Comedy of Errors*
1886	*Hindī vyākaraṇ*	Shiva Prasad	textbook/grammar	
	Gaṇitdarpaṇ	Sonibaldev	textbook/mathematics	
	Hindustān ke logoṁ kā saṅkṣipt itihās		textbook/history	
	Tulsī satsaī saṭīk	Tulsidas	devotional poetry	with a commentary by Baijnath Kurmi
	Tulsī pañcaratna	Tulsidas	devotional poetry	collection of works by Tulsidas
	Śaśimaulī	Lakhpatirai	devotional poetry	
	Saudāgar līlā	Caturdas	devotional poetry	2nd, rev. ed.
	Śivpārvatīcaritra	Orilal	devotional poetry	
	Banśīlīlā	Shyamlal Vajpeyi	devotional poetry	
	Rastaraṅg	Lakshman Prasad Pandey	devotional poetry	
	Rāmsudhā arthāt Sītārām tattva	Vrajcandra Jain	devotional poetry	
	Kavipriyā saṭīk	Keshavdas	poetics	with a commentary by Haricarandas
	Śṛṅgār pradīp	Harihar Prasad	poetics	

Appendix III (*contd.*)

Appendix III (*contd.*)

Year	Title	Author/Translator	Category	Remarks
	Vairāgyasandīp bhāṣā ṭīkā sahit	Harihar Prasad		
	Hafīzullāh Khān kā hazārā	Hafizullah Khan (comp.)	poetical anthology	
	Adbhut sṛṣṭi caritra	Pyarelal (trs.)	cosmology/natural philosophy	trs. of the Persian *ʿAjāʾib al-makhlūqāt*
	Sarasvihār mañjarī	Avadh Bihari Avasthi		
1887	*Anurāg latikā*	Shivraj Mishra	devotional poetry	
	Ṛtuprakāś	Jagmohan Singh Maharaj	devotional poetry	
	Rāmāyaṇ adhyātma vicār	Yamunashankar Pancoli	epic/philosophy	
	Kāvyakalpadrum	Baijnath Kurmi	poetics	
	Ṣaṭrtuvarṇan	Baijnath Kurmi	poetics	
1888	*Rājā bhoj kā sapnā*	Shiva Prasad (trs.)	textbook/reader	from the English of Henry C. Tucker
	Govardhanvilās	Brajvasidas	devotional poetry	
	Mādhavvilās	Madhav Prasad Tripathi	devotional poetry	
	Pīyūṣlahrī	Baldev Simha (trs.)	devotional poetry	trs. from the Sanskrit of Jagannath Trishuli
	Jñānprakāś	Prabhudayal	devotional poetry	
	Śṛṅgārsaṅgrah	Sardar Kavi	poetical anthology	
	Bhāṣā amṛttaraṅginī	Tikaram		

Appendix III (*contd.*)

Year	Title	Author/Translator	Category	Remarks
	Rūs kī tārīkh		history	transl. of Mackenzie Wallace's *History of Russia*
1889	*Mahābhārat*	Kalicaran et al (trs.)	epic	prose transl. of the *Mahābhārat*
	Rāmnivās rāmāyaṇ	Janakiprasad Mahant Rasik Bihari	epic/devotional poetry	
	Śrīrāmvyāhotsav	Bhuvankavi	devotional poetry	2nd edition
	Sāhitya yugalvilās	Radhakant Sharan	devotional poetry	
	Raghuvaṃśa kāvya	Raja Lakshman Simha (trs.)	poetry	from the Sanskrit of Kalidasa
	Bārahmāso	Benimadhav	poetry	
	Manmohinī	Hafizullah Khan (comp.)	poetical anthology	
	Ṣaṭṛtukāvyasaṅgrah	Hafizullah Khan (comp.)	poetical anthology	
	Mahipālsiṃha saroj	Mahipal Simha	poetical anthology	
	Anurāgvarddhinī	Matadin Pandey		
	Manmohan	Baldevprasad	devotional hymns	
	Bhajanmālā	Devanandan Simha	devotional hymns	
	Navaratnabhāṣya	Shyamsundar Lal	music	
	Rāgvinod	Mahadev Shukla	music	
	Banśīrāgmālā	Loknathkavi Dvivedi	music	
	Rāgsaṅgrah	Krishnacandra	music	
	Vaṃśīlīlā bhāṣā	Shyamlal Vajpeyi	music	
	Yugalsamvād bodhprakāś	Yugalkishor	religion/Vedanta	
	Jñāntaraṅg	Mangaldas	religion/Vedanta	

Appendix III (*contd.*)

Appendix III (*contd.*)

Year	Title	Author/Translator	Category	Remarks
	Kailās āgaman		religion	
	Varāhapurāṇa	Madhavprasad Sharma (trs.)	Purāṇa	
	Nāthsaṅgrah	Loknath Dvivedi	hymns and poems	
	Nāthsaroj	Loknath Dvivedi	hymns and poems	
	Rādhikā sukhmā	Loknath Caturvedi		
	Nibandhmālādarś	Gangaprasad Agnihotri (trs.)	collection of essays	from the Marathi of Vishnukrishna Shastri Chiplunkar
	Jñāndīpikā	Shridatt Simha		
	Dvārkāśram yātrādarpaṇ	Dudhdas	pilgrimage manual	
	Setubandhāśram yātrādarpaṇ	Dudhdas	pilgrimage manual	
	Śyāmkelī	Govind Sahai		
1890	*Rāmāyaṇ saṭīk*	Tulsidas	epic/devotional	with a commentary by Baijnath Kurmi
	Vinayapatrikā saṭīk	Tulsidas	devotional poetry	with a commentary by Baijnath Kurmi
	Śrī Sūrdās kṛt dṛṣṭikūṭ saṭīk	Surdas	devotional poetry	with a commentary by Sardar Kavi
	Kumārasambhava	Kalicaran (trs.)	poetry	from the Sanskrit of Kalidasa
	Premtaraṅginī	Hafizullah Khan (comp.)	poetical antholog	
	Rasprabodh	Sayyid Ghulam Nabi 'Raslin'	rhetoric	

Appendix III (*contd.*)

Appendix III (*contd.*)

Year	Title	Author/Translator	Category	Remarks
	Vijayviśāl	Hajarilal	Purāṇa	from the *Jaiminīpurāṇa*
	Muṇḍaka-upaniṣad	Yamunashankar Pancoli (trs.)	Upaniṣad	
	Māṇḍukya-upaniṣad	Yamunashankar Pancoli (trs.)	Upaniṣad	
	Śrīrāslīlā	Saryusharan (comp.)	devotional songs	
	Rasārṇav	Shukdev Mishra	alchemy	
1891	*Janakīmaṅgal saṭīk*	Tulsidas	devotional poetry	with a commentary by Baijnath Kurmi
	Barvai rāmāyaṇ	Tulsidas	devotional poetry	with a commentary by Baijnath Kurmi
	Chappaya rāmāyaṇ	Tulsidas	devotional poetry	with a commentary by Baijnath Kurmi
	Chandāvalī rāmāyaṇ	Tulsidas	devotional poetry	with a commentary by Baijnath Kurmi
	Chandprakāś	Ramprasad	poetics	
	Vinayamālā	Dayadas Svami		
	Śatpañcavilās	Shaligram Kavi		
	Aitareya-upaniṣad	Yamunashankar Pancoli (trs.)	Upaniṣad	
	Saṅgītśikhā	Bakhshram Pandey	music	
	Pañcatantra	Lala Sitaram (trs.)	tales	trs. from the Sanskrit
	Hanumānnāṭak bhāṣā	Ramanand Caturdas	drama	trs. from the Sanskrit
	Nāgānand nāṭak	Lala Sitaram (trs.)	drama	
	Mayaṅkamañjari	Kishorilal Gosvami	drama	

Appendix III (*contd.*)

Appendix III (*contd.*)

Year	Title	Author/Translator	Category	Remarks
1892	*Kuṇḍaliyā rāmāyaṇ saṭīk*	Tulsidas	devotional poetry	with a commentary by Baijnath Kurmi
	Vairāgya sandīpaṇī saṭīk	Tulsidas	devotional poetry	with a commentary by Baijnath Kurmi
	Rāmājñā praśn saṭīk	Tulsidas	devotional poetry	with a commentary by Baijnath Kurmi
	Hanumān bāhuk saṭīk	Tulsidas	devotional poetry	with a commentary by Baijnath Kurmi
	Nṛtya rāghav milan	Ramsakhe	devotional poetry	
	Jñānprabhākar	Baldevdas	devotional poetry	
	Sant mahimā saneh sāgar	Chedidas	devotional poetry/ hagiology	
	Nakhśikh battīśi	Ganeshdatt Mishra	poetics	
	Caitanyacandrodaya bhāṣā	Sitaram Sharma Upadhyaya	hagiography?	
	Rāmrāg	Mitrasen	music	
	Bhaiṣajyaratnāvalī bhāṣā ṭīkā sahit	Ravidatt (trs.)	medicine	from the Sanskrit of Govinddas
	Suśrutasaṃhitā bhāṣā	Ravidatt (trs.)	medicine	
	Nighaṇṭu ratnākar	Ravidatt (trs.)	medicine	
1893	*Nakhśikh hazārā*	Paramanand Suhane (comp.)	poetical anthology	
	Śrī Rādhākṛṣṇālīlā	Paramanand Suhane (comp.)	poetical anthology	

Appendix III (*contd.*)

Appendix III (*contd.*)

Year	Title	Author/Translator	Category	Remarks
	Sarvasārsaṅgrah	Paramanand Suhane (comp.)	poetical anthology	
	Pāvas kavittratnākar	Paramanand Suhane (comp.)	poetical anthology	
	Vacan taraṅginī	Bhavadev		
	Miṭhāī caritra	Chedilal Kolapuri 'Premcand'		
	Gītārāmāyaṇ	Mahavirdas		
	Śrī Rādhā Kṛṣṇa rāslīlā	Parmanand Sahai	devotional poetry	
	Lokendra brajotsav	Patiray Lakshman Simha	devotional poetry	
	Cikitsopadeśikā	Ganeshdatt Mishra	medicine	
	Vicitra caritra	Kunjbiharilal	mythology	
	Samar bijay	Tirthraj	astrology	
1894	*Śrīdhar bhāṣā koś*	Shridhar Tripathi	textbook/dictionary	
	Śivrājbhūṣaṇ	Bhusan Kavi	poetics	
	Kāvya kalāpinī	Sitaram Sharma Upadhyaya	poetics	
	Avadh bilās rāmāyaṇ	Indrajit	epic	
	Maṇḍalī maṇḍan arthāt Cānakya nīti darpaṇ	Sitaram Sharma Upadhyaya	ethics	
	Gharāū ghaṭnā	Bhuvaneshvar Mishra		
	Viṣṇupurāṇa padyānuvād	Bikharidas (trs.)	Purāṇa	
	Vairāgyavinod	Ganeshdatt Mishra	religion	
	Vivekdivākar	Svami Atmaram	religion	on the *Rāmāyaṇ*
1895	*Vinayavihār*	Ramvihar Vrindaban		
	Bhaktāmbunidhi	Jiyalal Tripathi	devotional poetry	

Appendix III (*contd.*)

Appendix III (*contd.*)

Year	Title	Author/Translator	Category	Remarks
	Bhaktisāgar	Charandas	devotional poetry	
	Anurāgsāgar	Kabir	devotional poetry/ hagiology	comp. by Nandkumar Lal
	Rāmāyaṇ rāmānurāgvalī	Vaidehi Sharan 'Baiju'		
	Adhyātma-rāmāyaṇ	Baijnath (trs.)	epic/philosophy	
	Padma-purāṇa bhāṣā	Maheshdatt Shukla (trs.)	Purāṇa	
	Chāndogya-upaniṣad	Yamunashankar Pancoli (trs.)	Upaniṣad	
	Īśa-upaniṣad	Yamunashankar Pancoli (trs.)	Upaniṣad	
	Siddhāntprakāś	Paramanand	religion/Vedanta	
	Tanurakṣak dharmprakāśak	Paramanand	religion/Vedanta	
	Śakuntalā upākhyān	Nevaj Kavi (trs.)	drama	from the Sanskrit of Kalidas

Appendix IV

Select Chronological List of NKP Urdu Publications

Year	Title	Author/Translator	Category	Remarks
1859	*Jām-e jahān numā*	Shiva Prasad	textbook /geography	
1860	*Risāla-e kusūr aᶜshāriya*	Baldev Bakhsh	textbook/arithmetic	
1861	*Jāmiᶜ al-favāʾid*	S. A. Abbott	textbook/mensuration	
	Svayambodh	Shiva Prasad	textbook/primer	
	Tārīkh-e baghāvat-e Hind	Kanhaiyalal 'Ashiq' (trs.)	history	comp. and trs. from the English
	Majmūᶜah-e qavānīn-e taᶜzīrāt-e Hind	Nazir Ahmad et. al. (trs.)	law	Urdu trs. of *Indian Penal Code*
1862	*Qiṣṣa-e Sūrajpūr*	Srilal (trs.)	textbook/reader	trs. from the Hindi
	Ṭilism-e Shāyān	Totaram 'Shayan'	romance	Urdu version of *Dāstān-e Amīr Hamzah*
	Mahābhārat manẓūm bā tasvīr	Totaram 'Shayan'	epic (versified)	abr. poetical version of Faizi's Persian *Mahābhārat*
	Muntakhab al-tavārīkh	Javahirlal Akbarabadi (trs.)	history	abr. version of *Makhzan al-tavārīkh*
1863	*Wāqiᶜāt-e Hind*	Karimuddin	textbook/history	
	Navā-e gharīb	M. Mardan ᶜAli Khan 'Raᶜna'	history/geography	

Appendix IV (*contd.*)

Appendix IV (*contd.*)

Year	Title	Author/Translator	Category	Remarks
	Tārīkh-e nādir al ʿaṣr	Naval Kishore	history/topography	
1864	*Muntakhabāt-e Urdū,*	M. Karimbakhsh (comp.)	textbook/reader	pts. 1–2
	Gulshan-e Faiẓ	Nandkishor Lal	textbook/reader	trs. of *Bhojprabandhsār*
	Tārīkh-e Inglistān	Faridbakhsh (trs.)	textbook/history	
	Intikhāb-e tārīkh-e pādshāhān-e Inglistān	Faridbakhsh (trs.)	textbook/history	trs. from the English of J. Sutherland
	Risāla-e ʿilm-e ṭabʿīyat	Sadasukh Lal	textbook/natural philosophy	
	Baḥr-e dānish	Muhammad ʿAbdul Rahman	textbook	
	Ẓabṭ-e ʿishq	M. Mardan ʿAli Khan 'Raʿna'	poetry	
	Tārīkh-e [mumālīk-e] Chīn	James Corcharan 'Karkaran'	history	
1865	*Jabr-o-muqābala*	Bamshidhar	textbook/algebra	
	Majmūʿah-e sukhan	Shiv Narayan (comp.)	textbook/anthology	
	Anīs al-saiyāḥīn, pts. 1–3	Durgaprasad	textbook/geography	trs. from the English
	Dastūr al-maʿāsh		textbook?	trs. from the English
	Padmāvat	Malik Muhammad Jaysi	romance	
	Tārīkh-e Rūm	Muhammad Qudratullah Khan	history	trs. from the Arabic
	Makhzan al-adwiyah	Muhammad Nur Karim (trs.) Shirazi	medicine	trs. from the Persian of Muhammad Husain Khan

Appendix IV (*contd.*)

Appendix IV (*contd.*)

Year	Title	Author/Translator	Category	Remarks
	Tashīl al-shifā	Asghar ʿAli Khan (trs.)	medicine	trs. of Ghulam Imam's *ʿIlāj al-ghurabā*
1866	*Gulzār-e dabistān*	Shivnarayan	textbook/reader	
	Majmūʿah-e wāsokhthā		poetry	
	Iksīr-e hidāyat	Fakhruddin Ahmad Qadri (trs.)	religion/ethics	trs. of al-Ghazali's *Kīmiyā-e saʿādat*
	Tārīkh-e ʿahdnāmajāt va iqrārnāmajāt, 7 vols	Kanhaiyalal 'ʿAshiq' (trs.)	history/agreements and settlements	trs. from the English
1867	*Maṭlaʿ al-ʿajāʾib (Mālumāt al-afāq)*	Mahdi ʿAli Khan (trs.)		
	Gulistān-e mutarjim	Sheikh Saʿdi	poetry	*Gulistān* with Urdu trs.
	Kulliyāt-e Mīr	Mir Taqi 'Mir'	poetry	
	Maṣnavī-e Ẓafar	Bahadur Shah 'Zafar'	poetry	
	Dīvān-e Rind	Nawab Sayyid Muhammad Khan 'Rind'	poetry	
	Hazār dāstān	Totaram 'Shayan' (trs.)	romance	prose version of *Alf Laila*
	Mujarrabāt-e Akbarī	Wajid ʿAli Muhani (trs.)	medicine	from the Persian of Muhammad Akbar
1868	*Wāqiʿāt-e Hind*	Ramchandra Sen	textbook/history	reprint
	Miftāh al-tavārīkh	Thomas Bailey	textbook/history	

Appendix IV (*contd.*)

Appendix IV (*contd.*)

Year	Title	Author/Translator	Category	Remarks
	Mufīd al-mubtadī	[teachers of the Normal School, Lucknow]	textbook/primer	reprint
	Taᶜlīm al-mubtadī		textbook/primer	
	Tashīl al-qavāᶜid	Karimuddin	textbook/grammar	reprint
	Inshā-e Urdū	Karimuddin	textbook/letter-writer	
	Arzhang-e cīn	Debi Parshad	textbook/calligraphy	
	Naẓm-e parvīn	Debi Parshad	textbook/calligraphy	
	Aqvām al-Hind	Kishorilal	textbook/caste histories	
	Karīm al-lughāt	Karimuddin	textbook/dictionary	
	Ḥaqāʾiq al-maujūdāt	Banshidhar (trs.)	textbook/natural philosophy	trs. of Shiva Prasad's *Vidyāṅkur*
	Mukhtaṣar al-maṣābat		textbook/survey	
	Risāla-e qavāᶜid-e Urdū	Mirza Nisar ᶜAli Beg Banarsi	textbook/grammar	pt. 1
	Islāḥ al-ḥurūf	Muhammad Abbas	textbook/primer	
	Dāʾira-e ʾilm	Muhammad Karimbakhsh (trs.)	textbook/ethics	trs. from the English
	Premsāgar	Shankardayal 'Farhat'	devotional poetry	reprint
	Rāmāyan-e Farhat	Shankardayal 'Farhat'	devotional poetry	reprint
	Jānakī bijai	Shankardayal 'Farhat'	devotional poetry	reprint
	Shīv purān manẓūm	Shankardayal 'Farhat'	devotional poetry/Purāṇa	reprint
	Ganesh purān manẓūm	Shankardayal 'Farhat'	devotional poetry/Purāṇa	
	Mahābhārat manẓūm	Sarbuddin Khan	poetry/epic	
	Dīvān-e Saudā	Mirza Muhammad Rafi 'Sauda'	poetry	

Appendix IV (*contd.*)

Appendix IV (*contd.*)

Year	Title	Author/Translator	Category	Remarks
	Kulliyāt-e Momin	Momin Khan 'Momin'	poetry	
	Maqtūl-e ʿishq	Ghafur Bakhsh	poetry	
	Alif laila nau manẕūm	Asghar ʿAli Khan 'Nasim'; Totaram 'Shayan'; Shadilal 'Caman'	poetry	
	Farhang-e ʿishq	Totaram 'Shayan'	poetry	
	Maṣnavī Mīr Ḥasan	Mir Hasan	poetry	
	Maṣnavī Gulzār-e Nasīm	Daya Shankar 'Nasim'	poetry	reworking of the *Gul-e bakāvalī*
	Sho ʿla-e jawwāla	Fida ʿAli 'Aish'	poetry	
	Shāhnāma-e Urdū	Gokul Parshad (trs.)	epic	
	Bāgh-o-bahār	Mir Amman	tales	
	Totā kahānī	Haidarbakhsh	tales	
	Qiṣṣa-e Sipāhīzāda	Sheikh Rahman	tale	
	Qiṣṣa-e gul-o-ṣanobar	Nemchand	tale	
	Gul-e bakāvalī	Nihalchand	tale	illustrated edition
	Baitāl pacchīsī	Mazhar ʿAli 'Vila'	tales	
	Zād al-ākhirat, Tafsīr-e Qurʾān	M. ʿAbdus Salam Badaʾuni	religion/commentary	4 vols
	Tuḥfat al-mominīn	Kurban ʿAli	religion	
	Nūr al-hudā	Sayyid Imdad ʿAli	religion	
	Miftāh al-jannat	Karamat ʿAli	religion	
	Āʾīna-e maẕhab-e hunūd	Jaidayal Singh	religion	

Appendix IV (*contd.*)

Appendix IV (*contd.*)

Year	Title	Author/Translator	Category	Remarks
	Sudāmā caritar	Girdhari Lal	religion	
	Subaḥ kā sitāra	Abbas ʿAli	religion	trs. of al-Ghazali's *Daqāʾiq al-akhbār*
	Zād al-ʿuqbā	Muhammad Qutbuddin Khan Dehlavi	religion	abr. trs. of ʿAbdul Haq Dehlavi's Persian commentary on the *Asmā-e ḥusnā*
	Aḥkām-e ṯaʿām-e ahl-e kitāb	Sayyid Ahmad Khan	religion	
	Qiṣaṣ al-anbiyā	Muhammad Tahir (trs.)	history/lives of prophets	also known as *Rauẓat al-aṣfiyā*
	Futūḥ al-shām	ʿInayat Husain	history	
	Tuḥfat al-aṭibbā	Musharraf Husain	medicine	
	ʿIlāj al-ghurabā	Asghar Ali (trs.)	medicine	
1869	*Risāla-e mushtahar al-faiẓ*	Gobind Lal	textbook/mensuration	
	Inshā-e Ṯāhir	Muhammad Tahir	textbook/letter-writer	
	Taḥrīr-e uqlaidas	Vamshidhar (trs.)	textbook/geometry	trs. of Euclid's Elements of Geometry
	Mirāt al-ʿarūs	Nazir Ahmad	textbook/female education	
	Bhāgvat	Jagannath Sahaʾe 'Khushtar'	devotional poetry	reprint
	Caman-e benaẓīr	Ibrahim	poetry	Persian and Urdu

Appendix IV (*contd.*)

Appendix IV (*contd.*)

Year	Title	Author/Translator	Category	Remarks
	Majmūʿah-e wāsokht	Nawab Muhammad Yusuf ʿAli Khan Bahadur	poetry	
	Wāsokht-e Amānat	Khvaja Hasan Amanat	poetry	
	Maṣnaviyat-e Shauq	Nawab Mirza Shauq	poetry	incl. *Bahār-e ʿishq; Zahr-e ʿishq, Lazẓat-e ʿishq; Fareb-e ʿishq*
	Dīvān-e Muʿīn	Khvaja Muinuddin	poetry	
	Dīvān-e Lutf	Muhammad Lutf ʿAli Khan	poetry	
	Wāsokht-e Shāyān	Totaram 'Shayan'	poetry	
	Maṣnavī Nal daman	Raghunath Rai (trs.)	poetry	
	Shāhnāma-e Urdū	Fida ʿAli 'Aish' (trs.)	epic	
	Indar sabhā	Amanat and Madari Lal	drama	two versions of the *Indarsabhā*
	Dāstān-e Amīr Ḥamzah nau manẓūm	Totaram 'Shayan'	romance (versified)	
	Dāstān-e Amīr Ḥamzah	Khalil ʿAli Khan	romance	
	Cashma-e Shīrīn		romance	
	Zulaikhā Urdū	Nisar ʿAli Figar	romance	
	Nau ratan	Muhammad Bakhsh	tales	
	Laila Majnūn	Mirza Muhammad Taqi Khan 'Hosh'	tales	
	Innahu la Qurʾānun karīm		religion	The Qurʾan with an interlinear Urdu trs. by Shah Rafiuddin

Appendix IV (*contd.*)

Appendix IV (*contd.*)

Year	Title	Author/Translator	Category	Remarks
				and selections from Shah ʿAbdul Qadir's notes in the margin
	Gulshan-e Ibrāhīm	Ibrahim	tales	
	Tafsīr-e sūra-e Yūsuf manẓūm		religion	
	Falāḥ-e dārain	Muhammad Qutbuddin Khan Dehlavi	religion	
	Tuḥfat al-aḥibba	Muhammad Qutbuddin Khan Dehlavi	religion	
	Tuḥfat al-zaujain	Muhammad Qutbuddin Khan Dehlavi	religion	comp. from various Arabic
	Sharḥ-e Muḥammadī	Muhammad Khan	religion	
	Maulūd sharīf shāhīd	Sheikh Wahid	religion	
	Ārāʾish-e maḥfil	Mir Sher ʿAli 'Afsos'	history	reprint
	Riyāẓ al-umarā	Rahman ʿAli Khan	history	
	Zubdat al-ḥikmat	Muhammad Qamar ʿAli	medicine	
	Qānūn-e ʿItrat	Itrat Husain	medicine	
1870	*Mufīd al-inshā*	Shivnarayan and Amiruddin	textbook/letter-writer	
	Saccī bahādurī	Shiva Prasad	textbook/reader	
	Mabādī al-ḥisāb	Banshidhar	textbook/arithmetic	

Appendix IV (*contd.*)

Appendix IV (*contd.*)

Year	Title	Author/Translator	Category	Remarks
	Risāla-e ᶜilm-e muṣallaṣ		textbook/trigonometry	trs. of Snowball's Trigonometry
	Amān al-lughāt	Aman al Haq	textbook/dictionary	
	Sadā suhāg	Mirza Nasiruddin	textbook/female education	
	Būstān-e ḥikmat	Faqir Muhammad Khan 'Goya'	philosophy	trs. of *Anvar-e Suhailī*
	Bārah māsah	Kanhaiyalal	poetry	
	Kulliyāt-e Ẓafar	Bahadur Shah 'Zafar'	poetry	
	Dīvān-e Nāsikh	Shaikh Imam Bakhsh	poetry	
	Fasāna-e ᶜajāʾib manẓūm	Bholanath	poetry	reprint
	Fasāna-e ᶜajāʾib	Rajab ᶜAli Beg 'Surur'	romance	
	Pāra-e ᶜām mutarjam		religion	
	Maẓāhir-e ḥaqq	Muhammad Qutbuddin Khan Dehlavi (trs.)	religion	trs. of the *Mishkāt al-maṣābīḥ*
	Miftāḥ al-qulūb	Lal Muhammad	religion	
	Tarjuma-e Futūḥ al-shām va Futūḥ al-miṣr	ᶜInayat Husain (trs.)	history	Urdu trs. of al-Waqidi
	Tārīkh-e sitāra-e Hind	Totaram 'Shayan'	history	
	Ṭilism-e farang yaᶜne Siḥr al-ḥalāl	Motilal (trs.)		trs. from the English of W. Gregor
	Mīzān al-ṭibb		medicine	trs. from the Persian of Muhammad Akbar Arzani

Appendix IV (*contd.*)

Appendix IV (*contd.*)

Year	Title	Author/Translator	Category	Remarks
	Ṭibb-e Akbar	Muhammad Husain Nanautawi (trs.)	medicine	trs. from the Persian of Muhammad Akbar Arzani
	Iksīr al-qulūb	Muhammad Nur Karim (trs.)	medicine	trs. from the Persian of Muhammad Akbar Arzani
	Kīmiyā-e ʿanāsirī, Urdu trs. of *Qarābādīn-e Qādirī*	Muhammad Nur Karim (trs.)	medicine	trs. from the Persian of Muhammad Akbar Arzani
	Mujarrabāt-e Raẓāʾī	Raza Hasan	medicine	
	Qarābādīn-e Shifāʾī	Muhammad Hadi Husain Khan (trs.)	medicine	
1871	*Miṣbāh al-masāḥat*	Banshidhar	textbook/mensuration	
	Āʾīna-e tārī<u>kh</u> numā	Shiva Prasad	textbook/history	trs. of *Itihās timir nāśak*
	Gyān prakāsh	Gulzari Lal	textbook	
	Bhagat māl	Tulsiram	hagiology	Urdu version of Nabhadas's *Bhaktamāl*
	Tālīf-e Hargobind	Hargobind	moral precepts	
	Kulliyāt-e Amīruʾllah Taslīm	Amirullah 'Taslim'	poetry	
	Kulliyāt-e Ātish	Khvaja Haidar ʿAli	poetry	
	Dīvān-e Zauq	Shaikh Muhammad Ibrahim 'Zauq'	poetry	

Appendix IV (*contd.*)

Appendix IV (*contd.*)

Year	Title	Author/Translator	Category	Remarks
	Maṣnavī Nal daman	Kaliparshad	poetry	
	Prahlād caritar	Girdharilal	poetry	
	Dāstān-e Amīr Ḥamzah Ṣāḥibqirān	Hafiz ʿAbdullah Bilgrami	romance	
	Sarosh-e sukhan	Muhammad Fakhruddin Husain	romance	
	Dīvān-e Ḥaẕrat Khvājah Muʿinuddīn Chishtī	Khvaja Muinuddin Chisti	religious poetry	
	Maulūd sharīf	Ghulam Imam Shahid	religion	
	Ẓafar-e khalīl	Muhammad Qutbuddin Khan Dehlavi	religion	
	Tārīkh-e Ḥabībullah	ʿInayat Ahmad	history	
	Tārīkh-e Napoliyan Bonāpārṭ	Mushtaq Husain (trs.)	history	trs. from the English
	Qarābādīn-e Zakāʾī	Muhammad Hadi Husain Khan (trs.)	medicine	trs. from the Persian of Zakaullah Khan
	Tarjuma-e Qānūn-e Shaikh Bū ʿAli Sīnā	Ghulam Hasanain (trs.)	medicine	trs. of Ibn Sina's *Qānūn*
	Rapaṭ-e Darbāb-e tijārat-o-paidāvār	Ajodhya Parshad (trs.)	trade report	trs. from the English of R.H. Davies
1872	*Tārīkh-e [Gulshan-e] Panjāb*	Debi Parshad	textbook/history	

Appendix IV (*contd.*)

Appendix IV (*contd.*)

Year	Title	Author/Translator	Category	Remarks
	Karīmā mutarjam	Shaikh Saᶜdi	textbook/ethics	the *Pandnāmah* with an interlinear Urdu trs.
	Khulāṣat al-manṭiq	Debi Parshad	textbook/logic	
	Dīvān-e Fidā	Fida Husain	poetry	
	Dīvān-e Ghāfil	Munavvar Khan 'Ghafil'	poetry	
	Dīvān-e Ẓafar	Bahadur Shah Zafar	poetry	
	Kulliyāt-e Saudā	Mirza Muhammad Rafi 'Sauda'	poetry	
	Maṣnavī Nālah-e Taslīm	Amirullah 'Taslim'	poetry	
	Jāmiᶜ al-akhlāq	Amanatullah (trs.)	ethics	trs. of *Akhlāq-e Jalālī*
	Tafsīr-e Urdū-e sūra-e fātiḥa	Ikramuddin	religion	
	Nūr al-hidāyat	Badiuzzaman (trs.)	religion	trs. of *Sharḥ al-Wiqāya*
	Safarnāma		history/travelogue	D. Forsythe's political mission to Yarkand
	Sair-e Sayyāḥ	Miyam Dad Khan 'Sayyah'	history/travelogue	also includes *ghazals* by Sayyah
	Sair-e Panjāb	Kali Raʾe & Tulsiram	history	pts. 1–2
1873	*Kīmiyā-e ḥikmat*	M. Auhaduddin	textbook/ethics	
	Waqāʾiᶜ-nigār-e Inglistān	Abul Hasan (trs.)	textbook/history	trs. of Collier's *British Empire*
	ᶜIlāj al-mavāshī	Abul Hasan (trs.)	textbook/veterinology	trs. of J.H.B. Hallen's *Treatment of Cattle Disease*
	Gulshan-e ghairat	Ghulam Haidar Khan	textbook	

Appendix IV (*contd.*)

Appendix IV (*contd.*)

Year	Title	Author/Translator	Category	Remarks
	ʿIṭr-e majmūʿah	Ghulam Hasnain 'Qadr' Bilgrami	textbook/anthology	commentary on *Majmūʿah-e Sukhan*
	Risāla-e qavāʿid-e Urdū, pt. 4	Muhammad Ahsan	textbook/grammar	
	Tahẕīb an-nisvān	Auhaduddin Ahmad Shefta	textbook/female education	
	ʿAql-o-shuʿūr	Sayyid Nizamuddin	textbook/reader	
	Umāpatī digbijay	Lalji Kakorvi	devotional poetry	
	Adbhut Rāmāyan	Shankardayal 'Farhat'	poetry/epic	reprint
	Gulzār-e Ibrāhīm	Mir Hasan	poetry	
	Anvar-e Suhailī	Bihari Lal (trs.)	poetry	trs. of the Persian *Anvar-e Suhailī*
	Dīvān-e Jarār	Mustafa Mirza Husain Beg 'Jarar'	poetry	
	Dīvān-e Ṣādiq		poetry	
	Dīvān-e Ghālib	Mirza Asadullah Khan Ghalib	poetry	
	Shāhnāma-e Urdū manẓūm	Mulchand	epic (versified)	
	Padmāvat-e Urdū	Muhammad Qasim ʿAli	romance	
	Ṯilism-e ḥairat	Hamid ʿAli 'Shevan'	tale	
	Maulūd sharīf manẓūm	Mirza ʿAli Bahar	religious poetry	2nd ed.
	Kathā Satya Narāyan	Jvalashankar	religious tale	
	Qiṣṣa-e māh-e ramaẓān	Muhammad ʿAbdullah Khan	religious tale	

Appendix IV (*contd.*)

Appendix IV (*contd.*)

Year	Title	Author/Translator	Category	Remarks
	Jawāhir al-qur'ān mutarjam	Imam ʿAli ibn Najaf ʿAli (comp.)	religion	selections from the Qur'an with an interlinear Urdu trs. by Shah Rafiuddin
	Kashf al-hājāt	Muhammad Nuruddin (trs.)	religion	trs. from the Persian
	Aḥkām al-dīn	Muhammad Qutbuddin Khan Dehlavi	religion	
	Manāhij al-nubūwat	ʿAbdul Haq Dihlawi	religion/life of the prophet	trs. of *Madārij al-nubūwat*
	Rāndoṁ kī shādī	ʿAbdul Rahim	religion/law	
	Sair-e maqbūl	Ghulam Haidar Khan	history/travelogue	
	Kārnāma-e Sikandarī	Gokul Parshad (trs.)	history	on the basis of the Persian *Sikandarnāma*
	Futūḥāt-e Hind	ʿInayat Husain	history	
	ʿAjā'ibāt-e rozgār	Master Ramchandra	history	reprint
	Camanistān-e Josh	Ahmad Hasan Khan Josh		reprint
1874	*Tashrīḥ al-ḥurūf*	Debi Parshad	textbook/primer	
	Taʿlīm an-nisvān		textbook/female education	
	Sirāj al-masāḥat	Karam Rasul Lakhnavi	textbook/mensuration	
	Misbāḥ al-masāḥat	Bamshidhar	textbook/mensuration	
	ʿŪd-e Hindī	Mirza Asadullah Khan Ghalib	letters	
	Zabān-e rekhtā	Abdul Ghafur Khan 'Nassakh'	poetry	

Appendix IV (*contd.*)

Appendix IV (*contd.*)

Year	Title	Author/Translator	Category	Remarks
	Daftar-e bemis̤āl	Abdul Ghafur Khan 'Nassakh'	poetry	
	Kulliyāt-e Nassākh	Abdul Ghafur Khan 'Nassakh'	poetry	
	Jogannāma	Batin	drama	Panjabi
	Lailā o Majnūn	Mirza Muhammad Taqi Khan	romance	
	Padmāvat-e Urdū	Amir Ziyauddin & Sayyid Ghulam Ali	romance	
	Qiṣṣa-e saudāgar baccā	Shah Rahman	tale	
	Maṯla alʿulūm va majmaʿ al-funūn	Zain al-ʿAbidin (trs.)	encyclopaedia	trs. from the Persian of Wajid ʿAli Khan
	Jangnāma-e Karbalā	Muhammad Fazil	religion	
	Khulāṣat al-maṣāʾib	Muhammad Hadi ʿAli	religion	
	Gulzār-e jannat	Muhammad Qutbuddin Khan Dehlavi	religion	
	Baḥr al-ḥaqīqat	Mir Hasan	poetry	
	Tārīkh-e ṯilism-e Hind	Totaram 'Shayan'	history	
	Futūḥāt-e Wāqidī, 4 vols.	Bashirat ʿAli Khan & Sayyid Mehdi Husain (trs.)	history	trs. of al-Waqidi's *Kitāb al-Maghāzī*
	ʿAjāʾib al-qiṣaṣ	Muhammad Fakhruddin (trs.)	history/lives of prophets	trs. of *Qiṣaṣ al-anbiyā*
	Tārīkh-e Firishtā		history	trs. from the Persian of Firishta
	Tārīkh-e Ṯabarī		history	trs. from the Persian of Tabari

Appendix IV (*contd.*)

Appendix IV (*contd.*)

Year	Title	Author/Translator	Category	Remarks
	Jāmiᶜ al-tavārīkh		history	trs. from the Persian of Faqir Muhammad
	Tarjuma-e Muntakhab al-tavārīkh	Ihteshamuddin (trs.)	history	trs. from the Persian of Badaʾuni
	Mirāt al-salāṭīn	Gokul Parshad (trs.)	history	trs. of *Siyar al-mutaʾakhkhirīn*
	Maqālāt-e Iḥsānī	Ahsan ᶜAli Khan	medicine	
1875	*Jughrāfiya-e avval Jughrāfiya-e dovvom*	Shivnarayan	textbook/geography	
	Urdū sarf-o-naḥv	Raja Shiva Prasad	textbook/grammar	
	Guldasta-e adab	Debi Parshad	textbook/reader	
	Ruqaᶜāt-e Urdū	Muhammad ᶜAta ᶜAli 'Khak'	letter-writer	
	Kathā Satnarāyan	Jagannath Sahaʾe	devotional poetry	
	Kulliyāt-e Niẓām	Muhammad Mardan ᶜAli Khan	poetry	
	Kulliyāt-e Ghālib	Mirza Asadullah Khan Ghalib	poetry	
	Kulliyāt-e Naẓīr Akbarabādī	Vali Muhammad Nazir Akbarabadi	poetry	
	Sarāpā-e sukhan	Sayyid Muḥammad ᶜAli (comp.)	poetical anthology	reprint
	Guldasta-e sukhan		poetical anthology	*mushāᶜiras* held at the NKP
	Shakuntalā nāṭak	Nevaj Kavi	drama	
	Tarjuma-e Mujarrabāt-e Dairabī	Basharat ᶜAli Khan (trs.)	religion	trs. of Al-Dairabi

Appendix IV (*contd.*)

Appendix IV (*contd.*)

Year	Title	Author/Translator	Category	Remarks
	Maẕāq al-ʿārifīn	Basharat ʿAli Khan (trs.)	religion/ethics	trs. of al-Ghazali's *Iḥyāʾ ʿulūm al-dīn*
	Miftāḥ al-jannat	Karamat ʿAli	religion	
	Hindū dharm kī sresthatā	Baijnath	religion	
	Ganj-e Shahīdān	ʿAli Ahmad	religion	reprint
	Gulistān-e be<u>kh</u>izān	Muhammad Qutbuddin Khan Dehlavi	collective biography	also known as *Naghma-e ʿandalīb*
	Tārī<u>kh</u>-e rāj parsastī	Debi Parshad	history	trs. from the English
	Āṣār aṣ-ṣanadīd	Sayyid Ahmad Khan	history/topography	
1876	*Miʿyār al-imlā*	Debi Parshad	textbook/orthography	2nd rev. ed.
	<u>Z</u>a<u>kh</u>īrah-e saʿādat	Lalji Kakorvi (trs.)	ethics	trs. of the *Bhāminīvilās* of Jagannath
	Kulliyāt-e Inshāʾallāh <u>Kh</u>ān	Insha Allah Khan	poetry	
	Marṣiyahā-e Dabīr	Mirza Salamat ʿAli Dabir	poetry	pt. 2
	Waqāʾiʿ-e rājkumār	Kevalkrishna (trs.)	fiction	trs. from the Bengali of Bankimcandra Chattopadhyaya
	Taqwiyat al-īmān maʿ taẕkīr al-i<u>kh</u>vān	Muhammad Sultan Khan	religion	
	Dah ma<u>kh</u>zan	Nasirullah	religion	

Appendix IV (*contd.*)

Appendix IV (*contd.*)

Year	Title	Author/Translator	Category	Remarks
	Ghāyat al-auṭar	Muhammad Ahsan Nanautawi and Khurram ʿAli	Islamic law	trs. of the *Durr al-mukhtār*
	Tūzuk-e Jarmanī	Bishambhar Nath	history	
	Risāla-e cahal javāb tārīkhī	Debi Parshad	history	
	Ṣaulat-e Afghānī	Muhammad Zardar Khan	history	
	Kāmīshan Barodā	Damodar Das (trs.)	history/politics	trs. from the English
	Murakkabāt-e Aḥsānī	Hakim Ahsan ʿAli	medicine	
1877	*Jughrāfiya-e ʿālam*	Isvari Parshad	textbook/geography	10th ed.
	Zubdat al-qavāʿid	Durga Parshad	textbook/grammar	
	Inshā-e Mādhorām	Madhoram	letter-writer	trs. from the Persian
	Inshā-e khirad afroz	Qamaruddin	letter-writer	
	Inshā-e Bahār bekhizān	Ghulam Imam Shahid	letter-writer	
	Inshā-e mufīd an-nisā	ʿAbdullah Khan	letter-writer for women	
	Lughāt-e Sarvarī	Ghulam Sarvar Lahori	dictionary	
	Gyān sāgar	Girdharilal	devotional poetry	
	Sudāman caritar	Jagannath Sahaʾe	devotional poetry	
	Dīvān-e Goyā	Faqir Muhammad Khan 'Goya'	poetry	
	Kulliyāt-e Ṣanʿat	Shaikh Karimuddin	poetry	
	Majmūʿah-e marṣiya-e Mīr Anīs	Mir Babar ʿAli Anis	poetry	vol. 4

Appendix IV (*contd.*)

Appendix IV (*contd.*)

Year	Title	Author/Translator	Category	Remarks
	Shabistān-e ʿāshiqī yaʿne Hemlatā nāṭak	Nagendra Nath Banerji (trs.)	drama	trs. from the Bengali
	Kalimat al-dīn		religion	principles of the Brahmo Samaj, trs. from various Bengali works
	Ṭariqāt-e ʿibādat		religion	Brahmo Samaj publication
	Injīl-e Dāʾūd	French	religion	
	Tārīkh-e Rājistān	James Tod	history	trs. of Tod's *Annals and Antiquities of Rajasthan*
	Tārīkh-e makhzan-e Panjāb	Ghulam Sarwar Lahori	history/geography	
	Makhzan-e ḥikmat	Ghulam Sarwar Lahori	history	
	Bahāristān	Ghulam Sarwar Lahori	history	also known as *Tārīkh-e Gulzārshāhī*
	Ḥaqīqat al-auliyā	Ghulam Sarwar Lahori	history/lives of saints	
	Tazkirat al-kāmilīn	Ramchandra	history/collective biography	3rd ed.
	Tazkirat al-khulafā	Amanat ʿAli	history/collective biography	
	Kāyasth dharm darpan	Lalji Munshi	caste history	trs. from the Sanskrit of Ramcaran
	ʿAjāʾib al-makhlūqāt	Gokul Parshad (trs.)	cosmology	trs. from the Persian, illustrated ed.
1878	*Mufīd al-ṣibyān*	Durga Parshad	textbook	

Appendix IV (*contd.*)

Appendix IV (*contd.*)

Year	Title	Author/Translator	Category	Remarks
	Inshā-e Safdarī	Ghulam Safdar	textbook/letter-writer	Persian and Urdu
	ʿŪd-e Hindī	Mirza Asadullah Khan Ghalib	letters	new edition
	Bhāṃvargīt	Surdas	devotional poetry	trs. from the Hindi
	Dīvān-e Walī	Shah Waliullah Gujarati	poetry	
	Dīvān-e Hindī-e Khvājā Mīr Dard	Khvaja Mir Dard	poetry	
	Dīvān-e ʿĀshiq	Kanhaiyalal 'ʿAshiq'	poetry	
	Būstān mutarjim manẓūm	Govind Parshad 'Fiza'	poetry	versified rendering of Saʿdi's *Būstān*
	Guldasta-e shujāʿat also known as *Urdū Sikandarnāma*	Ghulam Haidar	epic	trs. from the Persian of Nizami
	Gulshan-e Sarvarī	Ghulam Sarwar Lahori	ethics	
	Ak͟hlāq-e Sarvarī	Ghulam Sarwar Lahori	ethics	
	Naʿt-e Sarvarī	Ghulam Sarwar Lahori	religious poetry	
	Guldasta-e mukammal	Muhammad Mohsin Kakorvi	religious poetry	
	Muk͟htaṣar-e Sair-e gulshan-e Hind	Baburam	history	
	Ẓiyā-e Ak͟htar	Muhammad Hasan Bijnori	history/biography	life of Nawab Wajid ʿAli Shah
	Tārīk͟h-e farmān ravayān-e Avadh	Radhe Lal	history	

Appendix IV (*contd.*)

Appendix IV (*contd.*)

Year	Title	Author/Translator	Category	Remarks
	Wāqiʿāt-e panj hazār sāla	Radhe Lal	history	chronological tables
	Gulzār-e Inglistān va Kharistān-e Rūs	Laksmi Narayan	history/politics	
	Amritsāgar	Pyarelal (trs.)	medicine	trs. from the Hindi
	ʿIlāj al-amrāẓ	Muhammad Hadi Husain Khan	medicine	trs. from the Persian of Muhammad Sharif ʿAli Khan
	Zakhīrah-e khvārazmshāhī	Muhammad Hadi Husain Khan (trs.)	medicine	trs. from the Persian of al-Jurjani
1879	*Islāḥ al-ḥurūf*	Husain ʿAli	textbook/primer	pts. 1–4
	Maktūbāt-e Aḥmadī	Sayyid Ahmad Husain	textbook/letter-writer	
	Mabādī al-ḥisāb manẓūm	Gobind Sahaʾe	textbook/arithmetic	
	Jughrāfiya-e Hindustān	Ishvari Parshad	textbook/geography	
	Tashīl al-tarkīb	Zaimullah	textbook/grammar	
	Uṣūl-e ʿajība	Jamaluddin Khan	textbook/grammar	
	Guldasta-e ʿajam	Mujibullah Khan	textbook/grammar	
	Inshā-e Surūr	Rajab ʿAli Beg 'Surur'	letter-writer	
	Dastūr al-ṣibyān Urdū		letter-writer	trs. from the Persian of Naunidhi Raʾe
	Dīvān-e Bahār-e ʿarab	Muhammad Nazir Mustafai	poetry	
	Majmūʿah-e marṣiya-e Mīr Anīs	Mir Babar ʿAli Anis	poetry	vols. 1&2

Appendix IV (*contd.*)

Appendix IV (*contd.*)

Year	Title	Author/Translator	Category	Remarks
	Bāgh-e ʿĀshiq	Kanhaiyalal ‘ʿAshiq’	poetry	also known as *Qiṣṣa-e gul o sanobar manẓūm*
	Lāvnī Banārsī	Banarsi Das	musical drama	
	Alf Laila		romance	vol. 1
	Tafsīr-e Qādrī	Fakhruddin Ahmad Qadri (trs.)	religion/commentary	trs. of *Tafsīr-e Ḥusainī*
	Makhzan al-anvār tarjuma-e Ganj al-asrār	Muhammad Yusuf ʿAli Shah alias Banke Miyam (trs.)	religion	trs. from the Persian of Hazrat Khvaja Muʾinuddin Chishti
	Rāh-e najāt	Muhammad ʿAli of Panipat	religion	4th ed.
	ʿAnāṣir al-shahādatain	Muhammad Nasir ʿAli	religion	
	Kuch hāl-e janāb H.C. Ṭakar	Shiva Prasad	history/biography	life of Henry C. Tucker
	Savāniḥ-e ʿumri-e rājā Gopalkrishan	Kumvar Kartakrishan	history/biography	
	Qaiṣar al-tavārīkh	Kamaluddin Haidar	history	
	Savāniḥāt-e salāṭīn-e Avadh	Kamaluddin Haidar	history	
	Khvāb-e Rājistān	Debi Parshad	history/topography	
	ʿIlāj al-ghurabā	Asghar ʿAli (trs.)	medicine	trs. from the Persian of Ghulam Iman
	Zīnat al-khail	Muhammad Mehdi	medicine/veterinology	on the treatment of horses
	Braj ban yātrā	Natholal (trs.)	pilgrimage manual	

Appendix IV (*contd.*)

Appendix IV (*contd.*)

Year	Title	Author/Translator	Category	Remarks
1880	*Āʾina-e jahānnumā*	Ram Jivan	textbook/geography	
	Jughrāfiya-e Avadh	Durga Parshad	textbook/geography	
	Sharḥ-e sih naṣr-e Ẕuhūrī	Shaikh ʿAbdul ʿAziz	textbook/commentary	
	Lughāt-e Naṣīrī	Muhammad Nasir	dictionary	Persian and Urdu
	Pandnāma-e kāshtkārān	Motilal	advice for cultivators	
	Surma-e cashm-e baṣīrat	Lala Laksmi Narayan	on education	
	Taḥrīr-e ʿishq	Debi Parshad	poetry	
	Kulliyāt-e Wahbī	Shiv Parshad 'Wahbi'	poetry	
	Maṣnavī-e nairang-e ʿishq	Kamta Parshad 'Nadan'	poetry	also known as *Bahāristān-e Nādān*
	Wāsokht-e Gauhar	Gendan Lal 'Gauhar'	poetry	
	Qiṣṣa-e gopīcand bharthari	Lakshman Simha	musical drama	reprint
	Fasāna-e Āzād	Ratan Nath Sarshar	fiction	vols. 1-2
	Ek rūsī zamīndār kā qiṣṣa	Henry Fanthome (trs)	fiction	trs. from the French of Henry Greville
	Zīnat al-ʿarūs	Muhammad ʿAbdul Hamid	fiction	on the model of *Mirāt al-ʿarūs*
	Būstān-e rāḥat qiṣṣa-e shāhzāda Fitan	Bhagvant Rai 'Rahat'	tale	
	Wilādat-e Kanhaiyajī aur Narsingh avatār	Vamshidhar	religion	

Appendix IV (*contd.*)

Appendix IV (*contd.*)

Year	Title	Author/Translator	Category	Remarks
	Guldasta-e karāmat	Ghulam Sarwar Lahori	religion	
	Maʿdin al-javāhir	Muhammad	religion	
	Qutbuddin Khan	Dehlavi		
	Qiyāmatnāma o bihishtnāma	Fayyaz al-Haq	religion	trs. from the Arabic
	Tārīkh-e ʿajīb	Muhammad Jafar	history	historical account of the Andaman Islands
	Rumūz al-ḥikmat	Rajab ʿAli	medicine	
1881	*Chamelī aur gulāb kā qiṣṣa*	Shiva Prasad	textbook/tale	
	Khulāṣa-e tavārīkh-e Hind	Ram Narayan (comp.)	textbook/biography	
	Hidāyat an-nisvān	ʿAli Muhammad	moral precepts for women	reprint
	Guldasta-e Amānat	Amanat Raʾe	poetry	
	Sarāpā-e pīrī	Nasir ʿAli Bilgrami	poetry	
	Muntakhab-e kulliyāt-e Ẓafar	Bahadur Shah Zafar	poetry	reprint
	Majmūʿah-e marṣiya-e Mīr ʿIshq	Mir Husain Mirza ʿIshq'	poetry	
	Cashm-e shīrīn	Miskin	poetry	
	Muwajjah-e gham o Nāla-e Ḥazīn	Gopal Sahai 'Hazin'	tale	

Appendix IV (*contd.*)

Appendix IV (*contd.*)

Year	Title	Author/Translator	Category	Remarks
	Ṭilism-e hoshrubā	Muhammad Husain 'Jah'	romance	vol. 1
	Sūraj purān	Khudabakhsh	Purāṇa	
	Mirāt al-ḥikmat va ʿilāj al-jahl	Rai Murlidhar	philosophy	
	Ekādashī mahātmya	Ramprasad	religion	
	Cahal majālis	Sayyid Wazir Husain Rizvi	religion	
	Zewar-e īmān	Muhammad Anvar ʿAli	religion	
	Milād-e muṣṭafā	Sayyid Wazir Husain Rizvi	religion	
	Muẓhir-e milād	Shaikh Wazir ʿAli	religion	
	Zamān al-firdaus	ʿInayat Ahmad	religion	
	Tanbīh al-ghāfilīn	Sayyid Muhammad et al.	religion	
	Tuḥfat-e Sarvarī	Ghulam Sarwar Lahori	religion/Sufism	
	Dīvān-e ḥamd-e yazdī	Ghulam Sarwar Lahori	religion/Sufism	
	Kashshāf-e asrār al-mashāʾikh		religion/Sufism	trs. of John P. Brown's *Dervishes or Oriental Spiritualism*
	Kanz al-asrār	Ghulam Haidar (trs.)	religion/Sufism	trs. from the Persian of Sheikh Bu ʿAli Shah Qalandar
	Fālnāma-e manẓūm	Khwaja ʿAli Muztar	omens and auguries	also known as *Gulshan-e fāl*
	Tuḥfat al-aṭibbā	Musharraf Husain	medicine	
1882	*Avadh kā bayān*	Vishambharnath	textbook/history	
	Hindustān kā bayān	Vishambharnath	textbook/history	

Appendix IV (*contd.*)

Appendix IV (*contd.*)

Year	Title	Author/Translator	Category	Remarks
	Risāla-e minhāj al-manṭiq	Muhammad Raza Khan (trs.)	textbook/logic	trs. of Ballantyne's work on the principles of logic
	Majālis an-nisā	Khvaja Altaf Husain 'Hali'	textbook/female education	
	Banāt an-naᶜsh	Nazir Ahmad	textbook/female education/ fiction	
	Taubat an-Naṣūh	Nazir Ahmad	textbook/fiction	
	Sharḥ-e Gulistān entitled *Guldasta-e khayāl*	Razaq Bakhsh	commentary	commentary on Saᶜdi's *Gulistān*
	Musaddas-e Ḥālī	Khvaja Altaf Husain 'Hali'	poetry	
	Dīvān-e Bashar	Munavvar Husain	poetry	
	Majmūᶜah-e marṣiyahā-e Mirzā Dabīr	Mirza Salamat ᶜAli 'Dabir'	poetry	3rd ed.
	Marṣiyahā-e Mīr ᶜIshq	Mirza Sayyid Husain 'ᶜIshq'	poetry	
	Nūr al-bedār	Amjad Husain		
	Tarjuma-e Srīmad Bhāgavat	Mukund Lal	Purāṇa	trs. of the *Bhāgavata Purāṇa*, 2nd ed.
	Guldasta-e ḥaqīqat	Sital Parshad	Purāṇa	trs. of the *Bhāgavata Purāṇa*
	Muntakhabāt-e Maṣnavī-e Maulvī Rūm	Ghulam Haidar (trs.)	Sufism	extracts from Rumi

Appendix IV (*contd.*)

Appendix IV (*contd.*)

Year	Title	Author/Translator	Category	Remarks
1883	*Miṣbāh al-tavārīkh*	Kanhaiyalal and Kalicharan	textbook/history	
	Naṣīr al-lughāt	Nasiruddin Ahmad Khan	dictionary	trs. of *Ghiyāṣ al-lughāt*
	Bishnulīlā	Ramsahaʾe 'Tamanna'	devotional poetry	
	Rāmlīlā	Ramsahaʾe 'Tamanna'	devotional poetry	
	Dīvān-e Bakhtāvar	Bakhtavar Singh	poetry	
	Fasāna-e Āzād	Ratan Nath Sarshar	fiction	vol. 3
	Qiṣṣa-e ʿābid o shaitān o qiṣṣa-e ʿābid o muḥtālgān [?]	Mujib/Fasil	tales	
	Hanumān calīsā	Ramsahaʾe 'Tamanna'	religion/ritual	
	Kitāb al-ashrāf	Haji Muhammad Darabullah	religion	
	Naṣīḥat an-nisā	Haji Muhammad Darabullah	religion/advice to women	
	Fawāʾid an-nisā	Muhammad Zahiruddin	advice to women	3rd ed.
1884	*Ḥaqāʾiq al-maujūdāt*	Shiva Prasad	textbook/natural philosophy	trs. of *Vidyāṅkur*
	Savāl-o-javāb-e jughrāfiya-e ṭabīʿi		textbook/geography	trs. from the Hindi
	Sadā suhāg	Mirza Nasiruddin Muhammad	female education	
	Tazkirah-e Afghānī	ʿAbdul Muhammad Khan	collective biography	
	Insha-e dilrubā	Revati Prasad	letter-writer	
	Nāla āfirīn	Shaikh Imamuddin 'Murad'	poetry	

Appendix IV (*contd.*)

Appendix IV (*contd.*)

Year	Title	Author/Translator	Category	Remarks
	Afsūn-e Siḥr	Debi Parshad 'Sihr'	poetry	also known as *Tabdīr-e ʿishq*
	Majmūʿah-e marṣiya-e Mīr Ẓamīr	Mazhar Husain 'Zamir'	poetry	
	Rāmāyan-e 'Ufaq	Dvarka Parshad 'ʿUfaq'	poetry	
	Rāmāyan-e vālmīki	Parmeshavar Dayal (trs.)	epic	
	Ṭilism-e hoshrubā	Muhammad Husain 'Jah'	romance	vol. 2
	Gayā mahātmya	Lalji Munshi	religion	2nd ed.
	Mokshagyān	Jaigopal (trs.)	religion	
	Bajrang sāṭhakā	Ramsahaʾe 'Tamanna'	religion	
	Qiṣṣa-e ḥazrat Yūnus	Muhammad ʿAbdul Hamid Rafik	religion	
	Maṣnavī-e guldasta-e maʿnī	Muhammad Halb ʿAli Khan	religion/Sufism	
	Pandnāma-e jebī	Muhammad Halb ʿAli Khan	religion/advice	
	Mauj-e sultānī	Mirza Muhammad Raʾis Bakht Zabiruddin Gurgani	history/genealogy	
1885	*Uṣūl-e ʿilm-e ḥisāb*	Rai Brajbhukhan Lal	textbook/arithmetic	
	Qavāʿid-e Mannīlāl	Mannilal	textbook/grammar	
	Muraqqaʿ-e gham	Muhammad Raza Khan Raza	poetry	
	Burhān-e gham	Mirza Sayyid Husain 'ʿIshq'	poetry	
	Daryā-e taʿashshuq	Wajid ʿAli Shah 'Akhtar'	poetry	
	Majmūʿah-e rasāʾil			

Appendix IV (*contd.*)

Appendix IV (*contd.*)

Year	Title	Author/Translator	Category	Remarks
	Majmūʿah-e mars̤iya-e Dilgīr	Mirza Dilgir	poetry	vols. 1-3
	Taṣvīr-e g̲h̲am	Ashraf ʿAli Mast	poetry	
	Mas̤navī-e rumūz al-ʿāshiqīn	Talibshah	poetry	
	Mas̤navī-e gulshan-e ʿishq	ʿInayatullah Roshan	poetry	
	Gyāngīt manẕūm	Hira Lal	poetry	
	Miʿyār al-balāghat	Debi Parshad 'Sihr'	rhetoric	
	Sarosh-e suk̲h̲an	Muhammad Fakhruddin Husain	romance	illustrated edition
	Cār gulzār	Hargopal	tale	
	Qiṣṣa-e gulfām	Madhoram	tale	
	Qiṣṣa-e siyāhposh	ʿInayatullah Khan	tale	
	Nāṭak nal damayantī	Vinay Prasad	drama	
	Gulistān-e ḥikmat	Muhammad ʿUmar ʿAli	philosophy	
	Riyāẓ al-anwār	Muhammad Bashir	religion	
	Ṭilism-e rūḥānī	Husain Ahmad	religion	
	Dīvān-e naʿtiya	Ahmad ʿAli	religion	
	Risāla-e zubdat al-az̲kār	Ghulam Haidar	religion	
	K̲h̲ulāṣā-e muk̲h̲taṣar-e tārīk̲h̲-e ahl-e Hind	Rameshvar Prasad and Mevaram	history	pt. 1

Appendix IV (*contd.*)

Appendix IV (*contd.*)

Year	Title	Author/Translator	Category	Remarks
	Maṣāʾib-e ghadar	Nazir Ahmad (trs.)	history	from the English of William Edwards
	Kīrtisāgar	Lalji (trs.)	biography	trs. from the Hindi
	Āʾīna-e farang	Muhammad ʿUmar ʿAli	travelogue	
	Zād-e gharīb	Muhammad Hadi Husain Khan (trs.)	medicine	trs. from the Persian of Sadiq ʿAli Khan
	Majmūʿah-e kāghaẕāt-e kārravāʾi-e ʿadālāt		law	also in shikasta script
	Intik͟hāb an-nujūm	Mahtab Rai	astrology	
	Jādu prakāsh yaʿne jādū ke tamāshe kī tīsrī kitāb	Ghulam Nabi	magic	
	Kanz al-Ḥusain	Sayyid Ghulam Husain Ramal	magic	
	Taʿbīrnāma-e k͟hvāb	Basharat ʿAli Khan (trs.)	interpretation of dreams	trs. of *Taʿbīr al-rūyā*
1886	*Maẓāmīn*	Raja Shiva Prasad	textbook/literature	
	Muntak͟habāt-e urdū	Nisar ʿAli Beg	textbook/literature	
	Savāl o javāb uqlaidas musammā ba Gulshan-e uqlaidas	Ramcharan	textbook/geometry	
	Mensuration yaʿne maṣāṇat	Ram Ratan Lal	textbook/mensuration	

Appendix IV (*contd.*)

Appendix IV (*contd.*)

Year	Title	Author/Translator	Category	Remarks
	Jughrāfiya-e Hind shomālī	Sayyid ʿAli	textbook/geography	
	Fann-e zirāʿat kī pahlī kitāb	J.B. Fuller	textbook/agriculture	
	Bārahmāsā Sundarkalī	Sundarkali	poetry	
	Dīn Siṃh kā bārahmāsā	Parmeshvar Din Singh	poetry	
	Fighān-e Ḥaidar	Agha Haidar ʿAli Beg	poetry	
	Maṣnavī-e Yūsuf va Zulaikhā	Nandkishor	poetry	
	Maṣnavī-e ḥairat afzā	Muhammad Kasim ʿAli 'Kasim'	poetry	
	Maṣnavī-e ṭilism-e jahān	Farrukh Husain	poetry	
	Rāmāyaṇ-e Bahār	Banke Bihari Lal	poetry	
	Dīvān-e Ḥairat	Abdurrahman Khan 'Hairat'	poetry	
	Majmūʿah-e marṣiya-e Dilgīr	Mirza Dilgir	poetry	vols. 5-6
	Wāsokht sani namak	Ramji Mal 'Namak'	poetry	
	Kishkindha kand	Hafizullah Khan (ed.)	epic	
	Mehdīnāma	Mirza Muhammad Askari (trs.)	romance	trs. of pt. 1 of *Būstān-e khayāl*
	Qiṣṣa-e shāh-e Yaman va Sakhāvat-nāma	ʿInayat Husain	fiction	
	Pandnāma-e Wāḥid	Muhammad Wahid ʿAli	ethics	

Appendix IV (*contd.*)

Appendix IV (*contd.*)

Year	Title	Author/Translator	Category	Remarks
	Ṯilism-e akhlāq	Sri Kishan	ethics	
	Lāl chandrikā	Lal Singh (trs.)	ethics	trs. of Chanakya's *Nītiśāstra*
	ʿAmalnāma-e rūs yaʿni tarjuma-e tārīkh-e rūs	Ratan Nath 'Sarshar' (trs.)	history	trs. of Wallace's *Russia*
	Savāniḥ-e ʿumri Lārḍ Lārans	Zavvar Husain (trs.)	history/biography	trs. of Bosworth Smith's *Life of Lord Lawrence*
	Vakīl al-ghurabā	Sayyid Wazir Husain	religion	pilgrimage guide
	Kitāb-e islām va musalmān	Sayyid Muhammad Husain	religion	
	Qiṣṣa-e dāʾī Ḥalīmā	Shahid	religion	
	Khudā kī raḥmat	Muhammad Murtaza Khan	religion	
	Minhāj al-sālikīn	Maulvi Munir (trs.)	religion	trs. of al-Ghazali's *Minhāj al-ʿābidīn*
	Zikr al-shahādatain	Ahmad Khan Sufi	religion	
	Tarjuma-e Urdū-e Riyāẓ-e riẓvān	Muhammad Abul Hasan (trs.)	commentary	
	Baranda-e ḥujjat	Jaigopal	astrology	
	Taḥqīqāt-e nādir ṭibbī maʿrūf ba mufradāt-e Hindī	Bashir Ahmad (trs.)	medicine	Urdu and Sanskrit

Appendix IV (*contd.*)

Appendix IV (*contd.*)

Year	Title	Author/Translator	Category	Remarks
	Ṣafā᾽ī aur tandurustī	Lala Svamidayal (trs.)	medicine	trs. of Cuningham's *Sanitary Primer*
1887	*Qiṣṣa-e Sanḍfarḍ va Mārṭan*	Shiva Prasad	textbook/tale	trs. of Thomas Day
	Dil bahlā᾽o	Shiva Prasad	textbook/tales	
	Mashq-e nastaʿlīq		textbook/calligraphy	
	Inshā-e Surūr	Ahmad ʿAli 'Surur'	letter-writer	
	Dīvān-e Ghālib	Mirza Asadullah Khan Ghalib	poetry	
	Dīvān-e Sukhan Dihlavī	Muhammad Fakhruddin Husain 'Sukhan Dehlavi'	poetry	
	Kulliyāt-e Ẓafar	Bahadur Shah 'Zafar'	poetry	
	Maṣnavī-e shīrīn khusro	Gobind Parshad 'Fiza'	poetry	
	Tarjuma-e Ḥadā᾽iq al-balāghat	Imam Bakhsh Sahba᾽i	rhetoric	
	Bāl kand va sundar kand	Hafizullah Khan (ed.)	epic	
	Gusain caritar	Lalji Munshi	history/biography	Life of Tulsidas; Urdu and Hindi
	Tazkirah-e ilāhī	Muhammad Abul Hasan	collective biography	
	Tarjuma-e Ṭilism-e hoshrubā	Muhammad Husain 'Jah'	romance	vol. 2
	Muḥsanāt yaʿni Fasāna-e mubtalā	Nazir Ahmad	fiction	

Appendix IV (*contd.*)

Appendix IV (*contd.*)

Year	Title	Author/Translator	Category	Remarks
	Fasāna-e Āzād	Ratan Nath Sarshar	fiction	vol. 4
	Kuch bayān apnī zabān par	Shiva Prasad	on language	
	Kalām al-mulūk mulūk al-kalām	Binodi Lal Bhargava (trs.)	letters	trs. of Sir Alfred C. Lyall's speeches
	Minhāj al-sālikīn	Abul Hasan (trs.)	philosophy	trs. of the *Yogavāsiṣṭha*
	Guldasta-e akhlāq	Sadasukh Lal	ethics	
	Srimad bhāgvat manẓūm	Sardar Singh 'Nasim'	religion	
	Bodhprakāsh maᶜ farhang	Shivdayal	religion	
	Tavārīkh-e Ḥabībuᵓllāh	Muhammad ᶜInayat Ahmad	religion	
	Nāla-e ᶜāṣim	ᶜAbdul Halim	religion	
	Qiṣṣa-e jamjama	Muhammad ᶜAli	religion	
	Tarjuma-e Fawāᵓid Saᶜdīya	Abul Hasan (trs.)	religion/Sufism	
	Risāla- e taᶜrīf al-nabẓ	Mirza Bashir Ahmad	medicine	
	Mujarrabāt-e Bashīr maᶜrūf ba Risāla-e quwwat-e bāh	Mirza Bashir Ahmad	medicine	
	Āb-e ḥayāt	Kamta Parshad 'Nadan'	medicine	
	Davā al-ḥaiwān va al-ṭuyūr	Ahsan ᶜAli Khan	medicine/veterinology	
1888	*Tashrīḥ al-ḥurūf*	Debi Parshad	textbook/primer	

Appendix IV (*contd.*)

Appendix IV (*contd.*)

Year	Title	Author/Translator	Category	Remarks
	Ḥurūf-e tahajjī	Raja Shiva Prasad	textbook/primer	
	Cār bāgh tarjuma-e cār gulzār	Muhammad Yusuf Khan (trs.)	textbook/grammar	
	Miftāḥ al-qavāʿid	Sadasukh Lal	textbook/grammar	pt. 3
	ʿIyār al-qavāʿid	Muhammad Mumtaz al-Haq	textbook/grammar	
	Jughrāfiya-e duniyā		textbook/geography	
	Ārsī maṣāḥif	Muhammad Jamiluddin 'Nayyir'	textbook/female education	
	Tuḥfah-e Sarshār	Ratan Nath Sarshar	poetry	
	Sudāman caritar	Hara Narayan	devotional poetry	
	Ṭilism-e hoshrubā	Muhammad Husain 'Jah'	romance	vol. 3
	Qiṣṣa-e Ḥātim Tāʾī manẓūm	Sukhraj	tale (versified)	
	Majmūʿah-e qiṣaṣ		tales	
	Shirāz kī mihrbāno	Muhammad ʿAbdul Qadir	romance	
	Jām-e Sarshār	Ratan Nath Sarshar	fiction	
	Fasāna-e jamīl	Hamid Hasan (trs.)	fiction	trs. of G.W.M. Reynold's *Loves of the Harem*
	Halvā-e bedūd	Muhammad Husain Mahmud	ethics	
	Taḥqīqāt-e insānī	Kamta Parshad	philosophy	
	Dīvān-e nauḥajāt-e Ḥaidar maʿ munājāt	Agha Haidar ʿAli Beg	religion	

Appendix IV (*contd.*)

Appendix IV (*contd.*)

Year	Title	Author/Translator	Category	Remarks
	Gulzār-e khalīl	Ghulam Imam Shahid	religion	
	Mavāᶜiẓ-e Jaᶜfarī	Ghulam Haidar Khan	religion	
	Taḥqīq-e Jaᶜfarī	Ghulam Haidar Khan	religion	
	Risāla-e sair al-āftāb	Sayyid Muhammad ᶜAli (trs.)	religion	
	Gulzār-e gham	Sayyid Husain Mirza 'ᶜIshq'	religion	
	Milād-e sarvar-e anbiyā	Sarwar ᶜAli	religion	Urdu and Arabic
	Muhr-e nabūwat	Nizamuddin	religion	
	Shahādatnāma	Nawab ᶜAli Muhammad Khan	religion	also known as *Ghamkada*
	Tārīkh-e miṣr jadīd entitled *Tuḥfah-e miṣariyya*	Abul Hasan (trs.)	history	trs. of Mackenzie Wallace's *Egypt and the Egyptian Question*
	Sikkhoṁ kā ṭulūᶜ va ghurūb	Raja Shiva Prasad	history	
	Baḥr-e muḥīṭ	Asghar Husain	medicine	
	Dastūr an-najāt. Maṣāᵓib al-ḥummiāt	Asghar Husain	medicine	
	Makhzan-e manfaᶜat ẓarūrī al-maṭlab	Mahtab Rai	medicine	

Appendix IV (*contd.*)

Appendix IV (*contd.*)

Year	Title	Author/Translator	Category	Remarks
	Ṭibb-e Aḥsanī	Ahsan ʿAli	medicine	
1889	*Dīvān-e Farrukh*	Rao Shivdarshan Singh 'Farrukh'	poetry	
	Kulliyāt-e Turāb	Shah Turab ʿAli Kakorvi	poetry	2nd ed.
	Qaṣāʾid-e Ikrām	Mir Ikram ʿAli	poetry	
	Marṡiyahā-e Qais Bilgrāmī	Mir Nasir ʿAli 'Qais' Bilgrami	poetry	
	Daulat al-abār	Mirza Muhammad Askari (trs.)	romance	trs. of pt. 2 of *Būstān-e khayāl*
	Qiṣṣa-e shāh-e rūm		fiction	
	Sarāb-e bāgh	Sayyid Amjad ʿAli 'Kalk'	fiction	
	Linga purāna	Svamidayal (trs.)	religion	
	Zubdat al-maṣāʾib	Mirza Muhammad	religion	
	Ghazwa-e ʿarab tarjuma-e futūḥ al-ʿajam	Basharat ʿAli and Haidar Husain (trs.)	religion	
	Makhzan-e ʿulūm va funūn	Hira Lal Singh	miscellaneous	
	Tarjuma-e Dastūr al-ʿilāj	Muhammad Hadi Husain Khan (trs.)	medicine	
	Tarjuma-e Kāmil al-ṣināʿah al-ṭibbīyah	Ghulam Hasanain (trs.)	medicine	trs. of al-Majusi
	Tarjuma-e Qānūnchah	Ghulam Hasanain (trs.)	medicine	trs. of al-Jaghmini

Appendix IV (*contd.*)

Appendix IV (*contd.*)

Year	Title	Author/Translator	Category	Remarks
1890	*Bahāristān-e sukhan*		poetical anthology	
	Ṭilism-e hoshrubā	Muhammad Husain 'Jah'	romance	vol. 4
	Afsāna-e dilpazīr	Ahmad ᶜAli Khan	fiction	
	Kifāyah-e Manṣūrī	Muhammad Hadi Husain Khan (trs.)	medicine	trs. from the Persian of Mansur
	Qarābādīn-e Kabīr	Muhammad Hadi Husain Khan (trs.)	medicine	trs. from the Persian of Muhammad Husain Khan Shirazi
	Tarjuma-e Fatāwā-e ᶜĀlamgīrī, 4 vols.	Sayyid Amir ᶜAli Malihabadi (trs.)	Islamic law	trs. from the Arabic
1891	*Jāmiᶜ-e Tirmīzī maᶜ tarjuma-e Urdū*	Fazl Ahmad Ansari	religion	trs. of al-Tirmizi
1892	*Intikhāb-e kulliyāt-e Shāh Turāb*	Shah Turab ᶜAli Kakorvi	poetry	
	Jāmiᶜ al-lughāt-e Urdū	Ghulam Sarvar Lahori	dictionary	
	Būstān-e Avadh	Durga Parshad	history	
	Fasāna-e maᶜqūl	Ghulam Haidar Khan	fiction	
1893	*Dīvān-e Siḥr-e sāmirī*	Debi Parshad	poetry	
	Ṭilism-e hoshrubā	Ahmad Husain Qamar	romance	vol. 7

Appendix IV (*contd.*)

Appendix IV (*contd.*)

Year	Title	Author/Translator	Category	Remarks
	Ṭilism-e khayālāt	Hardayal Srivastav (trs.)	fiction	
	Laᶜbat-e farang	Ramnarayan (trs.)	fiction	
	Qurʾān mutarjam	Sheikh Rafiuddin	religion	Arabic and Urdu
1894	*Savāniḥ-e ᶜumrī*	Raja Shiva Prasad	autobiography	
1895	*Tafsīr-e Iksīr-e ᶜazam*	Ihteshamuddin Muradabadi	religion/commentary	

Appendix V

Select Chronological List of NKP Sanskrit Publications

Year	Title	Author/Translator	Category	Remarks
1868	*Bhāgavata-purāṇa*		Purāṇa	with the commentary by Shridhara
	Vaidyajīvana	Lolimbaraja	medicine	with the commentary '*Lolimmadīpikā*' by Sukhanandanatha
1871	*Manu-smṛti urdū bhāṣā anuvāda sametaḥ*	Manu	law	trilingual ed., with a Hindi and Urdu paraphrase
	Durgā-pāṭh saṭika		ritual/prayer	with a commentary by Nagesha Bhatta
1874	*Amarakośa prathama kāṇḍaḥ*	Amarasimha	dictionary	
	Satyanārāyaṇa-vrata-kathā bhāṣā ṭīkā sahita		ritual	
	Yamadvitīya kathā		religion	from the *Bhaviśyottara-purāṇa*
	Śārṅgadhara-saṃhitā vārtikā tilaka sahita	Sharngadhara Mishra	medicine	with a Hindi commentary

Appendix V (*contd.*)

Appendix V (*contd.*)

Year	Title	Author/Translator	Category	Remarks
	Śīghra-bodha bhāṣā ṭīkā sahita	Kashinatha Bhattacarya	astrology	with a Hindi commentary
	Sāmudrika bhāṣā ṭīkā sahita		palmistry	with a Hindi commentary
	Muhūrtta-cakra-dīpikā	Ramadayalu	astrology	also called *Muhūrttcintāmaṇisāriṇī*
	Pārāśarī bhāṣā ṭīkā sahita	Parashara	astrology	with a Hindi commentary
	Yājñavalkya-smṛti bhāṣā ṭīkā sahita	Yajnavalkya	law	with a Hindi commentary
1875	*Śrī-Bhagavad-gītā bhāṣā tilaka sahita*		religion	with a Hindi commentary by Harivamshlal
	Siddhānta-candrikā	Ramashrama	grammar/commentary	commentary of *Sārasvata-sūtra*;
	Dhātvarṇava	Keshavaprasada	textbook/grammar	collection of Sanskrit verbal roots with their Hindi meaning
	Muhūrtta-gaṇapatiḥ	Ganapati Raval	astrology	
	Śrī-Durgā-stotram		eulogistic hymns	
	Amarakośa sa bhāṣānuvāda	Amarasimha	dictionary	with a Hindi translation
	Sandhyā-paddhatī/Pañca-mahāyajña vidhiḥ bhāṣā - ṭīkā sahita	Dayanand Sarasvati	prayer book	at the instance of Raja Jai Kishen Das

Appendix V (*contd.*)

Appendix V (*contd.*)

Year	Title	Author/Translator	Category	Remarks
	Kāyastha-kula-bhāskara	Lakshminarayana	caste history	at the instance of Naubatrai, Tahsildar Nawabganj
1876	*Mārkaṇḍeya-purāṇa*		Purāṇa	
	Laghu-siddhānta-kaumudī	Varadaraja	textbook/grammar	rev. by Maheshdatt Shukla
	Laghu-jātaka bhāṣā ṭīkā sahita	Varahamihira	astrology	with a Hindi commentary
	Ṣaṭ-pañcasikā sa ṭīkā	Prthyuyasha	astrology	with a Hindi commentary
	Śrī-gopāla-sahasra-nāma		ritual/prayer	
	Mahimna-stotra		eulogistic hymns	
	Aparādha-bhañjanā-stotra		eulogistic hymns	
	Paramārtha-sāra	Abhinavagupta	Kashmir Shaivaism	with a Hindi commentary
1877	*Vratārka*	Shankara Bhatt	ritual	with a Hindi translation
	Vratārka	Shankara Bhatt	ritual	with an Urdu transliteration of the above
	Bhagavad-gītā saṭīka		philosophy/religion	with a Hindi transl. of Anandagiri's commentary

Appendix V (*contd.*)

Year	Title	Author/Translator	Category	Remarks
	Viṣṇu-sahasra-nāma saṭīka arthāt Hindī anuvād sahit		ritual/prayer	with a Hindi commentary and Urdu transliteration
	Mahimna-stotra artha sahita	Pushpadanta	eulogistic hymns	with a Hindi commentary and Urdu transliteration
1879	*Śrī-bhagavatī-gītā (Devībhāgavata)*		Purāṇa	at the instance of Raja Madhavsingh of Amethi
	Garuḍā-purāṇa bhāṣā ṭīkā sahita		Purāṇa	with a Hindi commentary
	Muhūrtta-mārttaṇḍ saṭīka	Ananta Narayana	astrology	
	Muhūrtta-cintāmaṇi saṭīka	Ram Daivajña	astrology	
	Jātakābharaṇa	Dhundhiraja	astrology	
	Bṛhaj-jātaka saṭīka	Varahamihira	astrology	with a Hindi commentary
	Horā-makaranda	Gunakara	astrology	
	Jātakālaṃkāra ṭīkā sahita	Ganesha	astrology	with a Hindi commentary
	Gokarṇa-māhātmya		panegyric	with a Hindi commentary
1880	*Muhūrtta-dīpikā*	Ramasevaka Trivedi	astrology	

Appendix V (*contd.*)

Appendix V (*contd.*)

Year	Title	Author/Translator	Category	Remarks
	Sāṃkhya-tattva-kaumudī bhāṣā tilaka sahita	Vacaspati Mishra	philosophy	with a Hindi commentary
	Yājñavalkya smṛti	Yajnavalkya	law	with an Urdu transliteration of Guruprasad's Hindi commentary
	Kāyastha-dharma-nirūpaṇ		caste history	
	Gītāgovindādarśa saṃskṛta aura bhāṣā	Jayadeva	*kāvya*	at the instance of Raja Shiva Prasad
1881	*Bhagavad-gītā ma' urdū tarjuma*		philosophy/religion	with an Urdu translation
	Līlāvatī	Bhaskaracarya	textbook/mathematics	
	Ṛjupāṭh	Gopala Bhandarkara	textbook/reader	
	Aparokṣānubhava bhāṣā ṭīkā sahita	Shankaracarya	philosophy	with a Hindi commentary
	Praśnottarī	Shankaracarya		
	Mādhava-nidānam	Madhavacarya	medicine	
1882	*Lagana-candrikā saṭīka*	Kashinatha Sharma	astrology	with a Hindi commentary by Rambihari Shukla

Appendix V (*contd.*)

Appendix V (*contd.*)

Year	Title	Author/Translator	Category	Remarks
	Karma-vipāka-saṃhitā		astrology	
	Viṣṇu-sahasra-nāmā		ritual/prayer	with an Urdu translation
	Ayodhyā-viṃśatikā	Umapati		
	Sudhā-mandākinī	Umapati		
1883	*Cāṇakya-nīti-darpaṇa bhāṣā ṭīkā sahita*	Canakya	moral and political philosophy	with a Hindi commentary
	Sad-ācāra-prakāśa	Sarayudatta (comp.)	ethics	
	Śrī-rāma-gītā saṭik		philosophy	with a Hindi commentary
	Kenopaniṣad		Upaniṣad	with a Hindi translation
	Kaṭhavallī-upaniṣad		Upaniṣad	with a Hindi translation
	Haṃsarāja-nidānam saṭīkā	Hansaraja	medicine	with a commentary
	Samāsa-cakra	Kanhaiyalal	grammar	
1884	*Mārkaṇḍeya-purāṇa saṭīka*		Purāṇa	with a Hindi commentary and Urdu transliteration thereof
	Garuḍa purāṇa bhāṣā ṭīkā		Purāṇa	printed in Mathura
	Mithilā-māhātmya saṭīka		Purāṇa/panegyric	with a Hindi commentary and Urdu transliteration thereof
	Mathurā-sabhā			
	Bṛhat-saṃhitā	Varahamihira	astrology	with a Hindi commentary

Appendix V (*contd.*)

Appendix V (*contd.*)

Year	Title	Author/Translator	Category	Remarks
1887	*Moha-mudgara*	attr. to Shankaracarya	Vedanta	with an interlineary Hindi trs. by Raja Shiva Prasad
	Arka-prakāśa	attr. to Ravana	medicine	with a Hindi commentary
1888	*Bhagavad-gītā-navala-bhāṣya*		philosophy/religion	with the commentaries by Anandagiri, Shridhara and Shankaracarya, and an abridged Hindi transl. of the later
	Sārasvata-vyākaraṇa saṭīkā	Anubhutisvarupacarya	grammar	with a Hindi commentary
1889	*Veda-vedānta-sāra-śiromaṇī*		philosophy	Bhaskaranand Sarasvati & Hariharanand Saraṡvati (comp.); with a Hindi transl.
	Stotra-saṃgraha		eulogistic hymns	
	Śrī Sārasvata-sūtra-pāṭhaḥ	Anubhutisvarupacarya	grammar	
1890	*Śrī Sārasvata saṭīka pūrvārddhaḥ*	Anubhutisvarupacarya	grammar	with a commentary called '*Siddhānta-ratnāvalī*' by Lokeśvara Śharmana Shukla
	Manu-smṛti bhāṣā ṭīkā sahita	Manu	law	with a Hindi commentary

Appendix V (*contd.*)

Year	Title	Author/Translator	Category	Remarks
	Adhyātma-rāmāyaṇa saṭīka		philosophy	with a Hindi commentary
	Kumārasambhava	Kalidasa	*kāvya*	with a Hindi translation
	Śiṣupāla-vadha bhāṣānuvād sahita	Magha	*kāvya*	with a Hindi translation
1891	*Māṇḍūkya-upaniṣad bhāṣā ṭīkā sahita*		Upaniṣad	with a Hindi translation
	Aitareya-upaniṣad bhāṣā ṭīkā sahita		Upaniṣad	with a Hindi translation
1892	*Matsya-purāṇa sa hindī bhāṣā ṭīkā*		Purāṇa	with a Hindi transl. by Kalicaran and Bastiram
	Upaniṣad-sāra		Upaniṣad	Selections from various Upaniṣads with Hindi commentary
1893	*Dṛṣṭānta-pradīpinī*			with a Hindi translation
	Vṛhaj-jyotiṣa-sāra saṭīk		astrology	with a Hindi commentary
	Jātakālaṃkāra saṭīk	Ganesh	astrology	with a Hindi commentary
	Vṛhaj-jātaka saṭīk	Varahamihira	astrology	with a Hindi commentary
	Mitākṣarā saṭīk	Vijnaneshvara	law	with a Hindi commentary

Appendix V (*contd.*)

Appendix V (*contd.*)

Year	Title	Author/Translator	Category	Remarks
	Rāma-gīta saṭīk		philosophy	with a Hindi commentary
1894	*Śrī Sārasvata-uttarārddhaḥ*	Anubhutisvarupacarya	grammar	with a Hindi commentary called '*Siddhānta-ratnāvalī*'
	Vaidyajīvana	Lolimbaraja	medicine	printed in Mathura
	Nirṇaya-sindhu saṭīk	Kamalakara Bhatta	ritual	with a Hindi commentary

Bibliography

Private Papers

ORIENTAL AND INDIA OFFICE COLLECTIONS, BRITISH LIBRARY

Dufferin and Ava Papers.

Proceedings etc., of the Government

ORIENTAL AND INDIA OFFICE COLLECTIONS, BRITISH LIBRARY

Proceedings of the Government NWP&Oudh.
Educational Department.
General Department.
Home Department.
Proceedings of the Government Punjab.
Educational Department.
Oudh Administration Reports.
Oudh Educational Reports.
Proceedings of the Public Service Commission.
Selections from Vernacular Newspapers (also called Native Newspaper Reports)
Catalogue of Books Published and Registered Under the Provisions of Act XXV of 1867, NWP, Oudh, Punjab (Quarterly Lists of Publications, QLP).

NATIONAL ARCHIVES OF INDIA, NEW DELHI

Home Department (Public and Educational) Proceedings.

UTTAR PRADESH STATE ARCHIVES, LUCKNOW

Proceedings of the Government NWP&Oudh.
Educational Department.
General Department.
Municipal Department.

Contemporary Journals and Newspapers

Avadh Akhbār.
The Hindoo Patriot.
Journal of the Asiatic Society.
Lahore Chronicle.
Tahzīb al-Akhlāq.
The Tribune.
The Pioneer.

Official Publications, Catalogues and Reference Works

Appendix to the Education Commission Report. Report by the North-Western Provinces and Oudh Provincial Committee. Calcutta: Superintendent of Government Printing 1884.

Arberry, A.J. 1937. *Catalogue of the Library of the India Office. Vols II–Part VI. Persian Books.* London: Secretary of State for India.

Blumhardt, J.F.1889. *Catalogue of Hindustani Printed Books in the Library of the British Museum.* London: Longmans.

———. 1893. *Catalogue of the Hindi, Panjabi, Sindhi, and Pushtu Printed Books in the Library of the British Museum.* London: Quaritch.

Census of the N.-W. Provinces 1865. Vol. I. General Report and Appendices. Comp. by W.C. Plowden. Allahabad 1867.

Census of the North-Western Provinces 1872. Vol. I. General Report and Statements and Tables Showing Details of Area and Population. By W.C. Plowden. Allahabad 1873.

Census of the N.-W. P. and Oudh in 1881. Supplement to the Report on the Census, comprising statistics of the tahsils . . . and detailed tables of the occupations. Allahabad 1882.

Census of India 1891. District Census Statistics NWP&Oudh. Aligarh District. Allahabad 1895.

A Collection of Statutes Relating to India. Vol. 1. 1899. Calcutta: Office of the Superintendent of Government Printing, India.

Dictionary of Indo-Persian Literature. Comp. by Nabi Hadi. Delhi: Indira Gandhi National Centre for the Arts and Abhinav Publications 1995.

Ellis, A.G. 1894–1901. *Catalogue of Arabic Books in the British Museum,* Vols I–II, London: Trustees of the British Museum.

Gazetteer of the Lahore District 1883–4. Lahore: Punjab Government 1883–4.

A Gazetteer of the Province of Oudh, 1877–8. Vols I–II. Reprint. Delhi: B.R. Publishing Corp. 1985.

Liotard, L. 1883. *Note Regarding Paper-Making Industry in India*. Simla: Government Central Branch Press.

Manual of Titles for Oudh, Showing all Holders of Hereditary and Personal Titles in the Province. 1889. Allahabad: Government Press.

Nesfield, J.C. and Deviprasad (comp.). 1874–93. *Catalogue of Sanskrit Manuscripts Existing in Oudh*. Calcutta/Allahabad: N.-W.P. and Oudh Government Press.

Nevill, H.R. 1909. *Aligarh: A Gazetteer* (District Gazetteers of the United Provinces of Agra and Oudh, Vol. VI). Allahabad.

The New Calcutta Directory for the Town Calcutta, Bengal, the North-West Provinces, Punjab, Arracan, Assam, Pegu, Tenasserim. Calcutta 1862–3.

Prana Natha and Chaudhuri, J.B. 1938. *Catalogue of the Library of the India Office, Vol. II–Part I. Sanskrit Books*. London: His Majesty's Stationery Office.

Rose, H.A. (comp.). [1911] 1978. *A Glossary of the Tribes and Castes of the Punjab and North-Western Frontier Province. Based on the census report for the Punjab, 1883, by the late Sir Denzil Ibbetson and the census report for the Punjab, 1892, by Sir Edward Maclagan*. Vol. II. Lahore: Aziz Publishers.

Report on the Census of the North-Western Provinces and Oudh and of the Native States of Rampur and Native Garhwal, taken on the 17th February 1881. By Edmund White. Allahabad 1882.

Reports on Publications Issued and Registered in the Several Provinces of British India. 1874–1895.

Selections from Educational Records. Part 1, 1781–1839. Calcutta 1920.

Selections from Educational Records of the Government of India. Vol. 1, 1858–71. Delhi 1960.

Selections from Speeches of the Lieutenant-Governors of the NWP from 1867–91. Allahabad 1890.

Sharma, Vinod Chandra. 1959. *Uttar Pradesh District Gazetteers*, vol. XXXVII. Lucknow: Government of Uttar Pradesh.

Storey, C.A. 1927–77. *Persian Literature. A Bio-Bibliographical Survey*. 3 vols. London: The Royal Asiatic Society of Great Britain and Ireland.

Thacker's Indian Directory for Bengal, the North-Western Provinces, the Punjab, the Central Provinces, the Rajpootana States, Oude and British Burma. 1885–(1960). Calcutta: Thacker, Spink & Co.

Thornton, Edward. 1857. *A Gazetteer of the Territories under the Government of the East-India Company and of the Native States of the Continent of India*. London: W.H. Allen & Co.

Published Works and Unpublished Theses in English

Abdus Subhan (ed.). 1986. *The Khudnawisht Sawanih Hayat-i-Nassakh (Autobiography of Abdul Ghafur Nassakh)*. Calcutta: The Asiatic Society.

Ahmad, Nazir. 2001. *The Bride's Mirror*. Mirāt ul-ʿarūs. *A Tale of Life in Delhi a Hundred Years Ago*. Trs. by G.E. Ward, with an afterword by Frances W. Pritchett. New Delhi: Permanent Black.

Ahmad, Nazir. 1985. *Oriental Presses in the World*. Lahore: Qadiriya Book Traders.

Alam, Javeed. 1999. 'The Composite Culture and its Historiography'. *South Asia* XXII. Special Issue: 29–37.

Alavi, Seema. 2003. 'A National Medicine in Colonial India? The Muslim Physicians and the Takmil-ut Tibb College at Lucknow.' (http://www.fas.harvard.edu/~asiactr/ archive/newperspectives/Text/Seema.htm./27.06.2003).

———. 2005. 'Unani medicine in the nineteenth-century public sphere: Urdu texts and the *Oudh Akhbar*'. *Indian Economic and Social History Review* 42 (1): 101–29.

Allen, Clarence E. 1897. *Publishers' Accounts. Including a Consideration of Copyright and the Valuation of Literary Property*. London: Gee Co.

Altick, Richard D. 1957. *The English Common Reader: A Social History of the Mass Reading Public 1800–1900*. Chicago: University of Chicago Press.

Amrit Rai 1991. *Premchand: His Life and Times*, trs. from the Hindi by Harish Trivedi, Delhi: Oxford University Press.

Anderson, Benedict. 1991 [1983]. *Imagined Communities. Reflections on the Origin and Spread of Nationalism*. 2nd, revised ed. London: Verso.

Arberry, Arthur J. 1960. *Oriental Essays: Portraits of Seven Scholars*. London: Allen & Unwin.

Arnold, David. 1993. *Colonizing the Body. State Medicine and Epidemic Disease in Nineteenth-Century India*. Delhi: Oxford University Press.

———. 2000. *Science, Technology and Medicine in Colonial India*. Cambridge: Cambridge University Press.

———. (ed.). 1988. *Imperial Medicine and Indigenous Societies*. Manchester: Manchester University Press.

Asaduddin, M. 2001. 'First Urdu Novel. Contesting Claims and Disclaimers.' *AUS* 16.1: 76–97.

Atiyeh, George N. (ed.). 1995. *The Book in the Islamic World. The Written Word and Communication in the Middle East*. Albany: State University of New York Press.

Atkinson, Edwin T. 1973 [1882]. *The Himalayan Gazetteer*, vol. 3 (2). Reprint. Delhi: Cosmo Publications.

Āzād, Muḥammad Ḥusain. 2001. *Āb-e ḥayāt. Shaping the Canon of Urdu Poetry*. Trs. and ed. by Frances Pritchett. In association with Shamsur Rahman Faruqi. New Delhi: Oxford University Press.

Azmi, Arshad Ali. 1970. 'The Decay of the City of Lucknow'. *Indian History Congress: Proceedings of the 32nd session*, vol. II: 168–72.

Bahri, Hardev. 1948. 'Contributions to Hindi Lexicography'. *Proceedings and Transactions of the All-India Oriental Conference, Twelfth session*. Vol. IV: 85–96.

Baijnath, Lala. 1886. *Social Reform for the N. W. Provinces: Proceedings of Public Meetings, with Two Papers and a Preface*. Bombay: Voice of India Printing Press.

Bailey, T. Grahame. 1932. *A History of Urdu Literature*. Calcutta: Association Press/London: Oxford University Press.

Banerjee, Sumanta. 1989. 'Marginalization of Women's Popular Culture in Nineteenth Century Bengal'. In: Kumkum Sangari and Sudesh Vaid (eds.). *Recasting Women. Essays in Colonial History*. Delhi: Kali for Women, 127–79.

Barnett, Richard B. 1980. *North India Between Empires: Awadh, the Mughals and the British, 1720–1801*. Berkeley: University of California Press.

Barns, Margarita. 1940. *The Indian Press*. London: George Allan & Unwin Ltd.

Barrier, N. Gerald and Paul Wallace (eds.). 1970. *The Punjab Press, 1880–1905*. East Lansing: Michigan State University.

Barz, Richard K. 1994. 'The Caurasi Vaisnavan ki varta and the hagiography of the pustimarg', in: Winand M. Callewaert and Rupert Snell (eds.). *According to Tradition. Hagiographical Writing in India*. Wiesbaden: Harrassowitz, 43–64 (Khoj, vol. 5).

Basak, N.L. 1959. 'Origin and Role of the Calcutta School Book Society in Promoting the Cause of Education in India, Especially Vernacular Education in Bengal (1817–1835)'. *Bengal Past and Present*, vol. 78: 30–69.

Bayly, C.A. 1971. 'Local Control in Indian Towns—The Case of Allahabad 1880–1920'. *MAS* 5.4: 289–336.

———. 1975. *The Local Roots of Indian Politics: Allahabad 1880–1920.* London: Oxford University Press.

———. 1992 [1983]. *Rulers, Townsmen and Bazaars. North Indian Society in the Age of British Expansion 1770–1870.* Delhi: Oxford University Press.

———. 1996a. *Empire and Information: Intelligence Gathering and Social Communication in India, 1780–1870.* Cambridge: Cambridge University Press.

———. 1996b. 'Colonial rule and the "informational order" in South Asia'. In: Nigel Crook (ed.). *The Transmission of Knowledge in South Asia: Essays on Education, Religion, History and Politics.* Delhi: Oxford University Press, 280–315.

———. 1998. *Origins of Nationality in South Asia. Patriotism and Ethical Government in the Making of Modern India.* Delhi: Oxford University Press.

Bayly, Susan. 1999. *Caste, Society and Politics in India from the Eighteenth Century to the Modern Age.* Cambridge a. o.: Cambridge University Press.

Bennett, Scott. 1990. 'The Golden Stain of Time: Preserving Victorian Periodicals.' In: Laurel Brake, Aled Jones and Lionel Madden (eds.). *Investigating Victorian Journalism.* Basingstoke: Macmillan, 166–83.

Bhatia, Tej K. 1987. *A History of the Hindi Grammatical Tradition: Hindi-Hindustani grammar, grammarians, history and problems.* Leiden a.o.: Brill.

Bhatnagar, Ram Ratan. 1947. *The Rise and Growth of Hindi Journalism (1826–1945).* Allahabad: Kitab Mahal.

Bhattacharyya, Amit. 1988. 'Swadeshi Paper Industry in Colonial Bengal'. *Bengal Past and Present,* vol. 107: 79–97.

Bhattacharya, Jogendra Nath. 1968 [1896]. *Hindu Castes and Sects.* Reprint. Calcutta: Ed. Indian.

Blackburn, Stuart. 2001. 'The Tale of the Book: Storytelling and Print in Nineteenth-Century Tamil.' In: Rachel Dwyer and Christopher Pinney (eds.). *Pleasure and the Nation: The history, politics and consumption of public culture in India.* Delhi: Oxford University Press, 115–37.

———. 2003. *Print, Folklore, and Nationalism in Colonial South India.* Delhi: Permanent Black.

Blochmann, H. 1869. 'Badaoni and his Works'. *Journal of the Asiatic Society* 3 (1): 105–44.

———. 1872. 'Koch Bihar and Asam'. *Journal of the Asiatic Society* I: 49–101.

Bool Chand, 1933. 'Urdu Journalism in the Panjab'. *JPHS* 2: 29–42.

Borthwick, Meredith. 1984. *The Changing Role of Women in Bengal, 1849–1905.* Princeton, NJ: Princeton University Press.

Bourdieu, Pierre. 1993. *The Field of Cultural Production. Essays on Art and Literature*. Ed. and intr. by Randal Johnson. Cambridge: Polity Press.

Brass, Paul. 1974. *Language, Religion and Politics in North India.* London: Cambridge University Press.

Brown, Lucy. 1985. *Victorian News and Newspapers*. Oxford: Clarendon Press.

Burton, Richard F. 1887. *The Book of the Thousand Nights and a Night*, vol. 13 [*Supplemental nights . . . with notes anthropological and explanatory*, vol. 3]. London: Privately printed at the Burton Club. (Literature Post. 2004. 1001 Nights. Vol. 13 by Burton, Richard. http://www.literaturepost.com/book/61.html./24 February 2004.)

Busch, Allison. 2006. 'Questioning the Tropes about "Bhakti" and "Rīti" in Hindi Literary Historiography'. In: Monika Horstmann (ed.). *Bhakti in Current Research, 2001–2003.* Delhi: Manohar, 33–47.

Carroll, Lucy. 1973. 'The Kayastha Samachar: From a Caste to a National Newspaper'. *Indian Economic and Social History Review* 10 (3): 280–92.

———. 1975. 'Caste, Social Change, and the Social Scientist: A Note on the Ahistorical Approach to Indian Social History'. *Journal of Asian Studies* 35 (1): 63–84.

———. 1978. 'Colonial Perceptions of Indian Society and the Emergence of Caste(s) Associations'. *Journal of Asian Studies* 37 (2): 233–50.

Chakraborti, Smarajit. 1976. *The Bengali Press, 1818–1868: A Study in the Growth of Public Opinion*. Calcutta: Firma KLM 1976.

Chandra, Sudhir. 1992. *The Oppressive Present. Literature and Social Consciousness in Colonial India*. Delhi: Oxford University Press.

Chartier, Roger. 1984. 'Culture as Appropriation: Popular Cultural Uses in Early Modern France'. In: Steven L. Kaplan (ed.). *Understanding Popular Culture: Europe from the Middle Ages to the Nineteenth Century*. New York: Mouton, 229–53.

Chatterjee, Partha. 1993. *The Nation and its Fragments: Colonial and Postcolonial Histories*. Princeton, NJ: Princeton University Press.

———. 1995. 'History and the Nationalization of Hinduism'. In: Vasudha Dalmia and Heinrich von Stietencron (eds.). *Representing Hinduism: The Construction of Religious Traditions and National Identity*. New Delhi/Thousand Oaks/London: 103–28.

Chauduri, S. (comp). 1956. *Index to the Publications of the Asiatic Society 1788–1953*. Calcutta: Asiatic Society.

Chunder, Bholanauth. 1869. *The Travels of a Hindoo to Various Parts of Bengal and Upper India*. Vol. 1. London: Trübner & Co.

Cohn, Bernhard S. 1983. 'Representing Authority in Victorian India'. In: Eric Hobsbawm and Terence Ranger (eds.). *The Invention of Tradition*. Cambridge: Cambridge University Press, 165–209.

———. 1997. *Colonialism and its Forms of Knowledge: The British in India*. Delhi: Oxford University Press.

Cole, J.R.I. 1988. *Roots of North Indian Shīʿism in Iran and Iraq. Religion and State in Awadh, 1722–1859*. Berkeley/Los Angeles/London: University of California Press.

Comfort, Alex (trs.). 1964. *The Koka Shastra. Being the Ratirahasya of Kokkoka. And other Medieval Indian Writings on Love*. London: George Allan and Unwin Ltd.

Cook, Andrew S. 1989. 'The beginning of lithographic map printing in Calcutta'. In: Pauline Rohatgi and Pheroza Godrej (eds.). *India: A Pageant of Prints*. Bombay: Marg Publications, 125–34.

Craig, Alec. 1963. *Suppressed Books. A History of the Conception of Literary Obscenity*. Cleveland and New York: The World Publishing Company.

Crooke, Willam. 1974 [1896]. *The Tribes and Castes of the North Western India*. Vol. 2. Reprint. Delhi: Cosmo Publications.

Cyclopedia 1908. *The Cyclopedia of India. Biographical-Historical-Administrative-Commercial*. Vol. II. Calcutta: The Cyclopedia Publishing Coy.

Dalmia, Vasudha. 1995. 'The only real religion of the Hindus: Vaiṣṇava self-representation in the late nineteenth century'. In: Vasudha Dalmia and Heinrich v. Stietencron (eds.). *Representing Hinduism: The Construction of Religious Traditions and National Identity*. New Delhi/Thousand Oaks/ London: 176–210.

———. 1997. *The Nationalization of Hindu Traditions: Bhāratendu Hariśchandra and Nineteenth-century Banaras*. Delhi: Oxford University Press.

———. 2004. 'Generic Questions: Bharatendu Harishchandra and Women's Issues'. In: Stuart Blackburn and Vasudha Dalmia (eds.). *India's Literary History: Essays on the Nineteenth Century*. Delhi: Permanent Black, 402–34.

Dalmia-Lüderitz, Vasudha. 1992a. 'Hariścandra of Banaras and the reassessment of Vaiṣṇava bhakti in the late nineteenth century'. In: R.S. McGregor (ed.). *Devotional Literature in South Asia. Current Research, 1985–1988*. Cambridge: Cambridge University Press, 281–97.

———. 1992b. 'A National Theatre for the Hindus: Hariścandra of Banaras and the Classical Traditions in Late Nineteenth Century India'. In: M. Offredi (ed.). *Literature, Language and the Media in India*. Delhi: Manohar, 181–206.

Darnton, Robert. 1982. 'What is the History of Books?' *Daedalus*, Summer 1982: 65–83.

Das, Rajani Kanta. 1941. *History of Indian Labour Legislation*. Calcutta: University of Calcutta.

Das, Sisir Kumar. 1978. *Sahibs and Munshis. An Account of the College of Fort William*. Calcutta etc.: Orion Publications.

———. 1991. *1800–1910: Western Impact—Indian Response*. New Delhi: Sahitya Akademi (A History of Indian Literature, vol. 8).

Das Gupta, Jyotirindra. 1970. *Language Conflict and National Development*. Berkeley: University of California Press.

Davis, Emmett. 1983. *Press and Politics in British Western Punjab 1836–1947*. Delhi: Academic Publications.

Desika Char, S.V. 1963. *Centralised Legislation. A history of the legislative system of British India from 1834 to 1861*. Bombay etc.: Asia Publishing House.

Diehl, Katherine Smith. 1964. *Early Indian Imprints*. New York & London: Scarecrow Press.

———. 1973. 'Lucknow printers 1820–1850'. In: N.N. Gidwani (ed.). *Comparative Librarianship: Essays in Honour of Professor D.N. Marshall*. Delhi etc.: Vikas Publishing House, 115–28.

Dittmer, Kerrin. 1972. *Die indischen Muslims und die Hindi-Urdu Kontroverse in den United Provinces*. Wiesbaden: Harrassowitz.

Eisenstein, Elizabeth L. 1980. *The Printing Press as an Agent of Change: Communications and cultural transformations in early-modern Europe*. Vols 1–2. Cambridge: Cambridge University Press.

Eliot, Simon. 1995. 'Some trends in British book production, 1800–1919'. In: John O. Jordan and Robert L. Patten (eds.). *Literature in the*

Marketplace: Nineteenth-Century British Publishing and Reading Practices. Cambridge: Cambridge University Press, 19–43.

Elliot, Henry M. 1976 [1859]. *Memoirs on the History, Folk-lore, and Distribution of the Races of the North Western Provinces of India: being an amplified edition of the original supplemental glossary of Indian terms*. Ed., rev. and rearranged by John Beames. Reprint. Osnabrück: Biblio-Verlag.

———. 1867–1877. *The History of India as Told by its Own Historians*. Ed. from the posthumous papers of the late Sir H.M. Elliot by John Downson. Vols 1–8. London: Truebner.

The Encyclopaedia of Islam. New Edition. 1960–1997. Vols 1–9, Leiden: E.J. Brill.

Farooqi, Musharraf. 2000. '*Dastan-e Amir Hamza Sahibqiran*: Preface to the Translation'. *AUS* 15 (1): 169–73.

Faruqi, Shamsur Rahman. 1998. 'Unprivileged power: The strange case of Persian (and Urdu) in nineteenth-century India'. *AUS* 13: 3–30.

Feather, John. 1994. *Publishing, Piracy and Politics: An Historical Study of Copyright in Britain*. London: Mansell.

Febvre, Lucien and Martin, H.-J. 1958. *L'Apparition du Livre*. Paris: Michel.

Federico, Annette R. 2000. *Idol of Suburbia: Marie Corelli and Late-Victorian Literary Culture*. Charlottesville: University Press of Virginia.

Fisher, Michael H. 1987. *A Clash of Cultures: Awadh, the British and the Mughals*. Delhi: Manohar.

———. 1993. 'The Office of Akhbar Nawis. The Transition from Mughal to British Forms'. *MAS* 27 (i): 45–82.

Forbes, Geraldine. 1996. *Women in Modern India*. Cambridge: Cambridge University Press (The New Cambridge History of India 4.2)

Garcin de Tassy, J.H. 1870–1. *Histoire de la Littérature Hindouie et Hindoustanie*, vols 1–3. Paris: Adolphe Labitte.

———. 1850–78. *La Langue et la Littérature Hindoustanies. Discours d'Ouverture du Cours d'Hindoustani/Revue Annuelle*. Paris: Librarie Orientale de Maisonneuve et Cie.

Gellner, Ernest. 1994. *Conditions of Liberty: Civil Society and its Rivals*. New York: Allen Lane.

Ghosh, Anindita. 1998. 'Cheap Books, "Bad" Books: Contesting Print-Cultures in Colonial Bengal'. *South Asia Research* 18 (2): 173–94.

———. 2002. 'Revisiting the "Bengal Renaissance": Literary Bengali and Low-Life Print in Colonial Calcutta'. *Economic and Political Weekly*, vol. XXXVII, No. 42: 4329–38.

Ghosh, Sunit. 1998. *Modern History of Indian Press*. New Delhi: Cosmo Publications.

Goldman, Robert P. 1977. *Gods, Priests, and Warriors. The Bhṛgus of the* Mahābhārata. New York: Columbia University Press.

Goody, Jack (ed.). 1968. *Literacy in Traditional Societies*. Cambridge: Cambridge University Press.

———. 1986. *The Logic of Writing and the Organization of Society*. Cambridge: Cambridge University Press.

———. 1987. *The Interface between the Written and the Oral*. Cambridge: Cambridge University Press.

———. 2000. *The Power of the Written Tradition*. Washington: Smithsonian Institution Press.

Graff, Violette (ed.). 1997. *Lucknow: Memories of a City*. Delhi: Oxford University Press.

Grierson, George Abraham. 1889. *The Modern Vernacular Literature of Hindustan*. Calcutta: Asiatic Society.

———. 1903. 'The Early Publications of the Serampore Missionaries'. *The Indian Antiquary*, June 1903: 241–54.

———. 1909. 'Gleanings from the Bhakta-Mala'. *JRAS*: 607–44.

Griffiths, Antony. 1996 [1980]. *Prints and Printmaking. An Introduction to the History and Techniques*. London: British Museum Press.

Growse, F. S. 1883. *Mathura: A District Memoir*. 3rd revised and abridged ed. Allahabad: Government Press.

Guha, Ranjit. 1988. *An Indian Historiography of India: A Nineteenth-century Agenda and its Implications*, Calcutta: K.P. Bagchi.

Gupta, Abhijit and Swapan Chakravorty (eds.). 2004. *Print Areas. Book History in India*. Delhi: Permanent Black.

Gupta, Charu. 2000. '"Dirty" Hindi Literature: Contests about Obscenity in Late Colonial North India'. *South Asia Research* 20 (2): 89–118.

———. 2001. *Sexuality, Obscenity, Community. Women, Muslims, and the Hindu Public in Colonial India*. Delhi: Permanent Black.

Gupta, Narayani. 1981. *Delhi between Two Empires, 1803–1931: Society, Government and Urban Growth*. Delhi: Oxford University Press.

Haidar, Syed Jalaluddin. 1981. 'Munshi Nawal Kishore (1836–1895): Mirror of Urdu Printing in British India'. *Pakistan Library Bulletin* XII (1): 12–23.

Hali, Khwaja Altaf Husain. 1997. *Hali's Musaddas. The Flow and Ebb of Islam*. Ed. and with an introduction by Christopher Shackle and Javed Majeed. Delhi: Oxford University Press.

Hall, David D. 1996. *Cultures of Print: Essays in the History of the Book*. Amherst: University of Massachusetts Press.

Hansen, Kathryn. 1989. 'The Birth of Hindi Drama in Banaras, 1868–1885'. In: Sandria B. Freitag (ed.). *Culture and Power in Banaras. Community, Performance and Environment, 1800–1980*. Delhi: Oxford University Press, 62–92.

———. 2001. 'The Indar Sabha Phenomenon: Public Theatre and Consumption in Greater India (1853–1956)'. In: Rachel Dwyer and Christopher Pinney (eds.). *Pleasure and the Nation: The history, politics and consumption of public culture in India*. Delhi: Oxford University Press, 76–114.

Hardy, Peter. 1960. *Historians of Medieval India: Studies in Indo-Muslim historical writing*. London: Luzac.

Harishcandra. 1954. *Bhāratendu granthāvalī*. Vol. 3. Ed. Brajratnadas. Benares: Nagaripracharini Sabha.

Harris, José. 1993. *Private Lives, Public Spirit: Britain 1870–1914*. Oxford: Oxford University Press.

Harris, Michael. 1990. 'London's Local Newspapers: Patterns of Change in the Victorian Period'. In: Laurel Brake, Aled Jones and Lionel Madden (eds.). *Investigating Victorian Journalism*. Basingstoke: Macmillan, 104–19.

Harrison, Mark. 1994. *Public Health in British India: Anglo-Indian Preventive Medicine, 1859–1914*. Cambridge: Cambridge University Press.

Hasan, Amir. 1990. *Vanishing Culture of Lucknow*. Delhi: B. R. Publ. Corp.

Hawley, John Stratton. 1984. *Sur Das: Poet, Singer, Saint*. Delhi: Oxford University Press.

Hay, Sidney. 1994 [1936]. *Historic Lucknow*. Reprint. Delhi/Madras: Asian Educational Services.

Haynes, Douglas E. 1987. 'From Tribute to Philanthropy: The Politics of Gift Giving in a Western Indian City'. *Journal of Asian Studies* 46 (2): 339–60.

Hoey, William. 1880. *A Monograph on Trade and Manufactures in Northern India*. Lucknow: American Methodist Mission Press.

Hohendahl, Peter Uwe. 1989. *Building a National Literature. The Case of Germany, 1830–1870.* Trs. by Renate Baron Franciscono. Ithaca and London: Cornell University Press.

Howsam, Leslie. 1998. *Kegan Paul—A Victorian Imprint: publishers, books and cultural history.* London and Toronto: Kegan Paul International and University of Toronto Press.

Hughes, Linda K. and Michael Lund. 1995. 'Textual/sexual pleasure and serial publication'. In: John O. Jordan and Robert L. Patten (eds.). *Literature in the Marketplace. Nineteenth-century British publishing and reading practices.* Cambridge: Cambridge University Press, 143–64.

Hurst, John F. 1887. 'A Native Publishing House in India'. *Harper's New Monthly Magazine* LXXV, June to November.

Husain, Yusuf (ed.). 1966. *Selected Documents from the Aligarh Archives.* Bombay: Asia Publ. House.

Ingham, Kenneth. 1956. *Reformers in India 1793–1833.* Cambridge: Cambridge University Press.

Irschick, Eugene F. 1994. *Dialogue and History: Constructing South India, 1795–1895.* Berkeley: University of California Press.

Isaac, Peter and McKay, Barry (eds.).1999. *The Human Face of the Book Trade: Print Culture and its Creators.* Winchester: St. Paulas Bibliographies; Delaware: Oak Knoll Press.

Johns, Adrian. 1998. *The Nature of the Book: Print and Knowledge in the Making.* Chicago: University of Chicago Press.

Jordens, J.T.F. 1978. *Dayānanda Sarasvatī. His Life and Ideas.* Delhi: Oxford University Press.

Joshi, Priya. 1998. 'Culture and Consumption: Fiction, the Reading Public, and the British Novel in Colonial India'. *Book History* 1: 196–220.

———. 2002. *In Another Country. Colonialism, Culture and the English Novel in India.* New York: Columbia University Press.

Joshi, Sanjay. 2001. *Fractured Modernity: Making of a Middle Class in Colonial North India.* New Delhi: Oxford University Press.

Kabir, Abulfazal M. Fazle. 1987. *The Libraries of Bengal: 1700–1947.* London/New York: Mansell.

Kalsi, A.S. 1990. 'The Influence of Nazir Ahmad's Mirāt al-ʿarūs (1869) on the Development of Hindi Fiction'. *AUS* 7: 31–44.

Kanhaiyalal. N.d. *The Late Pandit Mukund Ram.* Reprinted from Arjuna. Lahore: Mitra Vilas Press.

Karlekar, Malavika. 1991. *Voices from Within: Early Personal Narratives of Bengali Women.* Delhi: Oxford University Press.

Kaviraj, Sudipta. 1995. *The Unhappy Consciousness: Bankimchandra Chattopadhyay and the Formation of Nationalist Discourse in India.* Delhi: Oxford University Press.

Kerr, Ian J. 1979. 'Social Change in Lahore, 1849–1875'. *Journal of Indian History* 57 (2&3): 281–302.

Kesavan, B.S. 1989–1997. *History of Printing and Publishing in India. A story of cultural re-awakening.* 3 vols. New Delhi: National Book Trust.

Khan, Iqbal Ghani. 2000. 'A Book with two Views—Ghulam Husain's "An Overview of the Modern Times"'. In: Jamal Malik (ed.). *Perspectives of Mutual Encounters on South Asian History 1760–1860.* Leiden/Boston/Köln: Brill, 278–97.

Khan, Javed Ali. 1994. 'Beginnings of Historical Writings in Urdu'. *JPHS* 42 (1), 23–35.

———, 1995. 'Historical Writings in Urdu Under the Auspices of Dihli College (1825–77)'. *JPHS* 43 (4), 381–94.

Khan, Mofakhkhar Hussain. 1999. *The Bengali Book: History of Printing and Book Making 1667–1866.* Vol. 1. Dhaka: Bangla Academy.

Khan, Nadir Ali. 1991. *A History of Urdu Journalism (1822–1857).* Delhi: Idarah-i Adabiyat-i Delli.

Khan, Rasheeduddin (ed.). 1987. *Composite Culture of India and National Integration.* Simla: Indian Institute of Advanced Study in Association with Allied Publ., Delhi.

Khan, Shaukat Ali. 1981. *History and Historians of Rajasthan.* Delhi: Triveni Publications.

Khare, Prem Shanker. 1964. *The Growth of Press and Public Opinion in India (1857–1918).* Allahabad: Piyush Prakashan.

Khurshid, Abdus Salam. 1964. *Journalism in Pakistan: First Phase, 1845–1857.* Lahore: Publishers United.

Khurshidul Islam and Ralph Russell. 1994 [1969]. *Three Mughal Poets. Mir, Sauda, Mir Hasan.* Delhi: Oxford University Press.

Kidwai, Riaz ur Rahman. 1993. *Lucknow: The Lost Paradise.* Lucknow: S.R. Publications.

Killingley, D.H. 1981. 'Rammohan Roy on the Vedanta Sutras'. *Religion* 11: 151–69.

King, Christopher R. 1992. 'Images of Virtue and Vice: The Hindi-Urdu Controversy in Two Nineteenth Century Hindi Plays'. In: Kenneth W. Jones (ed.). *Religious Controversy in British India: Dialogues in South Asian Languages.* Albany: State University of New York Press, 123–48.

———. 1994. *One Language, Two Scripts: The Hindi Movement in Nineteenth Century North India*. Bombay: Oxford University Press 1994.

King, Ursula. 1977. 'True and Perfect Religion: Bankim Chandra Chatterjee's Reinterpretation of Hinduism'. *Religion* 7: 127–48.

Kopf, David. 1969. *British Orientalism and the Bengal Renaissance. The Dynamics of Indian Modernization 1773–1835.* Berkeley and Los Angeles: University of California Press.

Kumar, Deepak. 1997. 'Unequal Contenders, Uneven Ground: Medical Encounters in British India, 1820–1920'. In: Andrew Cunningham and Bridie Andrews (eds.). *Western Medicine as Contested Knowledge.* Manchester/New York: Manchester University Press, 172–90.

Kumar, Krishna. 1991. *Political Agenda of Education. A study of colonialist and nationalist ideas.* New Delhi/Newbury Park/London: Sage Publications.

Kumar, Nita. 2000. *Lessons from Schools: The History of Education in Banaras*. New Delhi: Sage.

Laird, M.A. 1967. 'The Contribution of Missionaries to Education in Bengal During the Administration of Lord Hastings, 1813–23'. *Bengal Past & Present* 86: 68–89.

Lakhanpal, P.L. 1960. *Ghalib: The Man and His Verse*. Delhi: International Books.

Latif, Syad Muhammad. 1981 [1892]. *Lahore: Its History, Architectural Remains and Antiquities.* Reprint. Lahore: New Imperial Press.

Law, Graham. 2000. *Serializing Fiction in the Victorian Press*. Houndmills etc.: Palgrave.

Lelyveld, David.1996. *Aligarh's First Generation. Muslim Solidarity in British India.* Delhi: Oxford University Press.

Llewellyn, J. E. 1993. *The Arya Samaj as a Fundamentalist Movement.* New Delhi: Manohar.

Llewellyn-Jones, Rosie. 1985. *A Fatal Friendship: The Nawabs, the British, and the City of Lucknow*. Delhi: Oxford University Press.

Lockyer, Dora. 1977. 'The provision of books and libraries by the East India Company in India, 1611–1858'. Unpubl. thesis submitted for Fellowship of the Library Association.

Long, James. 1848. *Handbook of Bengal Missions, in Connexion with the Church of England.* London: John Farquhar Shaw.

———. 1859. *Returns Relating to Publications in the Bengali language, in 1857, to which is added, a list of the native presses with the books printed at each . . ., with a notice of the past condition and future prospects of the vernacular press of Bengal, and the statistics of the Bombay and Madras vernacular presses. . . .* Calcutta: General Printing Department.

Losty, Jeremiah P. 1989. 'Sir Charles D'Oyly's Lithographic Press and his Indian Assistants'. In: Pauline Rohatgi and Pheroza Godrej (eds.). *India: A Pageant of Prints*. Bombay: Marg Publications, 135–60.

Ludden, David E. 1996. *Contesting the Nation: Religion, Community, and the Politics of Democracy in India*. Philadelphia: University of Pennsylvania Press.

Lütt, Jürgen. 1970. *Hindu-Nationalismus in Uttar Pradeś 1867–1900.* Stuttgart: Ernst Klett Verlag.

Lutgendorf, Philip. 1994a. *The Life of a Text: Performing the* Rāmcaritmānas *of Tulsidas*. Delhi: Oxford University Press.

———. 1994b. 'The Quest for the Legendary Tulsīdās'. In: Winand M. Callewaert and Rupert Snell (eds.). *According to Tradition. Hagiographical Writing in India*. Wiesbaden: Harrassowitz, 65–85 (Khoj, vol. 5).

Macaulay, Thomas. 1880. *Miscellaneous Writings*. Vol. 3. London: Longman's Green and Co.

Maclean, Ian. 1999. 'Adrian Johns: The Nature of the Book' (Review). *Times Literary Supplement* of 26 February: 12.

Madan Gopal. 1964. *Munshi Premchand: A Literary Biography*. London: Asia Publishing House.

———, 1972. *The Bharatendu: His Life and Times*. New Delhi: Sagar Publications.

Mahajan, S.G. 1984. *History of the Public Library Movement in Maharashtra*. Pune: Shubhada-Saraswat Publ.

Mainkar, T.G. 1977. *The Vāsiṣṭha Rāmāyaṇa: a study*. New Delhi: Meharchand Lachhmandas.

Malik, Jamal. 1997. *Islamische Gelehrtenkultur in Nordindien. Entwicklungsgeschichte und Tendenzen am Beispiel von Lucknow*. Leiden/New York/Köln: Brill.

Marzolph, Ulrich. 2001. *Narrative Illustration in Persian Lithographed Books*. Leiden/Boston/Köln: Brill. (Handbuch der Orientalistik, Section 1, vol. 60).

Mattausch, John. 1996. 'A "Penury of Bookes": The Printing Press and Social Change, in an Indian Setting'. *South Asia* XIX (2): 59–83.

McDonald, Peter D. 1997. *British Literary Culture and Publishing Practice 1880–1914*. Cambridge: Cambridge University Press.

McGregor, Ronald Stuart. 1974. *Hindi Literature of the Nineteenth and Early Twentieth Centuries*. Wiesbaden: Harrassowitz.

———. 1984. *Hindi Literature from its Beginnings to the Nineteenth Century*. Wiesbaden: Harrassowitz.

Mehta, Makrand. 1991. *Indian Merchants and Entrepreneurs in Historical Perspective: With Special Reference to Shroffs of Gujarat, 17th to 19th Centuries*. Delhi: Academic Foundation.

Menon, Dilip. 2002. 'No. Not the Nation. Lower Caste Malayalam Novels of the Nineteenth Century'. In: Meenakshi Mukherjee (ed.). *Early Novels in India*. Delhi: Sahitya Akademi, 41–72.

Metcalf, Barbara Daly. 1982. *Islamic Revival in British India: Deoband, 1860–1900*. Princeton: Princeton University Press.

———. 1990. *Perfecting Women. Maulana Ashraf ʿAli Thanawi's* Bihishti Zewar. Berkeley/Los Angeles/Oxford: University of California Press.

Metcalf, Thomas R. 1979. *Land, Landlords, and the British Raj. Northern India in the Nineteenth Century*. Berkeley/Los Angeles/London: University of California Press.

———. 1990. *The Aftermath of Revolt. India, 1857–70*. New Delhi: Manohar.

Meulenbeld, G. J. 2000. *A History of Indian Medical Literature*. Vols I–III. Groningen: Egbert Forsten.

Minault, Gail. 1998. *Secluded Scholars: Women's Education and Muslim Social Reform in Colonial India*. Delhi: Oxford University Press.

———. 1999. 'Delhi College and Urdu'. *AUS* 14: 119–34.

———. 2003. 'Master Ramchandra of Delhi College: Teacher, Journalist, and Cultural Intermediary'. *AUS* 18.1: 95–104.

Minkowski, Christopher Z. 2001. 'The Pandit as Public Intellectual: The Controversy over *virodha* or Inconsistency in the Astronomical Sciences'. In: Axel Michaels (ed.). *The Pandit. Traditional Scholarship in India*. Delhi: Manohar, 79–103.

Misra, Jogesh. 1979. *History of Libraries and Librarianship in Modern India Since 1850*. Delhi/Lucknow: Atma Ram.

Mohan, Surendra. 1997. *Awadh under the Nawabs: Politics, Culture and Communal Relations 1722–1856*. New Delhi: Manohar.

Mookerjee, Firoze. 1992. *Lucknow and the World of Sarshar*. Karachi: Saad Publications.

Muhammad, Shan (ed.). 1972. *Writings and Speeches of Sir Syed Ahmad Khan*. Bombay: Nachiketa Publications.

———. 1978. *The Aligarh Movement: Basic Documents, 1864–1898.* Vols 1–3. Meerut: Meenakshi Prakashan.

Mukherjee, Meenakshi. 1994 [1985]. *Realism and Reality. The Novel and Society in India.* Delhi: Oxford University Press.

———. (ed.). 2002. *Early Novels in India.* New Delhi: Sahitya Akademi.

Mukhtar, Ahmad. 1930. *Factory Labour in India.* Madras: Methodist Publishing House.

Nabhvi, Ramlal. 1993. 'The Rāmāyaṇa Literature in Arabic, Persian and Urdu'. In: K. Krishnamoorthy (ed.). *A Critical Inventory of Rāmāyaṇa Studies in the World.* Vol. II. Delhi: Sahitya Akademi.

Naim, C.M. 1984a. 'Prize-Winning *Adab*: A Study of five Urdu Books Written in Response to the Allahabad Government Gazette Notification'. In Barbara D. Metcalf (ed.). *Moral Conduct and Authority: The Place of* adab *in South Asian Islam.* Berkeley: University of California Press, 291–314.

———. 1984b. 'A Note on Šahr-Āšōb'. *AUS* 4, 42.

———. 2003. 'Ghalib's Delhi: A Shamelessly Revisionist Look at Two Popular Metaphors'. *AUS* 18.1: 3–24.

Naim, C.M. and Carla Petievich. 1997. 'Urdu in Lucknow/Lucknow in Urdu'. In: Violette Graff (ed.). *Lucknow: Memories of a City.* Delhi: Oxford University Press, 165–80.

Nair, P. Thankappan. 1990. 'Origin of the Persian, Urdu and Hindi Printing and Press in Calcutta'. *Indo-Iranica* 43: 8–69.

Narain, Kirti. 1998. *Press, Politics and Society: Uttar Pradesh, 1885–1914.* New Delhi: Manohar.

Narayana Rao, Velcheru; David Shulman and Sanjay Subrahmanyam. 2001. *Textures of Time: Writing History in South India, 1600–1800.* New Delhi: Permanent Black.

Naregal, Veena. 2001. *Language Politics, Elites and the Public Sphere.* New Delhi: Permanent Black.

Natarajan, J. 1954. *History of Indian Journalism* (Report of the Press Commission, Pt. II). Delhi: Government of India Press.

Nowell-Smith, Simon. 1968. *International Copyright Law and the Publisher in the Reign of Queen Victoria.* Oxford: Clarendon Press.

Oesterheld, Christina. 2004. 'Entertainment and Reform: Urdu Narrative Genres in the Nineteenth Century'. In: Stuart Blackburn and Vasudha Dalmia (eds.). *India's Literary History: Essays on the Nineteenth Century.* Delhi: Permanent Black, 167–212.

Ohdedar, A. K. 1966. *The Growth of the Library in Modern India: 1489–1836.* Calcutta: World Press Private.

Oldenburg, Veena Talwar. 1989 [1984]. *The Making of Colonial Lucknow 1856–1877*. Delhi: Oxford University Press.

Ong, Walter J. 1982. *Orality and Literacy: The Technologizing of the Word*. London a.o.: Methuen.

Orsini, Francesca. 2002. *The Hindi Public Sphere 1920–1940. Language and Literature in the Age of Nationalism*. Delhi: Oxford University Press.

———. 2004a. 'Detective Novels. A Commercial Genre in Nineteenth-century North India'. In: Stuart Blackburn and Vasudha Dalmia (eds.). *India's Literary History: Essays on the Nineteenth Century*. Delhi: Permanent Black, 435–82.

———. 2004b. 'Pandits, Printers and Others: Publishing in Nineteenth-century Benares'. In: Abhijit Gupta and Swapan Chakravorty (eds.). *Print Areas. Book History in India*. Delhi: Permanent Black, 103–38.

Peabody, Norbert. 1996. 'Tod's *Rajast'han* and the Boundaries of Imperial Rule in Nineteenth-Century India'. *MAS* 30.1: 185–220.

Pemble, John. 1979. *The Raj, the Indian Mutiny and the Kingdom of Oudh, 1801–1854*. Delhi: Oxford University Press.

Pernau, Margrit. 2003. 'The *Dehli Urdu Akhbar* Between Persian Akhbarat and English Newspapers'. *AUS* 18.1: 105–31.

Petievich, Carla. 1990. 'Poetry of the declining Mughals: The *Shahr āshob*'. *JSAL* 25 (1): 99–110.

Pinch, William. 1996. *Peasants and Monks in British India*. Berkeley: University of California Press.

———. 1999. 'History, Devotion and the Search for Nabhadas of Galta'. In: Daud Ali (ed.). *Invoking the Past: The Uses of History in South Asia*. New Delhi/Oxford: Oxford University Press, 367–99.

Pingree, David. 1981. Jyotiḥśāstra: *Astral and Mathematical Literature*. Wiesbaden: Harrassowitz.

Pollock, Sheldon. 2003 (ed.). *Literary Cultures in History. Reconstructions from South Asia*. Berkeley/Los Angeles/London: University of California Press.

Powell, Avril A. 1993. *Muslims and Missionaries in Pre-Mutiny India*. Richmond: Curzon Press.

———. 1999. 'History Textbooks and the Transmission of the Pre-colonial Past in North-western India in the 1860s and 1870s'. In: Daud Ali (ed.). *Invoking the Past: The Uses of History in South Asia*. New Delhi/Oxford: Oxford University Press, 91–131.

Priolkar, Anant Kakba. 1958. *The Printing Press in India: Its Beginnings and Early Development*. Bombay: Marathi Samshodhana Mandala.

Pritchett, Frances W. 1984. '"The World Turned Upside Down": 'Šahr-Āšōb' as a Genre'. *AUS* 4, 37–41.

———. 1985. *Marvelous Encounters: Folk romance in Hindi and Urdu.* New Delhi: Manohar.

———. 1991. *The Romance Tradition in Urdu: Adventures from the Dastan of Amir Hamzah*, New York: Columbia University Press.

———. 1995. *Nets of Awareness. Urdu Poetry and its Critics.* Karachi: Oxford University Press.

Qureshi, Hamid Afaq a.o. 1986. 'Political Factors Behind Socio-Cultural Changes in Lucknow During 1722–1856'. In: Y. Krishan (ed.). *Essays in Indian History and Culture.* New Delhi: Indian History and Culture Society.

Raghavan, G. N. S. 1994. *The Press in India: A New History.* New Delhi: Gyan Publishing House.

Rahbar, Daud (trs., ann.). 1987. *Urdu letters of Mirzā Asaduʾllah Khān Ghālib.* Albany: State University of New York Press.

Rahman, Tariq. 1996. *Language and Politics in Pakistan.* Karachi: Oxford University Press.

———. 2002. *Language, Ideology and Power. Language-learning among the Muslims of Pakistan and North India.* Karachi: Oxford University Press.

Rai, Lajpat. 1967. *A History of the Arya Samaj*, Bombay a.o.: Orient Longman.

Ransom, Teresa. 1999. *Miss Marie Corelli, Queen of Victorian Bestsellers.* Gloucestershire: Sutton Publishing.

Ransom, Will. 1963. 'What is a Private Press?'. In: Paul A. Bennett (ed.). *Books and Printing. A Treasury for Typophiles.* Cleveland and New York: The World Publishing Company, 175–9.

Rhodes, Dennis E. 1969. *India, Pakistan, Ceylon, Burma and Thailand* (The Spread of Printing. Eastern Hemisphere). Amsterdam: Vangendt.

Rizvi, Sayyid Mahboob (comp.) and Quraishi, Murtaz Husain F. (trs.). 1980. *History of the Dar al-Ulum Deoband.* Vol. 1. Deoband: Idara-e Ihtemam, Dar al-Ulum.

Robinson, Francis. 1973. 'Municipal Government and Muslim Separatism in the United Provinces, 1883 to 1916'. In: John Gallagher, Gordon Johnson and Anil Seal (eds.). *Locality, Province and Nation. Essays on Indian Politics 1870 to 1940.* Cambridge: University Press.

———. 1974. *Separatism among Indian Muslims. The Politics of the*

United Provinces' Muslims 1860–1923. Second Impression. London: Cambridge University Press.

———. 1993. 'Technology and Religious Change: Islam and the Impact of Print'. *MAS* 27.1.: 229–51.

———. 1994. 'An Intellectual Renaissance'. *The Taj Magazine. Lucknow: A Special Issue*. Vol. 23 (1): 120–4.

———. 1996. 'Islam and the Impact of Print in South Asia'. In: Nigel Crook (ed.). *The Transmission of Knowledge in South Asia: Essays on Education, Religion, History and Politics*. Delhi: Oxford University Press.

———. 1997. 'The Re-emergence of Lucknow as a Major Political Centre.' In: Violette Graff (ed.). *Lucknow: Memories of a City*. Delhi: Oxford University Press, 196–212.

———. 2001. *The ʿUlama of Farangi Mahall and Islamic Culture in South Asia*. Delhi: Permanent Black.

Rocher, Ludo. 1986. *The Purāṇas*. Wiesbaden: Harrassowitz.

Rohatgi, Pauline and Godrej, Pheroza (eds.). 1989. *India: A Pageant of Prints*. Bombay: Marg Publications.

Rose, Jonathan. 1995. 'How Historians Study Reader Response: Or, What did Jo Think of *Bleak House*?'. In: John O. Jordan and Robert L. Patten (eds.). *Literature in the Marketplace. Nineteenth-century British publishing and reading practices*. Cambridge: Cambridge University Press, 195–212.

Ross, Fiona G.E. 1999. *The Printed Bengali Character and its Evolution*. Richmond: Curzon Press.

Roy, Tapti. 1996. 'Disciplining the Printed Text: Colonial and Nationalist Surveillance of Bengali Literature'. In: Partha Chatterjee (ed.). *Texts of Power. Emerging Disciplines in Colonial Bengal*. Calcutta: Samya, 30–62.

Russell, Ralph.1992. *The Pursuit of Urdu Literature. A Select History*. Delhi: Oxford University Press.

Russell, Ralph and Khurshidul Islam (trs.; eds). [1969] 1994. *Ghalib 1797–1869: Life and Letters*. Delhi: Oxford University Press.

Ruswa, Mirza Mohammad Hadi. 1993. *Umrao Jan Ada. Courtesan of Lucknow*. Trs. by Khushwant Singh & M.A. Husaini. Mumbai: Disha Books.

Sadiq, Muhammad. 1995. *A History of Urdu Literature*. Second edition. Rev. and enlarged. Delhi: Oxford University Press.

Sangari, Kumkum. 1999. *Politics of the Possible. Essays on Gender, History, Narratives, Colonial English*. New Delhi: Tulika.

———. 2004. 'Multiple Temporalities, Unsettled Boundaries, Trickster Women. Reading a Nineteenth-century *Qissa*'. In Stuart Blackburn and Vasudha Dalmia (eds.). *India's Literary History. Essays on the Nineteenth Century*. Delhi: Permanent Black 2004, 213–50.

Sangari, Kumkum and Sudesh Vaid (eds.) 1989. *Recasting Women. Essays in Colonial History*. Delhi: Kali for Women.

Sarkar, Tanika. 1999. *Words to Win: The Making of* Amar Jiban, *a Modern Autobiography*. New Delhi: Kali for Women.

Saxena, Ram Babu. 1941. *European and Indo-European Poets of Urdu & Persian*. Lucknow: Newul Kishore Press.

———. 1990 [1927]. *A History of Urdu Literature*. Reprint New Delhi/ Madras: Asian Educational Services.

Scheglova, Olga P. 1999. 'Lithograph Versions of Persian Manuscripts of Indian Manufacture in the Nineteenth Century.' *Manuscripta Orientalia* 5.1: 12–22.

Schimmel, Annemarie. 1973. *Islamic Literatures of India*. Wiesbaden: Harrassowitz.

———. 1984. *Calligraphy and Islamic Culture*, New York: New York University Press.

Schmidt, Richard. 1922. *Beiträge zur indischen Erotik. Das Liebesleben des Sanskritvolkes*. Berlin: Hermann Barsdorf Verlag.

Seal, Anil. 1968. *The Emergence of Indian Nationalism: Competition and Collaboration in the Later Nineteenth Century*. London: Cambridge University Press.

Sen, Siba Pada 1973. (ed.). *Historians and Historiography in Modern India*. Calcutta: Institute of Historical Studies.

Sender, Henny. 1988. *The Kashmiri Pandits. A Study of Cultural Choice in North India*. Delhi: Oxford University Press.

Sharar, Abdul Halim. 1975. *Lucknow: The Last Phase of an Oriental Culture*. Transl. and ed. by E. S. Harcourt and Fakhir Husain. London: Paul Elek.

Sharma, S.P. 1996. *The Press: Socio-political Awakening*. New Delhi: Mohit Publications.

Sharma, Sanjay. 2001. *Famine, Philanthropy and the Colonial State: North India in the Early Nineteenth Century*. Delhi: Oxford University Press.

Shaw, Graham. 1981. *Printing in Calcutta to 1800: A Description and Checklist of Printing in Late 18th-Century Calcutta*. London: The Bibliographical Society.

———. 1989. 'The Beginnings of Printing in Bombay.' In: Pauline Rohatgi and Pheroza Godrej (eds.). *India: A Pageant of Prints*. Bombay: Marg Publications, 111–24.

———. 1994. 'The Introduction of Lithography and its Impact on Book Design in India'. *Vihangama. The IGNCA Newsletter* II (2).

———. 1997a. 'Printing in Devanagari'. In: B.S. Kesavan, *History of Printing and Publishing in India. A Story of Cultural Re-awakening*. Vol. 3. New Delhi: National Book Trust, 126–32.

———. 1997b. 'The Tanjore "Aesop" in the Context of Early Marathi Printing'. In: B. S. Kesavan, *History of Printing and Publishing in India. A Story of Cultural Re-awakening*. Vol. 3. New Delhi: National Book Trust, 140–8.

———. 1998. 'Calcutta: Birthplace of the Indian Lithographed Book.' *Journal of the Printing Historical Society* 27: 98–111.

Sheo Narain. 1916. 'The "Kohinoor" of 1851.' *JPHS* IV (1): 51–61.

Sherring, M. A. 1974 [1872]. *Hindu Tribes and Castes as Represented in Benares*. Reprint. Delhi: Cosmo Publications.

Singh, Anand Shankar. 1991. *Growth of Political Awakening in Uttar Pradesh 1858–1900*. Varanasi: Vishwavidyalay Prakashan.

Singh, Kuar Lachman. 1874. *Historical and Statistical Memoir of Zila Buland-shahar*. Allahabad.

Slaje, Walter. 1994. Vom *Mokṣopāya-Śāstra* zum *Yogavāsiṣṭha-Mahārāmāyaṇa*. Wien: Verlag der Österreichischen Akademie der Wissenschaften.

Smith, Anthony D. 1998. *Nationalism and Modernism. A Critical Survey of Recent Theories of Nations and Nationalism*. London/New York: Routledge.

Snell, Rupert. 1991. *The Hindi Classical Tradition. A Brajbhāṣā Reader*. London: School of Oriental and African Studies.

Spear, Percival. 1951. *Twilight of the Mughuls: Studies in Late Mughul Delhi*. Cambridge: Cambridge University Press.

Sprenger, A. 1854. *A Catalogue of the Arabic, Persian and Hindustany Manuscripts of the Libraries of the King of Oudh*. Vol. I. Calcutta: Baptist Mission Press.

Stark, Ulrike. 2000. 'Educating Women, Educating a Daughter: Babu Navincandra Rai, *Lakṣmī-Sarasvatī samvād* (1869) and Hemantkumari Chaudhurani'. In: Antony Copley (ed.). *Gurus and Their Followers: New Religious Reform Movements in Colonial India*. New Delhi: Oxford University Press, 33–56.

———. 2001. 'Lucknows Jalsa-i Tahzib: Urbane Elite, organisierte

Handlungskompetenz und frühe 'associational culture' in Britisch-Indien'. In: Harald Fischer-Tiné (ed.). *Handeln und Verhandeln. Kolonialismus, transkulturelle Prozesse und Handlungskompetenz*. Münster: LIT, 51–73.

———. 2003. 'Politics, Public Issues and the Promotion of Urdu Literature: *Avadh Akhbar*, the First Urdu Daily in Northern India'. *AUS* 18.1: 66–94.

———. 2004a. 'Towards a New Hindu Woman: Educational Ideals and Female Role Models in Shivprasad's *Vāmāmanrañjan* (1856).' In: Ulrike Roesler and Jayandra Soni (eds.). *Aspects of the Female in Indian Culture*. Marburg: Indica et Tibetica, 173–86.

———. 2004b. 'Hindi Publishing in the Heart of an Indo-Persian Cultural Metropolis: Lucknow's Newal Kishore Press (1858–1895)'. In: Blackburn/Dalmia (eds.). *India's Literary History. Essays on the Nineteenth Century*. Delhi: Permanent Black, 251–79.

———. 2007. 'Makkhanlal's *Sukhsāgar* (1846/47): The First Complete Version of the *Bhāgavatā Purāṇa* in Modern Hindi Prose?' In: J. Hartmann/K. Klaus (eds.). *Indica et Tibetica. Festschrift für Michael Hahn*. (Wiener Studien zur Tibetologie und Buddhismuskunde). Wien: 491–506.

Steinberg, S.H. 1996. *Five Hundred Years of Printing*. New ed., rev. by John Trevitt. London: The British Library & Oak Knoll Press.

Storey, Graham. 1951. *Reuters' Century 1851–1951*. London: Max Parrish.

Sukthankar, V.S. 1936. 'Epic Studies VI: The Bhṛgus and the Bhārata: A Text-Historical Study'. *Annals of the Bhandarkar Oriental Research Institute* 18 (1): 1–76.

Sundaram, V.A. (ed.). 1936. *Benares Hindu University 1905 to 1935*. Benares: Benares Hindu University.

Sutherland, John. 1995. *Victorian Fiction: Writers, Publishers, Readers*. Houndsmills: Macmillan.

Szrajber, Tanya. 1997. 'New Documents on Early Lithography'. *Print Quarterly* XIV (3): 290–302.

Taban, Faruqi Anjum. 1995. 'Population of Lucknow in 1857: From Records in a Contemporary Urdu Newspaper'. *Proceedings of the Indian History Congress, 55th session, Aligarh 1994*: 724–6.

Talwar, Vir Bharat. 1989. 'Feminist Consciousness in Women's Journals in Hindi'.In: Kumkum Sangari and Sudesh Vaid (eds.). *Recasting Women. Essays in Colonial History*. Delhi: Kali for Women, 204–32.

Tauer, Felix. 1968. 'Persian Learned Literature to the End of the 18th

Century.' In: Jan Rypka et. al. *History of Iranian Literature*. Ed. by Karl Jahn. Dordrecht: D. Reidel, 429–37.

Tavakoli-Targhi, Mohamad. 1993. 'Rediscovering Munshi Newal Kishore (1836–1895)'. *South Asia Library Notes and Queries* 29: 14–22.

Terry, R.C. 1983. *Victorian Popular Fiction, 1860–1880*. London: Macmillan.

Thairani, Kala. 1987. *Copyright: The Indian experience*. Ahmedabad: Allied Publishers.

Thiel-Horstmann, Monika. 1983. *Crossing the Ocean of Existence: Braj Bhāṣā Religious Poetry from Rajasthan. A Reader*. Wiesbaden: Harrassowitz.

Tønnesson, Stein and Antlöv, Hans (eds.). 1996. *Asian Forms of the Nation*. Richmond: Curzon.

Travis, Alan. 2000. *Bound and Gagged. A Secret History of Obscenity in Britain*. London: Profile Books.

Trivedi, Harish. 1993. *Colonial Transactions: English Literature and India*. Manchester and New York: Manchester University Press.

Twyman, M. 1967. 'The Lithographic Hand Press 1796–1850'. *Journal of the Printing Historical Society* 3: 3–50.

Vanzan, Anna. 2000. 'Medical Education of Muslim Women in Turn-of-the-Century India. The 9th Chapter of the *Bihishtī Zewar*'. *JPHS* XLVIII (1): 3–8.

Vedalankar, Sharda. 1969. *The Development of Hindi Prose Literature in the Early Nineteenth Century (1800–1856 A.D.)*. Allahabad: Lokbharti Publications.

Viswanathan, Gauri. 1989. *Masks of Conquest. Literary Study and British Rule in India*. New York: Columbia University Press.

Watt, Carey Anthony. 2005. *Serving the Nation. Cultures of Service, Association, and Citizenship*. Delhi: Oxford University Press.

Watt, George. 1892. *A Dictionary of the Economic Products of India*. Vol. VI (1). London/Calcutta: Government Printing.

Wood, Ananda E. 1985. *Knowledge Before Printing and After. The Indian Tradition in Changing Kerala*. Delhi: Oxford University Press.

Works in Hindi

Bhargava, Manhargopal [Bhārgava, Manhargopāl]. 1970. 'Munshī (Paṃ.) Navalkiśor jī kī vaṃś paramparā'. *Bhārgava Patrikā*, Farvarī: [24].

———. 1981. 'Navalkiśor pres kā saṃkṣipt paricaya'. *Uttar Prades* 9 (9): 31.

Caturvedi, Parasuram [Caturvedī, Parasurām]. vs 2021. *Uttarī bhārat kī sant paramparā*. Rev. ed. Allahabad: Bharti Bhandar.

Caturvedi, Shrinarayan [Caturvedī, Śrīnārāyaṇ]. 1981. 'Sāhitya ke unnāyak Munśī jī'. *Uttar Prades* 9 (9): 3–6.

Dvivedi, Mahavir Prasad [Dvivedī, Mahavīr Prasād]. 1928. *Vaicitrya-citraṇ*, ed. Premcand. Lucknow: Naval Kishore Press.

Dikshit, Bandidin [Dīkṣit, Bandīdīn]. 1895. *Jīvancaritra*. Lucknow: Naval Kishore Press.

Gupta, Balmukund [Gupta, Bālmukund]. 1994. *Gupta-nibandhāvalī*. Ed. by Jhabarmall Sharma and Banarsi Das Caturvedi. Delhi: Gaurav Gatha Sangam.

Gupta, Mataprasad [Gupta, Mātāprasād]. 1947. *Hindī pustak sāhitya, 1867–1942 īsvi*. Allahabad: Hindustani Ekedemi.

———. 1989. *Tulsī sāhitya sandarbh koś*, Kanpur.

Harishchandra [Hariścandra]. 1954. *Bhāratendu granthāvalī*, vol. 3, ed. Brajratnadas. Banaras: Nagari Pracharini Sabha.

———. 1989. *Bhāratendu samagra*. Ed. by Hemant Sharma. 3rd ed. Banaras: Pracharak Granthavali Pariyojna, Hindi Pracharak Samsthan.

Hasan, Anvarul [Hasan, Anvārul]. 1981. 'Rāṣṭrīya ektā ke pratīk'. *Uttar Pradeś* 9 (9): 10–11.

Hindī sāhitya koś. 1986. Vols 1–2. Ed. by Dhirendra Varma. 2nd ed. Varanasi: Jnanmandal Ltd.

Hindī-sāhitya-sāriṇī or Hindi Bibliography. Being a universal, classified and scientifically arranged record of Hindi books published up to the end of 1964. 1971. Comp. and ed. by Pitambar Narain and S. Bhaskaran Nair. Hoshiarpur: Vishveshvaranand Institute.

Krishnacarya [Kṛṣṇācārya]. 1966. *Hindī ke ādīmudrit granth*. Benares: Bharatiya Jnanpith Prakashan.

Mishra, Krishnabihari [Miśra, Kṛṣṇabihārī] 1985. *Hindī patrakāritā: Jātīya cetnā aur khaṛī bolī sāhitya kī nirmāṇ-bhūmi*. 2nd ed. New Delhi: Bharatiya Jnanpith Prakashan.

Mishra, Surendramohan [Miśra, Surendramohan]. 1987. 'Unnīsvīṁ sadī kī hindī pāṭhya pustakoṁ kā bhāṣik yogdān'. *Gaganāñcal* 20 (3): 45–7.

Nagar, Amritlal [Nāgar, Amṛtlāl]. 1991. *Amṛtlāl Nāgar racnāvalī*. Vol. 9. Ed. by Sharad Nagar. Delhi: Rajpal and Sons.

Sengar, Shivsimha [Sengar, Śivsiṃha]. 1966 [1878]. *Śivsiṃh saroj*. Ed. by Triloki Narayan Dikshit. Lucknow: Tej Kumar Press.

Sharma, H.N. [Śarma, H.N.] (ed.). vs 1993. *Sundargranthāvalī*. Calcutta.

Shukla, Ramcandra [Śukla, Rāmcandra]. vs 2051. *Hindī sāhitya kā itihās*. 29th ed., Kashi: Nagari Pracarini Sabha.

Siddiqi, Abdul Alim [Siddīqī, Abdul Alīm]. 1981. 'Pūrvī sabhyatā ko den'. *Uttar Pradeś* 9 (9): 15.

Simha, Bhagvati Prasad [Siṃha, Bhagvatī Prasād]. 1957. *Rāmbhakti meṁ rasik sampradāy*. Balrampur: Avadh Sahitya Mandir.

Singh, Dhirendranath [Siṃha, Dhirendranāth]. 1986. *Ādhunik hindī ke vikās meṁ Khaḍgavilās Pres kī bhūmikā*. Patna: Bihar Rashtrabhasha Parishad.

———. (ed.). 1991. *Sundarī-tilak. Viśleṣaṇātmak anuśīlan*. Varanasi: Jnanmandal.

Suzuki, Takeshi and Toshio Tanaka. 1981. 'Jāpān meṁ Navalkiśor pustakālaya'. *Uttar Pradeś* 9 (9): 9; 18.

Tandan, Hariharnath [Ṭaṇḍan, Hariharnāth]. 1960. *Vārtā-sāhitya. Ek vṛhat adhyayan*. Aligarh: Bharat Prakashan Mandir.

Uttar Pradeś. 1981. *Uttar Pradeś. Munśī Navalkiśor par viśeṣ sāmagrī, 1836–95*. Varṣ 9, aṅk 9, farvarī.

Works in Urdu

ᶜAbdul Hai [ᶜAbd al-Hayy]. 1923 [1342 ah]. *Gul-e raᶜnā*. Azamgarh.

ᶜAbdul Haq [ᶜAbd al-Ḥaqq]. 1945. *Marḥūm Dehlī Kālij*. Delhi: Anjuman-e Taraqqi-e Urdu.

Abrar, Hasan [Abrār, Ḥasan]. 1980. 'Urdū ṣiḥāfat kī ᶜahd āfirīn yādgār Avadh A<u>kh</u>bār'. *Nayā Daur* 35 (8–9): 39–42; 100.

Ahmad, Siddiq [Aḥmad, Siddīq]. 1937. *Tārī<u>kh</u>-e Anjuman-e Hind-e Avadh*. Vol. I. Lucknow: Naval Kishore Press.

Al-Hasan, Anvar [al-Ḥasan, Anvār]. 1980. 'Maṭbaᶜ Navalkishor kā shuᶜba-e taṣnīf va tarjuma'. *Nayā Daur* 35 (8–9): 74–80.

Al-Hasan, Riaz [al-Ḥasan, Riyāẓ]. 1980. '*Avadh A<u>kh</u>bār* aur uske cand eḍīṭar'. *Nayā Daur* 35 (8–9): 43–7.

Al-Hasan, Sayyid Zahir [al-Ḥasan, Sayyid Ẓahīr]. 1980. 'Munshī Navalkishor kā maulid aur <u>kh</u>āndān'. *Nayā Daur* 35 (8–9): 204–5.

ᶜAli, Chaudhari Sharvat [ᶜAlī, Caudharī Sharvat]. 1980. 'Lughat navīsī aur maṭbaᶜ Navalkishor'. *Nayā Daur* 35 (8–9): 90–4.

ᶜAli, Rahman [ᶜAlī, Raḥmān]. 1964. *Taẕkirah-e ᶜulamā-e Hind*. Trs. into Urdu by Muhammad Ayyub Qadiri. Karachi: Pakistan Historical Society (*TUH*).

Beg, Mirza Bismillah [Beg, Mirzā Bismi'llāh]. 1955. 'Munshī Amīrullah Taslīm'. *Proceedings and Transactions of the All-India Oriental Conference, Sixteenth Session*. Vol. II. Lucknow: 473–86.

Bilali, Sabah al-Hasan [Bilālī, Ṣabāḥ al-Ḥasan]. 1980. 'Maṯbaᶜ Navalkishor kī kahānī, munshī Navalkishor kī zabānī 1858 se 1862 tak'. *Nayā Daur* 35 (8–9):70–2.

Danish Lakhnavi [Dānish Lakhnavī]. 1996. 'Khushnavīsān-e Avadh: aḥvāl va āṣār'. In: Sayyid Amjad Husain (ed.). *Avadh: Āʾīna-e aiyām meṁ*. Lucknow: Mahkama-e Ittilaᶜat va Rabitah-e ᶜAmma-e Uttar Pradesh, 262–4.

Eᶜjazi, Tajassus [Eᶜjāzī, Tajassus]. 1980. 'Munshī Navalkishor kī ṣiḥāfatī tarbīyatgāh: Koh-e Nūr'. *Nayā Daur* 35 (8–9): 52–8.

Fihrist 1874. *Fihrist-e kutub maujūda maṯbaᶜ munshī Navalkishor vāqaᶜ Lakhnaʾū va Kānpūr*. Lucknow: Naval Kishore Press.

Fihrist 1879. *Fihrist-e kutub maṯbaᶜ munshī Navalkishor. Lighāyat yakum agast 1879 ᶜī*. Lucknow: Naval Kishore Press.

Haidari, Akbar [Ḥaidarī, Akbar]. 1980. 'Munshī Navalkishor aur Avadh Akhbār'. *Nayā Daur* 35 (8–9): 20–38.

Husain, Sayyid Amjad [Ḥusain, Sayyid Amjad] (ed.). 1996. *Avadh: Āʾīna-e aiyām meṁ*. Lucknow: Mahkama-e Ittilaᶜat va Rabitah-e ᶜAmma-e Uttar Pradesh.

Husain Akbarpuri, Anvar [Ḥusain Akbarpūrī, Anvār]. 1991. *Avadh ke tārīkhnigār*. Faizabad: Nishat Offset Press.

Kakorvi, Nazir [Kākorvī, Nāẕir]. 1939. *Urdū ke hindū adīb*. Lucknow: Anvar Book Depot.

Khan, Ashfaq Muhammad [Khān, Ashfāq Muḥammad]. 1979. *Naẕīr Aḥmad ke nāval*. Delhi: Maktaba-e Jamiᶜa Limited.

Khan, Nadir ᶜAli [Khān, Nādir ᶜAlī]. 1990. *Hindustānī pres 1556–1900*. Lucknow: Uttar Pradesh Urdu Akademi.

Khan, Kazim ᶜAli [Khān, Kāẕim ᶜAlī]. 1980. 'Ghālib aur Munshī Navalkishor'. *Nayā Daur* 35 (8–9): 136–54.

Khan, Sarvar Qaiyum [Khān, Sarvar Qaiyūm]. 1980. 'Munshī Navalkishor avadh rīviyū ke ā'īna meṁ'. *Nayā Daur* 35 (8–9): 185–9.

Khan, Shams Tabriz. [Khān, Shams Tabrīz] 1980. 'Munshī Navalkishor: qaumī yakjihatī ke peshrau'. *Nayā Daur* 35 (8–9): 172–4.

Khurshid, ᶜAbdussalam [Khurshīd, ᶜAbd us-salām]. 1963. *Ṣiḥāfat Pākistān va Hind meṁ*. Lahore: Majalis-i Taraqqi-i Adab.

Lalji Munshi [Lāljī Munshī]. 1903. *Jīvancaritar*. Lucknow: Naval Kishore Press.

Navalkishor. 1990 [1863]. *Tavārīkh-e nādir al-ᶜaṣr*. Reprint. Patna: Khudabakhsh Oriental Public Library.

Nayā Daur. 1980. *Munshī Navalkishor nambar*. Vol. 35 (8–9).

Nurani, Amir Hasan [Nurānī, Amīr Ḥasan]. 1982. *Munshī Navalkishor. Ḥālāt aur khidmāt*. Dehli: Idarah Akhvan al-Safa.

———. 1994. *Munshī Navalkishor aur unke khaṭṭāt va khushnavīs*. New Delhi: Taraqqi-e Urdu Byuro.

———. 1995. *Savāniḥ-e Munshī Navalkishor*. Patna: Khuda Bakhsh Oriental Public Library.

Nurjahan [Nūrjahān]. 1980. 'Munshī Navalkishor aur unkā khāndān'. *Nayā Daur* 35 (8–9): 206–13.

Rizvan, Mirza Muhammad [Riẓvān, Mirzā Muḥammad]. 1980. 'Munshī Navalkishor ke mutaᶜalliq cand mutafarriq bāteṁ'. *Nayā Daur* 35 (8–9): 231–4.

Sabiri, Imdad [Ṣābirī, Imdād]. 1953. *Tārīkh-e ṣiḥāfat-e Urdū*. Vols 1–3. Delhi: Jadid Printing Press.

———. 1973. *Urdū ke akhbār navīs*, Delhi: Sabiri Akademi.

Shams Badauni [Shams Badāʾūnī]. 1995. *Nizāmī badāʾūnī aur Nizāmī Pres kī adabī khidmāt*. Lucknow: nd.

Siddiqi, Ansar al-Hasan [Siddīqī, Anṣār al-Ḥasan]. 1980. 'Maṭbaᶜ Avadh Akhbār kī kahānī, Avadh Akhbār kī zabānī'. *Nayā Daur* 35 (8–9): 48–51.

Siddiqi, Muhammad Abul Lais [Siddīqī, Muḥammad Abu'l Laiṣ]. 1991. *Lakhnaʾū kā dābistān-e shāᶜirī*. Lucknow: Sarfaraz Qaumi Press.

Siddiqi, Muhammad ᶜAtiq [Siddīqī, Muḥammad ᶜAtīq]. 1956. 'Jalsah-e Tahẕīb Avadh kā pahlā aur qadīmtarīn kalcaral idārah'. *Urdū Adab* 5: 85–111.

———. 1962. *Ṣūbah shomālī va maghrabī ke akhbārāt va maṭbuᶜāt (1848–1853)*. Aligarh: Anjuman-e Taraqqi-e Urdu.

Zamani, Asifa [Zamānī, Āṣifa]. 1980. 'Munshī Navalkishor aur unkā naẓm-o-nasaq'. *Nayā Daur* 35 (8–9): 163–7.

———. (ed.). 2000. *Munshī Navalkishor aur unkī adabī khidmāt*. Lucknow: Rotashu Printers.

Name Index

Title Index

(For book titles see also Appendices III–V, which have not been indexed)

Subject Index